D1532670

# www.wadsworth.com

*wadsworth.com* is the World Wide Web site for
Wadsworth and is your direct source to dozens of online
resources.

At wadsworth.com you can find out about supplements,
demonstration software, and student resources. You can
also send e-mail to many of our authors and preview
new publications and exciting new technologies.

**wadsworth.com**

Changing the way the world learns®

# Inclusive Education
## for the
# 21st Century

## A New Introduction
## to Special Education

**Deanna J. Sands**
*University of Colorado, Denver*

**Elizabeth B. Kozleski**
*University of Colorado, Denver*

**Nancy K. French**
*University of Colorado, Denver*

**Wadsworth**
Thomson Learning

Australia · Canada · Mexico ·Singapore · Spain
United Kingdom · United States

*Education Editor:* Dianne Lindsay
*Assistant Editor:* Tangelique Williams
*Editorial Assistant:* Keynia Johnson
*Marketing Manager:* Becky Tollerson
*Project Editor:* Trudy Brown
*Print Buyer:* Mary Noel
*Permissions Editor:* Bob Kauser
*Production Service:* Strawberry Field Publishing
*Text Designer:* Carolyn Deacy

*Photo Researcher:* Melanie Field
*Copy Editor:* Thomas Briggs
*Illustrator:* Joan Carol
*Cover Designer:* Cuttriss and Hambleton
*Cover Images:* Jeff Greenberg, PhotoEdit; Kent Knudson, West Stock; Robin L. Sachs, PhotoEdit; PhotoDisc
*Cover Printer:* West Group
*Compositor:* TBH Typecast, Inc.
*Printer:* West Group

Printed in the United States of America

1  2  3  4  5  6  7  03  02  01  00  99

For permission to use material from this text, contact us by
**Web:** http://www.thomsonrights.com
**Fax:** 1-800-730-2215
**Phone:** 1-800-730-2214

**Library of Congress Cataloging-in-Publication Data**
Sands, Deanna J.
    Inclusive education for the 21st century / Deanna J. Sands, Elizabeth B. Kozleski, Nancy K. French.
        p.   cm.
    Includes bibliographical references (p.  ) and index.
    ISBN 0-534-23820-3
    1. Inclusive education—United States.  2. Handicapped students—Education—United States.  3. Educational change—United States.
I. Title: Inclusive education for the twenty-first century.  II. Kozleski, Elizabeth B.  III. French, Nancy K.  IV. Title.
LC1201 . S27 2000
371.9'046—dc21                                            99-057340

For more information, contact

**Wadsworth/Thomson Learning**
**10 Davis Drive**
**Belmont, CA 94002-3098**
**USA**
**http://www.wadsworth.com**

**International Headquarters**
Thomson Learning
290 Harbor Drive, 2nd Floor
Stamford, CT 06902-7477
USA

**UK/Europe/Middle East/South Africa**
Thomson Learning
Berkshire House
168-173 High Holborn
London WC1V 7AA
United Kingdom

**Asia**
Thomson Learning
60 Albert Street #15-01
Albert Complex
Singapore 189969

**Canada**
Nelson Thomson Learning
1120 Birchmount Road
Toronto, Ontario M1K 5G4
Canada

 This book is printed on acid-free recycled paper.

# Brief Contents

# Contents

## PART THREE

# Putting It All Together 371

# Preface

Every author, even while striving for a balanced presentation of all perspectives, has an underlying philosophical anchor. We come from research traditions that emphasize the importance of explaining the "lens" or viewpoint from which we gather and present information. Thus, in this preface, we will outline our underlying values and beliefs about education.

We are keenly aware that others hold different perspectives based on their own life experiences. Therefore, we have been careful to present accurate information and to show how that information supports inclusive education. We hope that as you read this book, you will develop your own vision of education for all students in the twenty-first century.

We believe that all individuals—regardless of their social class, socioeconomic status, ability, culture, linguistic background, gender, sexual preference, or religious beliefs—belong in our communities, and therefore, in our schools. There are probably other labels that could be used to categorize or separate groups. Whatever these other labels are, consider them as additions to the preceding list. Fundamentally, we believe that the act of including everyone in our public schools is vital for creating a strong and resilient society.

We recognize that inclusion poses a challenge to the status quo and that changes must be made in how we educate our nation's children in order to achieve this vision. Usually, an introductory textbook provides readers with an entrée into the existing conventions of a particular field. But this textbook introduces the existing norms in special education and also challenges them. Thus, we provide an alternative approach to traditional special education, one grounded in research and practice.

In this book, we question the educational system's focus on labeling, categorizing and, often, systematically excluding students with disabilities from access to the social rhythms and routines as well as the academic content of the general education milieu. Our goal is to engage you in exploring new ways of thinking about how students with disabilities can become active, engaged members of their schools. Thus, the structures, teaching technologies, and curricula that are presented will help you reconsider how schools can support the needs of other groups of students who have been traditionally excluded or marginalized. We also discuss at great length the kinds of knowledge, skills, beliefs, and attitudes it takes to create a community of learners among all those who reside in the larger community served by the school.

Although our vision for schools is challenging, our intent is to make this book as realistic, useful, and true to life as possible. We are keenly aware of the problems in today's schools, so we have presented scenarios that depict both the positive and negative outcomes of various educational practices. Many of our stories about teachers, para-educators, and families are based on real people we know and the way they work together. In many cases, we've changed their names to protect their privacy or have combined descriptions of events that actually occurred separately.

As you read this text, we encourage you to take advantage of the many learning opportunities contained in each chapter. Each chapter begins with a brief outline listing key chapter topics. Chapter introductory vignettes offer different perspectives on key educational issues. And the material in the boxes, figures, and tables in each chapter will enhance your understanding of the topic. We encourage you to stop reading when you come to an **Extending Your Learning** box and take time to reflect on the concept or do the activity. Throughout the book, **stories** are used to provide you with a mental image of classrooms in which the practices are used. We urge you to read each story critically, asking yourself how it illustrates the concept being discussed. You may find that there are some terms or concepts you don't understand. We suggest that you look first to the chapter glossary for a definition. If the word you seek doesn't appear in the glossary, you may want to consult a dictionary.

We have included an **Instructional Activity** in every chapter. These activities provide opportunities for you to learn in ways other than reading and listening to lectures. You can use the activities in class, as homework, or as an extra credit assignment. If possible, go into schools and classrooms as an observer. While you're there, compare what you see to the vignettes in the book. Ask yourself what kind of school professional you want to be, how you want to act, and how you want to relate to your colleagues and to the families of your students. Create your own vision as we have ours.

## Acknowledgments

We would like to thank the following people for helping make *Inclusive Education for the 21st Century* a reality: Doris Crist for fighting for Michael's future and his need for an education, knowing there would be a day when she would no longer be alive to take care of him; Michael Crist for helping us understand the value of every human life and to pursue teaching children with disabilities as my career; Sadie and Jimmy Lombardi for showing us how the presence of a disability isn't necessarily a handicap; Jane Vines for showing how the spirit can triumph; Charlotte Metz for teaching us that caring comes first; Jamie, Mark, Bobby, Brenda, Buddy, and many other students in our lives for helping us learn how to teach; Jane Ryan, Donna Sobel, and Joyce Waterhouse for modeling what good teaching is all about; Erminel Love for holding high expectations and providing supports necessary to achieve them; Nancy Steele for developing the Triad System and for letting us watch her in action and tell her story; Tom French for his dynamic work with thousands of kids and for sharing thirty-one years of school stories; John Kozleski for his enthusiastic support throughout this project; John Applegate, Christine Ramirez, Tiny Atencio, Paula Perrill, Mark Semmel, Kappy Hall, Loretta Gonzales for insisting that we answer their questions about how to manage the many roles of a special educator; Melissa Dyckes, Peter Kailus, Amber Waheed, and Holly Deresio for all their hard work reviewing the manuscript, and to the first three for their creativity in preparing the Instructor's Manual; Judy Heumann, Nancy and Bill Baesman, Anita Wagner, Mary Kiesau-Bramer, Cathy Krautkramer, Sandy Ruconich, Karen Watson, Kathy Herman, Pam Kniss, Amber Keith, Tom Bellamy, Amy Hickman, Joe Pope, Dan Vinyard, Rosemary Harrer, and Candy Vargas for telling their stories.

We would also like to thank the following reviewers: Beverley Argus-Calvo, New Mexico State University; Michael Banks, Missouri Southern State College; Gail Moorman Behrens, Upper Iowa University; Andrew R. Biegel, State University of New York, New Paltz; Lynn R. Caffrey, York College; George Calhoun, Jr., Southwest Missouri State University; David F. Conway, University of Nebraska, Omaha; W. Donald Crump, University of Alabama; Bruno D'Alonzo, New Mexico State University; Ronald Eaves, Auburn University; Eugene Edgar, University of Washington; Gerald Fain, Boston University; Jeannette E. Fleischner, Teacher's College, Columbia University; Joan Forsgren-White, Utah State University; Paula M. Gardner, California State University, Sacramento; Don E. Hagness, Eastern Kentucky University; Nancy Halmhuber, Eastern Michigan University; Edwin Helmstetter, Washington State University; Sydney W. Howard, Quinnipiac College; Asha K. Jitendra, Lehigh University; E. Ann Knackendoffel, Kansas State University; Maurice Miller, Indiana State University; Janice Olszowy, Cleveland State University; Eun-Ja Kim Park, California State University, Bakersfield; James S. Payne, University of Mississippi; Michael E. Pullis, University of Missouri, Columbia; Joyce A. Rademacher, University of North Texas; Rangasamy Ramasamy, Florida Atlanta University; Robert Reid, University of Nebraska, Lincoln; Brenda Scheuermann, Southwest Texas State University; Stuart E. Schwartz, University of Florida; Bill Sharpton, University of New Orleans; Deborah C. Simmons, University of Oregon; Bernita Sims-Tucker, University of Maryland, East Shore; and William J. Sweeney, University of South Dakota.

> *To be as much as we can be*
> *We must dream*
> *Of being more*
> —*Karen Ravn*

## PART ONE

# An Ecological Approach to Education

## CHAPTER 1

# Schooling in the 21st Century

# A Visit with Judy Heumann

*by Judith Heumann*

Looking back on my own educational experiences, while some were quite positive, I can see now that the teachers and administrators with whom my family and I interacted in the 1950s and 1960s gave little or no thought to the impact of my educational experiences on my future quality of life and my ability to contribute to society. At that time, education and rehabilitation for disabled children and adults were not at all outcome-oriented; they were driven more by stereotypical notions of disability than by a reality-based approach to potential achievement.

Despite the polio I acquired at the age of 18 months, my mother very proudly took me to enroll in the public school system in Brooklyn, New York, when I was old enough. It never occurred to either of us that she would be told to take me back home or that the school system instead would opt to educate me by sending a tutor to my home twice a week for four years. In the decades prior to the mandates and impetus of the **Individuals with Disabilities Education Act (IDEA),** no thought was given to my academic and socialization needs. Rather, a teacher came to my home twice a week for a total of two to five hours per week until I was 9 years old. I was not allowed to go to school because, due to my difficulties in mobility, the school administrators considered me a "fire hazard."

Though I finally got to go to public school at the age of 9, I was placed in a "health conservation" class located in the school basement. Some of the students in this class were as old as 21. We infrequently associated with "the kids upstairs," and we felt awkward and embarrassed when we did interact—almost as if we were freaks on parade. Concepts such as **appropriate education** and **least restrictive environment** were nonexistent during these years, and my educational process continued to be guided more by my disability than by my strengths and intellect.

I went to college and graduated from Long Island University in 1969 with a minor in education. My goal was to teach, but the vocational rehabilitation agency providing me with financial assistance would not allow me to major in education, since it was not considered a realistic employment goal for someone with a significant disability. Instead, I was steered toward one of the two majors identified as appropriate for young disabled women at the time: social work or speech therapy. I chose speech therapy and took all of the education credits I could. Sure enough, when I applied for a teaching job in the New York City public school system, school officials turned down my application because I couldn't walk. I took my case to court and won, becoming the first wheelchair user to teach in the New York City public schools. I taught for three years.

I now know that if I had docilely accepted the negative self-image the educational system of the 1950s and 1960s tried to impose on me, I would not be where I am today—the highest-ranking federal education official with a disability in the Clinton administration. Fortunately, the confidence instilled in me by my parents and other significant individuals throughout my life helped me through the rough spots; but other disabled people, even in these more enlightened times, have not been so fortunate. The educational community must recognize that its treatment of disabled children will either enhance or detract from the child's academic, social, and emotional development. Educators must not allow their fears of disabled people to restrict disabled children's development. Indeed, disabled children must be afforded meaningful and ongoing opportunities that foster the development of self-esteem and positive academic outcomes. As you read the chapters in this book, please reaffirm your commitment to achieving quality outcomes for *all* children. Your efforts will then be of maximum benefit and impact positively on the lives of disabled children and youths—the adults of tomorrow.

# Introduction

Calls for "educational reform" and "school restructuring" within the educational community are echoed in the popular media, in state legislatures, in local school boards, and in the chambers of the Senate and House of Representatives in Washington, DC. Increasing student diversity and changing economic and social conditions strain the capacity of our educational system to produce well-educated graduates. Many constituencies question the effectiveness of the current educational system's approaches to educating an increasingly diverse student population. More and more, the concept of "inclusive school practices" is discussed as a philosophical basis for reconstructing the manner in which we organize schools to meet the needs of all learners.

In this chapter, we give an overview of why schools need to focus on improvements to their policies, organizational structures, and practices, and how changing social and economic conditions challenge existing school organization structures. The analysis of the special education system and current concerns about that system will help you understand why many of our current school practices fail to be responsive to the needs of many students in our schools, as well as to broader social goals. We then provide a rationale for the use of inclusive school communities and inclusionary practices as a context for widespread educational reform. Within that context, you will learn how to address common outcomes for all learners and to apply quality-of-life standards as a means of assessing how well we do the work of schools. Finally, we review the changes that must be made if we are to reach our goal of inclusive school communities.

# Challenging the Status Quo

When you picture yourself as a teacher, what do you see? Many people enter the field of education believing they will work in a school building that has many classrooms, each with a single teacher working with the same group of students for a year. Your image of a secondary teacher might include five or six groups of students who come to your class for a subject like algebra, physical sciences, or American literature. You might see yourself facing your students as you teach. Your students may share the same or similar ethnic backgrounds, or they may come from backgrounds and experiences very different from one another's—and your own. Pay attention to what you imagine yourself doing as the teacher, and you may find that you are using the same instructional processes you preferred as a learner.

Whatever your image, there is growing evidence that traditional conventions of schools and classrooms are becoming outmoded as the educational, social, political, and economic needs of our society rapidly change (Apple & Beane, 1995; Elmore & Fuhrman,

1994; Goodlad, 1984; Daggett, in O'Neil, 1995). These changes challenge traditional models of school organizational structures, assessment, curriculum, instruction, and classroom management. Growing numbers of students from diverse ethnic, **linguistic,** cultural, and socioeconomic backgrounds and with diverse abilities attend our schools. The learning and social needs and skills of young Americans entering school vary tremendously. Schools and school professionals must stretch to meet these diverse needs.

Historically, our response to student diversity has been to create special programs, often separate from the scope of general education, to meet the educational needs of nonmajority students (Carlson & O'Reilly, 1996; Gartner & Lipsky, 1987). Schools have programs designed to support students who speak languages other than English, who have literacy problems, and whose disabilities affect their ability to learn. But intense criticism and calls for reform increasingly target such programs in bilingual education, Title I reading, and special education (A concern about, 1992; National Association of State Boards of Education [NASBE], 1992; U.S. Department of Education, 1993). Proponents of change urge construction of a unified educational system that responds to the needs of all children, despite their differences (Association for Supervision and Curriculum Development, 1992; Lipsky & Gartner, 1996; NASBE, 1992; National Center on Educational Restructuring and Inclusion, 1995; Wagner, 1997). These reform proposals recognize that *most,* not some, students have diverse learning needs.

## Changing the Vision of Schooling

As teachers alter their instructional methods in response to student diversity, they are also asked to change their practices in response to other social, political, and economic conditions. Information technology has expanded both the amount of information we access and the ways in which we access it (Dede, 1989). Also, the shift from national to global economics has resulted in a need for workers with new skills and attitudes (Daggett, in O'Neil, 1995). Changes in the world necessitate changes in what and how students are taught. As curricular and instructional methods evolve, traditional school organizational policies, structures, and practices must change to provide the necessary structural frameworks and supports (Sage, 1996). As a

A young man enjoys a game of tennis.

result, educational reform in the next ten years will be more exhaustive and better supported than in previous change efforts (Fullan & Stiegelbauer, 1991).

## Creating Inclusive Learning Communities

Many critics of our current educational system argue that the most logical response to our rapidly evolving social, economic, and political contexts is to create schools that are grounded in democratic principles and the constructs of social justice (Goodlad, 1984; Rifkin, 1997; Sarason, 1995; Skrtic, 1995b). These values are embodied in the concept of inclusive school communities designed to support the education of all students. The concept of inclusive schooling involves "the practice of including everyone—irrespective of

talent, disability, socioeconomic background, or cultural origin—in supportive mainstream schools and classrooms where all student needs are met" (Karagiannis, Stainback, & Stainback, 1996, p. 3). The basic premise of inclusive school communities is that all children, with or without disabilities, and including those with linguistic, ethnic, cultural, and socioeconomic differences, belong in school and should have access to similar broad educational outcomes. The challenge in inclusive school communities is to provide a diverse student body with access to these outcomes and to ensure, to the maximum extent possible, that all students have opportunities to achieve the highest possible quality of life. These challenges are met when we embody the concepts of inclusion, community, collaboration, democracy, and diversity and when "all children and members of the community have a future of fulfilled human and community potential, security, belonging, and valued interdependence leading to meaningful contributions" (Coots, Bishop, Grenot-Scheyer, & Falvey, 1995, p. 19). Inclusive school communities are synonymous with what many people mean when they call for school renewal and restructuring (Stainback & Stainback, 1996), so they serve as a vehicle for school reform. This text challenges you to develop the knowledge and skills needed to create and sustain inclusive school communities and thus to become a part of school reform and improvement.

For our purposes, we should distinguish between inclusive school communities and the concept of inclusion. While we certainly draw from the principles and values of inclusion, the term is often applied more narrowly than we intend here. Over the past several years, particularly within the field of special education, there has been much debate regarding the context in which students with disabilities should receive their education. Placements for students with disabilities vary from separate schools, some residential in nature, to general education classrooms (see Chapter 2). Often, discussions about "inclusion" focus solely on the goal of having students with disabilities attend their neighborhood schools and participate in general education classrooms with necessary supporting services. Our discussion is broader and propounds the idea that inclusive school communities are both a process for and an outcome of social justice, equity, and democracy within our educational system (Siegel, 1995; Skrtic, 1995a; Wlodkowski & Ginsberg, 1995). While we embrace the values and beliefs underlying earlier discussions about inclusion, we expand on discussions of placement to address issues of school organization, **governance,** assessment, curriculum, instruction, and classroom management that respond to the needs of all students, not just those with ability differences. Creating and sustaining inclusive school communities addresses calls for reform in both the general and special education communities (Lipsky & Gartner, 1998).

## Envisioning New Schools Through the Eyes of Students with Disabilities

In this text, we provide you with a framework for your career as an educational professional. As you begin to understand the concepts that will sustain inclusive school communities, you will read about Annie, Michael, Tanya, Kirk, and Kurume. All five of these students and their experiences are real. While all five students have disability labels, more importantly, they have ability differences. Like many students who receive special education services, these students and their families have had varying levels of success in working with educators to ensure that their individual needs were met. We have made a point of selecting case studies that reflect both the successes and the failures of the special education system. It is vital that professionals entering the system understand both its

strengths and its weaknesses so they can help improve the quality of services each student receives.

We use these five case studies to elaborate on concepts we introduce in subsequent chapters. The solutions we employ to meet the real-life challenges of teaching students with ability differences provide a template for the process of meeting the learning needs of all students. As you create classroom learning environments in which student diversity is supported, you, too, will be promoting inclusive learning communities.

## ■ SECTION SUMMARY

Recent research suggests that the traditional conventions of schools and classrooms are becoming outmoded. Growing numbers of students from diverse ethnic, linguistic, cultural, and socioeconomic backgrounds and with diverse abilities and educational needs are entering our schools, and school professionals must grow and adapt to meet these challenges. As part of this emerging vision, inclusive school communities grounded in democratic principles and the constructs of social justice for all support the concept of equal educational opportunities for all learners—including students with disabilities. Before we continue the discussion of schooling in the twenty-first century, let us take a detailed look at each of our five case study learners: Annie, Tanya, Kurume, Michael, and Kirk.

## CASE STUDY

### ANNIE  *A Student with Intensive Support Needs*

**A**nnie is nine years old. She lives in Fort Tipton, with her mom and dad, Debbie and Dave. Her older brother and sister, Dave junior and Emily, now attend Thomas Jefferson Middle School. Fort Tipton is not much bigger than it was at the turn of the century. About 5000 people live in town, but the town provides services to the surrounding ranchers and farmers. Dave manages the local supermarket, while Debbie volunteers at the local community hospital. Debbie also has been the den mother of Dave junior's Boy Scout troop and works at the elementary school library on Friday mornings.

Annie goes to school at Humphrey's Elementary School, the only elementary school in her rural community. Annie's classroom has five other children

who, like Annie, have been labeled as having multiple disabilities. This is called a self-contained classroom, since children without disabilities are not included.

Annie has a rare genetic disorder called Cornelia de Lange syndrome. Like other children who have this syndrome, she is small in stature, about 36 inches tall, and her fingers and toes are short and flat. Her face has the characteristic bushy eyebrows that meet in the middle, and she has particularly small facial features. The bridge of her nose is rather flat and her eyes are widely spaced.

Annie uses a walker or crawls to explore her environment. She is a responsive child who initiates all kinds of interactions with her family. As is typical of most children with Cornelia de Lange syndrome,

Annie has severe mental retardation. She communicates nonverbally, by pointing and gesturing, because she has not yet learned to speak. The thing that concerns her family the most is the way Annie often hurts herself. Her family reports how she might bite her hand as often as five or six times in a minute. She has open sores on her face where she has picked at her skin.

At home, Annie seems comfortable and loves to play with her sister. She crawls all around her trilevel home and often goes to her own room and brings her toys out to the family room to play. She communicates nonverbally but effectively with her family members.

The family is concentrating on helping Annie learn to dress herself, pick up her toys, and make her own bed. It's still hard to take Annie out to church or grocery shopping because of her skin picking and biting and because she cries loudly when she's unhappy. As a result, the whole family seldom goes out together. But the family hopes the school will help them develop effective ways to teach Annie the skills that would allow her to participate in her community along with the rest of her family.

Debbie is increasingly worried about the differences in Annie's behavior at home and at school. At school, Annie is a different child. Her five classmates range in age from 6 to 12, but she rarely initiates interactions with her classmates or with her teacher. Typically, she sits quietly and picks at her skin when she is placed in group activities like music or morning circle. Her teacher, Ms. Grady, works with Trudy, a para-educator in her classroom. School starts at 8:30 with calendar and morning circle. Then the speech therapist works with the children to encourage them in making sounds and words. At 10:00, the children practice taking their shoes off and putting them back on. At 10:30, when the rest of the children in the school have finished their recess, Ms. Grady and Trudy take Annie's class out to the playground. After recess comes snack time, music, and lunch. After lunch, the children listen to stories during rest time. The day wraps up with an art activity and classroom tidying. Trudy and Ms. Grady put the children on the special education bus at the end of the day, fastening their seat belts or harnesses. When Annie gets on the bus, she begins to make sing-song noises. She straightens her posture and looks out the window, smiling.

Dave doesn't attend the school meetings about Annie, but it's evident when he picks her up and hugs her that he loves Annie dearly. Although their marriage seems strong now, Debbie and Dave had difficulty when Annie first came home from the hospital. Dave didn't want people from the infant and toddler services coming into his home, and he even turned away the public health nurse. Debbie was afraid. Although she had successfully raised her two other infants, Annie's little body and her odd cries made Debbie question her parenting skills. Nor would Dave let her get help. By the time Annie was 6 months old, Debbie, fatigued and emotionally spent, was hospitalized for pneumonia. Dr. Turner, the family doctor, sat down with Dave in private and told him his family life was never going to be satisfactory unless he let his wife and Annie get the support they needed.

Fortunately, Dave was able to respond to Dr. Turner's advice. By working with the infant and toddler center, Debbie gained confidence in her skills in interpreting and responding to Annie's needs. Her confidence helped Dave junior and Emily develop active sibling relationships with Annie. Dave became more involved in the day-to-day care of Annie. Together, the family was able to create an environment that supported Annie and one another.

Now, however, the family is in jeopardy once more. Annie's depressed behavior at school is beginning to affect her health. She's not eating, and she's picking her skin even more. Both her weight loss and her skin picking are making her more vulnerable to infection. And the special education team at Humphrey's lacks the expertise to provide the kind of assistance that the family and Annie need.

## CASE STUDY

### TANYA  *Benefiting from Infant and Preschool Support Systems*

As Juanita was riding home on the bus one evening from her job, she noticed a mother and infant sitting across the aisle. She was reminded of the birth of her own child, Tanya, now 3 years old. Juanita was 16 and living with her mother and father when Tanya was born. The memory of that day still brought tears to her eyes.

Four days after Juanita and her parents moved into their new apartment, Juanita, only six-and-a-half months pregnant, awoke early in the morning with strong, forceful contractions. Her parents rushed her to their local community hospital. Juanita implored the Virgin of Guadeloupe, a patroness of Mexico, to help her endure what was to come. She was in labor for fifteen scary, painful hours. She was told that the baby would be extremely small and, its survival in jeopardy, would have to be transported to a hospital 70 miles away with an intensive care unit. Juanita cried and prayed. Her parents offered a *mandas* (a promise in return for God's intervention) to God and vowed to take Juanita and the baby (if the baby survived) to visit a shrine in Mexico. When Tanya was finally born, the nurse whisked her away and told Juanita that she could not hold her because "she is too small." Juanita felt crushed and bewildered.

Tanya weighed just 2 pounds, 6 ounces and had several medical complications, including a condition in which fluid collects in the brain, called hydrocephalus, and a breathing disorder, respiratory distress syndrome, caused by the immaturity of her lungs. The doctors and nurses told Juanita that her baby might not live because she was so small and had so many serious complications.

Tanya spent the first two months of her life in the hospital's neonatal intensive care unit. She had surgery to repair the hydrocephalus, but her lungs were still underdeveloped. Tanya was plugged into many different monitors and was given medication through an intravenous (IV) tube in her scalp. She looked fragile and helpless with the respirator tubes taped to her face and with needles and tubes everywhere. Many thoughts ran through Juanita's mind: "Will she ever come home? Is she in pain? How long will I have to drive 70 miles just to look at her through the glass of the isolette?" Juanita felt as if her baby belonged more to the nurses than to her; she felt so incompetent around the child. Meanwhile, the nurses were wondering why Juanita didn't visit her baby more often. The nursing staff didn't understand that being around this very sick, small baby only made Juanita feel more guilty and sad.

Juanita and her parents wanted to bring a *curandero* (healer) to see Tanya and seek a cure for the baby, but the hospital staff wouldn't permit it. Only family members were allowed in the unit. After two months, Tanya's lungs improved to the point that she was able to go home. Juanita was excited and pleased but apprehensive about her ability to take care of such a *cruatyra* (precious little one). On several occasions over the next three years, Juanita had to return to the hospital with Tanya due to infections and pneumonia.

And now? Juanita and Tanya still live with Juanita's parents, Elodia and Javier. Tanya has been late in her development due to her prematurity, the complications at her birth, and some recurring illnesses. Tanya didn't walk until she was 2½ years old. She has trouble figuring out how to use a door handle she hasn't seen before or how to find her clothes when they've been put in the wrong drawer. She just started putting two words together. And sometimes she combines Spanish and English when she talks.

Tanya loves to play "dress-up" and wears her mother's shoes, belts, and old T-shirts around the house. She often has her baby doll in tow and wants adults to help her dress and undress her "baby." Tanya is very good at helping with simple jobs in the kitchen. She dislikes getting her hands dirty and refuses to play with finger paints or to touch "gooey" things. One of her favorite daily events is to take a bubble bath and play with her toys in the bathtub. She goes to mass every Sunday with her mom and likes to sing when she's there.

Juanita is now 19 years old and single. She dropped out of high school when Tanya was born but earned her General Education Diploma (GED) by going to night school. When Tanya was 18 months old, Juanita learned from a friend at church about a center that offered early-intervention supports for infants and toddlers with developmental delays. The teachers who worked at the center interviewed Juanita and observed Tanya at home. Juanita and the teachers met and decided that Tanya would benefit by being involved in the activities of the center. Juanita enrolled Tanya and had a home visitor come to see her once a month to check-up on Tanya's development.

Not only did the home visitor check Tanya, but she made suggestions to Elodia, Tanya's grandmother, and to Juanita about activities that they could use to get Tanya to explore her environment and develop her language skills. Both Elodia and Juanita enjoyed the activities and ideas the home visitor suggested and thought they could see many improvements in Tanya's skills. Javier, the grandfather, thought that Tanya would improve without all the special attention, so he was usually working outside when the home visitor came.

Now that Tanya is 3, she attends a preschool in her neighborhood three mornings a week. Since Tanya had been labeled by the early intervention center as preschool disabled, it was important to find a preschool program that would meet her learning and social needs. Juanita also wanted to make sure that Tanya would go to a preschool with other children in the neighborhood, so she worked with the preschool intervention center to find the right school for Tanya.

Through early assessment and conversations with Tanya's home visitor, Tanya's preschool teachers have come to understand her need for individual learning supports. Juanita talks to the teachers frequently about the ways that they can all help Tanya learn. As a result, Juanita and the teachers are working with the child to learn concepts such as "over, under, and around." They want Tanya to increase her vocabulary and to speak in simple sentences. Both the teachers and Juanita are trying to encourage Tanya to use words instead of gestures to communicate. They are also encouraging Tanya to participate in activities that include lots of movement, such as running, swinging, climbing, and jumping, so that

she can confidently navigate and explore her home and classroom. Everyone agrees that communication and mobility are important tools that will help Tanya to develop her cognitive and social skills.

Now that Juanita is working, she depends on Tanya's *abuela* (grandmother) to make sure that some of the activities Tanya needs help with are being accomplished during the day. Juanita is proud of Tanya and believes that someday she will "catch up" to her peers.

## CASE STUDY

### KURUME *Preparing for the Transition to Adulthood*

"You know, Dad, I really worry about what I'm going to do with my life—maybe I should quit my part-time job at the car wash and find a job that would give me more experience with computers." At 18, Kurume, a young African-American man who has profound deafness, says this to his father because he has begun to realize that the transition he is about to face has to be more carefully planned for him than it usually is for other kids his age. His dad thinks, "We have come a long way—I just hope we can find our way through the next few years."

Kurume was born deaf, but no one suspected it because he was the first child born to Mattie and Ed, who had been married less than two years when he was born. They thought their new son was an angel—sleeping through loud noises and all kinds of commotion. His mother took a leave of absence from her job and stayed home with him for his first year. She began to suspect that something was wrong because his "babbling" stage lasted only a few weeks; then he stopped making many sounds. Mattie mentioned this to the pediatrician, who dismissed her as a nervous first-time mom. She stopped talking about it so much, but her fears were mounting. One day, at home in the kitchen, she walked behind Kurume while he was happily playing with some plastic bowls and lids and blew a whistle just to see what would happen. Kurume never noticed. When she later told the pediatrician about this incident, he ordered a hearing test. To her extreme dismay, the audiologist confirmed her worst fears.

The diagnosis was profound deafness. The pediatrician advised Mattie and Ed to keep Kurume at home until he was 5 and then to send him to a state school for students who are deaf and/or blind. Mattie and Ed never really considered that possibility and decided instead to search for a program that would help them meet Kurume's needs at home. Naturally,

they wanted their child to be like the other kids. So they decided to try an auditory training program in which Kurume would get speech therapy and learn to speak. At 18 months, little Kurume began going to "speech school," and he continued until he was 6 years old. The program helped him learn to produce speech sounds, taught him basic vocabulary, and seemed in some ways like a typical preschool program—except that none of the children in the program could hear or speak to each other very well. Kurume was taught to pay close attention to the speaker and to other signals in his environment. He was a bright and active child and was happy in school.

When Kurume turned 6, Mattie and Ed decided that he should go to St. Anne's kindergarten program, where most families in their church sent their kids. Kurume had a speaking vocabulary of about fifty words by then, and they thought he would learn more words by playing with children who talked all the time. The teachers felt that Kurume wouldn't be able to keep up with the class, however, and by the middle of the year, they advised Mattie and Ed to move Kurume to a public school program that emphasized oral skills for children with hearing impairments.

Kurume's next school was Porter Elementary, where he continued until he was 12 in what was called a "mainstreamed" class. Mainstreaming meant that the children were all in a separate special education classroom most of the day but went to physical education, music, art, lunch, and recess with other children their own age. The special education teacher for the deaf who managed Kurume's mainstreamed class said that as soon as she could be sure that he could use five- to six-word sentences and could understand 90 percent of what the classroom teacher said, she would allow him to attend regular grade-level classes. Kurume was happy at this school, but he never really got to know many of the kids his age because he couldn't quite keep up in the classroom.

Meanwhile, Mattie and Ed had two other children, and Mattie became a full-time mom. She volunteered as a den mother so Kurume could be a Cub Scout. Some of the other parents objected, but Mattie's presence at Cub Scout activities made it a little easier for Kurume to participate. She helped the other kids learn how to play and communicate with him.

As Kurume grew older, Mattie and Ed feared for his transition to junior high. They were concerned that his lack of language skills was limiting both his academic progress and his social development. They explored all the programs available in the city and found a "total communication" program at Grant Junior High that would teach Kurume both oral and sign language skills. Grant was referred to as a "center" school, but Kurume spent most of his day in a special education classroom with a special teacher for the hearing impaired. His school friends were mostly other boys with hearing impairments. He thinks back on that as a lonely time because he had to ride the bus across town to get to school and none of his school friends lived nearby. During these years, Kurume made some neighborhood friends because of his younger brother, Rashaan. Because Rashaan knew all the local kids, he was able to ease Kurume's entry into neighborhood games and activities. It also helped that Mattie, Ed, Rashaan, and his sister, Kaneesha, began to learn sign language, and, little by little, so did the neighborhood kids.

Kurume now goes to Kennedy High School near his home and, for the first time in his educational experience, attends regular classes most of the day. Coincidentally, his English teacher also has a hearing impairment, but having an interpreter has made the biggest difference for Kurume. With the help of the interpreter, he finds that he can take reasonably good notes during class and that they really help him when he does his homework and studies for tests. So far,

he has done reasonably well academically, earning B's and C's in most classes.

Kurume is a natural athlete and excels at swimming and basketball. His friendships with other athletes have grown, and he is often invited to parties and participates in many other school activities. As a photographer for the yearbook in his junior year, he developed an interest in camera equipment and was seen behind the camera at many high school sports events. Now, during the summer before his senior year, he has a part-time job at a car wash. Kurume gets along pretty well with his co-workers even though communication is sometimes difficult. Some of the kids at the car wash think it's "cool" to learn some basic signs, but Kurume relies on oral language much of the time at work.

Now that all three of her children are in school, Mattie has returned to work as a systems analyst and has shown Kurume quite a bit about the computers that she works on. Mattie and Ed were divorced a few years ago. Kurume lives with his mother but sees his father every weekend and relies on heart-to-heart conversations with both his parents. Kurume really loves computers and is saving to buy his own PC.

Kurume asks many of the same questions that other kids his age ask: "What do I want to do with my life? Could I go to college? Will I be able to get a job I like?" He is a little worried about taking on full responsibility for living on his own, but, like most 18-year-olds, he is very eager to be independent of his parents.

Kurume thinks he has a good chance at life because he had to "make it" in a regular high school and in a regular job. Kurume firmly believes that he's learned some things that he might not have learned had he gone to a school exclusively for students who were deaf. Kurume's family had high expectations for him and provided lots of guidance and support. Their attitude of seeing him as a person first, not a deaf child, allowed them to focus on helping him to develop his own skills, abilities, and interests, and not on his deafness.

## CASE STUDY

## MICHAEL  *Struggling to Get the Support He Needs*

"**M**om, I'd rather not turn in my work than get an F on something I turn in." Michael Lee and his mother Anita were having this conversation on their way back from a meeting at Skyview High School. Anita understood Michael's frustration, but she was

concerned that it might develop into a dropout mentality. She wondered if she would ever be able to get the supports Michael needed to stay in school; it wouldn't happen if today's meeting was any indication. Anita was amazed that, as an administrator for the state department of education, she was well aware of Michael's rights and knowledgeable about the special education process, and yet she and Michael continued to meet resistance when advocating for his special education services needs.

Michael started school and had difficulty in kindergarten with activities such as coloring, cutting, and skipping. Even though he was a young 5-year-old, Anita was assured by his day care providers and preschool teacher that he was ready for school. In first grade, he had trouble learning letter sounds and remembering sight words. And sometimes his teacher had trouble getting Michael to respond in class; he was obstinate and refused to do his work. A regular education, building-level referral meeting was held at which it was decided that he would receive assistance from the educational consultant. In second and third grade, Michael continued to receive individual or small-group remedial instruction from the educational consultant and remained on target with his reading, math, and written language skills.

By the end of third grade, Michael had used the maximum number of hours he could spend with the educational consultant without being placed into special education. Fourth grade began, and he was on his own. Within five weeks, both his teacher and Anita realized that there were problems. His teacher was having to individualize his spelling by having him repeat second- and third-grade mastery words. He often could not remember what he wanted to write (although verbally he was very expressive). And when he could remember, often he could not figure out how to spell the words. He also had difficulty comprehending what he *was* able to read, although his vocabulary was strong enough that frequently he was able to "make up" words that would fit in the context of what he was trying to read. Michael's teacher and Anita unknowingly initiated a special education referral within three days of each other. Michael was trying hard, but he was extremely frustrated and could not understand why he had so little success.

Michael was found to be eligible for special education in fourth grade with a primary disability label of "learning disabilities." He was placed in a resource room with small group and one-to-one instruction for forty-five to ninety minutes daily. His goals were to (1) improve spelling, written language, proofreading, and editing skills, (2) remediate skill gaps in math, (3) compensate for tracking and visual perceptual weaknesses, and (4) maintain legible handwriting over an increasing length of time. All went well for the remainder of the year.

Then Michael began fifth grade. Anita waited for almost three weeks, asking Michael daily if he was going to the resource room, but the answer was always no. Anita met with his teacher to discuss what services Michael was receiving. The teacher told Anita that she was team teaching with the regular education teacher during reading. When Anita asked what services Michael was receiving on written language, spelling, and math, the answer was, "none." The teacher explained that the school had decided to change its delivery model. The only services he would receive would be through team teaching in the regular classroom. Anita reminded the teacher that an individualized education plan (IEP) review had not been done and that there could be no change in services without one. Anita requested an immediate IEP review and the immediate resumption of resource room services. An IEP review was held, and the recommended placement was for the regular classroom plus the resource room 350–370 minutes weekly. The rest of the year went well.

A troublesome pattern of service delivery again emerged in sixth grade and continued through eighth grade. First, services on Michael's IEPs would not begin until three to four weeks into the school year. Second, there was little communication between his special education and general education teachers, to the extent that the regular education teachers did not even know Michael had been identified as needing special education support services. Third, Michael would move from going to the resource room to a team-teaching situation to receiving no support, all of this without a formal review of his IEP or without formal notification of and approval by Anita. Finally, whenever Anita requested meetings prior to the actual date of Michael's annual review (May), she was informed that the teachers simply did not have the time.

Michael's progress through junior high varied. The supports he received in the area of language arts seemed to help. But throughout those years, Michael experienced great difficulties in math. He failed basic skills tests and, at the end of eighth grade, was still having problems with basic computation procedures. The only way the school was willing to support his math needs was if he attended special education math classes; otherwise, he was on his own. Michael was struggling between admitting that he needed help and not wanting to go to a "special place" to receive it. He insisted on attending the general education math classes. By the end of eighth grade, however, Anita demanded that he be moved to the special education math class and agreed to have him take a "selected topics" math course at the high school next fall.

During March of his eighth-grade year, Michael had to register for high school. Anita, Michael's father Chen, and Michael received the registration packet and discovered that the selected topics math course was not being offered the following year. Anita called the counselor and was referred to the assistant principal, who was responsible for managing special education services at the high school.

At that meeting, Anita and Michael were told that Michael should sign up for geometry instead of the selected topics course, which would be followed in subsequent years by Algebra I and Algebra II, or for a new four-year course offering called the "Interactive Mathematics Program (IMP)." Anita asked what special education supports and services would be provided in either of these classes for Michael. The answer was, "none." Anita told the assistant principal that she did not think Michael could handle either class without support, since he basically skipped eighth-grade math. At that point, the assistant principal turned to Anita and said, "*You* really have a problem." The assistant principal then suggested that Michael enroll in one of these classes anyway, and if he could not do the work, they would

move him. Anita told her that this would set Michael up for failure and was unacceptable. Next the assistant principal suggested a special education math class, which is taught at about the fourth-grade level and would not qualify the student for college entrance. Michael told the assistant principal that he planned on going to college. At that point, the assistant principal suggested that perhaps Anita should help Michael understand that college was not for him.

Anita pressed for a description of the special education supports and services Michael could expect in high school. She discovered that for Michael to receive any special education support, he would have to sign up for an elective course called "Learning Strategies." Michael balked. Students were allowed two electives. He had been recommended to take Accelerated Spanish 101 and a band class because of his strengths in Spanish and music. Why should he have to give those up to receive supports to which he was entitled? The assistant principal had no suggestions other than to insist that a choice would have to be made to drop either Spanish or the band elective.

## CASE STUDY

### KIRK   *A Student Whose Behaviors Challenge His Teachers and Peers*

Kirk's mom and dad, General and Mrs. Grant, live in a neighborhood of large homes with lavish landscaping. Kirk's mother married the general twenty years ago, after the death of his first wife. When General and Mrs. Grant combined their households, they each had children from their previous marriages. Mrs. Grant's three sons had enjoyed a close relationship with their late father. General Grant's daughters both attended St. Agnes Episcopal Academy, where they were on the honor role. By the time Kirk was born, these children had gone on to college, so Kirk was essentially raised as an only child.

General Grant, now retired, has several consultation contracts with government agencies in the Middle East. While these jobs allow the family to continue its affluent lifestyle, Kirk's dad is gone for long periods of time, just as he was during his military career. As a result, Kirk's mom has had to raise her son more or less on her own. Kirk's mom is a soft-spoken woman who defers both to her husband and to school professionals. She has tried to carry out the recommendations of various teachers over

the years, but Kirk continues to challenge her leadership and guidance, as he does with his teachers at school.

At age 14, Kirk is very small in stature and has a disheveled appearance. A year ago, Kirk was removed from Bell Middle School after he was caught selling marijuana to other eighth-graders. By court order, Kirk was declared a delinquent and committed to a residential child care facility where he currently lives and attends school with other young men who have social and behavioral problems. To avoid a stricter sentence, General and Mrs. Grant agreed to remain involved with the school program and to work on improving their family communication and interpersonal dynamics.

Kirk's history of serious behavioral and attendance problems in school dates back to fourth grade. His school record indicates problems with lack of attention, impulsive behavior, difficulty with conforming to classroom rules, anxiety, lack of social skills, and arguments with authority figures. By fifth grade, he was diagnosed with attention deficit hyperactivity disorder (ADHD) and other conduct disorders and placed in a special education classroom for students with emotional disorders. Kirk was also prescribed Ritalin, a drug that physicians often use to control hyperactivity. However, his behavior continued to be problematic, and he was suspended five times that year for hitting other students, as well as teachers. From fourth through eighth grade, Kirk's grade point average (GPA) hovered around 2.0 even though his teachers and parents believed he was capable of much better performance. His records show that he missed an average of thirty-five days of school per year.

Now in ninth grade, Kirk's achievement test scores indicate that he is performing three years below his grade level on math, reading, and writing skills. His GPA is 1.5. Because he goes to school at the residential child care facility, his classmates are also students with serious behavioral problems. The curriculum focuses on basic math and reading skills, as well as programs in anger management and substance abuse. Kirk recently discontinued his Ritalin because, in his own words, "the counselor here doesn't believe in using drugs." His individual education plan (IEP) focuses on changing his behavior by using methods designed to decrease verbal outbursts, reinforce communicating in a respectful manner, and displaying positive social behavior.

His teacher thinks of Kirk as a problem youth who has made little progress in his academic and social behaviors despite living at the facility for almost a year. It's now time to revisit Kirk's plan for improvement. As part of planning to help involve Kirk in setting proactive goals for himself, he was asked to participate in the following interview with his counselor, Mollie. As you will read, Kirk remains loyal to his peers and angry toward the school. What is evident, unfortunately, is that Kirk is attached to a group of friends who promote and support violent behavior.

*Mollie:* If there wasn't any school tomorrow, what would you miss the most?

*Kirk:* Nothing! Well my friends, I guess, because that's where we hang out.

*Mollie:* Is there anything besides your friends?

*Kirk:* No, school sucks, I don't like it. The teacher's always on my case, he hates me. But I guess I would rather be there than in lockup. And I would miss my school points so I wouldn't make my level [in reference to the token economy behavior management system used in the school], so that's what I would miss the most. But I hate school.

*Mollie:* What makes you come to school and why?

*Kirk:* I have to come to school, it's part of my program. Anyway I don't want to hang out by myself all day. And sometimes we get to do all-right stuff like make up songs.

*Mollie:* Well, what made you go to your regular school before you got into trouble?

*Kirk:* My mom would make me go. It used to be all right—I mean, my friends would be there and it was just the place to go, so I went. Middle school was all right, the teachers were pretty cool there, and I liked going, but that was when I was a little kid.

*Mollie:* Is there anything that makes you feel like you belong to the school you go to? Think of things that make you feel comfortable in that way.

*Kirk:* Well, my friends, I guess. This is a cool school because me and a bunch of my friends are here. This is our school—we run it!

*Mollie:* Kirk, what kinds of things do you think other people say about you?

*Kirk:* That I'm headed for the state penitentiary!

*Mollie:* Why?

*Kirk:* Because I'm crazy and everybody knows that I'll go down with my friends eventually.

*Mollie:* Well, what do you think your teachers would say about you if I asked them?

*Kirk:* Well, my music teacher would probably say I was OK. She's pretty cool. My other teachers though, don't even ask them! They'll tell you I don't want to learn nothing. They hate me!

*Mollie:* Finish the following question for me. When I get angry I . . .

*Kirk:* Shoot them. Or make them hurt so bad that they'll never mess with us again.

*Mollie:* How do you feel about that?

*Kirk:* I feel good, I feel great!

*Mollie:* Well, what would you like to do when somebody tries to make you do something?

*Kirk:* Tell them that I'm not their slave. I'm my own person. I don't do stuff I don't want to do.

*Mollie:* Where do you think you fit in best? At school, at home, where?

*Kirk:* I fit in with my friends. I hate school, and I don't get along with my parents. I don't want to talk about my family. When are we going to be finished?

*Mollie:* What do you need from school in order to be successful?

*Kirk:* My GED.

*Mollie:* Well, what would it take for you to become a top-notch student?

*Kirk:* I'm not good in school. I can't understand stuff. I hate school.

*Mollie:* If you could wish for one thing in school, what would it be?

*Kirk:* That it didn't exist. I hate all f—ing schools and all teachers.

*Mollie:* If you were to give advice to another kid who has been caught or is being questioned by a police officer, what would it be?

*Kirk:* If the cop doesn't know you, then give another kid's name, birthday, and social security number. That way they can't check on your warrants. Always say that you didn't see what happened, and never admit to anything. That way they probably won't take you in.

*Mollie:* OK, last question. Is there anything that somebody who might want to work in a school needs to know about kids your age?

*Kirk:* Tell them that we would probably do better if they were understanding. It would make us want to try harder. I guess that's how it was at my old school, but that was a long time ago. Schools aren't like that anymore.

---

# The Need for Educational Reform

The foundations of school reform are embedded in vital political, social, and economic contexts that exceed the scope of this chapter. Educational reform undoubtedly is linked to the future well being of our society. Here, we focus on only three of the many compelling issues in school reform: (1) organization of schools, (2) changing **demographics,** and (3) changing economics. We have chosen these three topics, not necessarily because they present the most compelling moral reasons for reform, but rather because they pose the most immediate challenges to successful outcomes for students.

The changing demographics of the U.S. population have contributed to the unprecedented diversity in our school population and, along with social and economic conditions, have led to the need for changes in the purpose, function, and operation of our educational system. The goal of schooling has shifted from preparing a select group of students to pursue higher education to providing an education for all students. Our economy once required workers who could perform repetitive factory jobs, but now industry and business demand workers who have initiative, as well as problem-solving, interpersonal, and thinking skills. The Internet and other global communications have increased our access to information on a worldwide basis, relieving teachers from being the "be all, end all" source for student learning. Finally, advances in **cogni-**tive psychology and brain research have expanded our understanding of how we learn.

The organizational structures and policies of schools do not yet reflect all of the rapid changes in our demographic, economic, and social bases and in our knowledge about how humans learn. Here we provide a rationale for the failure of schools to meet the challenges of today and tomorrow. In doing so, we hope you will see that inclusive school communities represent a significant shift in the ways schools are organized and deliver educational services.

## How Schools Are Organized

While social and economic agendas shift rapidly and would seem to require related changes in the function and purpose of schools, most schools maintain the status quo (Cuban, 1996; Daggett, in O'Neil, 1995). Schools are so resistant to change partly because of their organizational schemata. One popular view is that schools should be organized and operated like a factory, with the ultimate purpose being to "produce" a standard program (MacKinnon & Brown, 1994). Ironically, the somewhat rigid organization and curricula of schools today originally arose as a direct response to the unprecedented economic growth of the latter half of the nineteenth century, which created jobs in an industrial economy. By 1860, the United States was manufacturing a variety of tools and interchangeable parts that enabled the proliferation of industry. Production

## Extending Your Learning

When you think about diversity, what do you think about? Probably you think about individuals' skin colors, their languages, their socioeconomic backgrounds, their religious customs, and perhaps even the kinds of food they eat. Have you ever thought to yourself, "How odd that he chose that color for his sweater?" or "Why is she spending all of that time bounding off rocks or jumping out of airplanes?" Diversity includes more than ethnic, cultural, socioeconomic, and linguistic differences; it also includes tastes, preferences, sexual orientations, gender differences, communication styles, and, most appropriately, differences in the skills and capacities of learners. Students who demonstrate differences in learning are often considered and labeled "disabled." Conditions that affect students' physical, cognitive, communicative, or **affective** skills typically serve as the basis for diagnosing their disabilities (see Chapter 5). Ask yourself questions like "What am I going to have to know and do in order to support all children in my school community?" While you read this chapter, track the changes that take place in your image of schools, classrooms, and professional roles as you consider and learn about inclusive school communities.

Talents

of these products required workers able to consistently perform repetitive tasks. Schools were capable of turning out individuals (usually white males) with these skills since it was relatively easy to add vocational training to the school curriculum. As Marshall McLuhan suggested in 1962, schools appeared to develop their curricula in the image of the mass production assembly line. In the educational system, our current five-day week, seven-hour day, and division of labor between disciplines, between teacher and student, and between administrator and teacher simulate the industrial schedule and pattern of interactions.

Schools have responded to students who were nonmale and/or nonwhite by creating subassembly lines for female children, children of color, and children with disabilities. Historically, students with disabilities have been educated through the special education system and placed in schools or programs separate from the ones their nondisabled peers attended. Some believe that this process of sorting oc-

curs because school organizations are based on the factory model and require consistency in their "raw materials" to turn out standard products. When students did not meet the standard or when they required extra help to achieve, they were systematically sorted, selected, and relegated to programs separate from the general education classroom and curriculum standards (Carlson & O'Reilly, 1996; DuFour, 1995; Grenot-Scheyer, Coots, & Bishop, 1995; Karagiannis, Stainback, & Stainback, 1996; Kozol, 1991). And the more different students were perceived to be, the farther they tended to be moved from the general education system and buildings. Specialized asylums, state schools, reformatories, and orphanages were used to address the needs of student populations that were deemed to be nonproductive or incapable.

Special education, as a subsystem of the broader education system, has its own policies and procedures, funding, organizational structures, personnel, and professional practices. It is an example of one subassembly line among many. Bilingual education, vocational education, and **Title I** literacy programs also take students who don't fit the standard system. Other categories of students who receive special programs from specifically trained personnel include children of migrant farm workers, children with limited English proficiency, children with special gifts and talents, and neglected and abused children (Carlson & O'Reilly, 1996). Through the traditional general education/special education approach to education, general educators are responsible for "typical" students while experts in the areas of learning, reading, language, physical needs, and mental health needs are responsible for identified groups of learners whose needs fall into one or more of those areas. Special educators are responsible for children identified as eligible for special education services.

When students demonstrate difficulties in learning conventionally, our educational system sorts them out into specialized subassembly lines. As the five case studies in this chapter show, these subassembly lines require personnel with specialized training. In Kirk's case, a special educator with certification in the area of emotional disorders assumes primary responsibility for his education. Similarly, Michael's special education needs would be supported by a teacher with certification in the area of learning disabilities. After leaving preschool, Tanya was served by a teacher who held a teaching certificate in the area of "moderate mental retardation."

Role differentiation among school professionals assumes that students' differences are more important than their shared traits and that one school professional cannot have adequate competencies to work with more than one type of child. The end result of **diversification** and expert-based models is that many school professionals believe they are able to work with only one type of student. Expert knowledge is necessary to work successfully with individuals such as those who have visual impairments or deafness. But when expert knowledge is translated into role-specific duties and responsibilities, the system becomes rigid. This rigidity makes it difficult to re-allocate resources in response to the shifting needs of learners and communities. An alternative to an expert-based role differentiation model would be collaborative, **transdisciplinary teaming,** in which professionals assume that it is their professional obligation to share their expertise and help others develop the skills to work effectively with students.

The organization of our schools has been described as a professional bureaucracy—one that focuses on performance and seeks standardization (Mintzberg, 1979; Skrtic, 1991, 1995b). Experience has shown that these professional bureaucracies will resist transforming their basic frameworks to respond to demographic, social, and global economic change (Cuban, 1996). However, the social and economic forces that have structured our schools are no longer the reality.

## How Changing Demographics Challenge School Organizations

The demographics of our school-age population are no longer consistent with a one-size-fits-all model of educational production. School professionals strain to meet the needs of a school population composed of individuals from ethnically, linguistically, and culturally diverse backgrounds, with varying levels of ability, as well as with the dynamics of alternative family structures and rising rates of children raised in poverty. The nearly 20 percent of children in our country who live in poverty (U.S. Department of Commerce, 1997) may come to school poorly fed and lacking access to books and the readiness skills that support their ability to function effectively in formal school environments. In 1996, over 30 percent of one-parent families had children under the age of 18 (U.S. Department of Commerce, 1997). Forty percent of Euro-American students and 80 percent of all African-American students reach the age of 17 with only one biological parent in the household (Olson & Hanson, 1990). In 1990, more than two-thirds of children had working mothers compared to 55 percent a decade earlier (Dunkle & Usdan, 1993). Figures 1.1–1.3 depict some of these changing demographic data. Demographics suggest that, by the year 2000, the majority of public school students in several western states, including California, Texas, New Mexico, Arizona, and Colorado will be His-

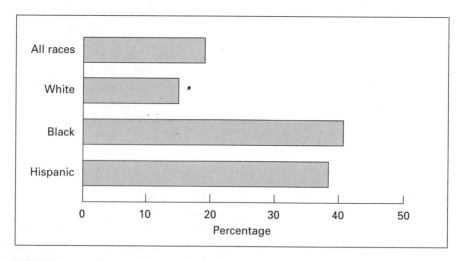

**FIGURE 1.1**  ■  Children Under 18 Living in Poverty, by Ethnicity
Source: U.S. Department of Commerce, 1997, p. 475.

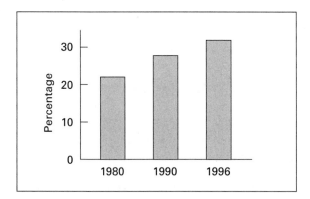

**FIGURE 1.2** ■ Change in Percentages of Single-Parent Families with Children Under 18, 1980–1996
Source: U.S. Department of Commerce, 1997, p. 63.

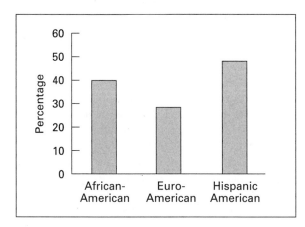

**FIGURE 1.3** ■ Single-Parent, Female-Headed Families in Poverty, by Ethnicity
Source: U.S. Bureau of the Census, 1998, pp. 60–201.

panic, Native American or African-American (Grossman, 1991). Nationwide, census projections indicate that, by the year 2010, 38 percent of the school population will be children of color (Hodgkinson, 1992). Over 4.5 million students in public schools speak a language other than English at home (Shannon & Hakuta, 1992). Finally, since 1975, children with disabilities, formerly excluded from public schools by and large, are now assured access to a free and appropriate public education through Public Law 94-142. As a result, the enrollment of students with disabilities has increased by 78 percent from the previous twenty years, with 5,373,077 served by special education during the 1993–94 school year (U.S. Department of Education, 1995).

These new educational consumers have values and beliefs about education, approaches to learning, sociocultural needs and expectations, and skills that create a conflict for an educational system formerly dominated by students who did not have disabilities and who were from a fairly homogenized sociocultural background—that is, from Euro-American, middle-class, two-parent families. Since educational systems are designed for **homogeneity,** they do not have the flexibility in their organizational schemata or professional roles to respond appropriately. The traditional sorting schema results in a bureaucracy of such complexity that it becomes redundant (different subassembly lines perform similar tasks), expensive (subassembly lines mean more specially trained and licensed professionals), and nonresponsive, and quality assurance becomes almost impossible (Sarason, 1990; Skrtic, 1995b).

The depth of the clash between the new educational consumers and existing school organizations is exemplified in studies that examine differences in teacher expectations, teacher bias, and teacher behavior toward students on the basis of ethnic, linguistic, economic, and ability differences (Cummins, 1986; Grant, 1984; Kozol, 1991; Matute-Bianchi, 1986; Moore & Cooper, 1984; U.S. Department of Education, 1991). For example, Montague and Applegate (1993) found that teachers concluded that students with learning disabilities could not handle problem-solving strategies without ever having given them a chance to try. In another study, Greenwood (1991) found that students' economic status was related to instructional time; specifically, students from schools in relatively affluent suburban areas received fifteen minutes more instruction per day than did students from schools in less affluent neighborhoods. While diversity has an impact on how schools are organized, how students are grouped for instruction, and how we choose to teach, economic agendas shape much of the content of what we teach.

## How Economics Challenge Our Educational Systems

As we have discussed, the educational system replicates the organizational schema of factories in that schools provide students with a standard set of information in an orthodox manner (MacKinnon & Brown, 1994).

Furthermore, the predominant set of information transmitted in schools is designed to prepare students to enter colleges and universities (Goodlad, 1984). When students fail in the college-bound track, they are assigned to classes that prepare them for a vocation. Common educational practices include instruction by telling, rote memorization, one-method instruction, one-answer response modes, memorization rules, template exercises, and routine worksheets (Steen, 1989). These practices grew out of an economic system that required workers who could pay attention to directions and complete repetitive tasks.

Unfortunately, the skills that high schoolers have acquired by the time they graduate and the needs of the marketplace are increasingly disconnected. Our economy requires highly skilled workers who can access, understand, and disseminate data from our information networks; work cooperatively in work groups; and interact with an increasingly diverse business community. Yet, business leaders tell educators that our high school graduates lack the ability to problem solve, think creatively, work effectively with others, and generalize solutions from one work task or environment to another, so they can learn new tasks. In a changing marketplace, organizations need workers who can retool quickly to fill new jobs, perform new skills, and even create jobs that have never before existed (Daggett, 1991; Rifkin, 1997).

Businesses and industries have learned that organizations with little or no hierarchy that matrix tasks across disciplines are more effective financially and more responsive to rapidly changing market forces (Peters, 1992). Workers must, accordingly, have skills in decision making, collaborative leadership, information analysis, and self-directed learning, and the emergence of a strong service industry requires that they have the social skills to work with one another and the public at large (Ford, Davern, & Schnorr, 1992). Major changes in school organization and curriculum offer-

ings are needed to foster student development and use of those skills.

## ■ SECTION SUMMARY

Schools need to find new ways of responding to the dilemmas posed by changing demographics and shifting economic agendas. No longer can schools afford to create bureaucracies that make their tasks more complex and hierarchical. Instead, schools must develop flexible organizational systems that can adapt to the changing needs of their consumers and yet still produce graduates with the skills to succeed in our socioeconomic system. Changes in the organizational principles of schools require school professionals who are willing to adjust their teaching methods and their curricula to meet the needs of their students. School professionals need to change not only what they teach but how they teach it. Educational reform is essential for schools to respond to the changing social, political, and economic realities of the twenty-first century. And special education provides us with a special case to study in depth. The issues special education faces are mirrored in the issues the educational system as a whole faces. By analyzing the special education system in greater depth, we may come to understand some of the broader aspects of educational reform that are so important for our society to adopt.

# Challenges to the Special Education System

## Special Education in Historical Perspective

References to children with disabilities have appeared in the literature for many centuries. One of the best-known accounts of such a child was written by Jean Marc Gaspard Itard (1775–1883). In his book *The Wild Boy of Aveyron,* Itard described his attempts to educate a child who had been abandoned in the woods of southern France. The boy was 12 when Itard met him, but he did not speak and had no social skills. The educational tasks Itard undertook on behalf of that boy are often identified as the beginning of special education.

By the mid-1800s, special schools had been created in the United States to educate students with deafness and blindness. State governments funded many of these while others were funded by local agencies and charitable organizations. By 1952, all but two states had legislation mandating education for some, but not all, persons with mental retardation. Although students with mild levels of mental retardation received public education, students with moderate or severe-to-profound levels were excluded and often were placed in state-run residential institutions (Beirne-Smith, Patton, & Ittenbach, 1994).

In 1975, this country made a formal commitment to the education of all students with disabilities with the passage of **Public Law (P.L.) 94-142,** the Education for All Handicapped Children Act. (Chapter 2 details the elements of this sweeping legislation.) In addition to assuring each child with a disability the right to an education, the law also provides funding for centers of research on disability, professional preparation to educate students with disabilities, and centers for parent information and training. As a result of the emphasis on research, we now know more about strategies that support learning for students with disabilities (Christenson, Ysseldyke, & Thurlow, 1989; Deschler, Ellis, & Lenz, 1996). We also know more about how to support their behavioral needs (Horner, 1994; Horner & Day, 1991; Savage, 1991). Through subsequent amendments to P.L. 94-142 (see Chapter 2), infants and toddlers can participate in early intervention programs and can receive early childhood special education. Now young children with disabilities and their families can take advantage of community-based preschool and day care services before they enter school (Vincent, 1995).

The system of special education services and programs that emerged as a result of P.L. 94-142 has provided educational opportunities for many children who would not otherwise have been educated. Judy Heumann, featured in our chapter-opening vignette, would have been able to attend school had she been of school age when P.L. 94-142 was passed. Despite the overall benefits, many special and general education reformers have suggested that P.L. 94-142 initially resulted in many unforeseen and unfortunate outcomes (Gartner & Lipsky, 1987; Kozol, 1991; Lipsky & Gartner, 1989).

In particular, three critical issues have been raised repeatedly (Skrtic, 1995a): (1) the benefits and drawbacks of categorizing and labeling students for specialized services, (2) the unintended overrepresentation of children from diverse ethnic, linguistic, and socio-economic backgrounds in special education, and (3) student outcomes from special education. As a result, serious policy debates have been about both the need for the **special education subsystem** and the way we respond to children with diverse learning needs (Gartner & Lipsky, 1987; Wang, Reynolds, & Walberg, 1989).

## Programming by Disability Labels

It's important to understand that school districts responded to the mandates of P.L. 94-142 by creating a separate, alternative educational subsystem with unique policies and regulations, funding, organizational structures, and personnel and professional practices (Swize, 1993). This was a logical response to a sweeping set of federal regulations that were charting unfamiliar territory for most school districts. Here we consider the unintended results of this bureaucracy.

"Inherent in the original approach to special education was the belief that appropriate services could be provided to children based on an identification of their major handicapping condition" (Swize, 1993, p. 3). In the initial implementation of the law, specialized programs were designed around each type of disability. Once students were identified and then labeled by disability, school systems assumed that their needs were being met, since services followed labeling (Reichler, 1980; Skrtic, 1995b). For example, when the label "learning disabled" was applied to Michael, the subject of one of our case studies, he was served in a resource room for students with learning disabilities. Similarly, because Kirk was labeled as "emotionally disturbed" (ED), he was served in a different classroom specifically organized for students classified as ED. It was assumed that all students with the same label had common educational needs and therefore could be helped by the same kind of program. Once a category was established, then a classroom or program could be created and the educational process begun (Reichler, 1980). As a result, most school systems had classrooms designed specifically for students with different levels of mental retardation (mild, moderate, or severe), specific learning disabilities, vision impairments, serious emotional disturbance, hearing impairments, and physical disabilities.

The use of labels and associated classification systems to provide special services to students with disabilities has come under attack. First, this categorical approach to education resulted from the belief that disability stemmed from deficits in the student rather than in the delivery of instruction, the configuration of schools, or social and economic conditions. Because they adopted competitive and intellectual goals as their product, schools were placed in a position of needing to sort students according to their potential for academic achievement. Yet, even the proponents of a labeling system for students served under P.L. 94-142 acknowledged that the by-products of labeling may well result in **stigmatization,** rejection, and exclusion (Hobbs, 1975; see also the chapter-opening vignette).

Second, despite extensive efforts to categorize and educate students by disability label, in practice there is little differentiation among educational objectives, instructional strategies, or curriculum content of the various **categorical-based classrooms** (Hocutt & Alberg, 1995; Sands, Adams, & Stout, 1995; Taylor & Racino, 1991; Ysseldyke, O'Sullivan, Thurlow, & Christianson, 1989). For instance, although Michael and Kirk had different labels and were sent to different types of classrooms to receive educational supports, research tells us that they probably worked on similar tasks geared toward the same outcomes, using similar types of teacher intervention (Ysseldyke et al., 1989). In fact, students within a given category probably differ as much from one another as they do from students in other categories (Meese, 1994).

Third, the system of labeling set up a continuum of placements that moved students with more significant disabilities farther and farther away from their home schools and/or their home communities. This isolated and constrained the opportunities provided to those students, and it contributed to a prevailing belief of people without disabilities that these places were necessary and desirable.

Finally, and perhaps most compelling, labeling and its accompanying demeaning perspectives have come under strong attack by the very people to whom they are directed—people with disabilities like Annie, Tanya, Kirk, Michael, and Kurume. While the law did not initiate the practice of labeling people, it codifies the practice. As a result, people with disabilities often are identified by their disability (for example, deaf kid, blind man, cripple) instead of being recognized individually. Most people with disabilities want to be recognized as people first, and not by their label, so there is now a preference for using references such as "students with mental retardation" as opposed to "re-

tarded students" (Williams & Shoultz, 1982). People with disabilities believe that the fact of their disability should be viewed as a natural part of their life and not used as a basis for exclusionary or discriminating actions (Colorado Developmental Disabilities Planning Council, 1995).

Debate persists regarding the relative merits and faults of labeling (see Table 1.1). In many respects, the positive aspects of labeling affect groups—of children, parents, and professionals associated with a particular category—but the negative aspects affect individuals (Heward & Orlansky, 1992). When groups of families rally around students who fit a particular disability category, they can influence school boards and state and federal legislators and obtain funding for increased services. Depending on how those services are organized and delivered, however, they may or may not improve things for the individuals. The challenge is to ensure the rights and resources necessary for an appropriate education for students with disabilities without also generating the debilitating social, emotional, and academic side effects.

## Overuse of Special Education

Although special education was created to support the unique needs of a special population, it may be used instead to provide a place for students whose learning needs and behaviors clash with school expectations. As a result, many students from ethnically diverse backgrounds have been staffed into the special education system. Many people believe these students end up in special education not because of true disabilities, but because their social and academic expectations and behaviors differ from the dominant school culture (Grossman, 1995). According to Grossman (1991), Hispanics, African-Americans, and Native Americans are overrepresented in programs for students with serious emotional disturbance, learning disabilities, behavior disorders, and developmental disabilities (for example, see Figures 1.4 and 1.5). When low socioeconomic status and gender are added to ethnicity, the likelihood of non-Euro-Americans being placed in special education programs is even higher. The apparent overidentification of students of color and low socioeconomic status as disabled suggests that, in the current process for determining eligibility for services, disability and cultural difference are synonymous. In

| TABLE 1.1 | Potential Merits and Faults of Classification-by-Label Systems |
|---|---|
| **Potential Merits** | **Potential Faults** |
| ■ Diagnosis may lead to specific treatment.<br>■ Labels help to organize and communicate research findings.<br>■ Funding is often based on specific categories.<br>■ Labels can assist special interest groups to promote specific programs, sponsor legislative action, or increase public awareness. | ■ Labels focus on negative aspects and cause others to think about the individual in terms of inadequacies or defects.<br>■ Because of labels, some people hold low expectations for others, resulting in a self-fulfilling prophecy.<br>■ Labels are often misused to explain all of the child's behaviors (for example, "Annie doesn't know any better than to hit because she is mentally retarded").<br>■ Because of labels, we tend to "blame the victim"—always ascribing faults to the student and not looking for instructional or curriculum variables that may be causing performance difficulties.<br>■ Labels and their associated reactions from others can contribute to an individual's poor self-concept.<br>■ Labels can lead peers to reject or ridicule students with disabilities.<br>■ Labeling is often permanent—once labeled, very few students ever regain their status as "just another kid."<br>■ Labels are used to exclude and segregate.<br>■ The time and resources spent to classify and label students could be better directed toward the planning and delivery of instruction. |

Source: Heward & Orlansky, 1992.

fact, difference, and not disability, may be the primary function served in the special education assessment process.

If overidentification continues at its present pace and if the demographic projections for the school-age population are correct, special education could eventually serve more students than general education (see the Pett cartoon) (Grossman, 1991; Kozleski, 1993). Moreover, the current overidentification of students from non-Euro-American backgrounds for special education services suggests that the future will bring increased underemployment and a large, unskilled labor market, because the outcomes for special education are less satisfactory than was originally projected. The use of special education and other federal entitlement programs as a social selection mechanism in the United

States is indefensible since the end result of educational exclusion and separation has been the domination of one group over others (Carnoy, 1974; Grossman, 1995). The shift in national demographics compels us to reexamine the purpose and function of special education and politicizes the debate about where students with disabilities should be served.

## Accountability for Outcomes

Traditional special education services are being reexamined in light of research findings that suggest separate programs and services may not support positive adult outcomes for students in special education (A concern about, 1992). First, students with disabilities

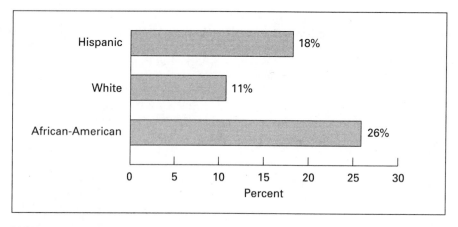

**FIGURE 1.4** ■ Special Education Students Classified as Retarded, by Race
Source: Shapiro, Loeb, & Bowermaster, 1993, p. 46.

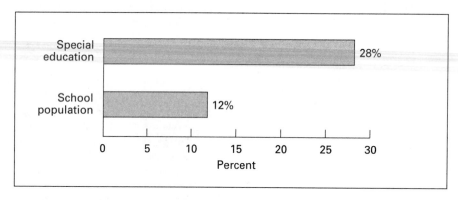

**FIGURE 1.5** ■ African-American Student Representation in Special Education
Source: Grossman, 1995, p. 4.

drop out of school more often than their nondisabled peers. Wagner (1989) found that 36–55 percent of students with disabilities, depending on type of disability and location, drop out of school as opposed to 14–29 percent of students without disabilities (Butler-Nalin, 1989). Follow-up studies of students with disabilities who do graduate document poor adjustment in the areas of employment, friendships, community access, ability to live independently from their families, and accessing posteducational environments (for example, Affleck, Edgar, Levine, & Kortering, 1990; DeStefano & Wagner, 1991; Fairweather & Shaver, 1990; Hasazi, Gordon, & Roe, 1985; Mithaug, Horiuchi, & Fanning, 1985). Only 30–40 percent of graduates with disabilities are typically employed, primarily in unskilled or semiskilled entry-level jobs. Nearly one-third of students with disabilities, primarily those with learning

and emotional disorders, like Michael and Kirk, are arrested at least once after leaving high school (Shapiro, Loeb, & Bowermaster, 1993). These postschool benchmarks of students served by special education have caused much debate about restructuring special education services (Karpinski, Neubert, & Graham, 1992).

## ■ SECTION SUMMARY

The system of special education has served an important function of putting into practice values, policies, and regulations that mandate the free and appropriate education of children with disabilities. Furthermore, special education has increased the capacity of our educational system to understand the types of strategies

necessary to support the educational needs of students who have disabilities. It is important to question, however, whether the manner in which the system has been organized and operated has led to unintended, unnecessary outcomes. Critics argue that when we classify and label children and exclude them from general education, we send a strong social message that is discriminatory and personally offensive. In addition, there is reason to question the long-term educational benefits and outcomes for students from specialized programs.

Special education is not exempt from the social and economic changes that are affecting the educational system as a whole. Increasing diversity means that more learners with different needs will enroll in our public schools. If special education continues its current organizational schemata, it will result in more and more subassembly lines with questionable results. And if the educational system as a whole continues to rely on subsystems like special education to deal with diversity, the outcome will be dismal for many. The factory model no longer serves its purpose. Instead, schools must evolve into organizations in which all learners become the responsibility of all school professionals. Restructuring the educational system to operate from an inclusive basis, using the expertise of

school professionals and related-services personnel in a collaborative way to meet the needs of all students, offers an important alternative approach (MacKinnon & Brown, 1994; Stainback & Stainback, 1996).

## Inclusive School Communities as a Context for Reform

If we are to respond to diversity and innovation, schools must move away from standardization and become flexible organizations that use the collaboration of professionals to solve changing environmental demands (Apple & Beane, 1995; Biklen, 1985; Lipsky & Gartner, 1996; Skrtic, 1991, 1995b). Students, not subject matter, instructional practices, or personnel issues, must be at the core of all reform efforts. School reform requires that the needs, abilities, capacities, and goals of children drive the decisions we make about the organization and conduct of our educational communities. "Unless and until we learn how to change how children . . . experience themselves and each other in the classroom—our schools will remain what they are or get worse" (Sarason, 1993, p. 144). When our organizational policies, structures, and practices respond to the needs of all students, our educational system will be better able to respond to broader social, economic, and ability issues.

Inclusive school communities can serve as the context for understanding and creating a system of education that is duly responsive to the challenges we face in general and special education (Schaffner & Buswell, 1996). Inclusive school communities are rooted in the philosophy that all children can learn and belong in the mainstream of school and community life (Stainback & Stainback, 1996). Creating inclusive school communities requires consideration of (1) the rights of students, (2) shared responsibility, (3) structural changes to schools, and (4) necessary changes in existing roles and school practices.

## Acknowledging the Rights of Students

Recall that, early in the chapter, we asked you to picture yourself as a teacher. We suggested that many teachers see themselves working with students who look similar, come from similar backgrounds, and learn in similar ways. But creating and sustaining inclusive school communities requires a shift away from that image. Children, even those who may share many characteristics, bring sets of unique, individualized learning strengths and needs to school.

> At issue is the entitlement of each child to life, liberty, and the pursuit of happiness. That right cannot be realized unless each child has a successful elementary and secondary school experience. Failure in school can be compensated for only by privilege of wealth or family. The child whose family is not influential or economically advantaged is doomed to an adulthood of poverty, disease, and early death with a certainty almost as high as if he or she were condemned by public decree. The issue of each child,

> not children collectively, needs emphasis. To obtain an affective as well as a cognitive response to this claim for entitlement, reformers need to have the real individual in mind. (Astuto, Clark, Read, McGree, & Fernandez, 1994, pp. 81–82)

The basic rights of children are at the heart of forming inclusive school communities. Those rights include not only a free and appropriate education but also the right to form relationships and participate in their home, school, and neighborhood communities. These **inalienable rights** constitute, in part, the core key conditions necessary for a democratic way of life: (1) concern for the welfare of others and "the common good," (2) concern for the dignity and rights of individuals and minorities, and (3) faith in the individual and collective capacity of people to create possibilities for resolving problems (Beane & Apple, 1995; Soder, 1996). In inclusive school communities, *all* students are considered to be full-fledged members, and when any student demonstrates a need for support, it is the responsibility of the entire community to respond. The principals of "community," "diversity," and "caring" are foundations to inclusive school communities (Sapon-Shevin, Dobbelaier, Corrigan, Goodman, & Mastin, 1998; Scherer, 1998). In real terms, this means that students like Annie need access to their typical peers in the classroom, the hallways, the cafeteria, and the playground. Students like Annie, Michael, and Kirk need to know how to include and accept, not shun, students who are different from themselves, too. All students have the right to learn skills that will make them good citizens of inclusive classrooms. They also have the right to express their own learning needs and interests and to participate in an accepting and warm school and classroom environment.

## Sharing Responsibility

In inclusive school communities, responding to and supporting student diversity becomes a shared responsibility of all school professionals. Rather than fitting students into categories that correspond to the roles of school professionals, the collective and individual needs and goals of students shape the daily decisions and actions of school professionals. That is, students, not professionals, drive the organization and use of educational resources. Refer to the motto "Each Belongs" in Figure 1.6. This motto is a shorthand representation

**Each Belongs**

- Here, every learner has the right to be involved in all the meaningful activities of the school.

- It does not matter what academic, behavioral, physical, or communicative capabilities or limitations you possess currently. Although not all behaviors are equally acceptable, all people are accepted and wanted.

- This is the place where we will support your weaknesses so you may capitalize on your strengths.

- We will not seek to "get rid" of you because you are too much trouble or because you are "unfit." Rather, we will collaboratively develop a functional plan to help you address your goals and needs.

- Your goals become ours and ours become yours. We are in this together—we sink or swim together.

- We will work together to meet the challenges of learning and living with one another.

**FIGURE 1.6 ■** The Motto of a School That Supports Inclusionary Practices

of the belief that all children, with or without disabilities, belong in school. Notice that, throughout this motto, the term *we* is used, meaning that everyone involved in the activities of that school is responsible for meeting student needs.

Along with school professionals, support personnel, families, and peers, community members are needed to support and respond to student needs and goals. These individuals and groups need to take responsibility for guaranteeing high achievement among all our children (U.S. Department of Education, 1995). Whether you plan to be a general education teacher, a school psychologist, a principal, a special education teacher, a school nurse, a counselor, or a **paraprofessional,** or whether you are a mother, father, or member of the business community, you have a set of interests and responsibilities for the education of all students, including students who have needs similar to or different from our case study students—Annie, Kurume, Tanya, Michael, and Kirk. It requires the active involvement and commitment of a wide range of individuals, including the students themselves, to make use of the strengths and to support the needs that our diverse

student population brings to inclusive school communities. (Detailed information about these roles and responsibilities is provided in Chapter 4.)

## Changing Organizational Structures

Inclusive school communities are organized and managed through shared decision-making structures, unlike the traditional hierarchical, authority-based models so often observed in schools (Educational Leadership, 1994/1995). Traditionally, discussions of important school outcomes have been conducted in private, by school administrators, curriculum specialists, and other "experts." In contrast, in inclusive school communities, children and youths, their families, and community members all participate in these important decisions along with school professionals and support personnel (see Boxes 1.1 and 1.2). Students' interests, needs, and goals become the focus for collaborative decision making and creative problem solving (Cessna & Adams, 1993), and they drive the way a school is organized and managed, as well as how resources (finances, personnel, materials) are allocated and used. Unlike the hierarchical professional bureaucracy, collaborative organizational structures expand our capacity to meet the best interests of our students.

To create collaborative organizational structures, schools must configure themselves as **adhocracies** instead of professional bureaucracies that seek to attain

**BOX 1.1**

### Who Are School Professionals?

Special education teachers

Classroom teachers

Social workers

Occupational therapists

Speech language therapists

Special subject teachers' consultants

Learning specialists

Counselors

School psychologists

School nurses

Physical therapists

Principals

standardization and performance goals (Skrtic, 1995b). The focus of adhocracies is on innovation through problem solving, so they nurture new patterns of thinking, learning, and working together among school professionals and support personnel (Senge, 1990). Adhocracies are not characterized by hierarchical, specialized divisions of labor; they are "flat" organizations in which members of interdependent, **multidisciplinary teams** work together to solve problems of practice (Skrtic, 1995b). To adopt these new roles and participate in collaborative decision making, you, as a school professional, will need a set of skills vastly different from those your first-grade teacher had when he or she began to teach.

## Changing Roles

The roles and responsibilities of school professionals, support personnel, families, community members, and students necessarily change as schools attempt to create inclusive school communities. Where general education teachers once planned lessons alone, they now collaborate with professionals in other specific areas of expertise (York-Barr, Schultz, Doyle, Kronberg, & Crossett, et al., 1996). The role of experts such as special education teachers, occupational therapists, and school counselors shifts from targeting small groups of students for extended pull-out services to providing a broader base of support for the needs of all learners. The *primary* context for these support services becomes the general education classroom. Inclusive school communities do not rule out responding to individuals or small groups of children with similar needs through flexible individualized or small-group

interactions planned and occurring in concert with the activities of the general education classroom. When Kurume's parents were divorced, he participated in a support group for students in a similar situation offered by the school psychologist. Similarly, Michael attended a group that met for eight weeks and focused on strategies for improving study skills. These activities were conducted outside the classroom because they were more effective that way. Michael and Kurume were not involved in these activities to the exclusion of their involvement in their own general education classrooms, though. The nature of inclusive school communities allows for these variations in service and support delivery.

Because of the gift of diversity that children bring to our schools, there is no recipe card, no "paint-by-number" canvas that will allow you to follow the steps or color in the blanks and achieve inclusive school communities. It takes the combined efforts of students, their families and peers, school professionals, support personnel, and community members (Alper, Schloss, Etscheidt, & Macfarlane, 1995; Falvey, 1995; York-Barr et al., 1996). Each individual has interests and responsibilities in making this work; Tables 1.2–1.4 highlight those that each brings to the school community. Kirk provides a good example of the need for students to assume responsibilities. He needs to learn to make responsible choices from a limited set of options and to balance his response to authority with the needs and interests of his group of friends. In contrast, Debbie and Dave, Annie's parents, need both to provide for Annie's needs and interests and to allow for their own and their other children's quality of life. You, as a school professional, will have responsibility for teaching your students both to recognize when they need help and to know how to get it. The interests and responsibilities of all the entities involved are different, and yet, without the fulfillment of each responsibility, inclusive school communities will remain only an ideal.

## ■ SECTION SUMMARY

Inclusive school communities are a response to the fundamental strains imposed on our current educational system. In inclusive school communities, the assumption is that all students belong and that the school must respond to the needs of the student. Inclusive

---

**TABLE 1.2** **Families' Interests and Responsibilities in Inclusive School Communities**

| Interests | Responsibilities |
|---|---|
| To improve their quality of life<br>To maintain family life<br>To make choices for themselves and their children<br>To control their environment<br>To provide security and safety for their children<br>To maintain productivity<br>To promote community participation and support for themselves and their children | To provide for their children's needs and interests that allow for their own quality of life and the quality of life of their children<br>To interact with school professionals and to advocate for the needs and interests of their own children, as well as all children<br>To support the efforts of school professionals when those efforts have the intention of increasing their children's quality of life or that of other children<br>To support school personnel in providing a secure, safe environment for their own children, as well as all children<br>To support their own children and other children in becoming caring individuals who can interact with and support the learning and social needs of their schoolmates<br>To continue to grow and learn and engage in change |

---

**TABLE 1.3** **School Personnel's Interests and Responsibilities in Inclusive School Communities**

| Interests | Responsibilities |
|---|---|
| To be effective and productive professionally and personally<br>To maintain their own dignity, safety, and security<br>To participate in a school community that fosters professional growth and development, that tolerates their differences, limitations, capacities, and needs<br>To initiate and sustain relationships with other professionals<br>To engage in life-long learning | To request the assistance and support they need to be professionally responsible and productive<br>To share knowledge with others and offer support<br>To teach students how to make choices and to allow (foster) real choices among limited options<br>To teach students how to exert control over their environment in socially acceptable ways<br>To provide basic skills to earn a living and acquire housing, clothing, and food<br>To teach workplace skills (cooperative work, conflict management, communication)<br>To provide normal environments and access to people with different capacities and limitations<br>To teach skills for establishing and maintaining relationships<br>To continually enhance their understanding of themselves as learners, to self-assess strengths and weaknesses, to engage in change, and to gain new information |

| TABLE 1.4 | Community Members' Interests and Responsibilities in Inclusive School Communities | |
|---|---|---|
| **Interests** | | **Responsibilities** |
| To have their tax dollars spent well | | To pay taxes that support public schools |
| To gain and maintain quality-of-life outcomes for themselves | | To exercise opportunities for input and support of public schools and all children |
| To know that schools are preparing young people to live independent lives and to become responsible, tax-paying citizens | | To support the efforts of school professionals who value quality of life as an outcome for all children—no matter what their disability, limitation, capacity, or need |

school communities operate from the student up in the decision-making process, so recognizing the rights of students and changing our responses to responsibility, organizational structures, and roles are critical conditions for the process to begin. These essential elements of inclusive school communities are predicated on the education of school professionals, like yourself, who have the capacity to reflect on their practices, change or modify their teaching techniques and curriculum, and participate in collaborative decision making (Educational Leadership, 1994/1995).

Now that you have an idea of what inclusive school communities are, we need to look at the desired outcomes of these practices. The following discussion defines the learner outcomes in inclusive school communities.

# Educational Outcomes for All Learners

Proponents of inclusive school communities call for broad, flexible core outcomes that target the skills and knowledge that provide students with opportunities to reach successful and satisfying adult lives (Ysseldyke, Thurlow, & Gilman, 1993; see also the chapter-opening vignette). By targeting outcomes, we can identify a series of indicators that help us assess whether our educational practices are helping students meet established goals. Given changing social and economic conditions, we propose five educational outcomes that help students to (1) develop and support family connections, (2) exercise choice and become self-determined,

(3) engage in lifelong learning pursuits, (4) enjoy socioeconomic security and productivity, and (5) participate in and support their school and neighborhood communities.

By specifying a target outcome rather than a process, inclusive school communities can choose the best fit among assessment, curriculum, instruction, and student needs in their school community (Goodlad, 1984; O'Day & Smith, 1993; Ysseldyke et al., 1993). Outcomes help us to avoid expending our energy on debate over preferred instructional methods. They focus our attention on ensuring that students achieve the outcomes that benefit their adult lives.

## Developing and Supporting Family Connections

In most cultures, the family is the fundamental unit of social order. Not only does the family provide nurturance and support for each of its members, it also constitutes the backbone of neighborhoods and communities. By ensuring that graduates of our educational system have the capacity to nurture, develop, and support families, schools can contribute to the well-being of both individuals and their neighborhood communities. But today's family structure may differ from the post–World War II nuclear family ideal; the number of single-parent families, blended families, and families with same-sex parents continues to rise. Tanya's mother, Juanita, still lives at home with her parents and has not seen Tanya's father since she discovered she was pregnant. Kirk has five half-brothers and -sisters, none of whom have ever lived at home with him. Kirk's and Tanya's families are not unusual, but their beliefs about the family and its predictability may be different from Michael's. (Chapter 3 examines how different family structures impact children.) Both the traditional and the newer family structures need support so that children raised in these settings can learn and thrive in schools and leave school prepared to accept family responsibilities.

Schools can play two critical roles in promoting positive family outcomes for students. First, schools can help family members develop the social skills that enable them to form and maintain significant, lasting relationships and create personal support networks for their children. Kurume's family received support and encouragement to learn **sign language** so they could communicate with him more effectively. Second, schools can focus their assessment, curriculum, instruction, and management practices on helping students develop and use social skills so they can help one another in school and, eventually, assume meaningful adult and family roles. Schools should be places for the entire family to connect with others, to learn, and to grow (Melaville & Blank, 1993). In addition to developing skills that support and enrich family structures, students also need skills, such as self-determination, that enhance their personal development.

## Exercising Choice and Becoming Self-Determined

It has become a cliché that the only constant in our lives is change. Jobs, people, relationships, knowledge, and laws change. Individuals can no longer rely on a predictable set of rules for behaving or for making decisions. They must have skills in assessing, planning, and executing strategic responses to immediate and long-term situations. This ability to act reflectively is one characteristic of self-determined behavior. **Self-determination** is defined broadly as "the capacity to choose and have those choices be the determinants of one's actions" (Deci & Ryan, 1985, p. 38). Self-determined people act based on knowledge of themselves and their competence to create situations and environments that ensure success in daily living. Kurume is beginning to think about life after high school. Specifically, he is asking questions about his interests in computer technology and his goal of living independently as an adult, and he is making plans to obtain the skills and experiences he needs to reach those goals.

Kurume is a good example of Wehmeyer's (1996) proposition that self-determination should be an educational outcome that refers to "acting as the primary causal agent in one's life and making choices and decisions regarding one's quality of life free from undue external influence or interference." More specifically, Wehmeyer (1996) suggests that self-determination encompasses four essential characteristics: (1) autonomy, (2) self-regulation, (3) self-realization, and (4) psychological empowerment (see Figure 1.7). In Wehmeyer's model, **autonomy** refers to the ability to make and act on choices based on self-selected preferences. **Self-realization** entails knowing one's own strengths and needs and striving to capitalize on these; **self-regulation** involves exerting control over one's behavior consistent with these preferences, choices, strengths, and strivings. People who act with **psychological empowerment** believe they have control over their lives, have the skills to get what they desire, and apply those skills when they choose. The emergence of self-determined behavior depends on the development of a set of subskills such as goal setting, decision making, problem solving, self-awareness, internal locus of control, and self-assessment (Wehmeyer, 1996).

Concern about a lack of self-determination among students with and without disabilities is widespread (Hoy, 1986; Meyer, 1991; Mithaug, 1996; Phillips, 1990; Ward, 1996) and is particularly directed toward students who are on the verge of exiting school to assume adult roles (Brown, Joseph, & Wotruba, 1989;

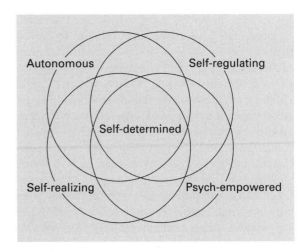

**FIGURE 1.7** ■ Characteristics of Self-Determination
Source: Sands & Wehmeyer, 1996.

Young children from different backgrounds and with differing abilities enjoy recess together.

Mithaug, Martin, & Agran, 1987). Furthermore, studies of adults with disabilities indicate that they generally have little autonomy in making life choices for themselves (Baker, Seltzer, & Seltzer, 1977; Kozleski & Sands, 1992; Stancliffe & Wehmeyer, 1995). Schools can serve as the critical socialization agent. But to do so, they must facilitate self-determination as an explicit component of the curriculum to help prepare children for the adult challenges of a rapidly changing society.

Students who are given opportunities to express their choices and make decisions can contribute to an understanding of, as well as responses to, their educational needs (Sands & Doll, 1996). As adults, they will also be more likely to advocate effectively for positive employment conditions and for access to governmental and community services (Fisher, 1985; McWhirter & McWhirter, 1990; Ness, 1989). The ability to express choices and make decisions emerges in very young children and continues to develop in adolescence and adulthood as individuals learn more of the necessary elements (Doll, Sands, Wehmeyer, & Palmer, 1996) and are provided with opportunities across many contexts (Mithaug, 1996). To promote the educational outcome of student self-determination, we must empower students to choose their own educational services and

supports. Schools, in partnership with families, must create environments in which student choice and decision making is both supported and valued.

## Engaging in Lifelong Learning Pursuits

Students exiting the education system in the twenty-first century can expect to change careers at least six times over the course of their adult lives (Daggett, 1991). Such changes require learning throughout the life span, and the skills and competencies associated with each career path will demand learning resources and capacities that tap differing abilities. Traditionally, students have been exposed to a transmission-of-information model (that is, lectures, seat work, and so on) of instruction. Unfortunately, this model tends to focus on memorization and knowledge of facts, and students often have difficulty applying what they have learned to real-life contexts (Daggett, in O'Neil, 1995). Another by-product of the transmission model is that learners become dependent on external sources for "knowing." In contrast, providing students with the skills and experiences to understand themselves as learners and to choose the best ways for learning new patterns of behavior and acquiring in-depth knowledge of emerging fields requires intimate knowledge of themselves as learners. Therefore, teaching students how to "discover" things for themselves and engaging them in reflection on and monitoring of their own learning is crucial in preparing students to cope with change in our rapidly evolving information age (see Chapter 10).

## Enjoying Socioeconomic Security and Productivity

The emergence of the middle class in the twentieth century has given way in the current postmodern society to a two-tiered economic stratification between the "haves" and the "have-nots." Unfortunately, the underclass is largely peopled by those who have long been **disenfranchised:** single mothers, people of color, and people with disabilities. Historically, people from lower socioeconomic strata have not been well educated (Ward, 1996), and many of the social services established to buffer their life circumstances were provided paternalistically, undermining their initiative and self-respect (Szymanski & Trueba, 1994). People in lower socioeconomic strata typically are undereducated, lacking knowledge and skills in literacy, mathematics, and technology; thus, they also frequently lack the skills they need to seek and retain jobs and to build long-term careers. Moreover, in our postindustrial economy, unskilled and low-skill jobs are rapidly disappearing (Daggett, in O'Neil, 1995; Rifkin, 1997). To ensure that our population can compete in a global economy, the educational community needs to focus on promoting the skills and attitudes that will permit individual socioeconomic security and productivity.

Recent federal legislation is providing the impetus and support for schools to attend to the long-term socioeconomic and occupational needs of students. In 1990, amendments to P.L. 94-142, the Education of All Handicapped Children Act (EHCA), mandated **transition services** for students with disabilities that promote movement from school to postschool activities such as vocational education and competitive employment (see Chapter 2). In 1995, Congress passed the School-to-Work Opportunities Act in an effort to (1) increase school-to-work opportunities for all secondary-aged youths, (2) reorganize learning opportunities so that all youths can achieve high academic and occupational

standards and are prepared for further postsecondary education and training and for high-skill, high-wage careers, and (3) build partnerships among schools, employers, labor, community organizations, and parents to develop and sustain school-to-work opportunities as part of a lifelong learning system (U.S. Departments of Education and Labor, 1994). Through initiatives such as these, students will have experiences that increase their chances to achieve socioeconomic security and productivity.

## Participating in and Supporting School and Neighborhood Communities

Active citizenship and involvement in the community have been goals of our educational system since the founding of this nation. Community participation is at the heart of a healthy democracy. "More than ever before, humankind is confronted with confusion regarding the nature of man, conflicting value systems, ambiguous ethical, moral, and spiritual beliefs, and questions about his own role in society" (Goodlad, 1984, pp. 53–54). In an era when **impermanence** characterizes our urban and suburban communities, the ability to form and maintain relationships with individuals whose values, beliefs, and cultural backgrounds differ from our own is essential to creation of a cohesive and stable environment. Data collected in studies by Sands, Kozleski, and Goodwin (1991) and by Kozleski and Sands (1992) indicate that involvement in community activities is highly valued by adults with and without disabilities and that it creates cohesion within a community that results in shared responsibility for achieving a high quality of life.

For students to achieve educational outcomes of community participation and support, it is critical to establish an emotional sense of community, caring, and belonging in inclusive school environments. Flynn (in Stainback, Stainback, & Jackson, 1992) defines this sense of community:

*When we describe school as being a community [we are referring to] a group of individuals who have learned to communicate honestly with one another, whose relationships go deeper than their composures and who have developed some significant commitment to rejoice together, mourn together, to delight in each other, and make others' conditions their own. (p. 5)*

When schools and classrooms are structured to promote a sense of "community" or "caring," students develop the skills necessary to learn, play, live, and work with people who are different in a variety of dimensions, including ethnicity, culture, ability, and socioeconomic status (Elias, Zins, Weissberg, Frey, Greenberg, Haynes, Kessler, Schwab-Stone, & Shriver, 1997; Nevin, 1993). But helping students achieve these goals is not always easy. Table 1.5 lists some of the conclusions one researcher drew in helping students develop relationships with peers who differed from one another. Applying these same lessons to your own work in schools will take conscious and sustained effort, but the importance of establishing a sense of community and belonging in inclusive school communities cannot be underestimated. "Associations with significant others have a direct and indirect impact on the manner in which we view ourselves and our world, and by which we meet a myriad of personal needs" (Abery & Fahnestock, 1994, p. 83).

Developing a sense of community and belonging requires that students with and without disabilities be taught to engage in many forms of interaction. Hamre-Nietupski, Branston, Ford, Gruenewald, and Brown (1978) suggested that these include helping, provision of service, and **reciprocal interactions.** According to Meyer (1987):

> Many forms of interactions enrich our lives and give us the chance to develop friendships and critical personal relationships that we will enjoy throughout our life span. We typically regard these interactions, relationships, and friendships as central to our personal well being. It is time for children with disabilities to share these experiences, so that they will no longer be isolated from what is perhaps the most essential component of what we elusively refer to as "quality of life." (pp. 251–263)

For some individuals with disabilities, mere access to others in a community offers opportunities for relationships that have not been available historically because they were often shielded from the rest of the community.

Community support and participation are an antidote to some of the problems we face as a society, including alienation, transience, and a loss of shared values. The contemporary philosopher Richard Roarty (1989) speaks of "solidarity" as the ability to view differences in such things as race, customs, and rituals as less important than the universal experiences of humanity, birth, loss, pain, joy, and death. Individuals can form inclusive school communities that become the bridges linking them across their differences.

## ■ SECTION SUMMARY

To produce individuals who can thrive in the twenty-first century, schools must work to ensure students' competencies in developing and supporting family connections, exercising choice and self-determination, engaging in lifelong learning, enjoying socioeconomic security and productivity, and participating in school and neighborhood communities. But having students achieve those broad educational outcomes cannot be the only standard by which we operate and evaluate our school programs. We must also be concerned with student and family quality of life. Schools must share a

---

**TABLE 1.5** **Lessons Learned from Promoting a Sense of Community**

- Community members cannot merely be tolerant; they must welcome new members who may be difficult to get to know and challenging to include.

- One key to developing a sense of community is to get individuals to open their eyes and hearts.

- The appropriate amount of support for a given individual may vary over time.

- Casual acquaintanceships are as much a part of a community as long-term, deep friendships.

- Even after much hard work, some situations simply may not work.

- Even long-term relationships may come to an end.

- In building a sense of community, it may be necessary to seek new connections.

- Surrounding an individual with community members enriches that person's life.

- Ordinary moments when people share daily life together make all the work worthwhile.

Source: Adapted from Bartholomew-Lorimer, 1993.

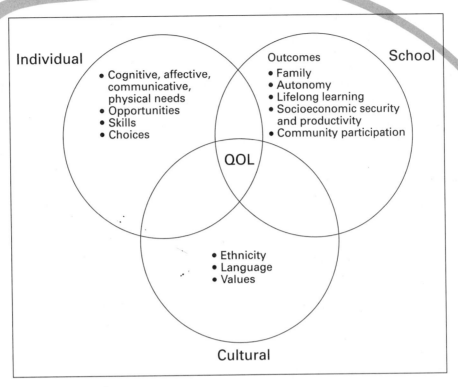

**FIGURE 1.8** ■ Influences on Quality of Life (QOL)
Source: Dennis et al., 1993.

universal commitment to quality of life as a primary goal for education. But what exactly is quality of life? We examine this question next.

## Quality of Life

Having common outcomes for students is one aspect of what we hope to accomplish through schooling. But we must not lose sight of a second important goal: the effect those outcomes have on the quality of students' lives. There is no single definition of quality of life (Taylor & Racino, 1991), but the essence of many definitions is that it is an ever-changing, personally defined construct that encompasses the ability to adopt a lifestyle that satisfies one's unique wants and needs and gives a corresponding sense of satisfaction, happiness, contentment, or success (Blatt, 1987; Karen, Lambour, & Greenspan, 1990; Stark & Goldsbury, 1990). Kirk's parents, General and Mrs. Grant, may not achieve a high level of quality of life if their general outlook on

life is negative. In contrast, an individual or a family like Annie's, with limited financial resources may nevertheless have a high quality of life if they have a positive view of their general circumstances. The perceived elements of quality of life change with age and experience. To a young adult, landing an upper-management position in a corporation may be the focus of economic security and result in a high quality of life. To a person approaching retirement, access to good health care may affect the quality of life more than job prospects.

Quality of life is complex and elusive; it is based on culturally specific, individual, and common values and needs (Dennis, Williams, Giangreco, & Cloninger, 1993). Three spheres intersect to influence it (see Figure 1.8): (1) individual characteristics, which reflect personally relevant values and experiences unique to an individual, (2) basic needs shared by all people, and (3) experiences and meanings that groups of people share. The influence of the individual and the interaction of these three components is context dependent (Dennis et al., 1993). Michael, Anita, and Chen Lee provide us with an opportunity to understand how these three spheres interact. Michael's quality of life is being influenced by his goal to become a doctor. His need for productivity is a common outcome that researchers suggest is a critical element of quality of life. His ability to reach his career goal is influenced by the cultural context of his Chinese-American heritage. With his mother as his chief advocate, Michael's progress in school has been facilitated by her willingness to attend meetings and seek necessary supports for her son. In addition, Michael's individual characteristics, including persistence, motivation, and difficulty in learning abstract concepts, have made achieving his goal both easier and more difficult.

Within school contexts, we must understand the dimensions of quality of life and the interrelationships among these dimensions. School professionals, by themselves, cannot determine quality-of-life outcomes. By measuring quality-of-life satisfaction among students, graduates, their families, and the larger community, however, schools can determine the effectiveness with which they are meeting student needs.

In this text, we propose a tight alignment between quality of life and educational outcomes. When students (1) develop and support family connections, (2) exercise choice and become self-determined, (3) engage in lifelong learning pursuits, (4) enjoy socioeconomic security and productivity, and (5) participate in and support their school and neighborhood communities, they accomplish important educational outcomes. These may not be sufficient, however, to confer quality of life. As a school professional, you must attend to quality of life and understand two influences on quality of life: culturally specific and individual characteristics.

# The Influence of Culture, Language, and Ethnicity

Because quality of life is inextricably meshed with an individual's cultural, linguistic, and ethnic background, any discussion of these issues must be entered with an understanding of the interactions among culture, context, and individuals. Identity, values, beliefs, and behaviors cannot be predicted based on any single cultural feature. It would be risky for a teacher to make assumptions about a student because of race, religious affiliation, or linguistic background. The following are some issues that may influence the choices school professionals make in their own practice.

Culture influences how individuals perceive themselves and their status both within their own group and in other cultural, linguistic, or ethnic groups (Heath, 1983). Children come to school understanding their status within their own family and cultural group. When their cultural/familial context is compatible with the dominant, Euro-American culture of schools, children make the transition to school relatively easily. But some children who grow up in the culture that dominates the rituals, routines, and language of schools and school professionals may have other intraindividual or intrafamilial issues that place them at risk for success in schools. Kirk, the student who has behavioral problems, grew up with an ostensible match between familial customs and routines and school customs and routines, but either family, individual, or school issues complicated Kirk's educational adjustment and success. Imagine the additional challenges if Kirk's family had spoken a different language or had immigrated to the United States from another country.

School professionals are predominantly from Euro-American, English-speaking, middle-class backgrounds, and their cultural dominates schools, although they may be teaching students who represent many other cultural, ethnic, language, and socioeconomic backgrounds. The Euro-American culture values linear, sequential thinking, and students are expected to learn what their teachers know and to demonstrate their knowledge through performance on tests. According to many researchers (Au, 1980; Heath, 1986; Ogbu, 1978; Ogbu & Matute-Bianchi, 1986), this type of learning is linked to the school culture of the United States and does not reflect the ways of learning familiar to children from Polynesian, Latino, or rural African-American cultures. School calendars follow the agrarian calendar developed during the nineteenth century, when students needed to work on their family farms during the summer growing season and the autumn harvest, and holidays continue to conform to the Christian religious calendar. English is the language of instruction, and for students with limited English proficiency, the primary focus of instruction often is on improving skills in English without preserving the development of competencies in the students' other language. According to Commins (1989) and Commins and Miramontes (1989), without careful attention to development of competency in both languages, the achievements of bilingual students can be limited in both English and their first language.

Educational and family achievement are also culturally defined. Information from school about a child's progress may have little relevance to some families. In the Euro-American culture, to be "well educated" implies such things as a knowledge of Western literature, competency in higher mathematics, knowledge of government and the global economy, and expertise in a profession such as law, medicine, education, or architecture. When a child is having difficulty learning to read, spell, write, or solve math problems, the family may be concerned if they define "well educated" in the Euro-American way. But if a family views "well educated" as being well mannered, respectful to elders, and willing to pursue family goals, competency in school skills may be of little concern. Traditional school-related reading or learning disabilities may cause little or no concern for families who value craftsmanship over literacy or navigation skills over computation skills. This is not to say that school professionals should ignore or diminish their focus on academic achievement. Instead, it suggests that, in forging relationships with families, school professionals must be aware of these different perspectives (Harry, 1992). Most schools assume that the best family environments operate with mainstream Euro-American values and behaviors, and when this is not the case, it complicates communication between school and home.

Where school and family values differ, assessing quality of life may be the only way to determine how schools are meeting learner needs. While family-determined quality-of-life outcomes should support family autonomy, they also need to support the types of autonomy and decision making that are valued by the student's surrounding culture. School professionals, support personnel, and community members must understand the subtleties of the linguistic, behavioral, and religious differences underlying the broad cultural categories into which students may be divided. The group labeled as "Asian" in the U.S. census comprises individuals from Polynesia, Indonesia, the Philippines, Southeast Asia, China, Korea, and Japan. People from these various countries and regions vary greatly in their religious beliefs; these may include Taoism, Confucianism, Zen and Shinto Buddhism, Hinduism, and Catholicism. Religious beliefs help to shape the relationship among generations, the value placed on eco-

nomic success, and the family response to the emancipation of children.

Lifelong learning, socioeconomic security, and community participation are quality-of-life outcomes that are shaped culturally, ethnically, linguistically, and economically. Knowledge of the cultures, ethnic groups, and languages represented in your classroom will help you understand how quality-of-life outcomes are viewed by your students' families. Some generalizations about a culture may assist you in learning to ask important questions, but assuming that all families from a particular region or culture operate from the same perspective will prevent you from personalizing the outcomes you develop for a particular student or group of students.

## The Influence of Individual Characteristics

The freedom to make choices and the independence to act on them are at the root of achieving quality-of-life outcomes, but not everyone wants or is able to achieve the same ones. Some people want to acquire cars, homes, and expensive clothing, while others prefer to limit their acquisition of possessions. Reality can constrain our freedom to act on our desires; our skills and opportunities largely define what we are able to do. Income level determines our options for where we live, and we socialize within our professional and personal networks (Janicki, 1990).

While external circumstances constrain the range of choice, individual characteristics also narrow options. We can organize these into four interactive elements: affective, physical, communicative, and cognitive (see Chapter 5). Motivation is an affective characteristic that profoundly influences an individual's ability to take risks, confront challenges, and engage in new and difficult tasks. Levels of motivation are balanced by capacities in the other areas. An individual who is highly motivated but takes longer to learn a new task may achieve a higher quality of life than an individual with greater cognitive skills but lower levels of motivation. The balance among all these characteristics is unique to each person and makes it difficult to predict individual outcomes. To help students achieve high levels of quality of life, school professionals must understand individual differences and personalize their responses to them.

Differences among individuals are accentuated by their abilities and disabilities. It is hard to know how to provide options for making choices to people like Annie, who have severe mental retardation and compounding communication disabilities. Not only do they have difficulty in formulating choices, but they often cannot communicate their choices. Kirk provides another example of how abilities impact choices. Let's suppose that Kirk has chosen to become a physician and has communicated that choice to his family and teachers. His choice may be complicated by the fact that, because of his emotional problems, he has difficulty managing frustration and stress; this could affect his ability to complete difficult premed courses. Think of a person with multiple physical and health issues who may have limited work endurance. While this individual may want to work full time, physical limitations could restrict him or her to part-time work.

The lessons learned from supporting the needs of persons with disabilities are applicable to learners as a whole. First, people with disabilities are prevented from achieving high quality-of-life outcomes more by our lack of collective creativity in developing alternative methods of teaching and accommodating their individual needs than they are by their own disabilities. Technology now enables many persons with disabilities to overcome traditional barriers to exercising choice and performing tasks. Communication systems on computers allow people to interact with their environment despite physical or cognitive limitations. Second, what constitutes performance need not be the same for all learners. For instance, balancing a checkbook can be done in a variety of ways. Some people enter checks and determine their new balance each time they write a check. Others collect a series of debits before they take the time to compute their account. Still others enter their outstanding checks onto a computer spreadsheet, let the computer do the computation, and simply record the balance reported. All of these methods accomplish the same result, but each suits different competencies and affective needs of individuals, and collectively they move beyond the expectation of standard, independent performances by all learners.

The dominant culture in the United States stresses independence, perseverance, and hard work (Baldwin, 1994). Independent people who can "do for themselves" and are self-sufficient are highly valued. Independence is important, but using independent performance as the primary criterion for success creates unnecessary roadblocks for individuals to achieve quality-of-life outcomes. When you understand that learners bring different strengths and needs to the classroom, you can personalize learning opportunities and learner outcomes and support individual quality of life. The development of compensatory skills, interdependence, and partial participation are equally viable strategies and assure that individuals are not unduly restricted by their learning preferences and abilities.

**COMPENSATORY SKILLS** Compensatory skills offer an individual alternative methods for getting a job done. Take the checkbook example. Not everyone needs to learn to compute his or her own balances. Technology can do it for us. Learning to use a computer to balance a checkbook is a compensatory skill for individuals who have difficulty with math algorithms. A person with severe physical limitations may learn to wear tennis shoes with Velcro closures as an alternative to shoes with laces that require tying. Some learners need to compensate for a lack of reading skills that limits their ability to understand a difficult text. For example, Michael relied on the **mnemonic** SQ3R —for *s*urvey, *q*uestion, *r*ead, *r*ecite, *r*eview (Robinson, 1961; see Chapter 10). This compensatory strategy helps him remember to check for understanding after each paragraph he reads.

**INTERDEPENDENCE** Interdependence refers to people depending on other people to perform for them or assist them in the demonstration of certain skills (Condeluci, 1991). The experienced bricklayer may help the novice complete the construction of a wall. This master craftsman may lack the vigor of the novice, while the novice lacks the experience of the master. The collective capacity of the team to complete the task is greater than the ability of either individual. This concept captures the spirit of collaboration that business and industry is increasingly calling on our schools to teach. The concept of interdependence recognizes both the strengths and the limitations that individuals bring to tasks. It promotes collaborative problem solving and deemphasizes attention to learning differences and abilities.

**PARTIAL PARTICIPATION** An extension of interdependence is the principle of **partial participation**

(Baumgart, Brown, Pumpian, Nisbet, Ford, Sweet, Messina, & Schroeder, 1982). This principle supports access to environments and activities for individuals with disabilities even when their contribution to a particular task may be minimal (Falvey, 1986). Physical limitations prevent some bowlers from grasping, holding, and releasing a ball on the bowling lane. In fact, the only thing some bowlers can do is push a ball perched at the top of a ramp adapted for their use, but these bowlers are still participating in the fun of bowling. In a cooperative science learning activity, a learner with significant cognitive limitations can be responsible for acquiring, distributing, collecting, and turning in group materials and equipment.

Compensatory skills, interdependence, and partial participation are important dimensions of independence. They show us ways of thinking about independence that support individuals with varying abilities in taking part fully in the routines and activities of daily living. School professionals face many decisions as to whether independence, compensation, interdependence, or partial participation should guide an individual's skill development and use. These decisions depend in part on variables such as personal choice, learning capacity, time, and resources. Assisting individuals in making these choices is critical for achieving personalized quality-of-life outcomes.

## ■ SECTION SUMMARY

The diverse characteristics of students, including their cultural and individual needs, will necessarily have an impact on our ability to support their achievement of similar school outcomes. While we strive to achieve family connections, self-determination, lifelong learning, socioeconomic security and productivity, and community participation for all learners, the manner in which they achieve and demonstrate those outcomes will be different because of their cultural and individual values, needs, and experiences. Economic security and productivity for Tanya might take the form of work as a lab assistant in a hospital, whereas Kirk may fulfill his dream of becoming a physician. Self-determination for Annie may consist of directing and requesting assistance from her friends and family through an augmentative computer-based communication system. The challenge for schools is to understand the individual characteristics of learners and respond flexibly. Schools face many decisions as they create learning environments for diverse students, but applying the principles of inclusive school practices can make those decisions easier.

## Chapter Summary

Our call for schools that promote democratic principles and place primary emphasis on the needs of children to guide the operation and conduct of education is certainly neither new nor unique. In his classic *Democracy and Education*, John Dewey (1916) promoted a society that had "a type of education which gives individuals a personal interest in social relationships and control, and the habits of the mind which secure social change without introducing disorder" (p. 115). Unfortunately, we concur with Apple and Beane (1995) that the gap between democratic values and school practices is as wide now as ever. But there is evidence throughout our nation that individuals and groups are striving to close this gap and create inclusive school communities that honor and incorporate the rights of all children (Blase, Blase, Anderson, & Dungan, 1995; Falvey, 1995; National Center on Educational Restructuring and Inclusion, 1994, 1995; National Education Association, 1994; Rogers, 1994; York-Barr et al., 1996).

Restructuring our educational system to promote inclusive school communities that reflect democratic principles and support the needs of all students requires attention to school governance, organization, roles for all players, and classroom practices. It also requires a strong commitment by and sharing of power among many constituencies. The work is neither easy nor time-limited (Morra, 1994). In a study of eight school principals who strove to establish school communities that operated according to democratic values, Blase and his colleagues (1995) discovered that this type of reform requires an ongoing commitment to the immense challenges of ensuring a voice for teacher and family and community, promoting equity, redefining roles, building trust, managing time, and challenging hierarchical, authoritarian, centralized administrative policies and procedures. In addition, school professionals face the ongoing challenge of implementing effective curriculum and instruction strategies that balance individual and group needs and promote an overall positive classroom community (O'Connor & Jenkins, 1996).

This chapter serves as the foundation for discussions that can lead to action by defining the values and beliefs that undergird inclusive school communities. First, students drive the educational decision-making process. Second, all students are valued participants of their school communities. Third, diversity requires flexible, fluid organizational policies, structures, and practices. Fourth, inclusive school communities require the collective, cohesive efforts of school professionals, support personnel, students, families, and community members. Fifth, collective, cohesive action is predicated on collaborative decision-making structures. These values and beliefs can be applied as school professionals, support personnel, families, students, and community members articulate a mission for their individual school community. Shared missions allow all stakeholders to understand what is important to their unique needs and how they will solve their problems.

We have proposed five broad, common educational outcomes for all learners. While each school community must conduct thoughtful discussions as to the outcomes that are most important to their needs, the outcomes presented here reflect essential components for high quality of life for all learners. Furthermore, the outcomes respond to the social, political, and economic needs of our nation. The principles that promote quality of life help guide daily decisions that are made in schools that help to meet the collective and individual needs of students, school professionals, support personnel, families, and community members. Throughout the remainder of this text, we provide you with further information and ideas about the organizational and procedural methods that can help you realize these important goals.

Now, take one last moment to reflect on your image of yourself as a teacher. In what ways is it similar to or different from the one you had when you started this chapter?

**INSTRUCTIONAL ACTIVITIES**

## The Media Portfolio

### Objectives

- To analyze the various ways that the media represent and influence society's perspectives on disabilities
- To work collaboratively to create a product under a time constraint

### Materials

- Current newspapers
- Radio talk shows
- Television shows
- Movies
- The Web

### Product

- A class portfolio

### Agenda

- Your instructor will assign students to the following work groups: product production, product organization, materials collection, materials editing, product dissemination.

- The *product organization group* will develop and present an overview of the product organization with timelines. For example, they will create the table of contents, the major sections, and sample formats for tables and charts according to the organizational schema of their design.

- The *materials collection group* will create a filing system to collect information and set up a process for in-class material collection.

- The *product production work group* will locate on-campus resources for desktop publishing and graphic design and make decisions about the electronic and hard copy forms of the product. For instance, on campuses where hypermedia is available, the work group may want to create hypermedia stacks as well as a print copy.

■ The *materials editing group* will create a rubric for evaluating the content of each media entry. This rubric will include criteria for the appropriateness of the media clip presented, the analysis of the meaning in terms of the objective of the clip, and a decision whether to return the product to the author for revisions or send it on to the product production group for inclusion in the portfolio.

■ As the product is in the development process, the *product dissemination group* will evaluate the possible outlets for dissemination of the product and bring at least two options back to the class for selection. This group must consider costs, audience, and marketing strategies.

■ In addition to belonging to one of the project groups, you must submit at least two media contributions.

## *Evaluation*

■ You are accountable for the timely submission and revision, if necessary, of your own media contributions. You either pass or fail these criteria.

■ Work groups are accountable to the class for timely completion of their assigned tasks. Work groups either pass or fail these criteria.

■ You must complete a self-evaluation of your own work group contribution that includes a list of the tasks you completed or assisted on, a judgment about the quality of your contribution to each task, and an overall narrative about the collaborative experience. Your instructor may choose to grade this on a pass/fail basis or to assign points or percentages.

# Understanding Disability Through Case Studies

## *Objective*

■ To identify the key needs of the students portrayed in the five case studies and to use this information to make recommendations regarding each student's individual educational needs and programming

## *Materials*

■ Case studies

## *Product*

■ A series of five briefs prepared by pairs of students

## *Agenda*

■ Your instructor will assign students to pair groups, making sure that they exchange e-mail addresses and phone numbers so that they can communicate between class periods.

■ This initial assignment will be reviewed for the completeness of their analysis of the case studies, although they may add to their briefs throughout the grading period.

■ The audience for the briefs will be the parents and family members of each student, as well as teachers and other school professionals who may need information about the five students.

■ The briefs should incorporate "people first" language conventions.

■ Follow this format: Each brief should begin with an introduction that describes the student in each case study. The introduction should be followed by an analysis of the student's strengths and learning needs. The brief should contain two to three paragraphs that describe the kinds of activities in which each student may engage in school.

■ Revisit these briefs after reading each chapter of the book, and revise the content of each brief based on new learning and understanding about students with disabilities.

## *Evaluation*

■ Each brief will be evaluated for evidence that they read the cases and identified details of individual student needs.

# Glossary

**Adhocracies** Organizations that are built on premises of innovation and problem solving.

**Affective** Involving emotion.

**Appropriate education** An education that addresses the identified needs of a student as determined by comprehensive assessment and input from the student, family members, and school professionals.

**Autonomy** Independence.

**Categorical-based classrooms** Classrooms organized and created according to a set of categories such as labels or functions. For example, a learning disabilities classroom is created to address the needs of students who have been labeled as having learning disabilities.

**Cognitive psychology** An area of study within the field of psychology that has to do with cognition or thinking.

**Compensatory skills** Skills that are taught to an individual to minimize the effect of a disability. For example, a student might be taught to use mnemonic strategies to make up for a problem in memorization.

**Demographics** Descriptors of a group or area of the country such as population size, ethnicity, age, population density, and primary language.

**Disenfranchised** A perception that one's rights or privileges as set forth by the government are no longer important or accessible.

**Diversification** The process of creating a variety of products, activities, or areas of expertise that are more specialized. For example, the field of special education was diversified by the creation of areas of expertise that coincided with specific disability labels.

**Governance** Having to do with the manner in which a group or body makes decisions and conducts itself.

**homogeneity** Of the same or similar kind or nature.

**impermanence** Not permanent.

**Inalienable rights** Rights that are guaranteed and cannot be taken away or denied.

**Individuals with Disabilities Act of 1997 (IDEA)** Federal legislation mandating the provision of a free and appropriate education for students with disabilities. This sweeping legislation was initially authorized in 1975 as Public Law 94-142 and sets forth the minimal provision of education for students with disabilities and their families.

**Least restrictive environment** The environment that is most similar to, if not the same as, the general education setting, in which a student with disabilities can receive an appropriate education.

**Linguistic** Having to do with language.

**Mnemonic** A strategy or device that assists memory.

**Multidisciplinary teams** Collaborative teams consisting of individuals who represent multiple disciplines such as medicine, education, social work, rehabilitation.

**Partial participation** Allowing a person to participate in only a portion of an activity and event because he or she is unable to carry out the activity or be involved fully in the entire event.

**Paraprofessional** An individual who serves as a support person to and is supervised by an educator.

**Psychological empowerment** The level to which individuals believe that they can control the events or direction of their lives.

**P.L. 94-142** The original piece of legislation, passed in 1975, authorizing and mandating educational rights for students with disabilities.

**Reciprocal interactions** Interactions between one or more people that are mutual or complementary.

**Self-determination** A characteristic of behavior that is self-directed, goal-oriented, and purposeful.

**Self-realization** An individual's knowledge of his or her strengths, needs, and capacities.

**Self-regulation** The process by which an individual is able to plan, monitor, evaluate, and change his or her own behavior.

**Sign language** A system of communication that involves the use of the hands and fingers to symbolize words or expressions.

**Special education subsystem** A system separate from the general education system for managing the education of students with disabilities.

**Stigmatization** The negative labeling of an individual or group by another individual or group as different based on issues such as a conflict in values, behaviors, or physical features.

**Title I** A component of the Elementary and Secondary Education Act that authorizes and mandates literacy education in schools for underprivileged students.

**Transdisciplinary teaming** Collaborative teams consisting of persons who represent multiple disciplines but who conduct the work of the team through a blending of roles and responsibilities.

**Transition services** A set of services that are targeted toward assisting students with disabilities to be prepared to move from high school to postsecondary environments such as college, technical schools, or jobs. These services might include work experiences, visits to college campuses, or curriculum experiences that help students develop the skills or attitudes expected in the future environment.

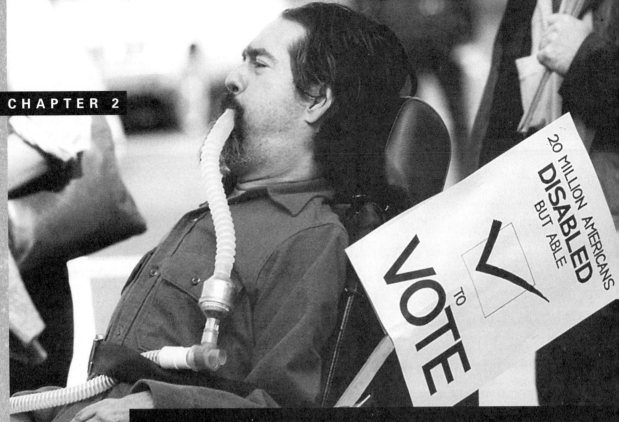

## CHAPTER 2

# Public Policy and Students with Disabilities

# Knowledge Makes a Difference for All

*by Nancy and Bill Baesman*

As parents of a beautiful young girl who began her life with some unique challenges, we believed from the start of her educational life process that she had a right to learn with her peers and to reach her full potential. Knowledge not only of our daughter's abilities and disabilities but also of the law was critical in obtaining an appropriate education for her. Being well versed in the law enabled us to become more involved in every aspect of her education because we knew we had a right to participate in the design and process. Our knowledge was also an asset to those professionals who lacked understanding of the law and who were able to benefit from our input.

Our daughter entered the school system in 1976, one year after Public Law 94-142 was passed. But instead of being sent to a segregated school for children with disabilities, she attended kindergarten in the public school across the street from our home, with the cooperation of school administrators, teachers, and parents. This happened because we knew the law and interpreted "least restrictive environment (LRE)" as meaning the neighborhood school. The success of this move not only changed our daughter's life forever but also changed our school district's attitude toward children with disabilities.

Our knowledge of the law also allowed us to contribute to the design of our daughter's **individualized education plan (IEP).** The educators were more attentive and receptive to our input, and this made the staffing less intimidating for all concerned. In fact, conveying to the staff that we were aware of the law and our daughter's rights made the parent/professional partnership work in the truest sense. It gave each member of the team an equal voice in the articulation and attainment of the ultimate goal—meeting the unique needs of our child. When the partnership was working, we saw the greatest growth in our daughter's achievements. However, when the educational process became defensive and uncertain, our daughter's educational supports broke down, and her potential was unchallenged.

Our knowledge of the law also changed the attitudes of the educators toward us as parents. One director of special education wrote us a letter nine years after we left his school district—and after a **due process hearing**—and said, "I'm proud to have known you and been a part of your life. I'm also happy with the impact you have had on special education in Grandview, especially our **occupational therapy (OT)** program, which is now a model for all schools." We had also started the first extended-school-year (ESY) program in that district. In another school district, we brought in a nationally known expert to consult with staff on how to provide community-based education. The staff was averse to this idea at first, but within a year, one teacher had thanked us, and another was coming to realize how important it was to listen to parents in order to foster her abilities as a teacher. When our daughter started high school, we once again tapped our knowledge of the law to insist that she attend her neighborhood school. Within two years, *all* high school students in the school district were attending their neighborhood schools. We believe that we were respected for the positive actions we took on behalf of our child. Parents who know the rights of their child can only increase the staff members' awareness of the law and help them through the process.

For us, due process is a way of resolving potential conflict, an avenue by which parents can exercise their rights to the fullest extent possible under the law. When parents know they are absolutely correct about their child's education but are unable to convince the educational system, due process may be their only recourse. But due process should be viewed as a positive means by which to resolve the dispute. Twice during our own child's educational life, we were able to assert her rights, and our efforts were not futile because a third party was compelled to decide. Due process was not easy, but it was definitely the right way to ensure our daughter's quality of education, and ultimately it proved to be successful for other students as well.

P.L. 94-142 was intended to help educators provide an appropriate public education with meaningful educational benefits in the least restrictive environment for all children. Because parents have pertinent information about their children, they need to participate as valued members of the team. *The child must always be the focal point, and that child's education must always be the primary concern.* We believe that our knowledge of the law and the steps we took to ensure our daughter's rights gave her the best possible inclusive, community-based education with her neighborhood peers, as well as all the **related services** necessary for her to succeed.

# Introduction

Public schools in this country have a remarkable history of being essentially locally controlled and managed public enterprises. Traditionally, schools and school districts or local administrative units have reflected the values of the communities and families they served. They have also mirrored the values of the school professionals who worked in the schools. In Chapter 1, we discussed the values that underlie much of our public school system—values that are institutionalized in school curricula and in methods of assessment, instruction, and evaluation. When we look at the policies, organizational structures, and practices of local schools, we can see that they, too, reflect community values. When communities are homogeneous, this congruence between community values and school practices smoothes the transition between home and school. However, as we also pointed out in Chapter 1, our communities are no longer mono-cultural or mono-linguistic or mono-ethnic. Yet many local and state educational policies remain rooted in the assumption that most students come from similar backgrounds and share common experiences. While students from the dominant culture may flourish in such a situation, other students are put at risk for succeeding and achieving because their backgrounds, experiences, and opportunities have not prepared them to succeed in this environment.

In the past, when schools and local school districts failed to accommodate the diversity of their student populations, there was little recourse. African-Americans, Hispanics, Native Americans, and students with disabilities experienced prejudice, separatism, inequality, and inadequate schooling (Karagiannis, Stainback, & Stainback, 1996). But, beginning with the **Brown v. Board of Education** ruling by the Supreme Court in 1954, the federal government has increasingly intervened on behalf of children and youths whose families have not been able to advocate for them.

This chapter tells the story of the federal laws that have been passed to protect the rights of individuals and minority group members who historically were excluded from receiving an education. These laws have influenced local educational practices when such practices and values have conflicted with national views of equity and access. The tension between individual and local values and the values promoted through federal legislation has been played out in many policy areas.

Some critics might assert that philosophy and ethics are the more appropriate disciplines to examine. But the remarkable, and perhaps unprecedented, influence of law in promoting access to education for marginalized groups of people, including children with disabilities, cannot be overstated.

Our values and our expanding knowledge base have had a significant impact on the development and implementation of law, which, in turn, has influenced local school practices. Changes in laws and policies that govern schools reflect how well graduates of the educational system perform in their jobs, their communities, and their families. This cyclical, interactive process means that while law constrains our behaviors, it also reflects the values that society wants to promote. In many respects, the passage of legislation that protects the rights of people with disabilities has pushed local communities to reevaluate how they have responded to the diverse needs of their local populations. Not surprisingly, disability law has affected the autonomy of local school districts, because laws that govern equity and access for persons with disabilities have emerged at the federal level. In some cases, states, school districts, and schools have been forced to respond to the needs of individuals with disabilities without any community consensus to do so. Consequently, values favoring diversity and inclusion are emerging, albeit slowly in some places, in all of our public school systems.

The history of disability legislation illustrates how litigation and legislation are active, ongoing processes. Each action in a court influences the work of legislators, just as legislation influences the work of the courts. As you read this chapter, think about the impact that this dynamic process might have on your professional roles and responsibilities. Knowing the law as it is presently constituted fulfills only part of your professional responsibility in assuring that legal mandates are implemented. As a school professional, you also must keep informed of changes in legislation, regulations, and case law, because developments in each of these arenas affect practices in schools.

Through federal mandates, the landscapes of classrooms and the lives of families and school professionals have been profoundly changed. As we saw in Chapter 1, students like Kurume, Kirk, Annie, and Tanya now attend schools with their more typical, same-aged peers. Classrooms have evolved because they include so many more types of students than ever before. The lives of families have changed because disability laws have empowered them to take the lead in determining the kinds of services and supports their children receive in public schools. And school professionals have expanded their vision of their roles in school and have learned to collaborate with families on an equal basis.

In this chapter, you will develop a historical and legal context for educating all learners, including those with disabilities, in the least restrictive environment possible. While some of this chapter introduces you to practices that are mandated by law, the essential message is that the values of communities influence the kinds of practices that occur in schools.

First, we examine the relationship between laws, regulations, and practices. Second, we introduce the laws that have had the greatest impact on how schools in the United States respond to the challenges of serving students with disabilities. These laws reflect a growing social concern for assuring equity in and access to public education for all students. Third, we discuss three pieces of federal legislation that have had a significant influence on our current educational system and the values it supports: Section 504 of the Vocational Rehabilitation Act, the Americans with Disabilities Act (ADA), and Public Law 94-142 (now known as IDEA 97). The spirit of these laws provides the context for our vision for schools of the twenty-first century as inclusive communities. Understanding how and why students with disabilities have come to have equal access to educational services in their local school systems through these legislative acts is essential to your understanding of special education. It will help you prepare both to meet the needs of learners who have disabilities and to work collaboratively with their families.

# The Relationship Among Laws, Regulations, and Practices

Laws are public policies that guide decision making, identify outcomes, and allocate resources to achieve specific goals. The public policies that inform our educational practices are developed through the legislative process by our elected legislators (senators, representatives, and so on) at the state and federal levels. Values undergird our most important laws and are translated

into law as elements or principles that guide implementation. In the educational realm, policy, or law, guides the design and implementation of programs and services for students and their families and regulates how families and school professionals will work together to accomplish this. Not all policies are laws, but laws like IDEA 97 form the basis of our public policy on the education of persons with disabilities. Not all policy is set at the federal level; some public policies are set at the state and local levels. For instance, the responsibility of real estate developers to set aside land for public schools is determined at the local level, while the type of taxes to be levied to support public education is determined at the state level.

## Regulations

Regulations or rules are written when a policy becomes codified as law through the legislative process. Once a law is enacted, the executive branch of government develops regulations that define or interpret the law. Regulations specify the procedures that must be followed in order to carry out the intent of the law. Regulations are governed by policy (law) set by the legislative branch of government, but the actual process of writing regulations is carried out by the appropriate executive branch of government, such as the U.S. Department of Education or the State Board of Education. If the policy is set at the local level, the school board or local school administrative unit may initiate the policy.

Regulations and their administration are one area in which the interpretation of law can be challenged; after all, regulations are themselves merely interpretations of law. For instance, one of the key elements of

IDEA 97 is that individuals with disabilities must be educated in the **least restrictive environment** possible. Let's look at how two hypothetical school districts respond to this legal mandate.

One school system, the Plutarch School District, may define the least restrictive environment as the environment in which other, typical students are educated. So, Plutarch creates a system where services to students with disabilities are delivered in general education classrooms with back up available, in other settings, only if needed. The Xertron School District, right next door, may interpret least restrictive environment in a very different way. Xertron assumes that students with certain types of disabilities are least restricted when their access to general education curriculum is provided in classrooms with low student: teacher ratios where other students with similar needs are educated. As a result, Xertron creates a system of services where children with disabilities are in resource rooms, special classrooms or schools. It allocates its resources based on these assumptions. Both systems may serve similar numbers of students with disabilities but in one system these students are most often in general education classrooms while in the other, students with disabilities are most often found in resource rooms and special classes.

It is in the translation of principles like least restrictive environment and individual need into a **service delivery system** that distortions of the intent of the law are created. School districts are systems that need to be able to anticipate what services their customers will need. As a result, they create programs and services in anticipation of that need. However, once the system is created, the bureaucracy has difficulty in adapting the system to serve the child whose special needs it may not have anticipated (Skrtic, 1995).

Look at what happens to the principle of least restrictive environment when two students, each with the same disabilities, enter our two hypothetical school districts. Plutarch and Xertron, like most school systems, have fairly rigid bureaucracies; staff is hired, budgets are set, and resources are allocated in predictable ways—assuming each district can predict how many and what kinds of students it will have in the next academic year and what schools those students might attend. And both Xertron and Plutarch, like other school systems, must address these organizational needs if they are to achieve stability over time.

The student who shows up in Xertron is placed in a special class for middle school students with disabilities like his. The student who shows up in Plutarch receives a middle school schedule like the other students without disabilities in her school. The student in the Plutarch system gets special support services from a special educator who visits his English class daily. The student in the Xertron system receives help and services from a special educator who teaches the special class. Xertron and Plutarch, like other school systems, respond best to the needs of students they are organized to work with. If the students in our example, each enrolled in a different school system, are a "match" for the services that the systems are prepared to provide, then they will benefit educationally. However, this scenario raises two questions: (1) Are the services provided a good fit for the individual students' needs? and (2) Are the services provided in the least restrictive environment possible?

Programs may not be the least restrictive. Additionally, IDEA 97 is concerned with services, not programs, that meet the individual needs of students. However, in an attempt to allocate resources, school districts create programs that may or may not meet student needs. Schools are caught in a conundrum in which they must meet the individual needs of students, which requires more flexibility than most schools' systems can accommodate. Therefore, when school district practices dictate that a student must participate in a particular program because he or she has a particular disability, then their regulations are vulnerable to criticism on the basis that the issue of the least restrictive environment is not adequately addressed. This criticism, at its most action oriented, plays itself out in court.

## Case Law

When the interpretation of an existing law is questioned, legal challenges help to define or clarify the issue. Service providers, families, persons with disabilities, school districts, and others all can challenge the interpretation and implementation of law. Challenges to existing practice are made through litigation in the courts, which interpret the law and scrutinize existing regulation. A series of challenges to a law or policy form the basis of case law. Case law provides a precedent for both writing and revising policy.

Protesters demand their legal right to full inclusion in the community rather than confinement to institutions.

An example from P.L. 94-142 (now IDEA 97) might make this dynamic clearer. When P.L. 94-142 was passed in 1975, parents were given many rights, including the right to contest student placement decisions made by school districts. The new law specified procedures by which parents who disagreed with a school district's decision ultimately could take the district to court. However, nothing in the original law stipulated who would bear the costs of the legal fees should the district be found at fault for not complying with the law. Therefore, although parents had an avenue to protest, few could afford to act because they could not afford attorney fees. After the courts ruled that attorney fees were to be paid by districts that lost

their cases, amendments to the law codified this practice in IDEA 97.

## Reauthorization of Laws

This cycle of drafting and passing legislation, writing regulations, and then challenging them through case law can lead to new laws that make explicit what may have been too vague in the original legislation. When bills are simply reviewed and revised based on public testimony and changing political and social values, case law can influence the outcomes of **reauthorization.** When bills are reauthorized, or extended, they receive a new number, denoting the session of the Congress in which the reauthorization occurred and the order in which it was passed. Because of the numbering convention, in 1990, P.L. 94-142, the Education of All Handicapped Children Act was reauthorized and renamed P.L. 101-457, the Individuals with Disabilities Act. Reauthorization of a bill on a regular basis helps to ensure that the intent of law and its execution are as closely aligned as possible. The 105th Congress of the United States reauthorized IDEA in 1997; this new bill, IDEA 97, is numbered P.L. 105-17. In the next section, we trace the development of federal educational policy over the recent decades.

## ■ SECTION SUMMARY

Laws, policies, and regulations inform our educational practices for all learners. Laws mandate the design and implementation of programs and services for students and their families and regulate how school professionals and families will work together to accomplish this. Regulations specify the procedures that must be followed according to specific laws. For example, according to IDEA 97, individuals with disabilities must be educated in the least restrictive environment.

## Historical Context: From ESEA to ADA

Until the 1950s, because education was not specifically addressed in the U.S. Constitution, educational policy was the sole responsibility of state and local governments. As a result, both access to and quality of education varied greatly from community to community. Gingerly, the federal government began to address educational policy in the 1950s, culminating in the passage of the Elementary and Secondary Education Act (ESEA) of 1965 (P.L. 89-10). The recognition that the federal government should, and would, pass policy addressing educational services in public schools paved the way for more specific legislation in the 1970s that addressed the needs of children with disabilities.

Factors such as changing values and beliefs about diversity, expanded responsibilities of public schools, national economic needs, and the numbers of children who were **disenfranchised** from their local schools converged on legislators at the federal level and created the impetus for new, ground-breaking legislation (see Table 2.1). In this section, you'll learn to identify some pieces of legislation by acronym (such as ESEA and ADA) and others by numbers (such as P.L. 94-142). In this text, we've used the referents that seem to be most commonly used. Each bill has a number that identifies the legislative session in which it was passed, as well as the number that the bill was assigned in that session; for example, P.L. 94-142 was the hundred-and-forty-second bill passed in the ninety-fourth session of Congress. P.L. 94-142 also has a name, the Education of All Handicapped Children Act, but traditionally it was referred to as P.L. 94-142. In the 1990 reauthorization of P.L. 94-142, it was renamed the Individuals with Disabilities Education Act (IDEA) to reflect changes in the language used to refer to persons with disabilities. In 1997, IDEA was reauthorized once again and became IDEA 97. Other bills, like the Americans with Disabilities Act (ADA), have come to be known by their acronyms; ADA is numbered as P.L. 101-336.

## The Elementary and Secondary Education Act (ESEA)

ESEA was a broad educational act that supported many federal initiatives. It provided funding to school systems so that they could offer free and reduced-price lunches to children whose parents' income was at or below poverty level. It provided additional teachers to schools in impoverished communities so that young children who were having difficulty learning to read would have the extra support they needed to become literate. ESEA targeted the children who—due to poverty, lack of opportunity, or disability—needed extra services and supports to benefit from their public school education. For instance, ESEA funded **vocational education** and education to students with disabilities. In ESEA, Congress also established a grant program to encourage states to initiate, expand on, and improve education for children with disabilities. In 1970, the grant program was revised as the Education for the Handicapped Act (P.L. 91-230). This act, like its predecessor, created incentives so that states that established programs for children with disabilities

**TABLE 2.1** **Key Federal Legislation Impacting Individuals with Disabilities and Their Families**

- *P.L. 89-10, the Elementary and Secondary Education Act of 1965.* This act established the role of the federal government in ensuring that underprivileged groups had access to high-quality educational programs and outcomes.

- *P.L. 93-112, the Vocational Rehabilitation Act Amendments of 1973.* This act contains Section 504, an antidiscrimination clause protecting the rights of people with disabilities.

- *P.L. 94-142, the Education of All Handicapped Children Act of 1975.* This act authorized and mandated educational rights for students with disabilities.

- *P.L. 101-476, the Education of the Handicapped Act Amendments of 1990.* This act changed the name of P.L. 94-142 to the Individuals with Disabilities Education Act (IDEA). It expands discretionary programs, mandates transition and assistive technology services in IEPs, and adds two new categories of disabilities: autism and traumatic brain injury.

- *P.L. 101-336, the Americans with Disabilities Act of 1990.* This law mandates access for individuals with disabilities in employment, public accommodation, transportation, state and local government services, and telecommunications.

## Extending Your Learning

What events in the 1960s influenced the passage of ESEA?

could receive money from the federal government that would defray program implementation costs. However, specific guidelines for program development were not included. ESEA today continues to provide financial support to school districts whose students come from lower socioeconomic classes, as well as to women's athletic programs.

## Section 504 of the Vocational Rehabilitation Act

At the same time that families of children with disabilities were impacting state and federal educational law through the court system, adults with disabilities were making their voices heard in the Vocational Rehabilitation Act of 1973. In 1973, many veterans of the Vietnam War were in need of support and services as they returned to civilian life. In particular, Section 504 of the act prohibits discrimination against anyone with a disability based solely on the disability. To this day, state and local government (including school districts), as well as any private organization that receives funds from the federal government, must comply with this mandate or risk losing the funds.

## P.L. 94-142

A flurry of civil rights litigation on behalf of individuals with disabilities culminated in the passage of P.L. 94-142, the Education of All Handicapped Children Act (EHCA), signed into law by President Gerald Ford. Since 1975, as a result of this law, public schools have been required to ensure that all children, "regard-less of their disability, be entitled to a free and appropriate public education from the age of 3 through their 22nd birthday." One of the law's chief achievements was to establish the role of families as critical in the process of determining appropriate services. Because of P.L. 94-142, families have been empowered to serve as advocates for their children's needs. You'll note that the Baesmans, the family described in the chapter-opening vignette, were strong advocates for their daughter from the time that she entered school.

Approximately every five years, P.L. 94-142 has been reauthorized. In 1986, Part H (P.L. 99-457) of the act extended the mandated age for services. Since 1986, services have been available for children from birth through an individual's twenty-second birthday. In 1990, P.L. 94-142 was renamed the Individuals with Disabilities Education Act (IDEA, P.L. 101-476). As part of the reauthorization, a mandate for planning for transition to adult life was added to the bill. In 1997, President Bill Clinton signed IDEA's reauthorization, IDEA 97.

IDEA 97 remains one of the most comprehensive education acts ever passed by Congress. The original special education legislation was passed to ensure that students with disabilities would get the services they needed to benefit from educational opportunities. In mandating services, the drafters of this legislation understood the need for educating professionals in a variety of areas to provide necessary services. Therefore, the bill authorizes spending on personnel preparation programs at the higher-education level, as well as expenditures to school districts to assist in providing the range of services necessary to guarantee equity of access for all infants, toddlers, and students with disabilities.

In the wake of P.L. 94-142, a series of other acts served to strengthen the intent of the original bill. Table 2.2 outlines the basic provisions of each of these laws. Perhaps the most important of the four measures is P.L. 99-457, mentioned previously as Part H, which extended the services in P.L. 94-142, originally mandated for children and youths ages 3 through 21 to infants and toddlers.

## Extending Your Learning

What act mandated free and appropriate public education for all children, regardless of their disability?

## The Americans with Disabilities Act (ADA)

The **Americans with Disabilities Act (ADA)**, passed in 1990, prohibits discrimination against individuals

| TABLE 2.2 | Other Federal Legislation Impacting Individuals with Disabilities and Their Families, 1986–1989 |

- *P.L. 99-372, the Handicapped Children's Protection Act of 1986.* This act mandates that when parents and guardians dispute a school system's provision of services to their children and prevail, they can be reimbursed for reasonable attorney fees and costs.

- *P.L. 99-457, the Education of the Handicapped Amendments of 1986.* Part H mandates services for preschoolers with disabilities and provides incentives to states for early intervention services for children up to age 3.

- *P.L. 100-407, the Technology-Related Assistance for Individuals with Disabilities Act of 1988.* This law assists states in developing programs of technology-related assistance to individuals with disabilities and their families.

- *P.L. 101-127, the Children with Disabilities Temporary Care Reauthorization Act of 1989.* This act funds respite care and crisis nurseries for children with disabilities and chronic illness, as well as for children at risk of abuse or neglect.

- *P.L. 101-392, the Carl D. Perkins Vocational and Applied Technology Education Act of 1990.* This act guarantees full vocational education opportunities for youths with disabilities.

with disabilities in both the public and the private sectors and mandates accessibility in all public transportation and accommodations. It has had far-reaching implications for employers, state and local governments, public services such as transportation and telecommunications, and entities that provide services to the public such as restaurants, bars, and shopping centers.

## ■ SECTION SUMMARY

ESEA, Section 504, IDEA, and ADA represent a new activism on the part of federal legislators. Through these acts, Congress translated the values of equity and access into public educational policy and practice. Whereas Section 504 prohibits discrimination against people with disabilities in any organization receiving federal funds, IDEA is an entitlement act mandating actual practices. For example, IDEA specifies how decisions will be made about which students receive special education services and how those services will be determined. In fact, schools must be able to show how they are in compliance with the act. Like Section 504, ADA is an antidiscrimination act, extending antidiscrimination provisions to all sectors of U.S. public and private industry. Now that you have a context in which to place these bills, let's take an in-depth look at Section 504 and ADA.

## An In-Depth Look at Section 504 and ADA

While IDEA mandates processes for determining what students are eligible for special education services in schools and how programs and services should be delivered and monitored, Section 504 of the Vocational Rehabilitation Act and ADA address the issues of equity and access in all segments of life. The Vocational Rehabilitation Amendments of 1973 contained an important provision, Section 504, that has wielded immense clout over the years. As new forms of disability have emerged, such as AIDS and **hepatitis B**, Section 504 has provided a guidepost to assist organizations in responding equitably to the practical issues raised by these infectious diseases. ADA has helped people with disabilities to obtain reasonable physical access in the private as well as the public sector.

### The Vocational Rehabilitation Act of 1973

The Vocational Rehabilitation Act and its subsequent amendments established federal support for rehabilitation services to adults with disabilities. Rehabilitation agencies, established in each state, were responsible for helping adults with disabilities find employment through assessment, training, and on-the-job support.

The act also set guidelines for the work of these agencies. For instance, in 1973, amendments to the act required rehabilitation agencies to give first priority to individuals with the most severe disabilities. For example, of our five students from Chapter 1 (Annie, Michael, Tanya, Kirk, and Kurume), Annie and Tanya might be prioritized over the three boys because their disabilities require more intense services. In addition to mandating the types of services that adults with disabilities might receive to become productively employed, the act also established guidelines for supporting employment of people with disabilities. In particular, Title V of the act has had a powerful, long-term impact on discrimination.

**TITLE V**   Title V of the Vocational Rehabilitation Act of 1973 contains five sections that provide protections to people with disabilities. Among other things, these sections mandate the following:

- That federal agencies have affirmative action programs to hire and promote qualified persons with disabilities
- That all buildings constructed with federal funds or owned or leased by federal agencies be free of any barriers that may affect persons with physical disabilities
- That any government contractor have affirmative action programs for persons with disabilities
- That the courts be permitted to determine who will pay the attorney's fees for a prevailing plaintiff in cases pertaining to discrimination against people with disabilities

The fifth section of the act, Section 504, is a deceptively simple piece of legislation. However, it has profoundly influenced the way in which individuals with disabilities have been treated since its inception. Of particular interest here is the increase in the number of students who are eligible for specialized accommodations, supports, and services. This highlights the value that Congress has placed on the need for individualized educational services based on the unique needs of each student.

**SECTION 504**   According to Section 504 of the Vocational Rehabilitation Amendments of 1973, "No otherwise qualified handicapped individual in the United States shall, solely by reason of his handicap, be excluded from the participation in, be denied the benefits of, or be subjected to discrimination under any program or activity receiving federal financial assistance" (29 U.S.C. 794). Because Section 504 applies to all persons with disabilities regardless of age, it has broader clout than IDEA, which applies only to individuals through age 21. Section 504 also has a more inclusive definition of disability than IDEA in that it does not list specific disability categories. Under Section 504, a person with a disability is defined as any person who (1) has a physical or mental impairment that substantially limits one or more major life activities, (2) has a record of such an impairment, or (3) is regarded as having such an impairment. Therefore, if a student can document that he or she has been labeled as disabled by a doctor using medical diagnostic procedures, then he or she may request that the school make appropriate accommodations. In contrast, under IDEA, a student may be given a specific disability label and receive special education services specified in an individual education plan (IEP) only after he or she has been assessed thoroughly and a multidisciplinary team has determined that the child's poor educational performance is due to the disability. It might help to think of Section 504 as ensuring access in schools and IDEA as ensuring that students who need it can get specialized educational services.

Section 504 has particular importance for general educators because students who may not qualify for special education services under IDEA may still qualify for modifications and accommodations under Section 504. This means that classroom teachers need to be able to modify their classroom environments, curricula, testing practices, behavior management strategies, and teaching methods to ensure that students who have disabilities, as defined by Section 504, are served.

An example might help you to understand the impact of Section 504 on your role in schools. Consider Chris, a student at Stapleton School who has been diagnosed by his family doctor as having an **attention deficit disorder** (ADD). While Chris's academic performance may not be poor enough to qualify him for

**Extending Your Learning**

What changes might classroom teachers need to make in their instruction and curricula as a result of Section 504?

**BOX 2.1**

## Southeastern Community College v. Davis (1979)

In 1979, the Supreme Court helped to define the meaning of the phrase "otherwise qualified" in Section 504. Francis Davis had a degenerative hearing impairment when she applied to Southeast Community College's nursing program. She was denied admission to the program after a hearing examination and a determination by the college faculty that she would not be able to perform her job safely for patients. Davis sued the college under Section 504, arguing that she had been discriminated against.

However, the Supreme Court disagreed, interpreting "otherwise qualified" to mean that an individual must be able to meet all of the requirements of the program as long as those requirements are reasonable. The Court ruled that the capacity to hear was a reasonable requirement to make to ensure that nurses would be able to respond to critical care situations. Therefore, the Court upheld the school's decision to deny admission to Davis.

services as a special education student under IDEA, he has a disability as defined by Section 504 because he is currently being treated by a medical doctor for an ongoing condition. The disability is such that Mr. Salazar, his fifth-grade teacher, under the provisions of Section 504, must modify his expectations for the number of minutes that Chris stays on task during reading. Without this modification, Chris may have difficulty sustaining his attention and end up distracting other learners in the classroom. Thus, as this example shows, a student may not qualify for special education services but still, because of a disability condition, require teachers to make changes in their classroom management, curricula, and instructional procedures.

**CLARIFYING SECTION 504**  The two cases in Boxes 2.1 and 2.2 help to explain how Section 504 influences organizations, like schools and school districts, that receive federal funding. The *Davis* case in Box 2.1 illuminates how the law supports the values of equity in and access to programs and jobs. The *Arline* case in Box 2.2 defines the concept of disability. It has particular implications for schools today because more and more students are testing positive for AIDS and HIV. In the *Arline* case, a public school teacher was dismissed because she had tuberculosis. Tuberculosis, like HIV, is a chronic disease. Chronic diseases are ongoing and impact the stamina of people who have them, perhaps resulting in absenteeism. When the Court concurred that chronic diseases constitute a disability, it conferred a protected status on individuals with these types of ailments. Dismissal from a job cannot result simply because a person has a disability. The disability must

prevent the individual from carrying out the essential functions of the job. And an employer has an obligation to provide accommodations to the employee so that he or she can carry out the functions of the job.

Similarly, students with tuberculosis, hepatitis, HIV, or other chronic disease are eligible to receive special accommodations that make the school curriculum accessible to them. For example, the school might have to adjust the student's schedule, shorten the school day, provide rest periods, adapt the physical education curriculum, provide a two-way telecommunications link between the home and the classroom, arrange for an adult tutor at home, or provide an extra set of textbooks at home. The list of potential modifications is lengthy. Remember that Section 504 places the burden on organizations to accommodate the disability of an individual.

**BOX 2.2**

## Board v. Arline (1987)

In 1987, the Supreme Court ruled that Arline, a public school teacher who had tuberculosis, was disabled, because she had a record of being hospitalized for treatment and expert testimony validated her disability condition. The school district, which had fired Arline, had to show that she was not "otherwise qualified" to hold a job as a teacher. Under Section 504, the district was prohibited from firing her simply because she had tuberculosis; having a chronic disease meant that she was in fact disabled.

| **TABLE 2.3** | **ADA Prohibitions Against Discrimination** |

- Employment
- Public services
- Transportation
- Public accommodations
- Services operated by private entities
- Telecommunications

- Housing
- Education
- Recreation
- Voting
- Institutionalization
- Health services

The *Davis* and *Arline* cases also demonstrate the importance of case law. In each case, the courts, and not regulatory agencies, helped to clarify the intent of the law. Note that the first case ruling occurred in 1979, six years after the 1973 Vocational Rehabilitation Act amendment was passed. The *Board* v. *Arline* ruling did not occur until thirteen years after the passage of the legislation.

Section 504 supports accessibility, including accessibility to public education for individuals with disabilities, and prohibits discrimination on the basis of disability alone. Because public schools receive federal funds, they must be in full compliance with Section 504.

## The Americans with Disabilities Act of 1990

The Americans with Disabilities Act of 1990 has been acclaimed as the most far-reaching civil rights legislation since the Civil Rights Act of 1964 (HEATH, 1990). Although schools had been required by law to meet the needs of students with disabilities since 1975, both private and public sector businesses and services responded to the needs of their clients or employees with disabilities as each organization saw fit. This occurred in spite of Section 504, because 504 applied only to organizations that received federal funds. ADA represented a response to the isolation of, discrimination against, and segregation of individuals with disabilities. For instance, architectural and transportation barriers prevented people with disabilities from participating in community activities. The lack of alternative communication access meant that people who were deaf or hard of hearing could not use the telephone or attend lectures. Overprotective rules and policies and exclusionary qualification standards and criteria meant that capable people who were limited in their physical

mobility might be disqualified from holding certain jobs. And having a disability sometimes meant that individuals were segregated or relegated to lesser services, programs, activities, benefits, and jobs.

ADA addressed these issues by prohibiting discrimination against individuals with disabilities in the areas of employment, housing, public accommodations, education, transportation, communication, recreation, institutionalization, health services, voting, and access to public services (see Table 2.3). Prior to passage of ADA, persons with disabilities had no legal recourse to redress such discrimination.

**OVERVIEW** ADA provided a clear and comprehensive national mandate for the elimination of discrimination against persons with disabilities. It also established clear, enforceable standards for identifying and avoiding discrimination. ADA provisions, like those of IDEA 97, ensure a strong federal government role in monitoring and enforcing antidiscrimination standards. ADA also gives Congress the power to address the discrimination faced by persons with disabilities.

Aware that compliance in all the areas in which discrimination against individuals with disabilities is prohibited would be difficult for most businesses and public agencies, lawmakers staggered the schedule for complying with each element. For instance, by July 26, 1994, all employers with fifteen or more employees had to comply with the antidiscrimination element of the law. However, the schedule for complying with transportation requirements ranged from August 26, 1990, to July 26, 2010. Yet another deadline was set for restaurants, hotels, and retail stores and malls, which had to meet antidiscrimination standards by January 26, 1992.

**ADA AND SCHOOLS** The principles and policies of the Americans with Disabilities Act serve as a basis for our national disability policy. "Under the ADA, disability is recognized as a natural part of the human

## Extending Your Learning

As you consider the various provisions of Section 504 and ADA, think about how these laws have impacted the lives of individuals with disabilities. How will Michael, Kurume, Annie, Tanya, and Kirk's lives be different because of these laws?

experience and in no way diminishes the right of individuals to live independently, enjoy self-determination, make choices, contribute to society, pursue meaningful careers, and enjoy full inclusion and integration in all aspects of American society" (United Cerebral Palsy Association, 1994). ADA regulations go beyond merely mandating services to students who qualify for special education. ADA also stipulates that people with disabilities have access to learning, to employment, and to recreation and leisure activities. As with Section 504, under ADA it is not necessary for a student's disability to be linked to poor educational outcomes in order for a school to have to address access issues. Accessibility to classrooms, bathrooms, lockers, athletic facilities, and transportation must be assured for all students. Libraries and media centers must have alternative ways for students to access print and electronic information. Teachers must provide alternative forms of instruction and assessment for students who need such accommodations, even if the students are not in special education. Because ADA applies to both private and public facilities, it influences what all schools must do, including **charter schools,** private schools, religiously affiliated schools, and vocational/technical schools.

## ■ SECTION SUMMARY

ADA and Section 504 were passed by Congress to ensure that individuals with disabilities would have equal access to public and private sector businesses, services, and employment. Both bills protect the rights of individuals with disabilities and provide sanctions against individuals and organizations that fail to comply with the legislation. Furthermore, both bills have important implications for the work of all school professionals, because they require that students who may not be labeled as disabled by the school system but who need special adaptations and accommodations receive those accommodations.

## An In-Depth Look at IDEA 97

The values that underlie IDEA 97 are basic to the American ideology: **egalitarianism** and inclusion (Turnbull, 1993). From our Declaration of Independence comes the premise that "all men are created equal." This principle has evolved over time through legislation and case law to mean women as well as men, people of color as well as Euro-Americans, people who speak languages other than English, and people with disabilities as well as those without. The principle of inclusion stems from the Fourteenth Amendment to the Constitution, which promises equal protection under the law. It was the Fourteenth Amendment that the attorneys for the plaintiff in the landmark 1954 case *Brown* v. *Board of Education* cited to challenge the separate-but-equal doctrine. As Justice Earl Warren wrote in the majority opinion:

> Today, education is perhaps the most important function of state and local governments. Compulsory school attendance laws and the great expenditures for education both demonstrate our recognition of the importance of education to our democratic society. It is required in the performance of our most basic public responsibilities, even service in the armed forces. It is the very foundation of good citizenship. Today it is a principal instrument in awakening the child to cultural values, in preparing him for later professional training, and in helping him to adjust normally to his environment. In these days, it is doubtful that any child may reasonably be expected to succeed in life if he is denied the opportunity of an education. Such an opportunity, where the state has undertaken to provide it, is a right which must be made available to all on equal terms.

In spite of the Supreme Court ruling, it was not until the passage of P.L. 94-142 twenty-one years later that all children with disabilities were assured access to a free and appropriate public education.

Continuing the tradition established by P.L. 94-142, IDEA 97 gives life to the basic constitutional values of egalitarianism and inclusion (see Table 2.4). IDEA 97 establishes a set of guidelines that govern the services and supports that students with disabilities and their families have the right to expect from their public school systems. But IDEA 97 is more than a set of guidelines. It also provides a mechanism whereby Congress can appropriate funds to the federal Department

| TABLE 2.4 | Key Elements of IDEA 97 |
| --- | --- |

- Access to free and appropriate public education (FAPE)
- The right to be educated in the least restrictive environment (LRE)
- Individualization of the educational program (IEP)
- Protection of student and parent rights
- Guidelines for the determination of a disability
- Provision of related services
- Implementation responsibilities at the federal, state, and local levels

## Extending Your Learning

As you read each section, think about how Tanya's, Michael's, Kurume's, Kirk's, and Annie's lives might have been different without IDEA 97.

amounts to a budget of about $3.1 billion per year (*Education Daily*, 1997).

The following discussion highlights the six key provisions of IDEA 97 that will affect your own practice in schools. Each section describes (1) a particular component of the law, (2) the case law that preceded IDEA 97 and led to the specific provision in the law, and (3) the case law that has helped to define the parameters of each provision.

## Free and Appropriate Public Education (FAPE)

Although it may seem difficult to imagine, there was a time when students with disabilities simply did not attend public schools. Around the turn of the twentieth century, a young psychologist named Alfred Binet was asked to create an exam that would help school officials select students who were able to learn and cull from classes students who were not able to learn at a typical rate and in a typical style. This was one of the first measures of intelligence designed to sort students. Based on the results of this test, certain types of students were excluded from public schools based on their difficulty in learning. Some families cared for these children at home, while others abandoned them or sent them away to institutions where they were sheltered, clothed, and fed. This system of sorting created a Euro-American cultural norm that was maintained by physicians, psychologists, and educators. It was commonly believed that a certain group of children were uneducable and, therefore, unlikely to benefit from any educational services. While this notion of who was educable broadened over time, even in the 1970s a sizable number of children in the United States were denied access to public education because of their perceived inability to learn and benefit from public education.

P.L. 94-142 profoundly revolutionized our cultural notions about disability and capacity by mandating educational services for all. Prior to the implementation of this law, children like Tanya would never have been

of Education to assist states and local school districts in implementing services and supports for students with disabilities.

IDEA 97 targets specific activities needed to provide educational services to every child with a disability. Although IDEA 97 contains the funding mandate to support the education of individuals with disabilities in local public school systems, it funds many other activities as well. For instance, IDEA 97 provides funding for research to develop our knowledge base about disabilities and their impact on learning and attaining quality-of-life outcomes. Additionally, IDEA 97 provides funding to support the education and training of school professionals to work with students with disabilities and their families.

Enforcement of the law occurs through a series of monitoring and evaluating activities carried out by the federal, state, and local education agencies. Data on the outcomes of special education services are reported to Congress each year. These data are collected by local education agencies and include the number and type of students served under the law and the types of placements students receive. Under federal law, up to 40 percent of the national average expenditure per student multiplied by the number of students with disabilities served in a state could be reimbursed by the federal government. However, Congress has never authorized enough money to meet this funding formula. Currently, Congress provides local education agencies with only 8.3 percent of the additional costs (those required in addition to the district's per-pupil costs) required to educate students with disabilities. This able to go to school. Most likely, Juanita would have been counseled to send Tanya away to a regional center or institution for children with mental retardation.

As you will recall, P.L. 94-142 mandated that all children, regardless of their disability, are entitled to a free and appropriate public education. Under this law, "free" was defined to mean that special education services would be provided at public expense, under public supervision and direction, without charging families for any costs incurred. "Special education" was defined as specially designed instruction that met the unique needs of each child with a disability. This instruction included classroom, physical, and home instruction, as well as instruction in hospitals and institutions. Educational instruction was to be supported by the services necessary to permit the child to benefit from the instruction. This meant that the state was responsible for assuring that all children received an education regardless of where they lived—at home, in a hospital, in a residential treatment center, or in an institution for children with emotional, mental, and/or sensory disabilities. Because most public education was provided through local educational agencies, this meant that each public school system had to provide services to the children within their district who had disabilities. Since passage of the original legislation, several important legal cases have defined its meaning.

**CASE LAW PRECEDING FAPE**   Although many cases contributed to the inclusion of the FAPE clause in the original Education of All Handicapped Children Act (P.L. 94-142), three cases are of particular importance: *Brown* v. *Board of Education*, *PARC* v. *Commonwealth of Pennsylvania*, and *Mills* v. *Board of Education*. Remember that, while the *Brown* case dealt with issues of racial segregation, it established a precedent that separate programs were not equivalent or equal. The other two cases, *PARC* and *Mills*, elaborated on and extended the *Brown* decision to students with disabilities. We will refer often to these two cases because many of the court's recommendations in the two were infused into the language of P.L. 94-142.

*PARC* v. *State of Pennsylvania*, 1971   In the early 1970s, thirteen children with mental retardation and the Pennsylvania Association for Retarded Children filed suit against the state of Pennsylvania on behalf of all children with mental retardation in Pennsylvania. According to the plaintiffs, the state had failed to provide access to a free, public education for children with

mental retardation. In the *PARC* decision, the Pennsylvania Supreme Court used the following argument to resolve the case:

1. All individuals with mental retardation can benefit from education and training whether the education results in self-sufficiency or the achievement of some degree of self-care.

2. The state of Pennsylvania stated that it would provide a free public education to all of its children between the ages of 6 and 21.

3. Because the state promised to educate all of its children, it cannot deny any child access to an education.

This ruling set a precedent with far-reaching implications. It meant that states have an obligation to place each child with mental retardation in a free public education program that is appropriate to the child's capacity. But the court went even further in this case by supporting the notion of least restrictive alternative. That is, children should be served in general education settings unless it can be shown that a child would benefit more from another setting that would restrict access to the general education environment. Because of *PARC*, students like Tanya and Annie can now attend school.

*Mills* v. *Board of Education*, 1972   Another landmark case involved the District of Columbia and seven children with learning and behavioral problems. In the *Mills* case, the District of Columbia had refused to continue paying for the education of these seven children because it could not afford to provide the kind and extent of services that these children needed. The families of the children sued. According to the district court, a school district cannot deny students access to a free public education because it cannot afford to pay for needed services. The court ordered the school district to provide services that were appropriate to the students' needs, regardless of the degree of mental, physical, or emotional impairment experienced by an individual child. The court also prohibited the school system from suspending a student for disciplinary reasons without a hearing and from discontinuing the student's education during a suspension.

The *Mills* case was an important landmark in that it extended the *PARC* decision to children with disabilities other than mental retardation. This meant that students like Kurume, Michael, and Kirk could now attend school. The *Mills* case expanded the *PARC* decision because, in this case, the school district claimed that it was willing to serve the students but lacked funds. The court held that the fiscal hardship on the district was an insufficient rationale for denying education to students.

In summary, the concept of FAPE places the responsibility for education on the school district. Districts cannot refuse to provide educational services because of the severity of the child's disability or because the cost of competent educational services is more than that needed to educate other, more typical students. Families of children with disabilities can expect that their children will receive educational services that are both free and appropriate to their needs.

**REGULATING FAPE** Once the law was passed, many questions had to be answered in order to define FAPE for state and local educational agencies. For instance, what children were eligible for special education? What types of services would constitute a free and appropriate education? If a child's family wanted to place her in a special residential school for developing alternative communications skills, who would pay? If a child was in a special education program when he was caught breaking and entering, would the school district have to pay for educational services while he is in a juvenile detention center?

The original legislation, passed in 1975, defined free and appropriate public education as special education and related services. It also defined related services to include

> transportation, and such development, corrective, and other supportive services (including speech pathology and audiology, psychological services, physical and occupational therapy, recreation, and medical and counseling services, except that such medical services shall be for diagnostic and evaluation purposes only) as may be required to assist a child with disabilities to benefit from special education, and includes the early identification and assessment of disabilities in young children. (P.L. 94-142, Section 602, 20 U.S.C. 1402)

In the most recent amendments to IDEA 97 (P.L. 105-17), orientation and mobility services were added to this definition. Now, teaching students to travel independently to and from school can be part of the services that schools provide. Students who have visual impairments may need this kind of instruction. Students with mental retardation also may need instruc-

tion to teach them to get from class to class or to and from school.

The law establishes that children and their families are entitled to services beyond what might typically be offered to a child without disabilities. This FAPE clause actually supports the notion of equal access. Furthermore, FAPE suggests that children with disabilities must have access to both the same resources as their peers without disabilities and additional resources and supports. These resources may result in the same outcomes as for their more typical peers but provide the opportunity to achieve those outcomes through varied methods. Therefore, disability law recognizes that not all children are able to achieve the same outcomes even when given the same opportunities.

Yet there are limits to FAPE. If a youth is sentenced to a prison term during his adolescence, he is entitled to special education services only if he was receiving special education services through an individualized education plan (IEP) before his conviction. If a young person between the ages of 18 and 21 enters the prison system and is identified as having a disability at that point, states are not required to provide special education services. Thus, FAPE does not extend to every individual in every situation.

IDEA 97 also constrains the amount of money local districts are required to reimburse parents who decide to send their child to a private school. If a hearing officer decides that equally suitable services are available in the local public school, then the school district may not be required to pay for tuition and services for a private school. This is a complex issue, but the law does establish conditions that must be met in order for tuition to be reimbursed.

**CLAFIFYING FAPE** Two important issues were unresolved in the regulations that fleshed out "free and appropriate public education." First, does "appropriate" mean the best possible services, or does it simply mean adequate? Second, was there ever the possibility that a student could be so disabled that he or she could not benefit from any form of educational services? Just what was the definition of an "education"?

*Hendrick Hudson School District* v. *Rowley* clarified the extent to which schools were responsible for implementation of state-of-the-art practices for children with disabilities. Amy Rowley, who was deaf, was attending fifth grade at a local elementary school in Peekskill, New York. Amy had minimal residual hearing and was an excellent lip-reader. She was fitted with an FM hearing aid that amplified words spoken by her teacher into a wireless receiver. Amy performed better than the average child in her classroom and communicated well with her fellow students. However, the lower courts ruled that she was not performing up to her potential, and therefore, the request of her parents to have an interpreter in the classroom was a justified expense to be borne by the school district.

In reviewing this case, the Supreme Court found that P.L. 94-142 requires states to assure that an education is provided for a child with sufficient support services to permit the child to benefit educationally. The Court's ruling hinged on two premises. First, the law does not require that the state or a local school system provide the best possible services. Instead, the standard is adequate services, like those to which other students have access. So, while Amy's education might have been enhanced by the interpreter, her performance in school was strong. Second, because her educational progress was apparently similar to her typical peers, the Court ruled that the district had no obligation to provide an interpreter to maximize her performance.

The *Timothy W.* case clarified the definition of "education" in "free and appropriate public education." In *Timothy W.* v. *Rochester School District,* the family of a 13-year-old boy who was **quadriplegic** and apparently had mental retardation sued the New Hampshire school district where they lived. The school district had refused to provide educational services to Timothy because they had decided that he could not benefit from special education because of the severity of his mental retardation. The first court that heard the case agreed with the school district. The judge in the lower court ruled that P.L. 94-142 was not intended to ensure the provision of educational services to all students with disabilities. However, in reversing the lower court's ruling, an appeals court held that the law applied to all students regardless of the severity of their disability.

**ASSESSING THE IMPLICATIONS OF FAPE**  Both the legislative and the judicial branches of government work to define, refine, and clarify the intentions of the law. The *PARC* and *Mills* cases influenced the work of legislators drafting P.L. 94-142. After the law was passed, the *Rowley* and *Timothy W.* cases helped to define the meaning of "appropriate" and "education." The decisions of courts across the country have affirmed that students with all types of disabilities have the right to a free, appropriate public education and

that no child can be excluded because of the nature or extent of his or her disability.

## Least Restrictive Environment (LRE)

Another basic premise of special education law has been that students should be educated in the least restrictive environment (LRE). Some special educators interpret LRE to mean the environment in which other, nondisabled students are educated; others interpret LRE to mean the environment that is the least restrictive for the student (Burton & Hirshhoren, 1979). When students with disabilities remain in settings with other children who are not labeled as disabled, this is referred to as mainstreaming, integration, or inclusion. Although each of these terms has a variety of permutations (Bogdan, 1986; Forest & Pearpoint, 1992), LRE has been cited as the legal rationale for all three practices. Turnbull (1993) discusses LRE in terms of the preference of the courts and the law for general education that is tempered by access to an environment that can provide the most appropriate education. IDEA 97 describes LRE in the following manner:

> To the maximum extent appropriate, children with disabilities, including children in public or private institutions or other care facilities, are educated with children who are not disabled, and that special classes, separate schooling, or other removal of children with disabilities from the regular education environment occurs only when the nature or severity of the disability is such that education in regular classes with the use of supplementary aids and services cannot be achieved satisfactorily. (20 U.S.C. 1412[5] [B])

**CASE LAW PRECEDING LRE**  Both the *PARC* and *Mills* cases established that children with disabilities have received inadequate and inappropriate educational services. Furthermore, these and other cases demonstrated that children with disabilities lacked access to educational opportunities alongside their more typical peers. In fact, as Congress noted in P.L. 94-142, inadequate services for children with disabilities tended to be the rule rather than the exception. In the *PARC* case, the court ruled that the presumption should be made that

> among the alternative programs of education and training required by statute to be available, placement in a regular public school class is preferable to placement in a special public school class and placement in a special public school class is preferable to placement in any other type of program of education and training.

In the *Mills* decision, the court also indicated that placement in a regular public school class with appropriate ancillary services is preferred to placement in a special school class. Thus, before passage of P.L. 94-142, case law established that LRE is where children without disabilities are educated. That means that classrooms in elementary, middle, junior, and senior high schools where students without disabilities are taught constitute the least restrictive environment for students with disabilities. Furthermore, case law established that school personnel must prefer such placement over other placements that remove children from interaction with their peers without disabilities. As with racial segregation, the courts presumed that separate educational facilities and programs are inherently unequal and that placement of a child in anything but the general education classroom is more restrictive.

**REGULATING LRE** Once a student is eligible to receive special education services, the options for service delivery often are prescribed by the school's existing structures. Over the past twenty years, the cascade model developed by Reynolds (1962) and Deno (1970) and refined by Reynolds and Birch (1982) has served as the primary format for structuring special education services (see Figure 2.1). In this model, a continuum of instructional delivery formats is conceptualized, from the least restrictive (instruction in a regular classroom) to the most restrictive (services delivered at home or in a hospital). The model is rooted in the notion that more students would be served at the base of the triangular structure and far fewer at the apex. As the triangular structure suggests, more students with disabilities should be served in the general education classroom. Theoretically, as their needs can be more adequately met in less restrictive settings, students move toward the base of the triangle. However, Figure 2.2 shows how that model has been actualized accord-

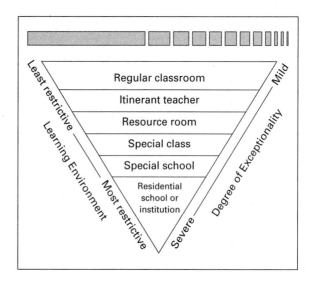

**FIGURE 2.1** ■ The Cascade System

ing to data from the U.S. Department of Education (1997). Although the regular classroom is considered to be the least restrictive setting, more students with disabilities are served in the resource room than in the regular classroom.

The cascade model of services may be seen as a legitimate response to the need to assign personnel resources and to ensure that all children's needs are met by personnel trained to work with a particular category of student. The unforeseen outcome has been the legitimization of a system in which most special education students (66 percent) are served for some portion of the day outside of the general education classroom, despite the spirit and intent of IDEA 97. Critics of the continuum-of-services model maintain that the existence of a continuum suggests that some individuals will be placed in each rung of the continuum regardless of their ability to flourish elsewhere (Taylor, 1988). In other words, if a continuum exists, it will be used.

**CLARIFYING LRE** More recently, many special educators have called for an integrated approach to serving students with special needs (Wang, Reynolds, & Walberg, 1988). This initiative was articulated in 1986 by Madeline Will, then assistant secretary of the Office of Special Education and Rehabilitative Services. She encouraged educators to create a partnership between regular and special education in order to serve students at risk for failure to learn and function effectively as participating members of their classroom communities

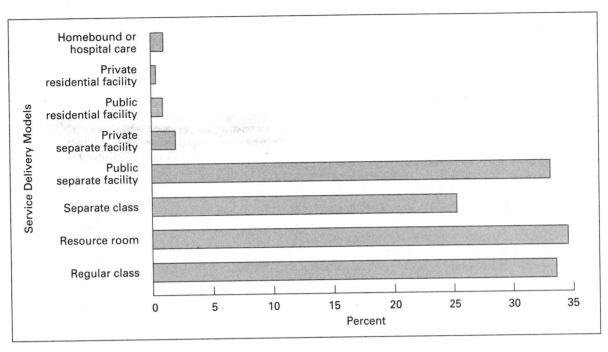

**FIGURE 2.2** ■ Percentage of Students Served by the Cascade Model

Source: U.S. Department of Education, 1997.

(Will, 1986). The Baesmans, authors of the chapter-opening vignette, believed that their daughter would learn best when she had the opportunity to work alongside her more school-able peers. As their story demonstrates, they needed the provisions of IDEA to push forward with their dream for their daughter.

Parents, family members, and professionals who work with students with intensive physical, intellectual, and behavioral challenges discuss this issue in terms of inclusion. Individuals with less challenging needs have been championed by persons supporting what is called the regular education initiative (Lilly, 1988; Reynolds, Wang, & Walberg, 1987; Stainback & Stainback, 1989). Inclusion and the regular education initiative assume that students attend school with their same-aged peers and are assigned with their peers to a general education classroom (Brown et al., 1989). Other terms, like mainstreaming or integration, imply that students come from another place (a special education classroom or school) to spend part of their educational day in a general education environment (Karagiannis, Stainback, & Stainback, 1996). Regardless of the terminology, many special educators are coming to believe that the strategies and teaching tech-

nologies that appear to be effective with special education populations (Brown & Palinscar, 1987; Bulgren, Schumaker, & Deschler, 1988; Ellis, 1994) must be delivered within the context of general education (Carnine & Kameenui, 1992; Kameenui, Carnine, & Dixon, 1995). Decentralization of administrative functions, flexibility in performing roles, building-level decision making, frequent and systematic evaluation of students, and support of general education teachers in general education classrooms—all are components of an inclusionary approach to serving students with diverse needs (Schaffner & Buswell, 1996).

The inclusionary practices approach is more than a passing fad. Rather it is the culmination of a twenty-four-year period of development of services for students with learning and behavioral problems, services based increasingly in the assumptions and value system of general education rather than special education (Lilly, 1988). An integrated model of service delivery assumes that all children will be served at their neighborhood schools. Furthermore, proponents of an integrated approach to meeting the needs of all students propose that all children be a part of general education and receive specialized services as needed rather than be part of a specialized delivery system that interfaces occasionally with general education. Although many professionals and parents of students with disabilities remain unconvinced of the benefits of serving children with disabilities in integrated settings (Kauffman, 1989; Kauffman, Gerber, & Semmel, 1988), this concept will continue to impact systems at the building level into the twenty-first century. As you will see, case law that affirms the values of inclusion continues to build.

In 1993, in the *Oberti* case, the Third Circuit Court affirmed that Rafael Oberti, a child with Down syndrome, had a right to an inclusive education, provided in a regular classroom in his neighborhood school. The judge wrote:

> The Act's strong presumption in favor of main-streaming . . . would be turned on its head if parents had to prove that their child was worthy of being included, rather than the school district having to justify a decision to exclude the child from the regular classroom. . . . We therefore hold that the district court correctly placed the burden on the School District to prove that the segregated placement proposed for Rafael was in compliance with the mainstreaming requirement of IDEA.

The court used three tests to make its decision—tests that will undoubtedly be used in other cases to decide whether an out-of-regular-class placement is necessary. First, evidence must show that the school district has taken more than token steps to modify and supplement the regular curriculum. Second, evidence must show that the child will benefit more from a segregated than an integrated classroom. Third, the impact on the education of other children must be considered. Therefore, we can predict that, increasingly, children with significant disabilities will be educated in the regular classroom. The kinds of curricula and strategies to be used will depend on the individualized education program.

## Individualized Education Program (IEP)

An individualized education program (IEP) is a tool that school professionals use to provide educational services tailored to the needs of children with disabilities. An IEP assures that the educational needs of a particular child, rather than those of a group of children, are addressed. In developing IEPs, school professionals focus on the needs, not the disabilities, of students.

Thus, for instance, even though Tanya and Annie may share the disability of mental retardation, their IEPs will be very different because their needs are different. The law stipulates that the educational services provided must be those specifically defined in the statute as comprising special education and related services. The law defines special education as "specially designed instruction, at no cost to parents or guardians, to meet the unique needs of a child with disabilities, including classroom instruction, instruction in physical education, home instruction, and instruction in hospitals and institutions" (20 U.S.C. 1401 [c][16]).

Every student receiving special education services must have an IEP that includes the following components:

- A statement of the student's current educational performance levels, including how the child's disability affects his or her progress in the general education curriculum. For preschool children, the IEP must describe how the disability affects the child's participation in appropriate activities.

- Measurable annual goals and short-term objectives or benchmarks that enable the child to participate in the general curriculum and help meet any other education needs resulting from the disability.

- Special education and related services.

- Program modifications or supports for school personnel that permit the student not only to attain annual goals and be involved in the curriculum but also to participate in extracurricular and other nonacademic activities.

- An explanation of the extent, if any, to which the child will not participate in regular education classes.

- Modifications in state- or district-wide assessments needed for the child to participate, or an explanation of why those assessments are inappropriate and how the child will be assessed instead.

- A statement of the extent to which the student will not participate in general education classes.

- A projected date for the start of services and their anticipated frequency, location, and duration.

- Appropriate objective evaluation criteria, procedures, and schedules for determining, at least annually, whether the short-term objectives are being achieved.

A student uses an augmentative device to promote his learning in the least restrictive environment.

- A statement of how parents will be informed as often as parents of nondisabled children of their child's progress toward annual goals, and the extent to which that progress is sufficient to enable the child to achieve these goals by the end of the school year.

- A statement of the transition services needed by students who are 14 years of age or older. This statement must focus on the child's courses of study, although services need not be provided until age 16.

Figure 2.3 shows an example of a completed IEP—this one for Michael. As it states on his IEP, all IEPs must be evaluated at least annually. Michael's case study illustrates how, each time that a change in services occurs, an IEP meeting must be held, even if it has only been a month since the last meeting. Furthermore, schools must respond to requests from students and their families for IEP meetings. Remember that in Michael's case such requests were ignored. His case study demonstrates how legal guidelines are sometimes ignored or misinterpreted by school systems, personnel, or families themselves. However, as you will read in the due process section, ignorance of guidelines

does not absolve districts and personnel from responsibility for failing to adhere to the regulations.

Even students who are in school programs in residential facilities like the one that Kirk attended must have an IEP that is developed, maintained, and evaluated annually. Students with disabilities who are attending private or parochial schools are also eligible for IEPs if they receive special education and related services from a public agency. Students are important members of the team that designs the IEP, and they should be involved in meetings that determine their educational goals and objectives. By law, the interests and goals of students who are 14 years of age and older must be represented in the IEP.

The role of families in the special education process is central. Families should be key members of the team that assesses and determines eligibility for special education services, and their hopes and aspirations for their children should be reflected in the educational goals and objectives that are developed for the IEP. In Michael's case, his mother referred him for special education assessment. Legally, one or both parents or the guardian of the child with disabilities may attend the IEP meeting. The Baesmans, the family from the chapter-opening vignette, were empowered by their

## INDIVIDUAL EDUCATION PROGRAM—STAFFING

Purpose: ☐ Initial Staffing    ☐ Annual Review    ☐ Triennial Review

Student Legal Name: _Michael Lee_ _____ Birth Date: _4/17/89_

Student No.: _719844_   School: _Plutarch_   Grade: _4_   Area: _South_

Parent Name: _Anita & Chen Lee_   Address: _2727 S. Pierce_   Phone: _900-4000_

---

**Presenting Problems**
(Annual review—state current disability only)

History of academic concerns

**Interventions**
(Annual review—state current special education services)

Specialized instruction with educational
   consultant
Modified assignments
Peer tutors

---

### Assessment Summary

#### Educational/Developmental

Michael's reading has improved and is not currently significantly below grade level (Woodcock-Johnson 34th percentile). He does need to use a marker to hold his place and he may need to be introduced to unfamiliar vocabulary. Michael did test significantly below his ability and grade level in math and written language (Woodcock-Johnson Math 2nd percentile and Written Language 25th percentile). His academic progress may be impeded by his difficulty staying on task, tracking, monitoring his own errors, handwriting, and poor sound symbol relationships. Michael assisted in determining his academic needs by choosing from a menu of those strategies that helped him solve problems in math and write more effectively.

#### Psychological

WISC-R scores: Verbal, 111; Performance, 95; Full Scale, 103. Average to high-average potential for academic achievement. A significant discrepancy between verbal and performance scores. Difficulty with visual–motor–perceptual tasks (low Block design, 6 errors on the Bender-Gestalt). Strengths in vocabulary, practical judgment and reasoning, and short-term memory.

#### Social

Michael comes from an intact, cohesive, and caring family. He becomes frustrated at times when he is unable to achieve the high goals which he sets for himself. Social interaction skills appear to be appropriate. Michael is able to express his feelings appropriately.

#### Communicative

*Peabody Picture Vocabulary Test:* Standard score, 105; percentile, 63rd
*CELF Receptive Language Score:* Standard score, 110; percentile, 75th
*Expressive Language Score:* Standard score, 115; percentile 84th
*Total Language Score:* Standard score, 114; percentile, 82nd

#### Physical

Visual screening at school: 20/20 both eyes. Hearing: passed. Red/green color blind. Needs to keep head at a distance from his paper.

*(continued)*

**FIGURE 2.3** ■ Michael's IEP

Student Legal Name: __Michael Lee_____  Birth Date: __4/17/89__  Student No.: __719844__

## Needs

Improve written language skills, including proofreading and editing skills

Remediate gaps in math skills, specifically computation

Compensate for tracking and visual perceptual weaknesses

Maintain legible handwriting over an increasing length of time

Reduce anxiety

Set goals related to his strengths and weaknesses

__X__  Curricular/Academic
__X__  Developmental/Compensatory
__X__  Social/Emotional
____  Prevocational/Vocational/Avocational
____  Physical Environment
____  Parent/Home/Family
____  Health
____  Transportation
____  Classroom Management
____  Extracurricular/Nonacademic

Is this student able to receive reasonable benefit from regular education?  Yes ____  No __X__
If no, is this due to a disability?  Yes __X__  No ____    Disability: *Specific learning disability*

## Annual Measurable Goals

Michael will learn at least three strategies that will enhance his written language skills in the areas of spelling, vocabulary, and text cohesion.

**Objective 1:** After writing at least one paragraph of narrative text, Michael will be able to identify and correct his own spelling errors with 90% accuracy over 10 trials.

**Objective 2:** Prior to writing tasks of at least one paragraph, Michael will use a context web to clarify the ideas that he plans to express and to order them logically. He will use this strategy without prompts on at least 9 out of 10 sequential occasions.

**Objective 3:** Using a spiral binder organized by class, Michael will keep a lexicon of vocabulary words that he learns in each subject, writing a complex sentence that defines each word. By the end of the year, Michael will have maintained this lexicon without prompt for at least one month.

## Characteristics of Service

**Nature:** Specialized academic instruction
**Scope:** Small group, 1:1
**Frequency:** On an as-needed basis

## Recommended Placement in the Least Restrictive Environment

Regular classroom plus resource room

## Placement Alternatives Considered

__X__  Regular classroom with consultative assistance
____  Regular classroom with assistance by itinerant specialist
__X__  Regular classroom plus resource room
____  Regular classroom with resource room plus itinerant specialist
____  Self-contained special class
____  Special day school/program
____  Other

*(continued)*

**FIGURE 2.3** ■ Michael's IEP *(continued)*

Student Legal Name: __Michael Lee__   Birth Date: __4/17/89__   Student No.: __719844__

Assessment of sufficient scope and intensity was completed to support the decision regarding identification of disability. The annual goals identified are designed to meet the educational and educationally related needs of the student. The characteristics of service herein are designed to meet the unique needs of the student and assure the least restrictive alternative for the provision of an appropriate education.

**Staffing Members (signature/title)**

_____
Special education director or designee

_____
Special education teacher

_____
Classroom teacher

_____
Parent

_____
Primary provider

_____
Date of staffing

_____
Principal or designee

_____
Speech/language teacher

_____
School psychologist

_____
Parent

**FIGURE 2.3** ■ Michael's IEP *(continued)*

role in the IEP meeting to advocate for their daughter. If the parents cannot be physically present at the IEP, other methods such as conference calls and computer linkages must be provided. And the local education agency must demonstrate that, when parents or family members were not present at an IEP meeting, good-faith attempts to include the student's family were made. Thus, when Kirk needed an IEP developed for his schooling at the juvenile detention center, his parents were included in the planning process.

Parent participation is such an integral component of the law that collaboration between families and professionals is not confined to planning for the individual child. The law mandates that families be given notice of meetings to develop and comment on plans by both local and state education agencies to serve students with disabilities. Mandated advisory panels to state and local agencies include families of children with disabilities. Families and the public in general are guaranteed access to information about the extent and quality of services to children with disabilities.

**CASE LAW PRECEDING IEPS**   In both the _PARC_ and _Mills_ cases, the courts ordered service providers to describe the curricula, objectives, teacher qualifications, and ancillary services for programs to students with unique needs. The language of P.L. 94-142 in defining and specifying what an IEP must contain was heavily influenced by these cases.

**REGULATING IEPS**   In general, because the components of IEPs are so clearly articulated in the law, assuring that these documents actually are written traditionally has been more easily accomplished than assuring that the quality of the IEP meets the spirit of the law. Unfortunately, the intended results and subsequent implementation of IEPs are not so neatly aligned. In a recent study in Colorado, Kozleski and Bechard (1991) found that, of the 150 IEPs examined by an expert panel, only a small percentage were written such that practitioners could readily implement the goals and objectives. The difficulty in assessing and identifying the needs of students and then translating those needs into IEPs continues to plague the teams that work to design these programs.

**CLARIFYING IEPS**   Since the passage of the original law, perhaps the most critical clarification of the IEP relates to the implementation of the principle of the extended school year. The courts have acknowledged in cases such as *Armstrong* v. *Kline* (1979) and *Alamo Heights* v. *State Board of Education* (1986) that each IEP must be designed to provide educational benefits to the child in accordance with his or her unique needs. Thus, for example, if it can be demonstrated that the gains in development made during the school year are jeopardized by a summer vacation, then the responsible educational agency is obligated to continue providing services during the vacation months. While IEPs have been an invaluable tool in clarifying the needs and educational goals of children with disabilities, families and professionals have not always agreed on their content. Accordingly, the due process component of this law has given families a measure of power in the decision-making process that has rarely been so clearly articulated in the law.

## Protection of Students' and Parents' Rights

The due process component of IDEA provides guidelines for notifying families and their children with disabilities about their legal rights in terms of determining eligibility and receiving services. Due process helps to protect the children and their families from being overwhelmed by the professionals and agencies that serve many children with disabilities; it helps maintain focus on the unique needs of children and their families.

According to due process, children and families have the right to be notified about any proposed assessment for determining eligibility for special education services. Due process provisions mandate that families receive information—in writing, in the family's native language—about what might happen if the assessment determines that a child is eligible for services. Notification must also include information about the family's right to consent or object to the proposed action, to have a hearing to voice its objections, and to obtain free medical, psychological, and educational evaluations.

Current federal law requires each state to establish a voluntary **mediation** system and to cover its costs. This allows parents to have access to a mediation process before filing a complaint and requesting a hearing. If a family requests a hearing, the hearing must be conducted promptly by an impartial hearing officer, at a time and place convenient for the family. The family has the right to examine school records, to be represented by an advocate or counsel, to present evidence, to cross-examine witnesses, to be furnished with transcripts of the hearing, and to receive a written statement of the findings.

Another component of due process deals with access to records. Confidentiality of records is guaranteed under the law. Families also have the right to review all records relating to the identification, evaluation, or placement of their child. Agencies must be prepared to interpret information for families when requested. And when families request amendments to their child's records, agencies must consider the request. If the agency disagrees with the request to amend the records, the family can contest the ruling in a hearing. The rights of parents and families are transferred to the student at age 18.

**CASE LAW PRECEDING PROTECTION OF STUDENTS' AND PARENTS' RIGHTS**  The *Mills* and *PARC* cases again played a critical part in shaping this part of the legislation. *PARC* provided the first precise process for determining eligibility and placement of children with mental retardation, while *Mills* broadened the process to encompass all children with disabilities. Some of the due process elements of IDEA were first articulated in the Family Educational Rights and Privacy Act (FERPA) of 1973. According to this bill, all records on individual students kept by educational agencies are open to review by parents, a right that is transferred to students when they reach age 18. FERPA regulations also stipulate that educational agencies must obtain parental consent in order to release records to any other agency.

**GUIDELINES FOR DETERMINING DISABILITY**
By law, special education students receive categorical labels in order to ensure that they receive services only for that segment of their education in which their physical, sensory, cognitive, or behavioral characteristics impede their ability to learn in the general education classroom. Table 2.5 lists the disability categories recognized under IDEA 97. It's important to remember that, although these categories are defined in IDEA 97, each state, and in some cases each local school district, has its own definition that may be more inclusive than the definition provided in the federal statute. For

example, in Colorado, the term "specific learning disabilities" is supplanted by the term **perceptual communicative disorder.** Both terms are used to label children with learning disabilities. However, because federal law supersedes state law, a state may not define a given disability more narrowly so that it prohibits students who would qualify for services under the federal statute from receiving them.

Many studies have shown that as the definitions for these disability categories change, so do the number of students who qualify for services under each category. For instance, when the definition for mental retardation was changed in 1985 to require a lower score on a test of intelligence to qualify for a label of mental retardation, more children were qualified for services as learning disabled (McMillan, 1988). Thus, the categorization of students according to various disabilities is more an artifact of cutoff scores, community standards, and tolerance for diverse learning styles than a finding of fact (Shepard, 1987). Infants, toddlers, and preschoolers have to some extent been exempt from this phenomenon because they may be labeled as having a disability without the need to categorize them according to a specific disability. Therefore, many states label young children as "preschool-disabled" rather than, for instance, "speech/language-impaired." This was the case with Tanya. However, once children move from preschool to elementary school, those who continue to qualify for special education services are identified with one of the disability categories established under federal statute.

The labels used in each state to identify students for special education services may vary. However, the disability categories listed in IDEA 97 must be subsumed in what each state uses to determine eligibility for special education services. For example, some states use **traumatic brain injury** as a separate disability category, while others include traumatic brain injury in the category "other health-impaired." It's important to remember that students may have impairments that do not interfere with their education. Disability labels

**TABLE 2.5  Federal Disability Categories in IDEA 97**

- "Autism" means a developmental disability significantly affecting verbal and nonverbal communication and social interaction.

- "Deafness" means a hearing impairment that is so severe that the child is impaired in processing linguistic information through hearing, with or without amplification, which adversely affects educational performance.

- "Deaf-blindness" means concomitant hearing and visual impairments, the combination of which causes such severe communication and other developmental and educational problems that they cannot be accommodated in special education programs solely for children with deafness or children with blindness.

- "Hearing impairment" means an impairment in hearing, whether permanent or fluctuating, which adversely affects a child's educational performance but which is not included under the definition of "deafness."

- "Mental retardation" means significantly subaverage general intellectual functioning existing concurrently with deficits in adaptive behavior and manifested during the developmental period, which adversely affects a child's educational performance.

- "Multiple disabilities" means concomitant impairment (such as mental retardation–blindness, mental retardation–orthopedic impairment, etc.), the combination of which causes such severe educational problems that they cannot be accommodated in special education programs solely for one of the impairments. The term does not include deaf-blind children.

- "Orthopedic impairment" means a severe orthopedic impairment, which adversely affects a child's educational performance. The term includes impairments caused by congenital anomaly (e.g., clubfoot, absence of some member, etc.), impairments caused by disease (e.g., poliomyelitis, bone tuberculosis, etc.), and impairments from other causes (e.g., cerebral palsy, amputations, and fractures or burns which cause contractures).

- "Other health impairment" means having limited strength, vitality, or alertness, due to chronic or acute health problems such as heart condition, tuberculosis, rheumatic fever, nephritis, asthma, sickle cell anemia, hemophilia, epilepsy, lead poisoning, leukemia, or diabetes, which adversely affects a child's educational performance.

- "Seriously emotionally disturbed" is defined as follows:
  (i) The term means a condition exhibiting one or more of the following characteristics over a long period of time and to a marked degree, which adversely affects educational performance:
    (A) An inability to learn, which cannot be explained by intellectual, sensory, or health factors
    (B) An inability to build or maintain satisfactory interpersonal relationships with peers and teachers
    (C) Inappropriate types of behavior or feelings under normal circumstances
    (D) A general pervasive mood of unhappiness or depression
    (E) A tendency to develop physical symptoms or fears associated with personal or school problems
  (ii) The term includes children who are schizophrenic. The term does not include children who are socially maladjusted, unless it is determined that they are seriously emotionally disturbed.

Source: 20 U.S.C. 1401(a)(1).

help local, state, and federal agencies provide funding for special education that targets students with disabilities and provides safeguards against the use of those funds for other purposes. A key issue is whether these safeguards accomplish their aim without harming the students who are labeled. It is only when the impairment interferes with their ability to benefit from education that students are identified for special education services.

## Provision of Related Services

When you think about the types of disabilities that Kurume, Tanya, Kirk, Michael, and Annie have, it's not surprising that they may need a variety of services to support their successful completion of school. As a result, in addition to educational services, IDEA 97 includes a provision that "related services" must be provided free of cost to children in order for them to

Source: 20 U.S.C. 1401(a)(17).

## BOX 2.3
### Related Services

As used here, the term "related services" means transportation and such developmental, corrective, and other supportive services as are required to assist a child with a disability to benefit from special education, and includes speech pathology and audiology, orientation and mobility, psychological services, physical and occupational therapy, recreation, including therapeutic recreation, early identification and assessment of disabilities in children, counseling services, including rehabilitation counseling, and medical services for diagnostic or evaluation purposes. The terms also includes school health services, social work services in schools and parent counseling and training.

receive reasonable benefit from their educational plan. Box 2.3 provides examples, listed in the law, of related services. Related services may be provided by another kind of school professional, such as a speech/language therapist, a school psychologist, a school nurse, or a social worker.

Of all our case studies, Annie and Tanya in particular have medical needs that require oversight and input from their pediatricians and school nurses. Both girls need some support and services from occupational and physical therapists to ensure that their muscles and coordination develop adequately. Kurume needs ongoing support from an **audiologist** to monitor any residual hearing and to gauge the usefulness of hearing aids. Because Kurume's, Annie's, and Tanya's communication systems have been impacted by their other disabilities, they need the assistance of a **speech/language therapist** to make sure that they have appropriate modifications and adaptations in their communication systems. For Kurume, this means that decisions about whether to sign, learn to read lips, or use a form of **total communication** must be made in conjunction with his family and the speech/language specialist. Annie's family needs guidance about what type of communication system to invest in. Tanya's mother, Juanita, needs to learn how to stimulate her daughter's oral language so that it can develop as typically as possible. Kirk's support system needs to include input

from a specialist who can help to develop, implement, and monitor a positive behavior support plan; Kirk's parents also may want some support to manage his behavior at home. Of course, the costs of these additional services are substantial. Since 1975, many disagreements between families and school districts have revolved around the provision of related services.

**CASE LAW ON RELATED SERVICES** What kinds of related services are districts really accountable for? An essential concern when students with significant health needs are served in schools is whether school districts are responsible for providing medical care. An important clarification occurred when the Tatro family brought suit against the Irving Independent School District. Eventually, the Supreme Court heard the case of *Irving Independent School District* v. *Tatro*. At issue was whether P.L. 94-142 requires a school district to provide **clean, intermittent catheterization** to a child with disabilities. Amber Tatro, who had **spina bifida**, needed to be catheterized every three to four hours to avoid injury to her kidneys. This simple procedure can be performed by a layperson with minimal training. The question was whether catheterization is a "related service" that helps a child benefit from special education rather than a "medical service" that serves a purpose other than diagnosis or evaluation. The Supreme Court concurred with the lower courts that clean, intermittent catheterization is a related rather than medical service because it can be carried out by laypersons rather than medical personnel and because it allowed Amber to benefit from educational services.

IDEA 97 stipulates that medical services must be limited to diagnosis and evaluation. Additional medical services are not the responsibility of schools. But psychological services are the responsibility of the school system when the services are necessary for a child to benefit from special education. These services can be provided by individuals in many roles, including counselors, psychologists, psychiatrists, and social workers. However, states mandate the licensing standards of these varying roles. Depending on the state, different personnel may actually offer counseling services.

Additions to related services made in the 1990 amendments include assistive technology, social work services, rehabilitative counseling, and transition services. Remember that, under IDEA 97, related services are available only to those students who need special education services. A glance back at Table 2.4 reveals

| **TABLE 2.6** | **Three Laws That Support Student Empowerment and Transition Services** |
| --- | --- |

- *Carl D. Perkins Vocational and Applied Technology Act (P.L. 101-392, (1992).* This act aims to increase the participation of special populations in secondary and postsecondary vocational education programs; it includes a broad requirement that schools provide transitional counseling for these populations (Kochar & Barnes, 1992).

- *Rehabilitation Act Amendments of 1992 (P.L. 102-569, 1992).* These amendments adopted the definition of transition services contained within IDEA; they also strengthen the language regard-ing interagency collaboration and require vocational rehabilitation counselors to become involved while students are in school (National Transition Network, 1993).

- *The Americans with Disabilities Act (P.L. 101-336, 1990).* This act provides greater accessibility to the work force, public buildings, and public transportation system, thereby enhancing life choices for students with disabilities exiting from high school (Whemann, 1992).

the seven basic components of IDEA 97; services to infants and young adults and transition services have been added in subsequent amendments (see Table 2.6).

## Services to Infants and Young Adults

Since the passage of P.L. 94-142, the bill has been reauthorized approximately every five years, with the most recent reauthorization in 1997. In the 1986 amendments to the original bill (P.L. 101-476), services were extended to individuals from birth through age 21. Because the needs of infants and young children differ from those of school-age children, the amendments introduced new terminology and procedures into special education. Chief among the features of the law that pertain to infants and toddlers was the provision for the **individualized family service plan (IFSP).** Then, in 1990, in response to data on student outcomes from special education, Congress mandated an additional component to educational planning called the **individual transition plan (ITP).** Currently, the provisions of IDEA 97 include an IFSP, an IEP, and an ITP (see Tables 2.7 and 2.8).

**EARLY INTERVENTION** According to the requirements of P.L. 105-17 (1997), service providers are not required to label young children by disability categories. For example, when Juanita found out that Tanya had disabilities, the early childhood special educators used the term "preschool disabled." They didn't label Tanya as "mentally retarded" or "language-delayed"; they simply noted that she had disabilities and was eligible for an early intervention program.

The law now allows more latitude in the types, intensity, and duration of services provided. Early childhood special educators may find themselves working in private preschool programs to help private providers modify and accommodate the needs of young children with disabilities. Alternatively, they may provide language enrichment activities for children from several programs.

Even more innovative is the component of the law focusing on infants. The provisions of the law support the notion of families rather than children alone as a focus of intervention, with an IFSP instead of an IEP mandated. The IFSP emphasizes working with the family's needs rather than developing a treatment plan only for the child. Since the amendments were first passed in 1986, much attention has been given to family involvement and the development of integrated preschool programs. This section of the law has also encouraged school systems to focus on early intervention. According to the most recent amendments to the law, the IFSP must include a statement about the natural environments in which early intervention services will be provided and a justification for the nonprovision of services in the natural environment, such as the home.

**TRANSITION SERVICES** Despite the reforms to special education in the 1980s and 1990s, the outlook for special education students moving into adulthood was discouraging. Repeatedly, researchers found that students with disabilities were leaving high school to face unemployment or **underemployment,** social isolation, and continued dependence on family and

| TABLE 2.7 | Sample Differences Between IFSPs and IEPs |
| --- | --- |
| **IFSP Objective** | **IEP Objective** |
| With coaching from the speech/language specialist, Tanya's family will spend at least half an hour, three times per week, reading simple picture books to Tanya, giving her a chance to turn the pages, point to pictures, and choose the books that she wants to hear. | At the snack table, when given a choice between an edible and nonedible object, Tanya will be able to say "eat cookie" to request a cookie with 90 percent accuracy over ten trials over a three-day period of time. |

| TABLE 2.8 | Sample Differences Between IEPs and ITPs |
| --- | --- |
| **ITP Objective** | **IEP Objective** |
| I will proof my own written work, making sure that my thinking is expressed in clear, logical order and my grammar and syntax are correct before handing in any written assignments, reaching an average of 9 to 10 proofed assignments during the last quarter from 0 right now. | After writing at least one paragraph of narrative text, Michael will be able to identify and correct his spelling errors with 90 percent accuracy over ten consecutive trials. |

friends for living accommodations (A concern about, 1992; Frank et al., 1990; Mithaug, Horuichi, & Fanning, 1985; Wagner, 1989).

**REVISING THE LAW** As a result of continued poor outcomes for students with disabilities, revisions to P.L. 94-142 culminated in 1990 with the mandate to include transition services for all students ages 16 through 21. In 1997, amendments to IDEA 97 specified that transition planning must begin by age 14. In IDEA 97, transition services are defined as

> a set of coordinated activities, based upon the student's interests and preferences, that promotes movement from school to post-school activities including post-secondary education, vocational training and education, integrated employment, continuing and adult education, adult services, independent living or community participation. The coordinated set of activities shall be based on individual student's needs, taking into account the student's preferences and interests, and shall include instruction, community experiences, the development of employment and other post-school adult living objectives, and when appropriate, acquisition of daily living skills and functional vocational education.

Like an IEP, an individualized transition plan (ITP) includes goals and objectives, timelines, and evaluations (Stowitschek & Kelso, 1989). Using an ITP, school professionals collaborate with students and their families to prepare the students for successful employment and independent living (Chadsey-Rusch, Rusch, & Phelps, 1989; Hardman & McDonnell, 1987; Miller, LaFollette, & Green, 1990; Rojewski, 1992; Stowitschek & Kelso, 1989).

Like the IFSP, the ITP involves the student and his or her family in determining and implementing goals. The language differences between the ITP and the IEP are apparent in the examples in Table 2.8. In the IEP, the student is referred to in the third person, and the objective seems to be framed in terms of the teacher's behavior rather than that of the student. In contrast, the ITP objective is in the first person. Michael is making a strong statement about the goal he is setting for himself in an effort to improve his written work. He specifies an outcome that can be measured, and he states how he measures up to that goal at the beginning of the process.

As you might imagine, planning for transition is a complex task because goals are set that are to be achieved over several years. And because adolescents

BOX 2.4

## Kurume's IEP

Kurume had his annual IEP meeting back in October. This year's meeting was particularly exciting for Kurume because it was his last meeting before graduating from high school in the spring. Prior to the IEP meeting, Kurume gave a lot of thought to his goals and objectives. He was certain that he wanted to pursue a career in computer technology, though he wasn't sure as to the specific area in which to develop his expertise—systems analysis, product design, marketing, or engineering. Kurume spoke with Ms. Howard, the head of his high school's business department, and identified a technology course that he could take during the final semester of his senior year. This course would give him an overview of the uses of technology. Kurume also found out that training programs were available at the local community college, state college, and university.

Kurume's preparation proved to be a valuable asset to his IEP planning team. Ms. Howard attended the meeting and agreed to modify the assignments in the computer class to allow Kurume to shadow three businesspersons in the local community who held various types of positions in the computer industry. Kurume could then gain a feel for the types of skills and demands required for the different jobs. Mr. Bradford, Kurume's special education teacher,

agreed to help Ms. Howard set up the job shadowing experiences and to arrange for Kurume's transportation. Kurume's rehabilitation counselor agreed to fund interpreters for each job shadow experience, as the information Kurume gained from these experiences could be used as a vehicle for gathering assessment data on his vocational interests. Kurume agreed to meet with his rehab counselor when he finished job shadowing in order to narrow his career goals. The rehabilitation counselor and Mr. Bradford then agreed to assist Kurume in contacting and meeting with representatives from the various postsecondary education facilities in order to help him determine which program would best suit his career goals. Kurume's mother agreed to make sure that Kurume would have transportation to get to the various schools. And Mr. Bradford agreed to teach Kurume how to access the Offices for Students with Disabilities on each campus in order for him to arrange for an interpreter for his interviews.

Each of the steps that had been agreed to were noted in Kurume's transition plan, and the names of persons who had accepted responsibility for each step were recorded as well. By the time he called his meeting to an end, Kurume was eager to implement his plan.

themselves are in a period of rapid development, their abilities, interests, and motivations change rapidly. At the same time, employment opportunities and connections among agencies and private businesses also change according to economic conditions and personnel moves (Stowitschek & Kelso, 1989).

**CLARIFYING TIME LIMITS FOR TRANSITION SERVICES** Let's suppose that, prior to graduation, Kurume had a transition goal of attending a community college to obtain a certificate in computer technology. However, Kurume's part-time job doesn't pay enough to cover the full cost of tuition and books. Because Kurume has not passed his twenty-first birthday, he may reconvene his IEP team and request funds from the school district to augment his salary to pay for college (see Box 2.4). At this time, neither the law nor its regulations specify any time limits regarding the reconvening of the IEP team

(National Transition Network, 1993). In fact, as the U.S. Department of Education has commented,

> the Act neither requires nor prohibits the provision of service to a student after the student has completed the State's graduation requirements. Thus, if a student is still within the eligible age range for FAPE within the State, the State, within its discretion, could continue to provide needed transition services to the student and use the funds under this part to pay for the transition services, or contribute to the cost of those services through a shared cost arrangement with another agency—provided that all applicable requirements of this part are met. (Federal Register, *1992, p. 44848*)

We anticipate that legal decisions over the next several years will help to define the extent to which local educational agencies are responsible for continued transition supports to students after their graduation from high school and prior to their twenty-second birthday.

# ■ SECTION SUMMARY

IDEA 97 is a complex law detailing both how school professionals are to plan and implement educational services to students with disabilities and what safeguards must be observed throughout the process. This act has had an immense impact on school policies, structures, and practices. The values that guide IDEA 97—those of equity and access—can and should impact the way schools respond to other, diverse student groups. By creating inclusive school communities that reflect the spirit of this law, schools will be able to respond to the needs of all learners.

When P.L. 94-142 was passed in 1975, special educators, parents of children with disabilities, and other professionals who work with persons with disabilities had high hopes for improvements in educational outcomes for people with disabilities. Children with disabilities were finally entitled access to the same educational systems as students without disabilities. The influx of aid to institutions of higher education helped train teachers, social workers, school psychologists, speech/language therapists, and physical and occupational therapists to provide needed services. Multidisciplinary teams of professionals were required to determine placement in programs and to determine the types and amounts of educational services. No child was to be excluded from services, and all educational services were to be determined on an individual basis. The due process component of the law allowed parents to participate in and to challenge educational decisions made regarding their children.

States were given the responsibility of overseeing implementation of the law in local school districts. Accountability for implementing all components of the law was established through on-site review of programs at the local and state levels. States that implemented P.L. 94-142 received funding; states that did not stood to lose funding. By the 1994–95 school year, nearly 11 percent of the 5.4 million students attending school were enrolled in special education programs funded by federal entitlement programs (U.S. Department of Education, 1997). By 1995, children labeled as learning disabled made up about 51 percent of the total number of students with disabilities being served; students with speech or language impairments made up about 20 percent of the total special education population; students with mental retardation accounted for about 12 percent of individuals ages 6 through 21 being served; almost 9 percent of special education students were labeled as emotionally disturbed. The remainder of the special education population in the 1994–95 school year consisted of students labeled as having multiple disabilities, hearing impairments, orthopedic impairments, other health impairments, visual impairments, autism, deaf-blindness, or traumatic brain injury.

According to the U.S. Department of Education (1997), the number of students within each category is changing, although the total number of students served seems to be growing by about 3 percent per year. This relative consistency in the overall percentage of students being served has been interpreted to mean that most students with disabilities have gained access to the system. The more difficult question is whether the quality of the educational experience has been sufficient to demonstrate that special education students have increased their abilities to function effectively as adult members of the community.

# Chapter Summary

Disability laws like Section 504, IDEA 97, and ADA constitute a bold and ambitious social agenda. According to the U.S. Department of Education (1997), there has been an increase in the educational achievements of individuals with disabilities. In 1986, 40 percent of students with disabilities did not graduate from high school; by 1994, this percentage had shrunk to 25 percent. In contrast, in 1986, 15 percent of the student population without disabilities failed to graduate from high school, a percentage that had decreased to 12 percent by 1994. Rates of work force participation have also increased since 1986. These statistics suggest that IDEA 97 is resulting in beneficial outcomes for individuals with disabilities and their families.

However, much work remains. When IDEA 97 was originally passed as P.L. 94-142, special educators were expected to have their own classrooms and to provide services independent of the general education classroom. But as special education policies have been refined, the role of special educators has been reconceptualized. Now, special educators must work with their general education colleagues in order to serve students with disabilities. This collaborative approach to service delivery helps ensure that students have both access (through special education supports) and opportunity (through the general education curriculum).

Like all laws, disability laws are living documents that are in the process of being defined and redefined even as you read this chapter. By maintaining current knowledge of educational legislation and case law, you will be able to respond to changing definitions of your roles and responsibilities as a school professional. For example, as a result of disability legislation, educators have a mandate to use practices that support free and appropriate public education in the least restrictive environment. The *Oberti* case helped to crystallize how schools could interpret the concept of least restrictive environment as the general education classroom, and not the self-contained special education classroom for children with particular types of disabilities. The way that we organize our classrooms, design curricula, and teach students is directed by an implicit philosophy and the values that inform policy. The challenge that disability legislation lays before us is to create learning environments that can accommodate the needs of all learners. In subsequent chapters, we will provide you with the building blocks of inclusive learning communities.

## INSTRUCTIONAL ACTIVITY

## Legal Bases for Access and Education for Individuals with Disabilities

### *Objectives*

- To gain an understanding of the legal bases for access and education for individuals with disabilities
- To develop a strategy for organizing and remembering key constructs about the legal bases

### *Product*

- An individual mnemonic

### *Agenda*

- Appendix 10.2 describes three procedures for remembering information. Choose the one that you find most useful, and create a strategy for remembering the key elements of IDEA, ADA, and Section 504.
- Share your mnemonic device with your classmates.

### *Evaluation*

- You should score 85 percent or better on an objective test that tests your knowledge of disability law.

# Glossary

**Americans with Disabilities Act (ADA)** A comprehensive 1990 law ensuring that individuals with disabilities, regardless of their age, have the right to access all services, facilities, programs, and job opportunities that are accessed by nondisabled individuals.

**Attention deficit disorder (ADD)** A diagnostic category used by the American Psychiatric Association to label a cluster of behavioral symptoms such as developmentally inappropriate over activity, impulsivity, and attention.

**Audiologist** A professional who specializes in testing and treating hearing impairments.

**Brown v. Board of Education** A landmark 1954 ruling by the Supreme Court that struck down the frequent practice of local school boards of segregating students of African-American descent from those of Euro-American descent in separate schools.

**Charter schools** Schools that are exempted from the typical local school district rules and regulations in order to offer an alternative set of educational experiences and programming for school-aged children.

**Clean, intermittent catheterization** A procedure to help individuals who cannot urinate independently.

**Disenfranchised** The term used to describe the marginalization of specific groups of individuals who may be excluded, purposely or not, from decision-making processes used to impact policy or services for a community, large or small.

**Due process hearing** A hearing conducted by an impartial, trained officer of the state to determine whether an individual's rights to an education under IDEA 97 have been upheld or violated according to the procedures set forth in IDEA 97.

**Egalitarianism** A philosophical position that supports equality among all people.

**Hepatitis** A viral infection affecting the liver with serious, long-term health consequences.

**Individualized education plan (IEP)** A plan mandated under IDEA 97 that specifies a student's current level of functioning, annual goals and objectives, and the necessary special education services needed to accomplish these goals and objectives.

**Individualized family service plan (IFSP)** A written plan developed collaboratively with the family and the service providers that details the types of services and interventions available to the family in supporting the development of their infant or toddler.

**Individualized transition plan (ITP)** A written plan, typically developed in conjunction with the IEP, that addresses a student's long-term goals and objectives for postsecondary education, vocation or employment, and community access.

**Least restrictive environment** Refers to the idea that students served in special education must receive their educational supports in the regular education classroom (the least restrictive environment) unless the student's education cannot be satisfactorily achieved in regular classes even with the use of supplementary aids and services.

**Mediation** A system of helping two or more parties with conflicting ideas to resolve a problem or issue.

**Occupational therapy (OT)** Therapy and interventions that focus on the development of skills for activities of independent daily living, such as eating, moving about, dressing, and writing.

**Perceptual communicative disorder** The Colorado label for students with learning disabilities. It implies that neurological factors have resulted in a student's inability to learn as his or her peers might. It also implies that language problems are at the base of the learning disability.

**Quadriplegic** A physical condition that involves paralysis of an individual's arms and legs.

**Reauthorization** The process of extending a law that was previously passed and that had a provision for future reexamination. Typically, there is a cycle associated with reauthorization. For instance, IDEA 97 is on a five-year cycle, such that every five years Congress must reexamine the outcomes of the law and change it as needed to improve its impact or its protections.

**Related services** Support services that address the developmental or remedial needs of students with disabilities. These services include special transportation; speech/language pathology; audiology; psychological, physical, and occupational therapy; counseling; school health; and medical and rehabilitation counseling.

**Service delivery system** An explicit system for how services are delivered. In school systems, a variety of service delivery systems exist. For instance, elementary, middle, and high schools deliver services based on chronological age and grade.

**Speech/language therapist** A professional who works with students who have speech and language problems.

**Spina bifida** A congenital condition in which the vertebrae do not develop completely prior to birth. Impairment varies from individual to individual depending on the extent of the malformation.

**Total communication** An approach to communication that involves the use of both verbal and nonverbal coding systems—for example, the combination of American Sign Language and speaking used simultaneously to communicate.

**Traumatic brain injury** A condition typically resulting from a major blow or injury to the head.

**Underemployment** Refers to when an individual is working in a situation for which he or she is overqualified.

**Vocational education** Educational programming and services directed to assisting students to develop the skills, habits, and attitudes needed to obtain and maintain productive work throughout their adult lives.

# Involving Families in School

## A Family's Story

*by Anita Wagner*

As parents of children who are now 16 and 13, we have been involved in many parent-professional partnerships over the years. I often think of how different things were after the births of each of our children. When Jamie, our daughter, was born, we had confidence in our ability to parent her. With the birth of Kevin, however, that confidence was greatly shaken, because Kevin was born with Down syndrome.

In those early dark days, we often felt out of control. It was as if our ability to manage our family and children had been taken away by the many "experts" working with Kevin. The experts believed that they knew better than we did about what our family needed. Essentially, the message we received was that our needs were now defined by Kevin's label and that we must follow the same trail as other parents who had children with Down syndrome. I remember suggesting to a friend that it suddenly felt as though many of the people working with us saw us as a "disabled family" because of Kevin. While it was very important for us to do whatever we could to meet Kevin's individual needs, we

also knew it was important for this to happen within the context of our family. We did not want Kevin's disability to completely consume or define our family.

As our family considers where we have been and where we are going with Kevin, we think of the experiences as a journey. This is a journey that many different service providers have shared with us over the years. The quality of the relationships we have had with service providers has varied over time and has depended on a number of factors. For example, our time, and Kevin's, is too precious to be taken up with those who do not share our dreams and respect the values of our family. We truly believe in the collaborative approach, with families having the right to make decisions for their children and themselves in harmony with professionals' responsibilities to share their knowledge and expertise. We have learned to be consumers and to look for these specific qualities in the professionals with whom we work.

In the past thirteen years, many teachers, therapists, and medical professionals have shared our journey with Kevin. One such individual is Kevin's occupational therapist, Margie. Margie started working with Kevin when he was 4 years old. As we reflect on our relationship with Margie, we see how she accepted our goals and priorities for Kevin. Margie has seen our family in every possible mood and stage as we have coped with and adapted to Kevin's needs. She helped us get back in touch with our competencies even during those times when we were not necessarily models of competence and confidence. She offered us a nonjudgmental sounding board and respected our lifestyle even though it may have differed from her own.

Margie continues to believe in and to share our dreams for Kevin. I believe the partnership we model has given Kevin the skills to become his own consumer and self-advocate. His dreams for himself reflect his sense of self-worth and self-confidence. Those dreams are possible when people like Margie believe in his abilities and offer honest friendship and a genuine sense of caring.

# Introduction

A picture is often worth a thousand words. Through pictures, children tell us about their families (see Figure 3.1). As you can see, the compositions of these families vary. Tanya's picture includes her mother, grandmother, and grandfather, as well as a guinea pig and a bird; Kirk's shows only his mother and father, despite the fact that he has three half-brothers and two half-sisters. These drawings represent the changing cir-

cumstances of families that we described in Chapter 1. Families vary in many ways—in their composition, in the ways they function and communicate, in their preferences and feelings.

Now imagine lines connecting the children's drawings to their school. The connections between families and school are lifelines that sustain inclusive school communities. In Chapters 1 and 2, we provided a rationale for the reliance on meaningful relationships among students, families, school professionals, and

**FIGURE 3.1** ■ Children's Conceptions of Their Families

support personnel. Understanding the complex and dynamic nature of changing family structures is a key to developing and maintaining these relationships and to keeping those lifelines connected.

By devoting an entire chapter to the complex dynamics of families, we emphasize the importance of sustaining and supporting relationships between schools and families. First, we explore family diversity by examining family membership and composition. Second, we examine socioeconomic and cultural influences on families. Third, we focus on the impact of a child with a disability on individual family members and on the family as a whole. Fourth, we address a variety of options for supporting families in their communities. Finally, we discuss how to develop collaborative partnerships between school professionals and families, so that families are not passive recipients of the services of school professionals but are equal partners in the educational process. Later, in Chapter 4, you will learn about the processes necessary to support these collaborative relationships. As you read this chapter, think about how you can work with families in ways that foster partnerships between families and schools.

# Understanding Families

While pictures help us to think about the different forms that families take, they can only illustrate what is observable. Pictures can show us how many members a family has, and they can tell us something about the sex, age, and ethnicity of family members. However, pictures do not tell us how family members are related to one another, nor do they tell us precisely about how family members feel or act toward one another. In this section, we explore both the more visible and the less obvious dimensions of family life.

## The Membership and Composition of Families

The concept of "family" conjures up many different images. Our students' drawings in Figure 3.1 reflect some of the important features of families in the United States. Kurume's picture, drawn when he was 6, included his father, mother, brother, sister, and cat. By the time Kurume reached 18 years of age, the features

of his family had changed because of his parents' divorce. However, because he values and relies on both of his parents' advice and because he spends equal amounts of time with his mother and father, Kurume's picture of his family remains the same. So, even though the features of his family have changed, his notion of family remains constant.

Annie's family picture was actually drawn by her best friend, Paige, because Annie's physical dexterity limits her ability to hold crayons and make marks on the paper. Paige talked to Annie while she drew, asking questions like "Is your father taller than your mother?" "Does Toby look like this?" and "Should I put a picture of Toby on your shirt?" Notice that Annie's family— her mom, dad, sister, and brother—reflect the image of the traditional nuclear family.

In contrast, Tanya's picture shows that her teenaged mother, grandmother, grandfather, guinea pig, and bird are all "family" to her. Tanya is an only child being raised in her immediate family of three adults—two woman from different generations and one man. She has had no contact with her father, so she didn't draw a picture of him. Though they are not pictured, Tanya's extended family also plays a significant role in her life. For example, the entire extended family, including aunts, uncles, and cousins, gathers every Sunday after church at Tia Elena's house to eat brunch, play cards, watch TV, and so on. In fact, Tanya spends so much time playing with her cousins that they seem almost like brothers and sisters. She sometimes takes her nap at Tia Elena's house and feels just as comfortable there as she does at home.

Kirk's picture shows only his mother and father— even though he has three half-brothers and two half-sisters. His half-brothers are his mother's sons with her previous husband; his half-sisters are his father's children with his previous wife. Although some of his half-brothers and sisters moved in and out of their home, the entire family never actually lived altogether at any time. Kirk refers to all of them simply as his brothers and sisters, but he chose not to include them all in his drawing. Now, he and his mother frequently live alone while his father is away working.

Michael's picture illustrates a family consisting of his mother, father, older sister, and himself. Both of Michael's parents work to provide for the family. Michael's dad, Chen, believes that getting children to school and tending to their education is a woman's responsibility. Thus, Michael has always relied on his mother to serve as intermediary at school and to help him register for classes and make important school decisions. He sometimes thinks of her as being the only person on "his side."

As you can see from these family portraits, the composition of the American family varies dramatically. Between 1980 and 1990, the number of families with "atypical" composition increased while the number of families with "typical" nuclear membership declined. Only about 6 percent of today's families fit the "Norman Rockwell" image of a family of two biological parents of similar religious, linguistic, and cultural heritage, one a wage-earner and the other a homemaker, with two children and a dog (Hodgkinson, 1991). We now have many more blended families: step-families, families of mixed ethnicity and religions, foster parents raising children who are biologically unrelated, grandparents raising children, and single-parent families. In fact, about half of children will spend a significant portion of their childhood in a one-parent home (Blankenhorn, 1991; Hodgkinson, 1991). And with changing family compositions come associated changes in the ways in which families function and carry out day-to-day responsibilities.

Changes in families and family behaviors mean that the traditional bridges used to connect families and schools have become less utilitarian. Even the language used by school professionals to describe families and their relationships needs to be sensitive to these changes. For instance, Kirk would be excluded if his school had a father-son potluck, but if the school organized an autumn potluck, he would be able to attend with his mother. However, it's not simply changing relationships that characterize today's families; it's the family systems themselves that are different.

## Family Systems and Functioning Styles

Families provide the primary care for their children, including those with disabilities (Perlman, 1983). School communities that include all children depend on strong connections with students' families. To establish these connections, school professionals must understand the roles, responsibilities, and communication styles of students' families. Bronfenbrenner's (1979) model of ecological units helps us to understand the interplay among various roles in our **social networks** (see Figure 3.2). His model describes units or subunits of

persons in society on whom the individual or family relies for aid, and it is frequently used as the basis for talking about families of children with disabilities. According to Bronfenbrenner, ecological units, or social networks, may be conceived topologically as a nested arrangement of concentric structures each embedded within one another.

As Figure 3.2 shows, at the innermost level is the developing child and his or her nuclear family members (mother, father, and siblings). This family unit is embedded in broader ecological subunits consisting of extended family, friends, and other close, personal acquaintances. These subunits are further embedded in even larger social units, including social organizations, the workplace, and professional agencies. This model helps us conceptualize the complexity of the family as a system and the way individuals function within that family and within society.

**FAMILY SYSTEMS** A **family system** is comprised of individual family members, each of whom has personal capabilities and skills (Dunst, Trivette, & Deal, 1988). Families may or may not contain members who are connected by genealogy. A family may consist of two or more generations, exist on a long-term or short-term basis, and be large or small. Regardless of the membership of the family unit, it is a social system that is structured by rules, patterns of communication, and positions of relative power. These structures allow families to function as a unit and provide support for each member's role (Goldenberg & Goldenberg, 1980). The roles that family members play are influenced by culture, tradition, social patterns, and family structure. In smoothly functioning families, these roles are mutually supportive and permit personal growth and satisfaction, self-expression, and development of a sense of **self-efficacy,** competence, and personal worth in all family members (Mason, Kruse, & Kohler, 1991). Family systems theory has been the basis for understanding families for the past thirty years. Kerr and Bowen (1988) believe that systems theory can explain many aspects of natural systems and that people and families are, indeed, natural systems.

According to Lambie and Daniels-Mohring (1993), there are four fundamental principles of family systems theory (see Table 3.1). First, no individual can be understood without looking at how he or she fits into the whole of the family. To understand a family system, you must consider all the individuals in the family, as

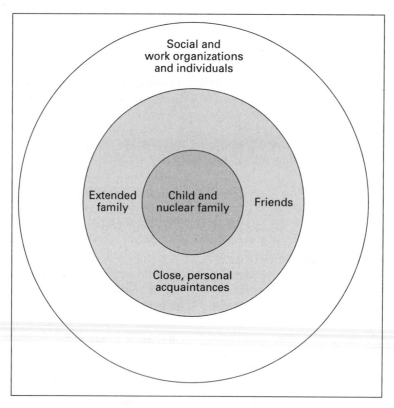

**FIGURE 3.2** ■ Bronfenbrenner's Model of Ecological Units

well as their interactions and their history. Second, families have both rules for structure and rules for change. The rules for structure are the rules that organize the day-to-day functioning of the family. For example, when Kurume's parents, Mattie and Ed, were first married, they both worked. Thus, they had to negotiate how they would run their household in terms of cooking, cleaning, and paying bills because their models for assuming these responsibilities were based on a division of labor whereby one adult stayed home while the other worked. The rules for change allow for adaptation to new circumstances. For instance, when Kurume was born and Mattie took an unpaid leave of absence to stay home to care for him, she and Ed had to renegotiate how they, as a family, would do the day-to-day tasks. The third principle of family systems theory states that the interaction of the family with the school, community, extended family, and friends is essential to the life of the family unit. Not all of the external systems are intimately linked to the details of

family life. But when one member of the family is a child with a disability, linkages with school and community supports and services, in particular, are vital. Finally, all families have both productive and nonproductive interactions. When multiple stressors in the environment converge on a family, individuals within the family, as well as the family as a whole, may react in less-than-productive ways.

The range and variety of capabilities and skills of individual family members are influenced by interactions with others, both within and outside of the family system (Dunst, Trivette, & Deal, 1988). A combination of skills of family members is often needed to achieve a desired goal. For example, all family members may participate in the preparation of dinner, with each individual fulfilling the role expected and performing certain tasks according to his or her proficiency.

When family members attempt to perform a function in which they are not comfortable, confident, or skilled, other members or outside sources may need

| TABLE 3.1 | Four Principles of Family Systems |
|---|---|

- No individual can be understood outside of the context of the family.
- Families have rules for structure and change.
- Interaction with external units is essential to the life of the family.
- All families have productive and nonproductive interactions.

to contribute to accomplish a desired outcome. The school is an important outside source of support and assistance available to families of children with disabilities. The lines we asked you to imagine between the school and the family represent one avenue for families to achieve their goals.

Consider the situation of Juanita and her mother, Elodia, and her father, Javier. Together, they decide that it is important that 3-year-old Tanya learn to be independent. Juanita and Elodia always prepare dinner together. When Javier gets home from his job at the public works department, he sits in the kitchen and visits with the women as they cook; it's a time for the family to talk while taking care of an important task. And when Tanya says, "Me do," and points to the dishes, they decide that she is ready to learn how to participate in this family activity. Specifically, they want Tanya to place the flatware and dishes on the table, but they need help in teaching her because her coordination isn't fully developed. So they call on her preschool teacher and her occupational therapist to help them achieve this goal by incorporating table setting into the preschool curriculum.

School professionals can obtain insight into the school behaviors and learning habits of a child by gaining a deeper understanding of the family as a system. By doing so, the professional is better equipped to work effectively with the student and to create productive partnerships with parents and other family members. Productive school-family partnerships often result in successful school experiences for children because the goals of the family create the direction for assessment, curriculum, and instruction.

**FAMILY FUNCTIONING STYLE** Each family has its own way of dealing with life events. Family functioning style refers to the unique combination of strengths that help a family access and use resources and that define the family's particular style of working together. In essence, family functioning style includes the strengths and capabilities of family members and the manner in which these abilities are used to secure or create resources. As Stoneman (1985) points out, "Every family has strengths and, if the emphasis is on supporting strengths rather than rectifying weaknesses, chances for making a difference in the lives of children and families are vastly increased" (p. 462). Capitalizing on a family's strengths and talents, rather than attempting to "fix" a family's deficits or weaknesses, enables establishment of a positive foundation. When the mindset is positive rather than negative, the initial and ongoing interactions between family members and professionals are more likely to be fruitful. As a school professional, you should be aware of the importance of seeking out and acknowledging the strengths and abilities of all families.

There are no right or wrong family functioning styles but rather differentially effective styles that are likely to be employed in response to various life events and situations. Think about the chapter-opening vignette, written by Anita Wagner, a mother who has had many experiences with school professionals. Anita remarks that Kevin's occupational therapist, Margie, never judges the decisions made by the family. Margie's lack of criticism implies a basic trust that the family can and will make reasonable choices and decisions for their child. And Margie gives support even when the family's choices and decisions don't coincide with her own professional judgment.

## ■ SECTION SUMMARY

"Family" can be used to describe every imaginable combination of natural and adoptive parents, stepparents, grandparents, brothers, sisters, stepbrothers, stepsisters, half-brothers, half-sisters, aunts, uncles, cousins, and others. Families that were once considered atypical are now very common in our society. Families are the most basic social units, providing, among other things, the primary care for children in our society. Systems theory helps us to understand families as a whole, as well as the linkages of the family to outside agencies and services. Family systems are composed of individuals who each contribute skills and capabilities to the family unit. School professionals who recognize and accept the variations in family membership, family systems, and family functioning styles will be better prepared to meet and collaborate with the families in their school community.

# External Influences on Families

By placing families within the context in which they live, we can fill in additional details of each family's picture. Socioeconomic status and culture are two important external influences on how families interact, which activities they choose, and what lifestyle they value.

## Socioeconomic Influences

Understanding the socioeconomic factors that affect families will help you understand how families function. Sometimes, family membership and composition affect the socioeconomic status of the family. For example, single parents maintain both caregiver and financial responsibilities for the family. Providing care to children is a significant challenge for single-parent families, and if economic stresses exist, the problem may be exacerbated (Demands, 1984). In 1990, the average income for single-mother families was within $1000 of the national poverty level. According to the

1990 U.S. census (Hodgkinson, 1991), females over the age of 25 with children to support account for the largest proportion of low-wage workers. Homelessness also affects children of all ages; many one- and two-parent families are homeless because of extreme economic distress. On any given night, it is estimated that nearly 100,000 children sleep in shelters for the homeless, and approximately 40 percent of shelter users are families with children (Hodgkinson, 1991).

At the same time, many families have multiple wage earners and various work schedules. Although several salaries in a family tend to diminish the problems associated with poverty, the likelihood increases that school-age children will return to a home in which there is no adult supervision for several hours after school. Hodgkinson (1991) reports that 14 percent of school-age children spend three or more hours a day home alone.

## Cultural Influences on Families

We all have a cultural heritage. However, many of us may not be aware of how our personal behaviors, preferences, and habits are culturally based. In particular, Euro-Americans, who are part of the dominant or mainstream American culture, may be least aware of the ways in which culture influences their customs and interactions (Lynch & Hanson, 1992).

The heritage of a family influences the behaviors, expectations, interactions, and communication styles of family members. The cultural backgrounds of families shape the members' beliefs and practices. Culture plays a role in defining who the individuals are, how they relate to one another in the course of their daily lives, and how they conduct their lives.

Remember the promise that Juanita's parents made just after Tanya's birth? In another family, the promise of a trip to Mexico to visit a shrine might not have been valued, but for Juanita it was comforting to know that her parents would make such a sacrifice for the baby's sake. Moreover, Juanita knows that her parents and extended family members will continue to help her raise her child. She values the wisdom and economic support that her mother and father will contribute throughout her child's life and the physical assistance she gets from aunts, uncles, and cousins. Cultural beliefs and values influence the thoughts and actions of the entire family.

## Extending Your Learning

1. Draw a picture of the family you grew up in. Think about your growing years. Who were the family members? Was the composition of your family typical of the families in your neighborhood? What was the socioeconomic status of your family? Was it similar to or different from that of the other families in your community?

2. "Discover" who you are, why you believe the things you do, and where your basic values come from by constructing a family tree or genogram. Ask your oldest family members to tell you stories of their early lives and the lives of their parents and grandparents. Also, spend some time going through old family albums and asking questions about the people in the photographs. Read any information (newspaper articles, journals from family members, letters, and so on) that is written about your family. Look up records of births and deaths. As you become more aware of your own heritage, continually ask yourself about how that heritage influences the person you are today. How did your upbringing impact your school experiences? How can you use this information to increase your own sensitivity to other families?

**CULTURAL INFLUENCES ON THE FAMILY'S VIEW OF DISABILITIES** Different cultures attach very different meanings to the presence of disabling conditions and thus affect the emotional and intellectual responses of the parents (Chan, 1986; Hourcade, Parette, & Huer, 1997; Morrow, 1987; Owan, 1985; Tung, 1985). Views related to disability and its causation range from those that emphasize the role of fate to those that place responsibility on the individual or his or her family (Hanson, Lynch, & Wayman, 1990). For example, Correa and Weismantel (1991) note that, in some Asian cultural belief systems, individuals may believe that they have little power to escape from their fate and seek mainly to achieve harmony in this life. In some cultures, blame may be attached to the parents for the child's disability. Some may see the disability as a punishment for sins or wrongdoings; others may view disability as the result of some action the mother or father took while the mother was pregnant; still others may believe the disability was caused by something the parents did after the child was born (Chan, 1986;

Kinzie, 1985; Morrow, 1987; Owan, 1985; Tung, 1985). For example, in the Ute tribe, mothers are instructed by the elders to avoid touching the baby's face during his or her first month of life, because this might have negative effects on the appearance of the child.

Differences in beliefs and practices may even occur among people who are sometimes presumed to share the same culture. For instance, some beliefs and practices that are common among people with Mexican origins are different from the accepted practices or beliefs of other Latin Americans, and yet they both might be globally referred to as Hispanic or Latino because they speak Spanish. The same is true of Native Americans: Navajo beliefs and values differ from those of the Apache and other tribal groups (Harrison et al., 1990).

**IDENTIFICATION WITH CULTURAL GROUPS** The degree to which individuals identify with their own cultural group varies. Factors that might influence an individual's or family's cultural identity may include length of residence in the United States or in a particular region of the country, the type of region (urban, suburban, rural), socioeconomic status, the person's age and sex, the amount and type of education, the number and type of resources or family support systems, isolation of the family from extended family networks, and, in the case of immigrants, the reason for the immigration and/or the "wave" of immigration with which the person was associated (Lynch & Hanson, 1992; Ramirez & Castañeda, 1974).

Leung (1988) offers a framework for understanding acculturation, or how certain minority cultural groups relate to the dominant culture of the area in which they reside (see Table 3.2). Red Horse (1988) has described a framework similar to that of Leung, with the additional distinction of a "pan-renaissance" group among Native Americans, which tries to "revitalize" traditional views and practices. A similar process among African-Americans was described by Jenkins (1982) as a search for a viable "black" identity and for the reclamation of respect for the African-American culture.

These frameworks help us to understand how families may relate to the dominant culture, but we also need to remember that, within a family, members may differ in the ways they relate to their cultural heritage. Tanya's mother, Juanita, and her grandparents would probably all be described as operating within Leung's category of traditionalism. Michael's parents might

| TABLE 3.2 | Leung's Acculturation Framework |
|---|---|

- *Traditionalism:* usually found among older adults who cling to the traditional culture
- *Marginality:* persons at the juncture of two cultures, accepting neither the old nor the new, and possibly experiencing alienation from both
- *Biculturation:* a level of efficient integration of both cultures
- *Overacculturation:* an extreme rejection of the ethnic culture, sometimes shown by young people

### Extending Your Learning

Think about the cultural heritage of your family. Where in Leung's framework would you place your parents, grandparents, siblings, and yourself? Are any of your family members trying to "revitalize" traditional views? What do family members do or say to convey their beliefs?

consider themselves at Leung's marginality level, while his grandparents could be categorized as traditional. But Michael and his sister are very comfortable in their ability to intertwine various aspects of both Asian and American cultures into their lives. Kurume's parents, who met and married in the mid 1970s, experienced the need to explore their own cultural heritage during those years. As a result of their interest in and study of their African-American cultural heritage, they selected names for their children—Kurume, Kaneesha, and Rashaan—that reflect their pride in their heritage.

### ■ SECTION SUMMARY

Economic circumstances may or may not be affected by family composition and membership. In any case, economic stressors can add a level of difficulty for families of children with disabilities. Cultural heritage may also affect the behaviors, expectations, and interactions of families, as well as the ways in which they cope with disabilities. Different families and different family members may identify with their cultural heritage to different extents.

## The Impact of Children with Disabilities on Their Families

There is little doubt that the birth or subsequent identification of a child with disabilities creates challenges, demands, stresses, and issues that the family must deal with day in and day out (Blacher, 1984; Combrinck-Graham, 1983; Leigh, 1987; Paterson & McCubbin, 1983; Shapiro, 1983; Turnbull & Turnbull, 1990). However, a focus on the distress that accompanies these issues and challenges traditionally has pervaded the research and literature on families of children with disabilities. Over the years, professionals may have created the stereotypical but erroneous view that these families are under so much stress that they cannot meet their challenges effectively.

Today, however, there is emerging recognition that the presence of a child with a disability may also strengthen families. The evidence of positive contributions lies in both the empirical literature and parent narratives and "stories" (May, 1993; Mullins, 1987). Recognition that there are both positive and negative aspects of raising children with disabilities creates a more accurate picture of the range of families' experiences.

The lives of families change when their children are born. This is particularly true for families with children who have disabilities. While the birth of a child with a diagnosed disability or chronic health problem may be a surprise to the family, the joy of a new addition to the family should not be forgotten. Professionals, friends, and neighbors may forget that an infant is first a new member of the family; any disability is secondary. Given this perspective, it is not surprising that a variety of emotions will surface for family members when a child with disabilities or special health care needs is born. One father's story is given in Box 3.1.

### Emotional Responses

**STAGES VERSUS STATES** Evidence suggests that parents of children with disabilities experience similar types of emotional responses and go through adjustment processes that bear similar characteristics (Eden-

---

**BOX 3.1**

**A Father's Story**

When Sean was born with spina bifida, friends and family grieved for us and described their sorrow. Some of our friends and family avoided us probably because they didn't know what to say and were uncomfortable with the thought of our baby having a disability. My favorite call came from a friend who said, "Congratulations, I heard you had a baby boy."

---

Piercy, Blacher, & Eyman, 1986; Featherstone, 1980). Many researchers have documented the series of emotions that parents report after discovering that their child has a disability. Blacher (1984) describes three stages of adjustment: (1) an emotional crisis characterized by shock, denial, and disbelief, (2) a period of alternating feelings of anger, guilt, depression, grief, lowered self-esteem, rejection of child, and overprotectiveness, and (3) acceptance. Anderegg, Vergason, and Smith (1992) also describe three stages: (1) confronting, (2) adjusting, and (3) adapting. These stages include all of the behaviors noted by previous researchers (Blacher, 1984; Bristol, 1987) and also represent erratic cycles that occur during movement within and between phases. Some of the emotions described in stage models are analogous to the emotions one would feel with the death of a loved one (Chinn, Winn, & Walters, 1978). These theorists presume that the mourning process assists parents in moving beyond the initial trauma and into acceptance.

Some authorities note that people do not necessarily move sequentially through a series of stages in a step-by-step fashion, with the final stage being adjustment (Turnbull & Turnbull, 1990). Now, family members and other authorities are questioning the validity of the stage theory approach (Allen & Affleck, 1985; Turnbull & Turnbull, 1990). It has become increasingly clear that family members should not be thought of as progressing through a series of stages with the final stage being adjustment or acceptance. Perhaps rather than stages, these emotional responses should be thought of as "states" that parents and other family members are experiencing. The notion of states allows for the many variations in the ways in and times at which families react to raising and living with a child

with disabilities. Yet it does not reject the idea that family members are experiencing some or all of the emotions described in the stages perspective.

Families have argued that their reactions are individualized and relate to a variety of factors. Even mothers and fathers frequently experience different emotions or states at different times. One parent may be actively grieving while the other parent is angered about the unexpected turn of events in their lives. Emotions may disappear and reappear or be triggered by events in the families' lives (Turnbull & Turnbull, 1990). For example, the birth of a child with a diagnosed disability may cause extreme sadness or depression; these emotions may reoccur when the child has a birthday or when the parents hear about a friend who has just had a new baby.

Complex emotions also emerge during transition periods when the child and family move from one set of services, supports, and routines to another. For instance, when Annie "graduated" to kindergarten, Dave and Debbie, Annie's parents, had to readjust their lives in many ways. They had to relinquish their secure relationships with staff, familiar classrooms, and established routines. They had to learn how kindergarten worked and to meet and get comfortable with a new set of people who were now working with Annie. For Debbie, in particular, it was a daunting process, and many of her buried emotions resurfaced.

Researchers also note that the type of disability may influence both the reactions of the family members and their interactions with their child (Beckman, 1983; Frey, Greenburg, & Fewell, 1989). For example, a father who is a sports fanatic may have a more difficult adjustment to a child with a physical disability than he might to a child who has a hearing loss. A mother who is a musician may struggle more with the effects of a hearing loss than she might from the loss of vision with a child who is blind. The various states that family members experience are unique to that person.

For Juanita, the feelings of guilt, bewilderment, and sadness were overwhelming. She was 16 years old while her baby daughter, Tanya, was in the Neonatal Intensive Care Unit (NICU). Juanita was nervous about being a mother. Sometimes it seemed that her daughter belonged more to the nurses than to her. Some days she was too tired to drive the 70 miles to see Tanya in the hospital. Yet, she felt guilty on the days she couldn't be there. She often thought, "Why me?" and sometimes wondered, "What did I do to make this happen?"

For parents of children who require extended hospitalizations, feelings such as Juanita's are quite common (Flynn & McCollum, 1989).

Annie's parents searched for years to find out why their daughter had been born with the rare **Cornelia de Lange syndrome,** sometimes blaming their families for passing on bad "genetics" and other times worrying that they had caused the syndrome by eating carelessly or being exposed to germs during the prenatal period. Even though the doctors explained the syndrome to them, they still did not understand why this had happened to them. They felt helpless in shaping Annie's future. And each year Annie's birthday filled them with melancholy; they viewed the birthday parties as milestones that marked the developmental levels of their other children and grieved that Annie couldn't do the same things.

Kurume's mother, Mattie, also went through times when she didn't want to know or believe that Kurume couldn't hear. She felt overwhelmed after the hearing test because it confirmed her worst fears, but she also continued to hope that his hearing would return and that he would be okay. Even after Kurume started school, each change in school placement brought new anxieties about how he would be accepted by the other children and by his teachers. Ed's concerns involved Kurume's ability to learn to speak. He worried about the future: "African-American males have enough trouble getting ahead in this world. How will Kurume handle the additional problem of communicating with the rest of the world?" At various times, he would think about his dream of being the father of a star athlete: "Could Kurume play sports if he couldn't talk to or hear his teammates?" Then, he'd realize that his biggest fear was about the long-term effects of deafness: "Would Kurume ever be able to get a job if he couldn't speak during an interview? How could he hold a professional position if he couldn't hear his co-workers?"

**TIMING AND EMOTIONAL RESPONSES** Sometimes, families first learn that their child has a disability during the child's school years. In some cases, school professionals identify issues, and then, through the special education process, a label is applied to the child for the first time. The parents may be frustrated and confused by the discovery of a disability in a child who seems capable in many ways (Harry, 1992). Other times, parents have long been aware that their child was having difficulties in school and have asked for

help in identifying and addressing the problem. And sometimes, parents are relieved to find out that there are reasons for the problems they have observed. In any case, families whose school-aged child is diagnosed with a disability may also experience a range of emotions upon learning that the word "disability" is being used in reference to their child (Vigilante, 1983).

Consider the situation from Kirk's mother's point of view. Marilyn knew that her son did not play with other children in the same ways that her other children had done when they were young. "But," she thought, "he's almost like an only child. His half-brothers and half-sisters are so much older, and no one has really taken the time to play with him. No wonder he behaves this way." When Kirk first went to school, his kindergarten teacher recognized that Kirk's behaviors were significantly different from those of the other children. Concerned, she spoke often to Marilyn about Kirk's behavior but did not refer him to special education. Later, after several years of school problems, extensive assessment confirmed that Kirk's social and behavioral needs warranted special education services. The team devised an IEP that permitted various school professionals to provide support for Kirk throughout his school day.

The process of providing special education services for Kirk required that a label naming a disability be applied to Kirk. As a result, at age 10, Kirk was labeled "seriously emotionally disordered," a statement for which Marilyn had no real preparation or time to adjust. She walked out of that meeting feeling dazed and shocked. "I walked in there thinking that we were going to find ways to help Kirk's behavior, but I never expected that they believed he was 'disabled.'" She cried herself to sleep that night, wondering where she had gone wrong and how she could have missed the signs. She felt guilty for not recognizing that he had a disability sooner, and she scolded herself for not doing something back in kindergarten. The next morning, she wondered if all those professionals could be wrong. "Maybe Kirk is just a little behind other kids because he was growing up without brothers and sisters," she thought. "Maybe he isn't really disabled." Her husband, Jerry, said that Kirk could "straighten up" if he wanted to, but Marilyn realized that her son really didn't know how to act in certain situations.

Michael was also well into his school years when his family began to recognize that his difficulties might be related to a disability. For Michael's family, frustration was the most common emotion. His mother,

**BOX 3.2**

## Research Findings on Families of Children with Disabilities

Abbott and Meredith (1986) found that parents reported positive contributions in the family because of their child. These included a stronger family (55 percent); personal growth, including more patience, compassion, and unselfishness (41 percent); and greater appreciation for the simple things (17 percent). Apparently, not only do parents perceive children with disabilities as making important contributions to their lives, but those perceived contributions are similar to perceptions about contributions of children without disabilities. In fact, more and more, evidence is emerging that suggests there are more similarities than differences between families with and without children who have disabilities (Turnbull, Behr, & Tollefson, 1986).

Out of 174 letters sent by families of children with disabilities to Congress in support of regulations concerning the treatment of newborns with disabilities, approximately two-thirds of the persons with disabilities and one-third of parents and relatives mentioned positive attributes of people with disabilities. Those positive contributions to family included being a source of (1) joy, (2) life's lessons, (3) love, (4) blessing or fulfillment, (5) pride, and (6) family strength (Turnbull, Guess, & Turnbull, 1988). And 18 parents of children with disabilities and 10 parents of children without disabilities agreed that their children provided them with opportunities for increased happiness, great love, strengthened family ties, expanded social networks, great pride and accomplishment, knowledge about disabilities and child rearing tolerance and sensitivity, expanded career development, and increased personal growth (Turnbull, Behr, & Tollefson, 1986).

Anita, initiated the referral to special education because she watched her otherwise happy, well-adjusted child agonize over his schoolwork. Each new school year and each proposed new solution brought new hope. And each time Michael failed another math test, she reentered the state of frustration. Anger surfaced as well when school professionals discouraged Michael's hopes for attending college.

**ADAPTABILITY AND QUALITY OF LIFE**   Parents of children with disabilities sometimes comment that they resent the implication that they are somehow superhuman or saintly. Such sanctification of families suggests that adaptation and acceptance require heroic efforts beyond those of "typical" families (Summers, Behr, & Turnbull, 1989). But families that cope successfully are simply made up of ordinary people who are doing the job of raising a child who poses some additional challenges because of her or his disability.

The implication that these parents are somehow saintly conveys another message: that the children who have disabilities will have lives of endless tragedy (Willette, 1987). Yet, children with disabilities are also sources of happiness and joy to their parents. The impact of the issues and challenges they present can no longer be seen as pervasively negative. In fact, many parents have reported that their lives were enriched and that raising a child with a disability made the family stronger (Abbott & Meredith, 1986; Wikler, Wasow, & Hatfield, 1983). Box 3.2 summarizes findings from studies investigating family perceptions about the impact of having a member with disabilities on their lives.

For example, Annie's parents, Dave and Debbie, are not saints, nor do they view their lives as endless tragedies. Although the caregiving responsibilities for Annie continues to place demands on the entire family, Annie's parents often comment to each other about all the wonderful people they have met across the country through the Cornelia de Lange Syndrome Association. They have become very close to four other families in their community who have children with disabilities, and they participate actively in their state's parent information and assistance center. Moreover, Debbie has learned that she has a natural aptitude for tending to Annie's health needs. In high school, Debbie thought she wanted to become a nurse. She never pursued that dream because, after working for a few years, getting married, and having children, it seemed unfeasible. But now Debbie has learned so much about Annie's medical condition that she has gained the confidence

## Roles of Mothers and Fathers of Children with Disabilities

Traditionally, mothers have been the primary caregivers for children. Mothers took children to the doctor, packed their lunches, took them to their piano lessons, signed their report cards, and generally were responsible for the entire range of daily tasks or chores related to the children. Because mothers were the primary caregivers, most early research on families of children with disabilities focused on mothers rather than fathers.

In today's world, many mothers are employed full-time and contribute financially to their families' well-being. As a result, work schedules (rather than tradition) may be a contributing factor in mothers' and fathers' levels of involvement (Turnbull & Turnbull, 1986). Parents with flexible work schedules may be more involved than parents with fixed work schedules. Thus, a parent's ability to attend school meetings or events may be limited by constraints of employment. Because most educational services are provided during the day, a parent's work schedule may limit his or her first-hand knowledge about the child's school experience. This has the potential to create a continuous information gap between schools and parents and between parents themselves (Davis & May, 1991).

Given the huge increase in the employment of women outside the home, fathers generally are playing a more active role in their children's lives than they did only two generations ago. The expanded role of fathers is evident in the presence of the father during the delivery of the child and in the day-to-day care of the child. It is not unusual for a father to take his child for a walk in the park, to prepare meals for his family, or to drop the child off at the day care center. The changing roles of both parents create different dynamics and expectations within the family—for families both with and without a child with disabilities.

The closer the relationship the father has with his children, the better understanding he has of those children. And when fathers understand their children better, they may feel more competent in caring for them (Lamb et al., 1987). There is also increasing evidence that a father's expectations for and acceptance of the child with disabilities may play a significant role in determining the family's attitudes toward the child (McLinden, 1990). Fathers who are more proactive in their child's life—whether in an advocacy role, as a

A father teaches a young boy how to throw a baseball.

to explore careers in the medical field. She believes that Annie was sent to her to give her the strength and self-confidence to pursue the dream that she otherwise would have lost.

Kurume's family is fairly typical of the families in their neighborhood, and Kurume is, in many ways, much like the other boys on his block. Mattie and Ed have served as scout leaders and have taken their fair share of turns in the car pools that transport the children to various athletic and after-school events. They differ from other families mainly in the amount of attention and energy they must give to Kurume's educational choices. They know that they have to be more attentive to all the available choices to ensure that Kurume gets the best education possible. Because of his deafness, they feel Kurume's career options are more limited than are the options for their other children.

scout leader, or as a coach—may be more accepting of and have higher expectations for their child because of their level of involvement. In this case, the family as a whole may benefit from the involvement of the father. Researchers (Frey, Fewell, & Vadasy, 1989) also have found that children's daily living skills are more advanced when the fathers' perceptions of the children are more positive. They hypothesize that the fathers' positive perceptions lead to more interaction with the children and thus promote child competence.

Several authors have reported that fathers express more concern than mothers over future issues such as the child's ability to be self-supporting, the cost of providing for the child, the social dependency of the child, and legal matters (Meyer et al., 1982). However, this does not mean that mothers are not also concerned about the high cost of raising a child with a disability and the implications for the child's future. Those concerns may simply not be a top priority concern for mothers, who reported more concerns about the friendships their child develops and their child's nutrition. Fathers tend to interact more with their children at home rather than going out into the community (Turbiville, 1994). In a survey conducted by Bailey and Simeonsson (1988), mothers reported twice as many family needs for services and supports as fathers.

These research findings suggest that both parents should be involved in professional-family interactions and be able to voice their concerns and solutions. Sparling, Biller, and Berger (1992) hypothesize that fathers may limit their involvement in their children's school experience because professionals lack knowledge about fathers' interests, priorities, and concerns for their child. Involving fathers from the beginning and letting them know how important they are can facilitate a more active role for fathers. Professionals are challenged to "get to know" fathers and their unique perspectives. By considering the priorities, interaction styles, and work schedules of fathers and mothers, school professionals can create opportunities for both parents to participate in vital decisions and in everyday school events.

## Relationships Between Parents

At one time, marriages were thought to be almost certain to fail if a child with disabilities were part of the family. Now, there is reason to question that idea. Re-search on divorce in families of children with disabilities is far from definitive. While an early study showed higher levels of divorce (Gath, 1977), later studies showed similar divorce rates and numbers of single-parent homes for families with and without children with disabilities (Landis, 1992; Williams & McHenry, 1981). The experience of parents whose marriage is sound and who are securely employed prior to the diagnosis of a child's disability may differ from that of parents whose marriages are unstable or who are experiencing unemployment at the time of the diagnosis (Trute & Hauch, 1988). Marriages that are already stressed because of other problems may dissolve with the additional pressures of raising a child with multiple or severe physical needs (Breslau, Staruch, & Mortimer, 1982). For example, families like Kirk's and Kurume's, which have the financial means to pay for special therapies or services for the child, may be less stressed by the costs and the demands than a family with fewer financial resources. Financial security and strong relationships between parents are two factors that provide stability as families focus on the needs of their children with disabilities. The time that it takes to support a child with disabilities, the emotional intensity that is focused on the child, and the potential for conflict over decisions on medical and educational supports also can strain relationships between parents.

Some children with disabilities have intensive daily needs that require constant vigilance from caregivers. If one parent assumes more of a caregiving role than the other, it may mean that the caregiver has less time and energy to spend on sustaining and nurturing the relationship between the parents. The caregiving parent's involvement with a child may be so great that the other parent may feel resentful. Ongoing caregiving demands thus could lead to tension and unresolved conflict in the marriage. The stability of the bond between parents can also be compromised by the number and variety of decisions that must be made about the medical, physical, educational, and health care of a child with disabilities. Parents may not agree on the needs of the child or the value of the available options. Because many parents have limited knowledge about the available options, these decisions may be made subjectively. And because subjective decisions often are based on assumptions, values, and previous experiences, spouses may arrive at different decisions. Additional energy is required to mediate and negotiate the decisions so that both parents feel comfortable with the decision-making process and the resulting decisions. While stresses associated with child care occur in most families regardless of the abilities of the children, these issues appear to be somewhat more intense in families with children who have disabilities.

## Siblings of Children with Disabilities

Building strong connections among schools, communities, and families of children with disabilities requires attention to the siblings of those children. Prior to the 1980s, the needs of siblings of children with disabilities were rarely addressed. The influence of a child with disabilities on nondisabled brothers and sisters can best be understood in the context of the entire family system (Cramer et al., 1997; Crnic & Leconte, 1986). Siblings of children with disabilities may experience arrays of emotions similar to those of the parents, as well as to those that characterize all sibling relationships. But the potential for more extreme reactions exists due to the increased complexities and stresses of having a family member with disabilities. Some siblings may have trouble adjusting while others appear to adapt quite easily (Cramer et al., 1997; Seligman & Darling, 1989; Senapati & Hayes, 1989).

**FACTORS IN SUCCESSFUL ADJUSTMENT** Research shows that many factors contribute to the successful adjustment of siblings of children with disabilities. For example, the sex and birth order of nondisabled siblings may be two important factors that contribute to their adjustment (Powell & Ogle, 1985). For example, Kirk was the youngest child in his family, and his half-brothers and half-sisters were much older. The impact of his disability on the family was less noticeable than in Annie's family, where she was the youngest but close in age to her brother and sister. The type and severity of the disability and the ages of the children may also greatly influence the sibling relationship. Annie's disability, unlike Kirk's, was noticeable from birth. Her health care needs impacted her family from the time that she entered it, whereas Kirk's needs, while intense, appeared when he was older. Siblings also have reported that they have concerns about the disability, uncertainty regarding the cause of the disability and its effect on them, uneasiness over the reactions of their friends, and feelings of being ignored or of being required to do too much for the child with

disabilities (Dyson, Edgar, & Crnic, 1989). For example, Kurume's siblings were concerned about his deafness; they wondered if they, too, would become deaf.

Certain feelings tend to surface at identifiable phases of the siblings' life. For instance, siblings are likely to be more compatible during the preschool years. While young siblings may be aware of some differences, they may not understand the nature or cause of the sibling's disability (Jewell, 1985). However, as siblings reach school age, the need for more specific information about their sibling's disability surfaces. Through the provision of detailed information, misconceptions from earlier years may be eliminated. By responding accurately to questions from siblings, family members are more likely to avoid providing misinformation, especially if the disability is viewed as only one of many characteristics of the child.

**CAREGIVING RESPONSIBILITIES** Older siblings may encounter an increased expectation to "look out for" the child with disabilities. Older sisters are most often asked to perform caregiving responsibilities (Stoneman et al., 1988). Parents may expect siblings to actively participate in caring for their brother or sister because of their familiarity with caregiving routines. In many instances, siblings actually may be more competent to provide care than adult outsiders who may need training and support. However, during adolescence, older sisters and brothers may develop resentment or negative attitudes because of child care expectations. These siblings' reactions are actually quite similar to those in families who expect older siblings to assume caregiving responsibilities for younger children even when the younger children have no disability.

Adolescence is a difficult time for most children. Teenagers become focused on how others perceive them and do not want to be seen as different by their peers. Having a brother or sister with disabilities may single out the adolescent as being different. Adolescents may place more importance on relationships with peers than on relationships within their own families (Crnic & Leconte, 1986), and so their willingness to continue giving care may dwindle. Yet, adolescents also are **egocentric** and want attention from their family members. They may feel neglected if their siblings with disabilities receive more attention from family members than they do. As nondisabled siblings approach adulthood, different concerns arise. In particular, siblings may be concerned about responsibility for financial support, living arrangements, and possibly guardianship (Stoneman et al., 1988).

**GENETIC IMPLICATIONS**  In some circumstances, particularly as they grow older, siblings become concerned about the genetic implications of disabilities (Cramer et al., 1997). Some conditions that cause disabilities are genetically transmitted from one generation to another. One example is fragile X, a chromosomal abnormality that is associated with distinctive physical features and, frequently, mental retardation. Although females carry the chromosome, fragile X is expressed mostly in males. Another genetic disorder is Tourette syndrome, a condition with symptoms that may include **motor or vocal tics**, sleep disturbances, learning problems, and/or temper outbursts. Both of these conditions (as well as many others) have the potential to be passed from generation to generation. Thus, if one family member has fragile X or Tourette syndrome, there is the possibility that other family members also may have or carry the **genetic markers** for fragile X or Tourette syndrome. Sometimes, it makes sense for all family members to be genetically tested to determine the presence or likelihood of the condition. The possibility that the siblings' children may inherit the condition needs to be considered. When genetic testing reveals that other family members carry the same genetic structures, families may choose to get genetic counseling to gain information about the likelihood of transmission of the condition to future children.

## ■ SECTION SUMMARY

When families have a child with a disability, the parents may have a range of emotional responses, now recognized as states that all family members experience at various times. Families may move cyclically through various emotional states of adjustment. In some cases, families report that their quality of life has been enhanced by the presence of a child with disabilities in their family. Much of the research on the emotional responses of families has focused on families in which a child's disability was identified at birth or in early childhood. Sometimes, however, children are identified as having a disability after they enter school, and then families experience many similar emotions. Fam-

ilies cope with and adapt to a child with a disability in many ways. Families are neither superhuman nor saintly, nor are they saddled with lives of endless misery. Although many researchers have identified the stressful aspects of parenting a child with disabilities, recent narratives and empirical studies show that parents are vitally aware of the positive contributions of their children with disabilities as well. Recent research on siblings shows that age, birth order, and sex influence siblings' responses to having a brother or sister with a disability. Caregiving and genetic issues also concern siblings.

# Family Support Systems

Support systems for families have many dimensions. Social support occurs through both formal and informal means and helps the family meet its emotional, instrumental, and informational needs (Barrera, Sandler, & Ramsay, 1981; Dunst, Trivette, & Cross, 1986; House, 1981; Thoits, 1982; Turnbull & Turnbull, 1986). One way that schools can create and sustain connections to families is to help them prioritize their need for formal and informal supports, as well as the resources and networks that will address their needs.

## Formal Supports

**Formal support** refers to the interaction between families and professionals from institutions or agencies that assist people with disabilities and their families to live in the community. Supports that are both formal and instrumental include a range of material goods and services, such as therapy delivered by a speech/language professional, assistance in filling out forms for Social Security benefits, provision of equipment, and legal advice on establishing guardianship. Formal, instrumental supports might also provide respite care or financial assistance via an insurance company. Formal supports that professionals offer to address the emotional needs of families may include empathic listening, respectful interactions, and perhaps family counseling. Supports that are both formal and informational may include the provision of oral or written details about a child's disability or about the kinds of community services available. School professionals may provide parents with a book to read about a particular syndrome, strategies to support behavioral change, or detailed information about the special education processes and procedures.

Formal supports are most effective when services are matched to the needs identified by the family. A good match enhances the functioning of the parents, the children, and the family as a whole. Barrera and Ainlay (1983) noted that parents' perceived satisfaction and perceived need for support are of fundamental importance to the success of a support system. Moreover, the level of satisfaction parents feel with their support network may directly influence the development of their child with disabilities (Dunst, Trivette, & Cross, 1986; Mahoney, Finger, & Powell, 1985). In other words, if parents are highly satisfied with the support they are receiving, their child may make greater developmental progress than if the parents are unsatisfied with their support. Because children with disabilities and their families are the primary recipients of formal support services, their perspective on the value and usefulness of support received is the standard against which professionals should measure their own behaviors. The perceived adequacy of support provided may be more important than the absolute amount of support provided for parents of children who are disabled or at risk of developing disabilities (Affleck et al., 1986).

The key to enhancing a family's capacity to cope with a child with disabilities lies in identifying the individual concerns, priorities, and resources of that family. Here, a school professional might help a family obtain information about a particular disability by providing written materials about the disability, giving a verbal explanation of the disability, offering the option to meet the parents of a child who has a similar disability, and facilitating involvement with an advocacy or support group. Working with families means going beyond the traditional four walls of the classroom and providing assistance that will positively influence the family and, thus, positively affect the child with disabilities.

For example, school professionals have provided various formal supports to Annie's family for managing her behavior at home. Annie's parents were very concerned when she went through a phase in which she resisted eating at mealtimes and threw her food on the floor. The school professionals and family members discussed techniques used at school during lunch and brainstormed other ideas for the family to try at home. They decided to gather information systemati-

cally about Annie's behaviors before, during, and after mealtimes both at school and at home to guide their discussions. The school team, including the school psychologist and special education teacher, helped analyze the data and formed an **intervention plan** to teach Annie more appropriate mealtime behavior. After observing Annie, her teacher and the school psychologist hypothesized that Annie was frustrated during mealtimes by her inability to hold her spoon and get the spoon to her mouth without spilling anything. So, she threw her food rather than eating it, thereby avoiding frustration.

The meal plan had three components. First, to make eating easier for Annie, the team located a special spoon designed to fit into a hand that had trouble holding typical spoons. Second, to make eating as enjoyable as possible, the team listed foods that Annie loved and that were hard to spill—such as mashed potatoes and gravy, celery with peanut butter, and carrots—and reduced Annie's portion size. Third, to make throwing food more difficult, the team gave Annie a small plate that was attached with Velcro to a place mat. Because Annie now had smaller amounts of food to eat and it was food she liked, eating became easier. And as soon as she ate her portion, she was able to be excused from the table. Over time, through the eating plan, mealtimes at Annie's house became pleasant once more.

## Informal Supports

**Informal supports** are naturally occurring events in life that address instrumental, emotional, and informational needs. Informal support refers to interactions with extended family, neighbors, church members, close friends, and other individuals and organizations that offer friendship and assistance in solving problems, recreating, or simply conversing about day-to-day happenings. Informal supports are not "professionalized" in that they are performed by individuals who do not necessarily possess any specialized education or training in a particular field.

There is an emerging recognition that informal sources of support are vital in helping families cope with the issues and stressors of having a child with a disability. Families report that the opportunity for their child to be involved with the Boy Scouts and 4-H clubs and to attend birthday parties frequently means more than the child's participation in the next therapy session. Parents often establish long-lasting friendships with other parents who have a child with a disability and rely on them as individuals who really "understand." We no longer live in a society in which our extended family necessarily lives in the same block, community, city, or even state. Yet, all of us need informal supports in our lives. Because of the importance of informal supports, many family support groups and networks have formed to provide instrumental, informational, and emotional support.

## Family Support Groups and Networks

Family support groups and networks are an emerging and popular response to a family's desire for support. Family support groups and networks may cross the boundaries between formal and informal support systems as defined by Unger and Powell (1980). Leaders, organizers, and members of family support groups may be professionals, family members, or both. Support groups may serve a number of functions that enhance a family's ability to cope, and they may fulfill an important advocacy function as well. Support groups and networks offer all the same types of support that formal and informal systems offer. In other words, emotional, instrumental and informational supports may come simultaneously from other families and from professionals who participate in the group. At the same time, family support groups and networks may avoid some of the pitfalls that the more formal supports may engender.

**BENEFITS OF FAMILY SUPPORT GROUPS AND NETWORKS** One important contribution of family support groups and networks is the validation of the feelings that a family experiences (Cramer et al., 1997; Oster, 1984). When family members meet other people from similar circumstances, they can share perspectives, learn from one another, discuss both positive and negative aspects, and even make jokes to help make difficult situations seem less traumatic and serious. Often, friendships evolve from sharing ideas with others who have common interests and struggles—friendships that may go beyond issues of disability and expand to include many other life interests. For example, an organization called "Family CONNECTS" is a general support group for families of children with disabilities living in the region where Annie and her family live. Annie's parents joined this group several years ago, and

they continue to value the friendships they've made with other families through the organization.

Other benefits of such support groups include (1) the opportunity to share information about resources and strategies to gain services or funding, (2) a decrease in the feeling of isolation that often accompanies the challenges of caring for a child with a disability, and (3) a chance to learn about both formal and informal advocacy, which can assist family members in achieving a greater sense of control and strength (Oster, 1984). Sometimes, adults with disabilities participate in the support group, and thus, families gain a unique perspective about current and future issues and priorities.

Shapiro (1989) reports that mothers who participated in support groups were less depressed, viewed their child as less of a burden, and utilized more problem-solving coping strategies than mothers who did not participate. Similarly, results from an evaluation of a bimonthly father's support group found that fathers demonstrated lower stress and depression and higher satisfaction with social support after one year of participation (Vadasy et al., 1985).

It is not unusual for families to provide instrumental types of support for one another. For example, one family that has some knowledge about the Social Security system may accompany another family to the Social Security office to provide moral support and advice. Or a support group member may accompany nervous parents to their first IEP meeting. Sometimes, families also share material goods, such as car seats, cribs, clothing, and even adaptive devices and equipment.

Families that share information, concerns, material goods, and strategies with one another may find greater satisfaction with life in general. Box 3.3 offers strategies for organizing and implementing a family support network. Frequently, family support groups and networks are organized among people who share concern about a particular condition, syndrome, or age. For example, Annie's parents belong to the national and regional chapters of the Cornelia de Lange Syndrome Association, which provides information about medical findings, legislation, litigation, and public policies that affect children with this syndrome. Other examples of family support groups or networks include the Epilepsy Foundation, the National Tourette Syndrome Association, the Learning Disabilities Association, the National Parent Network on Disabilities, and the Autism Association; many of these groups also have local and regional counterparts. Appendix 3.1

Source: Adapted by permission from Institute for Family-Centered Care (1994), *Advances in Family-Centered Care, 1*(1), 7.

**BOX 3.3**

## Guidelines for Facilitating Family Support Networks

1. Offer families opportunities to meet and talk with other family members who share similar experiences.
2. Give families who have just learned that their child has a disability the opportunity to meet families who are more experienced.
3. Provide opportunities for family-to-family support of *all* family members: Fathers and mothers, brothers and sisters, and grandparents or other extended family.
4. Consider a variety of settings in which families can meet others—for example, schools, child care and early childhood programs, local support groups and family-to-family networks, and com-munity and recreation programs for children and adults.
5. Hire family members as staff to facilitate family-to-family support.
6. Offer families opportunities to communicate with one another in a variety of ways—for example, family-to-family newsletters, phone networks, social gatherings such as coffee hours or pizza nights, spaces in school and community centers for informal conversations, and family-to-family bulletin boards.
7. Provide meeting space and logistical support, including child care and transportation, for family support groups.

contains a more comprehensive list of national disability organizations, associations, and foundations that provide support and advocacy to families and professionals.

**DRAWBACKS TO FAMILY SUPPORT GROUPS** For the most part, support groups have been documented to facilitate positive outcomes for family members. However, findings have been inconsistent in investigations of the benefits of parent participation in support groups. For example, one study of eighty-five mothers of children with disabilities enrolled in early intervention programs found that they evaluated their stress as less intense but showed no differences in the information they gained in comparison to mothers who did not participate in parent groups (Moran, 1985). Parent support groups may be more effective for parents who have a high need for support, but they may have adverse effects on parents with a low need for support. Affleck and colleagues (1989) found that a home-based support program for mothers of high-risk infants discharged from a neonatal intensive care unit produced beneficial results for the mothers whose expressed need for support was high and negative effects for those mothers who had infants with fewer difficulties and lower needs for supports. Qualitative data from interviews with 150 mothers of young children indicate that most of the mothers described positive benefits, but some mentioned stresses or problems attributed to parent groups, including discomfort in listening to other parents whose problems were more severe than their own, concerns about the competence of group leaders, and dominance of the groups by a few mothers (Krauss, Upshur, Shonkoff, & Hauser-Cram, 1993).

Family members may employ a variety of coping strategies when a child with a disability is part of their family. One of these strategies may include participation in a support group. The option of being involved with a support group or network should be made available to families, but it may not be desirable or useful to all families. This is a choice that individual family members must make for themselves.

**SUPPORTS SPECIFICALLY FOR FATHERS** Supporting fathers is challenging. Many men perceive that social supports from family members, co-workers, neighbors, and community groups are often limited (Ferrari, 1986; Turbiville, Turnbull, & Turnbull, 1995). Some men may believe that they must "be strong" at all costs, thereby limiting their potential for expressing concerns and fears. Fathers report feelings of isolation, fear of being misunderstood, uncertainty about the ramifications of their child's disability, and hesitation about reaching out to others for help (Davis & May, 1991; May 1993). At one fathers-only support group, several men noted that they had never talked to anyone about their true feelings before they became involved in the support group (Davis & May, 1991).

The shift in societal notions encouraging fathers to play a major role in raising their children is reflected in broad changes in our educational and health care programs. When fathers are not expected to play a primary role, they are less likely to be present. But when schools actively seek the participation of fathers, they are more likely to do so. However, many services and supports are not provided in contexts that enhance the participation of both parents. The time of day, types of activities, and location or setting of services and supports may create barriers that unintentionally exclude fathers. Therefore, school professionals must carefully plan activities that promote family involvement instead of limiting it. Both parents must be given the opportunity to be partners in making decisions and fully participating in the educational life of their child with disabilities. Also, professionals have a responsibility to encourage both fathers and mothers to take an active role in the educational experiences of these children.

**SUPPORTS SPECIFICALLY FOR SIBLINGS** Siblings of children with disabilities have many concerns, commonly asking, "Why did this happen?" "Is my brother contagious?" "Can I catch what he has?" "What will my friends think?" and "Am I going to have to take care of her all of my life?" Like their parents, siblings have information needs (Cramer et al., 1997; Wasserman, 1983). Also like their parents, siblings need to understand and manage their own feelings. A sibling's role in the family may be influenced by the brother or sister with disabilities, and support groups and special activities for siblings who have brothers or sisters with disabilities can provide these opportunities (Santelli et al., 1996). Connecting with another child who also has a sibling with a disability can be helpful. Another way of providing support for brothers and sisters involves developing a resource library of articles and books to be used by parents, siblings, and teachers

(Cramer et al., 1997). Support relationships and networks for siblings can occur informally or through formal support mechanisms.

## Neighborhood School and Community Supports

The inclusive neighborhood school and the local community provide the context for both formal and informal support services for families. The formal supports may include instruction by teachers and therapists, provision of cafeteria or food services, and transportation. The more informal supports may include extracurricular activities such as playing volleyball, working on the yearbook, or joining the Girl Scouts. Both formal and informal activities offer the opportunity for children to observe and interact with a diverse group of peers, interact with a variety of adults, and develop interests outside of the classroom. These activities help children to develop friendships among peers who have similar interests, which, in turn, creates a sense of self-esteem, belonging, and contributing. These supports become the underlying curriculum that prepares children for life by facilitating social development, decision-making processes, and leadership abilities.

When families participate in school and community activities, they may develop a greater sense of belonging. For example, the whole family feels pride when the school wins an athletic event, puts on a play, or gives a concert. Families may volunteer in school activities, which can enhance their feelings of achievement, affiliation, contribution, and self-esteem. Also, expansion of their social network provides family members with added opportunities for interactions with other children and adults and development of friendships and a sense of belonging. Therefore, the local school can become a central forum in which formal and informal supports are available for all family members.

## ■ SECTION SUMMARY

The lifelines you were asked to imagine at the start of this chapter represent the formal and informal support structures that families need to become vital partners in inclusive schools. When a family member has a disability, individuals within the family unit respond uniquely. Yet, each individual has instrumental, emotional, and informational support needs and priorities. Support groups and networks have emerged that address these concerns of families. Family participation in neighborhood schools and communities foster a sense of belonging and good working relationships.

# Family-School Partnerships

The connections between families and schools are made stronger when school professionals view families as partners. School professionals who communicate with and understand the families of their students facilitate more positive parental relationships with schools (Fiedler, 1993; Hulsebusch, 1989). In contrast, those who view families as deficient (particularly low-income or less educated families) continue to promote a barrier to home-school partnerships (Davies, 1988). In many situations, genuine partnerships are slow to develop (Mundschenk & Foley, 1994). Sometimes, school professionals and parents find themselves in adversarial positions, with the parents seeking a particular type of service or support for their child and the school unable or unwilling to provide that service. Unfortunately, mistrust sometimes forms the basis of the home-school relationship (Robinson & Fine, 1994). But new strategies for family supports were developed in the 1990s and continue as priorities for schools (Turnbull & Turnbull, 1990).

The emerging emphasis on families as equal partners promotes the concept of family members functioning as decision makers for their child and as stakeholders actively and intimately involved with planning, implementing, and evaluating their child's program and activities within the classroom, school, and organization. The shift from school staff as the sole "experts" to family members as viable experts about their child has challenged many professionals whose original training was antithetical to this current belief.

## Recognizing Personal Values and Beliefs

No matter what the composition of a family or the skills of the family members, the cornerstone of a successful partnership between school professionals and families is the professionals' acceptance of families as diverse, capable systems whose members form bonds and relationships in a unique fashion. The ways in which family members function, make decisions, and influence one another is unique to that family and should be respected and valued by professionals. Some decisions about services and supports for children and families are greatly influenced by a professional's personal values and beliefs. Those values and beliefs, in turn, are shaped by the personal history of the individual professional including his or her background, upbringing, educational experiences, and professional preparation. But one's beliefs may be so deeply ingrained that they are easily mistaken for truth or facts, rather than opinions or preferences.

There is the danger that, when you work with families whose values are significantly different from your own, you may inappropriately question their views of situations or their choices. Thus, your values may limit your ability to provide quality services and supports. If you allow your personal beliefs and values about children's and families' needs to prevent you from understanding what a family wants, your effectiveness as a school professional may be reduced. In addition, discordance between the beliefs and lifestyles of professionals and families may interfere with effective communication and, hence, the provision of meaningful, cohesive supports and services.

Perhaps one of your greatest challenges as a school professional will be understanding the value systems of the parents and families with whom you work. Recognizing and acknowledging your own personal values will help you understand or at least respect each family's unique set of beliefs and priorities (Hanson, Lynch, & Wayman, 1990).

## Becoming Cross-Culturally Competent

The changing demographics in our country dictate that professionals be both sensitive and competent when talking to and working with families from other cultures. The majority of school professionals who currently work with children with disabilities and their families are of Euro-American ancestry (Hanson, 1990; Hourcade, Parette, & Huer, 1997). In many cases, professionals and family members are not matched culturally. Of course, the cultures to which each adheres cannot be changed, but the ways in which professionals work with families can be altered.

## Extending Your Learning

Draw a picture of your current family—the family you live in now. What values are important to you and your family? Think back to the picture you drew of the family you grew up in. How do the beliefs of the family in which you grew up differ from the beliefs you have today? What situations or events in your life have affected the values that you hold today? How do your values affect the decisions you make in day-to-day life?

Working closely with a family requires respect for and knowledge and awareness of the family's cultural, ethnic, and linguistic heritage. Box 3.4 describes strategies that professionals can use to become more aware of and competent with members of diverse cultures. It is critical for school professionals to develop cross-cultural competence. No one can ever learn all of the beliefs and practices of all cultures. However, school professionals can (1) acknowledge that cultural differences as well as similarities exist, (2) avoid assigning values such as better or worse and right or wrong to cultural differences, and (3) recognize that differences are both healthy and appropriate. Professionals can become knowledgeable about the cultures represented in their school community and thus be able to work more competently with those families. In this process, it is paramount that no assumptions should be made about the concerns, priorities, practices, or resources of individual families due to their cultural backgrounds. Professionals should be particularly cautious about generalizing or stereotyping individuals or families according to cultural labels. Assumptions about an individual's or family's behavior based on their cultural background may result in inappropriate or inaccurate generalizations. Family-school partnership means respecting individuals and families, regardless of their cultural, linguistic, or ethnic background or any of the other social and demographic factors that influence their lives.

**BOX 3.4**

## Guidelines for Developing Cross-Cultural Competence

1. Develop cultural self-awareness by understanding your own customs, values, beliefs, and behaviors.
2. Learn about other cultures through readings, interactions, and involvement, and learn the language or some basic communication skills of another culture.
3. Be aware of the communication styles or level of context (high versus low) that families use, and adapt your personal style to one that is comfortable for the family.
4. Recognize nonverbal communication behaviors—for example, eye contact and facial expressions, proximity and touching, body language, and gestures.
5. Listen to the family's perspective, and respect family's choices.
6. View cultural differences as strengths rather than weaknesses.
7. Demonstrate awareness of different groups of people by using appropriate terms.
8. Develop characteristics of effective cross-cultural communicators. Specifically,
   a. Respect individuals from other cultures.
   b. Make continued and sincere attempts to understand the world from others' points of view.
   c. Be open to new learning—even if you don't agree.
   d. Be flexible.
   e. Maintain a sense of humor.
   f. Tolerate ambiguity.
   g. Approach others with a desire to learn.
9. Make no assumptions about concerns, priorities, or resources of individual families, regardless of their cultural background.

Source: Adapted by permission from E. W. Lynch & M. J. Hanson (Eds.) (1992), *Developing cross-cultural competence: A guide for working with young children and their families* (Baltimore: Brookes).

A teacher works with diverse learners to create an inclusive classroom community.

To fully understand and appreciate another person's culture, we must first understand our own culture. Cultural self-awareness is a first step toward achieving cross-cultural competence and developing skill in working with people from different cultural and ethnic backgrounds (Chan, 1990; Tiedt & Tiedt, 1990).

## Working with Families as Equal Partners

**THE FAMILY-CENTERED APPROACH** Schools increasingly are realizing the critical role they play in facilitating partnerships with family members. In the past, schools focused on parental involvement,

whereby parents were informed of the time and date of the IEP meeting and were encouraged to attend. Or perhaps a parent support group was formed by school personnel. Today, schools actively promote the development of collaborative, reciprocal relationships with families, working in partnership with the entire family, not only the parents, in what is sometimes referred to as a family-centered approach. For example, a brother might attend his sister's IEP meeting and offer suggestions and ideas that are valued as much as those offered by the physical therapist. This shift is reflected in the wording and thrust of legislation enacted over the past three decades.

The key principles of the family-centered approach originally were defined by health care professionals and parents of children with chronic illnesses or disabling conditions. The growing recognition of the importance of the family has extended into educational settings. Early childhood educators readily grasped and adopted the concept of family-centered services. Now, the family-centered theme is gaining popularity in the K-12 school system and the communities they serve. Figure 3.3 symbolizes the shift in thinking and practices related to families' participation across the life

## Extending Your Learning

Think about the beliefs you identified as important in the previous "Extending Your Learning." Do some of those values reflect your cultural background? How does your family heritage affect your current thinking?

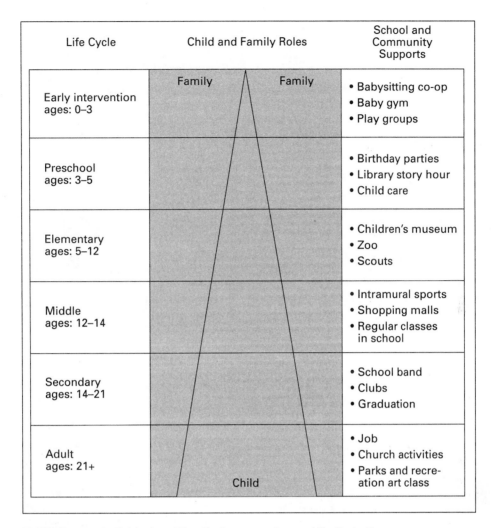

| Life Cycle | Child and Family Roles | | School and Community Supports |
|---|---|---|---|
| Early intervention ages: 0–3 | Family | Family | • Babysitting co-op<br>• Baby gym<br>• Play groups |
| Preschool ages: 3–5 | | | • Birthday parties<br>• Library story hour<br>• Child care |
| Elementary ages: 5–12 | | | • Children's museum<br>• Zoo<br>• Scouts |
| Middle ages: 12–14 | | | • Intramural sports<br>• Shopping malls<br>• Regular classes in school |
| Secondary ages: 14–21 | | | • School band<br>• Clubs<br>• Graduation |
| Adult ages: 21+ | | Child | • Job<br>• Church activities<br>• Parks and recreation art class |

**FIGURE 3.3** ■ Individual and Family Supports Across Life Cycle Stages

cycle stages of a child. Figure 3.3 also depicts the interaction among families, schools, and communities. When the child is very young, services and supports are focused on the concerns, priorities, and resources of the family related to the child within the context of that family. As the child enters preschool, the family remains the mainstay, but the child gradually increases participation in the school and community—perhaps going to child care three days a week and to the library for story hour once a week. As the child gets older, the family remains a constant in his or her life, but the school and the community exert ever-growing influences. When the child reaches adulthood, the family still has an influence, but the community is where this

person lives, works, and plays. The adult becomes responsible for his or her own planning and decision making.

School professionals and systems have modified their approach to focus on the family-school or parent-professional partnership. The key elements of a family-centered approach to supports and services (Shelton, Jeppson, & Johnson, 1987) are shown in Table 3.3. The table also provides a concrete set of recommendations regarding how to put these principles into practice in school settings.

It is important both to understand the individual components of family-centered services and to consider all of the elements as a whole. Any one element

| TABLE 3.3 Principles Underlying the Family-Centered Approach | |
|---|---|
| **Principles** | **Examples of Practices in Schools** |
| Recognition that the family is the constant in the child's life while the service systems and personnel within those systems fluctuate. | Family members play an active role in planning sessions as equal partners. |
| Facilitation of parent-professional collaboration. | Parents participate in the assessment, planning, and evaluation, providing information about their child. School personnel speak and write reports in understandable language without being condescending. |
| Sharing of unbiased and complete information with parents about their children on an ongoing basis in an appropriate and supportive manner. | Parents are included in all discussions and meetings about their child. Parents contribute information and observations about their child during assessment. |
| Implementation of appropriate, comprehensive policies and programs that provide support to meet the needs of families. | School personnel develop new policies and programs recommended by family members. |
| Incorporation of the behavioral and developmental needs of children and their families into service delivery systems. | Teachers talk to family members about the family's concerns, priorities, and resources, and jointly decide how schools and other programs can best meet family needs. Joint decisions are made by family members and professionals. |
| Encouragement and facilitation of parent-to-parent support. | School personnel provide opportunities for parents who have similar concerns to talk to one another through one-on-one or group interactions. |
| Recognition of family strengths and individuality and respect for different methods of coping. | School personnel do not judge or make comments about families that have uncommon values and beliefs. The positive aspects of families are highlighted by school personnel. |
| Assurance for the design of comprehensive, coordinated, multidisciplinary service delivery systems that are flexible, accessible, and responsive to family-identified needs. | Meeting times are arranged when family members, including fathers, can be present. School personnel communicate with family members in advance about the meeting time and place, the names and functions of participants, the proposed agenda, and the role of family members. |

can stand alone, but together the elements create a comprehensive approach to working with families. Each element reinforces and facilitates the implementation of the others. The influence of one element on another greatly enhances the strength of a family-school partnership.

**THE SHARED DECISION-MAKING PROCESS**
Engaging in a partnership means that all parties involved have responsibilities and play important roles. Families, too, share a responsibility in the education of their children. Complementary guidelines for par-

ents and for professionals on how to engage in collaborative educational planning are given in Table 3.4. The fundamental assumptions in the table reflect the emerging attitudes of the twenty-first century. The responsibility of parents to be active **advocates** for their child is as important as the development of the professional's skills in facilitating parent participation. However, the effort to create genuine partnerships must go beyond joint planning efforts between school professionals and families. School professionals should promote the active involvement of parents in leadership roles in the school and the community.

| **TABLE 3.4**  Guidelines for a Collaborative Educational Planning Meeting | |
|---|---|
| **Professional Roles and Responsibilities** | **Family Roles and Responsibilities** |
| Support parents in their preparation for the meeting. | Gather information that will help them prepare for the meeting. |
| Create an atmosphere that contributes to effective parental involvement. | Make sure they know who everyone at the meeting is and what their roles are. |
| Initiate strategies for involving parents in active decision making by ensuring they have a chance to voice their ideas. | Get and keep copies of everything the school has in the child's records. |
| Elicit special interests and concerns from parents related to the child and the child's welfare. | Share information about the child's functioning at home and in the community. |
| Create opportunities for parents to display competencies. | Specify what roles and responsibilities they are (and are not) interested in and willing to assume. |

And family members should be active in developing school policies, practices, and decisions about changes and improvements.

One way to promote family involvement in decision making is to offer the option of membership on committees, task forces, and boards. Families that participate in these kinds of activities should receive a thorough orientation and ongoing training so that they can contribute fully and comfortably. Table 3.5 lists some of the topics that could be covered in an orientation.

Not only must families be oriented to the group in which they will be participating, but the meetings and the organization as a whole must be structured to facilitate maximum participation from families. Box 3.5 contains guidelines for involving families as decision-making members of an organization. Each item in the list can serve as a way to measure an organization's competence in supporting family participation.

One rationale for family participation is the establishment of a sense of mastery and control for the family in the educational program decision-making process (Summers, Behr, & Turnbull, 1989). All of the principles related to parents' participation, to parental decision making, and to parent and child preferences take on an importance beyond mere legal compliance. The traditional conception of the professional as essentially in charge can have the effect of reducing families to the status of clients or helpless recipients of services. A parent's own educational experience may directly affect his or her level of comfort and willingness to contribute to the educational process. Strengthening family functioning creates a sense of independence so that families can "do for themselves"

| **TABLE 3.5**  Potential Topics in Orienting Families to Decision-Making Groups | |
|---|---|
| ■ The "culture" of the organization and its language, jargon, and acronyms | ■ Ways to communicate collaboratively: how to ask tough questions, how to speak so people will listen, what to do when in disagreement, how to listen to and learn from others' viewpoints |
| ■ The roles group members play | |
| ■ Ways to prepare for a meeting: what to wear, what to do ahead of time, what to bring | |
| ■ The procedures used to conduct the meeting, such as voting rules, report sequences, and time frames | ■ Encouragement to think beyond one's own child and family and to represent the perspective of all families of children with disabilities |

### BOX 3.5

## Guidelines for Involving Family Members in Decision-Making Groups

1. Develop a plan for identifying families to participate.
2. Support staff in developing an understanding of the value of family participation.
3. Provide orientation to both family members and staff about the issues, participants, and process.
4. Provide convenient meeting times and locations for family members.
5. Compensate families for their time, expertise, and expenses.
6. Clearly identify a staff person to be the primary contact person for reimbursement and other issues. Be sure she or he understands that timely reimbursement is essential.
7. Provide accurate, timely, clear, jargon-free, and appropriate information prior to meetings.
8. Provide clear information about the goals of the board, task force, or committee; the role of individual members; and the roles of family members.
9. Match veteran parents with inexperienced family members to ensure that new members feel sup-

ported in their roles as advisors and have the opportunity to share their new and fresh ideas.
10. Balance membership on committees between families and professionals. One family member on a committee is not enough.
11. Ensure diversity among the membership by recruiting from the community and the population the program serves.
12. During and after meetings, specifically recognize the value of family participation.
13. Consider incorporating a "family leave" policy into the practices of the committee so that family members can choose an inactive role but maintain their membership should family circumstances require some time off.
14. Consider sharing leadership-parent and professional co-chairs.
15. Recognize that some family members may require more support than others to participate in a meaningful way.

Source: Adapted by permission from Institute for Family-Centered Care (1994), *Advances in Family-Centered Care, 1*(2), 6.

rather than the professional "doing for families" (Dunst, Trivette, & Deal, 1988). A shift in attitude, practices, and policies that places the family in a central role alongside professionals can lead to "empowered" families that truly make a difference in the developmental and educational outcomes of their children (Turnbull & Summers, 1987). Table 3.6 summarizes the shifts in values and beliefs of families, professionals, and services and supports that have occurred.

Children's lives are enhanced when professionals believe that interaction with family members is one of active, shared decision making and learning. In other words, parents and professionals learn from one another how best to help a particular child. This process enhances both the self-efficacy and competence of parents. Treated as individuals with competencies, parents increase their self-efficacy and become more effective (Baker, 1984). Therefore, to facilitate the sharing of in-

formation by families, professionals need to clearly demonstrate respect for the expertise of family members and to explicitly acknowledge their role as active partners (Klein, 1993).

Look at Box 3.6, which offers ideas for including parents in their child's assessment. Even in the administration of a testing instrument, families can be active, involved participants. The role of family members is essential in creating and maintaining quality supports and services throughout the life of their child. Families should be intimately involved in decision making on their child's behalf and release that responsibility to them over time (Warren & Warren, 1989). You may be wondering about families that don't want to make or are uncomfortable making decisions about their child's education. Some families may feel that the professionals know best. The first step is to assure family members that you, as the professional, are not abdicating your role in planning for your students. Then highlight

| TABLE 3.6 | Value Shifts in Families, Professionals, and Services/Supports | |
| --- | --- | --- |
| **Traditional Values** | **Values for the Twenty-First Century** | |

**Parents**
- Involved
- Dysfunctional
- Denial
- Clients

**Parents**
- Partners
- Adaptive
- Different viewpoint or dream
- Experts

**Professionals**
- Paternalistic
- Holders of knowledge
- Discipline-specific approach
- Closed to dialog
- Deficit focused
- Goals created by experts
- Evaluation by experts
- Labeling children and parents

**Professionals**
- Supportive
- Shared knowledge
- Functional approach
- Seeking dialog
- Strength focused
- Mutually agreed-upon goals
- Joint evaluation process
- Absence of labeling

**Services/Supports**
- Monolingual/monocultural
- Product focused
- Exclusionary
- Hierarchical planning and decision making
- Euro-American orientation

**Services/Supports**
- Multilingual/multicultural
- Process focused
- Inclusionary
- Collaborative planning and decision making
- Multicultural orientation

the important contributions that families can make to the body of knowledge about the child. In addition, it is your role to continue educating families to make decisions and plans for their child.

Think about Annie's family. Annie's diagnosis is Cornelia de Lange syndrome. It took several months and even years for her family to understand her behaviors, likes, dislikes, and needs. Through a process of educating the family via written information about the syndrome, give-and-take discussions, review of a videotape about the syndrome, modeling of appropriate responses and interactions, demonstration of possible responses, and joint problem solving of issues, Annie's family became knowledgeable about the more technical aspects of her disability. Through these experiences, professionals promoted the family's expertise about Cornelia de Lange syndrome and options for their daughter. The family then felt more capable of making better decisions about what was best for Annie.

When professionals adopt perspectives that focus on the competencies and positive aspects of families, they increase the potential for both professionals and families to create the best education for the children. Now, let's look at some scenarios that highlight key moments in the lives of our case study children. In each case, parents and families felt more or less supported at different times.

## Actual Education Scenarios

**KURUME** Kurume's parents, Mattie and Ed, took active roles in deciding that their son would not be institutionalized, as recommended by one health care professional. Instead, they decided that he would live at home and be educated in programs that would help them meet Kurume's needs. Although definitive information about the outcomes of various approaches to

**BOX 3.6**

## Guidelines for Including Parents in Assessments

Assessment is a time of high stress for families. Children who may be eligible for special education services or are already receiving services are tested by professionals to determine their level of development and even IQ. For professionals, it is an everyday practice to assess children using an instrument designed to evaluate current knowledge and skills of the child. The process can be intimidating and overwhelming for parents. They are worried about the results of the test and what it might mean for their child. They might be thinking, "Does he have ADD?" or "Will she need medication every day?" We, as professionals, can support family members throughout the assessment process by actively including them. Here are some practical ideas for collaborating with parents during the administration of the assessment instrument.

1. Conduct the assessment in an environment that is comfortable for the child and family. For young children, home is often the best place.

2. Inform families you do not expect the child to be able to do all of the things you ask. You will take the child as far as he or she can go.

3. Ask parents to provide suggestions for ways to encourage the child to respond to individual test items.

4. Keep in mind that, the better families understand the purpose and intent of the overall test and individual items on the test, the more motivated they will be to carry out specific interactions later.

5. Understand that when parents contribute to the assessment process, it becomes more valid for them.

6. Encourage and be responsive to questions asked by parents before, during, and after the test administration.

7. Be aware that parents may be better able to elicit a response from the child, and ask them to administer test items when it is comfortable for them and appropriate for the child.

8. Talk with parents about their perceptions of how the child is doing and what skills he or she has.

9. Use the testing time to educate families about strategies that might be helpful with the child.

10. Encourage a give-and-take sharing of observations and information during the administration of the test.

11. Understand that every time a test is given to a child, parents have recurrent worries and anxieties about their child's current status and his or her future.

---

teaching a child with hearing loss was impossible to find, they read and talked to people about the options available. Throughout his school years, Kurume's family made many decisions about where he would be educated and what methods would be used. Because Kurume's cognitive, communicative, and affective needs are impacted by his deafness, they felt that their decisions would have a tremendous bearing on the outcomes of his education. Mattie and Ed found that they needed to go to the school fairly often—more often than they typically went to school on behalf of their other children. They were concerned that Kurume would miss out on important learning opportunities if they didn't stay well informed and actively involved. They were never completely sure that they were right in selecting oral programs that emphasized speaking rather than programs that included sign language as part of his total communication. Looking back, they sometimes wonder whether they did the right things. But whether their decisions were right or wrong, the key is that the people who were closest to Kurume—his family—played the central role in making decisions about his education.

As Kurume got older, Mattie and Ed relinquished some of their decision-making responsibility to Kurume himself. At that stage, they became his guides, allowing him to pursue his own options in terms of his education and extracurricular activities. As Kurume prepared to make vital career decisions, he looked to his parents, as well as outside sources, for advice and guidance.

**KIRK** In Kirk's case, Marilyn and Jerry also found themselves at school frequently. Often, it was because

Kirk was in trouble—on the playground, in class, in the hall, or at the bus stop. They wanted Kirk to have the best, but the school staff seemed to expect something of Kirk that wasn't reasonable. Also, from the parents' perspective, the staff seemed to expect them to have some control over what was happening at school. "What do they want us to do?" asked Jerry, after one meeting. "They're the trained professionals, and we can't control him when he's there at school." They found themselves less often in the decision-making role and more often in a defensive position. They knew that Kirk's behavior often posed serious problems at school, but they weren't very happy about it when they had to come to school to get him because he was being suspended for his behavior. When they asked Kirk about school, he told them that the teachers yelled at him all the time and were mean to him. But the school personnel they had dealt with didn't seem mean, so they didn't know what to think.

**MICHAEL** Michael often struggled with his academic work. Anita filed the paperwork to have Michael's skills assessed for possible placement in special education. She was able to do so because she had the background knowledge about the special education process. Anita's job at the State Education Agency was in the Special Services Department, where she worked on the funding for special education. As a result, she knew the law and had access to professionals in the department who helped her interpret the rules. Although she never expected to have to use her knowledge on behalf of her own son, when it became necessary, she did. Anita knew to call IEP meetings frequently; in fact, every time Michael failed to receive the support that she felt he deserved and that was agreed upon, she called a meeting. She knew the rights that her son had under the law, and she had the communication and problem-solving skills to be actively involved in obtaining those rights.

**ANNIE** Unlike Michael, who could tell his parents what he had trouble with and what his successes were, Annie couldn't speak for herself. Thus, Dave and Debbie had to find other ways to find out how she was doing at school. Dave and Debbie didn't go to the school as often as some other parents, but during kindergarten and first grade, they maintained a "back-and-forth book" about Annie. Figure 3.4 shows what

## Extending Your Learning

Based on our five students' experiences, try to apply the "Guidelines for Involving Family Members in Decision-Making Groups" (Box 3.5) and the "Principles Underlying the Family-Centered Approach" (Table 3.3). Where do the school professionals and families work well together, and where might they have worked more effectively? Why did the families and school professionals work as they did, and what they might have done differently?

Annie's back-and-forth book looked like during a few days in October of first grade. One day, when Annie was in third grade, Debbie was in the office supply store and noticed the hand-held, voice-activated tape recorders that businesspeople use to record notes and other messages. She bought an inexpensive one and decided to try asking the school professionals, the support personnel, and, especially, the other children to pull it out of Annie's daypack and speak into it about how Annie was doing, what she needed at school, and so on. Soon, Annie's tape recorder became the "hit" of the third grade. The other girls were eager to tell Debbie that Annie needed $3 for the field trip and that her field trip permission slip had to be returned by Friday. They told her when Annie cried or spent more time than usual picking at her skin. They also mentioned when she paid attention in the small-group lessons. In addition, the physical therapist spoke into the recorder to let Debbie know that Annie had used her **stander** successfully for forty-five minutes during math class. Annie's teacher found that it took only a minute to keep in touch with Debbie this way and preferred this solution over the back-and-forth book, because it was harder to write her thoughts than to speak them.

**TANYA** Juanita, Tanya, and her preschool teacher visited the kindergarten class when Tanya was preparing to make the transition from preschool to kindergarten. The kindergarten teacher showed them the tables and chairs in one part of the kindergarten room and the clay and paints in the art corner. Juanita and Tanya stayed while the teacher read a story to the children, and they took pictures of everything they saw. Meanwhile, Juanita and the preschool teacher both began

> 10/5
>
> Debbie -
> Annie stood in her stander today for 15 minutes. She
> didn't like it much and cried so we stopped.
> 10/6 Glad to hear she lasted so long. Debbie  Trudy
> 10/9
> Deb -
> Today Annie wouldn't eat much of lunch. It was spaghetti
> and I know she likes it and the celery sticks with peanut
> butter. Do you think she's coming down with something?
> Veronica
>
> 10/10 — Veronica
> I think she is getting something. She wouldn't eat
> much dinner last night either.
> Debbie
>
> 10/15 Debbie -
> Annie did a great job today. The children were drawing
> pictures of their families. Paige drew Annie's family for
> her and Annie stuck right with Paige the whole time!
> I'm so proud of her!  Trudy

**FIGURE 3.4** ■ Annie's Back-and-Forth Book

playing "kindergarten" with Tanya—at home and at school to prepare her for the change.

## ■ SECTION SUMMARY

Family-professional-community collaboration begins during the early childhood years, continues throughout the school years, and extends into adulthood. As service systems change, family members provide the personal information, history, and comprehensive knowledge that facilitates a smooth transition from one set of services, supports, and routines to another. No magical age exists at which parents cease to be concerned about and feel responsible for their child's happiness and welfare. The best reason to work at creating effective, meaningful relationships with parents and families is that children thrive when the adults in their home, school, and community environments work well together. Striving to create partnerships between family members and professionals in which all members of the team are equally valued and considered experts is a major change in the traditional role relationships between professionals and parents. Such a shift in practice requires reflection on and perhaps a reformation of personal and professional values and beliefs. It also requires that school professionals develop cross-cultural sensitivity and competence and actively solicit family members as resources, peers, and advisors. The synergy and reciprocity that occurs when school professionals and family members develop true partnerships is energizing and fulfilling for all those involved.

# Chapter Summary

The lifelines we asked you to imagine in the introduction to this chapter provide vital connections between families and schools that are strengthened or weakened by the work of school professionals with families. The changing characteristics of families in terms of membership and composition, as well as family systems and functioning styles, are crucial to the well-being of children with disabilities. External influences on families, including socioeconomic circumstances and cultural factors, have a significant effect on family functioning, choices, and attitudes toward disabilities. Children with disabilities have a major impact on their families, including the emotional responses associated with the presence of a child with a disability, the roles of mothers and fathers, and the relationships between the parents and among siblings. These families require both formal and informal support. The emergence of family support networks and groups, as well as the neighborhood and community supports available through an inclusive school community, have helped to provide that support. Family-school partnerships are built upon the personal values and beliefs of professionals, on cross-cultural competence, and on the fundamental assumption that families are equal partners in the educational process.

---

## INSTRUCTIONAL ACTIVITY

## The Family Panel

### Objectives

- To understand the issues that families face when raising a child with disabilities
- To develop a strategy for organizing and remembering key constructs about the legal bases of working with families

### Preparation

- Your instructor will invite at least three families to come to class. They should have children at different ages and with different learning abilities. Family members will share their personal experiences and respond to questions from students in the class.

### Materials

- A rubric for a reaction paper, distributed prior to class

### Product

- A two- to three-page reaction paper. The paper should highlight two issues that were raised by members of the family panel and compare the experiences reported by members of the panel to the information discussed in the chapter.

### Agenda

- Read Chapter 3 prior to the panel presentation, and prepare at least five questions that relate to issues raised in the chapter.
- Take notes and ask questions based on Chapter 3.

### Evaluation

- Your paper will be graded according to criteria such as thoughtfulness, application of concepts from the chapter to the content of the panel, selection of issues to discuss, use of language that is "people first," clarity of expression, and appropriate mechanics.

# Glossary

**Advocates** Individuals who defend or appeal on behalf of the cause of another person or group of individuals.

**Cornelia de Lange syndrome** A genetic disorder characterized by moderate-to-severe levels of mental retardation and self-injurious behavior and by slow growth of the musculoskeletal system.

**Egocentric** Viewing the world in relationship to oneself as opposed to taking others into consideration.

**Family system** The constellation of –individuals that constitute a family and the associated roles and relationships that exist among its members.

**Formal support** The interaction between families and professionals and agencies that assist people with disabilities and their families.

**Genetic markers** The patterns of chromosomes on genes that determine many of the unique features or conditions of human beings, including their physical and psychological attributes.

**Informal supports** Naturally occurring events in life that address instrumental, emotional, and informational needs—for example, interactions with extended family, neighbors, close friends, church members, and so on.

**Intervention plan** A document that identifies the types of programs, materials, or systems that will be put in place to support a student's needs.

**Motor or vocal tics** Small, uncontrollable body movements or vocal outbursts.

**Self-efficacy** An individual's belief about how well he or she performs a particular task or activity. For example, an individual's self-efficacy about math may be more positive than his or her self-efficacy about spelling.

**Social networks** The connections among individuals that exist for the purposes of communication and other types of interpersonal relationships.

**Stander** An adaptive device that is used to physically support individuals who have limited or no muscle control so they can stand in an upright position.

# National Disability Organizations and Agencies

**Alexander Graham Bell Association for the Deaf,** 3417 Volta Place NW, Washington, DC 20007-2778, 202/337-5220 V/TTY

**Alzheimer's Association,** 919 North Michigan Av., Suite 1000, Chicago, IL 60611, 312/335-8700 V, 312/335-8882, 800/272-3900

**American Association of the Deaf-Blind,** 814 Thayer Av., #302, Silver Spring, MD 20910, 301/588-6545 TTY only

**American Association of University Affiliated Programs for Persons with Developmental Disabilities,** 8630 Fenton St., #410, Silver Spring, MD 20910, 301/588-8252, 588-3319 TTY

**American Association on Mental Retardation,** 444 N. Capitol St. NW, #846, Washington, DC 20001-1570, 202/387-1968 V, 800/424-3688, Fax 202/387-2193

**American Council of the Blind,** 1155-15th St. NW, #720, Washington, DC 20005, 202/467-5081 V, 800/424-8666, Fax 202/467-5085

**American Diabetes Association (ADA),** Diabetes Info. Service Ctr., 1660 Duke St., Alexandria, VA 22314, 800/ADA-DISC

**American Foundation for the Blind,** 11 Perm Plaza, Suite 300, New York, NY 10001-2018, 212/620-2000 or 800/232-5463, 212/620-2158 TTY

**American Society for Deaf Children,** 2848 Arden Way, #210, Sacramento, CA 95825-1373, 916/482-0120 V/TTY, 800/942-ASDC V/TTY, Fax 916/482-0121

**American Speech-Language-Hearing Association,** 10801 Rockville Pike, Rockville, MD 20852, 301/897-5700; Consumer Affairs: 800/638-8255, 301/897-0157 TTY; Fax 301/571-0457

**Arc of the U.S.,** 500 E. Border St., #300, Arlington, TX 76010, 817/261-6003, 817/277-0553 TTY, 800/433-5255, 800/277-0553 TTY, Fax 817/277-3491

**Arthritis Foundation,** 1330 W. Peachtree St., Atlanta, GA 30309, 404/872-7100, 800/283-7800, Fax 404/872-0457

**Association of Birth Defect Children, Inc. (ABDC),** 827 Irma Av., Orlando, FL 32803, 407/245-7035 V, 800/313-2232 V, Fax 407/245-7087

**Association for the Care of Children's Health (ACCH),** 7910 Woodmont Av., #300, Bethesda, MD 20814, 301/654-6549 V

**Autism Society of America, Inc.,** 7910 Woodmont Av., #650, Bethesda, MD 20814, 301/657-0881 V, 800/3-AUTISM

**Bazelon Center for Mental Health Law** (formerly Mental Health Law Project), 1101-15th St. NW, #1212, Washington, DC 20005, 202/467-5730, 202/467-4232 TTY, Fax 223-0409

**Beach Center on Families and Disability,** Bureau of Child Research, University of Kansas, 3111 Haworth Hall, Lawrence, KS 66045, 913/864-7600, Fax 913/864-7605

**Better Hearing Institute,** Hearing Helpline, P.O. Box 1840, Washington, DC 20013, 800/327-9355, Fax 703/750-9302

**Brain Injury Association,** 1776 Massachusetts Av. NW, #100, Washington, DC 20036, 202/296-6443, 800/444-6443, Fax 202/296-8850

**Cancer Fax,** 301/402-5874 (National Cancer Institute)

**Cancer Information Service,** 800/4-CANCER

**Candlelighters' Childhood Cancer Foundation,** 7910 Woodmont Av., #460, Bethesda, MD 20814, 301/657-8401, 800/366-CCCF, Fax 301/718-2686

**Challenge (Attention Deficit Disorder Association),** P.O. Box 488, West Newbury, MA 01985, 508/462-0495

**Child and Adolescent Service System Program (CASSP),** National Institute of Mental Health (NIMH), Parklawn Bldg., 5600 Fishers Lane, Rm. 11C-09, Rockville, MD 20857, 301/443-1333

**Children with Attention Deficit Disorders (ChADD),** 499 NW 70th Av., #308, Plantation, FL 33317, 305/587-3700

**Children's Defense Fund,** 25 E St. NW, Washington, DC 20001, 202/628-8787, Fax 202/662-3510

**Cornelia de Lange Syndrome Foundation,** 60 Dyer Av., Collinsville, CT 06022, 800/223-8355, Fax 203/693-6819

**Council for Exceptional Children (CEC),** 1920 Association Dr., Reston, VA 22091-1589, 703/620-3660, 703/264-9446 TTY, 800/328-0272, Fax 703/264-9494

**Disability Rights Education and Defense Fund (DREDF),** 2212-6th St., Berkeley, CA 94710, 415/644-2555

**Epilepsy Foundation of America (and National Epilepsy Library & Resource Center),** 4351 Garden City Dr., Landover, MD 20785, 301/459-3700, 800/332-1000, 800/332-2070 TTY, Fax 301/577-2684

**ERIC Clearinghouse on Adult Career & Vocational Education,** 1900 Kenny Rd., Columbus, OH 43210, 614/292-4353 in OH, 800/848-4815, Fax 614/292-1260

**ERIC Clearinghouse on Disability & Gifted Education,** 1920 Association Dr., Reston, VA 22091, 703/620-3660 V, Fax 703/264-9494

**Estate Planning for Persons with Disabilities,** 2801 Hwy. 280 So., Birmingham, AL 35223-2407, 800/934-1929

**Families of Spinal Muscular Atrophy,** P.O. Box 196, Libertyville, IL 60048, 800/886-1762

**Family Voices,** P.O. Box 769, Algodones, NM 87001

**Federation of Families for Children's Mental Health,** 1021 Prince St., Alexandria, VA 22314-2971, 703/684-7710, Fax 703/836-1040

**HEAL (Human Ecology Action League),** P.O. Box 49126, Atlanta, GA 30359-1126, 404/248-1898 (for persons with environmental illnesses)

**HEATH Resource Center,** One Dupont Circle NW, #855, Washington, DC 20036-1110, 202/939-9320 V/TTY, 800/544-3284, Fax 833-4760 (national clearinghouse on postsecondary education for people with disabilities)

**Helen Keller National Center for Deaf-Blind Youths & Adults (HKNC)/Technical Assistance Center,** 111 Middle Neck Rd., Sands Point, NY 11050, 516/944-8900, 516/944-8637 TTY, Fax 516/944-7302

**Human Growth Foundation,** 7777 Leesburg Pike, Falls Church, VA 22043, 703/883-1773, 800/451-6434, Fax 703/883-1776

**Immune Deficiency Foundation,** 25 W. Chesapeake Av., #206, Baltimore, MD 21204-4820, 410/321-6647 in MD, 800/296-4433, Fax 410/321-9165

**Institute for Families of Blind Children,** P.O. Box 54700, MS 111, Los Angeles, CA 90054-0700, 213/669-4649 V, Fax 666-6283

**International Fibrodysplasia Ossificans Progressiva Assoc.,** P.O. Box 3578, Winter Springs, FL 32708, 407/365-4194 V/Fax

**Job Accommodation Network,** West Virginia University, P.O. Box 6080, 918 Chestnut Ridge Rd., #1, Morgantown, WV 26506, 800/232-9675 or 800/526-7234 V/TTY, Fax 304/293-5407

**Juvenile Diabetes Foundation International (JDF),** 120 Wall St., New York, NY 10005-3904, 212/785-9500, 800/223-1138 V/TTY, Fax 212/785-9595

**Learning Disabilities Association of America,** 4156 Library Rd., Pittsburgh, PA 15234, 412/341-1515, 412/341-8077 V, Fax 412/344-0224

**Leukemia Society of America,** 600-3rd Av., 4th Flr., New York, NY 10016, 212/573-8484, Fax 212/856-9686, 800/955-4654

**Lowe's Syndrome Association,** 222 Lincoln St., West Lafayette, IN 47906, 317/743-3634 V

**Lupus Foundation of America, Inc.,** 130 Piccard, Suite 200, Rockville, MD 20850, 301/670-9292 V, 800/558-0121, 301/670-9486

**March of Dimes Birth Defects Foundation,** 1275 Mamaroneck Av., White Plains, NY 10605, 914/428-7100 V/TTY, Fax 914/428-8203

**Muscular Dystrophy Association,** 3300 E. Sunrise Dr., Tucson, AZ 85718, 602/529-2000 V, 800/572-1717, Fax 602/529-5300

**National Alliance for the Mentally Ill,** 200 N. Glebe Rd., #1015, Arlington, VA 22203-3754, 703/524-7600 V, 703/516-7991 TTY, 800/950-NAMI, Fax 703/524-9094

**National Association of the Deaf,** 814 Thayer Av., Silver Spring, MD 20910-4500, 301/587-1788, 301/587-1789 TTY, Fax 301/587-1791

**National Association for Parents of the Visually Impaired, Inc.,** P.O. Box 317, Watertown, MA 02272, 617/972-7441, 800/562-6265, Fax 617/972-7444

**National Association of Protection and Advocacy Systems,** 900-2nd St. NE, #211, Washington, DC 20002, 202/408-9514 V, 202/408-9521, Fax 202/408-9520

National Association of State Directors of Special Education (NASDSE), 1800 Diagonal Rd., #320, Alexandria, VA 22314-2840, 703/519-3800, 703/519-7008 TTY, Fax 703/519-3908

National Autism Hotline, P.O. Box 507, Huntington, WV 25710-0507, 304/525-8014 V, Fax 304/525-8026

National Brain Injury Research Foundation, 14408 Newton Patent Ct., Centreville, VA 22020, 703/818-0078, 800/447-8445

National Captioning Institute, 5203 Leesburg Pike, 15th Flr., Falls Church, VA 22041, 800/533-WORD, 800/321-TTYS TTY

National Center for Clinical Infant Programs, 2000-14th Street N, #380, Arlington, VA 22201, 703/528-4300, 703/528-0419 TTY, Fax 703/528-6848

National Center for Education in Maternal & Child Health, 2200-15th St. N, #701, Arlington, VA 22201, 703/524-7802 V, Fax 703/524-9335

National Center for Law and the Deaf, 800 Florida Av. NE, Washington, DC 20002, 202/651-5454 TTY

National Center for Research in Vocational Education, University of Illinois, Rm. 345 Education Building, 1310 S. Sixth St., Champaign, IL 61820, 217/333-2609 V/TTY, Fax 217/244-5632

National Center for Stuttering, 200 E. 33rd St., #17C, New York, NY 10016, 800/221-2483, Fax 212/683-1372

National Chronic Pain Outreach Association (NCPOA), 7979 Old Georgetown Rd., #100, Bethesda, MD 20814, 301/652-4948 V, Fax 301/907-0745

National Clearinghouse on Family Support and Children's Mental Health, Portland State University, P.O. Box 751, Portland, OR 97207-0751, 800/628-1696, 503/725-4165 TTY

National Coalition on Deaf-Blindness, 175 North Beach St., Watertown, MA 02172, 617/972-7347

National Council on Disability, 800 Independence Av. SW, #814, Washington, DC 20591, 202/267-3846, 202/267-3846 TTY

National Cystic Fibrosis Foundation, 6931 Arlington Rd., Bethesda, MD 20814, 301/951-4422 V/TTY, 800/344-4823 V/TTY, Fax 301/951-6378

National Diabetes Information Clearinghouse (NDIC), 1 Information Way, Bethesda, MD 20892-3560, 301/654-3327 V, 301/657-2172 TTY

National Down Syndrome Congress, 7000 Dunwoody Road, Building #5, Suite 100, Atlanta, GA 30328-1662, 770-604-9500 V, 800-232-NDSC V, Fax 770-604-9898

National Down Syndrome Society, 666 Broadway, #810, New York, NY 10012-2317, 212/460-9330 V, 800/221-4602, Fax 212/979-2873

National Early Childhood Technical Assistance System (NEC*TAS), 137 E. Franklin St., 500 Nation's Bank Plaza, Chapel Hill, NC 27514, 919/962-2001 V, 919/966-4041 TTY, Fax 919/966-7463

National Easter Seal Society, 230 W. Monroe, #1800, Chicago, IL 60606, 312/726-6200, 726-4258 TTY, 800/221-6827, Fax 312/726-1494

National Fragile X Foundation, 1441 York St., #303, Denver, CO 80206, 303/333-6155, 800/688-8765

National Health Information Center (Office of Disease Prevention and Health Promotion), P.O. Box 1133, Washington, DC 20013-1133, 800/336-4797

National Hearing Aid Society, 20361 Middle Belt Rd., Livonia, MI 48152, 810/478-2610, 800/521-5247, Fax 810/478-4520

National Information Center for Children and Youth with Disabilities (NICHCY), P.O. Box 1492, Washington, DC 20013, 202/884-8200 V/TTY, 800/695-0285 V/TTY, Fax 202/884-8441

National Information Center on Deafness, Gallaudet University, 800 Florida Av. NE, Washington, DC 20002-3625, 202/651-5051, 202/651-5052 TTY, Fax 202/651-5054

National Information Clearinghouse for Infants with Disabilities and Life-Threatening Conditions, CDD/USC, Benson Bldg., 1st Flr., Columbia, SC 29208, 803/777-4435, 803/777-7826 TTY, 800/922-9234, Fax 803/777-6058

National Institute on Disability and Rehabilitation Research (NIDRR), Department of Education, 600 Independent Av. SW, Washington, DC 20202-2572, 202/205-8134 V, 202/205-9136 TTY, Fax 202/205-8515

National Library Service for the Blind and Physically Handicapped, Library of Congress, 1291 Taylor St. NW, Washington, DC 20542, 202/707-5100 V, 707-0744 TTY, 800/424-8567 V/TTY, Fax 202/707-0712

National Mental Health Association, 1021 Prince St., Alexandria, VA 22314-2971, 703/684-7722, 800/969-6642

**National Multiple Sclerosis Society,** 733-3rd Av., New York, NY 10017, 212/986-3240, 800/344-4867, Fax 212/986-7981

**National Organization for Albinism & Hypopigmentation,** 1500 Locust St., #1816, Philadelphia, PA 19102, 215/545-2322

**National Organization on Disability,** 910-16th St. NW, #600, Washington, DC 20006, 202/293-5960, 202/293-5968 TTY, Fax 202/293-7999

**National Organization for Rare Disorders (NORD),** P.O. Box 8923, New Fairfield, CT 06812, 203/746-6518, 202/746-6927 TTY, 800/999-NORD V, Fax 203/746-6481

**National Parent Network on Disabilities,** 1727 King St., Suite 305, Alexandria, VA 22314, 703/684-6763 V/TTY, Fax 836-1232

**National Rehabilitation Information Center (ABLEDATA),** 8455 Colesville Rd., #935, Silver Spring, MD 20910-3319, 301/588-9284 V, 301/495-5626 TTY, 800/346-2742, Fax 301/587-1967

**National Retinitis Pigmentosa Foundation, Inc.,** 11350 McCormick Rd., #800, Hunt Valley, MD 21031-1002, 800/638-5683 TTY

**National Spinal Cord Injury Assn.,** 8300 Colesville Rd., Suite 5515, Silver Spring, MD 20910, 301/588-6959 V, 800/962-9629, Fax 301/588-9414

**National Tourette Syndrome Association,** 4240 Bell Blvd., Suite 205, Bayside, NY 11361, 718/224-2999, 800/237-0717, Fax 718/279-9596

**National Tuberous Sclerosis Association,** 8181 Professional Place, Suite 110, Landover, MD 20785, 300/459-9888 V, 800/225-NTSA, Fax 301/459-0394

**Office of Civil Rights,** Region 5, Department of Education, 111 N. Canal Street, Suite 1053, Chicago, IL 60606, 312/886-8438 (region covering Minnesota)

**Office for Civil Rights National Office,** Department of Education, Rm. 5000, Switzer Bldg., 400 Maryland Av. SW, Washington, DC 20202

**Office of Special Education Programs (OSEP),** Switzer Bldg., 400 Maryland Av. SW, Suite 2651, Washington, DC 20202-2651, 202/205-5507 V, Fax 202/260-0416

**Office of Special Education & Rehabilitative Services (OSERS),** Rm. 3006 Switzer Bldg., 330 C St. SW, Washington, DC 20202-2500, 202/205-5465 V/TTY, Fax 202/205-9252

**Orton Society,** 8600 LaSalle Rd., Chester Bldg., #382, Baltimore, MD 21286-2044, 301/296-0232 (dyslexia)

**Osteogenesis Imperfecta Foundation, Inc.,** P.O. Box 24776, Tampa, FL 33623-4776, 813/855-7077

**People First, Inc.,** 800/433-5255 (self-advocacy group)

**Prader-Willi Syndrome Association,** 2510 S. Brentwood Blvd., #220, St. Louis, MO 63144, 314/962-7644, 800/926-4797, Fax 314/962-7869

**Protection and Advocacy for Mentally Ill Program (PAMI),** National Institute of Mental Health, Rm. 15C-21, 5600 Fishers Lane, Rockville, MD 20857, 301/443-3667, Fax 301/443-7926

**Resource Access Project (RAP),** Univ. of Illinois, Dept. of Spec. Ed., 403 E. Healey, Champaign, IL 61820, 217/333-3876, Fax 217/333-4293

**Schools Are For Everyone (SAFE),** 7800 Shoal Creek Blvd., #171-E, Austin, TX 78757

**Self-Help for Hard of Hearing People, Inc.,** 7910 Woodmont Av., #1200, Bethesda, MD 20814, 301/657-2248, 657-2249 TTY, Fax 301/913-9413

**Short Stature Foundation** (formerly Little People of America), P.O. Box 9897, Washington, DC 20016, 800/24DWARF

**Sick Kids Need Involved People, Inc.** (SKIP), 216 Newport Dr., Severna Park, MD 21146

**Spina Bifida Association of America,** 4590 MacArthur Blvd. NW, Suite 250, Washington, DC 20007, 202/944-3285, 800/621-3141, Fax 202/944-3295

**Technical Assistance on Training About the Rehabilitation Act (TATRA),** c/o PACER Center, 4826 Chicago Av. S, Minneapolis, MN 55417-1098, 612/827-2966 V/TTY, 800/53-PACER (for parents in greater Minnesota), Fax 612/827-3065

**The Association for Persons with Severe Handicaps (TASH),** 29 W. Susquehanna Av., Suite 210, Baltimore, MD 21204, 410/828-1306 V/TTY, 800/482-TASH, Fax 410/828-6706

**United Cerebral Palsy Association,** 1522 K St. NW, #1112, Washington, DC 20005, 202/842-1266 V/TTY, 800/872-5827

**Very Special Arts,** 1331 F Street NW, #800, Washington, DC 20004, 202/844-9040 V, 202/737-0645 TTY, 800/933-8721, Fax 202/737-0725

**Williams Syndrome Association,** P.O. Box 297, Clawson, MI 48017, 810/541-3630

**World Institute on Disability,** 510-16th St., #100, Oakland, CA 94612, 510/763-4100, 510/208-9493 TTY

## CHAPTER 4

# Tools for Constructing Inclusive School Communities

# Collaboration in the Classroom

*by Mary Kiesau-Bramer and Cathy Krautkramer*

Mary co-taught with Cathy for the first time twenty-two years after she earned her bachelor's degree and twelve years after she earned her master's degree in special education. She had just taken a class on collaboration and co-teaching and was eager to try out her skills. Cathy had been teaching since 1963 in elementary classrooms. Her goal was to incorporate a whole-language approach into her classroom to increase comprehension, fluency, and word recognition skills in the context of good children's literature.

## How Did It Work?

*Mary:* I wanted to work with Cathy because I think special education services should be provided in regular classrooms, and she had three special education students assigned to her class. I was new to the building and didn't know the students very well. Their assessment reports and goals indicated that they needed a lot of help with reading and written language.

*Cathy:* I was concerned about balancing the special needs of three students with those of twenty-four classmates. My students didn't like to be removed from the classroom for special education services, so I asked Mary about the possibility of her working in my classroom—rather than using a pullout system. She said yes.

*Mary:* At first, we set up a schedule and got to know each other. Cathy expects students to follow rules and know the consequences for their actions. Her reputation as a tough, no-nonsense kind of

teacher sounded good to me. However, I was concerned about the frustration level of the students in special education. Would the expectations be too much for them to meet? The three boys were all poor readers. Would they succeed?

*Cathy:* Since we had never worked together before, I was a little reluctant to put too much planning and teaching responsibility into Mary's hands at first.

*Mary:* I was also apprehensive about our relationship because we didn't really know each other, but we had just agreed to work together for an hour and a half every day. I didn't want to interfere in the way in which she ran the classroom, but I had to assure that the needs of the students were met. To be frank, I wasn't sure how the whole thing was going to work. Who would make the choices about reading materials? How much choice would the students have in selection of materials and activities? Who would be in control of classroom discipline? What exactly would my role be in the planning and execution of the daily plans?

*Cathy:* I was also concerned that our teaching styles might not be compatible.

*Mary:* Our method of operating was very simple, at first. Basically, Cathy did the planning and was the lead teacher, and I helped her carry out the plans.

*Cathy:* Our curriculum was also simple. We began the very first week of school. I placed each special education student in a different

group so they were not identified as a separate group. I led the daily lesson and set the guidelines, and Mary would fit in where she thought it was appropriate.

*Mary:* My contribution to get this off the ground was to offer to tape each selection in five-minute segments at a reduced speed to allow the less able readers to listen while they followed the written words.

*Cathy:* Sometimes, I asked students to dramatize a new end to the story. They planned, practiced, and presented their ideas to the rest of the class. Other times, we would read the story aloud in groups. Then we would use a creative activity such as acting out the story or parts of the story. Students sometimes played different characters. We made posters, puzzles, pictures, and plays. The most rewarding part was that all the students were loving it. We planned these activities because of the presence of the special education students, but now I realize that the other students benefited because they would have been less actively involved if we hadn't planned it this way. These ideas worked well for all the students. When I realized this, I began to trust Mary more.

*Mary:* As the year progressed, I often suggested ideas. As Cathy began to trust me more and more, I took the role of lead teacher more frequently. There was lots of flexibility in what actually happened each day. I knew that we had really gotten comfortable with each other the day Cathy said, "I'm not up to it today. Would you take over?"

## What Made It Work?

*Cathy:* After the first few days, I realized that Mary was astutely moving to all groups in my classroom and not just hovering over the special education students. This was the basis for her acceptance by all students. It wasn't long before all students would work with Mary just as readily as they would with me. Together, we met the academic needs of her students, and we helped them learn to get along in a fourth-grade classroom. I would often ask if she felt we were meeting their needs, and she always patiently pointed out that the goal for these students was to read and understand the literature, and that is what they were doing. As time progressed, Mary and I became very comfortable with the give-and-take of the classroom leadership. Sometimes, I would ask her to teach a lesson that came from her expertise; other times, she would see ahead of me and offer to lead a lesson or discussion. Almost daily I was thankful for another teacher to help me share the responsibility and teaching role.

By the end of the year, we had an extremely comfortable working relationship. We would build on one another's ideas and presentations. Students viewed us both as teachers in the classroom, and I never felt the students thought she was "reserved" for the special education students. We planned lessons with the special needs kids in mind, but they were modified for students of all abilities. I know several students frequently worked above their educational levels just because more was expected of them. Also, the special needs students participated in all class discussions and had lots of good ideas. If they were in a pullout program, this probably would not have happened.

*Mary:* My apprehensions about making our team work were soon put to rest. Cathy completely accepted me as a peer and co-teacher. There was no buildup time for the class to accept me. I was there, and here we go! I think the kids observed her attitude and accepted me as a co-teacher. We went into the experience with positive attitudes and a spirit of collaboration to do the best for all kids. If one plan wasn't as successful as we liked, we tried another.

*Cathy:* Fortunately, I had more than one student with special needs and could justify having Mary for so much time. But, since the three special education students were spread throughout the classroom, and because we planned our curriculum and instruction to automatically address their needs, I would sometimes forget that they had special needs. Mary and I are fortunate to work in a district that gives us that latitude. We are encouraged to try new things and make our own programs. We did not have to stick to a formula or to follow a set plan.

## What Would You Do Differently?

*Cathy and Mary:* Several things came up which we wanted to change or do differently. We used many activities that were planned or carried out in cooperative groups, but our evaluation of the students' cooperative skills was very subjective. We still need to create an instrument to monitor the cooperative groups accurately and efficiently. This would also help us to track student progress.

*Mary:* Students in special education need to be pre- and posttested using a curriculum-based assessment to document progress. Actually, all the students could benefit from such a practice. It would give us a much more accurate picture of each student and his or her progress.

*Cathy:* We agree that we need to spend more time in group processing—teachers with each other and students with their groups. This was the cooperative learning component that sometimes got cut in the interest of time. I think we cut ourselves out of some valuable learning time.

*Cathy and Mary:* We now realize that our planning time was way too flexible. It is important to have a consistent time and place set for meeting each week. Working together like this requires advance planning! This can be the deciding factor in whether co-teaching works or not.

*Mary:* Last, but very importantly, is the identification of relevant outcomes *before* you begin. It is critical to have a focus and also specific goals. In other words, you both have to know what you are trying to do.

## Conclusions

*Mary:* Quite by accident, a copy of the Colorado Assessment of Co-Teaching (CO-ACT), copyright 1993, developed by Lois Adams, Kay Cessna, and Marilyn Friend, appeared in my school mailbox one day. I gave a copy to Cathy, and we each filled one out. I was interested to learn that my scores were very close to Cathy's. I tended to score everything higher than she did, but we were never in disagreement. Overall, we rated lower than exemplary teams; however, the items helped us focus on areas for improvement. The instrument confirmed our analysis of what we did that worked and what we would do differently.

*Cathy:* I still have questions about this system. Would it work with more severely disabled students? I am not sure. Reading material would have to be tape recorded and presented in ways other than just reading. But if the goal is for the child to participate in a regular classroom, I think it can be

done. As I reflect on the year's accomplishments, I realize how much the students with special needs influenced our work and how much everyone benefited from the situation. We used many hands-on experiences, creative ideas, and discussions. No student in that class will ever forget our reading selections. They had fun immersing themselves in the literature.

*Mary:* I came away from this experience wanting to do it again. It was hard work but worth it. We had fun together, and I think the kids caught our enthusiasm. They were amazing in response to our expectations. Far from being too frustrating, the expectations that all were to meet the objectives minimized their differences in ability.

# Introduction

In the first three chapters of this book, you learned about the social and economic contexts that are imposing change on our schools, the way disability law supports equity and access for all learners in our schools, and the effects of families and their changing characteristics on the work of school professionals. This chapter focuses on how to create an integrated response to those conditions in the form of the inclusive school community. Remember, we use the word **"inclusive"** because we mean *all* students and families. And we use the term "community" because schools must rely on the involvement and support of everyone—professionals, support personnel, students, families—working toward a common end. Our notion of **schools as inclusive communities** is part of a new vision of education that expands the work of schools to serve a wider range of abilities, ages, interests, and needs.

In Chapter 1, we asked you to think about your role as a school professional. We reminded you of the traditional roles of teachers in schools where they typically have worked alone, behind closed doors. Little professional interaction occurred as people in different roles carried out their responsibilities. As you will read in this chapter, inclusive school communities are based on a foundation of collaborative, rather than unilateral, decision making, planning, teaching, and problem solving.

First, we describe inclusive school communities in terms of three fundamental characteristics: (1) an emphasis on belonging and meaningful participation, (2) the creation of alliances and affiliations among

members, and (3) the provision of mutual support. Second, we show how collaborative interactions contribute to the formation and maintenance of inclusive school communities while recognizing the diversity of community members and the complexity of their relationships. Finally, we delineate several of the interpersonal processes and skills that enable people to work collaboratively. By the end of this chapter, you will have gained insight into the ways that school professionals, support personnel, families, students, and community members can work together to achieve inclusive school communities.

# The Spirit of Community and Inclusion in Schools

Creating and maintaining inclusive school communities requires an emphasis on belongingness and meaningful participation, the creation of alliances and affiliations, and the provision of mutual emotional and technical support among all community members. Here, we discuss how these three elements are brought to life in inclusive school communities.

## An Emphasis on Belongingness and Meaningful Participation

Think about your own school or work experiences. Was there a time when you felt like an "outsider"—perhaps because you had moved to a new school or were taller than everyone else in your class or couldn't catch a ball? Or, was there a time when you felt that you weren't like everyone else, a time when being "alike" or "liked" or "popular" was what really mattered? Most of us, as children, had some school experience with exclusion from an activity or a group. The feelings that you experienced because of exclusion may be among the least pleasant of your school memories. We all have a basic need for a sense of **belongingness,** a need to participate in the larger group (Maslow, 1970).

For years, special education services were provided to students who needed them in a "special" place— down the hall, in a back room or a separate wing, or, in many cases, in a separate building. Although no malice was intended, students with disabilities were systematically excluded from many places and from many typical interactions that their peers experienced. Belonging to the school community and participating in the events and activities of the school community are equally important for all people. Refer back to Figure 1.6, which shows the "Each Belongs" motto of Bell Middle School. While no school philosophy or motto can prevent all the feelings of loneliness or isolation that students or adults may experience, the existence of such a motto or mission statement sets up an environment in which belonging is fundamental to the activities of the school community.

As you review the "Each Belongs" list, you may be thinking to yourself, "Sure, I would have liked to be in a place that would have accepted me that way, but aren't there some kids that are just too _____ [fill in your own adjective] to benefit from this policy?" Or, if you are thinking, "What about the _____ kids? How can any teacher be expected to handle the challenges they present?" But if every student is welcomed and included, then it is the responsibility of school professionals to collaboratively plan for and support the learning of every student. No individual school professional, support person, student, parent, or volunteer should have to handle significant challenges alone.

Let's take a look at the way a team of school professionals responded to a behavioral crisis at the beginning of Kirk's seventh-grade year. These professionals didn't have any magical solutions to the crisis, but you will see how, as a team, they worked together to find reasonable interventions that helped Kirk establish a sense of belonging to the school community.

Kirk sat waiting in the principal's office. His father was due home from his overseas duty in two days, and he was nervous every time his father came home. Then, about the time things began to settle down, his father left again. It was the first week of September, and Kirk had just been given a two-day suspension from school for inflicting a serious, skin-breaking bite on a classmate. Mr. Fairchild, the physical education teacher, never saw what started the incident, but he gathered that Kirk had some reason to be angry with the student he had bitten.

Needless to say, Kirk's name was on the agenda of the next "Red Team" meeting. As the instructional teams in many middle schools do, the Red Team got together weekly to plan instructional units, to evaluate student progress in academic and behavioral arenas, and to think collaboratively about the unique needs of individual students. The Red Team consists of six teachers—one each in math, science, language arts, social studies, physical education, and special education—as well as a para-educator, Mrs. Yelich, assigned to the special education program.

When Mr. Fairchild went home that night, the discussion from the team meeting nagged at him. Although all seven members had discussed what to do about Kirk, he felt that they had been divided in their approaches. When he spoke with Ms. Matheson, the special education teacher, the next morning, she agreed that they had gotten off track. They had started the meeting by discussing how to help support Kirk in his peer interactions and in class. But their conversation frequently lapsed into discussions about what to do *to* Kirk when he was disruptive (which, they discovered, was a problem in every class). Mr. Fairchild decided to call another meeting to point out the contradictions in their thinking.

At the second meeting, Mr. Fairchild reminded his teammates about the "Each Belongs" philosophy. This time, they used a collaborative problem-solving process to figure out how to help Kirk behave in ways that weren't violent or harmful to other kids so that he could gain a sense of belonging. By the end of the meeting, they had a plan that included the following components:

1. Teach Kirk to identify his own anger and to remove himself, if necessary, to avoid aggression.

2. Teach Kirk aggression control strategies, including preparing for provocation, avoiding confrontations, coping with arousal, and reflecting on the provocation (Novaco, 1975).

3. Teach some of his peers in phys ed how to help Kirk use his aggression control strategies to deal with frustrations in that class.

4. Select two or three kids in each of his other classes who can also encourage Kirk to use these skills.

5. Help Kirk develop a daily goal sheet to help him monitor his own use of aggression control strategies.

6. Have Mrs. Yelich check on Kirk at the beginning of each class to make sure he gets settled in and understands the class expectations for the day.

7. Teach Kirk to keep a daily journal on his behaviors and feelings.

They all went home that night feeling good about their plans for when Kirk returned to school. They knew, however, that their work had just begun.

## The Creation of Alliances and Affiliations Among All School Community Members

The collaborative work of the Red Team fostered strong alliances and a high level of affiliation among its members—a stark contrast to the feelings of school professionals who do their essential work alone. Their collaborative work also contributed to the ability of all the seventh-grade students to develop alliances and a sense of affiliation with one another as they included Kirk. The other students were quick to support Kirk because they realized that they, too, would be accepted and supported as needed. Kirk, of course, received the most benefit from their work. He had adults working on his behalf to actively engage him with his peers, to teach him new skills to manage his own aggressive behavior, and to help him gain acceptance. Brooks (1991) discusses the presence of "alliance" among children in classrooms:

> *Alliance implies trust and cooperation between teacher and student and among the students. It is reflected in students' feeling a sense of security and belonging, a comfort in knowing that they can reveal their vulnerabilities, that they can take risks, that they will not be demeaned or judged or accused, that they will be supported and encouraged for their efforts and that their individuality will be respected and accepted.*

Another example of the creation of alliances in a classroom can be found in the 1993 Academy Award–winning documentary *Educating Peter* (Goodwin & Wurzberg, 1992). The film presented glimpses into the third-grade classroom at Gilbert-Linkous Elementary in Blackhurst, Virginia, which included Peter Gwazdauskis, a child with Down syndrome. At the start of the film, the viewer notices that Peter is rather unruly—pushing, shoving, hitting, and generally bullying other children. In scenes filmed during the third week of school, the students and the teacher voiced their frustrations with Peter's action. Mrs. Stallings, the teacher, also spoke of her determination for Peter to succeed in her classroom. But she realized that, for the good of all the children, the physically aggressive behavior could not continue. How did Mrs. Stallings accomplish her goals? First, she admitted that she needed some help. She engaged the assistance of a special education teacher who helped her hold a series of class meetings. In those meetings, the students used a problem-solving process to address the real-world challenge they faced right in their own classroom. They hypothesized about why Peter acted like he did. They tried to figure out some ways to help him get what he needed in ways that didn't detract from their own welfare. And they joined together with one another and with the teachers to think about the supports that their own community of learners needed to function.

The opportunity to think through a challenging situation provided this third-grade class with one of the most meaningful curricular experiences available. Judging by the behaviors documented in the film at the end of the school year, the students, had, indeed, succeeded. Peter was selected for an award at the end of the school year. One member of that class summarized her feelings about Peter and her third-grade experience this way:

> *He changed because we changed. We changed our minds about him. You think you're teaching Peter things, but really Peter's teaching you things. We're teaching more how to do things. He teaches us more how to think—how to solve problems.*

This student's comments are especially poignant because they reveal a powerful sense of affiliation and alliance among students. Her comments also reflect a celebration of diversity within the school community, as well as a vision of how all students can belong and have meaningful participation in important school functions in spite of their differences in behavior, needs, and abilities.

## The Provision of Mutual Emotional and Technical Support

Mutual support is the third necessary element in inclusive school communities. School professionals historically have functioned autonomously and have been expected to handle the entire range of school circumstances with minimal support. Several decades ago, researchers noted that teaching was a lonely profession and that teachers were isolated from their colleagues (Sarason, 1971). Some teachers still go through the entire school day without speaking to another adult in a meaningful way (Eisner, 1988) and receive little support from anyone.

School professionals often find themselves in positions that are stressful and seemingly unmanageable. They have reported that their stress levels are related to professional isolation, lack of control over increasing demands, their own diminished effectiveness, and changes in work requirements (Fimian, 1982). Teacher stress also is linked with poor teaching performance and decreased sensitivity to the individual needs of students (Blase, 1986; French, 1991).

When isolation dominates and school professionals remain unsupported, the outlook for genuine responsiveness to the changing demands of students is bleak. The increasing diversity in schools, the growing intensity of students' needs, and the larger class sizes all contribute to a more demanding work environment for school professionals and support personnel. In addition, the explosion of knowledge in each of the traditional school subject disciplines places demands on school professionals that are substantially greater than they were in the past.

So, how can school professionals in the twenty-first century respond to the problems of isolation, stress, and increased demands? These circumstances necessitate more mutual sharing of technical expertise and more humane, caring interactions among school professionals than has ever been previously imagined. No single group of professionals can maintain the level of expertise or the emotional stamina to meet the needs of students. Nor can school professionals hope to address issues of diversity and unique educational needs without the support of parents, students, support per-

### Extending Your Learning

Review the story about Kirk and the Red Team. Notice how team members' work fostered an emphasis on belongingness and meaningful participation, on the creation of alliances and strong affiliations, and on the provision of mutual emotional and technical support for students and adults. Then recall places you've known where exclusion, lack of affiliation, and isolation were the norm. With a group of your classmates, make a list of suggestions for the schools that have not yet attained the spirit of community and inclusion.

sonnel, community members, and each other. If we are to provide effective education for all children and maintain the mental health of school professionals, then we must band together to accomplish that which none of us can do alone.

## Collaboration as the Key to Community and Inclusion

**THE TRANSDISCIPLINARY TEAM**   A **transdisciplinary team** is made up of individuals who work together with the child and family to support their needs (Alper et al., 1995). Team members bring different expertise to the group, but they share their expertise and ideas and support one another. In this sense, transdisciplinary teams display the three fundamental characteristics of community and inclusion: (1) They emphasize the belongingness and meaningful participation of all team members in spite of their differences in experience and training; (2) they work to create affiliations and alliances among team members, so that each team member feels a strong bond to the others; and (3) they foster the mutual emotional and technical support of one another. In this chapter, the phrases *team members, collaborative school community members,* and *collaborative team* all refer to people who use the transdisciplinary approach to working with students and families. The stories and examples in this chapter exemplify effective transdisciplinary teams. Even the Red Team that temporarily lost touch with its agreed-upon values worked as an effective transdisciplinary team.

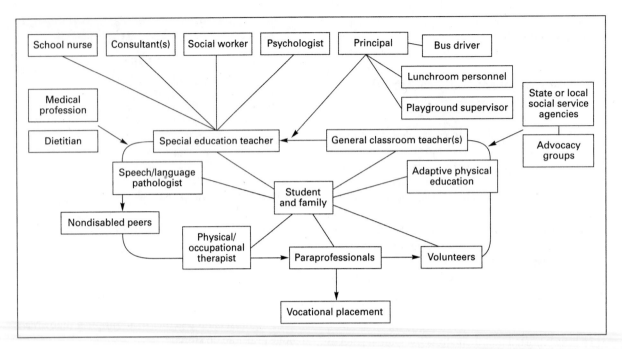

**FIGURE 4.1** ■ A Model of Potential Team Members for a Student in an Inclusive Educational Setting

Source: Adapted from S. Alper, P. J. Schloss, S. K. Etscheidt, & L. A. Macfarlane (1995), *Inclusion: Are we abandoning or helping students?* (Thousand Oaks, CA: Corwin Press), by permission of Corwin Press, Inc.

Figure 4.1 contains a model of potential team members in an inclusive educational setting. Developed by Alper and colleagues (1995), the model depicts the student and family as the focus of the team, immediately surrounded by the team members who are often closest to the student and family—teachers, paraprofessionals, related-services professionals, nondisabled peers, and volunteers. On the outer edges are several school community members who have important, but less direct, responsibilities for the student, such as the school nurse, the bus driver, lunchroom personnel, and playground supervisors. Finally, the school-based team may also be affected by professionals from other agencies and from the medical community.

Each student has a unique configuration of team members depending upon his or her specific needs and on the needs and preferences of the family. The team that works on behalf of a student may change over time. For example, the team that works on Annie's behalf while she is in her preschool and elementary school years probably will include every position in the model except for vocational placement. As Annie moves through her school years, a vocational specialist likely will join the team.

In contrast, Michael's needs probably require services by fewer providers. Michael clearly needs services from special and general classroom teachers, but he has never needed physical or occupational therapy, speech therapy, nursing, or other health care services beyond those that all children receive. He may, however, need the assistance of a paraprofessional in some of his classes, as well as additional assistance from a vocational specialist as he considers postsecondary education or career plans.

No matter which people and positions are represented on a student's unique team, collaboration is the critical attribute. Through collaboration, school professionals demonstrate leadership, support personnel carry out important functions, students attain a sense of fraternity, and parents realize legitimate power (French & Raven, 1959). Collaboration is at the heart of the inclusive school community.

Decisions that affect individual students, classrooms, families, and school professionals are made collaboratively by those most significantly affected. That is, the voices of all are heard and considered in order to reach agreement on action. This emphasis on collaborative decision making, planning, and problem solving is not unique to schools. Countries, businesses, industries, and human service agencies are all learning to use the power of collaboration to attain outcomes that are more productive than outcomes reached individually (Cook & Friend, 1993). Inclusive school communities, like other organizations, rely on the power of collaboration to achieve high-quality outcomes.

**CHARACTERISTICS OF COLLABORATION** Collaboration is a style of direct interaction between at least two co-equal parties, voluntarily engaged in shared problem solving, shared decision making, and shared resources as they work toward a common goal (Cook & Friend, 1993). The term *co-equal parties* does not infer that the individuals enter into the relationship holding the same sets of experiences, knowledge, or skills. Rather, it means that they each bring unique perspectives, experiences, knowledge bases, and personal belief systems that hold equal weight and value as they work together. Respect for diversity of experience and preferences is, thus, inherent in the definition of collaboration and vital to the achievement of high-quality outcomes.

People who work in a collaborative style also share responsibility and accountability for the outcomes of the work they do together. Each participant assumes full responsibility for the decisions that are jointly made and is fully accountable for the results of the endeavor. As collaborative relationships mature, they are characterized by an emergence of shared values and ever-increasing levels of trust and respect, even when shared values and high trust levels didn't exist early in the relationship. People engaged in collaborative relationships support one another and assure themselves that the outcomes of their work will benefit everyone involved. Through shared responsibilities, the emergence of shared values, higher levels of respect and trust, and mutual support and bene-

fits, each of the parties emerges stimulated, enriched, and better equipped to do their work (see Table 4.1).

**APPLYING THE COLLABORATIVE STYLE TO SCHOOL TASKS, PROCESSES, AND ACTIVITIES** Cook and Friend (1991) emphasize that collaboration is a style of interaction, not a program, a service delivery model, or an outcome. Collaboration doesn't exist in isolation; it exists only when people apply it to some specific task, process, or activity. In school communities, many tasks, processes, and activities may be handled individually or by groups of people operating in a collaborative style. The work of planning units and lessons, teaching groups of students, supporting the social and emotional growth of students, and meeting the physical and health needs of students may be approached collaboratively. Consider how the use of a collaborative style is applied to such tasks, processes, and activities on behalf of Kurume.

When Kurume was in the fifth grade, Mrs. Harind (the teacher of Kurume's hearing-impaired class) spoke to Mr. Aiello (the fifth-grade teacher) about working together on his thematic unit about the Aztecs. When she suggested that they include Kurume in the fifth-grade classroom, Mr. Aiello was surprised. He had assumed that students like Kurume should be with others "like them." Mrs. Harind explained that it would be valuable for the other fifth-graders to get to know Kurume and for him to get to know them. Mr. Aiello agreed that Kurume also stood to benefit from a rigorous unit on ancient cultures, but he wasn't sure that Kurume could keep up.

Mr. Aiello had received advanced materials from the museum regarding the upcoming exhibit on the Aztecs and was using them to plan a unit for his students. Mrs. Harind knew little about the Aztecs, but she did know a lot about the ways children with hearing impairments develop their language and concepts about the world. She had also learned about the benefits of cooperative

---

**TABLE 4.1  Characteristics of Collaboration**

- Co-equal parties
- Voluntary participation
- Shared responsibility
- Shared accountability
- Joint decision making
- Trusting, respectful relationships
- Mutual support and benefits
- Converging values

learning for oral language development. Perhaps most importantly, she knew a lot about Kurume because she had worked with him for two years in a row.

Mr. Aiello and Mrs. Harind agreed from the outset that they would assure that all their students would be successful and that each student would be challenged to meet very high expectations. To make that happen, they realized, they would have to work together to cover all the bases. They decided to structure the lessons cooperatively so that groups of students would work interdependently over the six-week unit and yet remain individually accountable for their own learning. As their plans took shape, they recognized that the real value in working collaboratively was the fact that they brought such different knowledge and backgrounds to the task.

Mr. Aiello and Mrs. Harind decided to require Kurume to **speech-read** much of the time and to use oral language extensively. But they also began incorporating some basic **American Sign Language** into the unit for all the students to enable his classmates to "speak" to Kurume and to emphasize the importance of language and symbol systems in the development of human cultures. As they planned, their enthusiasm grew, and they realized they wanted to co-teach portions of the unit—sometimes with both teachers in the classroom and other times with only one person in the room. However, their schedules were a bit of a problem, so they had to make many adjustments. For instance, they divided up some of the planning tasks but performed other tasks together. Even though they aimed for efficient use of their time, they found that the planning took longer than it would have if either one had done it alone. But they'll never forget how exciting it was to have another person giving detailed attention to the unit.

In this example, not all the organizational supports were in place for Mrs. Harind and Mr. Aiello to do their collaborative work. They decided to proceed knowing that there would be difficulties. Some of the schedule constraints and the problems they faced have been solved in some schools, but as this example shows, even when supportive structures are not yet fully developed, collaboration can occur.

However, school professionals who continue to work collaboratively in an environment that does not support collaboration by providing collegial planning time or other incentives for working together may find that they are working extra hard to accomplish their

## Extending Your Learning

With the definition of collaboration in mind, examine the nature of the relationship between Mr. Aiello and Mrs. Harind.

1. Was there direct interaction?
2. Was the relationship co-equal?
3. Was this a voluntary interaction?
4. Were they engaged in shared decision making?
5. Were they working toward a common goal?
6. Did trust and respect emerge?
7. What convergence of values is evident?

work. Some professionals have reported that they are working longer and harder just to keep up with the perceived demands of their positions—actions that may forecast complete burnout (French, 1991). Similar results have been documented among all types of school professionals and, indeed, among many professionals who work in helping agencies (Iwanicki & Schwab, 1981).

Yet, we have reason to believe that collaboration among school professionals and with parents, families, and community members will reduce stress and burnout. For example, Fimian (1986) demonstrated that the single most significant mitigating factor in relieving stress among professionals who worked with exceptional children was the social support they received from their colleagues. Information/media specialists, teaching specialists, counselors, psychologists, nurses, and occupational and physical therapists are all likely to suffer stress from the accelerating demands in schools, and they need the support that collaborative relationships provide (Iwanicki & Schwab, 1981).

## ■ SECTION SUMMARY

Inclusive school communities require a shift from exclusion, individualism, and isolation to an emphasis on belongingness, alliances, and mutual support. The latter elements form the basis of collaboration. Collaborative relationships are based on direct interaction among co-equal parties, who voluntarily participate, share responsibility and accountability, make decisions

Educators work collaboratively to solve problems about a student's learning and well-being.

together, grow to trust and respect one another, and begin to move toward more similar value positions. Collaboration requires that parties share in the relationship on a voluntary basis, enter the interaction as co-equal parties, work toward a common goal, and share responsibility for decisions and accountability for the outcomes of the interaction. Furthermore, the relationship is based on shared resources and characterized by increased levels of trust, respect, knowledge, and skills. Collaboration may occur even in environments that are not yet well organized to support it, but the additional planning and meeting time may require some professionals to work harder and longer. The next section elaborates by looking at how various groups of people use the collaborative style to create a sense of community and inclusion among the diverse groups of people.

# The Changing Roles of Team Members

Inclusive school community team members must respond to rapidly changing knowledge and technology. Their titles may remain the same, but their roles and responsibilities are evolving rapidly. Unfortunately, some school community members have continued to cling to outdated images of themselves performing the tasks and activities of education even as societal demands have dramatically altered the requirements.

To create inclusive school communities that respond to the complex needs of diverse students, school community members must assume new ways of doing their work. Specifically, families, students, school professionals, and support personnel face significant changes in their roles, responsibilities, and expectations.

 ## Families

As you learned in Chapter 3, families have experienced profound changes in the responsibilities they have in the educational process. Both at the individual level of advocating for their own children and at the organizational level in helping to clarify and carry out the mission of the school, the voices of families are necessary to inclusive school communities. In this chapter, we emphasize the role of families as partners.

The word **partnership** is now part of the terminology of the majority of school professionals as they work with the parents and families of students with special educational needs (Buswell & Martz, 1987; Lombana, 1983). **Parent-professional partnerships** can be defined as associations between a family and one or more professionals who function collaboratively using effective interpersonal skills in pursuit of a joint interest and common goal. Dunst and Paget (1991) describe the minimal requirements for such a partnership:

- Respect for mutual contributions of resources and expertise (knowledge, skills, time, and so on)

- Willingness to enter into a collaborative arrangement

- Loyalty, trust, honesty, and full disclosure of all "material facts" affecting the joint venture

- Co-equal status and power of the partners

How do school professionals and parents assure that these kinds of partnerships are possible? They begin by addressing each of the four minimal requirements and identifying ways to put them into practice. One way families formalize their contribution to partnerships is by preparing for meetings about their children (see Box 4.1). School professionals have typically come to these meetings with substantial documentation—test scores, **anecdotal records,** and **student products.** Yet, in the past, some parents entered such meetings armed with only their dreams and fears. While these may reflect important information, true partnerships are built on co-equal status. And to create co-equal status, parents must also have a vehicle through which they can contribute vital information about the performance levels their children demonstrate at home. Figure 4.2 contains one example of a form that may be used by parents to organize the information they contribute to the problem-solving process (Long, 1988). For parents who are unable to fill out such forms themselves, the form may become the protocol for an interview in which the school professional assists the family as members articulate their needs. When parents use a form (this one or any other) to preplan the information they will present at a meeting with school professionals, they have moved themselves into a position of parity with everyone else at the meeting. They hold the same advantages that the professionals have by bringing prepared documentation with them.

> **BOX 4.1**
>
> ## Guidelines for Families to Advocate for Their Children
>
> 1. Preplan for meetings.
> 2. Bring advocates to meetings.
> 3. Summarize their child's needs.
> 4. Observe their child in school.
> 5. Talk with their child to determine what he or she wants and needs.
> 6. Set meetings that fit their own schedules.
> 7. Attend conferences with school personnel.
> 8. Share ideas about the best practices with school personnel.

## Students

Because the educational outcomes of inclusive school communities encompass lifelong learning, socioeconomic security and productivity, self-determination, and community participation and support, students need to take on a more central, active role in their learning experiences. In particular, students must assume greater responsibility for their own learning and for that of their peers.

The role of students in creating and maintaining friendships in schools is also vital. Among the many reasons that full inclusion of special education students has been opposed is that the other "typical" students may not accept students with special needs or perhaps may even actively reject them. Apparently, much rejection has occurred in the past—particularly of students with emotional or behavioral challenges. Yet, we know of many examples of children who have shown extraordinary compassion and empathy toward students who have very different behaviors and come from very different backgrounds. At the end of the film *Educating Peter* (Goodwin & Wurzberg, 1992), the boy who had been kicked by Peter early in the year exclaimed, "Peter's one of my best friends now."

Nevertheless, many children with and without disabilities lack friends for a variety of reasons, including their personal appearance, sex, ethnicity, lack of opportunity to socialize, limited interest in or comfort with social interactions, or limited cognitive understanding of social situations (Asher & Renshaw, 1981).

# Parent's Assessment

Both pages to be completed before the IEP Staffing. Use additional paper as needed

Child's Name _____

| What are your child's strengths and areas of difficulty in each of the following areas? | Parent's Assessment (Current Levels of Achievement) | | |
|---|---|---|---|
| | **In Your Community** (at the store, park, church, neighborhood, etc.) | **At Home** (self-care, leisure-time, etc.) | **Working** (chores, responsibility, etc.) |
| **Physical Abilities** • current health status • vision • hearing • motor abilities (crawling, walking, writing, cutting, etc.) | | | |
| **Communication Abilities** • how well your child understands • method of communication (if other than speech) • how well your child makes his/her needs known • how well others understand your child | | | |
| **Thinking Abilities** (cognitive-psychological) • how long your child pays attention • your child's ability to remember • how quickly your child understands something new | | | |
| **Social and Emotional Abilities** • how well your child gets along with others • what your child likes or dislikes • your child's view of him/herself • your child's desirable and undesirable behaviors | | | |

**FIGURE 4.2** ■ Sample Assessment Form for Parents to Organize Key Information

Source: Developed through the Colorado Department of Education by parents of children in Special Education. Reprinted by permission.

| What are your child's strengths and areas of difficulty in each of the following areas? | Parent's Assessment (Current Levels of Achievement) | | |
|---|---|---|---|
| | **In Your Community** (at the store, park, church, neighborhood, etc.) | **At Home** (self-care, leisure-time, etc.) | **Working** (chores, responsibility, etc.) |
| **Developmental or Educational Growth** • how your child learns best • things your child has learned and not learned | | | |
| **Other** • how your child interacts with others who are not like him/her, or with others who do not understand him/her | | | |

| What would you like your child to be able to do in each of these areas: 3 years from now? 1 year from now? | | | |
|---|---|---|---|
| **Physical Abilities** | | | |
| **Communication Abilities** | | | |
| **Thinking Abilities** | | | |
| **Social and Emotional Behavior** | | | |
| **Developmental or Educational Growth** | | | |
| **Other** | | | |

**FIGURE 4.2** ■ *(continued)*

Any or all of these variables, as well as others, could contribute to a child's inability to form and maintain friendships. School professionals who recognize the need can actively promote friendships by encouraging students to engage one another.

During the fifth grade, Kurume had few friends at school because the school wasn't in his home neighborhood and because he had often been in classrooms that were separated from those of his peers. Mrs. Harind and Mr. Aiello used cooperative learning for the unit they collaboratively planned, but they didn't anticipate how difficult it would be for Kurume to gain real friendships with the other fifth-graders. He was a well-adjusted student and had perfectly appropriate interactions with other kids during class. Yet, on the playground, the other students might wave from a distance, but they rarely invited him to join their activities. One day, Mr. Aiello had playground duty and noticed Kurume standing off to one side of the basketball court. He asked Kurume if he knew how to play basketball and if he wanted to join in the game with the boys he knew from class. When Kurume said he did, Mr. Aiello asked the other boys to let him in. When the boys agreed, the ice was broken. Later, Mr. Aiello and Mrs. Harind talked about the playground incident. They decided to get more actively involved in helping Kurume make friends so that the positive results in the classroom could be extended to the playground. They decided to provide some direct instruction to all the students on how to ask to join activities, on what to do when they felt left out, and on how to deal with teasing. Their actions helped students accept greater responsibility for creating alliances.

## School Professionals

For school professionals who work in inclusive school communities, the tasks of assessing, planning, and implementing interventions, lessons, and therapies are only a portion of their role. All school professionals in inclusive school communities should be prepared to assume three major responsibilities—team member, co-teacher, and consultant—each of which depends on the use of a collaborative style.

**TEAM MEMBER** Participating in teamwork may be common now, but it was rarely seen as necessary twenty years ago. Historically, teaching and providing therapy have been individual activities, largely per-

| TABLE 4.2 | **Characteristics of Effective Teams** |
|---|---|

- Clear and elevating goals
- An organizational structure that facilitates the task
- Competent members
- Unified commitment
- A collaborative style
- High standards
- External support and recognition
- Principled leadership

Source: Larson & LaFasto, 1989.

formed alone behind closed doors. Virtually everyone has had some experiences with teams—sometimes frustrating, sometimes gratifying, and sometimes puzzling. You may have wondered why some teams develop a sense of team spirit while others never seem to. Researchers who have studied hundreds of teams have identified eight characteristics of highly effective, well-functioning teams; Table 4.2 lists those characteristics.

Perhaps most importantly, team members must be working toward the same goals, and these goals must be sufficiently clear, urgent, and worthwhile. Team members must be organized in a fashion that helps them get the job done. Good teams organize themselves differently for different kinds of tasks. Team members need to be competent at interpersonal skills, and they need technical competence as well. In education, technical competence translates into current knowledge of their area of specialization, the ability to perform the skills of their specialty, and the highest of ethical standards. In the best teams, members are committed both to the goals of the team and to their relationships with the other members. Team members consider the effects of their individual actions on the functioning of the team as a whole and on other individual team members. Trust emerges in well-functioning teams because members are reliable and have good communication skills. Teams that work well together have high standards for their work. They continually evaluate their outcomes and seek ways to improve how they work together and how they accomplish their purposes. The most successful school-based teams have "official" backing, such that common planning time and the basic resources they need to work together and to address their goals are provided. Finally, the leadership of the team may be provided by a designated member, by a person who emerges as a leader in the group, or collectively by all members.

What can team members do to ensure that the team has principled leadership? First, be aware school teams often operate without the benefit of a designated team leader. This circumstance is not inherently good or bad. In fact, leaderless teams may be quite effective as long as every member understands that numerous leadership functions must be performed by someone on the team. Defined this way, **leadership** is the act of performing one or more of the necessary functions that help the team complete its work while maintaining the relationships of the people who form the team. Well-known functions that help the group address the task at hand include initiating ideas, seeking and giving information, clarifying, elaborating, summarizing, and checking to see if others in the group understand the content of what is being discussed (Benne & Sheats, 1948). Examples of actions that promote healthy social and emotional functioning of the group include encouraging others, expressing feelings, harmonizing, compromising, seeing that silent members get a chance to speak, and applying previously agreed-upon standards to the group's functioning (Benne & Sheats, 1948). Various team members may perform a single leadership function or several of them.

**Principled leadership,** however, goes beyond the performance of leadership functions to include the values or standards held by those who provide the leadership functions. In inclusive school communities, the principled leader (1) helps create a sense of belongingness and meaningful participation among team members, (2) helps facilitate strong alliances and affiliations among team members, and (3) establishes a safe environment in which the team members provide emotional and technical support to one another. Among other things, principled leaders empower team members to be active, yet voluntary contributors; they promote a shared sense of responsibility and accountability and encourage joint decision making. In short, principled leaders in inclusive school communities promote collaboration (Blase et al., 1995).

**CO-TEACHER** Co-teaching is a collaborative arrangement between school professionals in which they create solutions and plan, teach, and modify lessons together—as in the case of Cathy Krautkramer and

## Extending Your Learning

1. What characteristics of effective teams are apparent as you review the story about the Red Team? You may not be able to infer all of the characteristics of the team members from their interactions during a single meeting or even several meetings. Try to use the evidence available, however, to make your best guess. Are their goals clear and worthwhile? What structure do they use? How competent are they? Are they unified in their commitment to their goals and to one another? Do they use a collaborative style? How would you rate the standards they set for themselves? Do they get the external support and recognition teams need?

2. Now, picture yourself sitting in with the leaderless Red Team. What forms might the various leadership functions take? Who initiates the discussion about Kirk? Who helps clarify the issues? What actions would keep the group focused on the problem at hand? What might group members do to encourage everyone's participation?

Mary Kiesau-Bramer in the chapter-opening vignette. School professionals choose to co-teach because it fosters the inclusion of special education students into general education classes (Bawrens, Hourcade, & Friend, 1987) and makes it possible to provide students with a more individualized and diversified learning experience (Friend, Reising, & Cook, 1993). Through co-teaching, school professionals jointly create units, plan lessons, modify lessons for individual needs, and carry out classroom instruction (Warger & Pugach, 1993). The intent is to create a classroom community in which all students are valued members and to develop innovative teaching strategies that would not be possible if only one teacher was present. Moreover, each of the participants in the co-teaching process benefits from the background knowledge and experience of the other. The participants have co-equal standing, with neither party taking a back seat to the other. As Mary and Cathy discovered over time, for co-teaching to work well, the focus of the instruction must provide opportunities for both professionals to be actively involved with students.

The experiences of Mrs. Harind and Mr. Aiello are another good example of co-teaching. Their relationship involved the creation of a unit of study for stu-

## TABLE 4.3    Co-Teaching Formats

- *One teacher, one observer.* One professional holds instructional responsibility while the other collects information on students in the class. Either person may take either role, and they may switch roles at any time.

- *One teacher, one provider of guided practice.* One professional provides individual help and guidance to students while the other provides instruction.

- *Simultaneous teaching.* The content is divided, and each professional provides instruction on one part to half the students at a time. Students then switch places, and each instructor provides the same content to the other group.

- *Parallel teaching.* Both professionals present the same content to portions of the larger group of students.

- *Remedial teaching.* One teacher instructs students who have mastered the material while the other takes students who have not and either re-teaches the material or adapts it in some way so those students are able to master a portion of it.

- *Tag team teaching.* Presenters take turns, with one on and one off. The person who is not presenting at the moment may fill a variety of roles (such as data collection or individual student assistance) or may even leave the room.

- *Speak-and-add teaching.* Both presenters are "on stage" at the same time, with one leading and the other supporting. The lead person is in charge of the content and makes process decisions. The support person adds examples, humor, or other perspectives.

- *Speak-and-chart teaching.* This format extends speak-and-add in that the support role consists of recording ideas on an easel, overhead projector, or chalkboard. Thus, the session has a neutral documenter.

- *Duet teaching.* This format represents the epitome of co-teaching and is possible only with skilled professionals who have done extensive collaborative planning. Both presenters talk, alternating or finishing sentences for each other. They use physical proximity as a tool. They choreograph the physical space; they avoid blocking the speaker and subtly cue each other with looks, proximity, hand gestures, voice tempo, and intonation. They stay focused all the time, with each attentive to the other and to the audience.

---

dents, collaborative lesson planning, discussions about the kinds of modifications needed to ensure success for Kurume, the presentation of lessons to students, and supervision of the work students did in their cooperative groups.

Co-teaching can take many forms; Table 4.3 lists numerous possible arrangements that co-teachers may use according to their purposes. Mary and Cathy applied several of these formats. When they were first feeling their way through co-teaching, they used the **tag team** format. Later, as they became more comfortable with each other and with co-teaching in general, they applied the **Speak-and-Add** and **Duet Teaching** formats.

There are numerous benefits to co-teaching, but there are also some costs (Gable, Arllen, & Cook, 1993). Benefits include increased flexibility to meet academic needs of students and increased innovative capacity through the sharing of materials, ideas, and energy. When school professionals co-teach, they have an enhanced ability to fluidly change student groupings, and they are better able to respond to other student needs. The costs of co-teaching may include an increase in planning time requirements. Also, successful co-teaching relies on a consensus between co-teachers on routines, procedures, rules, discipline, and grading practices. But it takes time to reach consensus in these areas when each of the teachers is used to working in more independent modes.

**CONSULTANT** Consulting is the third responsibility of school professionals in inclusive school communities. Sometimes, in the course of a school year, school professionals, parents, or students find themselves in need of some additional information in order to address instructional or behavioral challenges. In this case, they may seek out a consultant. A **consultant** is a person who engages in a process through which he or she provides information to an individual or a group in order to solve a problem or to learn more about some topic. The consultant works on behalf of a third party, the client.

Sometimes, the consultant is present within the school. School professionals possess unique knowledge and skills because of their preparation experiences, and any one of them may serve a consultant to others at various times. For example, school psychologists have important knowledge about the cognitive and mental health needs of students. School nurses hold specialized knowledge regarding certain physical conditions and health needs. Speech/language therapists, physical therapists, and occupational therapists all possess unique sets of information regarding the communicative and physical functioning of students. Special education teachers are experts in learning strategies and needs, while classroom teachers bring curriculum expertise and knowledge of group management.

Whether the consultant is a person who works in the same setting or one who enters the relationship from outside, consultation is defined as a process rather than a style of interaction because it consists of definable steps, which are listed in Box 4.2. When the consultant is external to the group seeking assistance, steps 1 and 2 are necessary and require substantial time. When the consultant is internal—for example, when Ms. Matheson, Kirk's special education teacher, works with other team members in the same building—these steps naturally are abbreviated. There are numerous variations in and perspectives on the consulting process (West & Idol, 1987) but the following characteristics are generally attributable to the process:

- *It is indirect.* The person in the consultant role provides no direct services to the third party (often the student). In the case of school personnel who consult with one another, the actions that result from the consulting episode are carried out by the consultee rather than the consultant.

- *It is triadic.* The work that is done during the consulting episode is done on the behalf of a third person. In the case of schools, the third person (client) is usually a student but could be a parent or other school professional.

- *It is voluntary.* The work that is done during the consulting episode is futile if the plans are not carried out or are in some way sabotaged. Although there are cases in which a well-intentioned administrator asks one school professional (or an outside consultant) to become a consultant to another

---

**BOX 4.2**

## Guidelines for the Consultation Process

1. Enter into the relationship.
2. Establish a personal working relationship.
3. Determine the nature of the consultative needs.
4. Give advice, information, materials, and services to the consultee that addresses his or her needs.
5. Exit the relationship.

---

who doesn't particularly want consulting services, such situations are rarely productive. Nonvoluntary relationships yield little.

- *It is based on an expert relationship.* The consultant must possess the knowledge and skill to address the problem, and the consultee must have respect for the consultant's expertise. Even if expertise exists, the lack of respect from the consultee negates the possible success of applying the expertise.

- *It addresses the consultee's problem.* The challenge, the rub, the problem, or dilemma "belongs" to the consultee. The consultant is outside the problem and does not "own" it.

- *It maintains differentiated responsibility and accountability for outcomes.* Because ownership of the problem remains with the consultee, there is no expectation that the consultant will actually carry out the intervention that has been proposed to solve the problem. A good consultant is conscientious about the quality of suggestions and the quality of the design of interventions, but ultimately implementation is beyond the consultant's control.

School professionals often find themselves playing the role of consultant. When they do, it is very useful to quickly review the characteristics of consultation and to recognize that the expectations of consulting are different from the expectations when one works collaboratively with others as a team member or in a co-teaching relationship.

Let's examine the variety of responsibilities that Mrs. Steele, the special education teacher in Annie's school, assumes during the course of her workday. Notice how often she has to shift between approaches. Sometimes, she provides individual instruction to Annie when Annie is in a general education classroom. Mrs. Steele sits beside Annie and works on a lesson that is quite different in content and approach from the lesson that the other third-graders are engaging in at the moment. When Mrs. Steele works this way with Annie, she is using an individual approach—the "I do" approach—because she holds full responsibility for the outcome of that instructional episode and she has full control over the planning and execution of the instruction. We traditionally call this role "teacher."

Later in the day, when Mrs. Steele meets with Annie's classroom teacher, Mrs. Stevens, to collaboratively plan lessons for Annie, she begins to share the responsibility for and control over the instruction and the outcomes. The role she now plays is the collaborative—the "we do"—one. When responsibilities for planning and instruction are shared between two or more school professionals, each gains in terms of his or her own sphere of professional influence, but each gives up some of the control that was typical of more traditional professional roles.

When Mrs. Steele provides a written lesson plan for Trudy, the para-educator, to carry out in the music class, she has surrendered a little more control over the situation, but again, she also has expanded her sphere of influence. This role of supervising and directing the work of para-educators falls into the "you do" approach. Even though Mrs. Steele has directed Trudy's work, she has little control while Trudy is out of her sight. During the times that Trudy provides direct services to Annie, Mrs. Steele is working elsewhere in the building providing special education services to another student.

Every other Tuesday, during lunchtime, Mrs. Steele meets with the group of students who have agreed to participate in Annie's **circle of friends.** They discuss all the ways that Annie can learn to do some of the things that typical kids do on the playground and in the lunchroom. Sometimes, Mrs. Steele participates as a team member—listening, sharing ideas, and providing principled group leadership. Other times, she shifts into the collaborative mode and uses her group facilitation skills to keep the discussion going. And sometimes, she serves as a consultant to the group, providing specific information and direction on how to address Annie's health or academic needs.

When students leave the circle meeting with new ideas about how to talk to Annie and how to interact with her, Mrs. Steele thinks to herself, "I need them to carry out their ideas in order to make Annie's day the most productive day that I can. I can't do it without them!" She knows that while she and the students are thinking and planning together, her role is characteristic of the collaborative approach. But when she sends the students off to do what they do best, she has very little control but lots of influence. Her approach has shifted, now, into a consultative one—she helps, but the students really do the work.

Finally, at the end of the school day, Mrs. Steele meets with the sixth-grade team during their planning hour to discuss curriculum-based assessment and its uses for providing individual supports to all sixth-graders. When she does so, she fully realizes that she is now serving in the role of a consultant and, as such, has moved into the "I help, you do" mode. She will not be the person to carry out the curriculum-based assessment procedures, nor will she have any control over how they choose to use (or decline to use) her ideas. Her sphere of influence at this point is great, but her control is very low.

In this vignette, Mrs. Steele shifts among the three approaches fluidly. She does so because her students require different types of interventions throughout her day. It is demanding for her to shift among these roles so frequently. But it was even more difficult for her five years ago when, as a newcomer to the school, she had to establish working relationships with many people while trying to gain a good grasp of her students' needs and the district curriculum. Over time, she has acquired both the skills and the working relationships necessary to most effectively address the educational needs of the students.

## Support Personnel

Several of the situations you have read about pertaining to Annie, Kurume, Kirk, Michael, and Tanya have involved paraprofessionals and other support personnel in schools, as well as school professionals and parents. Shifting responsibilities affect people who hold these other important positions in schools. In this section, we describe the responsibilities of paraprofessionals, school volunteers, clerical/secretarial workers, custodial and food service workers, and transportation workers/bus drivers. Historically, support personnel have not been viewed as having critical responsibilities in meeting the educational and social needs of students. However, without the focused work of all personnel involved, inclusive school communities cannot maximize the opportunities for all learners.

**PARAPROFESSIONALS** Paraprofessionals are paid school employees who assume substantial responsibility for the delivery of educational services to students in both general education classes and special education and remedial programs. The broad title "paraprofessional" is applied to a variety of school workers who provide essential instructional or other educational services alongside or under the supervision of a school professional (Pickett, 1984). In this book, we use the word **para-educator** to refer to a person who provides instruction to individuals or groups; supports students in classrooms; interprets from one language to another; monitors and supervises students in lunchrooms, halls, and bus loading zones and on playgrounds; and works under the direction of a school professional who holds ultimate responsibility for the outcomes of the instructional program (French & Pickett, 1997). In some places, the title of "teachers' aide," "educational assistant," or "instructional assistant" is used to identify these school workers, but these job titles are rapidly being replaced. Para-educators work in remedial programs, in bilingual and English as a second language (ESL) programs, in special education, and in typical classrooms. Some middle and high schools also employ people as locker room aides, job coaches, and transition assistants.

Another subgroup of school workers who fall under the general classification of paraprofessionals is sometimes called "paratherapists." Although the title is not yet widely recognized, Longhurst (1996) points out that paratherapists deliver various kinds of therapy to students under the supervision and guidance of certified speech/language therapists, occupational therapists, and physical therapists.

According to the 1997 reauthorization of IDEA, paraprofessionals may assist in the provision of essential, direct services (instruction and supervision) to students, but they must be appropriately trained and supervised. The law now recognizes the important roles that these workers have played for many years. Paraprofessionals provide such instructional services whether the professional to whom they report is or is not on the premises. Although some school districts insist on the physical presence of the professional, most do not. As in the medical profession, in which paramedics do their substantive work outside the physical presence of the supervising physician, paraprofessionals may do their substantive work without school professionals being present as long as a written plan guides their work and their work is directed, monitored, and evaluated by the professional.

Paraprofessionals have been employed in schools since the early 1950s, but their roles have changed substantially since then (Pickett, 1989). In the early years, their assignments were primarily clerical; they took attendance, graded papers, collected lunch money, and took field trip notes (Gartner, 1971). But this is rarely the case now. As the training, career development, and certification programs for paraprofessionals have increased, so have their levels of responsibility (Pickett, 1994).

Paraprofessionals' duties vary from district to district, from school to school, and from professional to professional because of differences in the community, district or school policy, and tradition, as well as differences in the preferences, talents, or needs of the supervising professionals. Often, the preferences and talents of the person who holds the paraprofessional position are the deciding factors in determining precise job duties. For example, Trudy feels confident in her ability to carry out Mrs. Steele's plans for Annie during music class. Mrs. Yelich has highly developed skills in managing disruptive behaviors and helping students (including Kirk) calm themselves, something Trudy would be very uncomfortable doing. Ms. Acquisto, the para-educator working with Ms. Nguyen, the second-grade teacher, goes into the second-grade classroom to teach the students there about sign language when she encounters children at the water fountain teasing Kurume about his use of sign. Margie, the health aide in Tanya's school, often performs health-related services for Tanya and other children there. Margie is supervised by the school nurse, who visits periodically and who has provided case-specific, on-the-job instructions and coaching related to Tanya's health needs and those of the other children. In each case, the transdisciplinary team determines the precise duties of the paraprofessional but considers the personal strengths and limitations of the individual and the particular training the person has received.

No matter what duties are assigned to a particular paraprofessional, it is the team of professionals that holds the ultimate responsibility for diagnosing instructional needs, prescribing and implementing teaching strategies and instructional environments, and assessing learning outcomes (Pickett, Vasa, & Steckelberg, 1993). It is the responsibility of the paraprofessional to carry out tasks under the supervision of one or more school professionals.

The intuitive good sense that most paraprofessionals display while working with students notwithstanding, paraprofessionals in schools still receive little formal preparation for the duties they assume (French & Cabell, 1993). IDEA now requires appropriate training for paraprofessionals who assist in instruction, and many professionals agree that preservice preparation programs are important to ensure the safety and welfare of students, but few ongoing, self-supporting preparation programs exist (French & Cabell, 1993; Longhurst & Witmer, 1994; Pickett, 1986). School districts, state offices of education, educational service units, and classified employees unions are each assuming more responsibility for the in-service training of paraprofessionals.

In spite of the increased use of paraprofessionals and the legitimate position they now hold in special education law, little is known about the impact of paraprofessionals on achievement or other student outcomes (Jones & Bender, 1993). Yet, paraprofessionals are being employed in increasing numbers across the country as the combined effects of immigration, inclusion, socioeconomic disadvantage, and teacher shortages continue to affect the personnel decisions made by school administrators (French & Pickett, 1997; Pickett, 1994).

**SCHOOL VOLUNTEERS**  In contrast to paraprofessionals, school volunteers work without pay. Yet, volunteers often create important linkages to the community and provide valuable services to students. The absence of pay implies that their attendance and performance is unregulated and that their services have been deemed nonessential in a legal sense, but volunteer workers contribute substantially to many school programs. At the elementary level, room "mothers" and parent and grandparent volunteers often read with children, providing a level of one-to-one adult contact that some children desperately need. At all levels, parents and other community volunteers provide enrichment for students by sharing their hobbies, their professional skills and knowledge, and their time. Many programs for intellectually gifted children rely on the mentoring provided by community volunteers.

Athletic, vocational, and fine arts programs also rely heavily on community resources for enrichment opportunities for students. Schools of the twenty-first century will continue to seek even more ways to bring the community into school and to expand the experiences of students outside the school.

**CLERICAL/SECRETARIAL WORKERS**  Clerical workers and secretarial personnel may also play vital roles in the delivery of services to special education students and in the education of all children in a community. They are paid employees who often provide the first point of contact between parents and school professionals. For example, secretaries and office clerks often know about the financial condition of a family because of their management of subsidized and free school meal programs. Also, they often are the only school workers who have complete information about attendance patterns for students and are more likely to hold an overall picture of a student's behavior over the course of a school day. They see the children who need to call home; they know who is sick that day; and they might be the only school employees to talk to the parents when they pick children up for doctor and dental appointments.

These workers are also in a unique position to support certain kinds of behavioral interventions because they tend to stay in certain locations in the building throughout the school day. Secretarial personnel frequently are included in the planning and decision-making meetings for students. For example, in Chapter 6, on classroom and behavior management, we mention the technique called **antiseptic bouncing.** This odd term simply means that a child is sent away from a potentially explosive or dangerous situation before someone gets hurt.

For example, an office worker at Deer Field Elementary, Charleen, has a prearranged, standing agreement with Ms. Pope, the classroom teacher, that any time Michael shows up in the office with a piece of paper clenched in his fist, she will ask him to sit down and wait for a reply. Michael thinks that his teacher has selected him to run an important errand for her, while Ms. Pope figures she has just avoided a confrontation with him over some classroom issue. By "bouncing" Michael out of her room, Ms. Pope has avoided losing time from instruction, prevented Michael from having an outburst, and averted an unnecessary confrontation. Charleen is the logical person to assist Ms. Pope because she is most consistently and readily available.

**CUSTODIAL AND FOOD SERVICE WORKERS** Although vital for reasons such as nutritional needs, health issues, school cleanliness, and personnel safety, these school workers also are potential contributors to the instructional process. Often, custodial and food service workers have job skills that can be used to illuminate math or physical science concepts. Like secretarial/clerical and transportation personnel, they can sometimes be called upon to support the behavioral intervention plans for students and may provide overall perspectives on students' behavior in hallways, restrooms, bus loading zones, and other campus locations.

For example, Virginia, the head custodian at Alsup Elementary School, made close friends with young Ryan when the third-grade team decided that he sometimes needed a safe "getaway" during the day to release excess energy. Once or twice a week, over the course of several months, Virginia and Ryan were seen mopping the lunchroom floor together. Ryan basked in the additional one-on-one attention and worked off some of his seemingly boundless energy doing physical tasks. Fifteen minutes of activity outside the classroom seemed to be enough to help him reapply himself to academic tasks. After Ryan's mother died, Virginia played an important "significant other" role for him as well. The third-grade team began to include Virginia in their discussions about Ryan because of the important part she came to play in Ryan's education.

**TRANSPORTATION WORKERS/BUS DRIVERS** Transportation personnel are integral to the programs of many special education students. They may provide a vital link between home and school. Sometimes, they relay messages from parents who bring their children to the bus stop to the school professionals or paraprofessionals who greet the buses. They may play active roles in the referral processes for special education, and they can help determine the effects of interventions. And they may be involved in individual behavior plans or extensions of classroom learning activities.

For example, Peggy, a bus driver at Deer Field Elementary, often stopped in to speak with Ms. Pope about Jason, who was sometimes disruptive on the way to school in the morning. Ms. Pope appreciated the advance warnings about Jason's emotional state. In turn, Ms. Pope gave Peggy some helpful tips on how to help Jason manage his own behavior on the bus. Peggy realized that supporting students like Jason meant that everyone had to communicate and partici-

pate in providing that support. Inclusive school communities must capitalize on the strengths of every support person in the school to provide appropriate role models and to play the role of significant other for students as needed. Teams of school professionals and paraprofessionals cannot do their jobs in isolation. Neither can support personnel alone. Together, however, they can work to support the education plans for all students.

## ■ SECTION SUMMARY

Expectations for families, students, school professionals, and support personnel have changed in recent years. In inclusive school communities, families and schools work in partnership to promote positive outcomes for students. Students provide support and friendship to one another. School professionals juggle the roles of team member, co-teacher, and consultant, all of which are founded on the principles of collaboration. And support personnel provide vital services to students, families, and school professionals. Although often untrained and/or unpaid, they are important to students' safety and welfare.

# Developing Collaborative Skills

Three vital processes permit families, students, school professionals, and support personnel to become skilled collaborators: (1) solving problems, (2) dealing with differences, and (3) managing ourselves and our time.

## Solving Problems

The need to join together to solve problems is the basis for many of the collaborative interactions school professionals experience. Teams function most efficiently and effectively when they have a preestablished problem-solving process. Waiting until the inevitable crisis occurs is the least effective way to decide how to proceed.

Some teams think that they are using a collaborative problem-solving process during their meetings,

## The Collaborative Problem-Solving Process

**Step 1:** Publicly recognize the existence of and define the problem.
  a. Describe what the problem is in terms of needs, not in terms of competing solutions. If insufficient data exist to define the problem clearly and completely, get more information. (If this is necessary, determine who will gather the data, what data will be collected, and when it will be done, and plan another meeting to review the data.)
  b. Write it down so everyone can see exactly what it is.
  c. Determine whom it involves.
  d. Describe when and where it happens.
  e. Decide how serious it is.
  f. Determine its causes and contributing factors.

**Step 2:** Decide whether to try to solve the problem, to address the need, or to disengage from the process. If you disengage, stop here; if you decide to try to solve it, go on to step 3.

**Step 3:** Decide on the criteria for a successful solution.
  a. Determine the standards that absolutely must be met.
  b. Be sure that the standards are consistent with the team's values.
  c. Identify circumstances or standards that would turn an acceptable solution into an ideal one.

**Step 4:** Generate possible alternative solutions.
  a. If only one solution is generated, stop and reexamine the problem, as stated.
  b. If any team member suggests that there is only one solution, sound the alarm!

  c. Generate a list of at least three alternatives without evaluating them.
  d. Employ every creative idea-generating strategy possible.

**Step 5:** Compare each alternative to the criteria.
  a. Either discard or redesign any solution that doesn't meet the standards.
  b. Decide which alternatives best match the desirable criteria.
  c. Decide whether the solutions might cause new problems.
  d. Examine and evaluate the risks the solutions pose. Is the potential outcome worth the potential risk?
  e. Examine the possible interactive effects of the solutions. Could a more powerful solution be achieved by combining alternatives? Would there be conflicts among alternatives if they were used together?

**Step 6:** Select one or more alternatives to implement.
  a. Write down the alternatives that are selected and the rationale for each selection. Be specific about what exactly is going to be done.
  b. Determine who will do what.
  c. Establish a timeline for implementation of the solution.

**Step 7:** Plan how to monitor, document, and evaluate the selected alternatives.
  a. Determine what data would constitute sufficient evidence that the solution is or isn't working.
  b. Establish a timeline for collecting that information.
  c. Establish a meeting time to examine the collected information.

only to find that feelings of mistrust and suspicion have cropped up. Often, the source of these ill feelings is a haphazard problem-solving process that leads to conflicting conceptions of what the problem is and what solutions are needed, judgmental views of who is at fault for the failure to solve the problem, and frustration that the problem still exists.

Box 4.3 contains a collaborative problem-solving process for team members to adopt before they reach the frustration point. This process is not an easy one to implement, nor can it be quickly implemented. Experienced teams can minimize the time it takes to complete the process, but even they will admit that it requires sustained effort. Let's examine the seven steps in greater detail and discuss the applications of each step to real-life situations.

**STEP 1: RECOGNIZING AND DEFINING THE PROBLEM** Many individuals want to ignore this step because they assume that everyone sees the problem in precisely the same way that they do. In most groups, however, nothing could be further from the truth. Rarely do two people see a situation in exactly the same way. Making erroneous assumptions about the nature of the problem early on can lead to major errors later on in the process. Albert Einstein once spoke of the importance of identifying the problem: "The formulation of a problem is often more essential than its solution, which may be merely a matter of . . . skill. To raise new questions, new possibilities, to regard old questions from a new angle, requires creative imagination and marks real advance in science" (cited in Getzels, 1982).

Conflicts and dilemmas that arise rarely present themselves as problems capable of easy resolution. They often have to be conceptually manipulated and formulated to enable any movement toward productive solutions. In every case, the quality of the problem recognition and definition precedes the quality of the solution that will be attained.

Sometimes school professionals make the mistake of breezing through the first step of the problem-solving process. Perhaps they assume that they know the nature of the problem or that they have enough information about the causes and the patterns of the problem to solve it.

Problems that are stated in terms of competing solutions or agendas also disrupt our ability to get to the heart of the issue. For example, in response to the biting incident that Kirk was involved in at the beginning of the school year, recall that the Red Team had some initial difficulty in getting started on this problem-solving process. They wasted an entire meeting discussing the challenges presented by Kirk's behavior in terms of the solutions that some team members secretly favored. Only when Mr. Fairchild and Ms. Matheson pointed this out were they able to get back on track.

Schools spend untold hours implementing solutions to problems that are poorly or erroneously defined. Problem identification is both the most frequently neglected and the single most critical step in the process. At the root of the answer to any problem is a clearly stated, well-defined question; at the core of every effective solution is a productively defined problem. Sometimes, students' problems are compounded by interventions that serve only to promote new behavioral or learning problems. At best, haphazardly applied and misplaced solutions waste time and frustrate students. At worst, poor solutions do significant damage to students.

## STEP 2: DECIDING WHETHER TO TRY TO SOLVE THE PROBLEM, TO ADDRESS THE NEED, OR TO DISENGAGE FROM THE PROCESS

Not every problem needs to be solved—or, indeed, can be solved. If the group defines the problem as one that is clearly outside its sphere of influence and control, then there is no point in continuing to fret about it. The team may choose at this point to redefine the problem as something that can be addressed by school personnel and then to continue through the problem-solving process, or it may decide simply to live with the dilemma.

## STEP 3: DECIDING ON THE CRITERIA FOR A SUCCESSFUL SOLUTION

Deciding the criteria by which solutions are to be judged is crucial in teams whose members have secret agendas or competing purposes. Yet, this step is often neglected. Knowing the criteria by which a solution will be framed is important even when team members get along well.

For example, as the Red Team members moved through the steps of the collaborative problem-solving process, they established criteria by which to determine which of the solutions they generated would be used to help Kirk. They agreed on only three: (1) that all supports and interventions had to maintain Kirk's dignity, (2) that all supports and interventions had to be nonaversive, and (3) that acceptable alternatives had to meet Kirk's needs.

The members of the Red Team are certainly very different people, but they do have some values in common. Other teams in which members hold drastically different values have more trouble with this step. The criteria that are selected are inevitably value-based. If any of the Red Team members had been convinced that punishment was an appropriate response to Kirk's behavior, this step would have taken much more time and effort. Negotiating agreement among people who hold conflicting values is difficult and time-consuming, but it is critical to the process. Without some level of shared values, agreement on acceptable solutions is impossible.

## STEP 4: GENERATING POSSIBLE ALTERNATIVE SOLUTIONS

There are numerous methods by which to generate possible alternative solutions. The most familiar (but not necessarily the most effectively used) method is brainstorming. In this process, group members suggest ideas as they think of them, facilitating their own thinking by listening to and building on the ideas generated by other group members. Effective brainstorming occurs when all the ideas that are offered are initially accepted and when lots of ideas are generated. Usually, all the ideas are written down, without editing, for all group members to see. Although there is obviously a point of diminishing returns, a greater volume of ideas and proposals generally leads to higher-quality decisions. The adventurousness of participants tends to be compromised by premature evaluation of ideas, so brainstorming processes are predicated on the initial acceptance of all ideas.

*Being Creative in Generating Alternatives* Schools cannot solve today's problems with yesterday's solutions or with yesterday's information. Many school professionals are virtual "warehouses" of information—they have collected vast quantities of facts. Although knowledge is essential to creative solutions, knowledge alone is not sufficient. Creative thinking about curriculum issues, instruction methods, classroom management, and behavior management requires a willingness to try various approaches. Sometimes, school professionals use foolish or impractical ideas as stepping-stones to practical new ideas; sometimes, they break the rules and hunt for ideas in unusual places (von Oech, 1983). In doing so, they set themselves up both for new possibilities and for change. For example, one special education teacher who enjoyed participating in contests on the radio got her whole team involved. Her medium may be unconventional, but she worked with her team to address several aspects of the language arts and math curricula in this way. Her students investigated the odds of winning such contests and used game show formats to quiz themselves on material in social studies and science.

*Breaking the Routine* We all have developed many routines in our lives, and for the most part, these routines serve us well. Sometimes, however, when we most need to be creative, remaining in routine thought patterns prevents us from exercising our creative capabilities. These routine thought patterns that hinder our thinking have been called "mental locks" (von Oech, 1983). We can release our creative energy as we think about the alternative solutions to school-related issues by breaking the routine and "unlocking" our thinking.

*Weighing Single Versus Multiple Alternatives* Nothing could be further from the truth than the idea that there exists a single right answer to any given problem. The

philosopher Emilé Chautier once said, "Nothing is more dangerous than an idea when it is the only one you have." More recently, Maslow (1970) added to Chautier's idea by saying, "When the only tool you have is a hammer, then everything starts to look like a nail." One of the ways that school professionals avoid this trap is by continuing to search for additional potential answers, sometimes rewording the question or problem in order to stimulate the process. For instance, when the Red Team reworded the problem from "What can we do to Kirk to get him to behave?" to "How can we help Kirk achieve successful peer relationships and acceptable academic outcomes?" they generated many more possibilities that met their criteria.

*Changing Patterns of Operation* One feature of human cognition is the ability to recognize patterns that help us to generalize and understand our environment. But sometimes these patterns inhibit creativity because people are reluctant to think beyond the recognized pattern. For example, when Kurume was about 7 years old, he was using the drinking fountain when another boy came out of the second-grade room. The boy began to make fun of Kurume by putting his thumbs in his ears, waving his fingers, and singing loudly, "Nyaa-na-na-na-na!" Young Kurume ran sobbing to Ms. Acquisto, the para-educator in the hearing impaired class. Later, Ms. Nguyen (the second-grade teacher), Ms. Jerzicky (the hearing impaired teacher), and Ms. Acquisto met to discuss the problem. At first, their ideas centered around ways to prevent children from the two classes from running into one another in the halls. But then it occurred to them that they could "break" the unspoken, unwritten rule of segregation. Just because they had always kept kids separate didn't mean that they had to continue to do so. They decided, instead, to find more ways to get the groups of kids together. Only when they decided to change the pattern of operation were they free to expand on the possibilities.

*Weighing Practicality* Given declining budgets and diminishing resources, teachers realize the futility of asking for additional assistance or materials if these are likely to cost much. Sometimes, they let this attitude of "impoverishment" influence the way they generate alternatives and prejudge school-related alternatives on the basis of practicality.

At a recent workshop on instructional adaptations, the school professionals at Humphreys Elementary (where Annie is a student) were asked to consider a

Diverse learners team up in small groups to enhance one another's learning.

new design for a soft drink can that featured a thin "leg" and a handle. The list of ideas related to its practicality the fifth-grade teachers generated included the following:

- Useful for camping—stick the bottom into the ground
- Practical for picnic tables—stick the bottom through the cracks
- More practical in the car than anything currently available—simply drill a small hole in the dashboard to support it
- Practical for airplanes or boats—simply drill a hole in the fold-down table

Their ingenuity was impressive. The workshop leader commented after the brainstorming activity that he anticipated that some participants would refuse to discuss the practical aspects of the can. He thought they might focus on all the things wrong with it. He reviewed all their lists and noted that, in many cases, the "practicality" of the mug depended on an adaptation to the environment. So then he asked three questions:

1. "How is it that you can think of practical aspects of a soft drink can in terms of adapting the environment, yet it is so difficult to think about adapting the environment for students who have hyperactivity disorder or who don't use oral language?"

2. "How is that you refrained from noting all the unsatisfactory aspects of the mug, yet you spend hours commiserating about the less desirable aspects of children who have attention problems?"

3. "Why not think about the practicality of alternative solutions in terms of changing the expectations, the supports, the structures, the organization, or the dynamics of classrooms, just as you thought about changing the surfaces, the environments, and the uses for the soft drink can?"

*Crossing Boundaries* As school professionals work together more closely, they are understandably a little nervous about crossing boundaries or stepping on one another's toes. It's no wonder. Specialization has become a fact of life. Because there is so much information available in every field, to become proficient, we must narrow our focus and limit our field of study. When a group of people is trying to generate new ideas, however, narrow perspectives can limit creativity. Problems may be stated too narrowly, and the group may neglect to appreciate the variety of knowledge or experience members have to offer.

In effective problem-solving groups, members depend on one another to contribute ideas that no one else would have thought of. For example, when Annie was in Mrs. Stevens' third-grade class, the team of people (some of whom had attended the instructional adaptations workshop) who were involved with Annie met to determine all the adaptations that needed to be made in Annie's learning environments. Trudy, the para-educator, mentioned that Annie often was left alone during math time because the other children were doing math activities that Annie couldn't do. This led to a lengthy discussion of all the typical third-grade things that Annie couldn't ever be expected to accomplish. Feeling a little discouraged, the team decided to start over with a fresh approach. Members began crossing boundaries by sharing information that allowed them to think about other skills that Annie could be working on that used the same types of math materials the other students used. Suddenly, the occupational therapist (OT), who had been silent up until this time, asked what materials they were using. Mrs. Stevens described the variety of **manipulative objects** they used, including popsicle sticks, interlocking plastic cubes, plastic pieces in geometric shapes, and beans. The OT offered to show Mrs. Stevens and several third-graders how those materials could be used to help Annie practice the very same skills that she worked on with Annie during their weekly session. The result of this planning session was that Annie's occupational therapy is now being enhanced by daily practice sessions—during math—monitored by people who are not licensed occupational therapists. The members of Annie's team crossed artificial boundaries and surmounted self-imposed limitations when they began to share knowledge and expertise with one another.

**STEP 5: COMPARING EACH ALTERNATIVE TO THE CRITERIA**   At this stage, the team applies the criteria that they have predetermined to the list of ideas they have generated. For example, the Red Team that worked on the challenges presented by Kirk examined each of the alternatives that had been generated and decided that each one met all the criteria. So, rather than eliminating anything at this point, they moved on to the next step. If any of their potential solutions had conflicted with the criteria, they would have discarded them.

**STEP 6: SELECTING ONE OR MORE ALTERNATIVES TO IMPLEMENT**   In this phase, the team decides among the remaining alternatives. Often, there are more ideas than can reasonably be implemented, so teams have to apply common sense in choosing those that will be easiest to implement and most likely to succeed. For example, the Red Team weighed the following alternatives:

■ The "peer coaches in PE" and **"peer assistants"** alternatives both met the criterion of providing Kirk with a sense of affiliation and belongingness. The team discussed the possible benefits of or drawbacks to using them in combination. Would there be too much overlap of energy and effort? Or would the use of one strategy end up enhancing the other? Could they achieve a more powerful effect by combining them? In the end, they decided to try both but established a priority order.

■ The "goal sheet" met the criteria but would require some additional work on Ms. Matheson's part.

■ "Self-removal" meant that Kirk might be leaving class temporarily. This made some team members very nervous, but others felt that it was worth trying. In the end, they decided to try it in some classes but not in others.

■ "Para-educators attention" not only met the criteria but also reassured the more reluctant teachers that they were not expected to implement all these ideas alone. Ms. Matheson would have to juggle her schedule a little to make it possible for Ms. Yelich to get to each of the classes, and she thought that it would take a few days to get this done. They agreed to start this intervention on the following Monday morning.

**STEP 7: PLANNING HOW TO MONITOR, DOCUMENT, AND EVALUATE THE SELECTED ALTERNATIVES**   Finally, the team must decide how it will know if its interventions are really working to accomplish the goals. Here, team members have to come to an agreement on what information needs to be collected, how that will be done, who will do it, and when they will meet to look it over. The Red Team's story illustrates how it accomplished this final step. When the Red Team reached this stage, various team members agreed to collect information and to teach Kirk how to monitor his own behavior.

# Dealing with Differences

Problem solving alone is not sufficient for collaborative processes to work. Collaborators need to be able to deal effectively with their differences. In schools, like anywhere else, it is easier to work with some people than others. School personnel tend to be quite good at recognizing good working relationships in schools when they see them, but they are often at a loss for words when asked to list the qualities that make them good. The more clearly school professionals are able to articulate the qualities that make a working relationship productive, the more likely they are to be able to duplicate those qualities as they work with others.

It is unrealistic to expect that school professionals, families, students, and support personnel will engage in the challenges of daily work in schools without disagreement. But people who deal well with differences tend to maintain a good balance between their emotional responses (like anger, frustration, joy, or excitement) to situations and their cognitive responses. They also tend to try to understand the other person's perspective and to possess good communication skills. In addition, they both do what they say they will do and can predict whether others will do the same. They are not easily deceived into expecting a level of dependability from others that is not likely to be forthcoming. Furthermore, they frequently use persuasion as a means of changing the minds of others, rather than attempting to force others' opinions or attitudes. Finally, people who work together and consistently manage their differences well are accepting of one another. They recognize both the strengths and the limitations of one another, and they work to compensate for them and to help one another improve.

While these characteristics of effective relationships are well documented (Fisher & Brown, 1988), variations in styles and personalities allow for a wide range of strategies that are effective in collaborative work groups. To assess the effectiveness of these strategies, ask the following questions:

1. *Is the strategy independent of disagreement?* A good strategy doesn't depend on shared values to work. Agreement makes working together easier and maybe more fun, but a good strategy works even when group members don't agree.

2. *Is the strategy independent of concessions?* One member should not have to give in or demand that others do so for a strategy to work.

3. *Is the strategy independent of partisan perceptions?* There are multiple perspectives to any situation, and seeing it from one perspective does not make the other perspectives wrong.

4. *Is the strategy independent of reciprocity?* Members should not wait for the other side to engage in exemplary behavior, nor should they assume that their example will be followed.

5. *Is the strategy independent of permanent "sides"?* Members should be open to persuasion and to revising their views about who is on their side. Former adversaries may become allies.

The strategy that passes all these tests can be said to be unconditionally constructive. Fisher and Brown (1988) emphasize that these guidelines are not about how to be "good" or "saintly" but rather about how to be effective. They explain that the guidelines "derive from a selfish, hard-headed concern with what each of us can do, in practical terms, to make a relationship work better" (p. 38).

By engaging in unconditionally constructive strategies for dealing with differences in teams, we stand a much better chance of addressing the pervasive problems that schools of the twenty-first century will face. Without unconditionally constructive strategies, teams often break down when disagreements arise, and they lose their ability to solve the problems. The number of possible problems that teams may experience as they attempt to work together and to deal with differences is staggering. Collaboration is possible only when people who work together are able to deal with differences. To accomplish this, they must monitor both the way in which they work together and the outcomes of their efforts.

# Managing Ourselves and Our Time

The third skill necessary for successful collaborative relationships involves attending to ourselves and our own responsibilities for setting goals and managing our time. Many school professionals sound the age-old lament, "There's just not enough time!" Some time management systems help people organize the tasks they have taken on, finding time for each task, without causing them to rethink their choices. The real challenge is to manage ourselves—our goals and priorities (Covey, 1990).

Consider Mrs. Matheson's experience. She was attending an after-school workshop on time management. The speaker asked the participants to turn to one another and "complain about what gets in the way of getting the results you want for yourself and your students." Without a moment's hesitation, Mrs. Matheson recited this list:

- Not knowing what to do first—multiple demands on my time
- Too many things to do
- Interruptions (from the office, phone calls from parents, students stopping me in the hall or dropping by my office)
- Behavior crises
- Paperwork
- My own procrastination
- Trouble saying "no"
- Home and personal life demands

If we want to create inclusive school communities, then community members should examine their self-management in light of that goal. What self-management skills help? Box 4.4 lists some suggestions; let's examine these guidelines in more detail.

**CONSIDERING YOUR PURPOSES** There always will be multiple demands on the time and energy of all school personnel, so it is critical to establish both a personal and a collective vision about what your inclusive community will look like. A clear view of what can be changed and what issues are beyond influence must be shared by people who work together in schools. The response to multiple demands depends on this vision of what can and should be done.

**KNOWING YOUR ROLES** Every school professional plays many different roles throughout the day in addition to the one of "teacher." In a previous section, you read about three roles that school professionals sometimes assume: team member, co-teacher, consultant. In addition, some school professionals supervise paraprofessionals by planning for and directing their work.

For example, Mrs. Steele, Annie's special education instructor, has initiated a system that she calls the **triad system** to manage her purposes and goals. She keeps a standing weekly appointment with every classroom teacher. She has found that this system helps her re-

---

**BOX 4.4**

**Guidelines for Developing Self-Management Skills**

1. Consider your purposes.
2. Know your roles.
3. Set priorities.
4. Consider what everyone needs.
5. Continue to grow and learn.

---

spond to a variety of educational needs. If you followed Mrs. Steele around on a Friday morning, this is what you'd see.

*7:45–8:15* Mrs. Steele assembles all the materials she'll need for her morning schedule. She speaks briefly with Trudy, the para-educator who will be with Annie in PE this morning, reminding her that the goals for Annie during these classes is to participate in as many ways as possible. Trudy explains that she feels a little left out in PE class, now that Annie can change into her gym shoes just as fast as the other children, without her help. She goes on to say that she spends more of her time helping the other children to know how to include Annie in their activities than she does actually helping Annie. Mrs. Steele smiles. She tells Trudy that she is on the right track.

*8:15–8:30* Mrs. Steele enters Mr. Chapman's fifth-grade classroom and goes directly to the table on the far side of the room. Tanya, a student who has an IEP and has been labeled as learning disabled, meets her there. Together, they wait for Mr. Chapman to finish giving the directions to complete the assigned story problem. Then the three of them review the objective they had established last week that Tanya should finish her homework and turn it in every day. Tanya first says that she had met her objective every day. Mr. Chapman pulls out his plan book with his notations in the margin and reminds Tanya that he had "prompted" her to get to work four times on Thursday and had checked her backpack to be sure she had her math book with her on Thursday night—and still she had not turned in her homework on Friday. They discuss what happened, why Tanya hadn't been able to meet her objective that day, and how they might help Tanya attain this objective. She decides that having a peer in her class call her up at home at night might help her remember to sit down to do her work. They have Julie come over to the table for a moment and ask if she will agree to do this. When she says she will, they plan out a sequence of events. They decide to repeat the objective for the following week.

*8:30–9:15* Mrs. Steele and Mr. Chapman teach a lesson on "Playing the Game of School" to the entire fifth-grade class. They focus on the planning and organization skills that students need to keep track of their assignments and be responsible for their homework. They divide the class into "homework base groups" and set up a contest in which every group whose members all turn homework in on time receives recognition on the homework chart. Tanya and Julie are assigned to the same group. As the fifth-graders get their science materials out for the next lesson, Mr. Chapman and Mrs. Steele chat for a moment at the door. Mr. Chapman says that he thinks this will help all his students learn to manage homework.

*9:15–9:30* Mrs. Steele enters the fourth-grade classroom to meet with Raul and Ms. Romani for their triad meeting. Raul's objective this week was to self-monitor the times that he shouted out in class, just as he had done last week, but to try to reduce the number of "shout-outs" by 5 percent. They examine his tally sheet and note Raul's success in reducing his "shout-outs" by 4 percent. Then they discuss ways that he could get attention when he felt a "shout-out" coming on without disrupting the flow of the class. They set a new goal for the week to come.

*9:30–10:15* Annie's third-grade class is now back in their own room. Mrs. Stevens has just finished a minilesson on the various ways that authors begin their stories, and she directs the children to continue with their reading and writing. Mrs. Steele arrives in time to see Annie's friend, Sharyn, invite her to come sit on the beanbag chair with her to read a book together. Mrs. Steele helps Annie with her walker and joins them on the beanbag to direct Annie's attention to the book that Sharyn reads to her. Mrs. Steele gives Sharyn a few tips for how to get Annie to notice the pictures. When Sharyn finishes, Annie's triad meeting begins. The adaptation they've made for Annie, because she doesn't speak, is that Annie picks someone to be her "speaker" at the meeting. This week it is Sharyn. Together, the four of them meet at the table to examine Annie's progress toward her objectives this past week. Sharyn points out that Annie now gets ready for gym

on time and does it independently, with only a few prompts from her friends. Mrs. Steele also notes that Annie paid attention to the entire book that Sharyn just read to her and that in recent weeks Annie generally has stayed on task for greater periods of time. They discuss how to continue encouraging her to attend for sustained periods of time. Mrs. Stevens registers her concern that Annie continues to pick at her skin and bite herself whenever she is left alone for more than three or four minutes. They discuss several possible interventions but agree that it will be helpful for Mrs. Steele to specifically observe when Annie is left alone for a short period to see if she can detect some pattern to the behaviors. They agree to be ready with more data by next week's triad meeting to explore this issue further.

*10:15–11:15* Mrs. Steele heads down to the second-grade room, where there are five children with IEPs. Today, she will have a triad meeting for Jeremy. She only holds one triad meeting a day with a particular teacher because it's difficult to take any more instructional time from the class. After Jeremy's triad meeting, Mrs. Steele works with a small group of students who are tape recording their stories.

**SETTING PRIORITIES** School professionals need to set priorities and have realistic time expectations. To do so, they must first understand two factors in the prioritization process. The two major dimensions of self-management are urgency and importance (Covey, 1990). Urgent tasks are those which demand attention immediately—for example, a ringing telephone. They create pressure and demand action. In contrast, importance is related to getting the results we want. Important tasks contribute to the overall purpose of the school or the individual. Planning for an upcoming instructional unit, thoughtfully examining a new student's file, and preparing plans for paraprofessionals are all examples of important tasks. Such tasks may lack urgency, but the cost of not doing them is high, as student outcomes may be compromised.

School professionals design personal time management strategies that are predicated on the particular goals that they have established for themselves in each of the roles they play. Mrs. Matheson began to realize that she had been using the "urgencies" of students as an all-too-convenient excuse to avoid a task that she didn't prefer. Once she recognized this, she found herself gaining an unprecedented degree of control over her own professional life. She tried to distinguish among true student crises and those interactions that could be delegated or delayed so she could make an informed choice about how to best use her time.

 **CONSIDERING WHAT EVERYONE NEEDS**  Seeking mutual benefit and mutual satisfaction for every dilemma, problem, or conflict is a way of thinking that requires, among other things, the maturity to realize that the best solutions to interpersonal disagreements or conflicts balance consideration for the other person's needs with consideration for one's own needs. It is the kind of thinking that we first discussed in the section on collaboration. Each person involved in good working relationships must perceive that his or her own needs can or will be met.

 **CONTINUING TO GROW AND LEARN**  School professionals, support personnel, families, and students who fail to keep up with new ideas do a disservice to the community and themselves. Collaborative work facilitates lifelong learning through the sharing of ideas and expertise (Joyce, Wolf, & Calhoun, 1993). In all of the situations we've examined in this chapter, school professionals demonstrated their ongoing commitment to their own learning. In some cases, they were learning from one another. Consider these examples:

- Mrs. Steele worked with many teachers in the school. In the process, she demonstrated her ideas and skills and simultaneously gained knowledge and skills by observing other professionals in action.

- Trudy explained the work she was doing with Annie in music class during one of their scheduled conferences, and Mrs. Steele learned more about how other teachers organize their classes.

- The professionals on the Red Team created new ways of supporting students by thinking out loud together.

- Mr. Aiello accepted Mrs. Harind's offer to work together, ostensibly for the purpose of enriching the education of one of their students, but in the process they learned many things from each other.

- Mrs. Yelich, the para-educator on the Red Team, received daily instruction and monitoring on behavior interventions and instructional methods from Mrs. Matheson.

### Extending Your Learning

Think about Mrs. Matheson's time management problems. Help her solve her problem by applying self-management skills. Make a list of things she could do to help herself. Compare your list with a classmate's, and add ideas you didn't think of.

- Ms. Acquisto, Ms. Nguyen, and Ms. Jerzicky shared ideas about how they could help children form some alliances and connections that had been missing in their school lives.

Formal learning experiences—classes, workshops, seminars, and study groups—are also of value. Some schools have begun to improve their connections with the community by offering courses that parents and teachers take together. For example, one school district employs teachers to offer evening classes for people who want to become fluent in conversational Spanish. Groups of people who have common learning needs and interests use one of the elementary schools to come together to learn. All are enriched by the experience. School professionals and support personnel also rely on information gained through outside resources, as these examples illustrate:

- Mrs. Harind used information about cooperative learning that she gained from her graduate courses at the university to enhance her work with other teachers.

- Mrs. Matheson attended a workshop on time management to learn to work more efficiently in all the roles her position entailed.

- Many of the faculty members at Humphreys Elementary attended a class on instructional adaptations to learn to be more creative in their approaches to instruction. They later worked together to figure out a better learning plan for Annie during math.

### ■ SECTION SUMMARY

To collaborate successfully, members of inclusive school communities need to develop skills in solving problems, dealing with differences, and manage themselves and their time. The collaborative problem-solving process consists of seven steps that team members use to arrive at good solutions to daily challenges. The skills for dealing with differences are based on the use of strategies that are unconditionally constructive. Self-management requires that members of inclusive school communities develop five important skills: considering their purposes, knowing their roles, setting priorities, considering everyone's needs, and continuing to grow and learn.

## Chapter Summary

Collaboration is the essential feature of inclusive school communities, in which everyone belongs and participates in meaningful activities, affiliations and alliances among community members are facilitated, and mutual support is the norm. Collaboration involves direct interaction between co-equal parties who participate voluntarily, share in decision making, plan resource allocation, and set common goals. Collaboration applies to numerous school tasks, processes, and activities, including planning the curriculum, assessing

students, setting schedules, defining staff roles, designing individual student support plans, and teaching.

In inclusive school communities, community members assume expanded roles. Families become full partners, and students accept increased responsibility for their own learning and for creating alliances. School professionals participate as team members, co-teachers, and sometimes consultants. Support personnel, including paraprofessionals, volunteers, clerical/secretarial personnel, custodial/food service workers, and transportation workers/bus drivers, each have knowledge and skills to offer the school community, and each benefits from participating in the school community.

The three sets of skills vital for all inclusive school communities are (1) solving problems collaboratively, (2) dealing with differences, and (3) managing ourselves and our time. The collaborative problem-solving process consists of seven steps and results in good solutions for instructional and other school-related concerns. Dealing well with differences is predicated on the use of a strategy that is unconditionally constructive. Finally, managing oneself involves the development of important skills: considering your purposes, knowing your roles, setting priorities, considering what every person needs, and growing and learning.

**INSTRUCTIONAL ACTIVITY**

## Problem Solving with a Transdisciplinary Team: The Fishbowl

### Objectives

- To understand the roles and responsibilities that different members of transdisciplinary teams bring to the problem-solving process
- To compare and contrast the problem-solving process used by an actual team with the problem-solving process provided in Chapter 4

### Preparation

- Your instructor will invite a transdisciplinary team to your class. This team should have as many different roles represented as possible—for example, special and

general educators, school mental health professionals, administrators, students, parents, para-educators, school health professionals, and other related-services professionals.
- The team will select a problem that it needs to solve (in other words, a real problem that is currently faced by the team).

### Materials

- A rubric for charting product distributed prior to class
- A one-page synopsis by the team that outlines some background issues and sets the context for the problem-solving process

## Product

- Compare and contrast the chart

## Agenda

- Observe and take notes as the transdisciplinary team conducts a meeting to discuss a problem they want to solve.
- At the end of the problem-solving process, ask process and content questions to members of the transdisciplinary team as time allows.
- As a homework assignment, reflect on the problem-solving process used by the transdisciplinary team.

- In the next class period, in pairs, engage in the pair and share portions of the Think/Pair/Share process outlined in Appendix 10.1. Produce a chart that reflects the process you read about and observed. Present your chart to the class.

## Evaluation

- Your instructor will collect the dyad charts and check for clear descriptions of each step of the problem-solving process and for congruence between elements of the process you observed and the process you read about.

# Glossary

**American Sign Language** Sign language in which signs represent whole words and complete thoughts rather than single letter.

**Anecdotal records** Written or recorded notes documenting certain actions, conversations, behaviors, or events that are kept by an adult about a student or group of students for the purpose of examining patterns in those actions, conversations, behaviors, or events.

**Antiseptic bouncing** A term used to describe a situation in which a student is calmly sent away to do something else to disengage him or her from a potentially explosive or dangerous situation before it escalates.

**Belongingness** A concept developed by Maslow to describe one of the basic human needs.

**Circle of friends** A group of similar-aged students intentionally assembled to establish relationships, and hopefully friendships, for students who have no friends.

**Consultant** A person who engages in a process of providing information to someone who seeks that information in order to solve a problem regarding a third party.

**Co-teaching** A collaborative arrangement between school professionals in which they create solutions and plan, teach, and modify lessons together.

**Duet Teaching** A format for co-teaching in which experienced co-teachers both present in a highly sophisticated manner.

**Inclusive** Including all students, families, and professionals in all the meaningful experiences of a school.

**Leadership** The act of performing one or more of the necessary functions that facilitates the completion of a task while maintaining the relationships of the people who are working together.

**Manipulative objects** Common objects used by students to help them understand mathematical concepts.

**Para-educator** A paid school employee who provides instruction and/or related services to individuals or groups; supports students in classrooms; interprets from one language to another; monitors and supervises students in lunchrooms, halls and bus loading zones and on playgrounds; and works under the direction of a school professional who holds ultimate responsibility for the outcomes of the instructional program.

**Parent-professional partnerships** Associations between a family and one or more professionals who function collaboratively using effective interpersonal skills in pursuit of a joint interest and common goal.

**Partnership** Associations in which people function collaboratively in pursuit of a joint interest or common goal.

**Peer assistants** Students identified and trained to support their peers academically, physically, emotionally, and socially according to need.

**Principled leadership** The performance of leadership functions based on a set of values or standards compatible with those of the team.

**Schools as inclusive communities** A concept that defines a new, greatly expanded role for schools, emphasizing belongingness and meaningful participation, creation of alliances and affiliations, and mutual support among all community members.

**Speak-and-Add** A format for co-teaching in which both presenters are "on stage" at the same time, with one leading and one supporting.

**Speech-read** A method used by persons with hearing impairments to decode lip movements and facial expressions in order to understand spoken language.

**Student products** Papers, recordings, tests, projects, or other materials that are made by students in the process of completing assigned academic work.

**Tag team** A format for co-teaching in which presenters take turns, with one on and one off.

**Transdisciplinary team** A team of people who are trained in different disciplines but who work collaboratively, sharing responsibility for a student's educational program.

**Triad system** A system by which a consultant meets with the consultee and the third party simultaneously.

## CHAPTER 5

# Schooling the Whole Child

# A Student-Centered Approach to Understanding Needs

Sandy earned her Ed.D. in education and now teaches in a state school for students who are blind. Sandy is, in her own words, totally blind.

*Interviewer:* What do you know about your own needs as a learner?

*Sandy:* Understanding my learning needs remains for me a work in progress. Learning styles and needs are as varied as the individuals who live them. Therefore, please consider the following comments merely as jumping-off places that will provide you with starting points from which you can make your own observations and discoveries about the interactions between visual impairments and learning. Also remember that they reflect my experiences as a totally blind learner.

*Interviewer:* What did you know about your needs as a learner when you were in school?

*Sandy:* During an introductory trigonometry unit, my eighth-grade algebra teacher saw I was having trouble distinguishing "opposite" from "adjacent" from "tangent," particularly when the triangle was rotated 90 or 180 degrees. Though he had no formal vision training, his solution was to make wooden triangles for me so we were sure we were both talking about the same geometric shape in the same orientation. I still found the concepts difficult to understand because I, like many other people who were born blind, have difficulty with spatial relationships. However, at least my teacher and I could now look at and discuss the same picture.

Sometimes you and your students may not be working from the same picture, and/or sometimes that picture must become a model. Take bowling, for instance. Based solely on what they can hear at a bowling alley, visually impaired students may assume that they walk a few steps down the alley and literally throw the ball at the pins as hard as they can. Thus, your first job is to let them feel that funny ball, to show them how to bend over and swing the ball during their approach (potentially requiring both verbal description and physical guidance) and use a rail or other physical guide down which they can walk independently to roll the ball toward the pins. However, your job is only half done. These experiences don't help students know what they're rolling the ball toward, and it's pretty tough to get the bowling alley pins for a hands-on inspection. An insightful PE teacher of mine modeled pin arrangement by gluing Lifesavers onto a card in the proper configuration. My score didn't improve, but I still remember what the pins look like.

During high school biology, I wish my parents, teachers, and I had all been more insightful. We all agreed that during dissection labs I would work with a partner who would do all the dissecting and describe what was happening. I was sure formaldehyde would ruin my hands and had no desire to examine frogs, worms, or anything else we'd dissect. As a result, I memorized my way through biology, receiving straight A's but only being able to verbalize dissection information. In retrospect, I wish I'd followed the pattern set by a blind biology student in a neighboring county who, unde-

terred by formaldehyde hands and animal innards, dissected everything and learned much more.

Some things can only be explained verbally because there is no equivalent sensory experience: the moon, the view from a mountaintop, the exchange of a romantic look. Verbal explanation is also necessary when information is written on a classroom chalkboard. This may seem foolishly obvious, but teachers often become so involved in talking and writing that they forget to verbalize everything. I encountered a graduate school statistics professor who liked to say, "Add this, subtract that, multiply by this, divide that, and there's your answer." At such times, I'd ask, "Dr. G. what's 'this'?" Apologetically, he'd explain—an explanation, I learned later, that clarified things for everyone in the class, not just me.

There are differences in how blind and sighted people do things. My mother and I had all sorts of problems in the kitchen because she tried to teach me cooking techniques like stirring. She wanted me to "flip" my wrist, which I couldn't do, and physical guidance only made the problem worse. Blind people also deal with objects differently. For instance, blind persons hooking up computer equipment may not turn the computer so that the back, where the connections are made, faces them. Rather, they will typically leave the computer in its normal orientation, connections facing away from them, and have no trouble hooking things up. As the blind person "sees" it, there's no reason to turn the machine around. Sighted people must make this accommodation because they don't feel things very well. We think the computer should be in the same orientation in which we typically use it, because it's easier to work with it in the normal position than when it's rotated 180 degrees.

*Interviewer:* How did your teachers support your needs?

*Sandy:* My teachers did many things right: providing tangible learning aids and adapting to my need for alternative learning channels (auditory and tactual instead of visual). In addition, they allowed me to use different learning media (abacus and typewriter as opposed to pencil and paper), and they held me to the same standards as their other students. I was expected to produce the same work and the same quality as everyone else, receiving genuine praise when I did well and genuine scolding when I got lazy. That was good training for the world of work, where it sometimes takes me longer to get things done, but my employer's expectations are the same for me as for any other employee.

*Interviewer:* Were there situations or times in which you did not feel as if your learning needs were supported?

*Sandy:* I wish my teachers had done three things differently. First, I wish they had initially thought about what I could do instead of what I couldn't do. By the end of the year, they virtually always saw more positives than negatives, but it took a while. Second, I wish my teachers had looked for my preferred learning style in a given situation and had capitalized on that style. In orientation and mobility (for instance, I've discovered I'm primarily an auditory learner), I feel I could have made more and faster progress in finding my way around if my teachers had taught me auditorily (verbal cues and explanation) in addition to the movement and mental mapping techniques they used. Third, I wish my teachers had allowed me to experience failure so I'd have understood how to deal with and learn from it. Obviously, students should succeed much more often than they fail, but always rescuing students before they fail doesn't prepare them well for adult life and the failure

they will inevitably know at some point. I didn't have my first failure experience until my second year of college when my voice teacher gently suggested I major in something other than music. I was devastated because I had no previous failure-overcoming experience to remind me that this setback was survivable.

*Interviewer:* What made it possible for you to graduate from school?

*Sandy:* I'm not sure I know why I'm successful. I do know that I had supportive parents and teachers who expected me to do my best, and those high expectations fostered high expectations in me. Together with teachers who made learning fun, I developed a sense of joy about learning and a desire to be a lifelong learner. However, my greatest gifts from parents and teachers were the inculcation of honesty and doing what's right regardless of the consequences. Anyone who lives by these and other good character traits will be successful, regardless of ability or circumstance. I believe character education is just as important as academic education for all students, but particularly for those with visual impairments.

# Introduction

Imagine a young music student. Her musical performance at school is influenced by the interaction between her cognitive, affective, communicative, and physical capacities and the environments in which she operates. A music teacher may provide instruction in how to play, say, the violin, but the degree of competence this young girl displays is a result of her own capacities and the quality of instruction she receives. This view of learning as a social and personal construction assumes that the educational needs of all learners can be met by creating environments in which learning occurs in multiple ways.

As school professionals, we guide and assist our students in becoming lifelong learners by helping them recognize their own abilities and set their own learning goals. We teach the skills that empower students to respond to their own needs, ambitions, and dreams within the constraints of their familial, political, economic, and social contexts. Initially, it is the responsibility of parents, working with school professionals, to identify the cognitive, affective, communicative, and physical needs of children. But this task of identifying learner needs and providing environments that address and support those needs is complicated.

In previous chapters, we set the context for understanding the complexity of the problem. Children come to school from different cultural, linguistic, and ethnic backgrounds and with different abilities. To respond to this diversity, school professionals must understand how these differing backgrounds and abilities impact learning. And to design vehicles for assessing instructional outcomes, they must first understand the characteristics of both learners and the learning process.

In this chapter, we examine the nature of learning and the ways in which it is impacted by four domains: cognitive, communicative, affective, and physical. As the chapter emphasizes, school professionals must address student needs across all of these domains in order to support the education of all learners and to ensure that our schools become truly inclusive learning communities. This chapter lays the foundation for subsequent chapters that detail the nuts and bolts of classroom life: classroom management, assessment, curriculum, and instruction.

## The Nature of Learning

The primary responsibility of teachers and other school professionals is to support learning. To learn, *Webster's* dictionary tells us, is to gain knowledge through experience (Woolf, 1979). Research indicates that learning occurs as information is received, acted upon, and organized in relationship to what individuals already know (Brown, Ash, Rutherford, Nakagawa, Gordon, & Campione, 1993). This process of **accommodation** between what individuals know and how experience transforms and expands their knowledge base and skills has been likened to an ecology of human development (Bronfenbrenner, 1973). That is, learning is a result of the interaction between the nature and ability of the individual and his or her experiences (Brooks & Brooks, 1993). Thus, even as the environment, and other individuals within the environment, transforms the learner, the learner's interac-

tion with the environment creates change (Stone & Reid, 1994; Vygotsky, 1978). This view of learning as an interactive process suggests that school professionals must attend to the learner, the learning environment, and the interaction between the two.

Teaching involves mediating learners' experiences by focusing learners' attention and activities on particular aspects of **knowledge construction.** By concentrating on some areas of learning, other areas are necessarily diminished or limited. Hence, discussions of the curriculum are important because they set the targets for learning outcomes. Targets can serve to expand or limit students' exposure to knowledge and skills development. Discussions of teaching techniques are important as well. Depending on the abilities, culture, and skills of each learner, the teacher role may range from facilitative and nondirective to prescriptive and direct. The "goodness of fit" between the teacher's instructional processes and the learning needs of students will result in optimal learning outcomes.

Although learning results from the interplay of the individual with the environment, it is profoundly influenced by the traits, capacities, skills, and limitations that the individual brings to any given learning opportunity. Learning is not simply a cognitive process. Rather, learning is influenced by personal attitudes, beliefs, and emotions about a topic or experience, as well as by the ability to use language to process and mediate the learning experience (Caine & Caine, 1994). For example, unlike Annie and Tanya, Michael, Kurume, and Kirk use language relatively well to mediate their learning. As a result, they have some well-developed academic skills; they can read and write and are able to express themselves orally. The physical capacities of students also contribute to their learning potential. For example, learners who are mobile, whose senses are acute, and whose physical health is robust are able to increase the number and ranges of experiences they have. Annie, who has limited capacity to explore her environment because she does not yet

| **TABLE 5.1** | **The Principles of Learning** |
|---|---|

- Learning occurs naturally.
- Learning processes change as a result of development.
- Individuals have different approaches to learning.
- Expressions of learning differ.
- Learning is strategic.

crawl, simply does not have the breadth of experiences to draw on that some of her classmates have. When school professionals think about the unique capacities of each of their students, they must remember that individuals' cognitive, affective, communicative, and physical abilities and skills all affect how, what, and how much they learn.

Table 5.1 lists five basic principles of learning to keep in mind when considering the interrelationships among cognition, affect, language, and physical capacities. These principles are (1) learning occurs naturally; (2) learning processes change as a result of development; (3) individuals have different approaches to learning; (4) expressions of learning differ; and (5) learning is strategic—it serves the unique purposes and intents of the individual. Let us examine each of these principles.

 ## Learning Occurs Naturally

Human learning is biologically rooted (Eisner, 1994). It occurs even without intervention or planning on the part of adults. Like other organs in the body, the brain has a biological function—it learns because it is programmed genetically to do so (Caine & Caine, 1994). From the beginning, without encouragement or intervention, babies use their five senses—taste, touch, vision, hearing, and smell—to gather information about the world around them and to understand, adapt to, and make demands on their environment. For example, they learn quickly that crying will evoke a response from their caregivers to feed them, change their diapers, or provide comfort. As toddlers, children explore their environments with a curiosity that needs no prompting or formal structure. They develop lan-

guage without being explicitly and purposefully taught and without conscious intention to learn. As a result of this naturally occurring phenomenon that we call learning, by age 4 or 5 children typically master thousands of abstract rules underlying spoken language (Zemelman, Daniels, & Hyde, 1993).

However, some children's opportunities to learn are limited, and they do not attain the milestones of early childhood development that are considered typical. These limitations may be imposed by conditions of poverty, abuse, neglect, and/or malnutrition, or they may be due to neurological malfunctioning of the brain, **cerebral palsy,** deafness, **mental retardation, autism,** or any of a number of other disabilities. Many disabilities restrict cognitive, affective, communicative, and physical functioning, and limitations in any one of these areas affect children's opportunities to learn. But these limitations do not mean that learning does not occur. Even children with the most severe disabilities learn in the sense that they respond to stimuli in the environment. The limitations may mean that a child spends a longer time mastering a particular way of interacting with the environment or practicing a particular skill many more times than his or her peers. Sometimes learning limitations mean that a student may not be able to learn a specific skill without direct instruction, even though he or she may be perfectly capable of learning other skills that are not part of the school curriculum.

This section of the chapter includes several tables that list some of the fourteen **learner-centered** psychological principles adopted by the American Psychological Association (1997) that highlight components of the learning process. For example, Table 5.2 lists three principles that support the notion that learning occurs naturally. These three cognitive and metacognitive factors represent principles about how central the learner is to the learning process. A dynamic relationship exists between children's experience of the world and the way that experience shapes their ability to learn new information (Piaget, 1971). While experience is critical in how young children learn, Piaget and others have suggested that the meaning that children make of their environment also results from the way they represent what they experience in their minds. With no formal instruction, young children are able to construct robust, serviceable theories of the world (Gardner, 1991). For instance, by the time that Kirk was 3 years old, he was able to predict when his mother would pick him

<table>
<tr><td colspan="2">

**TABLE 5.2**    The Learner-Centered Psychological Principles: Cognitive and Metacognitive Factors
</td></tr>
<tr><td>

■ *The nature of the learning process:* The learning of complex subject matter is most effective when it is an intentional process of constructing meaning from information and experience.

■ *Goals of the learning process:* The successful learner, over time and with support and instruc-
</td><td>

tional guidance, can create meaningful, coherent representations of knowledge.

■ *Construction of knowledge:* The successful learner can link new information with existing knowledge in meaningful ways.
</td></tr>
</table>

Source: American Psychological Association, 1997.

up at the day care center. Kurume was able to distinguish between Hondas and Camaros on the road, and he even knew that balanced wheels made his toy cars go faster. Kirk and Kurume learned these things without purposeful, planned instruction. Apparently, children learn information when they are developmentally ready to learn it.

## ⓑ Learning Processes Change with Development

Piaget (1971) suggested that children move through several stages as they learn to gather information and interact with objects in their environment. According to Piaget's developmental stage theory, as they mature, children have increasingly sophisticated abilities to use information, to think, and to act on their environment. Consider the different approaches to learning that Annie, Michael, Kirk, Kurume, and Tanya use.

Because of the mental retardation caused by Cornelia de Lange syndrome, Annie's learning occurs at what Piaget called the **sensorimotor stage,** which is characterized by physiological reactions and reflexive movements. She primarily uses her five senses to gain information from her environment but relies on crying, crawling, and noises to make her needs known and to influence her environment. Annie's problem-solving abilities can best be described as trial-and-error experimentation that allows her to discern predictable patterns in her environment. For example, she observes that, by touching a ball that contains a free-floating butterfly, the wings of the butterfly flap and sparkle—the beginning of her discovery of the concept of cause and effect. Instruction for Annie focuses on communication systems to help her fulfill her need to

investigate and make demands on her environment in socially acceptable and physically safe ways.

Even though Tanya is younger than Annie, she is functioning at what Piaget called the **preoperational stage,** which involves the child's ability to use symbol systems (like language) to investigate and explore the environment. Tanya primarily uses language to represent, remember, and act upon her environment. For example, she can use words to represent objects in her environment and so can ask for milk, juice, or cookies instead of having to pull on her mother's skirt or cry and point to get the items she desires. Furthermore, Tanya is increasing her ability to understand and solve problems in her environment. Her thinking now allows her to know that, even when a ball rolls out of view, it still exists. Juanita loves to play with Tanya by rolling a toy behind her and allowing her to "discover" it.

As middle schoolers, both Kirk and Michael function at the abstract level in some classes and at the concrete level in other classes. Learners who organize their learning in this way may be said to be operating at Piaget's third stage of learning, the **concrete-operational stage,** which involves the application of thinking skills and rules to tangible or concrete objects and events. When Kirk and Michael struggle in math to understand a symbol system that requires many mental manipulations, they are operating at the concrete stage. Although most of the other eighth-graders have no need for physical objects to illustrate word problems, Kirk and Michael need them to develop their understanding of the concepts involved.

In many ways, Kurume operates at a **formal operations stage,** which involves the manipulation of abstract ideas or constructs (Brooks & Brooks, 1993). In spite of the difficulties he had learning the subtle differences between words that have similar meanings, he

| **TABLE 5.3** | **The Learner-Centered Psychological Principles: Cognitive, Metacognitive, Developmental, and Social Factors** |
|---|---|

- *Strategic thinking:* The successful learner can create and use a repertoire of thinking and reasoning strategies to achieve complex learning.

- *Thinking about thinking:* Higher-order strategies for selecting and monitoring mental operations facilitate creative and critical thinking.

- *Context of learning:* Learning is influenced by environmental factors, including culture, technology, and instructional practices.

Source: American Psychological Association, 1997.

has a good understanding of concepts like liberty, responsibility, and justice. He engages in philosophical conversations about the meaning of life—reflecting on his own ability to think and make meaning of his experiences. Kurume demonstrates the characteristics of a well-developed, successful learner, as listed in Table 5.3.

Learning processes change as individuals develop, but some learners, like Annie and Tanya, may progress more slowly through these stages than their typical peers. Now that Annie is 9, her peers use concrete-operational strategies to learn while Annie continues to use the strategies of the sensorimotor stage. However, this does not mean that she is like a 1-year-old child. While her learning strategies may parallel those of a typically developing 1-year-old child, her experiences and her knowledge base are far vaster, she has been learning for a much longer period of time.

Learning processes also change with development due to the influence of social environments and social interactions. In the development process, the opportunities for social interaction and shared learning can enhance the content of what is learned and encourage higher-order learning processes.

The interaction between a child's development and his or her learning is complex, and no one theory adequately explains the phenomenon. The National Association for the Education of Young Children (NAEYC), like the APA, has identified some principles of child development and learning that inform what they refer to as "developmentally appropriate practice" (Bredekamp & Copple, 1997). These principles were drawn from a synthesis of three extensive research bases in the areas of (1) child development and learning, (2) individual characteristics and experiences, and (3) social and cultural contexts. Resources such as the NAEYC guidelines can be used as a guide to inform the instructional

practices and organizational decisions of inclusive school communities.

## Approaches to Learning Differ

As mentioned previously, babies first learn by touch, sight, sound, smell, and taste. Research on learning styles indicates that children demonstrate personal preferences for gaining information through one sense even when no impairment in other sensory systems can be detected (Sternberg, 1994b). As the APA learner-centered principles suggest, these preferences for using one sense over the others continue, even though we learn to use more complex thinking strategies. Learning style theorists argue that some children simply prefer to interact with their environment using their visual channels as their primary information source and thus prefer pictures, three-dimensional building materials, videotapes, and computer programs or graphics (Armstrong, 1994). Other children may favor auditory learning and therefore prefer listening to the teacher, an audiotape, or music. Still others may favor tactile and kinesthetic interactions within their environments and so prefer to see a demonstration of a skill than to read about it. Our interviewee from the chapter opener, Sandy, recalls the different approaches that she and her teachers and family used so that she could fully access critical information to develop concepts and skills. Though Sandy had a vision impairment, the types of accommodations made for her are typical of those needed by students both with and without disabilities.

Table 5.4 lists several factors in why individuals approach learning differently. The environment, experience, peers, adults, and the need to know all influence

| TABLE 5.4 | The Learner-Centered Psychological Principles: Individual Difference Factors |
|---|---|
| ■ *Individual differences in learning:* Learners have different strategies, approaches, and capabilities for learning that are a function of prior experience and heredity. | ■ *Learning and diversity:* Learning is most effective when differences in learners' linguistic, cultural, and social backgrounds are taken into account. |

Source: American Psychological Association, 1997.

learning. In other words, context has a significant effect on learning and performance (Sternberg, 1994a). Indeed, the basic elements of the learning process may be far more culturally influenced than previously thought (Serpell & Boykin, 1994). Researchers have found that the performance of the same individuals on the same tasks differs widely depending on the context (Ceci & Bronfenbrenner, 1985; Ceci & Liker, 1986; Lave, 1988; Nunes, Schliemann, & Carraher, 1993). For instance, children who performed poorly on a task at school could do the same thing well at home; other children who performed the task well at school were unable to do it at home. And in Brazil children who failed school math were able to do basic arithmetic as they sold things on the street. Learning, which looks so simple on the surface, is a complex process that depends on the abilities of the learner, the context in which learning occurs, and the relevance of the learning opportunity to the needs of the learner.

Morrison and Collins (1996) extend our conceptions of socially constructed knowledge. Like many contemporary cognitive researchers, they suggest that varying cultures and communities shape the strategies that their members use to learn. For instance, Delpit (1995) explains that in some Native American cultures it is a social violation to interpret the words (written or spoken) of others. As a result, when some children from Native American families are asked to explain what an author meant by a particular phrase or passage, they may not be able to responded successfully.

## Expressions of Learning Differ

Just as children are known to show preferences for how they interact with their environment, a growing body of research suggests that children have preferences for how they demonstrate their understandings and solutions. The differences among the outcomes and expressions of learning may be related to different capacities for learning. For instance, Gardner (1983) equates intelligence with the capacity to solve problems, interact with others, and fashion products in natural environments. Gardner describes seven basic intelligences: (1) linguistic, (2) logical-mathematical, (3) spatial, (4) bodily-kinesthetic, (5) musical, (6) interpersonal, and (7) intrapersonal. He asserts that all persons possess all seven intelligences, that people are capable of developing each to an adequate level of competency, that intelligences can work together in complex ways, and that there are many ways to be intelligent within each category. These "intelligences" are preferences that people have for constructing complex ideas about the world and for demonstrating their conceptions (Gardner, 1983). And Sternberg (1989) suggests that three interrelated processes contribute to learning and to the development of intelligence: (1) the internal models and knowledge of the individual, (2) the external environments experienced by the individual, and (3) the degree of experience the individual has with a given task, activity, or event.

These theorists help us to understand that people not only learn in different ways and have different **aptitudes** for learning but also demonstrate and express their learning in different ways. Differing capacities and contexts for learning will result in different expressions of learning.

## Learning Is Strategic

Children appear to learn what they need or want to know in order to understand and interact with their environment. Thus what they learn varies from one child to the next, depending on the particular environment and on the individual personality. Sometimes

## Extending Your Learning

What preferences do you have in teaching others? For example, how would you teach others about a new product? What limitations would your preferences impose on others?

children construct meaning from their environments to solve a problem, to avoid pain, or to gain comfort. For example, a child who grows up in a home that uses a wood stove as a heat source learns what distance to keep from the stove to avoid pain yet stay warm. A child who grows up in a home with a forced-air heating system may sit on the heat vent to get warm. Active teaching by a parent or other caregiver may or may not occur, but learning takes place in response to survival and comfort needs.

Similarly, children seem to learn skills or acquire information on a need-to-know basis. For example, when Kirk was younger, his parents controlled the money. As a result, in the second grade, when many other children knew how to make change for a dollar, Kirk had little experience and seemed uninterested in learning this skill. A few years later, however, when he had some money of his own, which he used for purchases at the local convenience store, he quickly learned how to make change.

Children have other purposes for learning as well. Early in life, even without language, they seek to understand or explain phenomena in their world—for instance, why an object hurled from a high chair follows a certain trajectory (Gardner, 1991). Children

may engage in cognitive activities, such as sustained attention to a task, simply for fun. Or they may remember information in a particular way because of their own styles or preferences. Given the importance of the affective and motivational dimensions of learning, the APA devoted three of its fourteen learning principles to these dimensions (see Table 5.5).

## ■ SECTION SUMMARY

Learning occurs as individuals construct meaning from the world around them through their interactions with others (Stone & Reid, 1994). Thus, learning is not simply a mental process but is inextricably linked to social transactions and the capacity to communicate (Wood, 1988). The content offered in most schools represents only one kind of learning opportunity. Therefore, formal "teaching" is not necessary for learning to occur, although most learners need some guidance to master complex content areas like reading or mathematics. Some learners may also need formal instruction in areas that many children pick up incidentally, such as the development of oral language skills during the early childhood years. The culture of the home and family plays a vital role in how familiar and comfortable children are with the learning routines and interactions that are used in most public schools (Delpit, 1995).

The strategies that typical individuals use to make meaning become more and more complex and efficient as they age. Teaching is connected to learning in that it may encourage, support, and foster learning. Alternatively, teaching may inhibit the learning process

---

| **TABLE 5.5** | **The Learner-Centered Psychological Principles: Motivational and Affective Factors** |
|---|---|
| ■ *Motivational and emotional influences on learning:* What and how much is learned is influenced by the learner's motivation. Motivation to learn, in turn, is influenced by the individual's emotional states, beliefs, interests and goals, and habits of thinking.<br><br>■ *Intrinsic motivation to learn:* The learner's creativity, higher-order thinking, and natural curiosity all contribute to motivation to learn. | Intrinsic motivation is stimulated by tasks of optimal novelty and difficulty, relevant to personal interests, and providing for personal choice and control.<br><br>■ *Effects of motivation on effort:* Acquisition of complex knowledge requires extended learner effort and guided practice. Without learners' motivation to learn, the willingness to exert this effort is unlikely without coercion. |

Source: American Psychological Association, 1997.

## Extending Your Learning

What impact do you think going to school had on Annie's learning?

if it fails to take into account the purposes, preferences, and developmental levels of students or the innate drive to learn. The key is to place the student, not the teacher, at the center of the learning process.

When children begin formal schooling, the regulation of learning processes through the standardization of curriculum and instructional practices alters the natural, strategic, and developmental aspects of learning. Consequently, formal schooling may impact children's preferred approaches to and expressions of learning. The structures of formal schooling also provide systematic guidance of children's learning and change the framework that guides the purpose of learning and the ways in which it occurs (Wood, 1988). Instead of allowing children to set their own educational direction, formal schooling structures their learning by setting up an environment in which groups of children are expected to learn the same thing, in the same way, at the same time. These impositions constrain the learning process that began as an individualized, self-directed, self-regulated process.

Learners respond and adapt to the environment in which they find themselves, developing more and more complex understandings of the world as they experience different environments and respond to different problems. Learners can be competent in many ways. The strategies that they develop and the ways that they express their competence will vary according to their individual strengths and their familiarity with the social context in which they find themselves. Learning also depends on the interaction between the environment and individual capacities. For school professionals to support learning in classrooms, they need to understand how the cognitive, affective, communicative, and physical capacities of individual learners affect their ability to learn. We've organized the next sections of this chapter to focus on the four domains of learning—cognitive, affective, communicative, and physical—because they are so intertwined in the learning process. By discussing the domains separately, we risk having you think of them as separate areas of functioning rather than complex, interactive components

of the whole child. However, separating them allows us to delve more deeply into the current research base. It also provides us with a way of discussing differences among individuals without resorting to the use of categories or labels.

## Learning and Disability

When individuals appear to have similar characteristics, they tend to be labeled by others and by themselves. For instance, "dropout," "rebel," "nerd," and "brain" are all labels that are used to describe some students. Classifying groups of individuals is a social phenomenon that exists within almost all cultures. In many businesses, categorizing customers or clients helps companies tailor their products to certain segments of the population. In medicine, individuals who share similar health concerns are often studied to identify ways of prolonging life, cure a disease, or understand how to teach lifelong good health habits. Similarly, within special education, many terms are used to describe the characteristics that students with disabilities bring to the learning situation. Disability labels categorize individuals according to the problems they have with learning. Unfortunately, many individuals with the same disability label learn very differently from one another. By viewing learning as an interactive construction between the individual and the environment, we can begin to understand why identifying a student's disability may not help us in creating a useful learning environment.

For instance, although Kirk has a disability label of "emotional disturbance," the label itself is not very useful in planning learning activities. But knowing that Kirk tends to stop interacting and problem solving when he thinks he will be wrong helps the teacher decide to provide Kirk with learning tasks in which he can be successful. Perhaps the teacher will develop lessons that cover only one or two concepts at a time, rather than a larger number. Or the teacher may decide to include a proofreading step in Kirk's learning units so that he has an opportunity for more feedback to correct errors before turning in a final product. Indeed, teachers can use a variety of strategies to support learners who are afraid of failing. But only by understanding how each individual learns can school professionals craft learning plans that support children's unique needs.

A young man enjoys downhill skiing.

By using domains to frame our understanding of individual children, we avoid the pitfalls associated with using categorical labels to identify students. Some labels are mandated in federal or state statutes; others have developed so that school professionals can communicate efficiently among themselves about the general characteristics of individuals. Each of the students featured in this book has been identified as having a specific disability. For example, Kurume is "hearing impaired." Annie and Tanya, in spite of vast differences in their capacities, limitations, and needs, have the same disability label: "mental retardation." Michael has " learning disabilities," while Kirk has been categorized as "emotionally disturbed."

## Extending Your Learning

What comes to your mind when you hear the label of "autism" applied to a child? As a teacher, what kinds of things would you want to know about a child with autism who may be assigned to your class? Are these questions different from the ones that you ask about other students without labels?

## ■ Section Summary

Unfortunately, the use of labels does not help school professionals provide competent educational services to students with disabilities—to plan curricula, instruction, or interventions. In fact, the labels may even lead professionals to believe that they know something about a student by knowing his or her disability label. Disability labels may identify problems within the learner, but they do not help school professionals teach, nor do they help students learn. Disabilities like mental retardation or autism are not diseases requiring "treatment"; instead, they are lifelong aspects of an individual. By understanding the needs of each learner within the cognitive, affective, communicative, and physical domains, we can better adjust the learning environment to promote optimal learning opportunities. The real educational needs of students may be masked when disability labels dictate the placement of students into specific programs or services. Think about Michael and Kurume. While their disabilities are different, they both have important needs in the areas of self-esteem and social competence. A focus on the capacities and limitations of students within the domains of cognition, affect, communication, and physical health will lead to educational practices based on what benefits each student.

# The Cognitive Domain

## What Is Cognition?

Part of understanding cognition is understanding the processes that are involved in how we think. *Webster's* dictionary defines *cognition* as "the process of knowing or the act of acquiring an idea" (Woolf, 1979). Broadly, **cognition** encompasses the acts involved in learning. When we refer to cognitive needs, we are concerned with the strategies, skills, and processes that interact to support learning. Interestingly, school professionals spend most of their time teaching students to memorize facts and to perform specific sequences of skills rather than enhancing students' ability to learn and make meaning from the information that they receive (Caine & Caine, 1994). Think about the processes at work when someone plays the violin. What we typically think of as musical ability draws its competence from all four of the domains. From the cognitive domain, the violinist relies on the memory process to produce the correct notes each time she plays. She relies on her **procedural skills** to sequence the order in which she plays. In fact, the cognitive processes help us to process, interpret, and use visual, auditory, olfactory, tactile, and sensory information (Atkinson & Shiffrin, 1968; Baddeley, 1981; Baddeley & Hitch, 1974).

## Cognitive Components

Our perspective on cognition is based largely on an information processing model that conceptualizes how sensory input is transformed, reduced, elaborated, stored, retrieved, and used (Neisser, 1976; Newell, 1980). Information processing theorists assume that information is represented internally and manipulated in real time by mental processes or strategies (Kail & Bisanz, 1992). It is critical to understand these processes and to link them to the broader notions of learning that encompass all four domains: the cognitive, affective, communicative, and physical.

Table 5.6 summarizes the functions and impacts of five cognitive components: (1) attention, (2) perception, (3) working memory, (4) long-term memory, and (5) executive control. Understanding how these components function helps us to identify areas in which students may excel or experience problems. Each cognitive process serves a precise function but does so only with the support of and in interaction with the others.

The principles of learning discussed earlier apply here. For instance, each of the cognitive processes are developmentally driven and change as children develop. In other words, as children grow, they become more adept and sophisticated in their abilities to carry out each of these functions. Furthermore, they develop elaborate cognitive skills that support interaction among the components. For example, toddlers at play spend short amounts of time doing one thing before they move on to another toy or experience. We might say that very young children have short attention spans. Because they are unable (or unwilling) to sustain their attention long enough to gather necessary information, they may fail to solve problems in their environment (Shaffer, 1993). With age, children become more persistent in solving problems and more purposeful in gathering or attending to necessary information. In addition, they develop strategies to filter out information that is not required to solve problems. Understanding the developmental nature of the processes and components that allow us to gather, store, retrieve, and operate on information is critical to the provision of educational programs that support student learning.

**ATTENTION**   Using our senses of sight, hearing, touch, smell, and taste, we attend to events in our environment. This sensory information is held in temporary storage so that it can be processed further (Gredler, 1992). Executive control processes allow us to direct and maintain our attention based on our understanding of the critical stimuli of an event or experience. In many cases, this requires us to filter out extraneous or unimportant information. For example, think of a time when you were listening to a lecture and the presenter was making use of an overhead projector. The lecturer's vocal qualities (tone, pitch, emphasis), words, and visual graphics represented the critical features of this experience. The hum of the projector fan, a cough from a member of the audience, or a passerby in the hallway were stimuli that could have redirected your attention momentarily. Your level of attentiveness also depended on your motivation for listening to the lecture and the meaning that you were able to derive from it. If for some reason you weren't interested in the topic or were unable to follow the lecture, your attention probably wandered. Our abilities to control selection of the appropriate stimuli within our environment and to maintain vigilance in attending to those stimuli are critical to our learning experiences.

| TABLE 5.6 | Characteristics of Cognitive Components | |
|---|---|---|
| **Component** | **Function** | **Impact on Learner** |
| Attention | Information from the environment is received through our senses and held in a short-term storage component. | The length of time that a learner can sustain attention impacts the amount of detail that can be absorbed as well as the length of time that can be spent in interacting with and solving problems. |
| | | Learners need to be able to attend to the salient details of a situation or problem. They must be able to shift their focus quickly if information changes rapidly. They must also be able to sustain their attention if the problem is complex but the environment is distracting. |
| | | If information is not presented in a way that matches students' preferences (visual, auditory, tactile, kinesthetic), they can miss critical features of the environment or learning activity. |
| Perception | Sensory information is transmitted neurologically and interpreted in terms of recognizable and meaningful patterns. | When learners fail to correctly identify and attend to critical features from their environment, then the meaning that they subsequently make of incoming information can be flawed or misdirected. |
| | Distinctive features such as depth, size, color, sound, patterns, and temperature are used to discriminate this sensory information. | |
| Working memory | Information is held temporarily, until it is interpreted, used, transferred, or forgotten. | As a result of perceptual interference, learners may have problems remembering information. |
| | | As learners process information in short-term memory, it stimulates long-term memory information banks. Poor linkages between short- and long-term memory mean that experiences may be forgotten. |
| | | Some learners may not be able to hold enough information in their working memory to make any meaning. |
| | | If capacity is not affected, then how well information in short-term memory is processed is influenced largely by a learner's previous experiences and background knowledge of a topic. |
| Long-term memory *Declarative knowledge* *Procedural knowledge* *Conditional knowledge* *Organizational structures* | Information from working memory is organized and stored until it is recalled or recognized for future actions and decisions. | Failure to link new information to previous understandings creates obstacles for students as they attempt to organize and, perhaps later, retrieve and use that information. |
| | Declarative knowledge is stored facts; procedural knowledge is memory of processes and procedures that are required to perform tasks; conditional knowledge is if/then knowledge sequences in which the learner must select a sequence or strategy that matches the presenting problem. | Lack of efficient strategies for storing or retrieving information results in loss of information, either because they forgot or because they can't retrieve what is still stored. |
| | | Linkages between procedures and their associated concepts help learners to select and use the right procedures for the right problems. |
| | Learners categorize, save, and retrieve information systematically. | |

*continued*

| **TABLE 5.6** *(continued)* | | |
|---|---|---|
| Executive control <br> *Metacognition* <br> *Self-regulation* | This cognitive component serves to monitor and drive both the individual functions of each component and the interactions among components. <br><br> Executive control processes such as evaluation, decision making, and judging allow us to gather, store, retrieve, and operate on information. | Many researchers believe that learning difficulties within individuals primarily result from learners' failure to activate and monitor strategic approaches to learning such as checking to see if they are solving the right problem, monitoring progress, or using the right strategy to solve the problem. <br><br> Strategic learners know when to ask for help and how to analyze their errors. |

**PERCEPTION** As we attend to incoming information, we begin to interpret and translate sensory stimuli. Perception is inextricably linked to and serves as a bridge between our attention processes and the meaning making that subsequently occurs in working memory. First, we interpret features of the environment to which we attend. For example, we identify from our sensory information characteristics, such as depth, size, color, sound, patterns, and temperature, and then assign meaning to these features in our working memory. If we fail to correctly identify and attend to critical features from our environment, then the meaning that we subsequently make of incoming information can be flawed or misdirected. For example, Kurume's teacher might notice that Kurume is adding when he should be subtracting. It's not that Kurume doesn't know how to subtract; he simply chose the wrong procedure because he didn't attend to all of the elements of the problem, including the signal to subtract (−) rather than add (+).

**WORKING MEMORY** As we attend to incoming stimuli and characterize the features of the information we hold that information in working memory for a short period of time. Simultaneously, we make decisions about the meaning of the information, the importance of keeping it, and ways to store it for future use. Alternatively, we disregard the information as superfluous and "forget" it. Information in working memory is held in "storage" while control processes are applied in order to hold on to or further process the information (Brainerd & Kingman, 1984; Ellis & Hunt, 1983). Working memory is thought to be associated with a short-term memory system that is regarded as a capacity-limited and time-limited storage system —we can hold on to four to seven bits of information that, unless processed further within several seconds, are typically "let go" or lost (Shaffer, 1993).

Our short- and long-term memories interact. The processing that occurs in working memory is directly related to and controls the flow of information to long-term memory systems. For example, suppose a friend gives you her telephone number but you don't have any paper to write the number on. It's important to you that you remember the number. Therefore, you may find yourself doing one of the following to help remember the information: (1) repeat the phone number over and over, (2) **chunk** the numbers into groups such as 526 62 89, or (3) connect familiar information to the numbers. This latter strategy might work as follows: If the telephone number is 526-6289, you may recognize the prefix as matching your own telephone number. Then, you may remember that your sister was born in 1962 and that your daughter was born in 1989. To recall the number, you string the three prompts—your prefix, your sister's birth date and your daughter's birth date—together. This technique of linking of new information to previously learned information is referred to as mnemonics. Cognitive processes applied within working memory, such as **rehearsal,** organization, **elaboration,** and mnemonics, allow us to hold on to information and provide a strategy for storing it in long-term memory (Swanson, 1991).

**LONG-TERM MEMORY** Long-term memory provides the ongoing storage of our conceptions of the world, impressions of past experiences and events, and strategies we use to process information and solve problems (Shaffer, 1993). While many people think of long-term memory as a "place" in our brains for storing information, recent research with persons who have sustained brain injuries suggests that our knowledge and memories can be found throughout the neurological networking systems within our brains (Marzano, 1992). Long-term memory involves the development and coordination of three knowledge systems—declarative, procedural, and conditional (Hresko & Parmar, 1991)—and depends on organizational "structures" that create connections between knowledge bits and knowledge systems.

*Declarative Knowledge*  The memory of facts, strings of associated words, characteristics of objects, and sequences of events are examples of **declarative knowledge.** Thus, when you recall the date of your sister's birthday, the words to the Pledge of Allegiance, the color of your mother's eyes, or the events of your summer vacation, you are drawing upon your declarative knowledge base. Recall from Chapter 1 that one of the criticisms of the current educational system is that most teaching focuses on amassing declarative knowledge. While a reliance on facts alone is insufficient, all learners need a repository of declarative knowledge. However, as you will see, simply having information does not guarantee that learners will be able to employ the information to solve problems.

*Procedural Knowledge*  **Procedural knowledge** refers to information regarding how to do things. For example, knowing the steps involved in carrying out a long-division problem is procedural knowledge. Procedural knowledge is guided by a set of concepts, rules, and steps (Gagne, 1984) that, with increased use over time, become automatic—requiring less overt cognitive processing. For example, think back to your earliest experiences learning to ride a bicycle. At first, you may have had to think overtly about each step you took as you carried out the physical responses necessary to set the bike in motion, begin pedaling, and steer. You may even have "talked" yourself through the steps ("Put one foot on one pedal, push with the other foot, lift my body on to the seat, steer the handlebars in a straight line, oops! shift to the left . . ."). Over time and with practice, however, you merely got on your bicycle and took off—without the need for conscious recall of the necessary steps.

*Conditional Knowledge*  Having information in our memory about facts and procedures is useful only if we know when to apply the knowledge to solve problems in our daily lives. **Conditional knowledge** refers to the ability to know when a particular procedure or bit of knowledge is needed to solve a problem (Hresko & Parmar, 1991). For example, when Michael took his American history test last semester, a question asked

him to compare and contrast the causes of the Civil War with the causes of the War of 1812. To answer that question, Michael had to have many kinds of information stored in his long-term memory. First, he had to call upon a substantial amount of declarative knowledge about both wars. Next, he had to decide which of the strategies in his procedural knowledge bank he should use. Finally, he had to recall the procedures for answering a compare/contrast question. Michael probably didn't actually do these three steps in this order; it's more likely that he thought about aspects of all three simultaneously. Thus, Michael used his conditional memory to pull out pieces of declarative and procedural knowledge at the very time that he needed to use those pieces of information and in the organizational format that was most useful to complete the task at hand.

*Organizational Structures*  The way that we access and use information in long-term memory is directly affected by the way that the information or knowledge is organized in memory. Organizing memory and organizing closets are not too dissimilar. Different people organize their closets in different ways. Some individuals may sort clothing by type—blouses/shirts together, jackets together, pants together. Others may organize by color—pastel clothing on one side, darker colors on the other. Some may choose warmth as the standard for the organizational system, so clothing is sorted by seasons of the year. Others may select the length of garments as the critical organizing feature. Some may not organize their clothing according to any particular feature and rely on remembering where they last placed an item to find it again. Others may rely on random searches to find something to wear. Similarly, each of us organizes our memories in unique ways. Some systems are more efficient than others if the goal is quick retrieval. Some systems may be a little more complex and take a little longer to use but have more categories in which to store information.

The analogy isn't quite complete, however, without considering the addition and removal of items. Sometimes the old organizational system fails to provide a particular location for a new or a novel item. In that case, a new category or feature must be created that allows for the introduction of the item into an ongoing system. For example, the purchase of an evening gown that is longer than any other items, that might be worn in any season, or that doesn't meet the characteristics of more common items requires some accommodations to the system. One approach might be to create a new category—fancy clothes. Another might be to add a new level of complexity to the clothing type system—with jackets, skirts, and dresses each organized by length.

As we store declarative, procedural, and conditional information within our memories, we apply various organizational strategies to enhance our remembering of that information and/or to connect new information to our existing storehouse of information. Frequently, we do so quite unconsciously, but sometimes a conscious decision is made to remember a particular piece of information in a particular way.

For example, many of the students in Michael's American history class memorized the causes of the Civil War along with the other information about the political and economic characteristics of the time. However, Michael remembered that the teacher had warned the class at the beginning of the semester that they would be expected to note the similarities and differences among each of the military incidents they studied. Because of this, when he studied the Civil War, he continually asked himself, "How is this feature similar to and different from the features of the War of 1812?" In short, he chose to remember information about one war in the context of another rather than as isolated pieces of information. Thus, when the question was posed on the test, he was prepared to answer. His thoughts and memories were organized in a way that was helpful to the required demonstration of the knowledge. Just as the organizational system in a closet affects a person's ability to readily retrieve desired garments, so does the organization of information in the long-term memory affect a person's ability to access remembered information.

Piaget (1971) called the organizational structures that people employ to remember bits and pieces of information **schemata**, collections of information that have some organizing feature unique to the individual. He then described two kinds of learning: (1) **assimilation**, in which information is integrated into the learner's existing knowledge base, and (2) **accommodation**, in which existing knowledge structures are changed. In the closet example, assimilation entails adding a jacket to the existing organizational plan because it makes sense to do so. Accommodation is required when the evening gown doesn't fit the characteristics of the other items neatly, forcing a rethinking of the system.

Other researchers and theorists have made similar distinctions. Rumelhart and Norman (1981) described three kinds of learning. The first two, accretion and tuning, deal with the gradual accumulation or addition of information and the expression of that information in more parsimonious ways. The third type, restructuring, involves reorganizing information so that it produces new insights and can be used in new situations.

Cognitive researchers and theorists tend to agree that learning is more than a simple matter of being "filled up" with facts, procedures, and skills that sit in little niches in the brain. Learning is dynamic. Once information is acquired and stored in long-term memory, it can be changed—and in the most effective learning situations, it is changed (Marzano, 1992).

**EXECUTIVE CONTROL** As we have discussed the various components and processes of cognition, we have implied that moving information between these components and processes is actively controlled and internally regulated. The executive control function of cognition is analogous to the conductor of an orchestra. It continually plans, monitors, adapts, or modifies our use of strategies; shifts resources for attention; prioritizes; and organizes our cognitive activities. The cognitive strategies that are used to solve problems in our daily lives are also applied internally to the processing, storage, and retrieval of information. Metacognition and self-regulation are primary components of the executive control system.

*Metacognition* **Metacognition,** or "knowing about knowing," refers to our awareness of our cognitive strengths and weaknesses (Brown, 1975) and the ability to think about how we are thinking. Consider the times that you have been reading a novel before drifting off to sleep and you flipped the page without paying attention or comprehending its contents. It is the metacognitive component of the executive control function that causes you to ask yourself about your attention to what you just read and to make a decision about whether to go back and read it again or to go on to the next page.

*Self-Regulation* Self-regulation involves taking deliberate control over our cognitive activity and modifying the way we are currently thinking about something. For example, when Michael was studying for his

American history test, he found himself drifting off and failing to pay attention to the words on the page of his text. He knew he was tired, but he decided that he needed to continue studying, so he used some **self-talk** to refocus his attention on the printed page. Efficient operation of the cognitive functions of attention, perception, working memory, and long-term memory depend on the ability to monitor and regulate the other cognitive functions.

## How Cognitive Needs Influence Affect, Communication, and Physical Health

Cognition is a complex, interactive process that can be better understood by looking at component parts. Although we presented these parts in a sequential fashion, they are interactive and operate simultaneously. The most efficient thinkers rely heavily on their executive control functions to manage and evaluate the way they use attention, perception, working memory, and long-term memory to respond to problems and tasks. When cognitive processes are working efficiently and clearly, individuals are able to manage their emotions, express their thoughts clearly, and make choices about how to manage their physical health. But disorganized thinking, memory loss, seizures, and a variety of other factors can impact mental health, the ability to express thoughts and feelings, and physical well-being. Nowhere is this interrelationship among cognition, affect, communication, and physical health more apparent than in the classroom.

To understand the relationship between cognitive processes and expectations for students, consider the vignette in Box 5.1 about Ms. Rahjad and her unit on ocean creatures. Ms. Rahjad used several teaching techniques that are supported by our knowledge base about cognitive processes. For instance, by asking students to talk about their experiences with the ocean, Ms. Rahjad helped them to focus on what they already knew by activating what was stored in long-term memory. Ms. Rahjad thus provided a support framework that enhanced the probability that her students would be able to elaborate on their long-term memories by adding new information in a logical, connected fashion to what they already knew.

When students do not have background knowledge about and experiences with a subject or are not aware of logical connections between new information and their previous experiences, they have extreme difficulties in assigning meaning to new information. As a result, they may "let go of" or "forget" the information or store it in an inefficient manner that is disconnected to previous knowledge, making later access and

---

**BOX 5.1**

### Ms. Rahjad and Her Unit on Creatures of the Ocean

Ms. Rahjad was about to begin a unit on creatures of the ocean. Because she was teaching in a land-locked state, she wondered what experiences her students had with oceans. She knew that, if she did not check this out, she could easily move through the unit without helping students fully understand the concepts and skills she planned to cover. She began by asking students, "What is it that you know about the ocean?" She was surprised to see several students waving their hands frantically in the air. One by one, the students she called upon told stories of personal experiences with the ocean. One student shared a story of a family vacation to San Diego and talked about swimming in the ocean, seeing jellyfish, and watching fishermen come to a wharf in the late afternoon with huge fish in the belly of a boat. Another student

remembered her father reading her *Pinocchio,* in which the puppet was swallowed by a whale. As each student contributed a story, it seemed to serve as a catalyst for other students to share their experiences, direct or indirect, with the ocean. As students recounted their experiences, Ms. Rahjad busily recorded their stories on a large piece of butcher paper. She knew that it would be critical to connect the new information from the unit to her students' previous experiences in order to provide a bridge between what they knew and what they would come to know over the course of the unit. She also knew that, even though this wasn't the right moment, she would have opportunities to correct the misinformation some had managed to glean from stories like *Pinocchio.*

## Extending Your Learning

How might Ms. Rahjad present the same activity if Annie were in her classroom?

retrieval unlikely. Students who are unable to connect with the topic often stop interacting in the learning environment; they simply lose the desire to engage in learning. If the vocabulary is unfamiliar, they may be unable to ask meaningful questions. Or, if the teacher doesn't make sure that all the students can hear and see the stimulus activity, they may lose interest.

For the processes of accommodation (Piaget, 1971) or restructuring (Rumelhart & Norman, 1981) to occur, teachers also must find out about the discrepancies in knowledge or the erroneous information that children currently have. Once teachers are aware of misinformation or misconceptions, they can help create in the child a sense of what Piaget called **disequilibrium**, whereby receptiveness to new information or to restructuring of old information is heightened. Thus, when the student in Ms. Rahjad's second-grade class brought up the story about a puppet-boy named Pinocchio being swallowed by a whale, she was given a unique opportunity. She found out one reason the children might have to explore the food chains among ocean creatures, and she found a way to create disequilibrium by having them "discover" the unlikeliness of whales swallowing boys.

Furthermore, our ability to make meaning from information has an impact on our ability to attend to important bits of information. If we have problems assigning meaning to information, it becomes more difficult to attend to important features of an experience. For example, have you ever noticed how easy it is to ignore environmental signs that you don't recognize? If you were to travel to, say, China, you might walk right past a teashop if the sign were written in Chinese characters. Lacking understanding of the language makes it easy to ignore the very information that would help accomplish the goal of purchasing jasmine tea. Likewise, Ms. Rahjad recognized that most of the children in her class needed help to attend to the information about what whales eat. By setting up two research questions—Do whales eat people? and What do whales eat?—she helped the children attend to written words and ideas about things with which they had little previ-

ous experience and therefore had little reason to comprehend, until now. Now every child in the class knows what whales eat and can describe what plankton is.

## ■ SECTION SUMMARY

Learning is not simply the processing of information. While information is processed, we think, feel, and respond emotionally and socially. Our hypothetical violin player experiences this same phenomenon. Her attitudes about practicing, her motivation to succeed, her enjoyment of different kinds of music, her beliefs about her competence as a violin player, her need to please others—all affect her learning and performance. The next section introduces you to some of the variables of the affective domain and the way they influence learning.

# The Affective Domain

## What Is Affect?

*Webster's* dictionary defines the word *affective* as "relating to, arising from, or influencing feelings or emotions" (Woolf, 1979). In this context, **affect** refers to the feelings, emotions, and motivational aspects of students, as well as to their social needs. Indeed, feelings, emotions, and motivations color the types of experiences that individuals choose to engage in and influence the meanings they make of those experiences (Tomkins, 1991). Thus, our feelings, motivations, and relationships with others interact with our cognitive and communicative skills, resulting in our unique view of the world (Bruner, 1986). Historically, however, the affective needs of students are those that have been most poorly addressed in schools (Swize, 1993). In fact, Goodlad (1984) describes schools as emotional deserts, places where few emotions, positive or negative, are evident. There is compelling evidence from the work of Vygotsky (1978) and others that the internal representations of reality that children construct are mediated by what they see and hear others do. More competent peers, older children, and adults provide models of the language and actions that help young children construct understanding and develop a repertoire of skills (Vygotsky, 1978). These social transactions with more experienced individuals are an essential element of the learning process.

Imagine, then, what might occur if children did not know how to approach others or if they were rebuffed by their peers. Any diminishment of social opportunities would negatively influence the scope of a child's cognitive development (Crockett, 1988). Conversely, limited cognitive schemas might negatively impact social interactions. Given that learning is a socially constructed phenomenon, school professionals must understand the facets of the affective domain so that they can support learning more effectively for each student.

Table 5.7 describes the components of the affective domain that school professionals should consider in their assessment, instructional planning, and curriculum for all students. We have organized the discussion of affect into two major categories, the internal or self dimension, and the external or social dimension. These categories reflect some of the thinking of Morse, Ardizzone, Macdonald, and Pasnick (1980) and Pullis (1988).

## Affective Components

The first dimension of the affective domain is the **internal self**, which comprises self-concept, self-regard, self-awareness, self-control, and motivation. The second dimension is an external or social one, which comprises social perception and social skills.

Before elaborating on each dimension, let us make four important points. First, the dimensions and their components are considered separately only for the sake of organizing your thinking about the topic. In reality, they are all complexly interrelated. Second, the affective dimensions change over time due to developmental and experiential factors. Self-concept, for example, emerges over time and shows greater complexity during adulthood than during childhood. For instance, Kurume improved his social skills as he had more and more contact with the other children in his neighborhood, developed a broader repertoire of skills, and learned to match and perform those skills in their appropriate contexts. Thus, Kurume learned to hail his friends with "Hey" while he greeted his friends' mothers with "Hello." Third, the affective domain is not distinct from the domains of cognition, communication, or physical needs; rather, the domains are intricately interwoven. How individuals feel, see themselves, control and explain their own behavior, get along with others, and deal with stress depends, in great measure, on their ability to think, to solve problems, to achieve physical comfort and safety, and to communicate with others. Finally, the principles of learning also apply to the affective dimensions. Our internal sense of self and our external expressions of self develop naturally and change over time. The formation and expression of these dimensions are unique to each individual, and the behaviors and emotions that individuals express are purposeful and functional.

**THE INTERNAL/SELF DIMENSION** Our hypothetical violin player has an internal set of beliefs and feelings about herself that constantly influence her learning and performance. We all have an internal self that monitors, adjusts, and regulates both our feelings and our behaviors. Let us examine the five elements of the internal self: self-concept, self-regard, self-awareness, self-control, and motivation.

*Self-Concept* Self-concept is the individual's understanding of the self as a player of different roles. For example, a person may see herself as a woman, a daughter, a mother, a sister, a friend, and a professional. These roles exist independently of one another, and yet, when one person plays all of them, they are enmeshed with one another. A well-developed self-concept allows for flexible, fluid movement between various roles. It also clarifies the boundaries between roles.

Maturity permits the development of increasingly complex yet differentiated self-descriptions and analyses of roles. For example, Kurume, at age 18, has a part-time job. This significant event in his life has caused him to develop a more complex understanding of his role as a son because his financial dependence is decreasing and he's more independent in making life decisions. He also is gaining a sense of himself as an employee and learning the appropriate boundaries between himself, his co-workers, and his boss. Kurume is also re-creating in his mind a sense of who he is as a person with a disability in the workplace—and how his identity affects his relationships with others. Thus, all the roles that Kurume has in life are nested in one another. He cannot leave his "son" role to become an employee or a co-worker. Kurume is all things simultaneously, but it is his sense of self that allows him to adapt his feelings and behaviors to each situation.

| TABLE 5.7 | Characteristics of Affective Components | |
|---|---|---|
| **Component** | **Function** | **Impact on Learner** |
| | **Internal / Self** | |
| **Self-concept** | Refers to the roles that an individual carries out in relationships with others—for instance, son, brother, co-worker, boss, athlete. | Understanding the expectations that these roles have within individuals' spheres of reference allows individuals to operate successfully without expending much mental effort on defining and critiquing performance of each role.<br><br>Clearly defined self-concept assists the learner in targeting mental effort on novel tasks rather than on routine interactions and behaviors. |
| **Self-regard** | Addresses the level of competence that an individual believes he or she has attained in each of the roles he or she holds. | When individuals believe that they are carrying out a particular role well, they are able to take risks within that role, are available to try new activities, and are more likely to attribute success to the effort that they expend.<br><br>When individuals assess their own performance of a role and find it inadequate, they tend to avoid new experiences and attribute success to factors beyond their control.<br><br>Individuals tend to acquire more information when their self-regard is positive rather than negative. |
| **Self-awareness** | Describes the ability of an individual to monitor thoughts, emotions, and behaviors. | Individuals who are aware of their own thoughts, emotions, and feelings are able to regulate them. Without self-awareness, self-regulation is difficult. |
| **Self-control** | Describes the regulation of thoughts, emotions, and behaviors. | In addition to being self-aware, individuals need to be able to alter their thoughts, manage their emotions, and reflect on potential behaviors. |
| **Motivation** | Describes the drive to act. | Motivation propels action. It is affected by the degree to which success is expected, the response of the environment to previous behaviors, and the response of the environment or people in the environment to the behaviors of others. |
| | **External / Social** | |
| **Social cognition** | Describes how the behaviors of others and the interactions among groups of individuals are understood and interpreted. | When learners can focus on the behaviors of others and interpret them, they are able to learn not only from their own actions but also from the actions of others.<br><br>Social cognition implies the ability to attend to subtle forms of communication and reinforcement that are provided in social groups.<br><br>Without these skills, learners find that their behaviors are often out of sync with the expectations and norms of a group. |
| **Social skills** | Refers to the repertoires of behaviors and performances that are used in interactions with others. | Proficiency in social skills implies both smooth performance of behaviors and also the ability to match the right repertoire to the social situation.<br><br>Limited repertoires or poor judgment in using the repertoires can lead to social isolation and exclusion. |

*Self-Regard*   Self-regard is closely related to self-concept. Through self-regard, we evaluate our sense of how well or how poorly we perform our roles and supports our ability to regulate our performance. The process of evaluation comes both from our own expectancy for success and our comparison of ourselves to others (Bandura, 1977). Evaluation comprises several interrelated stages of development. Initially, our sense of competence relies on the perceptions and feedback of others (Harter, 1983). For instance, Tanya looks to her mother for approval when she cleans her room or puts on her boots to go play in the snow. Tanya's sense of her own independence is supported by her mother's approval. As she matures, she will pay closer attention to her friends. If a friend is complimented on her haircut, Tanya will likely want a similar haircut. For Tanya to feel competent as a member of her peer group, she will want to match the appearance and behavior of her peers. The "thermostat" of self-regard is always on.

As people mature, their self-regard tends to rely on internal judgments. Kurume, for instance, is more likely to ask himself how well he is performing the role of a car-washer in his part-time job than he is to use the feedback of his peers. But self-regard is not generalized from one role to another. Thus, Kurume's assessment of his car-washer performance may be higher or lower than his assessment of his performance as a student. An important aspect of self-regard is the way that individuals relate their performance to events or other individuals in their environment. For example, Michael believes that his poor performance as a math student is related to his teacher's unfair grading practices. He attributes his learning problems to her behavior.

**Attribution** refers to the way that we create causal relationships between our performance and the context in which it occurs. When we attribute our performance to our own effort and ability, we tend to have greater control over the thermostat of self-regard. For instance, Kurume tends to attribute most of his success in school to his own effort and ability. As a result, when his grades go down, he will study harder and turn down invitations to party. By monitoring and evaluating his performance, Kurume regulates his effort in order to obtain the results he wants and to improve his own self-regard. In contrast, Michael, who attributes his poor math grades to his math teacher, has less control over changing his self-regard because, in his view, the person who has to change is his math teacher.

Weiner (1974) found that the ways that children explain the outcomes (success or failure) of their efforts tend to consist of one of four typical reasons: (1) effort ("I tried hard"), (2) ability ("I'm good at this"), (3) luck ("I just wrote something down and I guessed right"), or (4) task difficulty ("It was an easy test"). These four reasons, in turn, can be divided into two types of responses: (1) internal (effort and ability) and (2) external (luck and difficulty). Internal responses suggest that individuals believe that factors internal to themselves caused the outcome to occur; external responses suggest that they believe that factors external to themselves were responsible for the results achieved. Weiner (1979) also found that students who typically respond with internal attributions are more confident about achieving, actually achieve at higher levels, persist on tasks because they feel that they can score well, and believe they have control over achievement outcomes.

*Self-Awareness*   Like self-regard, awareness of one's own feelings and behavior is fundamental to being able to control or regulate those feelings and behavior. Self-awareness operates on several levels. First, individuals who are self-aware are conscious of their internal thought processes. For example, during a conversation with his calculus teacher, Kurume consciously reminded himself to maintain a calm tone of voice and to choose words that were conciliatory rather than inflammatory. Second, self-awareness requires the ability to identify emotions and their associated physiological characteristics. For instance, even Tanya knows when she is worried, telling her mother, "Tummy hurt," as she cried before her first day of preschool. Third, self-awareness requires the ability to observe and describe one's own behavior. For example, Kurume can tell his father about how he talked with his calculus teacher at school, both providing a verbatim description of the conversation and describing the tone of voice he used as he challenged his teacher's judgment of his work. The extent to which individuals are self-aware is related to their ability to regulate their own behavior. Regulating behavior also depends on self-control, the fourth element of the internal/self dimension.

*Self-Control*   Self-control is the ability to regulate emotions and behaviors. Self-control requires monitoring the relationship between emotions and cognition. For instance, Kirk has many complicated emotions about his family. In particular, his feelings about his father, whom he loves deeply, are conflicted because his father spends so much time away from home. In Kirk's case, when he criticizes his father by saying that he is uncaring, he is thinking about his father's reaction to some of Kirk's favorite rock music. But his conclusions, which are critical and possibly hurtful to his father, are driven more by his emotion of anger toward his father than they are by logical connections between his father's feelings about Kirk and his tastes in music. Thus, Kirk is allowing his emotions to override his logical thought processes. Kirk is experiencing difficulty in regulating his emotions and his cognitions.

*Motivation* Motivation is the fuel that propels our performance, that encourages us to expend effort or engage in a task. Motivation exists on many levels. According to Maslow (1975), the need for shelter, food, and safety constitutes the basic level of motivation. When individual needs for shelter, food, and safety are met, other types of motivation emerge. For instance, the need to form relationships and attachments with others is a fundamental human motivation. Several theorists suggest that beyond the basic drives for survival lie a set of psychological motivators such as the need for control, the need to feel emotions, the need for cooperation, and the need for psychological safety (Friedman & Lackey, 1991; Magai & McFadden, 1995; Tomkins, 1991).

Some types of motivation are external to the individual. These secondary sources of motivation include recognition, attention, prizes, money, position, and status. Other motivations or needs are internal, such as feelings of well-being, self-esteem, confidence, and identity (Butt, 1987). For example, Tanya's need to have relationships and attachments is internal. While Michael's performance on the football field is rewarded by his friends' admiration and a letter on his school jacket, he would continue to excel as a tackle without those external supports because his internal need to be competent is high.

According to Schunk (1996), motivation is optimized through high self-regard or **self-efficacy**. When individuals perceive themselves as being effective at a particular task, their motivation increases. Motivation, in turn, leads to attention to task, persistence, and increased effort. Meece, Blumenfeld, and Hoyle (1988) suggest that, when students specify learning goals, they become more active in regulating their own behavior to achieve success and are more intrinsically motivated to achieve their goals. Apparently, learners are motivated differently when they choose different kinds of goals. When students choose their own learning goals, they tend to challenge themselves and to use effective problem-solving strategies (Elliot & Dweck, 1988).

**EXTERNAL/SOCIAL DIMENSION** The external/social dimension of the affective domain determines social competence. Suppose our young violinist is playing in her first solo performance. When she makes a mistake, her sense of self-efficacy may allow her to ignore the mistake and move on. If her body language and facial expressions communicate competence and security to the audience, the error may go undetected by most listeners. This interplay between a sense of self-efficacy and outward calm diminishes the potential for communicating a sense of failure to others.

Social competence is the ability to read the social cues within specific contexts and respond to them effectively, matching the behavior to the cultural norms of the context. Social competence helps individuals to interact in a variety of groups using both social cognition and social skills (Pullis, 1988). Goldstein (1988) describes social competency as "the ability to use given skills or knowledge correctly at the proper time and place."

*Social Cognition* The first element of the external/social dimension, social cognition, includes the ability (1) to understand and interpret the meaning of social interactions and processes and (2) to select from a repertoire of social skills those that are most useful and appropriate for the circumstances. The ability to take more than one person's perspective in any social situation results in the ability to consider more than one potential outcome to the situation. For example, Kurume's experiences and maturity allow him to make inferences about the perspectives of all of the members of his transition planning team. He knows that Mr. Holloway, the principal of Kennedy Senior High, attends the transition meetings because it is an expectation of his role. But Kurume may not pay as much attention to Mr. Holloway's advice as he does to the advice of his special education teacher. She has had a long and supportive relationship with Kurume. Over the years, she has given him good advice, and he knows that she wants him to be successful as an adult.

Knowing that the behavior of others is linked to their cultural and familial experiences helps us to interpret the behavior and respond to it sensitively. For instance, when Juanita's family was so concerned about whether Tanya would live through the first two months of her life, the social worker who worked with the family was also Hispanic. Unlike the neonatal staff, she knew that their religious beliefs would help them to maintain their composure and ability to respond to Tanya's needs, even though they were scared and uncertain.

Finally, social cognition depends on the ability to judge the context in which an interaction occurs and choose sets of behavior that match the occasion. Thus, Michael is able to act differently in the locker room than he does at Sunday dinner. In contrast, Kirk shows poor judgment skills. Although he can engage in both polite and informal conversations, he lacks the skills that allow him to judge when and under what conditions he should choose one conversational style over another. It is social cognition that governs the use of social skills.

*Social Skills* The second of the two social competence dimensions is social skills, which consist of the behaviors, actions, and/or strategies that a person employs in social interactions. For instance, greeting an individual or group, joining a group, sharing with others, listening, and exchanging compliments are examples of social skills—the features of which can be taught (Goldstein, 1988). Social skills entail both the smooth execution of a set of skills and the ability to select the right set of behaviors for the particular circumstance. Some children may lack an adequate repertoire, while others have an adequate repertoire but fail to select the correct set of skills for the situation.

## How Affect Influences Cognition, Communication, and Physical Health

Student behavior has long been the subject of conversation among teachers and the community at large. Teachers see many student behaviors as "disruptive, confusing, and often just plain annoying" (Neel & Cessna, 1993). By understanding the developmental nature of both the internal and external dimensions of affect, school professionals can see their role in this area as teaching new skills rather than correcting or eliminating problem behavior. For example, Ms. Rahjad has learned to help her students judge the social

context and plan their own behavior. When she began the ocean creatures unit by asking students to tell what they knew about the ocean, she provided a few cues to help. Specifically, she asked the students how long a personal experience should be, how many details they thought they should share, and what happens when someone takes a long time to tell a story and puts in many details. By **cuing** her students to remember some guidelines for sharing experiences, she helped them to think about and plan their strategy for telling their stories. In effect, Ms. Rahjad drew on her knowledge about the affective needs of students to impact their learning process.

Feelings affect the way individuals communicate and the forms that their communication takes. For instance, Michael feels badly about himself in math class. He tries to avoid these feelings either by missing class or by participating as little as possible when he is in class. Both these strategies may help him avoid difficult emotions, but, by avoiding the learning situation, he only falls even further behind. His feelings are difficult for him to express. Therefore, his teacher sees defiant behavior rather than hearing a plea for understanding, support, and encouragement. In addition to the mixed communication signals that Michael sends, he has experienced stomach pains—typically right before math class. Michael's concerns about his math performance are probably related to his stomach pain. Michael's affective needs interact with his cognitive, communicative, and physical needs.

# The Communicative Domain

## What Is Communication?

*Webster's* dictionary defines communication as a "process by which information is exchanged between individuals through a common system of symbols, signs, or behavior" (Woolf, 1979). The extent to which we make meaning from the world around us, participate in social interactions, and exert control over events is predicated on our capacity to communicate effectively. As we discussed in relation to the cognitive and affective domains, the representation of our thoughts and feelings through language is an important facet of learning. Not all theorists agree about the nature of the relationship among cognition, affect, and communication, most agree that they are interrelated.

We communicate through our facial expressions, our body posture, our body language, and, for most of us, our verbal language. Some forms of communication, such as laughter, are universal and transcend differences in language and culture. Others, both verbal and nonverbal, rely on common culture or language for effective information sharing. We communicate both externally, to individuals or groups, and internally, to mediate and organize our own thoughts and behaviors. Music, drama, and the visual arts are also forms of communication. Thus, when our young violinist presents her first sonata, she communicates to her audience through her music. How well we communicate, externally and internally, is influenced by the avenues of communication that we are able to use and our level of sophistication in the use of each. For example, individuals like Kirk, Kurume, Tanya, and Michael, who use language to communicate, are more sophisticated in their communication than someone like Annie, who lacks a formal language system and uses gestures and sounds to communicate. Communicative competence, then, is a way of discussing the skills and abilities that an individual brings to the process of communicating. Let us elaborate on the various elements of communication that, when integrated, form the basis of communicative competence.

## Communicative Components

Most people use the words *language* and *communication* interchangeably, but they have very different meanings. Language is conceptualized as a set of rule-governed symbols developed for the purpose of communication. How these symbols are linked is mediated by rules or conventions of practice. According to this definition, English, Spanish, and American Sign Language are all languages. But Annie's gestures do not constitute a language even though they are communicative in nature.

While communication begins quite early in infants' lives when they learn to connect their crying to responses from the environment, language emerges at the end of the first year of life in the typically developing child. Bloom and Lahey (1991) suggest that language comprises three intersecting components: form, content, and use. Language is one of the primary vehicles for communicating because its conventions or rules for how symbols are put together are shared by

groups of individuals. Imagine how difficult it would be to communicate if we had to negotiate the meanings and form of our communication each time we interacted. As we discuss these three intersecting components, keep in mind that each applies to both the reception (oral and written) and the expression (oral and written) of communication. Table 5.8 provides an overview of the three components of language and the way these components are affected by the unique abilities of children.

**FORM**  The way that sounds are converted into words and sentences is governed by rules so that, when people communicate, their signals can be understood by one another. In English, we know that what we speak about, or the subject of our sentence, typically comes early in the sentence. We modify our nouns with adjectives that come before, not after, the word being modified—so we say the "wimpy dog," not the "dog wimpy." These conventions or rules about where certain types of words appear in sentences make up the syntax of a language. Often, we can identify nonnative language speakers, not by their accent, but by their unconventional syntax.

A formal language system is composed of building blocks that are used in various ways to form larger units of meaning. Languages are composed of a series of sounds, called phonemes, that are combined in a variety of ways to form words. One of the challenges of speaking more than one language fluently is mastering the phonemes for each language. For instance, the phonemes used in Japanese are different from the phonemes used in English. Learning new phonemes requires learning to form sounds in novel ways. Phonemes are represented visually as symbols such as the letters that we use in English. One of the tasks in learning to read is to understand the relationship between the sounds used in oral language and the written symbols that are used to represent these sounds.

In addition to conventions of sound for each language, or the **phonology** of a language, we create meaningful units out of the sounds through a set of rules that govern the way specific sounds are used to make or modify words. This is the **morphology** of a language. For instance, *bed* means one unit for sleeping, but *beds* means more than one unit. *S* is a morpheme that we use in English to indicate quantity, just as *ed* is used to indicate that an action occurred in the past. Language has both oral and written modes.

| | **Function** | | |
| **Component** | *Receptive* | *Expressive* | **Impact on Learner** |
|---|---|---|---|
| **Form** | Infants learn to pair sounds with objects or events—for example, words like *cookie* or *Mommy* with the real thing. | Infants begin their expressive use of language by naming. So they might use the word *mama* to mean "There's mommy" or to mean "I want mommy." Typically developing toddlers learn to put two words together as in "Go car." They learn the use of language, followed by its content and then form. | Hearing and vision assist infants in associating sounds and words with objects and events. Cognitive skills such as imitation need to develop so that infants begin to mimic the language they hear around them. Communication between mother and child occurs through crying and smiling. As the infant develops more complex forms of communication that rely on distinctions between sounds, the infant begins to employ language as a form of communication. When cognitive skills are delayed, the emergence of language is also delayed. A child's vision or hearing impairment may impede language development. In the case of deafness or partial hearing, the aural models for language development are limited, and the child may experience delays in constructing a formal language system, whether it is signed or verbal. Children with visual impairments will have difficulty with word meaning and with pragmatics. |
| **Content** | Vocabulary in children develops in relationship to the range and extent of experiences they have. | Children generally hear a new word before they use it. The richer the vocabulary of the language users in the child's environment, the more varied the vocabulary of the child. | Experiences can be limited by physical and sensory disabilities, just as impoverished environments limit the opportunities that children have for interacting with oral and written language. When infants have mental retardation or other disabilities that affect their capacity to construct and store information about their world, they may also be delayed or disordered in their use of language. The relationship between language and cognition is thought to be so intertwined because many researchers have found that individuals with mental retardation often display language disorders and/or delays (Mire & Chisholm, 1990). |
| **Use** | Caregivers respond to the sounds of infants—laughing in response to gurgling. Infants, in turn, respond to the laughter. These initial, interactive, reciprocal communications form the basis of the use of language. | Laughter, smiles, scowls, voice tone, and gestures are all examples of the use of expressive communication. | A child with very limited physical movements lacks the ability to make facial and physical gestures in response to caregivers. These initial experiences with turn taking are critical for the development of more complex pragmatic skills. A lack of reciprocal interaction sometimes causes caregivers to decrease the amount of language stimulation they provide. Infants with limited range of motion may be unable to use gestures to make requests for more or to show an object to a competent language user for comment, as in, "Yes, you have a big red block." |

**TABLE 5.8** **Characteristics of Communicative Components**

*Oral Language*  When we think about communication, we usually think about oral language. In early studies of language, researchers focused on how oral language developed. As a result, we have a relatively rich understanding of oral language and patterns of typical and atypical development. Research has demonstrated that infants and toddlers understand language at a more complex level than they are able to use it. Thus, we discuss both children's **receptive language,** or what they understand, and their **expressive language,** or what they are able to say. Typically, children are more advanced in understanding the language and communication that occurs around them than they are in expressing themselves. This lag between receptive and expressive tends to continue throughout childhood and into adulthood. If you think about your ability to speak a second language, you might note that you are more competent in understanding what is said than in expressing yourself.

*Written Language*  Written language has received an immense amount of scrutiny in recent years. Researchers now speculate that competent written language emerges the same way that oral language usage does. That is, understanding the purpose or need to write supports the development of the content of the written message. Reading is the receptive form of written language; writing is the expressive form. Thus, most students are able to read more complex material than they are able to produce in their own writing. As writers become more competent, they explore different forms of writing. As we will see in the methods chapters, understanding how skills in use, content, and form develop has important implications for how we teach the receptive and expressive forms of written language: reading and writing.

**CONTENT**  The second communicative function is content. **Semantics** (content) refers to the meaning contained in our communication. For example, when Juanita tells Tanya to look at the flowers as she points out the window, Tanya learns that a specific set of sounds together symbolizes the plants outside her window. As Tanya becomes familiar with one example of flowers, she will begin to apply the word *flower* to other, similar objects. Thus, tulips, roses, and pansies all become "flower" to Tanya. As we begin to think more deeply about semantics, we realize that words and sentences have multiple meanings. For example,

the words *skinny* and *thin* both describe a similar body size, but each word has an emotional as well as a literal meaning. The emotional meaning, or connotation, alters the literal meaning, or denotation, of a word. Similarly, the use of figurative language (metaphor, simile, analogy) complicates the meanings of our conversations. Consider the differences in these two sentences:

- I was saddened by the loss of my father.
- The sun stopped shining the day that my father died.

Both sentences tell the same story, but the second sentence has more impact because of the use of the metaphor. Such devices make our language richer, but they also challenge the listener or receiver to construct meanings that match the intent of the sender. In a way, figurative language veils the intended message. While competent language users flourish in this environment, individuals who have difficulty listening to an entire thought or remembering vocabulary or who tend to interpret sentences literally, struggle to make meaning.

**USE**  The third element of communication is use. Dictionaries serve as arbiters of word meaning, as well as pronunciation and spelling. However, as complete as a dictionary can be, it conveys very little information about the **pragmatics** of language. Dictionaries don't tell us what type of eye contact to use when making a request of a person in authority, nor do they give us the rules for how close to stand to a florist while discussing what flowers to buy. These nonverbal facets of communication are a component of pragmatics. In general, pragmatics refers to the contexts in which we communicate and our choices in how we communicate (Prutting & Kirchner, 1983). While we might greet both a prospective daughter-in-law and a good friend when we first see them, the formality of the greeting, the warmth in our voice, and our gestures might be very different. The use of figurative language, humor, and sarcasm are also considered to be part of pragmatics. Individuals who rely on literal interpretations or definitions of what is being said often miss the intended message. Both nonnative speakers and individuals with atypical language development may have difficulty with the pragmatics of a language because the rules that govern pragmatics are so subtle. Furthermore, the rules that individuals use in any communicative interaction vary according to the context and the motivations of the speakers (McCann & Higgins, 1988). For example, the manner in which adolescents make choices about the kind of communication they use to gain attention or make requests from peers may differ from that they use with parents or persons in authority.

Language usage becomes even more problematic when the complexities of culture and multiple languages are considered. The first language a child learns may be the same as the language used in the schools or a very different language constructed of phonemes and syntactical structures that vary drastically from the formal language of instruction. Imagine the difficulty in navigating between two languages, one that represents the birth community, and the other, the formal learning community of school. As a school professional, you must be aware of the difficulties that second-language learners have in schools.

## How Communication Influences Cognition, Affect, and Physical Health

The form, content, and use dimensions of communication help us to analyze the problems that students have with language. For instance, Michael may have mastered content but not form in expressing himself. So, when Michael told his teammates that he didn't want to play defensive back, the way he expressed it (the form) may have been offensive to some of them. He got his wish to play defensive line, but the side effect was that some of his teammates were angry with him. Additionally, the communicative competence of individuals directly impacts their ability to learn because complex cognitive schemata help individuals tailor their messages to the verbal and nonverbal capacities of others. Efficient storage and retrieval mechanisms are based on vocabulary. Cognitive schemata are elaborate to the degree to which individuals have the vocabulary to organize concepts into a coherent and connected knowledge base. Furthermore, because social interaction plays such an important role in the development of cognition and in the learning process itself, the need for individuals to be competent communicators is evident. Social interaction is predicated on the use of pragmatics. Similarly, cognitive development impacts the development and use of language and communication (Gerrig & Banaji, 1994). Form, use, and content also help us to understand other types

of communication, such as alternative and augmentative communication (AAC) systems.

## Augmentative and Alternative Communication

Most people use a verbal language system like English. But some individuals rely primarily on forms of communication that are not based on formal language systems, and others use formal language systems that are not verbal, such as the American Sign Language that Kurume uses for most of his communicative purposes. While the need for people who are deaf to use sign language is more apparent, in many other situations alternative or augmentative communication systems are necessary. Individuals with profound mental retardation may use a very limited range of signals to convey many meanings because they learn new behaviors slowly. Think about Annie, who has severe mental retardation. She uses crying to communicate hunger, fear, sadness, and a need for attention. Thus, she is able to communicate, but her repertoire of communication forms is so small that her ability to convey precise messages is limited and people around her must attend very closely to understand her. We can say that Annie uses an alternative communication system.

Some individuals with physical impairments may rely solely on eye blinks or the movement of their eyes to communicate, although what they communicate may be quite complex. For example, Stephen Hawking, the author of *A Brief History of Time* and a professor of mathematics and theoretical physics at the University of Cambridge, has amyotrophic lateral sclerosis (ALS), or Lou Gehrig's disease. For many years, he has had to communicate using an electronic communication system because he has lost neurological control over his vocal cords and can no longer form words that are intelligible to his listeners. Hawking uses an augmentative communication system.

Hawking's communication system also has a complex code with conventions for how he constructs his sentences. The symbols that his system is coded with are rule-governed; they follow predictable patterns that can be easily distinguished by listeners. In contrast, Annie's system is simple and does not require a complex system of rules for use. As a result, we might categorize her behavior as communicative but not language-based, because the contexts and forms that

Physicist and author Stephen Hawking uses assistive technology to communicate.

her communicative acts take are idiosyncratic rather than rule-governed. These two very different individuals both use AAC systems, but the systems vary greatly in their form, content, and use. Still, the needs that drive them—and us—to communicate are universal: making meaning, sharing our experiences, and controlling or managing our environment.

AAC systems like those that Hawking and Annie use can either substitute for or enhance the development of oral language. These systems can be aided by a piece of equipment such as a picture **communication board,** a voice output communication device, or a computer. Systems can also be unaided; that is, the user can use signs or gestures, but no devices, to communicate. AAC systems rely on a variety of symbol systems including Morse code, three-dimensional shapes, written words, manual signs, and objects (Lloyd & Karlan, 1984; Mirenda & Locke, 1989; Romski, Sevcik, & Pate 1988).

### Extending Your Learning

What if Kurume were a first-grader in Ms. Rahjad's class. What should she do to improve Kurume's opportunities to learn about the ocean?

### ■ SECTION SUMMARY

We introduced the term *communicative competence* at the beginning of this section to provide a way of talking about the capacities and skills that different individuals bring to the process of communicating. Communicative competence occurs not only as a result of the integration of form, use, and content but also as the result of complex interactions among cognition and affective arenas of growth and development. For instance, individuals who are able to store efficiently information in their long-term memory are more likely to have a richer vocabulary. Without a rich vocabulary, they may not be able to store and retrieve information. So, language usage governs memory processes, and memory processes simultaneously affect vocabulary. When different languages and cultures enter into this equation, it becomes even more complex.

In a similar dynamic, expression is more likely to occur in environments in which students are encouraged to try new words and forms of expression. Ms. Rahjad's classroom is such an environment. When she began the unit on ocean creatures, she played a tape of the sounds of the ocean. After her students listened to the ocean sounds, she asked them to describe what they heard. Every student had a chance to share ideas. By writing down the students' contributions, she encouraged their expression. And by encouraging students to share a new idea, she increased the chances that they will try new forms of expression. Motivation and self-concept are affective components that are linked to language usage. Teachers who are sensitive to the affective dimension of language usage increase the opportunities for students to develop their vocabularies.

Like cognition and affect, communicative competence continues to develop throughout life. There are a variety of causes for unusual patterns of communication development and use. What is critical to understand is that language and communication delays and disorders differ in their intensity and in the type of interventions required. Communication problems can range from a teenager who struggles with noun/verb agreement in written language to an adult who uses one or two gestures to communicate basic needs. Because communication problems vary so greatly, the intensity of intervention also varies to the same degree. But for individuals with significant language and communication disorders, developing alternative or augmentative communication systems is a necessity.

## The Physical Domain

Imagine once again our hypothetical violinist. Her cognitive, affective, communicative, and physical domains interact to influence her performance. For instance, her physical dexterity enables her to handle the bow and place her fingers on the frets of the violin to produce different notes. Her visual and auditory acuity helps her to see the notes on her music score and to discern whether she is playing them accurately. Her body's endurance level dictates whether she can play a long or short piece. To perform at peak levels, she needs to make sure that she has eaten enough of the right foods to maintain her concentration and stamina throughout the performance. If she has allergies or a cold, she needs to monitor her medication levels. And her brain and central nervous system need to communicate complex commands in order for all these physical systems to function. Competent performance occurs when all these components execute their routines effectively. In this sense, teachers and other school professionals need to understand not merely how we think, feel, and communicate but also how our brains and physical systems function.

Our bodies and brains support development in each of the other domains. Our physical ability to participate in activities is an essential element of our ability to adapt to, modify, and exert control over the environment. Our brains, in concert with other physical systems, govern how we move through space, grasp and manipulate objects, resist disease, eat, breathe, maintain physical comfort, avoid pain, rest, and dodge injury. The brain itself is composed of complex webs of neurons that send and receive electrical messages to all of the body's systems. Understanding how the brain operates in concert with the other physical systems is somewhat akin to reading the electrical schematic for a skyscraper. There are complex subsystems that operate the lights, run the generators, power the kitchens, and keep the elevators running.

### Physical Systems and Subsystems

How we use and maintain our physical systems and subsystems will, to a great degree, influence their level and length of functioning. As school professionals, you must understand the interrelationship of students' health and physical needs and their opportunities to learn and participate in school-related activities. The primary physical systems of the body are (1) the sensory, (2) the musculoskeletal, (3) the central nervous, (4) the immunological and metabolic, (5) the cardiovascular, and (6) the respiratory.

**THE SENSORY SYSTEM** The **sensory system,** you will recall, is composed of the five senses: vision, hearing, smell, taste, and touch. Sensory information enables individuals to perceive important differences in objects or events that contribute to an overall understanding and memory of the object or event. The memories that a person creates of an experience, an object, a procedure, or a skill may be stored temporarily in short-term memory and then be transferred to long-term memory. When one or more of these systems for input is absent or when a sensory input is limited in any way, the person must rely more heavily on other sources of sensory information.

All senses have a developmental component. Sensory systems are partially mature at birth and rapidly develop after birth. As indicated in Box 5.2, the sensory systems are critical foundations to learning. In fact, research indicates that, when all of the sensory systems are tapped for learning purposes, attention, perception, and memory are enhanced (Caine & Caine, 1994). Let us examine each sensory system and its impact on learners.

*Vision* The anatomy of the visual system is extremely complex, so our discussion here will focus on only the basic components and characteristics. Light rays reflecting off physical objects pass through several structures within the eye (the cornea, the pupil, the lens, and the retina) and then become a series of electrical impulses that pass through the optic nerves to the occipital lobes, which serve as the visual center of the brain. Children develop visual capacity rapidly as they mature through infancy and early childhood. Visual capacity consists of three functional aspects:

- *Visual acuity*—the ability to discriminate objects at near and far distances

- *Visual efficiency*—control of eye movement, discrimination of objects from the background, and attention to important details

- *Field of vision*—the ability to distinguish objects in a central field and in a peripheral field

Visual capacity is affected by the control and coordination of the muscles surrounding the eyes, by the shape and curvature of the lens and cornea, and by the functioning of the optic nerves and the cells within the occipital lobes of the brain.

Vision is one of the main channels used for attending to environmental information in order to construct, modify, and adapt our understanding of the world. For example, imagine you are driving to someone's home in a rural neighborhood. Your host understands that, to find your way there, you need visual cues—"landmarks" that help you orient yourself in space—as well as sequential, step-by-step directions. The more visual information that you have about the roads that lead to the neighborhood, the better you may be at constructing a **cognitive map** to the house. And the more sophisticated your cognitive map, the more likely you are to find your way even if you enter the vicinity from a different direction. When visual input is limited, mobility depends on the active engagement of all other senses to construct a cognitive map.

*Hearing* Hearing also functions as a main channel for accessing information from our environment. Hearing capacity consists of the ability to "collect" sounds from the environment, funnel them to the eardrum, and then conduct them into the inner ear. Sound waves move from the environment through the inner ear and are transformed into "excitation" in the cochlear nerves. From there, an electrical impulse is sent to the brain. Hearing capacity is defined by the frequency of sounds a person is able to distinguish and by the loudness of the sounds.

To make meaning from the sounds that we hear, we need to be able to identify the location of the sounds and to discriminate among environmental and speech sounds. Like vision, these abilities are developmental in nature. What the infant is able to locate and discriminate is far less complex and accurate than what the preschooler or 6-year-old is able to do. In addition to issues of acuity and discrimination, the capacity to sustain attention to sound affects learning.

Hearing is key to the development of our communication system. Formal language, a component of our communication system, is one of the primary vehicles for cognitive processing. According to Vygotsky (1962), cognition relies on language, particularly the early speech of children, which becomes "inner speech"— the equivalent of thought.

Because of the central role of language to cognition and hearing to language, hearing disabilities can have a critical impact on cognition. For many years, a belief persisted that, because cognition is so dependent on language and because language is so dependent on hearing, people with hearing impairments or deafness would necessarily have cognitive impairments. This belief was supported because most attempts to measure cognitive capacity were performed through the use of intelligence tests and associated intelligence quotients (IQ). However, IQ tests rely heavily on a per-

Through the use of Braille, a young student is able to tap into the world of books.

son's ability to speak standard English in order to perform well, so the validity of the tests is seriously compromised when an individual uses a communication system other than standard English.

Moores (1987) asserts that deafness alone does not impose limitations on the cognitive capabilities of individuals. However, the difficulties that individuals with hearing impairments or deafness can experience in developing communication and language skills can have secondary impacts on their cognitive processing and storage. Because language is one of the primary vehicles for processing and storing information, delays in language development can cause associated delays in learning.

In Kurume's case, his diminished hearing capacity was not detected in early infancy because his family had no reason to suspect it at birth or to believe their suspicions when they began to form in Kurume's infancy. As a result, Kurume had almost no access to language development through hearing his mother use speech. Helen was unable to begin teaching Kurume any language at all. If Helen and Ed had known about Kurume's condition, they could have begun learning sign language themselves and teaching Kurume the signs that parallel the early speech of other young children. Kurume did learn American Sign Language as his first language in preschool and early elementary

school; his parents learned along with him. Like other children with deafness (Allen, 1986), Kurume's academic achievement was notably poor in elementary school. He had difficulty reading and writing English, and there were many concepts that he couldn't easily understand because he lacked background knowledge and vocabulary. He had to engage in formal vocabulary study of basic English words in a way we might learn Russian or Italian. By high school, Kurume's hard work (hours of homework every night), extensive speech therapy, and support of his parents began to pay off. He began to be fluent enough reading, writing, and even speaking in his second language that other school subjects became a little easier. Although he earned many C's and D's in his first two years of high school, this year he is getting quite a few B's. By the time he graduates from high school, his grade average may be a high C.

*Smell and Taste* As with the other senses, smell and taste play important roles in our construction of perception and memories. These two senses, working in conjunction, transmit environmental information to the brain through sensors in the mouth and nose. Taste buds are located in the mouth and on the tongue, but the sense of taste also relies on the ability to smell the substance that is placed in the mouth. Infants show preferences, for example, for fragrant odors and displeasure for noxious ones and are able to discriminate the mother's smell. Newborns also can discriminate among sweet, acidic, salty, and bitter tastes and frequently show preferences for sweet tastes.

*Touch* The sense of touch is crucial to survival during the neonatal stage of development, in which the young infant responds reflexively to stimuli. The neonate is reliant on reflexive action. Tactile stimuli are necessary to trigger reflexes such as the suckling reflex and the grasping of fingers and toes. Initially, these reflexes are unrelated to issues of hunger, safety, or desire, yet they serve the important purpose of meeting the need to acquire nutrition, to manipulate objects, and to move. Infants gain a substantial amount of information about their own bodies and the environment surrounding them through the sense of touch. Tactile stimulation also plays an important role in the emotional development of infants (Ainsworth, 1973).

The role of senses such as smell, taste, and touch, like that of hearing and vision, is to provide multiple pieces of information that help children access, process, store, and retrieve information about their environments. When children are young, caregivers seem to capitalize on these three systems. That is, parents often go out of their way to provide children with toys and reminders to "feel," "smell," and "taste." Unfortunately, when children enter school, these senses are not attended to in the ways or to the degree that hearing and vision are (Caine & Caine, 1994). Recall that approaches to learning and expressions of learning differ. For example, some learners prefer information to be written; others prefer that it be spoken; still others prefer to touch and physically manipulate objects and information. "A safe general rule, therefore, is to ensure that all senses be engaged in the design of experiences for students and that students need to have deep and rich sensory experiences of whatever is to be learned" (Caine & Caine, 1994, p. 121).

**THE MUSCULOSKELETAL SYSTEM** The musculoskeletal system is formed by the structure of bones, muscles, and connecting tissues throughout the body, including the spinal column. Like other systems of the body, this system matures over time. In fact, the growth of bones and muscle continues through young adulthood. For most people, the degeneration of both bones and muscle slowly occurs throughout later

adulthood. Recent studies suggest that exercise and nutrition play a key role in developing and maintaining bone density and muscle mass throughout the life cycle. Development of the musculoskeletal system occurs from the spinal column outward. Thus, infants gain trunk and neck control before they gain control over their arms, legs, hands, and feet. Mobility and ambulation assist children in their exploration of the environment. Poorly developing or diseased musculoskeletal systems affect children's stamina, attention, and even the number of days that they are physically able to attend school.

The musculoskeletal and neurological systems play key roles in children's ability to manipulate objects in the environment, to be ambulatory, and to maintain sufficient endurance and strength to engage in movement and to maintain proper body posture. Exercise is crucial to the normal health and maintenance of the cardiovascular system. The abilities to manipulate objects and to move around also impact the ability of young children to explore and make meaning from their environment. As a result, children who are limited by the loss of a limb, a condition that changes muscular control, or the malformation of bone or muscle are developmentally compromised.

For example, Annie has Cornelia de Lange syndrome, which is associated with poor muscle tone. Although she can walk, she needs an assistive device (a walker) to move for any sustained period of time; otherwise, she becomes fatigued and has to crawl on the floor. Learning activities that allow for Annie's active participation must be presented to her in a format that she can access, either at a kidney-shaped table where she can stand with her walker or on the floor. Her ability to engage in these activities is also limited by her stamina—it takes so much effort to remain in an upright position that she can only do so for limited amounts of time, and then she needs to rest. The limitations imposed on Annie by her lack of stamina and mobility mean that she spends less time than other children engaged in learning.

**THE CENTRAL NERVOUS SYSTEM** The neurological system, also known as the **central nervous system,** is centered within the brain and spinal cord. Think of the telephone system in New York City. It's composed of innumerable networks of phone lines running through individual apartments, which are connected to a central access locale in the apartment house, which, in turn, is connected to a substation that feeds into a regional station and then travels to a central switching station. The central nervous system can be conceptualized in the same way. Messages from the brain direct muscles, govern autonomic processes such as breathing, and travel both to and from the brain and spinal cord through intricate neural pathways.

The analogy to the telephone system in New York extends to understanding how a neurological system can be compromised. If a line is damaged, then messages cannot travel over their typical routes. Alternative routes must be found, slowing the messages. Thus, a subsystem can be damaged without compromising the functioning of the whole. In some cases, the line is so heavily damaged that messages cannot get through. Individuals who have neurological impairments can fall into either or both of these camps.

Messages are sent over the central nervous system by electrical impulses, which are generated within tiny structures called neurons. To send an electrical impulse from one neuron to the next requires the presence of important chemicals called neurotransmitters. The neurotransmitters create a chemical environment that allows an electrical impulse to pass from one neuron to the next. Neurotransmitters have to be present when messages need to be sent and absent when messages should not be sent. For instance, when Tanya wants to reach out to get a cookie, she needs her brain to send electrical impulses to the large muscles of her shoulders and arm so that she can move her hand toward the cookie. But when she wants her arm to be still, she needs the neurons that govern its movement to be still. When the chemical environment between neurons is disturbed, it causes too much or too little activity.

Because neurons are formed into neural pathways and clusters of activities, some sections or portions of the brain may perform as expected while other portions of the brain and central nervous system may not function adequately. By analyzing images of the brain, researchers have discovered that different parts of the brain generate more electrical activity when particular activities are occurring (Sprenger, 1999; Sylwester, 1995). For example, when a person is speaking, some parts of the brain produce high levels of electrical activity while other parts appear dormant.

Recent research suggests that the brain is malleable—that is, that neural pathways can be changed and redirected by a variety of means (Sprenger, 1999; Sylwester, 1995). Individuals who sustain physical harm to their brains through a blow to the head are subject to a wide range of damage to their various neural pathways. These pathways also change their activity levels when various chemicals are ingested. For instance, the chemical that is widely prescribed to decrease hyperactivity, Ritalin, is thought to alter the chemical environment in the brain by changing the balance of neurotransmitters. Even more interesting is the discovery that brain activity can be changed or redirected by exposing individuals to new experiences and activities.

**THE IMMUNOLOGICAL AND METABOLIC SYSTEMS** The **immunological system** protects the body against disease and other harm like infections from cuts or scrapes. This system is incomplete at birth, but infants are somewhat protected by some of the antibodies produced by the mother's breast milk. The typically developing human body then begins to develop antibodies to various organisms present in the environment. Individuals whose immunological systems are compromised are vulnerable to various infections that, in the case of AIDS, may ultimately result in death. In preschool and elementary schools, it is common to see many children with sniffles and to see frequent absences due to flu, colds, ear infections, sore throats, tonsillitis, pink eye (conjunctivitis), and other contagious diseases. Resistance to these common infections allows children greater amounts of time and energy to spend on learning activities and to engage in activities that require attention and stamina.

The **metabolic system** transforms raw fuel (food) into chemical compounds that provide energy or act as catalysts for other complex chemical interactions. The capacity of the metabolic system to transform food into its various chemical properties and then transmit those chemicals to the various locations where they are needed is vital. For example, in order for cognitive processes to operate to their full potential, the metabolic system needs to ensure that various chemicals are produced and available for use. Metabolic dysfunction compromises the ability of individuals to get all the needed nutrients to their organs and may result in growth deficiencies and even mental retardation. Some metabolic problems are often degenerative, leading over time to convulsions, paralysis, and blindness.

**THE CARDIOVASCULAR SYSTEM** The **cardiovascular system** is the highway system of the body. It consists of the heart, veins, arteries, and capillaries and is vital to the functioning of muscles and neurological tissue because it supplies oxygen and nutrients to the internal organs (including the brain), as well as to the extremities. The presence of oxygen and nutrients enables neurons and other somatic tissue cells to perform their natural functions. The cardiovascular system also removes the waste products from the cells to the respiratory or the digestive system. Even minor impairments to the cardiovascular system have devastating and traumatic effects on cognitive, communicative, affective, and physical functioning. For example, inadequate oxygenation or nutrition or the buildup of waste products in the bloodstream can seriously impair a person's ability to attend to tasks, to code information for short-term memory, and even to remember information stored in long-term memory.

**THE RESPIRATORY SYSTEM**  The **respiratory system** extracts oxygen from the air and delivers it to the cardiovascular system. Compromises to the respiratory system include conditions such as cystic fibrosis and asthma. Children with cystic fibrosis have shortened life expectancy. Chronic infections may damage the lungs and may prevent digestive enzymes from operating properly. Depending on the severity of the condition, children with asthma may have to learn to manage their environment and use medications to prevent asthma attacks.

## How Physical Systems Influence Cognition, Affect, and Communication

The interdependence among the four domains should be clear by now—not only do these domains not operate independently, each contributes to the development and maintenance of the others. The physical system is critical to children's development, providing ongoing support for their cognitive, affective, and communicative needs. Without acute sensory systems, cognitive, affective, and communicative competence becomes more problematic. For example, consider Helen Keller. Although she was a gifted individual, she endured long years of isolation and experienced intense difficulties in learning, in communicating what she was capable of knowing and doing, and in developing meaningful relationships.

Annie's situation helps us understand the critical role that the neurological and musculoskeletal development plays in cognition and learning. Annie's neuro-

logical and musculoskeletal systems were slow to develop, and so she didn't learn to walk until she was about 6 years old. Because of her limited mobility, she explored fewer objects in her environment. When we assess her developmental abilities, we can see that she lacks information about how to play with some toys simply because she never had those experiences. Her limited physical movement also means that the way that she learns, by touching and feeling, is compromised by the range of objects with which she can interact.

Now think about the important role that our sensory systems play as we develop and refine skills and knowledge within the affective domain. Again, the use of vision is critical. For example, vicarious learning through observation of what others do and what results they achieve facilitates the imitation of selected social behaviors (Bandura, 1977). Many physical mannerisms that contribute significantly to a person's ability to interact in socially appropriate ways are learned through observation. For instance, the observed subtleties of nonverbal communication may significantly alter the meaning of spoken words. Other social skills, like smiling, are readily learned by infants as they observe and then respond to their caregivers. "For people with limited visual capacity, learning appropriate physical mannerisms as well as when and how to direct their smiles results from conscious effort [rather than incidental observations]" (Hull, 1990, pp. 202–203). Our emotions are often recalled or surface because of certain olfactory memories. For example, when Tanya visits her best friend's house, the smell of fresh sapodillas (a fruit) reminds her of happy times with her grandmother when she was young. These happy feelings then generalize to the moment at hand of playing with her friend. Similarly, if you are shopping for new clothes, the touch of a silky scarf or the pile of a furry coat may evoke memories of happy times in a special childhood outfit, and you may choose to buy the scarf or coat in anticipation of experiencing similar feelings.

In addition to the language delays that we have already discussed, hearing impairments may have an impact on the ability to ascertain the pragmatic or social aspects of communication and of everyday life. Language barriers between hearing and hearing-impaired persons often lead to loneliness among those who do not speak the dominant language very well (Charlson, Strong, & Gold, 1992). In typical classroom settings, children with hearing impairments are sometimes excluded from both casual and more formal interactions among students because of language barriers (Gaustad

& Kluwin, 1992). As a result, they often miss out on opportunities to learn some of the pragmatic aspects of communication like taking turns or politely interrupting an ongoing conversation. You may recall reading about how much time Kurume spent in the classroom at recess break, how he had difficulty joining the other boys on the basketball court, and how he was segregated from the other neighborhood children at a separate school. In addition, Kurume missed out on the serendipitous learning of much of the subtle "in-group" posturing and gesturing of typical children because he had been taught to focus all his attention on the adults in the classroom. He had to switch his attention back and forth between the teacher and his interpreter—leaving little attention capacity for looking around at other students.

The affective domain can also be deeply influenced by an individual's physiological capacities and limitations. The self dimension of the affective domain is directly influenced by the physical domain. People who have physical anomalies or limitations may recognize their differences at an early age and develop low self-regard. Sometimes, children and adults, intentionally or unintentionally, allow an individual's overt physical anomalies to influence their willingness to engage and dictate the nature of their interactions with him or her. This can have a devastating effect on that person's self-regard. Furthermore, when students' immunological systems are compromised, they often miss many days of school. As a result, they do not have the sustained opportunities to form and maintain friendships like their peers. Over time, lack of friendships can influence many components of the affective domain including self-concept, self-regard, and social competence.

The communicative domain can also be affected by limitations in the physical domain. A pat on the shoulder or a hug at a vulnerable moment can communicate more than words possibly could. The role of touch in the development of communication is subtle yet substantive. The intertwined relationship among cognition, communication, and hearing capacity has already been discussed. For sighted children, speech and language development occurs primarily through the integration of visual experiences and the symbols of the spoken word. Non-language-based communication also occurs readily through observation of the adults and other children with whom they interact. Smell, too, plays a part in communication. The smells of an environment communicate if that environment is inviting or offensive, and they provide cues as to how a

person will choose to interact within that environment. For example, when Annie's mom takes her to the bakery on Saturday morning for cream-filled donuts, upon entering the bakery Annie immediately recognizes where she is because of the sweet smells. She breaks into a wide grin and giggles because she is happy to be there. Finally, the development of the musculoskeletal system impacts the development of the structures of the oral cavity such as the hard and soft palate. How these palates are formed affects the production of speech. Similarly, the formation of cartilage in the nasal passages affects the amount of air that is taken in to produce speech.

## ■ SECTION SUMMARY

As with cognition, affect, and communication, a student's physical system is complex, interdependent, and fundamental to learning. If a student cannot hear or see well, his or her access to information is limited. If a student does not get enough sleep, his or her brain will not be alert and ready to attend to classroom activities and information. If a child comes to school hungry, his or her attention and physiological states will be compromised. Attending to students' physical needs is critical in making decisions about classroom environments and managing curriculum and instruction.

# Addressing the Four Domains of the Whole Child

We have explained components of each of the four domains and discussed the complex interdependence of the domains. Remember that a focus on the capacities and limitations of students across all four domains is necessary to support responsive educational practices. Although we chose to organize our thinking about human needs around four different domains, there is a very real danger in doing so. By focusing on only one domain, we may lose sight of the "whole child" or ignore equally pressing needs in other domains. We must never forget that a child is, in a sense, an ecosystem; when we address one part of the system through curriculum or instruction, we must take care not to ignore the dynamic interplay among all the parts.

We begin to understand individual children's needs through our interpretation of the actions and behaviors we observe and through our interactions with them. Interpretation is the key that opens the door of understanding. Why is it important for us, as school professionals and parents, to interpret learners' behaviors and actions? Without this level of analysis, we may miss the important messages that learners' behaviors convey. Understanding learner needs permits teachers and parents to foster students' internal abilities to speak for themselves—to recognize and explain their needs to others.

However, to engage in a comprehensive and accurate analysis of learner needs requires that we hold a conceptual model of each of the areas of human functioning. Having a conceptual model permits us to keep in mind an array of possible explanations for any particular behavior or interaction. We then construct working hypotheses, based on empirical evidence in the context of a conceptual model, that lead to an understanding of how an individual student meets his or her own needs. Armed with a thorough understanding of how a student's needs are currently being met, we can plan a curriculum and provide instruction and learning environments that help the student increase his or her sophistication in getting needs met.

## Avoiding Unintended Side Effects

Devising approaches to instruction and learning that focus on certain behaviors or needs without considering potential side effects may introduce problems that are even more difficult to solve. For example, at Deerfield Elementary School where Michael attended third and fourth grades, he was unable to use cursive writing adeptly enough to complete typical assignments on time. But his teachers believed that he should be held to the same academic standards as the other students. Thus, they insisted that he complete each assignment in full, in spite of the extraordinary amount of time he needed to painstakingly form the cursive letters on his papers. To finish his work, Michael spent most of his morning and afternoon recesses at his desk. Now, when people ask Michael what he remembers

about third and fourth grades, he says, "Those were lonely years. I never got to talk to other kids on the playground because I had to write all the time. The other kids must have thought I was stupid." Michael had little opportunity in those years to develop the social relationships and skills that students typically do at that age, and he also began to have many doubts about his own capabilities as a student.

## Masking Real Needs

Another danger is that ill-considered interventions (particularly those that seek to halt certain annoying or unacceptable student behaviors) may have the unintentional effect of masking the real need that was being fulfilled. For example, when Annie was seriously damaging her skin by picking at it, school professionals were so concerned about the possibility of infection and pain and the need for a more normal appearance that they created a behavior plan to eliminate the skin picking behavior. The plan was to say "NO" loudly and firmly as soon as she put her fingers together in the characteristic pincer motion. After several days of intense intervention, Annie did, indeed, stop picking at her skin, but there were some unfortunate side effects. She also had begun to use some spontaneous hand gestures, and the school professionals thought that she might be attempting to tell them that she wanted something. Unfortunately, when she stopped picking her skin, she also stopped using the hand gestures. The hand gesture behaviors that might have led to productive ways for Annie to fulfill some of her communication needs were prematurely inhibited. Moreover, in their determination to end the skin-picking behaviors, the school professionals failed to consider what basic human needs were being fulfilled by the behavior. For instance, Annie may have been trying to communicate about some need she had through skin picking. Perhaps skin picking meant that she was upset over a change in routine or an unfamiliar face in the room. Alternatively, she could have been bored and been seeking additional stimulation. Or she may simply have wanted recognition. If Annie had been using skin picking as a way of expressing some other need, she had now lost the only way that she knew to convey that need. And if she spontaneously developed a new way of communicating her need, school professionals who had not looked at the communicative intent of her behavior might repeat their error.

Kirk's elementary school experience also illustrates the point that behavior management methods may mask the real need that is being fulfilled by student behaviors that adults cannot condone. Throughout elementary school, there was much concern about the disruption caused by Kirk's outbursts, as well as the number of absences resulting from his school and bus suspensions. The special education services he received were carefully designed to suppress his outbursts. They developed a **behavior modification** plan and created changes in the classroom environment that were intended to minimize the likelihood of outbursts. For example, in fifth and sixth grades, Kirk's desk was separated from his classmates, placed in a corner of the room behind a makeshift screen made from a large appliance box. His teachers found that they could minimize the number of outbursts by keeping him separated from other kids and by giving him rewards for every half-hour in which he stayed there. School professionals were so concerned about simply maintaining his presence in school that they paid relatively little attention to his academic progress and even less attention to his need to forge and maintain peer relationships. In fact, the efforts they made to reduce his outbursts functionally excluded him from the incidental interactions with other students that most kids experienced throughout the school day. In short, Kirk's ability to fulfill his affiliation needs were blocked by these interventions. The unanticipated outcomes of this intervention in all likelihood negatively affected his self-concept. His outbursts may have been a way of avoiding academic expectations that he thought he couldn't handle. This experience may have taught him to choose an outburst when the difficulty level was high. Additionally, he lost the opportunity for valuable, naturally occurring experiences that would have helped him meet his affiliation needs. As a result, his tactics for avoiding unpleasant situations in the future may interfere with his social competence. In fact, this well-meaning intervention may have increased Kirk's limitations in the affective domain to the extent that the limitation became a disability.

### Looking at the Whole Child

These examples illustrate how crucial it is to look at all the needs of the child simultaneously. In each case, the school professionals failed to consider what their students were already capable of doing as they tried to plan how to teach them the skills and processes they still needed to learn. Annie had a way, albeit an inefficient one, of telling others what she wanted, but no one knew how to interpret what she meant. Michael's limited capacities to write were allowed to overshadow the needs of a little boy to fulfill his affiliation and communication needs. Kirk demonstrated a capability to achieve his own outcomes, but because his outcomes differed from the expected norm in the classroom, his behaviors were misinterpreted. The school professionals lost an opportunity to teach him more socially acceptable and efficient ways to get his needs met, and Kirk acquired a set of habits that would prevent him from attempting difficult tasks.

School programs and individual educational plans must build on the strengths that students hold and/or the methods they have developed to get their own needs met. Curriculum and instruction must also provide developmental supports and teach the specific skills that will enhance students' ability to get their own needs met in increasingly effective and efficient ways. To do this, school professionals need to inform their work with children with a conceptual understanding of all domain areas.

## Chapter Summary

In Chapter 1, we introduced the notion of inclusive school communities as a response to diversity. In Chapter 2, we discussed how policies and regulations work to support the work of inclusive school communities by ensuring access for all students. In Chapters 3 and 4 we examined how the collective work of families, school professionals, support personnel, students, and community members is necessary for inclusive school communities to function.

In inclusive school communities, student diversity is a given. The logical response to student diversity is to understand how learning is impacted by the domains of cognition, affect, communication, and physical needs, integrated uniquely for each individual. This means that school professionals begin their work by considering individual needs and then create learning environments that address those needs and capacities. Because individual needs can vary so greatly, school professionals must work together to identify student needs and develop appropriate learning environments.

Learning is affected by the way that individuals function in each of the four domains: cognitive, affective, communicative, and physical. By careful analysis of individual learner needs in each domain, we can plan learning environments that meet the learning needs of each student. Understanding the cognitive, affective, communicative, and physical demands of classrooms and schools helps us to match those environments to the needs of individual students. This approach alters our perspective on ability and disability.

It moves us from a model of repairing what is disabled within a learner to a model of optimizing the learning environment for all.

Assessment, curriculum, instruction, and classroom management practices must be viewed through an interactive learning lens in order for us to optimize learning in schools. The second half of this text supplies the nuts and bolts for successful practices in inclusive school communities.

**INSTRUCTIONAL ACTIVITY**

## Self-Analysis of Learning Preferences

### Objective

■ To use current learning theories to analyze your personal learning strengths, abilities, and needs across the domains of cognition, affect, communication, and physical health

### Preparation

■ Review Tables 5.6–5.8, which summarize the components of the cognitive, affective, and communicative domains.

■ Review Box 5.3, which lists the steps in a direct instruction procedure.

### Materials

■ A rubric for self-analysis, distributed prior to class

■ Transparency copies of each domain table

■ Student copies of blank domain tables

### Product

■ A self-analysis paper in which you summarize your learning abilities, strengths, and needs for each of the four domain areas and then provide a rationale for at least three types of supports that would assist you in the teaching/learning process

### Agenda

■ Using Box 5.3, your instructor will prepare a lesson that walks the class through a self-analysis of each member's learning strengths, abilities, and needs.

■ Your instructor will motivate you by using at least one of the rationale in Box 5.3. For instance, the utility value of the task is that you will be able to apply what you know about your own learning strengths to improve your performance in school. Alternatively, it will give you a way of applying theory to your own learning.

■ Using an overhead projector, your instructor will walk the class through each element of each domain, talking aloud (cognitive coaching) about his or her own personal preferences, skills, and needs. In addition to giving the verbal model, your instructor will list his or her preferences on the transparencies.

■ At the end of your instructor's presentation about each domain, take notes about your own learning strengths, abilities, and needs, as well as the types of questions that can be used to conduct a self-assessment in that domain area.

■ As you take notes, your instructor will randomly call on students to give examples of the types of notes and questions they have recorded.

### Evaluation

■ Criteria include thoughtfulness, accuracy of the learning processes identified, and the completeness of the response.

**BOX 5.3**

## A Direct Instruction Procedure

1. Motivate students by linking the lesson objective to at least one of three rationale:
   - The importance of achieving success on the task because of personal needs fulfillment.
   - The intrinsic enjoyment of the task—fun, opportunities for socialization, reflection.
   - Utility value, with task success a step toward a future goal.

2. Provide a model of the performance or product.
3. Isolate and teach the steps in the performance or product development:
   - Check for understanding of each step.
   - Ensure that students can perform each step.
4. Provide guided practice.
5. Provide independent practice.
6. Assess and reteach (if necessary).

# Glossary

**Accommodation** A learning process described by Piaget in which an individual changes an existing mental schema.

**Affect** Refers to one's feelings, emotions, motivational aspects, and social needs.

**Aptitudes** Capacities or talents that an individual possesses—for example, for throwing and catching balls.

**Assimilation** A learning process described by Piaget in which an individual incorporates new information into an existing mental schema.

**Attributions** Values or thoughts that create linkages between individual performance and the context in which a performance occurs.

**Autism** A behaviorally diagnosed condition in which communication, social behavior, and learning are compromised. Individuals with autism frequently exhibit developmental delays.

**Behavior modification** The science of changing behavior through close observation and the careful use of classical and operant conditioning procedures.

**Cardiovascular system** The network of arteries and veins that lead to and from the heart, as well as the functioning of the heart muscle itself and the accompanying oxygenation of the blood.

**Central nervous system** The complex internal network of neurons and synapses that organize the functions of the brain and the spinal cord.

**Cerebral palsy** A condition involving damage to the central nervous system, typically occurring during the birthing process. Individuals with cerebral palsy have a wide variety of symptoms related to control of their limbs, speech apparatus, and other bodily functions.

**Chunk** Grouping information into sets in order to allow working memory to handle more pieces of information.

**Cognition** Encompasses the acts involved in learning.

**Cognitive map** A mental representation of physical topography.

**Communication board** A device that represents typical speech through the systematic display of pictures or symbols. Depending on the skills and abilities of the individual, the board can be used by pointing or, in some way, indicating the picture or symbol that represents a word.

**Concrete-operational stage** The third stage of Piaget's theory, in which learners are thought to need physical and observable objects that can be manipulated in order to learn new concepts or understand the relationships among objects, events, or physical phenomenon.

**Conditional knowledge** Refers to information that is dependent on specific conditions.

**Cuing** A technique for supporting student learning in which the teacher uses clues or prompts to help students remember to use a particular strategy or select a particular answer.

**Declarative knowledge** Refers to information that is composed of facts.

**Disequilibrium** In Piaget's theory, a mismatch between what an individual knows and new information that is being presented in the environment, such that he or she is motivated to move to equilibrium by either assimilating the new information into existing mental schemas or accommodating existing schemas to account for the new information.

**Elaboration** Expanding upon information in order to attach sufficient meaning for the purposes of memory storage.

**Expressive language** The use of language as a medium for expression.

**Formal operations stage** The final stage in Piaget's developmental constructivism, in which learners use symbols and other abstractions to represent complex associations and connections and to solve problems.

**Immunological system** The system within the body that prevents and fights infection.

**Internal self** The thoughts and feelings that an individual experiences but may not reveal to others.

**Knowledge construction** The notion that understanding occurs as individuals develop their own interpretations of an idea or concept and relate it to other, similar concepts that they may already have experienced or learned about.

**Learner-centered** A term used to describe an approach to teaching and learning in which the lead for what to teach is provided by the learner rather than the teacher or the curriculum.

**Mental retardation** A condition in which the mental capacities of individuals fail to develop at the same pace or to the same extent as typical peers. There are varying degrees of mental retardation, and a variety of factors influence the presence of this condition, ranging from cultural/familial and environmental conditions to inborn errors of metabolism and chromosomal factors.

**Metabolic system** The system within the body that turns food into its component chemicals for the purpose of fueling various functions of the body.

**Metacognition** The process of thinking about the thinking process.

**Morphology** The organizational system for putting sounds together to make words.

**Musculoskeletal system** The complex structure of bones and muscles that support the human anatomy.

**Phonology** The sounds that form the building blocks for words in a language.

**Pragmatics** The aspect of language that is social and interactive in nature, involving the contexts in which and our choices of how we communicate.

**Preoperational stage** The second of Piaget's stages of learning, in which individuals begin to use symbols such as pictures and language to represent, remember, and act on their environments.

**Procedural knowledge** Refers to information regarding how to do things.

**Procedural skills** Skills that are sequenced in a specific order to complete an activity, perform a task, or construct a product.

**Receptive language** Refers to understanding and comprehending language rather than producing it.

**Rehearsal** The practice of repeating information in order to commit it to memory.

**Respiratory system** The system in the body that extracts oxygen from the air and delivers it to the cardiovascular system.

**Schemata** Collections of information that are categorized mentally into meaningful units that explain or help to organize a set of facts, events, or skills.

**Self-efficacy** The act of judging oneself as effective or capable in specific situations.

**Self-talk** A strategy that is often employed to rehearse and memorize information. It can either be audible to others or occur internally.

**Semantics** The meaning contained in language.

**Sensorimotor stage** The first of Piaget's stages of learning, in which individuals use their five senses to explore and make meaning of their environment. Typically, this stage is experienced by infants.

**Sensory system** The five senses—vision, hearing, smell, taste, and touch—through which individuals make meaning of their environment.

## PART TWO

# Strategies for Inclusive Schools

## CHAPTER 6

# Developing and Building Classroom Strategies to Support All Learners

# Introduction

By now, it should be apparent that we take the perspective that learning is constructed through the interaction of the individual with the environment. Cognitive, affective, communicative, and physical needs interact both within the individual and with the environment to create a unique set of skills and understandings that, in turn, support continued learning. Learning alters the individual's internal repertoire of skills and abilities, which then influence what and how the individual continues to learn and adapt to the demands of the external environment. Nature, through genetics, provides the initial building blocks of capacity and temperament (Thomas, Chess, & Birch, 1967). However, as infants and young children interact within their families and neighborhoods, learning becomes a spiral of external influences and internal mediation that results in the unique development of each individual. The cultural, economic, linguistic, ethnic, and racial pluralism of our society means that the children who enter school will bring with them many different learning spirals. This chapter provides a set of strategies that can be applied to creating learning environments that support the diverse, individual needs of learners in inclusive school communities.

The challenge for school professionals is to create inclusive school communities in which learning, not sanctioning, consumes the time of students and teachers (Kameenui & Simmons, 1990). It takes a whole school to make this happen because learning environments are a cultural construction (Brice Heath, 1983; Ogbu, 1993). That is, classrooms and schools have sets of formal and informal norms designed to support both social and academic interactions. These norms highlight the outcomes and behaviors that are valued in the school. As Brice Heath (1983) and Ogbu (1993) have noted, the preferred rituals and patterns of behavior are clearly delineated in schools and enforced by school professionals. Careful thought about what school communities value and what rituals and routines can be developed to support those values can provide the foundation for the work of inclusive school communities. Moreover, as Delpit (1995) asserts, when children from nonmajority cultures attend schools, they need explicit instruction so they can successfully navigate the school culture. Often, these expectations vary from those of nonmajority cultures. Consider the example that Delpit provides from a young teacher in an urban elementary school. Delpit notes that the teacher used many of the most current strategies for teaching literacy to emerging readers, including providing opportunities for children to draw pictures and write stories. One young student who was a gifted oral storyteller rarely wrote anything on paper, although his pictures were elaborate. This student's handwriting was legible and fluent, but he would not write his stories down. Finally, the parents were called in for advice. The young student's mother said, "Tell him to write his words first." Immediately, the student's stories went from one sentence to one page in length. Because the teacher had not been explicit in what he wanted, the student had been producing what he thought was the most valued element of the assignment.

Classrooms are only one aspect of a school's learning environment. Individual teachers may achieve high on-task student behavior because of their skills, but these individual efforts rarely spill over into all classrooms. Each teacher must develop a set of skills that promote students' self-regulation and self-management. Without collective effort across multiple environments and contexts, however, schools may fall short of creating inclusive learning communities and attaining optimal learning outcomes. Recesses, between-class periods, and the time before and after school must be seen as opportunities for developing a coherent environment for the use and practice of prosocial skills that support community building among students. Learning in inclusive school communities is a product of both classroom- and building-level support systems.

Inclusive school communities are ecosystems in which macro-features like building-level supports influence how classroom supports are organized. Classroom supports, in turn, affect the kinds of individualized support strategies that are selected. The most efficient support strategies are the ones that are created at the building level (Horner, 1994). While building-level supports require the involvement of everyone, they also require the least amount of individual time because they are employed universally. Classroom strategies for supporting learning require the work of school professionals and paraprofessionals who are responsible for particular groups of students. The use of whole-class strategies will limit the amount of time required for individual intervention. At times, of course, students need individual support. Although this is time-intensive, positive individual support helps to teach students the skills they need to be self-regulated learners.

| **TABLE 6.1** | The Dynamics of Learning and Behavior |
|---|---|

■ All behavior is learned (Wolery, Bailey, & Sugai, 1988).

■ Responses to behavior, both desirable and undesirable, encourage or discourage the behavior (Ferster & Skinner, 1957).

■ Behavior helps students meet their own cognitive, affective, communicative, and physical needs (Neel & Cessna, 1993).

■ Classrooms operate as ecosystems (Lazlo, 1972).

■ School professionals can orchestrate the ecology of the classroom (Wolery, Bailey, & Sugai, 1988).

■ Patterns of behavior can disrupt learning opportunities (Kameenui & Simmons, 1990).

In this chapter, we outline strategies that promote learning at the building and classroom levels. These strategies address the cognitive, affective, communicative, and physical aspects of the environment. First, we discuss some fundamental assumptions about students' behavior. Second, we examine actual strategies for both the classroom and the building. Finally, we look at the issue of individualized behavioral intervention strategies.

# Fundamental Assumptions About Students' Behavior

Because each new year brings a new and different group of students to your school and classroom, building and classroom environments need to respond to the unique needs of the new groups. No one book, video, or consultant can provide you with enough options to meet the needs of every group of students. You must be able to construct a classroom environment that supports learning for each group of students you encounter. To become confident in your own ability to create healthy, productive learning environments for all your students, you need to understand what motivates and maintains students' performance over time. Performance is one important way that you can observe what students have learned. This section develops several crucial premises that help to explain how individuals come to produce the preferred kinds of behaviors and performances. Recall the five basic principles of learning discussed in Chapter 5: (1) Learning occurs naturally; (2) learning processes change as a result of development; (3) individuals have different approaches to learning; (4) expressions of learning differ; and (5) learning is strategic. Table 6.1 summarizes the dynamics that support these principles.

Learning is supported through the environment in that students learn the behaviors and interaction patterns they display. Implicit in this statement is the corollary that alternative patterns of behavior can also be learned, if teachers know what they are and how to teach them. Also, students' behavior helps them to meet their own needs. Consequently, teaching new forms of behavior involves identifying what needs students are meeting through their current interaction patterns. Finally, patterns of behavior can support or disrupt learning. In every classroom, some students will have sets of behaviors that disrupt learning either for themselves or for others. At issue is whether the patterns of behavior need to change or whether the classroom norms need to be modified to accommodate differences among students. Because students are so diverse in their cultural and linguistic backgrounds and learning abilities, teachers need to be able to juggle their management systems to meet the needs of their students.

## All Behavior Is Learned

Students display many different kinds of behaviors in the classroom. They perform academically by answering questions verbally, participating in discussions, writing in their journals, and taking tests. They perform socially by greeting one another, offering to help someone, and making jokes. They use their communication skills to speak, write, and infer meaning from discourse and text. And if we think about behavior in terms of something that individuals learn to do (Wolery, Bailey, & Sugai, 1988), then changing behavior becomes an act of teaching.

This notion that behavior is learned is very powerful because it will drive much of what we do in the classroom to develop learning environments that are productive for all students. However, the premise that all behavior is learned does not reject the role of genetic inheritance. While individuals are born with specific genetic predispositions that shape their capabilities in the cognitive, affective, communicative, and physical domains, the kinds of behaviors that they produce are learned. Kirk, for example, is impulsive. He angers easily at slight provocations and expresses his anger by using threatening language ("You better give me that hamburger, or you'll be sorry"). Kirk may have a genetic predisposition to produce emotions quickly. However, the emotional responses and language patterns that he uses are learned, and he can learn new ways of managing his emotions that will assist him in developing and sustaining relationships with others (Scanlon, 1996).

## Responses to Behavior Encourage or Discourage the Behavior

Kirk, like the rest of us, learns his behaviors in several ways. First, responses to his behaviors are encouraged or discouraged by what happens as a result of his behavior. If his threats succeed in cowing others, he may be encouraged to continue to express his anger in this way. Skinner (1969) developed a set of principles to explain how behavior is influenced by **contingent responses** in the environment.

According to Skinner and other behaviorists, one way that behavior emerges and is maintained is through the processes of reinforcement and punishment (Skinner, 1969; Sulzer-Azaroff & Mayer, 1991). In this process of **operant conditioning,** reinforcement consists of the events, feelings, and thoughts that occur immediately after a behavior is produced and cause the behavior to continue or increase. Events, feelings, and thoughts that increase the likelihood of a behavior being produced again are called reinforcers. Punishment consists of the events, thoughts, and feelings that occur immediately after a behavior is produced that decrease the probability that the behavior will be produced again. The catch is that the individual producing the behavior must regard what happens right after the behavior as something to be avoided. It's not punishment unless behavior that it is designed to change or eliminate actually decreases.

What reinforces or punishes one person may not have the same effect on another individual. As a result,

it's important to analyze the relationship between behaviors and the events that immediately follow to understand what events strengthen or diminish behaviors (Haring & Kennedy, 1992). For example, Kurume, with his hearing impairment, often eagerly responds to shouting, because his **residual hearing** allows him to receive some loud sounds. Thus, when his football coach yells at him for missing a tackle, he may perceive the yelling and attention positively. In contrast, Michael is intimidated by yelling and will go to great lengths to avoid it. Thus, when his coach shouts in excitement because of a slick move Michael made carrying the football, he may stumble because yelling is so punishing for him, regardless of the context. As a school professional, you must remember that your behaviors or responses to students can have unintentioned effects. Therefore, choosing responses to students' behavior requires careful reflection on past interactions.

Operant conditioning is not the only way that behavior is learned. Kirk may have learned to express his emotions quickly and intensely if he observed others doing so and benefiting from that type of interaction. Bandura (1989) has developed a complex model of learning called **social learning theory.** Like other behaviorists, Bandura (1986) agrees that behavior is strengthened through contingencies that occur after a behavior has occurred. Bandura suggests that observing the contingent application of reinforcement and punishment to the behavior of others can also result in learning. Observational learning occurs most frequently when the person being observed is valued by the observer. In Kirk's case, as a young child, it may have been his father interacting with his mother. As Kirk matured, his role models probably shifted to other boys who achieved status and power through bullying others. Thus, Kirk may have learned to express his anger by observing others who profited from that type of interaction and by being reinforced himself for making his demands through threats and intimidation.

Operant conditioning and social learning theory explain how many behaviors and behavior patterns are learned, but behavior also develops and is maintained through other mechanisms. Some behaviors are produced because they have been associated with a particular kind of stimulus (Watson & Tharp, 1993). A stimulus or antecedent is the event, feeling, thought, or circumstance that occasions a certain kind of behavior (Wolery, Bailey, & Sugai, 1988). For instance, the smell of freshly baked bread may trigger hunger pangs even

## Extending Your Learning

Think about responses to your own behaviors that maintain or increase something that you do. What affective responses do you have to the person who provides you with those reinforcers? Now consider responses that have caused you to stop a particular behavior or pattern of behaviors. What affective responses do you have to the person or event that caused you to stop?

in an individual who has recently eaten. People who are trying to quit a habit like smoking may find that their desire to smoke increases in certain settings, such as bars, or in the presence of certain individuals with whom they have smoked. Physiological responses such as adrenaline secretion in an anxious airplane passenger prior to boarding an airplane are conditioned responses; even though danger is not imminent, the person has become conditioned to feel anxious in this situation. Recognizing the role of antecedents in producing behavior is vital to understanding how behavior is learned. Because antecedents are defined so broadly—as thoughts, feelings and external events—the triggers for behavior are abundant (Watson & Tharp, 1993). School professionals have some strategies that can be used to mediate the antecedents that trigger behaviors in the classroom. One of these strategies is called "self-talk." Most individuals employ some kind of internal language or self-talk that helps to modulate or interpret external events. For example, some world-class athletes have learned to heighten their performances by talking to themselves or visualizing certain kinds of motor movements. Students can learn to identify healthy and supportive self-talk such as "I know this is going to be challenging but I am prepared" or "I used to get angry when Mr. Bond corrected me, but I know he's helping me to do better." Through modeling the use of self-talk, school professionals can also influence the way students use internal language to mediate their own behavior.

We can influence and be influenced by the kinds of reinforcement and models that are available to strengthen or encourage particular kinds of behavior. Understanding how behavior is developed through social learning reminds us that, when we encourage behavior in one student through reinforcement, we may be encouraging or discouraging that behavior for oth-

ers. This is one of the twists of reinforcement principles. Reinforcement is highly idiosyncratic, and what reinforces or encourages one individual may be painful and punishing to another. Because of social learning, when school professionals chastise or correct one student, they influence all the students who witness the episode. School professionals are also reinforced and punished through the responses of their students. They increase certain kinds of teaching behaviors and decrease others because of the results they achieve. Depending on the school professional and his or her needs, what is punishing and reinforcing will differ.

Because the educational environment is so complex and multifaceted, it is virtually impossible to exert control over all of the possible sources of reinforcement and modeling. For instance, Annie is reinforced not only by her teacher's smile but by her own physiology. When she picks at her skin, she may experience a pleasant physiological sensation. As a result, in spite of the infections that result from the frequent scabbing of her skin, Annie continues to pick at her skin because she is reinforced physiologically for doing so. Likewise, unbeknownst to her mother, Juanita, Tanya's grandfather has been laughing for years when Tanya blows bubbles with her own spit. When Juanita scolds Tanya for blowing bubbles, she may discourage Juanita from blowing bubbles when she is around, but Tanya will continue to blow bubbles in other circumstances because she has been reinforced powerfully for doing so. Although Michael is not a fluent reader, he has learned many things in school. For instance, he knows that if he doesn't write the answers on his social studies worksheet, someone else, perhaps even his teacher, will do it for him in the guise of helping or providing assistance. Therefore, Michael has learned not to try to answer because he can find someone else to do it.

As young children mature, they use increasingly complex processes and structures to store what they have learned. For example, initially, because crying produced opportunities for feeding and holding, infants cried to get fed and held. However, because infants do not have language or a system for storing events in their long-term memory, their learning is maintained over short periods of time. Parents of young infants often dislike traveling because patterns established at home may be disrupted. This is because infants lose track of the patterns of reinforcement that are established through regular schedules. Of course, as most parents also know, these patterns are readily reestablished when they return home. As language, thought, and memory develop, individuals become able to store information about what is reinforcing both internally and externally. Some reinforcement comes from their own bodies (for example, being full), some comes from their own thoughts (for example, figuring out how to remember a security code), and some comes from their own feelings (for example, feeling joy because they can see the Big Dipper in the night sky).

## Behavior Helps Students Meet Their Own Cognitive, Affective, Communicative, and Physical Needs

Human beings do what they do—perform, behave, or act purposefully—to gain desired outcomes or results (Neel & Cessna, 1993). These purposes or outcomes include (1) freedom, (2) survival/safety/ security/protection, (3) recognition, (4) fun, (5) affiliation, (6) power, and (7) expression of self (Moore & Kozleski, 1990). As we discussed previously, these purposes or outcomes become the reinforcers for our behavior. The higher the probability that we will meet our needs in one of these seven areas, the more likely we are to perform the behavior.

Freedom refers to our ability to make choices, within social constraints, about such things as daily activities; to decide short- or long-term life goals; and to speak or act or not to speak or act. People need to make choices that reflect their interest in the task, activity, or subject at hand. Interest is based on a combination of prior experiences and knowledge, similarity to other known activities, relationships to other persons, and adeptness at some aspect of the task or topic. Choice is the fundamental issue because students are a captive audience in schools. The lack of student choices in instructional methodology, curriculum, and activities may contribute to the all-too-common lament, "I'm bored."

Survival/safety/security/protection describes our need to be secure in both the emotional and physical arenas. Being able to predict or depend on what will occur under certain circumstances contributes to a sense of security and reduces anxiety. When we are emotionally secure, we are able to focus on tasks rather than allocate mental resources to attending to potential threats in the environment. Thus, the need to survive and be secure has implications for the cognitive domain, although we may think of it in terms of the emotional arena.

Recognition refers to the need to gain the attention of other persons, to be at the center of things. People have various levels of need to be the focus of a situation, to be in the foreground. Fun refers to the need for basic gratification—the need to smile, to feel pleasure, and to engage in pleasurable activities—but this gratification must be self-determined even when others have played a role. Affiliation refers to the need to connect and relate to others. It implies the expression of intimate feelings or of a sense of mutuality or belonging (Dinkmeyer, McKay, & Dinkmeyer, 1980; Dreikurs, Grunwald, & Pepper, 1980; Kunc, 1992; Maslow, 1970).

Power is the ability to control external events or situations outside ourselves. It also involves the need to believe that we can exert enough control over situations so that outcomes match expectations. Finally, expression of self reflects the need to communicate to ourselves and to others about our own perceptions, feelings, and thoughts. It is the ability to display through actions or words our own uniqueness.

These purposes or outcomes build on the work of Maslow (1970), Glasser (1986), Butt (1987), Tomkins (1991), Magai and McFadden (1995), Friedman and Lackey (1991), and Burger (1992), who agree that human motivation is based on a hierarchy of drives such that only when a more basic need is satisfied is the person motivated to reach for or seek satisfaction on the next. Like Maslow and Glasser, Goldfried (1988) suggests that two basic motivations underlie many of our troubling behaviors: (1) the need to be loved and (2) the need to be perfect. Other researchers, such as Horner (1994), suggest that individuals with significant cognitive needs have several functions for their behavior, including (1) escaping or avoiding certain antecedents, (2) getting attention, (3) requesting something from the environment, and (4) achieving physiological stimulation. Another group of researchers focus on the communicative function of behavior, suggesting that behavior occurs because individuals are trying to express themselves (Donellen, Mirenda, Masaros, & Fassbender, 1984). But all of these theorists and researchers seem to agree on one key point: Behavior results from individuals trying to meet their own needs.

Because we have these needs, events in the environment can strengthen our behaviors by supporting our needs. Conversely, events that diminish our ability to meet our needs will weaken or eliminate certain types of behavior. We produce behaviors on the basis of analyzing a situation to determine what needs can be met, how much effort it will take to benefit from the activity, how likely we are to succeed in the activity, and what our attributions are for successful outcomes (Bandura, 1989, 1991; Bandura & Wood, 1989). As school professionals, you can use these principles of human behavior to create opportunities in your classrooms for students to determine their own needs and choose patterns of behavior that will achieve those needs.

The problem behaviors that students display give us important information about student needs, task demands, the social context, and the clarity of directions. When behaviors occur that trouble students or school professionals, a careful analysis of the behavior will help to identify the needs that students are trying to meet (Colvin & Sugai, 1988). Solutions to such problems may lie in how and what instruction is being provided, in the ways that students interact among themselves, or in the individual needs of students. By looking for solutions in many arenas, we can identify the right solution for the problem.

Sometimes, students need to learn strategies that will enhance their ability to meet their own needs. Some of these strategies will be affective. That is, students may need to learn how to give and receive attention or how to get their own need for power met in a conflict situation. Other strategies will be cognitive. That is, students may need to learn how to talk to themselves—to self-talk—to provide the security they need to tackle difficult problems (Watson & Tharp, 1993).

The forms of behavior that students assume are influenced by the behavioral demands and expectations of peers and school professionals (Walker & Bullis, 1991). Where school professionals may expect compliance and on-task behavior, peers judge one another on the basis of the ability to initiate and maintain friendships and play interactively. These expectations may compete and cause students difficulty as they develop strategies that both fulfill their own personal needs and satisfy external demands.

## Classrooms Operate as Ecosystems

By operating from a model that assumes that all behavior is learned through interaction with the environment and serves a personal function, school pro-

fessionals can enhance the opportunities for learning in classrooms. Think of the classroom as an ecosystem. The establishment of order through routines, procedures, explicit expectations, and reinforcers will ensure that the residents of this ecosystem—students and teachers—can flourish and learn. As students learn and alter their behaviors, the classroom culture changes to accommodate their changes. Because school professionals do not have the time to create separate systems for each student, they must create opportunities for reinforcement in the classroom that reaches the greatest number of students. By creating classroom systems, teachers reduce the time spent on managing conduct and make it possible to spend more time on academic learning. The reciprocal relationship between school professionals and their students that is played out through reinforcement, punishment, and social learning means that changes in any aspect of the classroom routine cause change in other aspects of the classroom.

According to Lazlo (1972), an ecosystem has one characteristic that is particularly apropos to the classroom: As the complexity of the system increases, so does its fragility. This means that each new student who enters the classroom has the potential to compromise the classroom system. As a result, school professionals must expect that they will need to change their systems of management over the course of an academic year. One way to keep track of when to make changes is by keeping information about the number of times that instruction must be interrupted to mediate behavior problems. When shifts in this key variable occur, this may be a sign that the four elements of the classroom ecology—the instructional, the cultural, the **psychosocial,** and the environmental—should be scrutinized.

## School Professionals Can Orchestrate the Ecology of the Classroom

Some teachers have learned how to organize their classrooms so that they spend most of their time and energy on instruction rather than discipline. There is no one way to do this. Some teachers do it by hooking students on the subject matter and being great content teachers (Froyen, 1988). These students are so engaged in learning that they have no time to create problems. Other teachers build relationships with their students that personalize students' commitment to the tasks of learning (Good & Brophy, 1994). Still others create supportive learning environments by setting norms, being consistent in responding to problems, and providing incentives for improved behavior and learning (Froyen, 1988).

Kauffman (1997) reminds us that, in the development of classroom ecologies, school professionals may unwittingly foster undesirable patterns of behavior. He points to six areas in which school professionals can make mistakes:

- Insensitivity to children's individuality
- Inappropriate expectations
- Inconsistent structure and routine
- Instruction in nonfunctional and irrelevant skills
- Inattention to the principles of reinforcement and punishment
- Undesirable models

These common mistakes remind us of what to monitor in our own performance. For instance, what reinforces Michael may not be the same for Kurume. Kurume may prefer more individual talk time with the teacher, while Michael may prefer being recognized through public praise. Alternatively, it may be appropriate to expect that Tanya can line up at the door with her peers, while Annie's teacher has to remember to stand near Annie when she gives the line-up cue. Finally, teachers and other school professionals have to remember to model the social interactions and intellectual habits that they want their students to emulate.

Good and Brophy (1994) remind us of four elements of successful classroom environments. One, students are more likely to follow rules that they understand and accept. Two, when learning activities are meaningful, students will be involved in their learning and be less inclined to create problem behaviors. Three, rather than emphasize how to control problem behaviors, teachers need to focus on creating a productive learning environment. Four, students need to develop the skills to mediate and regulate their own behavior. Therefore, classroom environments should create opportunities for self-regulation to emerge.

## Patterns of Behavior Can Disrupt Learning Opportunities

Many problems in the classroom can be classified into five categories: (1) conduct disorders, (2) socialized aggression, (3) attention problems, (4) anxiety-withdrawal, and (5) motor excess (Quay & Werry, 1986). Students who display attention problems like hyperactivity, distractibility, and impulsivity may have difficulty in organizing or acting upon information they receive (Pennington, 1991). However, there are many reasons that students are unable to concentrate, frequently change the target of attention, and show impulsive, responsive behavior unmediated by internal language or thought. Some children may exhibit these symptoms because of fatigue, others because of emotional stress, and still others because of their fear of failure with schoolwork. Children who are aggressive create safety issues in the classroom and disrupt the learning of others. Withdrawn and immature students often fail to keep up with the classroom curriculum. Because withdrawn students are not disruptive, however, classroom teachers often overlook their needs. Finally, socialized aggressive students may operate within a gang or peer group that encourages antisocial behavior. These students frequently have difficulty making developmentally appropriate judgments about ethical dilemmas.

Typical students may display any of the problems of hyperactivity, aggression, withdrawal, immaturity, and socialized aggression. When the frequency and the intensity of the problems increase, classroom teachers will need the support of many school professionals to work successfully with the students who exhibit these patterns of behavior. However, because these behavior patterns will appear in almost every classroom, proactive classroom management strategies will help to ameliorate the amount of disruption (Emmer, Evertson, Sanford, Clements, & Worsham, 1984). An important part of proactive classroom management is teaching students to develop patterns of self-regulated behavior (Catania, Matthews, & Shimoff, 1990).

## ■ SECTION SUMMARY

Because behavior is learned, how we respond to our students will encourage or discourage certain kinds of behavior. To teach students to meet their own cognitive, affective, communicative, and physical needs, we need to understand what needs drive their behaviors. By understanding that needs underlie behaviors, we move from models of managing behavior to models of supporting the behaviors and social connections that students need to learn. Classrooms operate as ecosystems in which changes in one element affect all other elements. When teachers focus their attention on making learning relevant, authentic, and meaningful for their students, they decrease the probability that problem behaviors will occur. When patterns of behaviors disrupt the learning environment, they become problems. Most teachers will encounter problem behaviors that fit into one of four categories: hyperactivity, aggression, withdrawal, and socialized aggression. Understanding the underlying causes of these behaviors and teaching students how their behaviors affect the overall ecology of the classroom will support the development of prosocial behaviors and a socially connected classroom environment in which learning is a shared and valued activity.

# Building-Level Supports

Because teachers and the classrooms they create vary, students need a set of norms that establish the standard for their interactions outside the classroom. Buildings in which school professionals and staff have consistent expectations for and responses to students can lead to a connected community among their students (Aleem & Moles, 1993). This community climate helps students to share values and expectations among themselves (Anderson, 1985). As some students become more and more vulnerable to school failure, dropping out, and violence, the schools must work harder to prevent the contexts in which these problems occur. Literature that focuses on risk and resilience in children has adopted models from the public health arena that focus on the creation of whole-community efforts to support the health and education of all children (Simeonsson & Thomas, 1994)

Students pass on the building tradition for belonging, learning, and caring from the older to the younger grades. Being explicit about the values of the community will support effective learning behaviors in the

building and in classrooms (Ladson-Billings, 1994). Based on our own work (Kozleski, Sands, French, Moore, & Roggow, 1995) and that of others in the field (Bellamy, 1994; Coots, Bishop, Grenot-Scheyer, & Falvey, 1995; Schelecty, 1990), we have identified several buildingwide support systems that can help school professionals meet the cognitive, affective, communicative, and physical needs of students. By creating these support structures, school professionals can develop a coherent approach to meeting student needs and move closer to achieving the outcomes for schooling introduced in Chapter 1. Students in buildings where these support structures are implemented effectively receive the benefits of consistent adult responses to their needs. This section provides some ideas about what building-level supports and processes need to be in place to create a connected, learning community.

## A Shared Mission

One element of building-level supports is the development and use of a shared mission (Jones & Jones, 1995). According to the work of several researchers (Biklen, Bogdan, Ferguson, Searl, & Taylor, 1985; Fox & Williams, 1991; Gursky, 1990; Villa & Thousand, 1992), when school professionals share both a common set of expectations for students and a commitment to ensuring that those expectations are met, time and energy spent on responding to poor behavior rather than supporting prosocial behaviors is minimized. A shared mission means that all school professionals, along with families, agree on a set of principles that articulate the values, beliefs, and educational goals that the faculty and families want to address in the school. Sharing values around expectations for students' behavior can be captured in an explicit mission statement for a school (see Box 6.1). For instance, the staff at Martin Luther King High School might ask themselves if their new approach to discipline will help students to become self-directed. When mission statements are developed by the staff of a school, working in concert with families, students, and community members, the result is a shared purpose. School professionals use the mission statement to guide their responses to the needs of students.

In its mission statement, Golda Meier Elementary School tells how it will ensure learning success for all students (see Box 6.2). This provides a road map for

**BOX 6.1**

## Martin Luther King High School's Mission

The mission of Martin Luther King High School is to prepare our students to be self-directed, literate, critical thinkers who are participating citizens of the community and the world.

**BOX 6.2**

## Golda Meier Elementary School's Mission

The mission of Golda Meier Elementary School is to ensure learning success for all students by offering alternative program models, sharing expectations with parents and students, designing multiple teaching strategies and learning experiences, grading for success, and providing many opportunities for mastery by progressing through skills at each child's individual learning pace.

**BOX 6.3**

## Thomas Jefferson Elementary School's Mission

Thomas Jefferson School shares the district mission to develop to the maximum the potential of all students to live fully contributing and satisfying lives in a rapidly changing world, and for the school district to be widely recognized as having caring, personalized, high-quality small schools.

the school professionals in that building to follow as they reflect on their own performance. The emphasis in this mission statement is on meeting all students' needs. In contrast, Martin Luther King focuses on the outcomes for students rather than the processes. Thomas Jefferson Elementary School identifies outcomes for students and goals for the school district (see Box 6.3). While each school identified its central purpose differently, the discussions that produced this statement focused the faculty's and staff's effort. To achieve a shared sense of purpose, mission statements must be discussed frequently. When decisions are made about new curriculum or discipline procedures, faculty and staff can ask themselves how the new idea will help them achieve the school's mission (Ellis & Fouts, 1994). A mission statement by itself is simply a bunch of words. A mission statement that guides the decisions a learning community makes about its own governance, inquiry, and learning activities strengthens the sense of community.

## Quality-of-Life Outcomes

Another element of building-level supports is a focus on quality-of-life outcomes for all students. Ultimately, students' experiences in schools should result in quality-of-life outcomes. As Vernita told us in a focus group of young urban high school students, "It's not the school that's important, but what you learn because you need to prepare yourself in order to be somebody in life. If you don't make an effort to learn something, you will never do anything."

The mission statements for Thomas Jefferson and Martin Luther King schools identify some of the features of quality-of-life outcomes for their students. To achieve these outcomes, students need to learn the appropriate skills. Specifying quality-of-life outcomes

helps school professionals teach prosocial behavior that will achieve these outcomes. For instance, for Kurume to become self-determined, he will need to be able to manage and mediate his emotional responses in difficult situations so that he can choose responses that support his learning or social goals. Annie needs to learn skills to communicate with others so that she can continue to be included within classroom and, eventually, workplace environments.

## A Focus on Sharing the Responsibility for All Learners

A third element of building-level supports is a shared responsibility among all staff for all learners. When school professionals and staff share the responsibility for all learners, they tacitly agree to mentor and coach all students. Thus, students receive support and guidance from faculty and staff in hallways, assembly

A high school student participates in a conference on how to develop classroom- and building-level supports, attended by school professionals, support personnel, parents, students, and community leaders.

rooms, playgrounds, lunchrooms, and all the other places where students congregate and interact outside of the classroom. This means that the staff need to share information about students who may need extra support. Translating this information into practice is complicated. For instance, most school professionals tend to rely on their own style to manage all student behavior (Froyen, 1988). These styles range on a continuum from highly authoritarian to highly collaborative. While these styles have advantages and disadvantages for the school professional, no one style can meet the needs of all students. School professionals need to be able to shift their own style to meet the needs of each learner rather than expect all learners to accommodate to their style (Froyen, 1988).

Rigid adherence to a specific classroom management style can be a barrier to sharing responsibility for all learners in a building (Grossman, 1995). For example, without adequate information, a teacher with a highly collaborative management style may approach a student who responds only to explicit rules and try to encourage a problem-solving approach to deal with misbehavior such as spitting in the hall. In response to the teacher's conversational initiative, the student may decide that the teacher is open to being manipulated. The student may then escalate the behavior and verbally threaten the teacher or other students. As a result, the teacher may have to provide a more restrictive consequence, such as sending the student to the office, than the original behavior warranted. Because of the poor match between the teacher's style and the student's need, the student receives more intensive discipline. School professionals need skills in a variety of management styles, as well as the ability to shift their styles to accommodate the developmental needs of students.

Developmentally, infants and young children typically need support and models in learning to mediate and manage their self-regulating behaviors (Vygotsky, 1978). As children become adolescents, they need occasional support and guidance as they mediate their own behavior and set goals for their future (Watson & Tharp, 1993). Students are able to internalize more and more of the processes that help them to mediate and manage their emotions, their interactions with others, and their ability to understand and respond effectively to the behavior of others as their cognitive, affective, and communicative skills develop. Because we know that the emergence of these skills operates on different timetables for different students, school professionals need to be fluent and fluid in their use of a variety of styles to assist students.

## Family Facilitation

A fourth element of building-level supports is an emphasis on encouraging families to become involved in their children's school communities. Families are central members of the school community even though they're not present during the day. Families' attitudes about the importance of learning and the value of rule

---

**BOX 6.4**

## A Parent Talks About the Urban High School Experience

*Interviewer:* Are parents happy with the school?

*Parent:* The parents in this district feel like they have no say, and what they do say is made fun of or squashed because they're going to do what they want to do anyway. Parents in this district feel like they are stupid or beneath the administration. They have school board meetings. You go that night because you think it's at 7 or 7:30. Oh well, they had that earlier today. When parents do go, then what happens is well, "It's not time for you to talk." If they got up there, go in their car and took the time to drive up there, they should be allowed to speak and should be listened to.

Many times, I've been in school board meetings where the school members drink coffee, look at each other, pick their nails, whatever, when the parents are still talking. That's why you have underinvolvement in this district. Parents are very uncomfortable in this district. They're afraid to. It's like when you were a kid and you walked into the principal's office. The principal is like "oh my God, mighty thing" in their huge desks and you sit down and, huh, that's how these parents go with the administration in this district. They're afraid, they're not actually afraid, but they feel beneath them, intimidated by them.

---

conformity permeate each student's attitudes in school (Wang, Haertel, & Walberg, 1993–94). Some families are very connected to academic learning because the parents themselves have a history of academic success in schools. They value the opportunity to learn yet may be unable, because of work, to serve on committees and attend class activities. Yet, these families want to support and share in the continued improvement and support of classroom activities (see Box 6.4). Some parents may be so involved in struggling to provide basic support to their families that they cannot spare the energy to come to committee meetings. When these families don't participate or forget to sign a permission note, then school professionals may feel unsupported. Other families, for a variety of reasons, are distrustful of school professionals. Perhaps they had a bad experience in school themselves. They may feel that their cultural values or lifestyles are not accepted by school professionals. Or, in the past, they may have heard only bad news about their child's progress in school and want to avoid hearing about any more problems.

More and more, the traditional events that connected families to school don't meet the needs and preferences of families. For example, back-to-school night, daytime parent-teacher conferences, and choir recitals or band performances may not appeal to the families who need most to be connected to schools. Because traditional activities may not provide the needed linkages, each building needs a small group of school professionals who will work with families to create activities that respond to the cultural, linguistic, and ethnic and time constraints experienced by families whose children attend their school. Rioux and Berla (1993) have compiled strategies for family involvement from model programs around the country; Boxes 6.5 and 6.6 list a few of these strategies.

---

**BOX 6.5**

## Strategies to Involve Families of Preschoolers

1. Schedule activities in which parents come together to learn about and discuss specific topics.

2. Organize group meetings in which parents can share experiences, discuss topics related to child development, and participate in learning activities with children. Issues may include discipline, toilet training, tantrums and fears, and stress levels of parenting.

3. Hold workshops to demonstrate educational toys and discuss how parents can use them to interact with their children.

4. Schedule monthly activities that provide families with a wide range of experiences such as visiting the zoo or museum, attending a play or football game, or going to the library.

Source: Rioux & Berla, 1993.

BOX 6.6

## Strategies to Involve Families in Schools

1. Offer monthly family field trips for elementary age children and their parents.

2. Provide satellite tutoring centers in the community (at a local church) guided by teachers and staffed by parents and outstanding high school students.

3. Involve the broader community—for example, by asking senior citizens to teach students a skill or having employees from local businesses talk with students about their work.

4. Develop video report cards for students to take home to their families.

5. Schedule family-school workshops throughout the school year driven by parent interests and requests and/or workshops designed and organized by parents.

6. Publish a book of family stories. This would be especially useful in a diverse community, in which both students and parents would have the opportunity to learn about other cultures by reading the "stories" of other families.

7. Ask older members of the community to serve as foster grandparents and to help in the classroom, working with children on assignments, playing games to reinforce skills, and reading to children.

8. Increase recruiting efforts for school activities. One program found that a personal invitation from a child impacted a parent's decision to attend a school activity more than a flier or printed invitation from the school.

9. Host Family Nights at school once or twice a month.

10. Create family networks for homework support.

11. Make class visits to classmates' homes.

12. Tour parents' work sites.

13. Use voice mail at school.

14. Get schools on the Internet so families can communicate via computer.

15. Use faxes, newsletters, and back-and-forth notebooks.

16. Host workshops on family-focused topics such as planning for summer break.

17. Encourage local recreation departments to host activities at the school once a month.

18. Travel to neighborhoods in vans outfitted with computers so that children and families can learn to use computers together.

19. Provide literacy workshops for families.

20. Send out tips for families via news bulletins—for example, five questions to ask children when they get home from school.

21. Tape record a parent-designed radio show in the evenings that is played over the intercom at the beginning of each week.

Source: Rioux & Berla, 1993.

## Student Assistance

Another element of building-level supports is a buildingwide system for supporting students' affective needs. While daily mediation and coaching require the involvement of all school professionals, some student problems warrant a more intensive support effort. Schools need a formal process for assisting students to cope with the life crises that they experience—whether it be violence at home, threats by a peer, or difficulty managing anger. When problems arise, students need an opportunity to process their emotions before they can get on with the business of learning. Often, however, processing is explosive, as students lose control of their emotions and lash out in anger, frustration, or fear before they can rationally dissect the situation. Unfortunately, in many schools, there is no opportunity to process the issues, nor is there a team of school professionals trained to provide assistance and support to students in crisis.

Given the complicated lives that many students lead, such a team is critical. When buildings have teams in place ready to respond to crises, they are better equipped to handle them with a minimum of disruption to other students and faculty. Serving as part of a student assistance response team gives school professionals an opportunity to hone their communication and problem-solving skills. And rotating these

**BOX 6.7**

**Steps in a Student Assistance Team Crisis Response Plan**

1. Agree on a shared definition of a crisis.
2. Ensure that all school professionals and other staff know how to request assistance and from whom.
3. Ensure that all school professionals know when assistance should be given.
4. Agree on the outcomes of any crisis response.
5. Understand how student needs will be met.
6. Identify the ways that other students' needs will be met.
7. Agree on how the teacher's needs will be met.
8. Evaluate and, if necessary, refine the plan.

**BOX 6.8**

**Steps in a Life Space Intervention**

1. Focus on the incident.
2. Help the student to describe the incident.
3. Select a goal for the interview.
4. Decide on a resolution for the incident.
5. Plan and rehearse the resolution.
6. Make the transition back to the classroom.

Source: Wood & Long, 1991.

roles among school professionals on an annual basis can foster professional development.

Box 6.7 contains steps for planning for a student assistance process. The steps include defining what a crisis is so that school professionals know when they have a crisis on their hands. This step is vital because school professionals have varying tolerances for problematic behavior. Without agreement on what constitutes a crisis, some student assistance teams find themselves with many referrals that could have been handled through basic classroom management techniques. School professionals need to know what the process is for requesting assistance, whom to request assistance from, when it should be given, and what it should accomplish. Without this shared awareness, some staff may expect services that the student assistance team is not prepared to provide. The process of assistance will include a system for identifying and addressing the needs not only of the student in crisis but also of his or her classmates and the teacher. Finally, the student assistance process should have a systematic method for refining and improving services.

Wood and Long (1991) provide a six-step life space intervention model for helping students to work through their crises (see Box 6.8). This process can be extremely effective in helping students learn how to identify their emotions and express them in appropriate and socially acceptable ways. The process requires that the practitioner combine effective listening skills with an ability to analyze the function of the student's crisis. The practitioner also must select a goal for his or her interaction with the student that will meet the student's needs. These goals might include (1) providing emotional support to the student, (2) getting the student to accept some responsibility for his or her role in the incident, (3) helping the student to debate his or her own rationalizations for behavior, (4) promoting the development of self-regulation, (5) supporting the use of appropriate interaction skills, and (6) gaining insight into and perspective on the motivations of others (Wood & Long, 1991). The work in any one interview focuses on one task. After planning for the intervention, the practitioner meets with the student to conduct what Wood and Long (1991) call an interview. When a student has some resolution on or insight into the incident, the interviewer helps him or her plan what to do when the next incident arises. Before ending the session, the interviewer helps the student to rehearse going back to the classroom so that the transition into the group is eased.

## Child Study

An important element of building-level supports is the use of a systematic process for school professionals to reflect on and plan for the individual needs of students who are having learning difficulties (Jones & Jones, 1995). While student assistance teams focus on immediate crisis response, some students have ongoing problems that remain unresolved in spite of the efforts of classroom teachers and the student assistance team. These students, and their teachers, need the attention of a problem-solving team (Fuchs, 1994). After listening to the issues presented by the classroom teacher about a particular student, this team can recommend changes in teaching strategies, disciplinary responses, and the curriculum. The team also may make recommendations to the student to change some of his or her learning strategies or school conduct. Typically, these problem-solving sessions occur before or after school when the classroom teacher and the student can meet with the group.

Schools that use child study teams are often able to provide the support that is necessary to keep students in general education (Graden, Casey, & Bronstrom, 1985). Child study teams reduce the number of children who are referred on to special education eligibility processes. As a result, there are fewer situations in which a student is assessed and denied access to special education services.

## A Buildingwide Approach to Developing Prosocial Skills

The final element of building-level supports is a shared focus on developing prosocial skills. Prosocial skills such as sharing, taking turns, proposing activities, persuading others, verbally mediating conflicts, and understanding differences among people help students to function effectively in groups (Scanlon, 1996).

Some buildings pick particular prosocial skills to work on across all grade levels; others allow teachers to work on specific skills that students in their class need. The key in each case is a buildingwide investment in the development of skills that help students to interact successfully in learning and social situations. Disciplinary procedures that are designed to correct poor behavior by providing a consequence assume that students can choose an effective or socially appropriate behavior. A prosocial skills approach assumes that problem behavior occurs because students lack appropriate skills to meet their own needs (Kameenui & Simmons, 1990). Aggressive behavior, for instance, may be one student's means of gaining attention from peers. A prosocial skills approach predicts that, if the student is taught an alternative set of attention-getting skills, such as telling jokes, then he or she will decrease the aggressive behavior and adopt the new set of skills. Therefore, staff invests time in teaching the behaviors that students need to interact successfully with their peers and their teachers.

Selecting the right skill to match the needs of the learner takes forethought and knowledge of some diagnostic assessment tools. Once a student need has been linked to the problem behavior, school professionals have to select the right skill or skills to teach. Although disciplinary procedures may still be in place to correct misbehavior, students have the opportunity to learn socially acceptable forms of behavior.

## ■ SECTION SUMMARY

Solving the learning and behavior problems that students exhibit in school is more complex than simply sanctioning certain types of behavior and disciplining individual students. Students choose particular patterns of behavior because they have been rewarded for the behavior over time. Changing behavior involves creating supports at the classroom and building level that help school professionals address the needs of students. At the building level, these supports include sharing a mission for the work of school professionals that guides the allocation of resources and the development of curriculum and activities. At the same time, school professionals need to focus their curricula on quality-of-life outcomes. In buildings where school professionals share the responsibility for all learners, students are supported throughout the day both in their classrooms and in hallways, assembly rooms, playgrounds, and gyms. Teams of school professionals enhance their own professional development as they work together to provide peer assistance, family connections, and individual student support. An essential building-level support is a cooperative effort by school professionals to teach their students the social skills they need to contribute positively to the social climate of the school. These collective supports help school professionals to organize their time efficiently by sharing the responsibilities. However, once the classroom door closes, each school professional needs a set of skills that will support the learning environment in each class. The next section addresses these classroom supports.

# Classroom Community Supports

The classroom is a community in which adults and students together find a way to accomplish learning tasks (Noddings, 1992; Peterson, 1992; Schapps & Solomon, 1990; Solomon, Schapps, Watson, & Battistich, 1990). These learning tasks are the vehicles for a variety of learning events. Some of these events are intended. For example, suppose a group of students is learning to solve quadratic equations in math class. Even though the subject matter is math, many types of learning occur within that experience. Students learn to recognize their skills as mathematicians and as members of a group. Some students are good at re-

membering processes, others are good at solving novel problems, and still others provide levity that relieves tension. Students also learn to identify one another's goals. While some students want to be the best, others merely want to be competent. Some students are more invested in becoming members of the group than in mastering the content; others are more focused on their relationship with the instructor. All of these agendas are played out within the context of the math classroom. Astute school professionals understand this as the subtext of their classroom. They weave their students into a cohesive group that has its own unique culture based on the cognitive, affective, communicative, and physical needs of its members.

In this section, we address the supports that can enhance the classroom community by looking at the cultural, psychosocial, and physical environments. (Remembering that all these environments are intertwined with the instructional environment, we have saved the discussion of the instructional environment for Chapter 10.) But first, read the scenario in Box 6.9. By framing her task in four arenas—the cultural, psychosocial, physical, and instructional—Ms. Simmons can achieve her curricular goals. Table 6.2 provides an overview of the features of each of these environments.

---

**BOX 6.9**

## Ms. Simmons' Ninth-Grade Math Class

Picture a classroom of 30 students and one teacher, Ms. Simmons, who has been teaching algebra for five years. This class is in a comprehensive high school in a large urban area. Of the 30 students, 17 are Anglo, 10 are Latino, and 3 are African-American. Three of the Latino students have immigrated from Guatemala in the last year and speak limited English. Another 4 Latino students are third-generation Chicano who speak no Spanish. The remaining 3 have been in this country for five years and continue to learn best in Spanish, a language Ms. Simmons does not speak. Of the 3 African-American students, one is the son of a locally prominent newspaper columnist. He is a scholarly, serious, and competent student who plans on applying to several prestigious liberal arts colleges on the East Coast. The second African-American is a young woman who plans on becoming an astronaut. She needs to do well in her math and science courses to be accepted in a program that will

prepare her for her career goal. The third African-American is Kurume, who is taking this math class as a transition back into the high school mainstream. Of the 17 Anglo students, 4 have been identified as having learning disabilities, and one has physical challenges and is in a wheelchair.

All of the students in this class plan on completing high school. Some of them intend to go on to college while others plan to enter vocational programs. Ms. Simmons is excited about her curriculum. She has a series of community activities and group projects that will show students how to use algebra to solve real-life problems. The students know little about one another and are concerned about their ability to do well in this class. While Ms. Simmons knows a lot about how to teach math, she is intimidated by the linguistic, cultural, and ability diversity of her students. How she deals with this diversity can support or confound her instructional task.

| TABLE 6.2 | Contextual Features of Classroom Environments | |
|---|---|---|
| **Classroom Environment** | **Feature** | |
| Cultural | Communication | |
| | Rituals and customs | |
| | Roles | |
| | Expectations | |
| Psychosocial | Warmth | |
| | Acceptance | |
| | Inclusiveness | |
| | Rules | |
| | Classroom structure | |
| Instructional | Clarity of instruction | |
| | Match between learning targets and approaches to teaching | |
| | Ratio of teacher to student talk | |
| | Types of questions asked | |
| Physical | Time management | |
| | Routines and procedures | |
| | Sensory needs | |
| | Materials | |
| | Physical layout | |
| | Student-teacher ratio | |

Using Ms. Simmons' classroom as an example, let us examine the kinds of decisions that Ms. Simmons can make to enhance the cultural, psychosocial, and physical features of her classroom environment.

## The Cultural Environment

Culturally, Ms. Simmons must deal with three elements: (1) the cultural roles and expectations that she and her students bring to the classroom, (2) the rituals and patterns of life in the classroom, and (3) the communication patterns that are used to express feelings and thoughts and to describe events. Box 6.10 contains some comments by a high school teacher who lives in the same area where she teaches. She discusses some of the expectations that people have of the schools and the students who attend the school where she works. Her concerns mirror the observations of qualitative researchers like Mehan (1993) and Eisenhart and Graue

(1993), who suggest that culture is a social construction that is mediated and interpreted through discourse and through patterns and rituals of behavior.

**CULTURAL ROLES AND EXPECTATIONS OF TEACHERS AND STUDENTS** Rituals and customs in the classroom may support individual achievement or group accomplishment. Simple, everyday activities such as lining up for recess can convey important messages about gender, achievement, behavior, and personal responsibility. For instance, if teachers use "first in line" as a reward for accomplishment, they may be teaching that being first is more important than simply accomplishing the task. Even lining up itself, a technique for managing transitions between activities or events, conveys important information about personal responsibility. By having students go in lines from activity to activity, teachers may lose important opportunities to teach students how to get from one place to another, by themselves, on time.

**BOX 6.10**

## A Teacher Talks About Her High School

*Interviewer:* Tell me about the school community.

*Teacher:* I'm probably more tunnel visioned than anybody else in here because I went to school through this school district from elementary on. I lived in this district so I'm very tunneled in what I see. I think the number one problem we have is the reputation of the community. Our kids come to school here, and they've been told all their lives that it smells bad, it's a bad place to live. People expect our students to be thugs. When you grow up and listen to the radio, our area is the butt of jokes. You grow up your whole life caring about that, and you begin to believe it. I think one of the biggest things that we fight in this community is the reputation. We just talked about how they don't see themselves as being good. We fight that all the time, I think it's one of the biggest things.

In different classrooms, different attributes are valued. For example, Mr. Espinoza may value compliance and appearance while Mrs. Bellamy may value autonomy and creativity. Mr. Espinoza may value questioning while Mrs. Bellamy may value timeliness. Value is assigned when these attributes become part of a grading rubric or the teacher verbally recognizes the occurrence or nonoccurrence of one of these attributes. Mr. Espinoza might say, "Sarah, who's the teacher here? You or me? That's right, I am. That means that you need to follow my directions." This verbal recognition of noncompliance gives value to the concept of compliance. When a pattern of comments around compliance arises in the classroom ("Hey, thanks, Ripley, nice job of following directions"), it indicates that importance is given to compliance. Similarly, an observer in Mr. Espinoza's classroom might see him setting up his students to increase the number of questions they ask: "Okay, class, for the next half an hour, I'm going to see how many questions we can generate. Any question goes. Ready, begin." Later, another observer might note the number of times that Mr. Espinoza reinforces questioning ("Wow, that was a great question. I wonder how we can begin to answer it?"). While the attributes mentioned in these examples represent some of the characteristics of competent performance, knowing what is valued in the classroom creates the possibility that teachers can change what is valued depending on the needs of their students.

The role expectations for teachers, other school professionals, paraprofessionals, administrators, students, and parents are part of the culture of the school and the classroom. For instance, if students are consumers of knowledge, then they primarily play a role of recipient. If students are explorers of the knowledge base, then they play a more active role in determining what is to be learned. Similarly, if teachers are disciplinarians, then they will create and enforce rules. If teachers are guides, then they may assist students in determining what the rules should be and how to enforce them. Role expectations often determine the kinds of structures that are created in classrooms and buildings. Often, school professionals who work within the culture are unaware of the shape that it has taken. Assessment of classroom culture can occur through observations and interviews.

Teachers are valued differently in different cultures and societies (Grossman, 1995). For instance, the role of teacher in Southeast Asia is highly valued. Families and students defer to the judgment of the teacher, and students are taught not to challenge the ideas or content of a teacher's presentation. In contrast, in the Western European intellectual tradition, students are expected to engage their teachers in argument and disputation. Teachers challenge students to demonstrate their knowledge, and students who don't engage in this process may be labeled as slow learners or underachievers.

Gender roles also influence how students and teachers are expected to behave (Englehard & Monsas, 1989; Fennema & Peterson, 1985). In some cultures, males are expected to lead, and females to follow. Difficulties can emerge during parent conferences when a female teacher attempts to lead a discussion with a father who is culturally bound by his beliefs about the lesser status of women. Student-teacher, faculty, and teacher-administrator interactions are impacted by each individual's beliefs about the roles and status that gender confers.

In the Western European tradition, the knowledge base is grounded in the study of the emergence of

Western Europe and, later, North America as dominant economic, social, and political forces in the world. The disciplines of mathematics, philosophy, economics, history, and language all have an accepted core knowledge base. The notion of a knowledge base leads to the belief that the role of the teacher is to impart this knowledge base. Therefore, the teacher is the dispenser of knowledge, and the student is the recipient. Students from some non-Western cultural backgrounds have difficulty with this **dialectic** relationship between the teacher and the learner. The dialog in many classrooms revolves around teachers asking questions for which they already know the answer. Some students may cease their involvement in these dialogs when they perceive that the teacher already knows the answer to questions posed.

Furthermore, the nature of reprimands differs from one culture to another. In typical North American classrooms, teachers tend to explain why a behavior is problematic using cause-and-effect logic. For instance, a teacher might explain to a young child that going in the street is dangerous because he or she might get run over. In one kindergarten classroom of children primarily from Haiti, Ballenger (1992) found that she needed to engage in a disputation sequence in which children first acknowledged their misbehavior (Teacher: "Did I tell you to go?" Student: "No"). Then the teacher needed to relate the appropriate behavior to a relationship (Teacher: "Why am I telling you this?" Student: "Because you like us"). Attending to these subtle but important cultural differences in teacher-student interaction can support students, foster the development of increasingly complex and self-determined behaviors, and enhance student outcomes.

More recently, the information age has challenged our traditional dispenser/vessel model of teaching. In cyberspace, more information is accessible than any one person can store, retrieve, and offer. The teacher's role as dispenser may be usurped by computers. As a result, the role of the teacher in the classroom may change from one of dispenser to one of facilitator and motivator. Finding your own metaphor for your role in the classroom is critical to framing your behavior in the classroom. The metaphor you select will also impact the kinds of skills and behaviors that you expect of your students. Recognizing that they may not understand your expectations will alter your behavior. You will become explicit in identifying the learning behaviors you value and reward in your classroom.

**RITUALS AND PATTERNS OF LIFE IN THE CLASSROOM** Rituals are used to mark events within a culture—beginnings and endings, celebrations and mournings, individual accomplishments and group events. Rituals and their absence highlight what is valued within a culture. In a class like Ms. Simmons', in which there is a great deal of diversity, the teacher needs to establish a set of rituals that will highlight what is valued within the community. Box 6.11 illustrates the way that subgroups can emerge in schools that do not attend to rituals that promote a sense of community and cooperation. Care must be taken not only to celebrate learning accomplishments but also to appreciate individual presence.

For instance, Ms. Simmons could establish a student-of-the-week celebration. If she picks students who have achieved some learning goal, she may always miss a group of students within the class. If, however, she uses the student-of-the-week award to highlight individual capacity, it allows her to highlight anything that is unique about a particular student: language, learning accomplishments, challenges the student has overcome, ethnic heritage, community contribution.

Ms. Simmons also can use the beginning and ending of each session to establish a ritual that is unique to the class, perhaps involving the whole class in selecting a ritual. The ritual could use an emblem from a group of applied mathematicians who solved an important problem, or it could come from a cultural group that is not represented in the classroom. The key is establishing a ritual that is used consistently to indicate the onset of the class. For example, Ms. Simmons could use "Einstein's glasses" to begin each class. After telling a

**BOX 6.11**

## A Spanish-Speaking Student Talks About His Urban High School Experience

*Interviewer:* Describe the kinds of students who come to school here.

*Student:* I would say there's a variety because all kinds of students come to the school. Americans come from everywhere, Orientals, Mexicans, from El Salvador, Germans. It would be difficult to describe them because many of them dress very bad, in my taste. I think that's also one reason there's discrimination because almost the majority of us come, for example, from Mexico or other parts in the South. Those who are from here dress, I don't know, with their big pants and they see us who just came here

and we don't dress like that, then they discriminate—"look how they dress, like this and like that." The way of speaking, the way of dressing, the way of thinking, it's all very different between Hispanics and Americans. Americans think everything is easy. On the other hand, we Hispanics are always thinking of how to better ourselves and all that, and we think how we can improve in school, how to be better, but not the Americans, because they're always going to have help. That's why the way an American and a Hispanic think is very different.

story at the beginning of the semester about how the glasses came into her possession, she could give these glasses to a different student each day. By selecting someone to experience Einstein's legacy for a day, she would focus the attention of the class and give students the opportunity to take on the mantle of a mathematics wizard. Similarly, some activity that is used to mark the end of class will provide a focus at a time when attention tends to drift.

The rituals chosen for use in a particular classroom could follow a shared tradition in the whole school. For instance, a school could choose to use the rituals of a Native American tribe or of a particular country, such as Denmark or Mexico or Nigeria, for a year. The creation of rituals and traditions helps the class to coalesce, to create its own identity. It may be the highest achieving, the closest knit, the most community sensitive, the most industrious, the most diverse, the most politically aware, the most critical. By developing this class identity, the culture of the classroom takes on its own life, no longer orchestrated by the architect (the teacher) but instead generated by the students themselves.

**COMMUNICATION PATTERNS** Successful learning environments hinge on the relationships that we form with students and that students form among themselves. We nurture and support relationships through our patterns of communication. These linguistic patterns are crucial vehicles for conveying a sense of car-

ing and support for students and their learning. Paying close attention to how we listen to and talk with students can forge powerful connections to them. Teachers' language is not merely a conduit of information; it is also a bridge to motivating students to work at their learning. Mehan (1993) states that "because language is action, different uses of language constitute the world differently. Events in the world do not exist for people independently of the language people use to make sense of them" (p. 262). The patterns of interaction that we choose can encourage or discourage student effort. Because learning requires effort, teachers need skills in the strategic selection and use of communication patterns and modes.

*Communication Between Teachers and Students* Culturally, it's important to identify not only the dominant language spoken in a classroom but also the other languages or dialects used by learners in the classroom. Teaching may occur in one language while social interactions are conducted in another. When teachers speak only the language of instruction, they may be unaware of or unable to access the informal communication channels in the classroom. Use of language is also critical. In many public schools in the United States, teachers ask questions whose answers they already know. Students who are prepared for this teacher probe technique enter into the dialog comfortably. However, in some cultures, questions are used only to gain information that is unknown. Students who come from these cultures into the American classroom culture may be confused about the questioning ritual they observe. The teacher may appear unknowledgeable to these students. Basic channels of communication in which the teacher is fluent may result in alienation or confusion for some students.

Roles and relationships between teachers and their students are created through a variety of symbols. For instance, some teachers may signal their role as an authority figure by referring to themselves as Mrs. Bellamy or Mr. Espinoza. Other teachers may provide a signal that they want to be considered as a peer, asking students to call them by their first name. Students who share similar cultural knowledge may interpret the signals accurately, but other students may miss the subtle signals or interpret them in another way. Because we use language to create boundaries, construct meaning, telegraph roles, and manage behavior, understanding how language is being used and received in the classroom is critical.

Language use needs to match the ability of students to understand. This means that teachers must pay attention to their syntax and semantics. Elaborated comments and directions may work for one group of learners but not for another. Simple, unadorned sentences, accompanied by gestures and notes on the blackboard, may be more effective vehicles for communication. And remember that verbal language is not simply interpreted literally but also is interpreted at an affective level. Each individual interprets the information he or she hears idiosyncratically; that is, while some features of a verbal message may be interpreted similarly, listeners may interpret the whole message differently. Suppose Ms. Simmons says, "I'd like you to look at this problem on the board." Some students may interpret her comment as a redirection while others may feel that she is instructing them to attend because they have been talking to each other. Language is cloaked by nonverbal cues that include the choice of words, metaphors, facial expressions, body postures, gestures, proximity to the listener, and voice tones. These features of a message give it power. By understanding the complexity of communicative interactions, Ms. Simmons can select words, gestures, and a voice tone that will result in a message in which the content can be attended to rather than masked by the students' affective responses. Feedback should be encouraging rather than discouraging, and encouragement should support improvement, not perfection. Avoid negative comments

by supporting effort, emphasizing strengths, and being optimistic. Let students know that you have faith in their abilities, and encourage them to monitor and reward their own performance.

*Communication Between Students* The pragmatics of communicating are among the most difficult skills for students to master (Bryan, Donahue, & Pearl, 1981). Recall that pragmatics are the strategies that speaker and listener use to engage in communication. Skills such as taking turns speaking, perceiving sarcasm, initiating new topics, providing feedback, encouraging each other, and recognizing differences are all pragmatic skills. Students in public schools are learning to master the pragmatics of their own cultural group (Pearl, Bryan, Fallon, & Herzog, 1990). Students who have had little experience in different cultural milieus may be very critical of the pragmatic skills of new students. Cliques at the middle and high school level have their own pragmatic rules. Students who perceive these subtle differences and accommodate them are able to move among several groups. Students who are unable to modulate their own pragmatics find it difficult to become accepted by any group.

Knowing how difficult it can be for students to belong to or affiliate with a group, Ms. Simmons must create a context for supporting student-to-student communication in her own room. By doing so, she will be able to support reciprocal learning interactions among her students. Strategies for supporting positive student interactions include using dyads (pairs of students) as work groups initially, before increasing the size of the work groups, so that different students learn to work cooperatively with each other. Dyad tasks could include interviewing each other, developing a set of activities for class use that promote homework completion, developing a set of catchy phrases to encourage problem solving, creating a telephone tree for the class, developing a list of classmates' birthdays, and selecting a set of dates for class celebrations. Dyads can change from day to day so that, by the end of the first month of school, all the students have had an opportunity to get to know one another. Dyads are a great way to have students review procedures taught to the whole class. Given that dyads are created to encourage appropriate pragmatic skills, members should have the opportunity at the end of each task to provide feedback to each other. This feedback should focus on listening skills, the use and misuse of humor, and perception and celebration of differences in communication styles.

*Communication Between Adults in the Classroom* With the increasing use of para-educators, team teaching, and collaborative coaching, adults in classrooms have an opportunity to model the kinds of communicative behaviors that they want their students to emulate. Using effective listening, saying "please" and "thank you," making eye contact, joking, and picking appropriate times to have difficult discussions will assist adults in creating appropriate models.

## The Psychosocial Environment

While culture creates the environment in which students and school professionals construct what is valued, individual students have different internal needs that teachers need to address. Thus, supporting the psychosocial environment means identifying and attending to the developmental needs of learners so that they have the emotional and social support needed to concentrate on learning. The psychosocial environment is created through interactions among teachers and students. Classrooms are social organizations in which interactions can support both group cohesion and individual development. How school professionals stimulate, orchestrate, and reinforce social and individual behavior creates the context for the psychosocial environment of the classroom. While students bring individual experiences and beliefs about their own capacities to the classroom, school professionals can mediate these beliefs through example, classroom structures, and rules. Furthermore, by grounding observations of students' behaviors in their experiences and developmental levels, school professionals can respond to behaviors through instruction rather than discipline (Kameenui & Simmons, 1990).

Organizing students into categories can help us to respond to their differing needs more efficiently. One model that helps us to identify the kind of psychosocial environment that may address the needs of a particular group of students comes from the work of Hunt (1975, 1979; Hunt & Gow, 1984). While Hunt postulated that students' cognitive processes can be categorized developmentally into three subsets, we hypothesize that a similar model for understanding the affective development of students is useful. In our model, summarized in Table 6.3, we organize our thinking about students' affective development into three stages. In the Western European tradition, as students develop, we expect them to move from stage A

through B to C. Maturity is associated with independence and self-regulation, and external controls are dissipated as children progress from being parent-directed to being self-directed. However, the suggestion of progression has cultural implications because different cultures may value adults who function within any one of these stages. Therefore, identifying a student within a given stage does not imply that teachers must or should encourage the student to move from one to another. Instead, matching student behavior to a given stage helps teachers to know what types of supports and incentives they need to create in their classrooms to meet the psychosocial needs of individuals. Because most classrooms will host an amalgam of students operating in stages A, B, and C, school professionals need to be able to create classwide systems that support all three groups of students. Box 6.12 lists specific strategies that teachers can employ to enhance the psychosocial environment.

**STAGE A** Students operating in stage A are tied to external sources of reinforcement and value. They hear the voice of the authority figure or the community more loudly than they hear their own. They evaluate their activities and behavior using the framework of the community. Their value system tends to be dichotomous. Students in stage A rarely engage in negotiating rules or punishments. Rather, they assume that rules, rewards, and punishments are nonnegotiable and that right and wrong are immutable. They expect teachers and other authority figures to reward valued behavior and to punish transgressions, and they tend to be frustrated when their peers escape or avoid punishment.

Students in stage A display the characteristics that Swift and Spivack (1969) found typical of low-achieving students at the elementary and secondary levels. At the elementary level, these characteristics included the following:

- Engaging in behavior that requires teacher intervention and control
- Being overdependent on the teacher
- Having difficulty concentrating and paying attention
- Entering the classroom with fewer ideas and materials than higher-achieving children
- Becoming upset under the pressure of academic achievement more often than higher-achieving children

| TABLE 6.3 Characteristics of Stages A, B, and C and Possible Teacher Responses | |
| --- | --- |
| **Characteristics** | **Teacher Responses** |
| **Stage A** | |
| Externally directed | Explicit rewards and consequences |
| Dichotomous thinkers | Frequent rewards |
| | Predictability and consistency |
| | Reliance on goals for good behavior |
| | Shaping of new behaviors |
| | Development of social reinforcement as the prevailing system for maintaining behaviors |
| | Emphasis on skill development |
| **Stage B** | |
| Emerging internal regulation | Emphasis on development of self-regulation and conflict mediation |
| Able to negotiate rules and rewards | |
| Able to take the perspective of others | Development of group governance through democratic procedures |
| | Less reliance on external systems of control |
| | Use of discussion and example to develop codes of conduct among students |
| | Development of self-reinforcement strategies |
| **Stage C** | |
| Altruistic | Emphasis on self-evaluation |
| Self-determined | Problem solving through discussion |
| | Service curriculum to help other students |
| | Experiments in models of self-governance |

- Doing sloppy work or responding impulsively
- Becoming involved in teasing, annoying, or interfering with the work of other children

Swift and Spivack (1973) also found that secondary students who are low achievers are characterized by eight factors:

- General anxiety
- Quiet and withdrawn
- Poor work habits
- Lack of intellectual independence
- Dogmatic and inflexible
- Verbal negativism
- Restlessness
- Expressed inability to complete tasks or reach goals

Teachers of students in stage A respond to their students' need for external structure by creating explicit systems of reward. These teachers teach, review, and reward positive behavior frequently during the day. Providing that structure reassures students that the classroom is a predictable, well-managed environment. It relieves students of having to check whether the rules are being followed and provides the opportunity for them to engage in learning. Teachers of students in stage A can expect to spend time mediating conflicts and consistently applying rewards and consequences.

---

**BOX 6.12**

### Strategies for Enhancing the Psychosocial Environment

1. Encourage exploration and questioning.
2. Support failures as learning opportunities.
3. Share laughter with students.
4. Provide students with opportunities to make choices and to learn from them.
5. Teach students to work and play with their peers.
6. Model and reinforce appropriate social interactions with peers and adults.
7. Provide opportunities for students to evaluate the social atmosphere of the classroom.
8. Refine teaching and learning opportunities based on feedback from students.
9. Use logical and natural consequences to help your students learn to manage their own behavior.
10. Model the management of your own emotions so that your students can learn to communicate effectively and appropriately even in times of emotional distress.
11. Use your role with your students to promote communication that respects their feelings and abilities.
12. Evaluate the effectiveness of your systems at least twice during the school year by asking for feedback from students and their families.
13. Respond to issues that emerge from the feedback and change your system if necessary.

---

**STAGE B** Students in stage B understand that rules, rewards, and consequences are constructed rather than imposed. They want to negotiate and to individually tailor rules that will support their own goals. They can participate effectively in conflict mediation, although the outcomes are more likely to be judged successful when outcomes produce personal benefits.

Teachers of students in stage B play a more facilitative role. They can expect to teach students how to mediate their own conflicts, facilitate group meetings, and help students learn to use a democratic approach to creating class rules and procedures. When disciplinary problems or emotional crises arise, these teachers can help students design their own solutions to the problems.

**STAGE C** Students in stage C are altruistic. They are willing to set aside their own needs for the good of the group. They are competent at taking the perspectives of others into account as they view a conflict or event. They need to understand why a rule or procedure is necessary before they can accept its application. They worry about whether the needs of all their peers are being addressed, and they are learning to be involved in solving inequities that others may experience. They are ready to engage in long-term efforts to change both

systems and rules. They tend to operate according to an internal set of rules or principles that govern the decisions that they make. When questioned, they are able to provide a rationale for their behavior.

Teachers who work with students in stage C help them to learn how to evaluate the goals of their own and others' behavior. When disciplinary problems or emotional crises arise, they use conversation to help solve the problem. When a large portion of a class is operating predominantly at stage C, these teachers support self-governance and community involvement.

## The Physical Environment

Students have learning preferences that can be supported through the way the physical environment—space and time—is managed in the classroom (Becker, 1981; Weinstein, 1979). For example, traffic patterns in classrooms should be thought out so that work can be accomplished with minimal disruptions. Materials storage and access should fit the instructional goals and reflect the independence levels of the students. The rhythm and pace of activities in the classroom will contribute to learning accomplishments. For instance,

## Extending Your Learning

The danger of categorizing students by stages is that you may pigeonhole students by using a few incidents to typecast an individual. Thinking about students in terms of stages can be a way of choosing effective supports and interventions quickly, but you need to use data about student performance to verify, refine, or reexamine your initial assumptions. Think about your own affective development. To what extent do you operate within a particular stage? What kinds of events cause you to operate within some of the other stages? How might this also apply to other students?

managing time so that students have ample opportunity for practicing new skills and for learning both individually and in small- and large-group situations helps to sustain interest over the course of a day. The noise, temperature, and paint color in a room can contribute to or detract from learning, just as the sheer numbers of students in a space can enhance or detract from the learning environment. Even furniture and seating arrangements support learning. For instance, in kindergarten and first grade, the physical cues provided by carpet squares or chairs help students to monitor and regulate their movement. By using space and equipment thoughtfully, school professionals can reduce the amount of group management they do verbally and thus increase time on task. Box 6.13 lists a few strategies for enhancing the physical environment.

**BOX 6.13**

### Strategies for Enhancing the Physical Environment

1. Arrange tables, desks, chairs, and work spaces so that students whose behaviors are less well controlled are nearer the teacher.
2. Allow students whose activity levels are high to listen and do work in flexible seating arrangements (sitting on the floor, standing, using a table rather than a desk).
3. Create private spaces for students where they can withdraw from the group to regroup psychologically.

**PHYSIOLOGICAL NEEDS** Learning preferences affect the efficiency with which learning occurs. If learning is occurring efficiently, then the learner is exerting less effort. Learners can probably sustain attention and learn more when learning is occurring efficiently (Sternberg, 1994). The physical environment (space, lighting, materials, activity patterns) and the physiological needs of the learner significantly impact individual learning efficiency and effort. Remember Ms. Simmons' class? The student in the wheelchair has a spinal cord injury and is paralyzed from about the middle of his back down. This means that he has control over his arms, neck, upper torso, and head. Sitting for even an hour at a time in one position is extremely fatiguing for him. Before Eric let Ms. Simmons know that he needed to change position at least once during class, he spent the last fifteen minutes of class agonizing over whether he would make it to the end of class without flopping over or sliding out of his chair. So, for the first quarter of algebra, Eric missed over an hour of instruction each week. It was no wonder he got a C his first quarter. After a conference at the end of the first grading period, Eric was paired with two other boys in algebra, who lift him into a padded chair about fifteen minutes after the beginning of class each day. This chair has supports for Eric's lower body and positions him back into the seat so that he uses a different set of muscles to support his note taking. About ten minutes before class is over, the two boys place Eric back in his wheelchair. In this way, Eric is able to avoid the fatigue that compromised his ability to attend in class.

While Eric's situation is a bit easier to understand than ones involving less obvious disabilities, the principles are the same for all of us. Hunger, muscle fatigue, time of day, and amount of sleep affect our ability to perform. Teachers must account for these physiological needs as they plan the pace and rhythm of instruction. For instance, it's important to schedule times during each hour when students have the opportunity to move around the room. Simple tasks such as having students work on the blackboards, exchange seats, and distribute materials offer opportunities for classroom movement.

**SOUND** Some of us can sit in the middle of a busy airport terminal and read a technical report, respond coherently to e-mail, and not hear any of the commotion around us. Other travelers may be unable to even read the comics without being distracted by passers-by. Many learners lack an ability to screen out sound successfully. As a result, classrooms in which student work groups are busily engaged are often difficult environments for some students to be productive. Teachers need to understand these learner preferences and design their classroom space so that visual and sound screens are created to lessen the potential for distraction.

Some students fail to retain what they read, relying instead on aural transmission to understand a new concept or strategy. Therefore, teachers need to create opportunities for sharing new information aurally so that all students have an opportunity to incorporate new information. Teachers who work with students with hearing impairments may be asked to wear and use special amplification hardware that directs high-quality sound into receivers worn by the students with hearing impairments. Sometimes, this software is also used with students who are easily distracted from listening.

**SIGHT** Some learners may be easily distracted visually. They may have difficulty listening to a lecture while sitting next to a window or under a mobile hanging from the ceiling. Having students complete a brief learning preference questionnaire at the beginning of the year can help teachers make decisions about how to set up the classroom to screen out visual and auditory distractions. Lighting also effects students' ability to sustain attention to a task. For instance, dim lighting impedes reading while fluorescent lighting fatigues the eyes. A combination of natural and artificial light is probably the best solution to lighting a classroom adequately. For students with vision impairments, the classroom must be properly illuminated to optimize the use of any **residual vision** the students have. Most students benefit from the use of some visual materials during the presentation of new information. Using well-designed overhead transparencies, graphs, charts, slides, and notes on the board provides a format for students to develop a coherent perspective on a new topic. And alternating among visual aids helps students to focus their attention, because they are more likely to attend to novel stimuli.

**DESIGN** Learners have physiological needs that teachers can translate into design principles as they lay out their classroom. These design features pertain to classrooms at the secondary as well as primary level.

For example, tables and chairs need to fit students. Asking 15-year-olds to sit in chairs and tables designed for 8-year-olds is a recipe for a poor learning environment. Tables and chairs should be flexible so that they can be moved into more than one configuration. Tables can be put together for cooperative learning groups or separated so that pairs of students can work side by side without bumping elbows or knees.

Teachers should be able to conduct learning groups in more than one place in the classroom. Flip charts and overhead projectors enable the teacher to provide instruction from more than one place in the classroom. And carpets buffer sounds and make the floor another potential working space.

Using space to structure activities diminishes the role of teachers as traffic police. Plants, bookcases, file cabinets, and storage closets can be used to create boundaries that separate activity areas. But teachers should be able to maintain visual contact with most areas in their rooms. Scanning the environment frequently and acting before a surface behavior becomes disturbing is an essential element of effective classroom management. Also, students need to be able to store their own belongings. Cubbyholes, lockers, closets, and bins can be used to provide private storage space for each student. Materials that are not in use for a particular unit should be put away. Furthermore, classrooms should have plenty of places to hang student work, and displays should be changed frequently. Bulletin boards should be changed at least once every two weeks. Finally, the teacher's desk is an organizational model for students. It's difficult to ask students to be organized when the teacher's space is not. Thus, teachers can provide models for organizing space in the ways that they organize their own materials.

## ■ Section Summary

Teachers can create a culture that supports learning in their classrooms through the use of rituals, patterns, and styles of communication. These activities create a context in which students become members of the classroom community.

Most classrooms will contain students at all three stages of psychosocial development. As a result, teachers need to be able to respond to the needs of students for more or less external controls, for more or less verbal mediation, and for more or less feedback and praise. How teachers respond to the psychosocial needs of individuals is a critical aspect of students' ability to exert an effort to learn. Students achieve in environments that encourage them to be involved, that provide them with boundaries for their behavior and that of others, and that reward effort and achievement. How teachers encourage participation will differ depending on whether they are responding to the needs of students in stages A, B, or C. Teachers need to plan the physical environment as carefully as they plan curriculum and instruction. Doing so will eliminate learning problems for some students. Remember, it's more important for the physical design of the classroom to meet the needs of learners than to please the teacher's aesthetic sensibilities or those of his or her colleagues.

# Proactive Behavioral Supports

While careful choices in the instructional strategies that you use will prevent many behavior problems from occurring, you also need a set of behavioral strategies that, if implemented, will help students to manage their own needs without disrupting their peers or the learning environment. These strategies include the incentive system that you set up for reinforcing appropriate behavior, the curriculum that you use to teach process skills, and the investment you make in teaching students to mediate conflicts and negotiate differences. Classroom researchers have found that, in classrooms in which students and teachers are able to focus on learning rather than behavioral problems, teachers spend a great deal of time teaching the strategies and behaviors that students need to manage their own behavior (Brophy & Evertson, 1976; Emmer, Evertson, & Anderson, 1980; Evertson, 1987; Kounin, 1970; Weinstein & Mignano, 1993). These findings add support to one of the basic premises of this chapter—that behavior is learned. When school professionals operate from this premise, they teach students the behaviors that they need to have to function effectively in the classroom. While behavior skills and learning strategies are important for students whose needs are typical, they are essential for students with unique learning needs. By setting goals for behavioral expectations and teaching students the skills they need to meet those goals, you can ensure that all students have the opportunity to succeed in your classroom. This section addresses three key components of proactive behavioral support:

(1) the use of incentives to strengthen learning, (2) a focus on teaching procedures and routines, and (3) direct instruction in social and cognitive skills that support learning and prosocial interaction. By addressing these three elements, school professionals will find that students can manage their own behavior more effectively and rely less on teacher direction and cueing. This means that teachers and students can spend more time on learning and less time on discipline.

## Providing Expectations and Incentives

Incentives help students know what is valued in a classroom. Incentives can range from flashing a smile to providing opportunities to participate in activities that are highly valued by the students. There are many naturally occurring reinforcers in the classroom that compete for students' time and interest (Paine, Radicchi, Rosellini, Deutuchamn, & Darch, 1983). Creating a system of incentives means capitalizing on the naturally occurring reinforcers that promote the behaviors you want.

Beginning the first day of class, school professionals should establish norms for the kinds of behaviors that support learning in the classroom. In a class meeting, a set of expectations for student and teacher behaviors can be established (Emmer & Aussiker, 1990). The list of expectations should be brief but comprehensive. For instance, an expectation might be that the teacher will provide a daily, weekly, and monthly calendar of events for the class. Another teacher expectation might be that all work will be graded within two days. Expectations for students might be that they will treat each other and their teachers with respect, be prepared to work and study, and agree to follow classroom rules and procedures. Rules that govern playground behavior, lunchroom behavior, and classroom behavior all can be specified.

Teaching students how to follow classroom rules, providing incentives that make following the rules attractive, and providing feedback during each class, then, promotes these expectations (Good & Brophy, 1994). Teachers influence students' behaviors through the climate they create, the frequency and quality of the feedback they give students, and the time they allow for students to question and respond to instructional activities (Good & Brophy, 1994). By focusing on the behaviors that promote effective learning envi-

A teacher reviews a list of expectations—not rules—for supportive, proactive behavior with his young learners.

ronments and ensuring that students are reinforced and encouraged to develop those behaviors, teachers and other school professionals can maximize the probability that those behaviors will dominate their classroom environments (Webber & Scheuermann, 1991). Box 6.14 lists some strategies for helping students learn to manage their own behavior.

## Developing the Procedural Curriculum

Many routine activities occur in a classroom and a school on a daily basis. School professionals often assume that, because these routines occur so frequently, students learn them through their execution. While students may be able to conform to the behavioral expectations, they may never develop the internal procedural and conditional knowledge that will enable them to re-create these routines in the absence of external cues to do so (Scanlon, 1996). Many of these routines can help students regulate their own learning (Graham, Harris, & Reid, 1992). Think about the skills that are required to learn effectively: study habits, note taking, prioritization of goals, time management, and the allocation of mental resources, to name but a few. Without explicit instruction, the habits of self-regulation are dif-

ficult to establish (Brigham, 1989; Cervone, Jiwani, & Wood, 1991).

The procedural curriculum also includes learning basic routines such as making sure that students know how to head papers, what writing instruments to use, and whether it is appropriate to use both sides of the paper. Furthermore, procedures are imposed for handling incomplete work, late work, makeup work, and missing work. And students are taught to correct their own work. We create these rules and routines so that students can complete their learning tasks. To ensure that students can follow these rules and routines, we teach them.

In general, teaching procedural skills involves a few simple steps. Students need a model for correct performance. They also need to hear the rationale for why the rule or procedure makes sense. Next, they need to see and hear the steps for creating the performance. Then they need to practice the steps themselves, with coaching from someone else to make sure that they practice the right procedure, in the right order. Finally, they need to perform the skill independently, with feedback on their finished product or performance. In first grade, the procedural curriculum might include teaching students how to carry sharp scissors from one part of the classroom to another. In fifth grade, the

---

**BOX 6.14**

## Strategies for Helping Students Learn to Manage Their Own Behavior

1. Set the standards for behavior in your classroom and make sure that students and their families know what the standards are.

2. Create incentives for students to meet those standards.

3. Use structure, consistency, reinforcement, feedback, consequences, and cues to assist students in meeting those standards.

4. Reward the behaviors that meet classroom standards.

5. Understand that your students differ in their ability to meet standards, and modify your expectations based on those individual abilities.

---

procedural curriculum might include teaching students how to choose and carry out an independent research assignment. To address the habit of self-regulation, teachers may describe aloud their own mental processes for planning ahead, monitoring their progress, and evaluating the results (Watson & Tharp, 1993).

Teaching the procedural curriculum also means teaching students to self-regulate their time, their behavior, their interactions with others, and their priorities and goals. When we teach these skills, students are able to respond effectively to differing learning environments (Agran & Martin, 1987; Kameenui &

**BOX 6.15**

## Strategies for Establishing Routines and Procedures

1. Post routines and adhere to them.

2. Notify students in advance when routines will be interrupted.

3. Schedule activities, small- and large-group instruction, and other classes in such a way that the attention spans of students are accommodated.

4. Teach the routines and procedures that students need to make the transition from large- to small-group activities and from the classroom to the lunchroom, to resolve conflicts, to ask for help, and to refresh their memories.

5. Create opportunities to practice routines and procedures.

Simmons, 1990). Box 6.15 lists some strategies for establishing routines and procedures.

## Teaching Social Skills

**HOW TO TEACH SOCIAL SKILLS** When we investigated learning in Chapter 5, we discussed learning as a social construction. That is, learning occurs as students construct their understanding through interaction with others. When students lack the skills to interact among themselves, they limit their opportunities to learn (Scanlon, 1996). Thus, teaching social skills becomes an important element of the learning environment (Wentzel, 1991). Students need to be able to interact effectively with one another to optimize learning. The key to teaching social skills is seizing the opportunities that arise during the daily interactions in school. Students will use new skills when they have a need to do so. Informal or incidental learning occurs when students are reinforced for using previously taught skills. In group learning, these may be skills like performing roles (for example, encouraging or recording), following rules (for example, speaking softly, taking turns talking), meeting expectations (for example, working on attentive listening), and processing progress toward fluency in a skill (for example, selecting a cooperative skill to practice and describing how one is improving). Every activity, every lesson, and every unit can be enriched by providing clear, informal, feedback on emerging social skills.

Most formal social skills instruction can be encapsulated into five carefully planned components (see Box 6.16). First, the teacher creates the situation so that

**BOX 6.16**

## Components in Formal Social Skills Instruction

1. Establish the need.
2. Directly teach the skill.
3. Create cueing systems to remind students when to use the skill.
4. Have students practice in context.
5. Reinforce the skill over time.

students understand the need and value of the skill. Next, the teacher directly teaches (by telling, giving examples of the behavior, showing video examples, and so on) the desired behavior. Now, the teacher helps the students figure out the guidelines or cues that help them remember when to use the skill. Then the students practice the skill and get feedback from the teacher until they can do it with minimal guidance. Finally, the teacher continues to reinforce that skill so that students will persist in refining the skill until it becomes automatic.

For example, Annie's fifth-grade teacher, Mrs. Harper, took time at the beginning of the year to teach students how to gather needed materials and move into their groups. She established the need for the skills simply by telling students to form into groups. She didn't forewarn them about what they'd do when they got there. She also had the video camera on hand to film the students' first attempt at forming groups. When they viewed the tape, they laughed at all the clowning around, and they commented on the confusion and the amount of time it took. But they also noticed, for the first time, that no one helped Annie, sitting in a chair, to join a group. She asked them to compare their behavior to that of efficient offices where business gets done. She also had students tell how they felt when they weren't sure where to go and when they found out that they didn't have the needed materials and couldn't participate in the activity without them.

Then, when students saw that there was a need for orderly movement and planning for materials, she demonstrated, step by step, how they should get up from their chairs, ask themselves what they would need

at the new location, retrieve the materials they would need, walk over to the new place, wait until it was vacated, and then sit down. She videotaped herself doing the demonstration, and the students reviewed it a few times, commenting on what she did. Then they tried again, as a whole class, videotaping the results and viewing and critiquing each repetition of the transition process. They talked about how "awkward" it felt to do things differently than they had done in the past. Eventually, they established an automatic routine. After that, Mrs. Harper reminded them periodically to remember their skills, and she rewarded their success.

**WHAT SOCIAL SKILLS TO TEACH** How did Mrs. Harper decide what social skills to teach? She based her decision on the needs of her students. Table 6.4 lists some of the skills that may need to be taught. In Mrs. Harper's case, she wanted to ensure that students had the skills they needed to work in cooperative learning groups.

*Group Stages* Students typically go through four stages in the formation of long-term formal cooperative work groups, and each stage demands a set of corollary skills (Johnson, Johnson, & Holubec, 1991). The first of the stages, forming, is easily recognized as the stage at which students are just beginning to participate in cooperative learning activities. These students need to know how to get up from their seats, move into their groups, and move from one group to another. Once they are in an assigned group, the next set of skills has to do with staying there and participating appropriately. So the next set of skills to teach has to do with taking turns talking, controlling the volume of their voices, keeping their hands and feet to themselves, making eye contact, looking at the speaker, and attending to the task.

As students improve in these fundamental skills in the forming stage, the teacher begins instruction in the functioning stage, teaching skills that students need to manage the group's work. Functioning skills include giving direction to the group work by stating and restating the purpose of the assignment, setting time limits, offering procedural suggestions, expressing support and acceptance of others' ideas, asking for help or clarification, offering explanations, paraphrasing, energizing through humor and enthusiasm, and describing one's own feelings as appropriate.

| TABLE 6.4 | Social Skills That Students May Need to Learn | |
|---|---|---|
| ■ How to give and receive feedback | | ■ How to join in activities |
| ■ How to give positive feedback | | ■ How to ask questions |
| ■ How to negotiate | | ■ How to follow directions |
| ■ How to solve problems | | ■ How to converse |
| ■ How to resist peer pressure | | ■ How to self-evaluate |
| ■ How to participate in a job interview | | ■ How to self-monitor |
| ■ How to explain a problem | | |

Source: Scanlon, 1996.

The third stage, formulating, requires students to engage in the mental processes that promote high-quality reasoning and learning. These skills include summarizing, seeking accuracy, elaborating on ideas, employing memory devices, understanding the reasoning of other group members, and sharing one's own explanations and reasoning with others. Finally, the fermenting stage requires that students engage in academic debates to stimulate their conceptualization and to promote depth of understanding. The skills required to engage in this stage include the following:

■ Criticizing ideas, not people

■ Distinguishing areas of agreement and disagreement

■ Integrating numerous ideas into a single position

■ Asking for supportive reasoning

■ Extending other's answers by adding more information

■ Probing to gain deeper understanding of ideas

■ Generating multiple ideas and answers

### Extending Your Learning

Think about an activity you engaged in with a group of youngsters. Perhaps it was in a classroom or during a field trip or in church or some other community setting. Think about the routines that you might have been taught prior to engaging in the activity. What kinds of routines needed to be taught? How could you make the teaching of the routines interesting and motivating?

■ Comparing the group's work with criteria or other information

*Individual Needs*   Decisions about which skills to teach and at what level of complexity also depend on the developmental level of students. Young children, or those with underdeveloped social skills, may need more time and instruction on the basic forming skills. For example, Kirk always has difficulty working in groups because he is still unskilled in knowing how to join groups and to relate to other students once he gets into groups. His age suggests that he should benefit from instruction in the skills of formulating and fermenting, as the other students in his classes do. Keep in mind, however, that he really needs to continue receiving individualized formal instruction and continued informal support on the most basic of social skills in addition to the skills that are being taught to the entire class.

## ■ SECTION SUMMARY

While spending valuable instructional time on teaching students classroom routines may seem a poor choice given all the demands on their time in the classroom, teachers who invest in teaching, rather than telling, these skills, are able to spend more time on instruction during the course of the school year. A second component of proactive behavioral supports includes careful and thoughtful selection of incentives that increase student motivation to meet classroom norms and expectations. Finally, most students need support in learning the social interaction skills that make group learning possible. Incentives, the procedural curriculum, and social skills development are critical components of a proactive approach to managing student behavior.

# Individual Behavior Support Plans

Even though schools are organized at both the building level and the classroom level to provide support for learning, there will always be one or two students who have learned to get their needs met in ways that disrupt learning for other students, create safety problems for other students, or impede their own ability to connect with their peers and learn efficiently. For these students, an individual behavior support plan will help school professionals identify the environmental and curricular supports that students need to progress.

Typically, individual behavior support plans are complex to construct and consist of several steps. To develop these plans, a child study team is formed that consists of family members, the student, the classroom teacher, and other school professionals skilled in the functional analysis of behavior. The team examines the relationship between events in the environment that may shape and maintain the problem behavior and tries to establish the function or communicative intent of the behavior or pattern of behaviors (Day, Horner, & O'Neill, 1994; Horner & Day, 1991; Kern & Dunlop, in press). Then the team develops a set of hypotheses linked to interventions that teach alternative and acceptable behaviors (Horner, Sprague, & Flannery, 1993). In keeping with the basic assumptions about behavior that we made at the beginning of this chapter, behavior support plans assume that behavior is learned, that behaviors can be strengthened or diminished by what occurs immediately after a given behavior is produced, and that the ecology of the environment can be changed to support the learning needs of students. In essence, a behavior support plan is a teaching plan that outlines the context in which new behaviors will be developed and what behaviors will be taught.

Figure 6.1 shows a completed behavior plan. Using Kirk as an example, we completed the plan using the following steps:

1. We compiled basic demographic information to keep a record of when we began to work systematically on a plan to improve Kirk's behavior. Notice that Kirk is part of our planning team, as is his mother.

2. We listed the behaviors we felt were creating the most problems for Kirk and for his teachers. Notice that we named the behavior and then described it in observable terms. Then we described how often the behavior happened, how intense each episode was, and how long each episode lasted. There are many ways to systematically collect data. We have included some observational formats in Chapter 7. Additionally, you may want to investigate the work of Kern and Dunlap (in press) and Wieseler and colleagues (1997).

3. We brainstormed some of the strategies that have been used in the past to control, manage, and improve his behavior. We also made brief notes about how effective each strategy has been. For the most part, these strategies have been unsuccessful.

4. We isolated the functions of Kirk's behavior in terms of the needs that he meets by using those behaviors. We completed this step after members of the team had completed their direct observations of Kirk in several settings.

5. We interpreted his behavior and made some careful, reflective hypotheses about why he might have been behaving in a particular way.

6. We began developing an implementation plan by discussing ecological modifications.

7. We looked at what Kirk could be taught to replace his problem behaviors.

8. We reviewed the menu of interventions listing options for skills that could be taught.

9. We discussed and developed a set of strategies designed to encourage Kirk to replace his old skills with the new ones.

10. We agreed on a plan that could be put in place when a crisis arose. We defined crises in Kirk's case as situations in which someone, including Kirk, might get physically hurt.

11. We listed the personnel responsible for carrying out each element of the plan and the resources and training that they would need for the various interventions.

12. We developed a plan for monitoring and refining the plan based on data collected during intervention.

# Student Support Plan

**Date of Plan:** February 1, 1996     **Planners:** Deanna Sands, Elizabeth Kozleski, Nancy French, Kirk, Chloe Barnsky, School Counselor, Mrs. Grant

**Student's Name:** Kirk        **Date of Birth:**        **Current Age:**

**Parent's Name:**                        **Phone #:**

**Parent's Address:**

**Teacher's Name:** Mrs. Barnsky        **Student's Grade:** 9

**School Name:** Thomas Jefferson High School

## I. Priority Behavior List. Describe the student's behaviors.

| Behavior | Frequency | Intensity | Duration |
|---|---|---|---|
| Angers quickly and with little provocation: verbally rages and walks quickly around the classroom | 2 or more times per school day | Is restrained from throwing furniture daily | 10-20 minutes at a time |
| Bullies: through verbal taunts, shames peers into giving up belongings, materials, place in line, activities | 3 times per day | Raises voice, moves close to peers | Brief, 3-5 minute episodes |
| Physically aggressive: hits peers with fists or legs | 2 times per week | Raises voice, moves in to confront peers, hits hard enough to cause bruising, has broken skin and an arm | 2-3 minute episodes |

| Behavior | Prior Strategies | Strategy Effectiveness |
|---|---|---|
| Angers quickly | Time-out, reinforcement for no anger | Time-out increased anger, reinforcers were ineffective |
| Bullies | Group contingency for no bullying | Kirk doesn't have allegiance to a group so he didn't care what happened to the group |
| Physically aggressive | Anger awareness training suspension (in-school) | Maintains same level of aggression |

## II. Functional Analysis of Behavior(s)

| Background | Cognitive Needs | Communicative Needs |
|---|---|---|
| History of absent father; only child at home; mother has difficulty imposing rules; Kirk is a juvenile status offender | Needs support to maintain attention, monitor and regulate problem-solving skills, self-evaluate | Has difficulty expressing needs under emotional stress |

**FIGURE 6.1** ■ Kirk's Individual Behavior Support Plan

| Physical Needs | Affective Needs | Right and Wrong Reasoning Skills | Ecological Analysis |
|---|---|---|---|
| Needs physical exercise to decrease physical stress | Monitor physiological signs that accompany emotion | Has egocentric value system and bases judgments of right or wrong on whether it gratifies his needs | Tends to exhibit problem behaviors in classes with male teachers, and with peers who are less assertive and easily cowed |

## III. Interpretation & Hypotheses

1. Behavior is maintained by Kirk's need for power and control in his life

2. Kirk's lack of communication skills leads to acting out his anger rather than verbalizing it

3. Kirk lacks adequate moral reasoning skills to mediate his behavior

## IV. Ecological Modifications

**Schedule**: Make sure his class schedule has a mix of physical activities like PE and band as well as academics

**Rules & Procedures:** Teach Kirk to leave the class when he needs to express his anger and visit the counselor

**Academic**: Teach problem-solving skills

**Surface Management**: Seat Kirk near the door – provide him with 2 passes per class for cooling off

**Group Dynamics**: Give Kirk leadership roles in class

**Other**: Communicate weekly with his mother about his progress

## V. Functional Equivalents

### Student Needs

1. Power and control

2. Communication

3. Moral reasoning development

### Instructional Strategies

1. Teach Kirk to recognize his anger triggers

2. Teach Kirk to mentally list at least 3 choices for negotiating

3. Teach Kirk to negotiate behavior and academic performance contracts with each teacher

### Menu of Interventions

__X__ Conflict Mediation

_____ Self-regulation

_____ Choice Making

_____ Rational Emotive Therapy

_____ Goal Setting

__X__ Communication Skills

__X__ Anger Response Training

__X__ Moral Reasoning

**FIGURE 6.1** ■ Kirk's Individual Behavior Support Plan *(continued)*

## VI. Motivational Strategies

Ignore/Redirect/Reinforce:

Reframing Negative Behavior:

**Successive Approximations**: Set targets weekly for anger management, bullying, and aggressive behavior

**Differential Reinforcement Schedule**: Have Kirk create a menu of reinforcers that he can choose from when he makes his behavior targets

## VII. Crisis Plan

What circumstances warrant requesting assistance? Physical aggression

Who is called for assistance? School Counselor

How do you get assistance? Page Counselor

What does that person do? Counselor pages Kirk on his beeper to prompt Kirk to come to his office

## VIII. Implementation Plan

| Intervention Strategy | Personnel Responsible | Resources Needed | Training Needs |
|---|---|---|---|
| Schedule | Advisor | None | None |
| Leadership roles | Classroom teacher | Collaboration | None |
| Anger response training | Special Educator | Resource period | Readings and coaching from school psychologist |
| Rational emotive therapy | School Counselor | Biweekly meeting | Readings and coaching |
| Moral reasoning | Special Educator | pagers | |
| Crisis intervention | Special services team | pagers | |

## IX. Coordination Strategies

| Questions | Strategies and Comments |
|---|---|
| How often will coordination meetings be held? | Once per month |
| Who will convene them? | School psychologist |
| Who will keep minutes? | Rotation schedule |
| What communication strategies will we use? | Crisis updates, weekly e-mail |
| How consistent are we in implementing our strategies? | Weekly feedback sheets |
| How effective are our ecological modifications? | Data collection by Special Educator |
| How effective are the incentive strategies? | Data collection by Special Educator |
| How effective are the functional equivalents? | Data collection by Special Educator |

**FIGURE 6.1** ■ Kirk's Individual Behavior Support Plan *(continued)*

## ■ SECTION SUMMARY

The planning necessary for this level of individualization should not be undertaken without the team effort of a variety of school professionals and family members. This complex process involves a number of steps, including forming the team, examining the relationship between events in the environment and the problem behavior, and developing interventions to address the problem.

# Chapter Summary

Supporting successful learning and behavior in the classroom encompasses several dimensions. It requires a collective agreement among school professionals throughout a building to work on the buildingwide

supports that will involve families, support students in crisis, and provide a focus for teaching students to become managers of their own behavior. It also requires careful thought and planning to manage the classroom community supports to help students target learning as their primary goal in school. Finally, school professionals need to become adept at identifying the functions of students' behavior and developing the curricula and supports to help students learn prosocial ways of getting their needs met. Buildingwide supports are complex because they require shared values and attitudes on the part of all school professionals in a building. But in the long run, a commitment to buildingwide supports frees up time to work on academic learning. The most person-intensive supports occur when a student needs an individual behavior support plan. Working together as a team will help to ensure that most students are able to get their needs met within the building and classroom communities.

---

**INSTRUCTIONAL ACTIVITY**

## Creating an Action Plan to Improve Peter's Classroom Community

### Objectives

- To analyze classroom communities in light of the information in the text on culture, social environments, and proactive behavioral supports
- To create action plans for improving the classroom using community observational data

### Materials

- Classroom observation checklist
- Action planning form

### Product

- Completed classroom observation checklist
- Action plan for further improving Peter's classroom community

### Agenda

- Watch the video "Educating Peter."
- Using the classroom observation checklist, tally the types of activities, teacher talk, feedback, and questions you observe.
- In groups of three, discuss discrepancies in your observations and critique the classroom interactions.
- Develop an action plan for Peter's classroom, including ideas on how to enhance the classroom community, who will be responsible for implementing the plan, and how to conduct ongoing evaluation of the classroom culture.

### Evaluation

- Criteria include coherence and completeness.

# Glossary

**Contingent responses** Reactions to behaviors or events that occur as a result of the observed behaviors or events.

**Dialectic** Refers to the interaction between two individuals or ideas.

**Operant conditioning** A construct that behaviorists use to describe why some behaviors persist and others decay, depending on the presence or absence of reinforcers and punishments.

**Psychosocial environment** The psychological and social contexts—expectations, responses, and interactions among or within individuals—that compose the perceived emotional and social climate.

**Residual hearing** Condition in which a person who is hearing impaired can still make meaning from limited bits of sound.

**Residual vision** The condition in which, as a person loses sight, the retina and optic nerves retain some functionality, allowing whatever light that can be perceived to be coded into meaningful visual information.

**Social learning theory** A model of learning in which behavior is strengthened through the observation of others.

## CHAPTER 7

# Using Assessment to Make Instructional Decisions

# Assessing Students

*by Karen Watson*

At the beginning of the school year, I give students an attitude survey in each subject area. This gives me an idea of what they value, what is difficult for them, how they like to learn, what strategies they have for learning this subject, and how they problem-solve in a particular subject. During the last half of the year, I do an interview that essentially hits the same questions. These tools, when compared, help the student, parents, and teacher see progress, identify strengths and needs, and note changes in attitudes and thinking.

The benefits of assessing students at the beginning of the year are apparent when I tell you about Nick. He was a fifth-grade student who was conferencing with his mother. He was going over his attitude survey in written language from the beginning of the year. He was so amazed at how he had changed. He told his mom that he would never answer these questions the same way now. He liked writing and could identify from his written products all the improvements he had made this year. Nick really enjoyed expressing himself through a written medium, whereas, at the beginning of the year, this was definitely an area in which he felt little confidence.

In addition to encouraging students to evaluate their own progress in writing, other evaluations of written language may come from parents, the student's peers, and the teacher. My students' portfolios include information from all of these sources. Each of these instruments looks different. Because we assess with so many different instruments, students need to know what the content and form of any evaluation will be. Then, highlighting the essential elements in a lesson will help students to know what to concentrate on in a particular writing assignment.

Rubrics can be used to assess writing. They specify the criteria for spelling, handwriting, mechanics, grammar, syntax, and use of higher-level writing elements such as metaphors, similes, and hyperbole. Other forms of writing assessments include reflective responses to a writing sample completed by the student, parent, or teacher. These reflective responses should note and emphasize student strengths to ensure that students maintain those elements of writing that they are close to mastering. Depending on the student, peer assessment may focus on only one or two areas.

Writing samples from each quarter along with the portion showing the editing process are kept in a **portfolio.** The samples are revisited to note changes, progress, and continuing needs of the student. This does not mean that there isn't room for standardized or criterion referenced tests. In fact, these become just one more part of an overall examination of a student's achievement in a particular area.

Generally, tests in reading are either informal or formal assessments that give vocabulary, comprehension, and/or word analysis information. Alternative assessments in reading can focus students on inferring meaning at a deeper level. This may be done through book clubs, **Socratic dialog,** and interpretive read-ing as in reader's theater. I have students focus on supporting their conclusions based on their own experiences, passages in the selection, or passages from other works they have read. It is also important to find out what questions they have. What puzzles, surprises, or feelings are evoked? What are their responses to these?

I have had students throw me out of their book clubs because they didn't need me. They argue, defend, support, and question one another and their conclusions! I come in when invited and occasionally help them refocus by asking them different questions. Watching and recording anecdotes from this process is a valuable, alternative tool to assess student's ability to read and understand concepts.

Math assessments are also changing. It is a delightful experience to give students a problem and watch the number of different strategies they use to solve it! I watch students while they are interacting in cooperative groups and look for the strategies that they use. Are their computation skills accurate? Do they have the tools to figure out what resources they may need to solve the problem? I make sure they have the materials and supplies they need to use manipulatives to solve the problems.

No longer is math strictly a matter of "sit at your desk and do paper and pencil figuring." There can and may be movement, research, discussion, arguments, logical defenses, and displays. Students need to think about how they solve problems. When I first started asking children about how they solved problems, many of them could not answer. The thinking can be done orally or in writing. I include written pieces as well as pictures of how they solve problems. The reflective instrument may need to be geared to help students task-analyze their problem-solving process in the beginning. As students become more proficient, they will be able to identify and report the strategies they use, detail how they solved the problem if there may have been other ways to solve it, and state if and why they feel they may have a correct or incorrect answer. The metacognition of solving math problems becomes as critical (or more) in the evaluation as the actual answers. The portfolio should reflect the changes the student is making in problem solving throughout the year.

Spelling continues to be a challenge for many students. How we evaluate students can also give them a chance to improve their retention of spelling. Typically, teachers give students a test at the end of the week by having students write the words in a list after the word is given in a sentence. Although I do this about nine times a year, there are other, much more application-appropriate methods for spelling evaluation.

Students are given their spelling words in dictated sentences. These sentences include words from lists of previous years. All words must be spelled correctly. This is also a good time to give students sentences that allow them to show if they know mechanics such as conversational punctuation, capitalization of proper nouns, or use of commas in a series. The spelling test not only shows retention of past and current words but can be used as a diagnostic tool in written language.

Giving students sentences in which they need to find and correct the spelling of their weekly words is also a strategy that indicates whether the student has mastered his words. Standardized tests often give a list of four ways to spell a word, of which only one is correct. Doing this with some of the child's spelling lists reinforces the visual memory for the spelling words and gives the student practice in this type of test.

During the last quarter, after affixes, their meanings, and the concepts of base words have been taught, students can be given tests that take the words from the spelling lists and turn them into other correctly spelled word forms. One of the best ways to ensure student retention of words is to vary the types of tests students take. This keeps them well prepared each week for any option.

The content of science and social studies is generally not addressed when it comes to looking at alternative ways to assess. Because science and social studies can be taught in a discovery milieu, the techniques for testing should include a reflection of students' learning styles and strength areas in the multiple intelligences. Portfolios may include these learnings. My students have reflective pieces with attached photos of how they went about solving science or social science problems. I have seen cooperative learning teams debate with each other the best way to solve a problem and support their conclusions. Tapes of these debates may also be included in portfolios.

Finally, another way to evaluate student achievement is through a showcase presentation. This is usually done in front of parents and can take the form of a celebration of stu-

dent learning. Showcases can include performances, demonstrations, books students have made, videos, products, and oral and written reports.

Assessment practices in schools have changed with the introduction of the use of portfolios by students. Portfolios themselves can serve as an overall evaluation of the student throughout the year. However, portfolio assessment can and may include showcase material, process information, and/or comparative growth evaluations. The portfolios may include student products, videos, pictures, written information, oral tapes, and so on.

For the portfolio to be truly effective, it should be a springboard for students to self-evaluate their progress, accomplishments, strengths, and needs. It can be used as the instrument that guides their thinking about how they think, problem-solve, and learn best. Students need daily access to their portfolios and should be able to use them when they conference with their parents and teachers.

When I look at the whole arena of assessment, I want to know not only where my students are with their skills in each subject area but how they learn, what their attitudes are, and what strategies they presently have at hand. More importantly, I want them to know these same things about their own learning. Once students are able to identify their own strengths and needs, their learning takes on a measure of joy and confidence not previously seen. They are able to take charge and direct their own learning. After all, isn't this where we want our students to be?

# Introduction

This chapter is designed to provide you with a framework for assessment. Table 7.1 illustrates a framework for categorizing the kinds of information and skills you will need in order to feel competent about assessment. Some of the knowledge and skills you will need are simply declarative. Remember that declarative knowledge is basic, factual information that you store in long-term memory and use when the occasion calls for it. You will also need procedural knowledge—the skills and steps that you use to conduct and analyze the results of your assessment. Additionally, you will use conditional knowledge, which helps you to choose among many approaches to select the right assessment for the kind of information that you need. First, we explore precisely what assessment is and why we do it. Next, we discuss assessment in inclusive classrooms. Finally, we examine a variety of informal assessment tools.

# What Is Assessment, and Why Do We Do It?

To most people, assessment and testing are synonymous. Because we associate being tested with being anxious, we are skeptical of, and sometimes resistant to, our classroom role as assessor or evaluator. Testing is certainly one way that school professionals assess, but it is only one part of a broad, comprehensive, and continuous process. While we can't promise that this chapter will relieve your test anxiety, it will provide you with a framework for engaging in assessment that will inform your decisions about what and how to teach.

It is almost impossible to work with students without assessing. We look at how our students relate to one another and make judgments about their skills, capacities, and limitations. We label our students according to the gains they make and the challenges they attempt. We identify the overachievers, the slackers, the athletes, the rowdies, the scholars, the artists, and so on. We apply these labels by observing and interacting with our students in all the contexts that we know them. Although our judgments are filtered by our own biases, this process that we engage in is really informal assessment. We assess, and then we act on those assessments by assigning certain responsibilities, by calling on some students and not others, and by making many other classroom decisions. In fact, assessment is the cornerstone of achieving effective outcomes for students.

Karen Watson, the teacher in the chapter-opening vignette, exemplifies this approach to assessment. As we hear her story, it becomes apparent that assessment involves more than merely evaluating how much information a student has about a particular content area. **Assessment** tells us what students want to know, what they already know, and what they need to know. Through the assessment process, school professionals obtain the information they need to choose the right curriculum for their students. Because assessment also reveals how students learn best and what motivates them to achieve, the assessment process helps to define the kinds of instructional approaches that will be most successful with students. The framework from Chapter 5 that laid out the four domains of learning—cognitive, affective, communicative, and physical—is integral to the information that school professionals seek from assessment. By understanding where students' needs are in each of the four domains, school professionals can refine instruction and curriculum to meet those needs.

In the Introduction, we presented a dynamic model of assessment, instruction, and curriculum. With students at the center of this process, we assess, choose curriculum and instruction on the basis of assessment, and then assess the outcomes of our teaching. Ongoing assessment allows us to refine and modify our instructional techniques and choice of content so that students can be as successful as possible (Fuchs & Fuchs, 1986). This model empowers school professionals to think strategically about the content and instruction offered to students. Without well-planned and well-executed assessments, school professionals have little information about which curricula and instructional methods will help their students to learn. Why should we assess? The answer is clear. We assess so that we can maximize the learning opportunities in classrooms and help students learn at their optimal levels.

## ■ SECTION SUMMARY

Assessment is crucial to achieving optimal outcomes for all learners. The next section is designed to help you structure the assessment process. By extending the principles of assessment to many contexts, you will be able to select assessment strategies that help you make informed curricular and instructional decisions.

| TABLE 7.1 | A Framework for Conducting Assessments |

| Declarative Knowledge | Procedural Knowledge | Conditional Knowledge |
| --- | --- | --- |
| What is assessment? | What are the steps to conduct a miscue analysis? | When do I use informal assessment? |
| What is the basic process for determining eligibility for special education? | When do we use formative assessment? | Under what situations would I use a standardized test? |
| What are informal assessment tools? | What are components of a critical review of a child's current level of functioning? | What are criteria for selecting norm-referenced tests? |
| What are tests of intelligence? | What are the steps in writing an IEP? | If I want to evaluate a student's progress, do I have to use a standardized tool? |
| What's the difference between behavior rating tools and adaptive behavior tools? | What responsibility do I have for the objectives written on a child's IEP? | When should I involve specialists like school psychologists in assessment of a particular student? |
| What kinds of tools should I use to explore language skill? | | Under what conditions can families challenge the educational decisions made about their children? |
| What are tests of achievement? | | What's the relationship between quality of life and information from a student interview or a standardized test? |

# Assessment in Inclusive Classrooms

## Formative Versus Summative Assessment

School professionals must engage systematically in both formative and summative assessments. **Formative assessment** helps school professionals to gather information about how a student is progressing. This assessment is formative because it helps to shape or form the instructional process. With formative assessment data, teachers either continue to use the same methods and pace in covering a content area or make adjustments in the curriculum or the instructional processes. When school professionals engage in formative evaluation, they make choices about the kinds of information they need. Refer again to Karen Watson's story. Her approach to assessment in her classroom informs her about what to teach next. She uses assessment as a formative process.

Information about how students learn based on the four domains is paramount to sound instructional practices. School professionals need to know about students' cognitive, affective, communicative, and physical needs. As students progress through a curriculum, school professionals assess their progress. Some-

times, teachers want to know how students compare to themselves. For example, how much have they learned in the subject area? Did they learn as quickly and efficiently as they are capable of? Are they motivated to learn? Do they have the self-regulatory skills to handle the homework assignments? Are they able to sustain attention over time? Do they have the vocabulary to handle the material? Is the teacher providing enough opportunities to practice new skills? Is sufficient attention being paid to the students' needs to change activities and positions frequently?

Alternatively, a teacher might want to know how students compare to a standard or criterion. For instance, which students are ready to move to the next level of complexity in the subject area? Which students need to continue to work on the same topic? A third kind of decision that teachers make involves comparing students to one another. For instance, who's the best writer in the class? What students should be grouped for direct instruction on the use of adverbs? Are the writers in Ms. Pope's fourth grade as competent as those in Mr. Barrett's class who are using writer's workshop? Choosing the right form of assessment helps us to make informed instructional and curricular decisions.

**Summative assessment,** in contrast, tells us how much has been learned. It occurs at the end of a unit,

## Extending Your Learning

Schools in Colorado are required to report the results of standardized tests administered in the second, fourth, eighth, and eleventh grades to the State Department of Education. Is this an example of summative or formative evaluation?

grading period, or school year. For example, report cards provide summative information. The grades that a student earns are measures of what has been accomplished; they are the sum or result of what has occurred. Judging a finished product is a complex task because the reasons that it is being judged will probably vary. When we make summative decisions, we may be judging whether a particular student will be accepted into a specific program or activity. Other summative decisions include passing a student on to the next grade or declaring that a student can graduate.

Measuring outcomes requires identifying the critical tasks that must be performed rather than the skill sets that need to be mastered to accomplish a task. Think about carpenters. While they need to know how and when to use their hammers, screwdrivers, drills, and saws, they also need to know what it is that they are building. If we made decisions about which carpenter to hire (a summative decision) based solely on the competence of tool use, we would be making only partly informed decisions. Similarly, if we assessed carpenters on their ability to design products, we would know what they intended to produce but would have no ability to discriminate between skilled and unskilled execution. Critiquing a carpenter's finished product might be a better way of making a decision about which carpenter to employ.

In fact, assessment is a continuous formative and summative process that requires critical thinking to select the right tools from among a menu of choices: observation, anecdotal records, classroom tests, portfolios, rubrics to evaluate performances and products, standardized tools, and curriculum-based measurements. Sometimes, decisions involve low stakes. For example, it won't damage a student's chances of attending college if the student doesn't move to the next reading level until next week. Low-stakes decisions mean that the teacher can make these decisions rapidly, and in the long run, these decisions don't harm or impede student progress toward a subsequent environ-

ment. Instead, low-stakes assessments assist primarily in orchestrating the accomplishments of a particular group of students.

In contrast, decisions based on assessment data can involve relatively high stakes; that is, the decisions have a more profound impact on what will happen to a student. For instance, assessment data are used to move students to the next grade or to hold them back. High-stakes assessment plays a key role in decisions about whether a student needs and is eligible for special education services.

## Considerations in Assessment

Regardless of whether you are engaging in formative or summative evaluation, you should keep several issues in mind as you proceed. You need to involve families in gathering assessment information and in interpreting what is collected. You need skills in translating assessment information into curriculum and instruction that meets your students' needs rather than suit your own teaching preferences. You need to choose a measurement unit that will yield meaningful information. And you need to select the right assessment strategy to meet your assessment purposes.

**FAMILY INVOLVEMENT** Families are most often the recipients of information about how well their children are doing in school. However, involving families in collecting information about how their children use academic skills at home can help to focus their support of student learning. As a result, when students begin to experience difficulty, families will be familiar with information-gathering processes that will aid in the development of a plan for improvement. Families are the best source for information about how a student is functioning outside of school. Families can help school professionals translate students' behaviors so that the meaning behind patterns of behavior can be uncovered. (Figure 3.4 showed a form that families can use to report information about their children.) When plans for improvement do not result in desired outcomes, a student may then be referred for assessment to determine whether a disability is present. When a decision is made to assess a student for special education services, families must be notified and must give their permission for testing to occur.

**CURRICULUM** When school professionals ask questions about their students' progress, they are asking about curriculum (what to teach) and instruction (how to teach). Chapter 9 elaborates on the issues of curriculum. In inclusive school communities, many curricula operate simultaneously. A child with significant health care needs may be learning about how to monitor her own medications, while a student like Kurume may be learning about how to care for his hearing aids. Most students are engaged in curricula that support their literacy and that are tailored to the individual needs of students through the assessment process. Later in this chapter, we examine assessment techniques that help us to track students' progress in basic academic content areas and to identify their learning needs.

**INSTRUCTION** Decisions about how to teach a particular unit of study rest on the teacher's knowledge of how a specific group of students learns. Because learning occurs through integration of the four domains of cognition, affect, communication, and physical health, teachers need this information about each of their students. For example, if Michael's teacher knows that he has a difficult time starting new assignments because he has trouble focusing his attention, she may choose to stand near him at the beginning of each silent reading assignment to cue him to attend. Similarly, Mr. Bacon, Kirk's social studies teacher, may make specific references to battles that were fought in specific geographic regions because he knows that Kirk's motivation to remember information is increased when he connects places to military campaigns. This interest of Kirk's helps him to feel closer to his father. In Annie's fourth-grade classroom, the teacher often uses the overhead projector with the classroom lights off because this helps Annie to focus on the skill being demonstrated. School professionals who engage in the process of assessment will have this information and be able to adjust their instruction accordingly. Chapter 10 provides an overview of instructional strategies.

**MEASUREMENT** To make meaning from data, you need to know the metric, or the kind of measurement that was used to provide the data. For instance, a carpenter needs to know if the plans being used to build a house were designed using centimeters or inches. Knowing the metric that was used in the design en-

sures that the object built will match the envisioned design. You will also want to know if the metric used was reliable. That is, did the measurement tool warp over time or stay true? This concept is referred to as the **reliability** of a measuring device. Information about a student gathered through the use of assessment tools should be reliable. That is, the same score should be obtained regardless of who grades the test (**interrater reliability**). Additionally, the student should be able to score about the same on the same test whether it was taken on Thursday or Friday (**test/retest reliability**). Finally, a test is said to be reliable when similar test items result in similar performances for an individual (**alternate-form reliability**).

Similarly, if a teacher wants to know whether a student can correctly compute the answers to two-digit multiplication problems, she must provide such problems for the student to answer. If the question is whether the student can translate an applied problem into an algorithm that can be solved, the teacher must provide a story problem with a familiar scenario and then ask the student to write the algorithm that must be solved. So, measurement tools must have **validity**; that is, they must measure what they are intended to measure. Suppose a teacher develops a test to determine which of her students can grow sunflowers most quickly. This test requires that each student run the 50-yard dash, recite the words to the theme song from the television show *Gilligan's Island*, and, using crayons, draw a replica of van Gogh's famous sunflower painting. Students receive three scores on this test: a time score, an accuracy score for the percentage of words correctly recalled, and a competency score for the number of features from the sunflower painting that were accurately replicated. This test could have high interrater reliability, high test/retest reliability, and high alternate-form reliability and yet not be valid. Its validity would be in question because the ability to grow sunflowers does not rely on running, memorization of songs, or drawing abilities.

Three types of validity generally are considered: content, criterion-related, and construct validity. Assessment texts such as Salvia and Ysseldyke's (1991) provide extensive information about how reliability and validity can be measured. As a consumer of testing information, you have a responsibility to ensure that the tests you select will provide information about students that is both reliable and valid. To do so requires careful reading of test manuals to ensure that reliability

## Extending Your Learning

Is it valid to measure physical strength of students by finding out how long they can stand on one leg?

and validity documentation are available and that the information provided is sufficient to make an informed decision.

Salvia and Ysseldyke (1991) recommend that reliability **coefficients** of .60 or better are sufficient for group-administered tests. However, when test data are to be used for making decisions about individual students, the stakes are much higher, and reliability should be .90 or better. In addition to careful analysis of reliability and validity, school professionals must consider the kinds of individuals, or the sample population, on which a test was normed. Even when a test's reliability and validity features are adequate, the test scores may not be valid if the norm sample is not representative of the entire population of individuals taking the test (Chamberlain & Medinos-Landurand, 1991).

Teachers and other school professionals must also determine whether they want accuracy or power in determining arithmetic proficiency. Accuracy may mean that a teacher allows the student to take as much time as needed to solve the problem. Power may be determined by how many problems a student can answer correctly within a time limit. When we assess, we need to understand the metric because it will help us to analyze the performance we observe. Determining the metric and then applying it consistently helps teachers to analyze how a student's learning is progressing.

Alternatively, a teacher might want to know how students compare to one another. Using the comparison approach, the teacher may want to know who is the best at two-digit multiplication problems. Teachers may also need to know which students are ready to move to the next level of complexity in the subject area and which students need to continue to work at the current level. Using this criterion approach, the teacher may need to know which students can compute at least 10 two-digit multiplication problems within two minutes. Those students that meet the criterion may be ready to move on to three-digit multiplication problems. Knowing when to move on versus when to continue to work on a specific skill is an important tool for teachers in allocating instructional time wisely.

Another question that school professionals frequently ask is whether the instructional strategy they are using is the most efficient for their students. Not only should learning occur, but it should occur at optimal levels. Matching the type of instruction to the content and the learner also requires assessment. To make all these decisions, the teacher needs to know how to design measurement tools that maintain objectivity across all students by keeping the context and the metric the same for all students.

Measurement is an important part of the assessment process. Making sure that the tools you use are reliable and valid is an important first step in assessing. As you can see, assessment involves more than the act of measuring. It also requires competent analysis and interpretation of the information gathered from the assessment procedures. These data are only as useful as the user's skills in making meaning from them. The meaning is constructed by knowing the kinds of questions that need to be answered.

## Selecting the Right Assessment Strategy

School professionals need to know when to obtain information about how an individual student is progressing through the curriculum and why he or she may be encountering difficulties. School professionals also need to consider the situations in which they may want information about how their students compare to other students who have similar needs and characteristics. Because the purposes of assessment vary, there are also many types of tools and strategies for assessment.

**COMPARING STUDENTS TO THEMSELVES OR TO A STANDARD** School professionals choose their assessment methods based on how the information from the assessment will be used. Suppose Mr. Tyler, Kurume's social studies teacher, needs to know what competencies Kurume brings to reading a textbook. Specifically, Mr. Tyler wants to know that, if he assigns a chapter to Kurume to read over three days, Kurume has the reading and comprehension skills to answer application, synthesis, and evaluation questions based on the text. Mr. Tyler can best answer this question by assessing Kurume's skills on the text that he intends to use for his course. Because the results of the assessment affect instructional decisions, Mr. Tyler is best advised to assess close to the arena in which Kurume is expected to perform. Similarly, a teacher who wants information about students' skills in writing should assess writing performance. In general, when school professionals need to make instructional decisions about what to teach next, informal assessments should be used.

In standards- or criteria-based assessment, a student is assessed against a clear objective standard of performance. Teachers can use the information they gather as a student completes a performance assessment to identify areas in which the student is having problems. This can lead to more targeted teaching as the teacher supports the student to meet the performance standard.

## COMPARING STUDENTS TO ONE ANOTHER

School professionals sometimes need information about how a student compares to other students on particular skills or ability levels. The comparisons among students help school professionals set their expectations for each student and identify each student's capacities. Furthermore, well-constructed formal assessments can help school professionals identify underlying cognitive, affective, and communicative needs that students have that may impede their performance on academic tasks. These needs emerge as the assessment tools reveal the relative strengths and weaknesses of each learner. Subsequent analysis of these strengths and weaknesses lead the assessor to a fuller understanding of the learner's needs. Typically, comparing students to one another requires that the measurement tool not only be reliable and valid but also be administered in a standard form. That is, the person giving the test will give it in the same way, using the same administration format, each time. An example might help to explain the use of a standardized assessment tool.

Students who excel in academics are adept at symbol manipulation, whether the symbols are language-based or numerically based. Other students may learn most efficiently when symbols are converted to objects that they can manipulate and experiment with in order to understand properties and relationships and to create connections between various elements. Teachers guide learning for the first type of student by using symbols. However, symbols without accompanying objects would frustrate the second set of learners.

Remember Annie? Annie learns in a third way. She does not use language, she communicates with cries

and gestures, she picks her skin when placed in unfamiliar settings, and she does not initiate interactions with her teachers or peers at school. One of the first questions that Annie's teacher asked is, How does Annie learn?

By comparing Annie's performance on a number of tasks to the performance of other learners, her assessor could make an educated guess about how Annie learns and modify teaching approaches accordingly to provide information to Annie in the form that she will best understand. Annie's performance on a formal test showed that she was able to complete only those items that were typical of infants and toddlers. As items became more difficult, Annie began to fail. Closer analysis of the patterns of Annie's strengths and abilities showed that, when she could touch and feel the test items, she was able to demonstrate her ability to problem solve. From observing these samples of Annie's behavior, her assessor hypothesized that Annie learns through touching and feeling. From this hypothesis, her teachers were encouraged to teach Annie by moving her through sequences of behavior so that she can memorize the motor sequences. Other learners can use language to mediate and memorize new information. Because Annie's language is still emerging, she needs other methods for learning new information. For instance, her teacher might instruct Annie on how to go to the bathroom at school by taking her to the bathroom and actually moving her body through the sequences of opening the door to the bathroom, walking to the toilet, opening the stall door, walking inside, and locking the latch. These chains of behaviors form behavioral repertoires. For Annie to learn them, she needs to repeat the repertoire many, many times. Similarly, her teacher might instruct her on how to use a swing by physically taking her through the entire sequence of swinging, including learning the phrase "going outside," finding the swing, and so on. Or her teacher might teach her to ask for more cookies at the snack table by physically taking her through each step of the process.

Teaching Annie involves repeating the same sequence of activities in the same way, over and over again. In this way, a sensorimotor learner like Annie can learn many sequences of behavior. A formal assessment tool, one that provides a comparison of Annie's behavior to that of other, more typical children, helps the assessor hypothesize about how Annie processes information. A formal assessment tool assists in developing those hypotheses because it has a standard form for administration, is reliable and valid, and provides a set of norms against which a child's performance can be measured. When school professionals have had many opportunities to observe students on the same set of tasks, they become increasingly proficient at understanding the processes that create certain types of performance.

## Standards-Based Assessment

Most of the previous discussion has covered assessment concepts that teachers can apply within their classrooms. It is also critical for school professionals to understand something about the standards-based assessment movement that is so influential today. Many states have adopted some form of statewide assessment whereby districts and individual schools within each district report results of student achievement testing annually. For the most part, at the time of this writing, these assessments provide information about which students are able to meet state standards for a particular grade in terms of literacy, math, science, or whatever content area the individual state has identified for assessment purposes. In most cases, these statewide assessments are tied to state standards in content areas.

**WHAT PURPOSES DO THESE ASSESSMENTS SERVE?** There is wide variation in the purposes for which district- and statewide assessment processes are designed. Assessment for accountability must be differentiated from assessment for educational growth. Assessment for accountability means that data from state assessments are used to examine the extent to which schools and school districts are educating their students effectively. In essence, schools and school districts are accountable to the public for ensuring the quality of educational outcomes.

Another kind of large-scale assessment, such as that done in some states, can also be construed to be a high-stakes process for students. In some cases, the outcomes of statewide assessment programs determine whether an individual student can progress to the next grade or graduate from high school. These assessments exist not only for accountability purposes but also as measures of individual student progress. In both scenarios, accountability and student outcomes, the statewide assessments systems are summative, pro-

viding outcome data on what has already occurred. But these assessments are not sensitive enough to help teachers understand what they could do to improve the quality of their instruction.

Furthermore, accountability systems may serve multiple agendas. For instance, accountability systems that determine eligibility for graduation have much higher stakes for individuals than do accountability systems that primarily inform policymakers at the local, state, and national level. These agendas are not mutually exclusive. However, because there are multiple purposes being played out locally and regionally, the potential for generalized assumptions about the outcomes of assessment systems are limited.

According to IDEA 97, all students with disabilities must be part of the assessment process. This means that the standardized assessment processes used can be accommodated to meet the needs of students with disabilities. A variety of difficult issues must be addressed regarding the accommodations and adaptations of standardized testing. Different states approach the task from very different perspectives. You will need to understand the implications for the students in your classroom, because accommodations and adaptations will be given only to students who receive the same accommodations and adaptations during instruction. Beginning in the summer of 2000, even students with the most significant disabilities will be assessed. This means that alternative assessments may be developed and used.

Embedded in this discussion is the issue of whether alternate assessment is merely a different method to achieve the same purpose as the typical assessment. In other words, given that students who will take alternate assessments will have unique educational needs, can the alternate assessment be designed to answer different, more individualized sets of questions? For instance, if the typical assessment system is designed to answer questions about equity of outcomes for all students, can the alternate assessment system be designed to determine the degree of growth experienced by individual students? In this hypothetical scenario, the design purpose of the typical assessments would be very different from the design purpose of the alternate assessment. In the typical assessment scenario, the assessments attempt to determine whether the current educational system results in similar educational outcomes for all students. In the alternate assessment scenario, the assessment looks at whether students are making progress on their IEPs. These hypothetical examples illustrate the potential range of responses to the mandate for the participation of children with disabilities in state- and districtwide assessments. In brief, the degree to which alternate assessment mirrors the design, purpose, and use of the general assessment has consequences for how the data are used in policymaking.

**HOW ARE STUDENTS SELECTED?** There is considerable debate about who would select students for alternate assessments. While the teams that design and monitor IEPs under the guidelines of IDEA 97 have considerable knowledge of individual student skills and abilities, the potential for erring either by failing to select eligible students or by selecting too many students for alternate assessment is magnified because of the pressures that teams may face at schools where the possibility of school reconstitution exists within the accountability system. Yet, the responsibility for making decisions about eligibility must reside locally because the most information about student performance and ability is held by the individuals who work with students. Therefore, the process to determine eligibility for alternate assessment must shelter or protect decision makers from undue repercussions.

**WHAT ISSUES SHOULD ALTERNATE ASSESSMENT DESIGNERS CONSIDER?** An alternate assessment process should not be confused with the function of the IEP, which we will discuss in more detail in Chapter 8. That is, an alternate assessment must provide information about policy issues such as ensuring that all students have opportunities to learn and access to effective educational supports and services. In addition, the alternate assessment process should hold systems accountable for the performance of all students. To design a meaningful alternate assessment, designers must ensure that the results of the assessment will provide information to schools, school districts, and states about how effective they are in providing educational services for all students.

■ **SECTION SUMMARY**

Formative and summative assessment require attention to similar issues. Knowing the depth and breadth of the curriculum in which you are assessing your students will help you design the types of tools that will best serve your purposes. Likewise, identifying your measurement metric and your standards will help you design an assessment tool that has internal consistency and that measures what you mean to measure. Finally, specifying the type of comparisons that will be most helpful to you will assist you in matching your tools to your outcomes. As statewide assessment becomes more and more prevalent, you will need to understand its implications for your own students with disabilities. You will need more and more formative assessment information as you teach to make sure that your students are mastering the necessary content.

The following discussion provides greater detail about the various kinds of informal, classroom assessment processes. By understanding the form and purpose of different types of assessment tools, you will be able to choose the right ones for the job. Recall that the value of a tool rests in its ability to give you information about the type of instructional decisions you need to make. If the tool doesn't help you make a particular decision, then the tool is not useful. Remember our carpenter? If he needs to hammer a nail and has only a level, it doesn't matter how precisely his level measures. In this situation, the level is useless.

# Informal Assessment Tools

Table 7.1 includes the question, "What are informal assessment tools?" This section introduces some informal assessment tools that are typically designed by teachers and other school professionals for use in classrooms. Developing and measuring students' progress informally is the most common form of assessment in classrooms. Understanding how to design assessments, measure the outcomes, and use the information to inform teaching is an important part of each school professional's responsibility. Informal assessment tools are informal because they have not gone through the same rigorous analysis as informal tools of their reliability, validity, and standardization of the methods used to administer them. Because of their elasticity, informal tools provide opportunities for teachers to analyze and interpret student performance based on the four domains of learning. Interpreting individual performance helps teachers to improve the match between their curriculum and instruction and the needs of their students. A growing body of research on dynamic

An elementary school student proudly displays her chart assessing her accomplishments of school and home tasks.

assessment supports the use of assessment tools that permit the tester to teach the student a way of solving a problem or enhancing performance (Campione, 1989). As assistance is given to the student, the tester is able to analyze the student's potential for change on a given task (Palinscar & Brown, 1991).

Assessment can be either quantitative or qualitative, or both. **Quantitative** measurement involves computing percentages based on the ratio of correct responses to the total number of possible responses and then using scoring devices such as rubrics to judge the quality of the product or performance. This kind of information helps to track progress. **Qualitative** assessment involves making judgments about the meaning of the errors and interpretations of tasks that individual students make. Interviews and conferences about student work are examples of qualitative approaches to measuring student growth. Through these qualitative

assessments, school professionals can make judgments about the cognitive, affective, communicative, and physical needs of students.

This section provides basic information about informal classroom-based assessment. Specifically, you will become acquainted with the notions of authentic and performance-based assessment and will learn about the use of observations and interviews. This section also outlines the use of teacher-designed tools for curriculum-based assessment.

## Authentic Assessment

One of the advantages of informal assessment is that school professionals can create an assessment task that closely resembles what a student might do outside of the school environment. The more real or authentic the task, the greater the likelihood that students will be able to meet the challenge in their nonacademic lives. In some arenas, this is relatively easy to achieve. For example, in athletics, running, jumping, catching, and throwing are skills that can be measured off the playing field. While track-and-field athletes directly transfer their skills to competition, athletes who play, say, football or basketball or baseball must embed their technical skills into actual plays made on the field or court. Although coaches can measure technical skills, the authentic assessment occurs when athletes are on the field reacting and responding to the competition and using their technical skills to prevail. One measure of competence is in the outcome of the game. However, because there are many variables that the athlete may not be able to control (such as the weather, the calls made by the umpire or referee, and the competence of team members), an authentic assessment of an individual's performance might include the number of hits or the number of touchdown passes or the number of blocked shots. Thus, authentic assessment involves observing and evaluating performances or products that are created under conditions that approximate reality or are themselves authentic.

When school professionals translate this principle to the academic realm, they are challenged to make the connections between the content they teach and the conditions under which a student might use the skills outside of school. For instance, if eleventh-grade English teachers are teaching expository writing, they may want to assess competence by involving students

| TABLE 7.2 | **Examples of Authentic Assessment of Expository Writing** | | | |
| --- | --- | --- | --- | --- |
| | Grade Level | | | |
| **Writing Task** | **Second Grade** | **Fifth Grade** | **Eighth Grade** | **Eleventh Grade** |
| Notifying someone of a change in plans | A note to their mothers about a change in the time for the Christmas play | A memo to the transportation department to explain the itinerary for a field trip | A plan for making the transition to senior high school, including goals for classes, extracurricular activities, a part-time internship, and involvement in athletics | A plan for graduating from high school, including goals for senior classes, extracurricular activities, postsecondary educational goals and timelines, and career plans |
| Persuading someone to volunteer | An ad in the school newsletter asking for volunteer story tellers | A letter to the local senior citizen activity center asking for volunteers for the school's grandparent program | A letter soliciting donations from local business for a dance dedicated to supporting relocation for immigrants from a developing nation | An open letter to the community discussing the need for volunteers for a school improvement program |
| Telling a story | An audiotape of the student telling a fairytale to a kindergartner | An audiotape of the student telling about family customs and rituals to other fifth-graders | An audiotape of the student telling one of O. Henry's short stories | An audiotape giving a biographical sketch of a famous writer |
| Reflecting on something that has happened | A journal entry | A journal entry | A journal entry | A journal entry |

in a writing activity that they might face in their jobs or their lives. This might include an article for the company newsletter, a letter to an attorney explaining the background on a legal issue, an editorial for the local paper, or a letter to the editor. An authentic assessment task might be to set up a menu of possibilities for a graded writing assignment (see Table 7.2 for an example). Students could pick among several options, write for a purpose, and submit their writing both for grading by the teacher and for submission to the authentic source.

## Performance Assessment

Assuring that an assessment task is authentic helps us verify that our students will be able to tackle real-life problems. While we should measure all assessment against those criteria, not all learning can be measured authentically. However, performance assessment is one way of approximating authenticity. Performance assessment occurs when the "what" that is being measured is something a student must do to show competence. Examples of performance assessment might include evaluating a dance, an essay, a skating routine, a tennis serve, a debate, or a skit. While these tasks may be performed, they may not always occur within an authentic setting. So, while a student may dance for the teacher, the setting may not be a recital open to the public.

Although students "perform" when they complete a multiple-choice, paper-and-pencil task, this is not an example of performance assessment. In performance assessment, the student demonstrates a skill under conditions that approximate reality but that may not actually be authentic. In performance assessment, a

**BOX 7.1**

## Steps in Performance-Based Measurement

1. Outline the essential performance for the unit. (*Example:* Write, direct, and produce at least one performance of a one-act play to an audience of peers.)

2. Construct a matrix that has the knowledge, skills, and conditional knowledge required to master content in the unit. (*Example:* knowledge: the ability to write dialog; skills: the ability to assign roles and manage production of costumes and sets; conditional knowledge: the ability to adhere to timelines by managing set crew and actors effectively.)

3. Identify tasks that learners can complete that will demonstrate their mastery of the unit content. (*Example:* Develop a timeline for rehearsals, set development, and actual performance of the play.)

4. Identify measures of effectiveness, specifying quantity and quality. (*Example:* adequate time allotted for recruitment and selection of actors, realistic timeline for set construction, and detail of timeline allowing for slippage in the schedule.)

student's ability to do a task, rather than know about it, is measured. In performance assessment, the criteria for poor, competent, and excellent performance are set by the evaluator, ahead of time. The student is asked to demonstrate a skill or routine. In this case, getting it right entails the process of execution rather than provision of a correct answer. Fine arts and athletics have long recognized and used performance-based assess-

ment, but it is now becoming more prevalent in the academic realm as well. For instance, watching a student conduct an experiment might help the teacher evaluate the student's knowledge of the scientific method more completely than having the student tell or write the five steps of this method in response to a written question. Box 7.1 provides the steps for creating a performance-based measure.

**TABLE 7.3** **A Rubric for a Persuasive Speech**

You must give a three-minute speech to a group of senior citizens convincing them to vote for increasing the mill levy to support improvements in the schools. A score of 4 or 5 is considered mastery.

| Score | Criteria | Score | Criteria |
|---|---|---|---|
| 1 | You run over the time limit. You have no logically constructed argument. You use a monotone inflection. | 4 | You use only your allotted time. You excite the audience with an introduction that provides an overview of your position. You introduce at least one cohesive argument for the mill levy. Your conclusion is gripping and to the point. |
| 2 | You run over the time limit. You fail to outline your case initially or offer a strong conclusion. Your intonation patterns do vary. | 5 | You use only your allotted time. You set up audience members to reconsider their own position. You provide them with at least two ways of thinking about the issue. You vary your voice tone and gestures to drive your points home. You finish with a compelling rationale for voting for the mill levy. |
| 3 | You use only your allotted time. You offer a strong conclusion but lack an initial outline. Your intonation patterns are interesting and paired with appropriate gestures. | | |

Performances are evaluated against a set of criteria that are determined prior to the execution of the performance (see Table 7.3 for an example). Usually, performances are scored for technical competence (such as having a introductory and closing statement that provides a general framework of a presentation's content) and for creativity (such as presenting information on the geologic formation of the Grand Tetons in Wyoming through a skit rather than lecture).

## Observation

There are many ways to observe students. Some forms of observation are anecdotal in nature while others provide quantitative information about a student's performance. Commonly used forms of observation include field notes, frequency counts, and time samples (Wolery, Bailey, & Sugai, 1988).

**FIELD NOTES** When school professionals want to understand the context in which a student is operating, they might choose to use field or anecdotal notes to record what they observe. Anecdotal notes are simple to make because they are written descriptions of what is occurring in a particular setting. An example of anecdotal notes is shown in Table 7.4. Notice how the anecdotal notes allow Mrs. Huang to reflect on Melissa's affective needs. While Mrs. Huang hasn't developed an intervention plan yet, by keeping anecdotal records on Melissa, she will be able to develop a strategy as she pays attention to the patterns of behavior her anecdotal notes track. Anecdotal notes provide an opportunity for school professionals to reflect on the cognitive, affective, communicative, and physical needs of their students.

**FREQUENCY** Frequency counts provide a quantitative measure of how often certain behaviors occur in

### TABLE 7.4  Mrs. Huang's Anecdotal Notes

| Date | Time | Narrative |
|---|---|---|
| November 11 | 10:30 to 10:45 | Melissa came back from music about three minutes late. When I asked her where she had been, she said that she didn't know. I didn't want to confront her then so I asked her to be sure to take a few minutes at lunch to talk with me. She replied angrily that she didn't have to. I ignored her outburst and returned to working with a small group on fractions. |
| | | Melissa walked back to her desk and picked up the worksheet that had been distributed. She ripped it up and looked angrily at me. I tried to ignore the behavior and directed my group to their task. I then gave them a simple problem to work on and left the group to talk quietly with Melissa. |
| | | As I approached her, she sat down and began to rummage through her desk. On my way over to her desk, I picked up another copy of the worksheet. I handed it to her when I got to her desk, and she took it from my hand. I touched her on the shoulder and said, "You look like you've been having a bad hair day. I'd like to hear all about it when the others go to lunch. I'm looking forward to spending some time with you. Can you look over this worksheet and make sure that you don't have any questions about what to do?" Amazingly enough, she actually looked at the worksheet, and shook her head no. I breathed a sigh of relief and headed back to my workgroup. |
| November 12 | 3:30 | During my lunchtime meeting with Melissa yesterday, I discovered that she has been having some problems with one of the cliques in the classroom. Stephanie, Crystal, and Sheridan are the arbiters of fashion in the classroom. Melissa wants to join them but really doesn't have the verbal skills to engage in their repartee. As a result they reject her cruelly, making fun of her appearance and what she says. During music, the clique gossiped continually, glancing at Melissa and giggling. She was late to class because she went into the bathroom to cry. I'm not quite sure what to do at this point since I can't mandate friendships. |

A school professional conducts an informal assessment to inform her instructional decisions.

the classroom. Mrs. Huang could keep track of the number of outbursts that Melissa has in the classroom. An occasional outburst may be typical for a third-grader. But when a teacher senses that the number of times that a student has difficulty managing his or her emotions or releases them unexpectedly or out of context, then keeping track of how often that happens helps the teacher to communicate with other school professionals. Frequency alone is a measure of the intensity of a problem.

**TIME SAMPLING**   Sometimes, a behavior happens so often that it's hard to count it accurately. In that case, another form of recording is helpful. Let's sup-

pose that Stephen seems to be out of his seat more often than in it. Tracking how often Stephen is out of his seat will help his teacher and other school professionals decide what kinds of intervention they need to use to get him in his seat and on task more often. Using a time sample involves selecting both a time period in which to observe and an interval of time within that time frame to observe the student. For instance, Stephen's teacher might decide that she wants to watch him during reading for ten minutes each day, so she sets up a schedule for her observation. Each minute for the ten minutes she has designated for this task, she will look up at Stephen, note what he's doing, and write down what she sees. If she does this for five days in a row, she should have a good overview of Stephen's activities during reading time.

## Interviews

Interviews are important, but often overlooked, forms of collecting information about students and families. Table 7.5 provides an example of interview questions to ask about reading preferences. Students are frequently the best source of information about what motivates them to learn, what areas of study they are

### Extending Your Learning

Try keeping anecdotal records on a student in a classroom that you are observing. After each description of what you observe, reflect about what the behaviors you observed might mean in terms of the student's cognitive, affective, communicative, and physical needs. Share your observations with an experienced teacher.

| TABLE 7.5 | Sample Questions in a Reading Interview |
| --- | --- |

- Tell me about how you use your reading skills.
- What kind of a reader do you think you are?
- If you could read as much as you wanted, what things would you read about?
- What makes someone a great reader?

| TABLE 7.6 | A Summary Checklist for Writing Test Questions |
| --- | --- |

- Do the test questions measure knowledge and skills in key elements of the curriculum?
- Are the test questions unambiguous?
- Does each test question evaluate a single idea or concept?
- Do essay questions evaluate higher-order thinking (application, synthesis, or evaluation)?
- Are the questions based on solving novel or interesting problems?
- Is a key for scoring each essay question created prior to grading?

Source: Bloom, Madaus, & Hastings, 1981.

interested in, and even why they may misbehave. An interview can be structured around questions like the ones in Table 7.5 to focus on a particular skill or content area, or it can be a more general interview about a student's preferences and dislikes. Interviews are tactically important because they can accomplish several purposes simultaneously. While skillful interviewers are collecting comprehensive information, they also convey to the student being interviewed that the student's opinions and preferences are important. Thus, interviews are a key strategy for uncovering the affective needs of students, particularly in the areas of motivation and self-regulation.

## Teacher-Designed Protocols

Teachers often design tests over units of learning. They help the teacher gauge the knowledge and skills individual students were able to master. Objective tests consist of written test items: multiple choice, matching, true/false, and short answer. Typically, tests are designed to ensure that students know terminology, facts, rules, and principles; have skills in using processes and procedures (an algorithm for addition, for instance); can translate a principle to a novel situation; and are able to apply their knowledge base. How teachers use information from their tests determines whether the tool is summative or formative.

If teachers use tests at the end of a unit of learning to determine a grade, then they are testing for summative purposes. However, if they design a set of test items that they administer frequently during the course of a unit and use the information to reteach or find another way of teaching content, then the test is being used for formative reasons. Table 7.6 provides a checklist for ensuring that the tests you design will provide you with

the information you need to make curricular and instructional decisions.

Objective and essay tests are not the only form of teacher-designed protocols. Ecological inventories and miscue analyses can be used to measure progress in the curriculum and help school professionals make decisions about what techniques or instructional strategies to continue to use, to refine, or even to discard.

**ECOLOGICAL INVENTORIES**  Ecological inventories provide a format for looking at the performance demands of a particular setting and evaluating the competence of individual students on each demand. Ecological inventories are developed by school professionals through careful observation of a particular setting. Like a task analysis, an ecological inventory organizes what occurs in the environment into a set of sequentially occurring sets.

Let's suppose that Kirk's out-of-seat behaviors are occurring frequently during math. Kirk's teacher might design an ecological inventory of math, listing all of the performance demands of math, from the transition into math to the transition out of math to the next activity. The list might include items like sitting at the student's desk, listening to directions, waiting for the work sheet, participating in group activity, sharing results of the activity with the class, listening to other's reports, taking a written skill drill on fractions, solving an estimation problem with a math buddy, handing in work, clearing the desk, and getting in line for recess.

Once the teacher has constructed a complete list of all the task demands, she observes Kirk using the ecological inventory. For each performance demand, the teacher checks either "No, Kirk did not do the task" or "Yes, Kirk did complete the task at the same time as and with similar accuracy to his peers." If Kirk was unable to complete a task correctly, the teacher notes how Kirk was prompted to complete that step. If he was unable to complete it independently, she notes whether she used an indirect verbal or nonverbal prompt to correct his performance. For instance, if the teacher said, "I'm looking for good listeners," and Kirk began

listening, this would be considered an indirect verbal prompt. It's less intrusive than if the teacher said, "Kirk, put on your listening hat," which would be a direct verbal prompt. If the verbal prompts did not work, then the teacher might try a gestural prompt. For instance, by moving closer to Kirk and pointing to her own ears, she might prompt Kirk to attend. A partial physical prompt would involve the teacher putting her hands on Kirk's shoulders and pointing to the blackboard.

After scoring Kirk on each performance element, the teacher needs to consider what possible reasons might exist for Kirk's prompted responses. This is called a discrepancy analysis. The issue is why Kirk's perfor-

**TABLE 7.7** **A Sample Ecological Inventory**

| Class Routines and Procedures | Student Performance | Reason | Possible Instructional Supports or Adaptations |
|---|---|---|---|
| Write draft, edit report | Does not write, will scribble on paper, skips letters on computer | Does not know how to write | Pair student with other student in the room, teach student to select research material when prompted by peer |
| Sit and listen quietly to instructions/directions | Sits for two minutes, gets out of seat, walks around room | Is looking for attention from the teacher | |
| Select/review topic for writing, gather reading research materials from room or library, read | Sits, waits, or wanders around room; will select book, magazine with gestural prompt; scans book and demonstrates interest with verbalizations | Has short attention to task | Have the teacher stand close to the student and periodically (less than every two minutes) put a hand on the student's shoulder |
| Remove paper, pen, English book | Same | Looks at others, models taking out materials | None needed |
| Read report to class | Cannot read/verbalize | Is unable to read | Distribute group report, use overhead projector to present findings |
| Locate and sit in assigned seat | Follows natural cues | Models other students' behaviors | None needed |
| Greet teacher | Same | Waits, looks, will wave hand when cued with gestural prompt | None needed |
| Enter class prior to bell ringing | Enters wrong room | Using other students as cues, selects a student in another room to follow | Teach student to locate a fellow student from the same class to follow to class |

mance is discrepant from that of his peers. The conclusion from the discrepancy analysis might be (1) he doesn't understand the directions from the teacher, (2) he's not paying attention, (3) he sits too far away from the teacher, (4) he doesn't seem to know where his materials are, or (5) he's more interested in getting attention from his peers than participating in the lesson. Depending on the student, the explanations will differ. Considering possible explanations for the behaviors observed helps school professionals identify the type of supports they need to give a particular student.

After completing the discrepancy analysis, the next step is to identify what needs to be taught and what accommodations need to be made. Examples of curriculum (what needs to be taught) might be strategies for paying attention, for organizing materials, or for identifying appropriate and inappropriate times for socializing. An example of an accommodation might be creation of an incentive system for paying attention.

Table 7.7 provides an example of a completed ecological inventory. Ecological inventories are useful because they help school professionals identify both the problem and some possible solutions. They're of ongoing value because they can also be the measure of how successful a set of curricular and support strategies can be. In Kirk's case, his teacher might observe him once a week for six weeks to see if the number of tasks that Kirk can perform without prompting increases. The ecological inventory can help teachers to observe and make decisions about what to teach and to figure out why a student may not be able to perform as expected. Applying their knowledge about the cognitive, affective, communicative, and physical domains helps teachers interpret student behavior and refine their instructional strategies.

**MISCUE ANALYSIS** Listening to students read aloud and scoring the accuracy of their reading helps teachers to recognize the kinds of strategies students use to read and helps guide teachers in making decisions about what needs to be taught (Fuchs & Fuchs, 1988). A miscue analysis should assist the teacher in establishing how much of what is read is understood by the reader and how many words are correctly identified. Assessing reading by listening to a student read has several components. First, the reader should have the opportunity to prepare by reading the selection silently. The reader might even be encouraged to read aloud to him- or herself prior to reading aloud for the assessor. When the reader and the assessor sit down

> **BOX 7.2**
> ## Ms. Martinez Begins a Miscue Analysis
>
> *Ms. Martinez:* Michael, I want to listen to your reading today. I'm not going to stop you or correct your reading. I want you to do the best that you can. As you read, I'm going to be making notes on my copy of your reading passage. When you finish, I'm going to ask you some questions about the selection. Do you want to ask me any questions about your reading?
> *Michael:* Am I going to miss recess?
> *Ms. Martinez:* No, we have plenty of time to finish this before recess. Why don't you begin?

together, the assessor should let the reader know what to expect. The dialog might sound something like the one in Box 7.2.

Now refer to Figure 7.1, which shows a sample miscue assessment form for reading. As Michael reads, Ms. Martinez will mark the words that Michael miscues on her copy of Michael's reading selection. The words that are miscues are circled, with Michael's actual miscues written above the circled words. If Michael corrects himself, that is also noted. The number of words correctly read are divided by the number of words in the passage. For example, if Michael read a 100-word passage and read 80 words correctly, then his score would be 80 percent accuracy.

In addition, other analyses should be completed. For instance, in how many sentences was the meaning changed by Michael's miscue? Let's suppose that Michael read the passage in Box 7.3, which is excerpted from Frank Baum's *The Road to Oz.* Look at paragraph 7. If Michael read that sentence and substituted "behind" for "next," then he would have changed the meaning of the sentence. For each word miscue, the assessor writes the word that was used to replace the actual word. Typically, students omit or insert words, substitute different words, or create nonwords by sounding out the letters in an unfamiliar word. Each of these types of errors is carefully noted because substituting a word with similar meaning suggests that the student is reading for meaning. In contrast, the student who substitutes a word that sounds like the unfamiliar word but makes no sense in the sentence is concentrating on word identification rather than comprehension.

Errors provide an opportunity to evaluate how the student is thinking about the task that he or she is engaged in. When the student finishes reading the passage, an accuracy percentage is calculated based on the ratio of the number of words read compared to the number of words read correctly.

The assessor also determines whether the miscue changed the meaning of the sentence. The student receives both a meaning score and a total word score. Finally, the assessor asks Michael to explain what happened in the passage. Some of the questions might deal with basic, knowledge-level matters such as, "What

characters were introduced in this passage?" Some of the questions might be interpretive such as, "Do you think the Shaggy Man is in a hurry?" or "Do you think it's safe for Dorothy to help the Shaggy Man?"

Miscue analyses, like ecological inventories, rely on the ability of teachers to interpret student behavior. If students are unable to recall passages, have difficulty making competent word substitutions, or have difficulty with vocabulary, teachers who know about the cognitive, affective, communicative, and physical domains can make reasoned interpretations of which of these areas may be affecting student performance.

---

# Classroom Reading Miscue Assessment

The checklist is designed to help teachers identify what reading strategies a student uses and with what degree of frequency. The instrument will guide teachers to plan instruction that will improve students' proficiency with effective reading strategies. In this assessment procedure, a child reads a whole story to a teacher while the teacher records how effectively the child strives to make sense of the story. Say to the child, "I need to learn what you know about reading and what more you are ready to learn about reading. To do that, I'd like you to read this story/article/information out loud while I make some notes. As you read, do what you normally do when you are reading by yourself. Pretend I am not here. When you finish I'll ask you to tell me what you read."

## Directions:

Fill in child's name, the date the child reads, the child's present grade level assignment, and your name.

There are two options in selecting material for the child to read.

1. A complete story from the basal in which he or she normally reads. List the publisher of the basal, the level of the basal, and the title of the story the child reads.

   *Or*

2. A children's literature (a story) or content (an expository text) selection. To select the appropriate level of difficulty, use this guideline: the child should not

make more than *one* meaning-changing error in ten words, i.e., the child should not read a word that changes the meaning of the text and leave it uncorrected more than once in every ten words. List the title of the story the child reads.

## Part I

The goal of proficient readers is to make sense. The analysis of Part I will indicate to what degree the child has the goal of making sense.

As the child reads, tally if each sentence makes sense or does not make sense as the child last read it.

■ This does not mean that a child has to read every word in a sentence correctly. If the child maintains the meaning of the sentence, even though some words are not read exactly, the sentence should be counted as semantically acceptable. For example, if the text states, "He had a hard time getting into *his* house at night," and the reader reads, "He had a hard time getting into *the* house at night," the sentence is semantically acceptable. If the text states, "He was *hungry* enough to eat anything," and the reader reads (without self-correcting), "He was *hurry* enough to eat anything," this sentence is not semantically acceptable.

■ When marking whether a sentence is semantically acceptable, consider the sentence as the child finally reads it. Children may read words initially that don't

---

**FIGURE 7.1** ■ Sample Miscue Assessment Form

make sense but correct them before going on to the next sentence. Give them credit for these rereadings and corrections if the sentence subsequently makes sense. For example, the sentence, "Soon the table was so full that *he* began to put them on his bookshelves," was first read as "Soon the table was so full that *the* began to put them on his bookshelves." As the child discovered that the miscue didn't make sense with what followed in the sentence, he went back and read it with the correct wording. This sentence should be marked semantically acceptable.

■ Often a child makes more than one miscue in a sentence. If he or she corrects one or more of the miscues but still leaves one or more miscues that disrupt meaning, the sentence is still semantically *un*acceptable. (However, do keep in mind the self-corrections the child is making so that you can include that information in Part II.)

■ In marking whether a sentence is semantically acceptable, also consider proper intonation and punctuation. For example, if a child disrupts meaning by running through a period without adding an acceptable conjunction or by turning a statement into a question, the sentence is not semantically acceptable.

Count the number of tallies in each row and list the sum in the Total box. Then add the two Total boxes to determine the total number of sentences read.

To predict how well the child was comprehending the story while reading, compute the percentage of sentences that made sense as the child read.

## Part II

This section lists four strategies proficient readers use to make sense of a text and three behaviors that interfere with comprehension of a text. Observing the child's use of each strategy helps you plan instruction for the reader.

■ With what frequency does the reader give some indication that the text doesn't make sense as s/he reads, even though s/he isn't able to do anything about it?

■ With what frequency does the reader replace words in the text with other words that make sense?
   Example: "Goldilocks ran like lightning out of the three bears' *house.*"
   Reader: "Goldilocks ran like lightning out of the three bears' *home.*"
   "Home" is a meaningful substitution for "house."

■ With what frequency does the reader go back and self-correct miscues that changed the text meaning?

■ With what frequency do the child's eyes take in pictures or other visual clues? For example, the child can't use information from pictures if his or her hand is covering the pictures while reading.

■ With what frequency does the child replace words in the text with other words that do not make sense in the sentence or in the story and give no indication of being uncomfortable with the lack of meaning?
   Example: "He liked to cook and *could* make good things to eat."
   Reader: "He liked to cook and *cold* make good things to eat."

■ With what frequency does the child leave out words that carry meaning for the sentence or story and give no indication that meaning is lost?

■ With what frequency does the child use graphophonic information to the exclusion of information about what would make sense, might be expected, or would sound right in English?

## Part III

One of the best measures in comprehension of the reader's ability to make sense of text is a child's unaided retelling of what has been read. When the child finishes reading, say to the child, *"Tell me everything you remember about what you read."* After the child has told you what he or she can, use the probe, *"Is there anything more you remember about the story?"* Only *after* the child has totally finished the unaided retelling should you consider asking questions to further probe what the child remembers. (Questioning should be considered optional.) A complete retelling of narrative text should include information about character, setting, events, plot, and theme and indicate the child's grasp of the text structure. A complete retelling of expository text should include major concepts, generalizations, specific information, and logical structuring. A partial retelling may reflect the broad sense of the text but lack structure or detail. A child who makes no attempt to reconstruct what he or she has read likely indicates an inability to retell the text or a lack of comprehension.

**FIGURE 7.1** ■ Sample Miscue Assessment Form *(Continued)*

# Classroom Reading Miscue Assessment

Reader's Name _____ Date _____

Grade level _____ Teacher _____

Selection read _____

---

I. What percent of the sentences read make sense?

|  | Sentence by sentence tally | Total |
|---|---|---|
| Number of semantically acceptable sentences | _____ | _____ |
| Number of semantically unacceptable sentences | _____ | _____ |

% Comprehending score:

$$\frac{\text{Number of semantically acceptable sentences}}{\text{Total number of sentences read}} \times 100 = \text{_____} \%$$

II. In what ways is the reader constructing meaning?

|  | Seldom | Sometimes | Often | Usually | Always |
|---|---|---|---|---|---|
| A. Recognizes when miscues have disrupted meaning | 1 | 2 | 3 | 4 | 5 |
| B. Logically substitutes | 1 | 2 | 3 | 4 | 5 |
| C. Self-corrects errors that disrupt meaning | 1 | 2 | 3 | 4 | 5 |
| D. Uses pictures and/or other visual clues | 1 | 2 | 3 | 4 | 5 |

In what ways is the reader disrupting meaning?

|  | Seldom | Sometimes | Often | Usually | Always |
|---|---|---|---|---|---|
| A. Substitutes words that don't make sense | 1 | 2 | 3 | 4 | 5 |
| B. Makes omissions that disrupt meaning | 1 | 2 | 3 | 4 | 5 |
| C. Relies too heavily on graphophonic cues | 1 | 2 | 3 | 4 | 5 |

III. If narrative text is used:

|  | No | | Partial | | Yes |
|---|---|---|---|---|---|
| A. Character recall | 1 | 2 | 3 | 4 | 5 |
| B. Character development | 1 | 2 | 3 | 4 | 5 |
| C. Setting | 1 | 2 | 3 | 4 | 5 |
| D. Relationship of events | 1 | 2 | 3 | 4 | 5 |
| E. Plot | 1 | 2 | 3 | 4 | 5 |
| F. Theme | 1 | 2 | 3 | 4 | 5 |
| G. Overall retelling | 1 | 2 | 3 | 4 | 5 |

If expository text is used:

|  | No | | Partial | | Yes |
|---|---|---|---|---|---|
| A. Major concepts | 1 | 2 | 3 | 4 | 5 |
| B. Generalizations | 1 | 2 | 3 | 4 | 5 |
| C. Specific information | 1 | 2 | 3 | 4 | 5 |
| D. Logical structuring | 1 | 2 | 3 | 4 | 5 |
| E. Overall retelling | 1 | 2 | 3 | 4 | 5 |

**FIGURE 7.1** ■ Sample Miscue Assessment Form *(Continued)*

**BOX 7.3**

## Chapter One: The Way to Butterfield

1. "Please, miss," said the shaggy man, "can you tell me the road to Butterfield?"

2. Dorothy looked him over. Yes, he was shaggy, all right; but there was a twinkle in his eye that seemed pleasant.

3. "Oh, yes," she replied; "I can tell you. But it isn't this road at all."

4. "No?"

5. "You cross the ten acre lot, follow the lane to the highway, go north to the five branches, and take—let me see—"

6. "To be sure, miss; see as far as Butterfield, if you like," said the shaggy man.

7. "You take the branch next to the willow stump, I b'lieve; or else the branch by the gopher holes; or else—"

8. "Won't any of 'em do, miss?"

9. "Course not, shaggy man. You must take the right road to Butterfield."

10. "And that the one by the gopher stump, or—"

11. "Dear me!" cried Dorothy; "I shall have to show you the way; you're so stupid. Wait a minute till I run in the house and get my sunbonnet."

12. The shaggy man waited. He had an oat-straw in his mouth, which he chewed slowly as if it tasted good; but it didn't. There was an apple-tree beside the house, and some apples had fallen to the ground. The shaggy man thought they would taste better than the oat-straw, so he walked over to get some. A little black dog with bright brown eyes dashed out of the farmhouse and ran madly toward the shaggy man, who had already picked up three apples and put them in one of the big wide pockets of his shaggy coat. The little dog barked, and made a dive for the shaggy man's leg; but he grabbed the dog by the neck and put it in his pocket along with the apples. He took more apples, afterward, for many were on the ground; and each one that he tossed into his pocket hit the little dog somewhere upon the head or back, and made him growl. The little dog's name was Toto, and he was sorry he had been put in the shaggy man's pocket.

## Extending Your Learning

Use the miscue analysis form in Figure 7.1 as you listen to a student read. Keep track of errors, and conduct an interview with the student when the reading passage is complete. How might you interpret your results?

**CURRICULUM-BASED ASSESSMENT** Curriculum-based assessment (Fuchs & Fuchs, 1987) incorporates several strategies to ensure that it is both reliable and valid. Like observations and performance-based assessments, curriculum-based assessment is based on observing the behaviors of students on tasks that are typically required in the classroom. Because curriculum-based assessment is derived from the curricular activities of the classroom, it assists school professionals in refining and strengthening their instructional strategies. Curriculum-based measurement focuses on individual student progress through the curriculum. Reliability is achieved by measuring the same skills repeatedly over time (Fuchs & Fuchs, 1986). Because curriculum-based assessment is designed to take place in the instructional environment, it provides information about how students are performing in the environments in which they are learning.

Designing a curriculum-based assessment requires four steps: (1) targeting or outlining the essential curriculum outcomes, (2) developing a list of skills that need to be learned to meet the curricular outcomes, (3) identifying tasks that learners can complete that will demonstrate their mastery of skills, and (4) specifying what skills are to be measured for each task (Tindal & Marston, 1990). In our example, we used knowledge of short story elements as the curricular outcomes (see Box 7.4). A curriculum-based assessment might entail selections from each of the targeted authors. Students would be asked to identify types of sentence construction, story structures, and subject matter for each selection. This task may be repeated on a weekly basis as students engage in the unit on early twentieth-century

**BOX 7.4**

## Steps in a Curriculum-Based Assessment

1. Outline the essential learnings for the unit. (*Example:* Identify common elements of the short stories of Edith Wharton, F. Scott Fitzgerald, and Dorothy Parker.)

2. Construct a matrix that has the knowledge, skills, and conditional knowledge that are required to master content in the unit. (*Example:* knowledge: identification of simple and complex sentences, story structures, and content analysis; skills: critical analysis of style and genre; conditional knowledge: selection of an approach to story

construction based on perspective and values to be conveyed to the audience.)

3. Identify tasks that the learners can complete that will demonstrate their mastery of the unit content. (*Example:* Describe a farewell scene at a train station written in the style of each author.)

4. Identify measures of effectiveness, specifying quantity and quality. (*Example:* Use of sentence construction, choice of adjectives, cohesion of description, and length of sentence.)

short stories. Changes in performance on the task will help the teacher to identify what students need to study during the next week. Each student's progress through the unit can be charted on all four facets of analysis.

Ecological inventories and miscue analyses are two tools that school professionals can use for curriculum-based assessment. The key to competent curriculum-based assessment is ensuring that the measurement device identifies specific knowledge gaps, helps teachers to know what and how to teach next, and can be used repeatedly to gather pertinent information. Miscue analysis meets these criteria because it helps school professionals identify the types of reading errors a student is making. As a result, instruction can be altered to address the problem. Ecological inventories help teachers identify the cues and prompts a student currently needs to complete a task, as well as help to understand why a student may be making the kinds of errors that are observed. The teacher might graph a student's miscue scores over time to chart progress. For example, the teacher might chart comprehension scores, word substitutions, nonsense words, and non-meaningful substitutions. This would help the teacher know whether what he or she was doing was making a difference in the student's learning.

## Portfolio Assessment

Portfolio assessment is a method for archiving student products so that progress on several fronts can be observed over time. Imagine the struggling artist trudging from gallery to gallery in Manhattan, portfolio

in hand, trying to get someone to show her work. What's inside that portfolio is a collection of the artist's best renderings. Similarly, a student's portfolio is a thoughtfully selected collection of his or her best work. It demonstrates competence in specific areas such as writing, drawing, public speaking, report writing, critical analysis, field notes, and book reports. Products and performances can be captured in written documents, evaluations written by others who worked with the student, videotapes or audiotapes of performances, photographs, electronic files, and so on.

Portfolios can be constructed in various ways. However, we have found that specifying projects, as well as the rubrics for evaluating products, helps students to focus their work on products that match the content and activities in which they are currently engaged. Portfolios should contain a brief description of how the student selected materials for inclusion in the portfolio. It should also contain criteria for judging the merits of each product. Finally, portfolios should contain a section of students' reflections about what they have learned and its value to them. Portfolios are most useful when they are frequently used in the learning process as a focus for teacher-student conferences.

## ■ SECTION SUMMARY

Informal assessment tools ground the practitioner's work. With these tools, practitioners can attend to the nuances of student needs and effectively scaffold instruction so that students can reach critical academic learning goals. Without these tools to collect evidences about how and what students are learning and to reflect on what they mean about the teacher's practice, instruction will be a hit-or-miss proposition.

## Chapter Summary

Assessment is an essential component in the classroom. Whether formative or summative, assessment should involve the family and focus on issues of curriculum, instruction, and measurement. The goal of assessment is to provide valid, reliable measures of student learning as it relates to the cognitive, affective, communicative, and physical domains. Teachers should be able to implement several assessment processes, including authentic assessments, performance assessments, observations, interviews, and portfolio assessments. Using some simple assessment tools, teachers should be able to design their own protocols, identify the effects of their instruction on student performance, and, as a result, continually refine their teaching activities to optimize student learning. Practitioners must assess with student outcomes in mind, informing the teaching/learning cycle.

**INSTRUCTIONAL ACTIVITY**

## Assessing Your Assessment Skills

### Objective

- To promote your understanding of the assessment process

### Procedure

- Refer back to Table 7.1 and answer as many of the questions as you can.
- List the questions you cannot answer and use them to guide your reading of Chapter 8.

## Glossary

**Alternate-form reliability** The process of ensuring that a test, given in alternate forms, yields information about an individual's knowledge or skills that is consistent across the forms.

**Assessment** The process of collecting evidence about student learning, student knowledge, and student skill and making inferences about how the student learns and understands, is able to do, and knows.

**Coefficients** In statistics, the numerical result of comparing two sets of scores to determine the degree to which one set can predict the other.

**Formative assessment** Assessment for the purpose of refining and improving the learning environment so that students can maximize their learning outcomes.

**Interrater reliability** The process of determining the degree of measurement accuracy across performance judges or raters.

**Portfolio** A collection of student work designed to help others assess or judge the student's current level of competence within a content area.

**Qualitative** Refers to the use of measurement tools that describe performance.

**Quantitative** Refers to the use of numbers to describe a performance or compare among performances.

**Reliability** In testing, refers to the degree to which repeated measures yield the same results.

**Socratic dialog** A teaching technique in which the teacher facilitates discussion through the use of questions designed to engage the group in the critical analysis of text and/or ideas and concepts.

**Summative assessment** Assessment for the purposes of determining student outcomes and their relationship to a set of preordained criteria or to a knowledge base.

**Test/retest reliability** The process of ensuring that a test yields consistent results about a learner.

**Validity** In testing, refers to the degree to which any given test measures what it claims to measure.

## CHAPTER 8

# Assessing for Eligibility and Program Planning

## Kathy Herman Remembers Her Staffing

This interview was completed with a high school student who received special education services and participated in her own staffing. At the time of this interview, Kathy was 19 and a high school senior. She was a veteran of several years of attending her own staffings. Kathy had been identified as a student with mild cognitive impairments.

### What Was It Like to Be Part of Your Own Special Ed Staffing?

I thought it was great because everyone was there, and I got to say what I wanted. It was good for me. If they said something that I didn't want, I had the right to say that I didn't want it and I didn't want to be in that situation.

### What Did You Learn About Yourself as a Learner?

I sat down with someone and they went through my stuff, and we decided what goals I needed to work on and decided what I needed to accomplish before finishing high school. I learned that I needed more time to learn new things. I also learned that I like to learn new things. It challenges me. When I am successful, I feel better about myself. By talking with my teacher, I learned that she thought I was a good student because I try so hard. I didn't know that my teachers thought that I was good.

### What Did Your Teacher Do to Prepare You to Participate in the Staffing?

They got me talking about what I need, and my strengths. They went down a list and asked if I agreed with [goals and suggestions]. I wanted to make sure that they were going to help me get an apartment. I really want to be able to move out of my house.

### What More Could Your Teachers and Parents Have Done to Prepare You to Participate in Your Staffing?

Nothing really. I felt well prepared because I had talked about what I wanted to do with my teachers and my mom. It's hard sometimes with my mom because she doesn't always want me to learn new things.

### What Was It Like to Be Known as a Special Ed Student?

I thought it was fun because I got to do more things and got more help to understand. The teachers help you make choices and all that.

### How Did It Make You Feel About Your Chance of Success in School?

I could do better in school because of the support that I got from the special education teachers. But I still felt like other students, just trying to do my best.

### Any Advice for Other Students Who Need Support and Assistance?

It kind of depends on their disabilities and what they need and what they are struggling with to get help to do better.

# Introduction

In Chapter 7, we introduced the basic concepts of assessment, including the linkages among assessment, curriculum, instruction, and student evaluation. In this chapter, we introduce the elements of assessment that lead to the formal identification of students who are eligible for special education services.

In the general education arena, when a student who is experiencing difficulty with learning is identified, a team of educators is assembled to discuss the needs of the student and to suggest some strategies to address the problem. The classroom teacher is then asked to apply these strategies to support the needs of the student. If the strategies or interventions work, then the student remains in the general education arena, supported by the classroom teacher in consultation with the prereferral team. This team operates under many different titles, such as prereferral team, care and concern team, or child study team.

In the event that the prereferral team's suggestions are not effective, another meeting is held to decide what the next steps might be. The team may recommend that the student be assessed to determine potential eligibility for special education services. In that case, the family of the student in question is contacted for permission to assess the student formally. However, only if the family agrees and gives permission for assessment does the process move forward. The assessment is conducted by school professionals from different backgrounds such as school psychology, speech/language, special education, and other related professions, but families play a critical role in this process.

In this chapter, we introduce you to the special education arena through the eligibility and individualized educational planning process. Second, we examine formal assessment measures, because some of the tools used to determine the special educational needs of students are considered to be formal assessment measures. Finally, we discuss tests that might be used to assess the cognitive, affective, communicative, and physical needs of students. By the end of this chapter, you should have a good idea of how students are evaluated for special education services. An important emphasis in this chapter is the inclusion of students, as well as their adult family members, in the staffing and program planning process (refer back to Kathy Herman's interview).

# Eligibility Assessment for Special Education

Even when classroom teachers pay close attention to the cognitive, affective, communicative, and physical needs of their students, some students will need additional supports from special education services in order to learn effectively. This section addresses the elements of special education eligibility determination that are common from district to district and state to state (see Figure 8.1).

As a school professional, you will be involved in making eligibility decisions. The information you obtain from your informal and formal classroom assessments is an essential part of the process. The more information you bring to the eligibility process, the more you can help the team determine what needs and services the student may require. Your careful use of informal and formal assessments and documentation of the results lends validity to the process of determining eligibility for special education services.

At the heart of the special education eligibility process is the **staffing**—a meeting of school professionals and family members who represent a variety of perspectives and backgrounds. At the staffing, the determination whether to serve a student through special

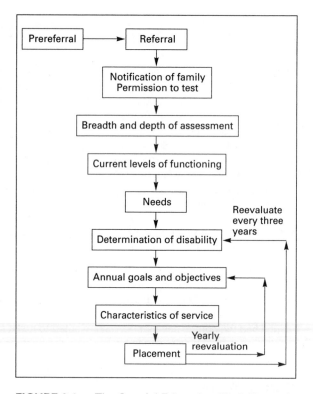

**FIGURE 8.1** ■ The Special Education Eligibility and Retention Process

education services is made. Although students who are presented at a staffing may have a disability, the eligibility decision is based on whether the student's disability interferes with his or her ability to access and benefit from the general education curriculum. In essence, this is a decision about educational disability. It's important to understand how the eligibility process unfolds and what role you might play in making decisions and delivering services to students.

## Prereferral

While not mandated by federal law, many schools have instituted a process of **prereferral** that occurs prior to any formal assessment for special education. Basically, a team of school professionals who have volunteered to serve on this committee for a school year monitor the progress of any student referred to them. The committee may recommend changes in classroom management practices, instructional strategies, or curriculum to assist the classroom teacher in finding effective ways to respond to the needs of a student. Parents should be involved in providing information about their child at this point. This committee typically is composed of one or two classroom teachers, a special services provider (reading specialist, special educator, school psychologist, social worker), and a building administrator. It meets weekly to discuss new cases, review the progress of ongoing cases, and determine if all available and appropriate strategies have been implemented reliably. Where satisfactory student outcomes have not been attained despite the prereferral committee's interventions, the committee may then recommend a complete assessment to see if the student qualifies for special education services.

The prereferral committee is crucial in several ways. First, a complete assessment for special education is expensive because it requires a multidisciplinary team of school professionals to complete reliable and valid assessment of each child referred. By using a prereferral process, many schools have reduced the number of students who are actually referred to special education because classroom teachers are able to modify their instructional environments to meet the needs of unique learners. Second, the prereferral committee assists in increasing the knowledge and skills of classroom teachers because the solutions that meet the needs of one student often benefit other students as well. Finally, if a student needs to be referred for assessment for special education services, some information has already been collected informally to assist the staffing team in making its decisions about whether a student qualifies for those services. Classroom teachers are vital to the success of the prereferral step. Careful, ongoing informal classroom assessment will provide the committee with crucial information on the cognitive, affective, communicative, and physical needs of students. The recommendations this committee makes to the classroom teacher rely heavily on the integrity of the information collected by classroom teachers.

## Permission to Test

Families are key members of the staffing team and bring vital background information to the team. Because families have critical information that will assist other members of the staffing team in making recommendations for eligibility and retention, families need to be notified at the beginning of the process so that they can give their permission for assessment to occur and provide information about their child. By law, notification to families must be in the family's native language, in written as well as oral form. An adult family member who has custody of the child being referred must give written permission prior to initiating any formal assessment. When a family is asked to give permission for their child to be assessed, it creates an opportunity to provide the family with information about the purpose of the assessment and the kinds of information and decisions that can be made at the staffing meeting. Many teams now provide families with informal assessment forms that the family can fill out prior to attending the staffing (see Figure 4.2 for an example). No more than twenty working days may elapse from the time the family gives permission to assess to the time of the formal staffing meeting. Families must be given assurances that the information collected to determine whether their child is eligible for special education services is confidential. This means that only members of the staffing team can access the files. Because staffing team membership includes the family, this ensures that the family has complete access to the files, the records of their child's performance on all assessments, and the written reports of the staffing team members.

At the staffing, decisions are made about the student's current abilities across all domains, including the affective, cognitive, academic, physical, medical, and communicative. Typically, the team includes family members, educators (both special and general), school psychologists, social workers or school counselors, a nurse, an occupational or physical therapist, and an administrator representing the school district. When needed, speech/language pathologists, vision specialists, and audiologists may join the team. Increasingly, students themselves are attending these meetings.

## The Breadth and Depth of Assessment

According to IDEA 97, any decision that places a child in special education must be made on the basis of more than one assessment. For instance, a child may not be placed in special education or labeled with a disability on the basis of his or her score on a test of intelligence. The law is quite clear on this point. Tests must have been developed and field-tested using a group of individuals whose characteristics are similar to that of the child being assessed. Also, tests may only be given for the purpose for which they were intended. In other words, a **behavior rating scale** may not be used as a measure of **adaptive behavior;** a test of **language competence** may not be used to obtain an **intelligence quotient.** A comprehensive, in-depth assessment must include careful identification of cognitive, affective, communicative, and physical needs, using tools designed for that purpose. Additionally, a complete analysis of students' current academic skills is essential for identifying any discrepancies between what students are *capable* of doing and what they actually are *accomplishing*. This analysis of discrepancies between capacity and accomplishment assists the multidisciplinary team in understanding the problems that underlie a given student's performance in school.

## Current Levels of Functioning

At the staffing, the multidisciplinary team is responsible for providing information about the student's current level of functioning in the affective, cognitive, academic, physical/medical, and communicative domains. If the school professionals share information from their assessments with one another prior to the staffing, they must also provide that information to the family. Without access to the assessment data, families may be unprepared to contribute at the formal staffing. Current levels of functioning should be descriptive as well as quantitative. That is, school professionals need to provide detailed descriptions of the student's current level of performance in each of the domains. Refer back to Figure 2.3, which shows Michael's IEP. Notice how the "Assessment Summary," which describes current levels of functioning, provides more than test scores. (One of the skills you'll need to develop is the ability to translate the jargon of special education from one district to another and from one state to another. Michael's IEP is a good example of the use of localized jargon that can be translated into other language.) For instance, under "Educational/Developmental," the classroom teacher has provided observational data about how Michael uses a marker to hold his place while he reads. The teacher also reports that Michael had difficulty staying on-task, tracking, and relating alphabetic symbols to sounds.

## Identification of Needs

From the assessment information, the staffing team generates a list of the student's needs. These can range from the need to develop more than one strategy for correctly identifying words in a text to the need to have a set of skills for mediating conflicts on the playground. As you can see, these needs are quite specific, yet they relate to the domains of the whole child introduced in Chapter 5. The first need relates to both the cognitive and the communicative domain; the second relates to the affective domain. The staffing team must determine students needs in the cognitive, affective, communicative, and physical areas. At this point in the staffing process, however, the student's needs are identified without relating them to a specific disability category. Michael's IEP provides additional examples of needs statements (see Figure 2.3).

## Disability Labels

When all the needs have been brainstormed, the team must then consider whether some or all of the student's needs are related to a disability. If the staffing team determines that the student meets the criteria for a disability, the student is so labeled. It is this act of labeling that determines whether the student is eligible for special education services. Depending on the state, the criteria used for making these determinations vary. As Congress reviews and renews IDEA 97, disability labels and their criteria change. Chapter 2 provides the current definitions for disabilities from IDEA 97, while Table 8.1 lists the disability categories recognized in IDEA. Here, we describe some of the disability categories in greater detail.

**SPECIFIC LEARNING DISABILITIES**  Even as the existence and the causes of learning disabilities continue to be hotly debated, this remains the disability category with the greatest number of students. Students who have specific learning disabilities, like Michael, typically score within the average to above-average range on tests of intelligence. However, their scores on math, spelling, reading, and writing achievement tests may be low on one or more of the tests. Differences between potential and achievement suggest that these students have difficulty processing, mediating, and responding to learning tasks in school. Thus,

| TABLE 8.1 | Disability Categories Included in IDEA 97 |
|---|---|

- Autism
- Deaf-blindness
- Deafness
- Hearing impairment
- Mental retardation
- Multiple disabilities
- Orthopedic impairment
- Other health impaired
- Seriously emotionally disturbed
- Specific learning disability
- Speech or language impairment
- Traumatic brain injury
- Visual impairment including blindness
- Early childhood disability

intervention typically involves improving the teacher's presentation skills (Kissam & Lenz, 1994), reteaching skills to students individually or in small groups (Palinscar & Brown, 1988), or, alternatively, teaching strategies for learning so that students can improve their capacity to focus on the important elements of a learning task (Burlgren, Deshler, & Schumaker, 1994; Graham & Harris, 1993; Schumaker, Nolan, & Deshler, 1985; Stoddard & MacArthur, 1993).

**SPEECH/LANGUAGE IMPAIRMENT** Students who have language and/or communication disorders have difficulties in the comprehension and expression of the meaning and content of language. Problems might include voice, **articulation,** and **fluency disorders.** Some students may stutter or stammer; others may have difficulty pronouncing certain sounds so they have speech lisps; still others may have difficulty in managing the flow of air as they speak, so that their voices are hoarse, harsh, or hypernasal. Some students have the capacity to create appropriate speech sounds but are unable to recall language they may already have learned. Other students have difficulty connecting the right word sounds to objects. As students mature, their language problems may be more subtle. For instance, reading comprehension, writing, and spelling difficul-

ties may occur because of underlying difficulties in language processing.

**MENTAL RETARDATION** By definition, people with mental retardation experience substantial limitations in their intellectual functioning that exist concurrently with limitations in two or more adaptive skill areas, including communication, self-care, home living, social skills, community use, **self-direction,** health and safety, **functional academics,** leisure, and work (AAMR, 1992). In the realm of cognition, mental retardation is characterized by related problems in the areas of attention (Zeaman & House, 1963), **mediational strategies** (Spitz & Webreck, 1972), memory (Ellis, 1970), **executive control** and metacognition (Bruer, 1993; Sternberg & Smith, 1985), and **transfer/generalization** (Ellis, Lenz, & Sabornie, 1987). As a result, they have difficulty in adjusting and accommodating to the daily fluctuations of life. Both Annie and Tanya fit this description, yet the degree to which they experience difficulty differs. We talk about limitations in adaptive behavior because it is in the application of problem solving to real-life situations that the disability becomes especially apparent.

**EMOTIONAL DISTURBANCE OR BEHAVIORAL DISORDERS** Depending on the state, students who fit within this category may be called emotionally disturbed, behaviorally disordered, or a combination of the two—emotionally and/or behaviorally disordered. As Kozleski, Cessna, Bechard, and Borock (1993) demonstrate, the label itself is not as important in the identification process as the criteria used to categorize students so labeled. Quay (1986) isolated four distinct subtypes within this disability: (1) conduct disorder, (2) anxiety-withdrawal, (3) immaturity, and (4) socialized aggression. As you will recall, Kirk was labeled as emotionally disturbed because of his **conduct disorder.** These four patterns of behavior appear to encompass components of disordered behavior seen in students who are labeled as either emotionally or behaviorally disordered. Students who qualify under this category generally require services to (1) help regulate and express their emotions, (2) learn socially acceptable forms of social interaction and friendship development, and (3) develop socially appropriate skills in conflict mediation and self-advocacy. By assisting students with behavioral and emotional disabilities to learn these skills, they are able to participate in and learn from the general education curriculum.

**DEAFNESS AND HEARING IMPAIRMENT**   Students who are deaf or hard of hearing, like Kurume, have difficulty learning language through hearing. Hearing loss is measured by an audiologist, who can estimate the degree of hearing that an individual has. Because verbal communication is the most frequently used vehicle for information transmission in schools, students with hearing loss or deafness are at a disadvantage in accessing most public school curricula. As a result, oral and written language development is often compromised. Hearing aids, amplification systems, computer programs, telecommunication devices, and sign language may assist individuals with hearing losses to access information in a hearing society. However, people who are deaf support the use of sign language and enjoy their own rich cultural heritage.

**BLINDNESS AND VISUAL IMPAIRMENT**   This category includes students who are blind and those who have some vision. Legal blindness is defined as 20/200 vision in the better, seeing eye after correction.

Students who are blind or visually impaired may have difficulty with the nonverbal aspects of communication and, because of limited sight, be constrained in their exploration of their environments. Supports for students in this category might include special training in orientation and mobility and specialized equipment to increase information gathering through sight, such as the use of optical scanners and readers and computerized **Braille** machines.

**PHYSICAL AND HEALTH DISORDERS**   Physical and health disorders comprise a wide range of conditions including cerebral palsy, spina bifida, cystic fibrosis, HIV and related illnesses, juvenile diabetes, anorexia, and spinal cord injuries. A physical disability may or may not result in difficulties in functioning in cognitive, affective, communicative, and physical/health domains. However, needs in these areas may emerge over time if limited mobility or manipulation exists or if limitations in the ability to acquire nutrition, to breathe, to rest, to avoid pain or injury, or to resist disease exist. Students with physical and/or health disorders may not need alterations to the curriculum, but they may require modifications to the physical environment.

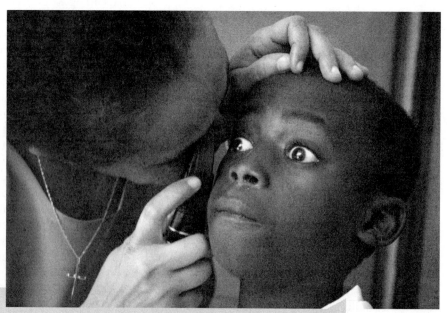

A young student undergoes an eye exam as part of the process of physical/health assessment.

**AUTISM** Autism occurs approximately in one out of every 2500 children and often is not diagnosed until the infant reaches his or her first birthday or beyond. Individuals with autism are identified by their withdrawal, lack of social behavior, severe language and attentional problems, and display of unusual, repetitive behaviors (Schreibman, Koegel, Charlop, & Egel, 1990). Many theories purport to explain the causes of autism, but each lacks consistent evidence to support its contention (Schreibman, 1988). As a result, families of children with autism often visit many specialists seeking an explanation and treatment for their child's problems. Currently, behavioral interventions that focus on teaching children with autism how to interact socially, use language to communicate, and focus on prompts and cues appear to have the most promise in helping them reach developmental and educational milestones (Schreibman et al., 1990).

**TRAUMATIC BRAIN INJURY** Traumatic brain injury refers to a type of disability that can affect functioning in the areas of cognition, affect, communication, and physical health (Brooke, Uomoto, McLean, & Fraser, 1991). Traumatic brain injury, or what physicians term a "closed head injury," occurs when an individual receives a blow to the head (Battan, 1994), which then may result in a loss of consciousness. Head injuries are classified into three levels of severity: mild, moderate, and severe (Rosenthal & Bergman, 1989). Mild head injuries result only in slight headaches and dizziness. Moderate head injury is associated with loss of consciousness, amnesia, seizures, vomiting, and possible listlessness (Rosenthal & Bergman, 1989). In addition to having the symptoms of moderate head injury, individuals who experience disorientation, an inability to follow directions, loss of focus in the eyes, and decreasing levels of consciousness are said to have severe head injury. Common causes of injuries to the brain include motor vehicle accidents and, in school-age children, accidents that occur while bicycling, skating, horseback riding, and fighting (Beukelman & Yorkston, 1991). The numbers of individuals who survive traumatic brain injury are increasing due to improvements in emergency medical care. As a result, more and more individuals with traumatic brain injury are returning to school (Beukelman & Yorkston, 1991). When individuals demonstrate signs of injury to their cognitive, linguistic, and affective capacities, it is difficult to predict the degree to which they will recover. Interventions for persons with traumatic brain injury range from speech/language retraining, to the development of strategies to deal with short-term memory loss, to the management of volatile emotions and poor coordination (Beukelman & Yorkston, 1991).

## Annual Goals

Only after determining if a student meets the criteria for a particular disability label is the staffing team able to set annual, measurable goals that address the student's needs. For instance, one of the needs identified for Tanya, the 3-year-old who was born prematurely, was that she develop her ability to express herself. On the basis of that need, Tanya's staffing team set a goal for Tanya to achieve in one calendar year. The written goal stated that, at home and at her preschool, Tanya be able to use speech to request attention and make her basic needs for toileting, eating, and drinking known. Under this general goal was listed a set of measurable objectives or benchmarks. One was that, at school, during snack, Tanya be able to request verbally at least three of the food items available at the snack table with 100 percent accuracy over a ten-day observation period. This meant that in April or May one of the preschool staff needed to observe Tanya and record the number of requests that she made verbally for food. This number was then divided by the total number of requests that Tanya made for food. For instance, at the beginning of the year, Tanya made her requests by pointing at the food she wanted. The objective required that Tanya say the name of the food she wanted (cookie, cracker, cheese, pretzel). This objective focused teacher attention on teaching Tanya to name the foods and to use the names as requests. The objective also was designed around a daily activity that might generalize to the kitchen at home or to the cafeteria in first grade. Goals are not written to encompass the entire curriculum for a particular child; rather, they focus effort in the classroom on the child's most essential needs.

## Characteristics of Services

The next step in the staffing process is to decide what kinds of special education and related services need to be in place for a particular student to be able to meet the goals and objectives set by the staffing team. In Tanya's case, ensuring that the preschool teacher and her paraprofessional were using effective techniques in teaching Tanya to use her food words was critical. A speech/language consultant also might be assigned to come into Tanya's classroom at least twice per week and observe the interactions between the teaching staff and Tanya at snack time. The speech/language consultant could then provide feedback and modeling to the teaching staff to make sure that they were providing the most efficient context for Tanya to develop her speech capacity. As you can see, all school professionals involved in Tanya's school program have some responsibility for ensuring that Tanya has ample opportunity to learn the skills that will help her meet her educational goals.

Similarly, in kindergarten through sixth grade, a special educator may come to the classroom on a regular basis to observe the kinds of modifications and adaptations being made to ensure that students with identified disabilities are receiving the kinds of instruction that will meet their needs. Services might also involve team teaching, brief tutorial sessions outside the classroom, or counseling support groups. Characteristics of services must fit the needs of the student rather than be one of a set of preordained service options.

Targeting educational goals and objectives for individual students includes specifying the classroom, curricular, and assessment modifications and adaptations that need to be in place so that the goals and objectives can be met. Classroom teachers must be familiar with the IEPs of their special education students and be prepared to make the modifications and adaptations necessary to prevent disabilities from being handicaps. While the modifications and adaptations are as numerous as the individuals for whom they are made, we have chosen to provide some lists of the general kinds of modifications and adaptations that are frequently used (see Table 8.2). Admittedly, lists have some negative side effects. Sometimes, lists constrain individual creativity; other times, they are used as the standard rather than as the guideline. By using Table 8.2, you can first select an area that you know a student has a particular need in and then select the accommodations or skills that you might need to teach and the adaptations to the instructional procedures that you already use.

## Placement

Students should be placed in the least restrictive environment possible. If schools feel that they cannot adequately meet the needs of the student within the context of the general education program, then they must have evidence that sufficient accommodations were made in the general education classroom prior to making a decision to serve the student in a more restrictive environment. Placement decisions may not be made on the basis of how or where other students with similar disabilities receive services. It is a common practice to place children with the same disability labels in the same classroom because it helps the school system to organize and plan for resource allocations. In one school district, all the children with severe communication needs are placed in a classroom with a teacher and an aide. However, this practice is educationally questionable unless individual student needs dictate that a student be placed in such a setting. In most districts, placement options range from the general education classroom to home-bound instruction. The full continuum of placement options listed in Chapter 2 are generally available. According to the provisions of IDEA 97, parents must be involved in the placement decision.

Annual reviews of goals, objectives, and placements must be conducted with each student's family. Adequate notification and scheduling of conferences that accommodate the family must be assured. At the end of the third year of special education services, a complete multidisciplinary assessment and staffing should occur for reevaluation purposes. At this time, a review is conducted to consider whether the student is still eligible for special education services under one of the disability categories. The review also includes an analysis of the annual goals, objectives, and placement to determine if they continue to meet the educational needs of the student. Families must be kept apprised of their child's progress as frequently as parents of children without disabilities are notified of their children's learning achievements. This means that, when children without disabilities bring home report cards, children with disabilities should also bring home reports of their progress.

## Due Process

Families have guaranteed due process rights under IDEA 97. They may request that an independent evaluation, paid for by the school district, be conducted for their child. They may also request a review of the staffing team's decision. The review process typically

| TABLE 8.2 | Some General Kinds of Accommodations and Adaptations | |
|---|---|---|
| **Cognitive Component** | **Skills to Teach (Accommodations)** | **Teaching Strategies (Adaptations)** |
| **Motivation** | Internal locus of control<br>Identification of motivators<br>Self-motivation<br>Time management<br>Self-reinforcement | Content/materials suggested by students<br>"Know, want, learn" charts<br>Independent projects |
| **Logical reasoning: Application** | Generalization skills<br>Extraction of principles<br>Evaluation skills<br>Sequencing skills<br>Critiquing skills | Construction of schemata<br>Highlighting of concepts<br>Rules application<br>Explicit strategies<br>Discovery learning |
| **Coping with novelty** | Identifying features of environment<br>Identifying social relationships<br>Identifying problems<br>Generating possible solutions<br>Evaluating solutions<br>Implementing solutions<br>Checking for efficiency, quality, and effort | Experiential educational opportunities<br>Cooperative learning groups<br>Team teaching<br>Community volunteering<br>Job shadowing<br>Peer tutoring |
| **Automaticity** | Independent study skills<br>Rehearsal skills<br>Planning skills<br>Planning for practice | Drill and practice<br>Redundancy |
| **Cognitive style: Impulsive to reflective** | Formulators<br>Implementors<br>Evaluators | Webbing |
| **Developing expertise** | Identifying interests<br>Identifying cognitive strengths<br>Identifying cognitive demands of interest areas<br>Taking risks<br>Predicting<br>Evaluating<br>Trying again | Variation in outcomes by interest level<br>Contract grades<br>Pre- and postassessment |

occurs at the central administration level when the director of special education services reviews a contested decision. If the director decides to support the decision of the staffing team, the family can request an independent, impartial due process hearing. The due process hearing officers are trained by the state education agency and must not have a vested interest in the district or the family's case. Each state also must have a voluntary mediation process available at no cost to families that can be used to negotiate differences of opinion prior to engaging in a formal hearing process. In any event, the family's right to counsel is assured. In cases in which the family's position is upheld in the hearing process, legal fees typically are paid by the district.

The process for determining whether a student is eligible for special education services follows a set of specific procedures. School professionals need to adhere to these procedures because violations of any part of the process may create the possibility that families can successfully challenge decisions of the staffing team. Although due process is an important safeguard, it is preferable for challenges to be substantive (Is this the right service or label for a student?) rather than procedural (Did the team remember to notify the family in a timely fashion?). Due process adds more cost to an already expensive proposition. It is reasonable to invest in that process when families and school professionals differ in terms of what needs to be done to meet the needs of the student. But it is wasteful to enter due process simply because proper procedures were not followed.

■ **SECTION SUMMARY**

Students must be classified according to one of the IDEA 97 disability labels in order to receive special education services. The precise qualifications for each disability vary from state to state, so you will want to familiarize yourself with the guidelines for determining eligibility in the district in which you work. Understanding the roles and responsibilities of each member of the staffing team is important (see Chapter 4). The key elements to remember include shared, transdisciplinary decision making, family involvement, the procedural steps for notification and maintenance of confidentiality, and the steps to identify the needs and services for a particular student. As a competent consumer of assessment data, you also need to understand the kinds of tools that are used to gather information about each of the needs areas. Table 8.3 summarizes the use of many of the assessment techniques introduced in this chapter. Notice that screening, in particular, relies on the work of the classroom teacher to collect observations, curriculum-based assessments, and standardized test scores (for example, from year-end, group-administered achievement tests). You will also want to be able to critique the quality of the information that is shared during the staffing process. The next section provides information that will help you make informed decisions about the quality and accuracy of information that is shared at the staffing and

design effective and appropriately targeted intervention plans for each student's needs.

# Formal Assessment Tools

Formal assessment tools are generally considered to be those tools designed to be administered in a standard way to each student who takes the test. Most of us have taken a formal assessment test at some point. In school, tests like the Metropolitan Achievement Tests (Farr, Prescott, Balow, & Hogan, 1986), the Iowa Test of Basic Skills (Hieronymus, Hoover, & Lindquist, 1986), and the California Achievement Test (CTB, 1985) are administered in the spring of each year to students at specific grade levels. These tests are formal because they are given in the same way to all students; their administration is standardized. Furthermore, scores earned by individual students are compared to the scores earned by a sample group of students who have already taken the test (see Box 8.1). In this way, individual students are compared to a group of their peers. Formal assessment tests typically yield some type of score that communicates a student's standing relative to others who have taken the same test. These scores might be expressed as percentiles or as standard scores such as z-scores or stanines.

**BOX 8.1**

### Kirk and the 40th Percentile

Kirk is the student with behavioral challenges. Even as he raises our concerns about how to manage his behavior in the classroom and keep him engaged in the activities of the classroom, we have to continue to worry about what he's learning. Kirk's school district tests all learners in the second, fourth, eighth, and eleventh grades using the California Test of Basic Skills. Kirk's test scores indicate that he scored at the 40th percentile in language arts. Percentiles provide a measure of relative standing. They indicate the percentage of people or scores that occur at or below the score that a given student earned. Thus, 40 percent of the students at Kirk's grade level who took the test scored at or below Kirk's score and 60 percent scored above.

**TABLE 8.3** The Assessment Grid

| Domain | Assessment Technique | | | | |
| --- | --- | --- | --- | --- | --- |
| | Screening | Eligibility | Planning | Placement | Progress |
| **Cognitive** | Observations of problem-solving approaches, attention to task, memory strategies in classroom<br><br>Achievement test scores from standardized test scores | WISC III<br><br>Anecdotal notes<br><br>Interview with student<br><br>Observation of student at independent work | Metacognitive interview on writing and reading process<br><br>Miscue analysis<br><br>Authentic assessment | Metacognitive interview on writing and reading process<br><br>Curriculum-based measurement | Portfolio of writing samples<br><br>Self-evaluation of strategy use<br><br>Curriculum-based measurement of content area progress<br><br>Time-sampling of attention to task<br><br>Miscue analysis |
| **Affective** | Frequency count of anger outbursts | Behavior Rating Profile<br><br>Direct observation<br><br>Parent interview | Ecological analysis behavior plan | Outcomes analysis | Frequency count of anger outbursts<br><br>Anecdotal notes |
| **Physical** | Latency data on how long it takes student to copy five sentences from board | Hearing, vision, and occupational therapy tests<br><br>Doctor's physical<br><br>Parent anecdotal records | Observational checklists | Observational checklists | Observational checklists<br><br>Performance assessment |
| **Communicative** | Language sample | Clinical evaluation of language functions<br><br>Classroom portfolio | Samples of written and oral language<br><br>Reading interviews | Samples of written and oral language | Samples of written and oral language<br><br>Standardized assessment |
| **Educational achievement** | Curriculum-based measures of written language in at least three content areas | Woodcock-Johnson Revised, Part II<br><br>Classroom work samples | Miscue analysis<br><br>Classroom, curriculum-based measures | Reading interview<br><br>Miscue analysis<br><br>Student interview | Miscue analysis<br><br>Writing sample<br><br>Anecdotal records<br><br>Products |

## Standardized Achievement Tests

Individual, standardized educational achievement tests provide different information about students than do informal systems for assessing educational achievement: curriculum-based assessment of performances (plays, speeches, experiments) and tasks (writing an essay, listening to a speech, reading aloud, doing desktop publishing). Informed school professionals understand that formal, commercially available tests such as the Woodcock-Johnson Test of Educational Achievement (revised) or the Peabody Individual Achievement Test (PIAT) provide comparative data about students. Unlike ability testing such as tests of intelligence, achievement testing should indicate the knowledge, skills, and processes that a student has in a particular content area: literacy, **numeracy,** computer technology, social studies, and so forth. Formal, standardized achievement tests do provide comparative data, but they are very limited in their ability to supply in-depth information about a student's knowledge base in a content area. This is because only a few questions are asked at each comparison point. And because most group-administered, standardized tests are based on multiple-choice responses, it's difficult to uncover the reasons that a student may have missed the correct response on any particular question. Furthermore, knowing that the student answers questions comparably to other students at the fourth-grade level doesn't provide the in-depth information needed to make instructional decisions (How does this student retrieve information? What preferences does the student have for learning?).

## Norm-Referenced Tests

Norm-referenced tests are based on a model of distribution called the normal curve. This model assumes that scores on a given test will assume the shape of a bell curve in which most scores line up near the top of the "bell," or around the mean, with fewer and fewer scores the farther away from the mean we get. In Figure 8.2, this model is demonstrated by charting the weight of the faculty in a fictitious school of education. The bars represent the number of faculty whose weight falls within narrow bands, such as the nine faculty whose weight falls between 150 and 155 pounds. Using a set of standard statistical procedures, we can compare individual scores to the distribution of weight for this normed sample. This concept is applied much more rigorously when comparing scores of individuals to normed samples.

This example should help you understand why you need to know something about the sample on which a test is normed. While comparing faculty from other schools of education in the United States to our fictitious sample might be acceptable, the fact that the normed sample of faculty is composed totally of white males ranging in age from 45 to 73 will make a difference in the analysis of a comparison group. Faculty from other schools of education can compare their weight to this distribution and find out if their weight is typical (falls in the highest part of the curve) or atypical (falls on either end of the curve). However, it would be difficult for a woman to compare herself to this norm because she may weigh less than the norm for the men but still be somewhat heavier than the

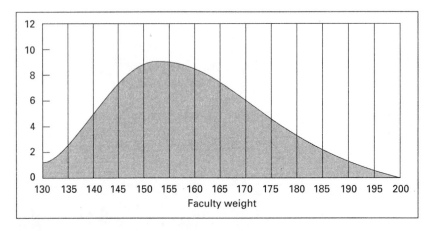

**FIGURE 8.2** ■ Weight Distribution of School of Education Faculty

norm for her female colleagues. A great deal of information is needed if the normed sample is to be compared to the individuals being measured and compared. For instance, gender, age, ethnicity, cultural background, linguistic preferences, and the distribution of ability differences among the normed sample might change the applicability of the normative data.

The sample group serves as the norm against which other scores are referenced. One way of judging the validity of a test is to evaluate the similarities between the norm-referenced group and the students taking a test. Where the norm-referenced group is similar to members of the group taking the test, scores on the test may be valid. Suppose, for instance, that scores of a group of white, female teenagers from upstate New York were compared to a normed sample of multi-ethnic, urban, male teenagers from three major southern cities. Differences in experiences, gender, and culture might mean that scores on the same test would result in a very different distribution of scores (Fuchs & Fuchs, 1987).

■ **SECTION SUMMARY**

Typically, school professionals use the informal assessment tools we discussed in Chapter 7 to make decisions about what and how to teach. Examples of informal assessment include performance assessments, observations, interviews, teacher-designed protocols, and portfolio assessments. For all of these approaches to assessment, designing assessment tasks that are as authentic as possible helps ensure that learning outcomes are applicable in real-life settings, as well as in the world of school. In contrast, formal assessment helps us to determine how the struggling student in a specific classroom compares to his or her peers in a broader sample than is possible in that classroom. Formal assessment also helps us to identify students who may be unusually gifted. School districts use data from formal assessment measures to provide one measure of the success that their students are having in meeting community standards for schooling.

For most students, the informal assessment measures that are based on school tasks will provide school professionals with a wealth of information about their students' current levels of performance and identify the areas of curriculum and instruction that should be employed. The next section of the chapter will help

you to integrate formal and informal approaches to educational assessment with the four domains of cognition, affect, communication, and physical needs.

# Assessment of Cognitive, Affective, Communicative, and Physical Needs

It's important to know how to link observations and performance data to the domain needs of students. Some of the tools that we discuss here are used to determine whether a student has a disability and is eligible for special education services. Many more of the tools are informal measures that lend themselves to use in classrooms in which teachers are working with diverse groups of learners. Table 8.4 summarizes the various assessment tools and processes.

## Assessing Cognitive Needs

Assessing cognition is complex because it is conceptualized differently by different theorists, practitioners, and test developers. In this text, we have taken the approach that practitioners need information about the cognitive developmental level and the information-processing capacities of the learner. To answer questions about cognitive development, we turn to informal assessment measures. We also introduce two frequently used formal assessment tools to reveal information about how a learner processes information: (1) WISC III and (2) the Stanford-Binet. While these tools are most often used by school psychologists, you need to become good consumers of the information that these tests can reveal.

**INFORMAL MEASURES OF COGNITIVE DEVELOPMENT** When school professionals look at cognitive development, they are asking, "How does this child learn?" From the cognitive developmentalists, we have learned that people have vastly different systems for making meaning from the world around them. By observing differences among children at different ages, the developmentalists speculate that learning occurs first via the sensorimotor system, then via interaction with the environment, then by observation and anticipation of the results of physical phenomena, and,

| TABLE 8.4 | Assessment Tools and Processes | |
|---|---|---|
| **Tools** | **What They Tell Us** | **Domain Linkage** |
| **Observations** | Provide data that tells us how often or how long a student engages in particular behaviors | Provide information about cognitive, affective, communicative, and physical health needs |
| **Interviews** | Provide us with the interviewee's perspective on a particular topic | Provide information about cognitive, affective, communicative, and physical health needs |
| **Anecdotal records** | Provide us with a complete description of how a student behaved during a particular activity or event | Can provide information about cognitive and communicative skills in particular |
| **Classroom tests** | Tell us how much information a student has retained about a particular process or knowledge base | Can provide information about cognitive and communicative skills in particular |
| **Portfolios** | Provide examples of products that the student has completed that demonstrate the quality of the student's performance (papers, reports, math exams, hypercard stacks) | Can provide information about cognitive and communicative skills in particular |
| **Rubrics** | Provide a yardstick for measuring products or performances | Judge performance against a set of predetermined standards, usually for achievement purposes |
| **Standardized tools** | Tell us how a student's responses compare to those of other students on the same set of problems | Can provide information about achievement, intelligence, social and emotional functioning, language and linguistic skills, and physical abilities |
| **Curriculum-based measurement tools** | Tell us to what extent a student's skills have improved on the same type of task | Provide information about cognitive, affective, communicative, and physical health needs |

finally, through the use of symbols (language or math) to represent reality.

Children can be observed completing a set of developmentally sequenced tasks to see how they interact with and make meaning from the environment. How children respond to these tasks helps the assessor identify children's cognitive developmental levels. Table 8.5 highlights the Uzgiris and Hunt Ordinal Scales of Psychological Development (Uzgiris & Hunt, 1975). This commercially available assessment product provides a series of sequentially arranged activities that are used to identify a child's level of sensorimotor development. There are six stages of development within the sensorimotor development level. Within each stage, the authors of the tool have designed tasks that become

developmentally more challenging. Let's imagine that Table 8.5 shows the results of Annie's performance on the test tasks. For object permanence, she was able to complete task 7, which, according to the test manual, placed her in stage V on object permanence. Her performance on the other subscales (means-end, vocal imitation, gestural imitation, causality, space, and schemes) are also listed in Table 8.5.

Similar rubrics that look at preoperational, concrete, and abstract reasoning on specific tasks can be used for older or more cognitively sophisticated students. Interviews with students also reveal information about their learning strategies and ability to regulate their own learning processes. Performance assessments that ask students to solve real-life problems give an op-

| TABLE 8.5 | Sample Uzgiris and Hunt Results | | |
|---|---|---|---|
| **Scale** | **Highest Developmental Attainment** | **Scale Step** | **Stage Place** |
| **Object permanence** | Secures object hidden under one of three screens, hidden alternatively | 7 | V |
| **Means-ends** | Uses string vertically; pulls object up from floor | 10 | V |
| **Vocal imitation** | Shows positive response to familiar babbling sounds | 2b | II |
| **Gestural imitation** | Imitates simple familiar gestures | 2 | III |
| **Causality** | Uses procedure as causal action in response to behavior created by an agent using a toy | 3d | III |
| **Space** | Places objects in cup; dumps out contents | 8 | V |
| **Schemes** | Drops or throws objects; visual monitoring of results of action/terminal location of object | 7 | IV |

Source: Adapted from *A Clinical and Educational Manual for Use with the Uzgiris & Hunt Scales of Infant Psychological Development* by C. J. Dunst, 1980, Austin: Pro-ed. Copyright 1980 by Pro-ed.

portunity for teachers to analyze the ways that students respond to novel problems. This information can provide insight into a student's cognitive developmental level. As a result of assessing students' cognitive developmental levels, teachers may decide that they need to provide concrete examples to students when they present new ideas and concepts. Alternatively, teachers may discover that they can present ideas in more abstract terms and move more quickly through the curriculum. The key here is creating ways of understanding the cognitive developmental level of students so that instructional techniques and curricula match the capacities of the learners.

**FORMAL ASSESSMENT OF INTELLIGENCE AND COGNITION** The relationship between intelligence and cognition is complicated and, often, misunderstood. In broad terms, intelligence can be viewed as individuals' capacities to learn to adapt to and shape their environment (Sternberg, 1986). Cognition encompasses the mechanisms used to process, mediate, store, and retrieve declarative, procedural, and conditional knowledge. However, as Sternberg (1986) suggests, intelligence is not simply the end product of cognition. Instead, it is cognition impacted by individuals' motivations, personalities, values, and individual expectations of themselves and their experiences in the world. Measuring intelligence, then, is an inexact science be-

cause so many of our formal measures focus exclusively on a narrowly defined set of cognitive abilities. Box 8.2, which discusses Annie's case, illustrates how misled teachers can be when they rely solely on intelligence tests to determine a student's cognitive needs.

Typically, intelligence tests measure only a portion of the competencies involved with human cognition. Usually, intelligence tests yield a score called an intelligence quotient (IQ). IQ scores are most highly correlated with predicting performance in school and reflecting the degree to which children have mastered middle-class cultural symbols and values (Reschly, 1981). Intelligence tests do not measure innate genetic capacity, nor are the scores fixed. Intelligence tests provide a measure of individual attention, memory, and verbal skills. Some persons do exhibit significant increases or decreases in their measured IQ (Reschly, 1981). The following discussion highlights some of the most commonly used intelligence measures and critiques their use with unique or diverse populations.

*Group-Administered Tests of Intelligence* Some formal intelligence tests are designed to be given to groups of individuals, such as the Cognitive Abilities Test (Thorndike & Hagen, 1986) and the Otis Lennon School Ability Test (Otis & Lennon, 1989). Like all group-administered tests, they can provide information about many individuals efficiently. However, they

**BOX 8.2**

## The Case of Annie Nin

Assuming Table 8.5 describes some of Annie Nin's abilities, her teachers now know the kinds of skills she has to solve simple tasks. This, in turn, helps them to understand what kind of teaching techniques to use to teach Annie to ride the bus or purchase some food at McDonald's. Annie's teachers know that she can't get to McDonald's all by herself. But, once there, Annie can use her communication board, can point to the picture of the burger that she wants, and can remember to ask for a shake instead of a coke. By understanding that Annie needs to be placed in situations in which she is expected to perform, and by teaching her through repetitions of the same task, her teachers can help Annie acquire new skills.

Cognitive tests can help teachers to understand the nature and needs of learners. What teachers need to avoid is teaching the learner to do the tasks *on the test*. Over the years, some of Annie's teachers have been confused. They thought their job was to make Annie smarter by teaching her to do the test tasks so that her scores would improve. They didn't understand that the test information should inform *how* they taught the tasks that were critical for Annie to achieve the best possible quality of life.

have many drawbacks because group tests rely on students' abilities to read, follow directions, and sit for at least twenty minutes. Because of language differences, age, and disabilities, many students may not be able to take such a test. Therefore, group-administered tests have limitations and are best used as screening devices. When a student's score appears unusual, then an individually administered intelligence test may provide a more balanced picture of ability.

*Individually Administered Tests of Intelligence* The KABC (Kaufman & Kaufman, 1983) is designed to measure both intelligence and achievement. The authors of this test define and measure intellectual ability in terms of the individual's capacity to perform problems that require both processing of information in sequential fashion and processing multiple bits of information simultaneously. Like other individually ad-

ministered intelligence tests, the test is divided into subtests. The KABC has 16 subtests in the battery; three measure sequential processing, seven measure simultaneous processing, and six measure achievement. Students receive scores for each subtest and for each type of processing—sequential and simultaneous. Another composite score is given for achievement.

The WISC III (Weschler, 1993) is another example of a widely used, individually administered test of intelligence. Like the KABC and the Stanford-Binet, this test is given to one student at a time by an examiner who has been carefully trained to administer the test. This test may be administered to children ages 6–16. As a child takes each of the subtests, his or her responses are scored according to a key. Based on the number of correct answers and the child's age, three scores are given: (1) performance, (2) verbal, and (3) full-scale. The scores show how the child who took the test compared to his or her peers at the same age. This test includes fourteen subtests, seven verbal and seven performance oriented. The scaled score on each subtest ranges from 3 to 16 with a mean of 10 and a standard deviation of 3. The full-scale score has a mean of 100 and a standard deviation of 15.

The WISC III is based on the idea that individuals must be able to handle tasks and solve problems using very different kinds of skills. On the one hand, individuals must act on their environment when they are confronted with such tasks as wrapping a box or building a bridge. These tasks rely less on language and more on the ability to visualize the task and use materials efficiently to solve the problem. The performance tasks on the WISC III involve visual/spatial abilities such as putting picture puzzles together or copying patterns using blocks. The subtests that comprise this portion of the test yield the performance score on the WISC III.

On the other hand, individuals also face a set of tasks or problems that require the use and manipulation of language. On the WISC III, these are the verbal subtests. In these subtests, individuals are scored on their ability to perform tasks such as repeating sequences of digits, defining words, and explaining specific behaviors and customs. For instance, a student taking this test might be asked, "Why is it important to wear boots after a large snowfall?"

The Stanford-Binet (Thorndike, Hagen, & Sattler, 1985), another frequently administered test of intelligence, is designed to be given to individuals ages 2–23. Fifteen subtests are grouped into four major areas:

verbal reasoning, quantitative reasoning, abstract/visual reasoning, and short-term memory. The overall score on this test has a mean of 100 and a standard deviation of 16.

*Formal Intelligence Tests for Students with Diverse Needs*
The KABC, the WISC III, and the Stanford-Binet are frequently used to measure intelligence because they are generally thought of as well-constructed tests with broad normed samples and relatively respectable reliability and validity coefficients. However, they are not normed on individuals who represent a variety of diverse situations. For instance, children who speak another language or whose home language is other than English may be at a disadvantage on either of these tests. Alternatively, while some of the subtests on both the Stanford-Binet and the WISC III do not require verbal language either in the administration or the response, the scores have not been normed on people in the deaf community. Because the socialization and acculturation of children who are deaf may differ from that of individuals who hear, the norms are not appropriately used for the individual who is deaf. This same argument may be used for other unique populations. Therefore, when scores for students with diverse needs are reported, care must be taken to ensure that the socialization and acculturation of these individuals was similar to the population on which the test was normed.

In addition to being concerned about the equivalency between the normed population and the child to whom a test may be given, examiners should be concerned about the kinds of responses required on particular tests. If, for instance, a subtest requires a pointing response and the child taking the test has cerebral palsy that affects the accuracy of his or her fine motor movements, the test is not "response-fair" to that individual (Salvia & Ysseldyke, 1991). One way to solve this problem is to become familiar with tests that have been developed with unique populations in mind. Table 8.6 provides a sample of these tools. Before choosing to use any of these tools, however, pay careful attention to their reliability and validity.

## INTERPRETING COGNITIVE ASSESSMENT DATA

Large discrepancies between verbal and performance scores are thought to be indicative of learning disabilities. However, as we have cautioned several times, it would be inaccurate to label a child as having a learning disability, or any other disability, based solely on his or her performance on one test. Performance on informal classroom assessments, as well as on intelligence tests, reveals information about how students approach learning. Unfortunately, some school professionals pay more attention to the scores than they do to the information gleaned through observing a student's patterns of performance on a series of subtests. The "Extending Your Learning" boxes that appear in the next few sections highlight questions that school professionals should ask as they observe students completing tasks in the classroom or on formal, standardized tests.

Using the cognitive domain table developed in Chapter 5, observant school professionals will watch as students complete each item on a test. They will look for clues that show how students initiate, sustain, and monitor their attention to a task. When a student begins to struggle, the school professional will watch for clues that tell what kinds of strategies the student is using to solve difficult problems. After the test is over,

| **TABLE 8.6** | **Intelligence Tests for Diverse Populations** |
| --- | --- |
| **Test Title** | **Appropriate Populations** |
| Nebraska Test of Learning Aptitude (Hiskey, 1966) | Deaf children between 5 and 12 years of age |
| Blind Learning Aptitude Test (Newland, 1969) | Blind children between 6 and 12 years of age |
| Test of Nonverbal Intelligence (Brown, Sherbenou, & Dollar, 1982) | Individuals who are unable to read or write and/or who have impaired language abilities (learning disabilities, aphasia, mental retardation, deafness) |

## Extending Your Learning

Questions to Ask About Learning Preferences

1. Does the student respond best to verbal instructions, demonstrations, gestural cues, pictorial cues, physical guidance, or repeated instructions?
2. Do you need to break down activities by guiding the student one step at a time?
3. Does the student learn best in groups or individually?
4. Does the student prefer to read information or hear it, or both?
5. Does the student have strategies that support learning weaknesses?
6. Can the student solve everyday problems in school, on the playground, and at home?
7. Is the student's performance consistent from day to day?
8. Does the student seem to know information one day and not the next?
9. How does the student function in environments that are active, bright, and busy?
10. How does the student function in environments that are quiet and focused?
11. Does the student perform best in the morning or afternoon, before or after eating?
12. How long is a student able to concentrate on a task?

## Extending Your Learning

Questions to Ask About Listening Skills

1. Does the student talk to him- or herself frequently or read aloud?
2. Does the student sing often and remember words and tunes?
3. Can the student tell you his or her address, telephone number, or other bits of information?
4. Does the student have a rich speaking vocabulary?
5. Does the student play with words, creating rhymes?
6. Does the student like poems, riddles, jokes, and can he or she remember and retell them?
7. Does the student follow oral directions well?
8. Does the student have good word attack skills?

### BOX 8.3
### Cognitive Assessment of Michael

Michael's overall cognitive ability is in the average range for his age, but this is not a good predictor of his performance on any one task because of the large discrepancies in his procedural knowledge. At this point, two factors impinge on his academic success at school. Michael has no strategies to deal with math concepts, and his knowledge of basic math facts is extremely weak. His lack of math strategies suggests that he will also have problems in science and social studies since measurement and estimation are skills that support knowledge building in both of those subject areas.

Michael has problems conceptualizing quantities that are larger than he can visualize. He has a hard time with 2-step problems and doesn't know how to ask for information or strategies to solve problems. He needs to learn to compensate for poor auditory skills through note taking and mapping. His visual abilities are strong as evidenced by his performance on the memory for names subtest, memory for sentences, and picture vocabulary.

the school professional might ask questions such as, "What did you do well on? What were you unsure of? If you were going to take the test over again, what would you do differently? What did you do when you began to feel unsure?"

A complete report will provide written, descriptive information about how each child approaches and solves the problems he or she is presented with during a test. Boxes 8.3–8.5 provide excerpts from actual reports that provide information about how students approach tasks. This information can assist classroom teachers in making decisions about how to introduce new material, how much time to allot for practice and drill before moving on to a new task, and how often to review previously mastered material. The strategies that a student has for learning new material, maintaining current skills, and matching the right skill to the right problem are critical. For example, preferences that a student may have for hearing new information versus seeing diagrams and maps that present new information schematically can be observed during assessments.

---

**BOX 8.4**

## Cognitive Assessment of Tony

Tony was cooperative during the assessment. He was shy and quiet. While testing, he seemed to need reassurance. As the test items became more difficult, he often looked at the examiner and asked, 'Is that right?' or asked questions to clarify the task he needed to do. During the applied problems subtest, he hurried to work his solutions and seldom used the paper provided to set up the problems. Even though he scored low on every test when compared to other students at his grade level (eighth grade), his strengths seem to be in comprehending and responding to visual information as his scores indicate from the matching for names, the visual closure, and the visual matching subtests. He consistently scored lower on the subtests that required declarative knowledge (picture vocabulary and letter-word identification), auditory processing (incomplete words), and procedural knowledge and reasoning (applied problems and analysis and synthesis).

---

**BOX 8.5**

## Cognitive Assessment of Shirley

In the design sequences subtest, many of Shirley's errors were due to her experimentation with different memorization strategies. At times, she would look at the first one, place it, then look at the second one, place it, and by the time she got to the third one, the design sequence was removed from view. Later she tried using all the available time to memorize the sequence, then start placing them afterward. By the end she demonstrated preference for the first method, with the added feature that she would search through for repeating shapes. Shirley was able to remember the shapes more easily than their order. In four of the twelve items, she got all the items correct on the first trial but reversed the order of the third and fourth design, and on another item, her final trial was correct except designs 3 and 4 were reversed. This suggests the possibility that she needs extra processing time to avoid errors of sequence. The brief processing time she was able to give to designs 3 and 4 according to the strategy she used resulted in reversed order. The reversed-letter subtest suggested that Shirley is able to hold and work on two to three items in short-term memory. Though she developed a strategy to remember all the items, she consistently got the first two or three right, then missed the rest.

---

How students respond to novel problems is indicative of their cognitive style. Some students are impulsive and select responses without considering all the variables; others are more reflective and spend considerable time thinking through their responses prior to answering. Some students persevere even when they are unsure of their answers; others stop trying to problem-solve when they are uncertain. Some students have only one strategy for problem solving; others employ many strategies. Understanding these differences among students assists school professionals in individualizing instruction.

## Ⓑ Assessing Affective Needs

Complete assessment in the affective needs area requires attention to social, emotional, and behavioral functioning. In each of these areas, school professionals assess whether a student's behavior is atypical in its frequency, duration, and/or intensity (Nelson & Hayes, 1986). In the social realm, school professionals need to know how a student is fitting in with his or her peers. Questions to ask revolve around the student's ability (1) to make and keep friends, (2) to interact effectively and appropriately with the various adults in the student's life, and (3) to retain membership in the student's family system.

School professionals also need information about their students' emotional lives. Information about how a student interprets, regulates, and communicates about his or her feelings plays a key role in understanding the student's motivation, stress level, and interest areas. School professionals also assess the patterns of behavior that they see students establishing, because these patterns can reveal the kinds of affective needs students have. For instance, students who tend to create situations in the classroom that demand teacher attention may be creating these situations because they lack attention in other areas of their life.

The behaviors we observe occur as a result of the interaction between students and the environments in which they function. Therefore, both the student and

## Extending Your Learning

Questions to Ask About Behavior

1. What kinds of problems does the student exhibit across various settings?

2. Who is concerned with the problem behaviors, and why?

3. Are there differences in the behavioral expectations in each setting?

4. Are some people more effective in managing the student's behavior?

5. Are there differences in cultural norms and values that explain discrepancies in both expectations for and responses to the student's behavior patterns?

6. Do some activities or events tend to trigger or encourage certain kinds of behavior?

7. What kinds of reinforcement exist for the inappropriate behavior?

8. What reinforces the student's appropriate behaviors and self-control?

9. Is the student aware of and able to monitor his or her own behavior?

the environments in which problem behaviors occur should be assessed. Through assessment, school professionals can better understand the underlying needs that students have and orchestrate activities and opportunities that will assist individual students in meeting their needs.

Affective assessment tends to take three forms: (1) behavior-rating checklists, (2) projectives or interpretations of student responses to pictures, and (3) direct observation of student behavior. As a classroom teacher, you will probably be asked both to complete behavior-rating checklists and to conduct direct observations of student behavior. As we saw in Chapter 6, collecting enough information to develop an adequate understanding of the functions of a student's behavior helps teams develop effective behavior support plans.

**BEHAVIOR-RATING CHECKLISTS**  Behavior-rating checklists such as the Behavior Rating Profile (Brown & Hammill, 1983), the Revised Behavior Problem Checklist (Quay & Peterson, 1983), and the Child Behavior Checklist (Achenbach & Edelbrock, 1986) have

more than one form so that information can be obtained from teachers, parents, and individual students. These checklists contain statements such as "The student is sent to the principal for discipline." To complete the checklist, a person must select from among four or five levels of agreement—for example, "The statement is (1) very much like the student, (2) like the student, (3) not much like the student, or (4) not at all like the student." After these checklists are completed and scored, it is possible to compare the student who was rated with the normed population to see if the student has atypical behavior in any of a number of areas. For instance, with the Child Behavior Checklist, which takes about fifteen minutes to fill out, students are rated on the degree to which they exhibit depression, social withdrawal, hypochondria, and anxiety. The checklist also yields ratings on externalizing behaviors such as aggression, delinquency, hyperactivity, and cruelty. Each behavior area is scored on a 3-point scale ("0 = Behavior is not true of the child; 1 = Behavior is sometimes true of the child; or 3 = Behavior is very true or often true of the child").

Another type of checklist that is used to assess affective needs is the self-report checklist. Examples include the Perceived Competence Scale for Children (Harter, 1982). This checklist asks the student to read a set of statements that describe children in general and to select the statements that best represent the student him- or herself. For instance, one statement reads: "Some kids often forget what they learn." To respond, the student must select descriptors such as "really true [of me]" or "sort of true [of me]." Students receive high scores when they report positive perceptions of their abilities. In the example given, a student would receive a higher score for reporting "sort of true" rather than "really true."

**PROJECTIVES**  Some school professionals use tools that are called "projectives." Although they continue to be used in many states, these tools are particularly vulnerable to questions about their reliability and validity (Mash & Terdal, 1981; O'Leary & Johnson, 1986; Salvia & Ysseldyke, 1991; Swanson & Watson, 1989). Most projectives use drawings or pictures that can be interpreted many ways. The student taking the test is asked to explain what he or she sees in a picture. In the Education Apperception Test (Thompson & Somes, 1973), students are assessed on their reaction toward authority, their reaction toward learning, their peer relationships, and their attitude toward school. Other projective tests include the Rorschach Psychodiagnostic Plates (Rorschach, 1921), the Children's Apperception Test (Bellak & Bellak, 1974), and the Draw-a-Person (Urban, 1963).

**DIRECT OBSERVATION OF BEHAVIOR**  In contrast to both checklists and projectives, direct observation relies on measuring behavior that is observed by the examiner (Wolery, Bailey, & Sugai, 1988). Behavioral observations typically follow a set of conventions during the observation sequence (Mash & Terdal, 1981). First, behaviors of interest are operationally defined so that they can be reliably observed by any number of observers (Nelson & Hayes, 1986). Second, the type of data to be collected is determined prior to the observation. For instance, if a student is off-task frequently during a lesson, the observer makes a decision prior to the observation about how long to observe the student. If the off-task behavior occurs almost continuously, an observation period of ten minutes might be sufficient. The observer also decides what system to use to record behavior. For instance, the off-task behavior may be difficult to measure precisely, but a time sampling approach will estimate its frequency quite accurately. Table 8.7 describes commonly used systems for recording behavior.

School professionals may want to know more about what occurs during a particular class than simply the frequency of a particular behavior. In that case, they may design a form for recording classroom behavior like the one shown in Figure 8.3. This type of recording system provides information about the frequency of both appropriate and inappropriate classroom behavior. In the example shown in Figure 8.3, the observer checks in on Tanya at ten-minute intervals to see the kinds of activities she engages in.

**ANALYZING BEHAVIORAL DATA**  After data from checklists and observations are collected, then decisions can be made. In Tanya's case, over a period of approximately three hours, she was engaged in appropriate classroom activities only 53 percent of the time, with the rest of her time spent on a variety of off-task activities. And observing Tanya over four or five sessions should reveal patterns in her behavior that will assist in determining the intensity, frequency, and duration of her off-task classroom behaviors. These data, in turn, can be used to help determine eligibility for special education services. Where patterns occur, behavior plans can be developed to increase prosocial behaviors. Strategies for increasing social and affective competence are too numerous to list here. However, matching student needs to specific curricular and reinforcement strategies is essential for effective behavior change to occur.

**OUTCOME ANALYSIS**  While behavior checklists help us to identify students whose behaviors may occur more often, be more intense, or last longer, they do not provide insight into the causes of the behaviors. Projectives, while designed to help us identify internal, affective disturbances, have poor reliability and validity and, hence, limited applicability. Behavioral observations can provide much information about how often and intense and under what conditions behaviors

---

**TABLE 8.7  Types of Direct Observation**

- *Frequency:* Record whether a specific behavior or event occurred.
- *Time sample:* Record whether a specific behavior or event occurred at a particular moment in time. Time sampling intervals are uniform in length, such as every 10 seconds, every minute, or every 5 minutes.
- *Whole interval:* Record whether a specific behavior or event occurred throughout a specific and uniform unit of time, such as a 10-second interval, a 1-minute interval, or a 5-minute interval. This requires continuous observation.
- *Partial interval:* Record whether a specific behavior or event occurred at any time during a specific and uniform unit of time, such as a 10-second interval, a 1-minute interval, or a 5-minute interval. This requires continuous observation.
- *Latency:* Record the length of time that elapses between the presentation of a cue or prompt and a student's response to the cue.
- *Duration:* Record how long the behavior lasted. Begin timing when the behavior begins; stop timing when the behavior ceases.

| | Appropriate | | | | | | Inappropriate | | | | | | | |
|---|---|---|---|---|---|---|---|---|---|---|---|---|---|---|
| 10-minute Intervals | Attend | Work | Volunteer | Read | Ask | Answer | Talk out of turn | Noise | Off-task | Rocking | Aggressive | Harrasses | Perseverates | Other |
| 8:40 | | | | | | | | ✔ | ✔ | | | | | |
| 8:50 | ✔ | | | | | | | | | | | | | |
| 9:00 | ✔ | | | | | | | | | | | | | |
| 9:10 | | | | | | | | | ✔ | | | | | |
| 9:20 | | | | | | | | | ✔ | | | | | |
| 9:30 | | | | | | | | | | | ✔ | | | |
| 9:40 | | ✔ | | | | | | | | | | | | |
| 9:50 | | ✔ | | | | | | | | | | | | |
| 10:00 | | | | ✔ | | | | | | | | | | |
| 10:10 | | | | ✔ | | | | | | | | | | |
| 10:20 | | | | | ✔ | | | | | | | | | |
| 10:30 | | | | | | | | | ✔ | | | | | |
| 10:40 | | | | | | | | ✔ | | | | | | |
| 10:50 | | | | | | | | | | | | | | |
| 11:00 | | | | | | ✔ | | | | | | | | |
| 11:10 | ✔ | | | | | | | | | | | | | |
| 11:20 | | | | | | | | | | | | ✔ | | |
| 11:30 | | | | | | | | | | | | | ✔ | |
| 11:40 | | | | | | | | | | | ✔ | | | |
| 11:50 | | | | | | ✔ | | | | | | | | |
| 12:00 | | | | ✔ | | | | | | | | | | |
| Total Number | 3 | 2 | 0 | 3 | 1 | 2 | 0 | 2 | 4 | 0 | 2 | 1 | 1 | |
| Percent of Observations | 14 | 10 | 0 | 14 | 5 | 10 | 0 | 10 | 19 | 0 | 10 | 5 | 5 | |

**Student:** Tanya
**Setting:** Fifth Grade Classroom
**Start Time:** 8:30
**Date:** 2/25/96
**Observer:** Mitchell
**Stop Time:** 12:00

FIGURE 8.3 ■ A Form for Observing Classroom Behavior

occur. School professionals must then take that data and develop informed hypotheses about why the behaviors occur. For instance, does Tanya cry to get attention, to express her anger, or to manipulate her mother into giving her an extra cookie?

In Chapter 6, we learned that patterns of behavior are produced by internal needs or drives. Figure 8.4 provides a format for developing an understanding of the needs that may be driving certain types of behaviors. Understanding what needs are being addressed helps school professionals to target skills that can be taught, conditions that can be altered, and behaviors that need to be encouraged or reinforced.

## Assessing Communication Skills

Direct observation and interviewing strategies used to assess students in the cognitive and affective areas can be transferred to the assessment of communication skills. Direct observation of communication skills in authentic situations provide crucial information for school professionals if they know what to observe and how to analyze it. Additionally, interviewing students after they have completed a task requiring the use of communication skills can reveal a great deal about how they organize and plan for communication. Commercially available, norm-referenced tools also help us to make these observations.

In Chapter 5, you learned that the communicative domain can be clustered into two categories: (1) receptive needs and (2) expressive needs. Students need to be able to understand information and situations in order to learn. Likewise, they need to be able to express

their own feelings, control the environment around them, and initiate interactions with others. Typically, students engage in these activities of making meaning through oral and written communication or through alternative forms of communication such as sign language or electronic communication devices. Generally, students use hearing and reading for receptive language. However, students with hearing impairments use their vision for receptive language because they see sign language rather than hear it. Students with other types of language impairments may need pictures or line symbols to receive information.

Assessment questions in the communicative domain revolve around how students use their preferred communication mode to express and receive various types of information. Most children follow a similar sequence for acquiring communication skills. We refer to this as a developmental progression. Knowing where a student is in his or her communication development helps school professionals understand the kinds of communication activities that should be planned. In addition to assessing the developmental level of students, school professionals also want to know what kinds of communication processing strategies individual students use. Both kinds of information will guide curricular and instructional decisions. This section discusses the strategies for assessing receptive and expressive skills in terms of developmental levels and processing capacities.

**RECEPTIVE COMMUNICATION SKILLS** School professionals need to be aware of the different languages that students speak or hear spoken at home as well as at school. Interviews with students themselves and with their families should reveal information about which languages are native to the student and which are second or third languages (Chamberlain & Medeiros-Landurand, 1991). This information should be gathered prior to engaging in any assessment based on the language of the classroom. School districts are required by law to identify children whose dominant language is other than English (Oller & Damico, 1991). Where appropriate, students' communication skills should be evaluated in both their dominant language and the language of the classroom. The basic issue remains, What competencies does the student have in managing the form, content, and use of his or her dominant language system? The tools that you learned about earlier in the chapter—observation, interview, and performance-based assessment—will

| Student Name | | | | | | Date of Completion | | | | | |
|---|---|---|---|---|---|---|---|---|---|---|---|
| Grade | | | | | | Setting | | | | | |
| School | | | | | | Name of Rater | | | | | |

Circle the number that is closest to your perception of the conditions in which the behavior occurs. One (1) means the behavior never occurs under those conditions. Five (5) means that the behavior always occurs under those conditions. Follow the directions at the end of the questionnaire to score your responses.

| | Never | | | | Always | |
|---|---|---|---|---|---|---|
| 1. Would this behavior occur continuously, over and over, if this person was left alone for long periods of time (at least an hour)? | 1 | 2 | 3 | 4 | 5 | DK |
| 2. Does this behavior improve after the student has eaten lunch or had a snack? | 1 | 2 | 3 | 4 | 5 | DK |
| 3. Does the student seem tired or lethargic during certain times of the day? | 1 | 2 | 3 | 4 | 5 | DK |
| 4. Is the student unable to hear directions being given? | 1 | 2 | 3 | 4 | 5 | DK |
| 5. Does this student seem restless and need to move after periods of seatwork or other quiet activity? | 1 | 2 | 3 | 4 | 5 | DK |
| 6. Does the behavior elicit laughter or other indicators of pleasure from the student? | 1 | 2 | 3 | 4 | 5 | DK |
| 7. When the behavior is occurring, does the student seem calm and unaware of anything else going on around him or her? | 1 | 2 | 3 | 4 | 5 | DK |
| 8. Does the behavior occur repeatedly at the same time during the day in spite of changes in routine or activity? | 1 | 2 | 3 | 4 | 5 | DK |
| 9. Does this behavior escalate when the student is under stress from a new situation or new learning task? | 1 | 2 | 3 | 4 | 5 | DK |
| 10. Does the student's behavior escalate when new adults or peers are present? | 1 | 2 | 3 | 4 | 5 | DK |
| 11. Does the student resist interacting with unfamiliar peers? | 1 | 2 | 3 | 4 | 5 | DK |
| 12. Does the behavior occur following a request to perform a difficult task? | 1 | 2 | 3 | 4 | 5 | DK |
| 13. Does the behavior occur when any request is made of this person? | 1 | 2 | 3 | 4 | 5 | DK |
| 14. Does the student seem to do the behavior to upset or provoke someone engaged in interaction with the student (especially when the student is being asked to do something)? | 1 | 2 | 3 | 4 | 5 | DK |
| 15. Does the behavior stop shortly after a task or person demands are removed? | 1 | 2 | 3 | 4 | 5 | DK |
| 16. Does the behavior seem to occur in response to talking to persons in the room other than the student? | 1 | 2 | 3 | 4 | 5 | DK |
| 17. Does the behavior occur when no one is attending to this student? | 1 | 2 | 3 | 4 | 5 | DK |
| 18. Does the student perform the behavior to upset or annoy someone when he or she is not being paid attention to? | 1 | 2 | 3 | 4 | 5 | DK |
| 19. Does the student try to isolate him or herself from classroom peers during play activities? | 1 | 2 | 3 | 4 | 5 | DK |
| 20. Does the student try to isolate him or herself from classroom peers during work activities? | 1 | 2 | 3 | 4 | 5 | DK |

**FIGURE 8.4** ■ An Observational Rating Scale of Student Needs

| | | Never | | | | Always | |
|---|---|---|---|---|---|---|---|
| 21. | Does the behavior put down the accomplishments of peers? | 1 | 2 | 3 | 4 | 5 | DK |
| 22. | Does the behavior occur to victimize or single out students who are less academically or socially capable? | 1 | 2 | 3 | 4 | 5 | DK |
| 23. | Is the behavior a rejection of attempts by peers to offer emotional or academic assistance? | 1 | 2 | 3 | 4 | 5 | DK |
| 24. | Is the behavior resistant to group reinforcement? | 1 | 2 | 3 | 4 | 5 | DK |
| 25. | Does the behavior occur when the student's performance or product is being critiqued? | 1 | 2 | 3 | 4 | 5 | DK |
| 26. | Does the behavior occur when an opportunity for verbal problem solving is presented? | 1 | 2 | 3 | 4 | 5 | DK |
| 27. | Does the behavior ever occur to get an object, person, or event that the student has been told is unavailable? | 1 | 2 | 3 | 4 | 5 | DK |
| 28. | Does the behavior occur when something valuable to the student has been taken away? | 1 | 2 | 3 | 4 | 5 | DK |
| 29. | Does the behavior stop when the student gets a valued object, person, or activity? | 1 | 2 | 3 | 4 | 5 | DK |
| 30. | Does the behavior seem to occur when the student has been told that he or she can't do something he or she had wanted to do? | 1 | 2 | 3 | 4 | 5 | DK |
| 31. | Does the behavior provide a role or roles that sets the student apart from classmates? | 1 | 2 | 3 | 4 | 5 | DK |
| 32. | Is the student's dress unusual for his or her peer group? | 1 | 2 | 3 | 4 | 5 | DK |
| 33. | Is the behavior viewed as unconventional by the student's peer group? | 1 | 2 | 3 | 4 | 5 | DK |
| 34. | Is the student off-task frequently during the day? | 1 | 2 | 3 | 4 | 5 | DK |
| 35. | Does the student frequently withdraw or refuse to participate in particular subject areas (as opposed to all subjects)? | 1 | 2 | 3 | 4 | 5 | DK |
| 36. | Does the student do the behavior only in the presence of particular peers? | 1 | 2 | 3 | 4 | 5 | DK |
| 37. | Does the student frequently seek out and cling to specific peers or adults? | | | | | | DK |
| 38. | Does the behavior distinguish this student in some unique way? | 1 | 2 | 3 | 4 | 5 | DK |
| 39. | Does the behavior occur apparently without environmental prompts or instigation? | 1 | 2 | 3 | 4 | 5 | DK |
| 40. | Does the behavior distract the teacher from her interactions with others? | 1 | 2 | 3 | 4 | 5 | DK |
| 41. | Does the behavior occur in spite of continued directions from the teacher? | 1 | 2 | 3 | 4 | 5 | DK |
| 42. | Does the behavior result in interactions or responses from peers? | 1 | 2 | 3 | 4 | 5 | DK |
| 43. | Does the behavior divert the attention of others from what is occurring in the classroom? | 1 | 2 | 3 | 4 | 5 | DK |
| 44. | Does the behavior elicit approval from peers? | 1 | 2 | 3 | 4 | 5 | DK |
| 45. | Is the behavior patterned after that of peers? | 1 | 2 | 3 | 4 | 5 | DK |
| 46. | Does the behavior occur when the student is asked to participate in an activity or event? | 1 | 2 | 3 | 4 | 5 | DK |
| 47. | Does the behavior occur exclusively with one other, select, peer? | 1 | 2 | 3 | 4 | 5 | DK |
| 48. | Does the behavior occur in apparent random fashion? | 1 | 2 | 3 | 4 | 5 | DK |

**FIGURE 8.4** ■ An Observational Rating Scale of Student Needs *(continued)*

| | | | |
|---|---|---|---|
| 49. | Does the behavior result in changes in the student's affect? | 1  2  3  4  5 | DK |
| 50. | Does the behavior result in getting additional information when faced with complex or difficult tasks? | 1  2  3  4  5 | DK |
| 51. | Does additional information reduce the behavior? | 1  2  3  4  5 | DK |
| 52. | Is the behavior sustained over the course of a complex or difficult task? | 1  2  3  4  5 | DK |
| 53. | Does peer or teacher attention reduce the behavior during the completion of a task? | 1  2  3  4  5 | DK |
| 54. | Does the behavior support the completion of a high quality product? | 1  2  3  4  5 | DK |
| 55. | Does the behavior appear to support the student's attention to a task? | 1  2  3  4  5 | DK |
| 56. | Does the behavior increase during activities in which the student's affect is positive? | 1  2  3  4  5 | DK |
| 57. | Does the behavior occur during activities that the student has chosen? | 1  2  3  4  5 | DK |
| 58. | Does the behavior occur in response to positive peer interactions? | 1  2  3  4  5 | DK |
| 59. | Is the behavior continuous during activities in which the student demonstrates positive affect? | 1  2  3  4  5 | DK |
| 60. | Does the student frequently follow group norms at the expense of personal safety and/or personal values? | 1  2  3  4  5 | DK |

## Scoring

To score this questionnaire, place the rating that you circled for each question in the box that corresponds to that question number. Add the ratings together in each column. Divide by the number of questions in each column. Put that number in the mean score row. Then rank your need areas from the highest to the lowest. High means (over 3) are areas that you need to address through curriculum and environment supports. Lower ranked means (3 or below) are areas that you may initially ignore or for which you may want to develop environmental strategies.

| | Physio-logical | Safety-Security | Recog-nition | Belonging & Love | Power | Expression of Self | Under-standing | Fun |
|---|---|---|---|---|---|---|---|---|
| | 1 | 9 | 16 | 37 | 13 | 25 | 35 | 6 |
| | 2 | 10 | 17 | 38 | 14 | 32 | 36 | 48 |
| | 3 | 11 | 18 | 45 | 23 | 33 | 51 | 49 |
| | 4 | 12 | 19 | 46 | 24 | 34 | 52 | 50 |
| | 5 | 15 | 22 | 61 | 26 | 39 | 53 | 57 |
| | 7 | 20 | 27 | | 28 | 40 | 54 | 58 |
| | 8 | 21 | 41 | | 29 | | 55 | 59 |
| | | 47 | 43 | | 30 | | 56 | 60 |
| | | | 44 | | 31 | | | |
| | | | | | 42 | | | |
| Total Scores | | | | | | | | |
| | sum/7 | sum/8 | sum/9 | sum/5 | sum/10 | sum/6 | sum/8 | sum/8 |
| Mean Score | | | | | | | | |
| Rank | | | | | | | | |

**FIGURE 8.4** ■ An Observational Rating Scale of Student Needs *(continued)*

A teacher takes notes as she observes young children at play.

help reveal the communicative skills of your students in these areas.

*Form* Because form refers to the rules that govern how we put sounds together in a language, one aspect of assessment is ensuring that students can discriminate between words that sound similar but are not, such as *pen* and *pin*, *Ellen* and *Alan*, *Ginny* and *Jenny*, and *boy* and *toy*. Prefixes, suffixes, and word endings change the meaning of words—for example, *boy* versus *boys* or *bury* versus *buried*. School professionals can create informal assessment tools that analyze students' ability to hear changes in morphemes that change word meaning. Alternatively, they can create written tests that ask students to distinguish between pictures that depict changes in word meaning. Because we know that curriculum-based assessment directly translates to instruction, creating tools that measure vocabulary used in the content area makes more sense than creating tasks that are not relevant to the class curriculum. Similarly, curriculum-based assessment of language functions such as the ability to follow oral and written directions will assist the classroom teacher in designing appropriate independent study activities. Syntactical knowledge can be measured by creating sentence completion activities so that students can demonstrate

their knowledge of syntax either orally or in written form.

*Content* Semantic knowledge is critical for students to read in the content areas. Knowledge of vocabulary can be checked both orally and in writing through objective vocabulary tests and completion of analogies. Reading comprehension tests provide important information about students' ability to make meaning from text.

*Use* According to Halliday (1975), language usage has seven functions: (1) informative, (2) imaginative, (3) heuristic, (4) personal, (5) interpersonal, (6) regulatory, and (7) instrumental. That is, we use language to inform others about internal and external events and to construct hypothetical situations and move beyond our current reality. Furthermore, we use language to explore the unknown, to catalog our personal experiences, to communicate with others, to regulate our learning and affective states, and to control the world around us.

Students vary in their ability to use language for each of these functions. One way that we can assess their competence in using language to express themselves is to complete a language sample. But we also need to know how students think about and regulate their use of language. When we measure language usage receptively, we are measuring the student's knowledge about when and where to use certain forms. One way of assessing a student's receptive language usage is to provide examples of the seven functions of language and ask the student when and where he or she might use those examples.

Here are two key issues to consider when assessing usage: (1) Does the student discriminate among the language functions? and (2) Does the student have the opportunity and motivation to make use of different functions of language frequently? Asking students to report on both their usage and their opportunities to use the different functions of language provides valuable insight for the teacher in making decisions about the kinds of activities to provide in the classroom.

**EXPRESSIVE COMMUNICATION SKILLS** While we need to know about how students process and understand language, we also need to analyze their ability to produce it. The basic issue in expressive language mirrors that for receptive language: What competencies in form, content, and use do students have in their language or communication system production? Both oral and written language can be measured using form, content, and use as a framework (Moran, 1987). Language samples are probably the most comprehensive method for analyzing expressive oral communication, but they require sophisticated knowledge of language systems to analyze the data effectively.

Classroom teachers can analyze the language competence of their students by noticing how individual students handle pragmatic interchanges involving humor, metaphor, and analogy. Typically, students with language problems will have difficulty distinguishing ironic or sarcastic comments from straightforward statements. Also, paying attention to how students initiate conversations, take turns in the conversation, maintain topics during turn taking, and exit interactions helps distinguish students who may be experiencing problems with their language development. In written forms, look for thematic maturity, the elaboration of ideas, the use of figurative language, syntactic knowledge, and spelling proficiency. By comparing students in these categories, teachers can identify those who may need additional assessment and support through special education services. Table 8.8 provides a list of formal language assessment tools. Typically, these tools will be used by speech/language specialists to identify children with language disabilities.

**TABLE 8.8  Formal Language Assessment Tools**

- Goldman-Fristoe Test of Articulation
- Auditory Discrimination Test
- Test of Adolescent Language 2
- Test of Auditory Comprehension of Language
- Test of Language Development 2, Primary
- Test of Language Development, Intermediate
- Carrow Elicited Language Inventory
- Northwestern Syntax Screening Test

## Assessing Physical and Health Needs

In inclusive classrooms, school professionals attend to the physical and health needs of their students through the way they design the classroom environment. After ensuring that safety features, lighting, seating arrangements, and temperature are appropriate for most of their students, school professionals may notice that some students have individual needs that require more attention. For instance, students who squint or fatigue quickly during silent reading may need a vision screening. Screenings of vision and hearing occur annually in most schools, but these screenings may not pick up all students who have needs in this area. As a result, school professionals need to collaborate with related services personnel to rule out problems in these and other physical and health needs areas before they look elsewhere for the source of problems.

Thorough observation in the classroom includes watching students as they copy from the board, listen to lectures or storytelling, and read directions from texts or from the board. Consider whether errors or inattention may be symptoms of vision, hearing, nutrition, or fatigue problems. Conferences with families at the end of grading periods can uncover critical information about chronic health problems such as diabetes, asthma, affective mood disorders, hyperactivity, hypoglycemia, and any substance abuse. Phys ed teachers are good sources of information about students' stamina, muscle tone, posture, grip strength, reflexes, flexibility, and coordination. Classroom teachers can observe students' fine motor coordination primarily through handwriting samples. Prereferral assessments can answer questions in these areas. Other types of assessment are best carried out by specialists such as occupational and physical therapists.

## Assessing Adaptive Behavior

When we measure adaptive behavior, we are measuring how well individuals are able to integrate their cognitive, affective, communicative, and physical skills into intricate repertoires of behavior that respond to the complexities of real-life demands. Adaptive behavior is most closely aligned with the quality-of-life factors outlined in Chapter 1: (1) family membership, (2) autonomy, (3) lifelong learning, (4) socioeconomic security, (5) productivity, (6) community participation, and (7) support. We measure adaptive behavior to understand what skills students currently have that support their successful adjustment in each of these arenas and what skills they need to develop to achieve successful life outcomes.

Typically, school professionals give grades for "good citizenship" and conduct. Also, students' quarterly reports may contain written comments such as "needs to learn to complete assignments on time." The behaviors that teachers list under the category of good citizenship—like volunteerism, initiative, personal responsibility, timeliness, and care and concern for others—are features of adaptive behavior. Accordingly, adaptive behavior as defined by Grossman (1983) encompasses "the effectiveness or degree with which an individual meets the standards of personal independence and social responsibility expected for his or her age and cultural group" (p. 157).

Adaptive behavior scales such as the Vineland (Sparrow, Balla & Cicchetti, 1984) and SkilSak (Sands, 1993) usually include checklists that focus on skills and behaviors such as money management, community competences, legal awareness, family responsibility, health and hygiene, sexual behavior, judgment, and social/interpersonal skills. As with affective needs, assessing adaptive behavior is based primarily on data from checklists. Typically, school professionals interview parents or caregivers, using the checklist as a guideline. Scores earned on adaptive behavior inventories are based on these interviews. Table 8.9 lists some of the common categories used in adaptive behavior instruments. Remember that scores on adaptive behavior measures, in addition to IQ scores, are used to categorize students as mentally retarded.

Students make a series of transitions during their public school experience—from preschool to kindergarten, from kindergarten to elementary school, from elementary to middle school, from middle to high school, and finally from high school to postsecondary environments such as college or the work world. Successful transitions depend for the most part on social competence and the ability to respond effectively to novel situations. Thus, attention to the development of adaptive behavior that will support successful transitions is important. Unfortunately, school professionals sometimes lack the perspective necessary to identify the skills that are essential for success in subsequent environments. Measuring adaptive behavior skills helps to focus attention on critical adaptive behaviors.

## ■ SECTION SUMMARY

Intelligence tests yield IQ scores that correlate highly with academic success in school, but individuals'

| TABLE 8.9 | Adaptive Behavior Categories Found in Commercially Available Assessment Tools | |
|---|---|---|
| **SkilSak (Sands, 1993)** | **Vineland (Sparrow, Balla, & Cicchetti, 1984)** | **Adaptive Behavior Inventory (Brown & Leigh, 1986)** |
| Health/Hygiene | Communication | Communication Skills |
| Family Responsibility | Daily Living | Academic Skills |
| Money Management | Socialization | Occupational Skills |
| Community Awareness | Motor Skills | Self-Care Skills |
| Legal Awareness | Maladaptive Behavior | Social Skills |
| Social/Interpersonal | | |
| Maladaptive Behavior | | |

scores on these tests can change. The best use of group-administered intelligence tests is for screening. While results of individually administered intelligence tests are often reduced to scores, student performance on these tests can reveal a great deal about how individual students solve problems. Careful observation and questioning of students involved in classroom activities can also reveal information about how students approach learning and problem solving.

Assessing affective needs requires the collection of data by classroom teachers, special educators, school psychologists, family members, and school counselors. These data should be collected on three dimensions: social, emotional, and behavioral. Analysis of the data should lead to hypotheses about what is driving particular patterns of behavior and lead to interventions that support student improvement and development.

Communicative needs encompass both receptive and expressive systems. Reception includes listening and reading; expression includes oral, sign, and other augmentative or alternative methods of expression and writing. Assessment in these areas entails analyzing knowledge and skills in the form, use, and content of communicative interactions. Samples of written and oral language provide a rich context for analyzing communicative skills, while reading aloud and asking comprehension questions can provide data on listening skills. Interviewing students about their own use of language will provide additional information on their metalinguistic knowledge.

Adaptive behavior, together with intelligence and social and communicative competence, is thought to provide a framework for predicting successful life adjustment. Adaptive behavior is assessed primarily through checklist interviews with family members or others who have knowledge of the targeted student.

Both formal and informal assessment tools can be used to gather information in each of the domains. Although some of the tools are used by specialists trained to administer and score the instrument, all school professionals need to understand what information the tools can and cannot provide. To create learning environments that maximize the learning potential for each student, careful assessment in each of the four domain areas is crucial.

## Chapter Summary

Both families and classroom teachers play an important role in providing information and observations about the skills and abilities of individual learners. Determinations of eligibility for special education are grounded in the use of carefully selected formal and informal tools that help to uncover the cognitive, affective, communicative, and physical needs of students. Once a team of family members and school professionals determines that a student is eligible to receive special education and related services, an individualized educational plan is designed. This plan contains measurable annual goals and objectives. During each school year, parents and other family members receive updates on the progress of their children toward the agreed-upon goals and objectives. In the next chapter, specific instructional strategies that support the needs of students in the cognitive, affective, communicative, and physical domains are discussed.

### INSTRUCTIONAL ACTIVITY

## Identifying Individual Student Needs

*Objective*

■ To observe a student in an actual classroom to help determine his or her skills, behaviors, and needs

*Materials*

■ Copy of Figure 8.4

*Product*

■ A student eligibility assessment for curricular and environmental supports

*Agenda*

■ Visit a classroom in a local school armed with a copy of Figure 8.4.

- Observe one student in the classroom for at least two hours—in a group instructional setting, in a small-group instructional setting, in independent seatwork, in an informal student gathering, and in the lunchroom or other building setting.
- As you observe, jot down notes about what you see.
- See how many of the questions in Figure 8.4 you can answer and which questions require more observation, interviews, or other data.

- In class, share your data and analysis with another student. Discuss what other information you might need, who might provide it, and what needs the student's behavior might address.

### Evaluation

- Criteria include completeness and coherence.

# Glossary

**Adaptive behavior**  Refers to the set of skills and behaviors that individuals use to engage in and cope with the social milieu.

**Articulation**  The clarity with which an individual pronounces sounds and words.

**Behavior rating scale**  A tool used to judge a student's behavior against a set of normative criteria.

**Braille**  A way of writing letters consisting of patterns of raised dots, pressed into paper, that represent letters and words, so that an individual who is blind can "read."

**Conduct disorder**  Behavior that is purposefully oppositional, defiant, or resistant.

**Executive control**  In information processing theories, describes the way in which the brain regulates mental activity, allocating attention and memory effort to salient stimuli.

**Fluency disorders**  Disorders that involve the production of speech—for example, stammering and stuttering.

**Functional academics**  The sets of skills that encompass activities of daily living such as reading signs, reading a bus schedule, and handling money.

**Intelligence quotient**  A numerical value assigned to individuals who take tests of intelligence. The quotient compares individuals to one another on the basis of their ability to perform a set of standard tasks.

**Language competence**  The skills required in the usage of language.

**Mediational strategies**  Skills that can be used to enhance or regulate impulsive or thoughtless behavior.

**Numeracy**  The content area of mathematics.

**Prereferral**  In special education, the problem-solving activities that school professionals and family members en-

gage in to improve a student's academic or social/emotional performance in order to avoid a more thorough process that may result in referring a student to special education.

**Self-direction**  Describes the constellation of skills and behaviors that are used in regulating one's own behavior.

**Staffing**  In special education, a meeting of school professionals and family members who determine the educational needs of students and eligibility for special education services as well as the student needs and characteristics of services.

**Transfer/generalization**  The ability to apply a set of skills in a novel situation, modifying and accommodating the skills so that they are useful but without retaining all of their original fidelity.

## CHAPTER 9

# Developing Responsive Curricula for Diverse Learners

# Views of a Special Education Teacher

*by Pamela Kniss*

In 1971, as a first-year teacher of junior high students with mental retardation, I approached the curriculum from a life experience perspective. I believed my students could not be successful in regular education classes. As a result, my curriculum was oriented toward the skills I thought were necessary for meeting the requirements of the adult world. In 1974, I began to teach students who were labeled as having learning disabilities. These students were expected to be successful in regular education classes. Consequently, the curriculum in their special education classes was based on a prescriptive diagnosis of their perceptual abilities/disabilities. My task was to cure the disabilities and return the students to regular education. At this time, all classroom work was individualized; every student had a different daily lesson that was planned with specific academic needs in mind. When it became clear that a learning disability could not be cured, the focus of the curriculum became teaching compensatory skills that would allow the students to pass their regular education classes. High school graduation was the desired outcome. However, research demonstrated that learning disabled students were not keeping jobs and often experienced unhappy personal lives. Thus, the outcome for the curriculum became transition from high school student to citizen. Again the units taught emphasized the skills and attitudes necessary for achieving vocational and personal success.

Today, I am moving more students into general education classes in response to our district's mandate for inclusion. Dealing effectively with both the curriculum in regular education and the curriculum I still feel is essential in special education has caused me to rethink my beliefs about my role as a teacher.

My journey through the world of special education began with my academic focus on mental retardation. I remember the moment I first fully understood my charge as a special education teacher: to find the keys to unlock each individual's potential. Thus, I knew I must thoroughly understand why and what I chose to teach. Pursuit of my master's degree in special education for the educationally handicapped, along with my teaching and a lifetime of study, have refined my understanding of learning and thinking. My experiences have further intensified my commitment to search for the best way to meet individual student needs. The vehicle I use to meet these needs is the curriculum. My perception of students' needs has changed over the years, but I have always been the one to drive this vehicle and to determine its destination. I often agonized over the route and wondered if students shared my commitment to reaching their destination. And as I fought my way through this transition, I realized that I no longer needed to be the driver. I could relinquish responsibility for driving to the student and sit next to him or her and provide guidance. Now my students take themselves down roads of their own choosing. Where they meet roadblocks, we create detours. When they reach dead ends, we retrace our path and begin again. I have found that, when students map their own destinations, they are more willing to make the necessary sacrifices to reach them.

I have begun to define for myself that which is special about special education. Faced with a curriculum with so many subjects, delivered in so many different ways, and supported by so many different materials, special educators have the opportunity to create a very "special" educational experience for students. Whether supports are provided by special educators or general educators, we begin individualizing the curriculum by determining, with the student, the modifications and adaptations necessary for successful achievement. However, in my opinion, this does not set us apart from any other very good teachers. To create a unique niche for ourselves, we must be able to use any curriculum as a vehicle for teaching the important life lessons unique to each student. We cannot expect ourselves to have an in-depth knowledge of all curricula offered at any or all levels, but we must have an in-depth knowledge of the learning characteristics of our students. Only when they and we know that information can we facilitate their inclusion in the mainstream of society as productive citizens and self-actualized individuals.

# Introduction

When most teachers hear the term *curriculum,* they think of lists of objectives or topics to be taught. However, these lists merely represent the most obvious symbol of a complex, ongoing decision-making process. What goes into the curriculum and what is left out is the essential issue. To resolve the issue, decision makers must agree not only on a definition of curriculum but also on philosophical orientations, management approaches, and design frameworks. In inclusive school communities, families, students, community members, and school professionals are all curriculum decision makers. Curricular decisions involve, and are influenced by, competing social, cultural, political, and economic forces, as well as the differing orientations at the national, state, and local level. Because there is no single way to create a curriculum, it is imperative to understand the comprehensive issues involved in the processes of curriculum development and implementation. Reflection and open discussion of these issues allows individuals or groups of persons to make sound curriculum-related decisions; Box 9.1 lists some key questions to ask in developing a curriculum.

In this chapter, we address the key curriculum-related issues that face our educational systems. First, we define *curriculum*—what it is and what it is not. Second, we discuss the major problems related to curricular practices in general education and special education. Third, we describe the types of curriculum decisions that must be made at the building level. The results of these decisions lay the foundation for and guide the curricular practices of school professionals, support personnel, students, families, and community members at both the building and classroom levels. Finally, we provide an overview of classroom-level curriculum decisions in inclusive school communities.

# An Overview of Curriculum Theory

Understanding what we mean by "curriculum" is critical to how we think about it and how we plan it (Morrison, 1993). As we discuss curricula in inclusive school communities, it is important that you understand our own perspective on curriculum and the reasons we made the choices we did—about definitions,

---

**BOX 9.1**

## Questions to Ask in Developing a Curriculum

1. How might a narrowly defined curriculum impact our ability to support a community of learners with diverse needs?

2. Why should we construct a curriculum so that it encompasses all of a student's experiences in schools?

3. In what ways do our beliefs affect our planning of curriculum?

4. How might student failure be related to current curricular frameworks?

5. What are the characteristics of a curriculum that supports student diversity?

6. Why must building-based school professionals assume greater responsibilities for creating and implementing a curriculum?

7. How are building-level decisions critical to the process of implementing a curriculum that is responsive to student diversity?

8. Why is it important that we provide students with opportunities to achieve the same broad outcomes but allow them a personal signature in the demonstration of their accomplishments, as opposed to working to ensure that all students achieve the exact same outcomes in the exact same way.

9. Should school outcomes vary significantly for students with diverse needs? Why or why not?

10. What is the relationship between curriculum and school outcomes?

11. What steps are necessary to ensure that the means of achieving school outcomes do not supersede the outcomes themselves?

12. What are the features of curricular units that respond to student diversity?

about how curriculum should be constructed, about who should be involved, and so on. In this section, we address two key issues related to curricula: (1) whether we view the curriculum narrowly or broadly and (2) how we distinguish between curriculum and instruction. But before you begin this section, reflect on questions 1–3 in Box 9.1.

## Courses Versus Sets of School Experiences

Magnitude is a frequently debated aspect of a curriculum. Magnitude refers to the breadth of the curriculum. For instance, should a course in Western civilization contain both contemporary and historical perspectives on spirituality? What should be taught, and what should be left out?

In the literature, curriculum has been narrowly defined as "(a) a plan for the classes offered by a school; (b) materials used to present information to students; (c) the subject matter taught to the students; (d) the courses offered in a school; and, (e) the planned experiences of the learners under the guidance of the school" (Hass & Parkay, 1993, p. 3). According to this narrow view, the curriculum typically is discussed in terms of courses such as English, math, and science or activities that take place in classroom settings. In contrast, individuals who hold a broader perspective believe that all of a student's school experiences, including those that occur outside of the classroom, constitute the curriculum.

We view curriculum broadly and subscribe primarily to Hass and Parkay's definition of the curriculum as "all of the experiences that individual learners have in a program of education whose purpose is to achieve broad goals and related specific objectives, which is planned in terms of a framework of theory and research or past and present professional practice" (1993, p. 3). We favor this definition for several reasons. First, we believe that learning occurs across all school environments, including playgrounds, assembly rooms, libraries, and cafeterias, as well as in students' home and community environments. Second, for students to succeed in school and in later life, they need multiple opportunities to develop and apply their knowledge and skills across all of those environments. Third, a broad view of the curriculum allows us the latitude to develop the physical, affective, cognitive, and

communicative skills necessary to support the development of the whole child (see Chapter 5). Like Hass and Parkay, we believe that curriculum development and implementation should involve the following:

- It should be based in theory, research, and professional practices.

- It should include the collective voice of the school professionals, support personnel, families, students, and community members.

- It should be flexible so that collaborative teams of professionals have a major role in deciding the curriculum of a classroom and that those teachers' decisions take into account the interrelatedness of individual, class, school, district, state, and national goals for students.

- It should acknowledge the difference between planned curriculum and experienced curriculum —with experienced curriculum, the set of actual experiences *and* learner perceptions of those experiences, constituting the bases of what is important to monitor and support in our schools (From Hass and Parkay, *Curriculum Planning* 6/e, © 1993 by Allyn & Bacon. Adapted by permission.)

The following scenario illustrates the practical benefits of a broad-based curriculum. Kirk was walking down the hall to his fourth-period science lab when he accidentally bumped into another student, knocking him to the floor. Before Kirk had a chance to register the sequence of events and apologize, the other boy jumped up and began to shove and berate Kirk. Given Kirk's difficulties in impulse control, he immediately retaliated by shoving back. Ms. Tanner, a school custodian, happened upon the scene and immediately separated the boys. She concluded that this event warranted her use of the schoolwide conflict mediation curriculum. She asked each student to retell in his own words what he believed had happened. She then walked the boys through the steps of conflict mediation until they were able to arrive at a satisfactory resolution. The boys agreed that the event was accidental, that they had both contributed to the problem, and that neither of them had used his best problem-solving skills to mediate the situation. Both boys then stated more acceptable and positive ways to have handled the problem and agreed to try those alternatives should a similar event happen in the future. At that point, the boys shook hands and were sent on their way. Ms.

Tanner stopped by the school office to document the event on her way to the gymnasium.

Even though this event took place in the hallway and Ms. Tanner did not have a "lesson plan" in hand, the conflict mediation process that she facilitated was a planned program of education. In fact, parents, community members, school administrators, teachers, school support staff, and student government representatives at Kirk's school had spent six months during the previous school year drafting a schoolwide conflict mediation curriculum and training to implement it. Their efforts were a direct response to a stated goal at the district and school levels that students would leave school ready to assume the responsibilities of citizenship. In addition, a group of school professionals, support personnel, family members, and student government representatives at Kirk's school had created a vision statement that documented a belief in the need for students to be taught and use prosocial skills. All this work was grounded in social learning theory and promoted self-determined, self-regulated learning.

What did Kirk and his peer learn? They had the opportunity to learn or to reinforce their abilities in (1) using a process for handling conflict, (2) acknowledging that all persons are valued, and (3) effectively communicating their needs to peers. This incident might have been handled very differently in a school that subscribed to a different view of the curriculum. Suppose, for instance, that Kirk and the other boy had engaged in this type of behavior in a school that believed that a curriculum consisted only of the courses offered by classroom teachers. We do not know of a school that offers a course in "hallway interactions." A building operating from this perspective would tend not to have a schoolwide policy or curriculum on conflict mediation. Most likely, this incident would have been perceived as outside the realm of the curriculum and viewed simply as a discipline problem. And Ms. Tanner, as the school custodian, might not have considered it her role to intervene. Instead, she might have contacted a teacher, who would then have sent the boys to the office to the assistant principal in charge of discipline. Typically, the assistant principal would deliver some sort of reprimand for misbehavior. Given this scenario, the boys might have learned some other lessons, such as that (1) misbehavior leads to punishment, and (2) it really does not matter how you treat one another as long as you don't get caught. Certainly,

the boys would have missed the opportunity to learn constructive ways to deal with conflict.

When school professionals, support personnel, families, peers, and community members consider the curriculum from a broad perspective, they expand the ways in which they can support and respond to students' diverse needs, goals, and interests. They must then plan curriculum experiences that extend from the classroom and building to the home and community. When we purposefully plan student experiences, we minimize the chances of incidental experiences intruding on the curriculum.

## Instruction Versus Curriculum

It's also important to distinguish between curriculum and instruction. For management and organization purposes only, this text reflects the view that the curriculum is the "what" and instruction is the "how" in the development and conduct of students' educational experiences (Goldstein, 1986; NICHCY, 1993; Pugach & Warger, 1993). The outcomes you hope to achieve and the content you present to achieve those outcomes constitutes "curriculum" of schools. In fact, the purpose of a planned curriculum is to assist learners in achieving school outcomes (Hass & Parkay, 1993). The ways in which that content is presented or the methods used to achieve those outcomes constitute "instruction."

However, this differentiation is arbitrary and often misleading. To illustrate, consider the following scenario: In Michael's ninth-grade history class, his teacher was planning a lesson on the social, political, and economic factors that led to World War I. She decided to present the lesson using Jigsaw, a cooperative learning tool that requires the teacher to restructure both the "what" (curriculum) and the "how" (instruction) of the lesson. For this lesson, Michael's teacher assigned each member of the group with a reading that provided information on the social, political, or economic factors that led to the war. Each student was expected to read his or her article and prepare a one-page summary of significant factors leading to the war. The format of the page was open-ended; students could draw, type, collage, or use other forms to represent their data. Once members completed their portion of the task, the group had to decide on the top or most important factors across the social, political, and economic domains that led to the war. In order for students to critically analyze and reach a consensus on the top five factors (a cooperative group goal), they had to use their best communication and collaboration skills.

As this scenario indicates, the teacher's choice of **cooperative learning** as an instructional format provided students with an opportunity to learn, develop, or apply skills of collaboration, effective communication, and peer support. These skills reflect a planned curriculum in the domain areas of affective, cognitive, and communicative needs. Thus, it becomes difficult to differentiate cooperative learning as either an instructional strategy or a curriculum content area. In this sense, although we distinguish here between curriculum (refers to outcomes or content) and instruction (relates to methods), remember that they are not mutually exclusive. Also, recall from Chapter 8 the integral role of assessment in formulating students' school experiences. If the purpose of educational programs is to achieve both broad goals and related specific goals, assessment must be ongoing and purposeful, informing teachers and students about individual progress, successful and ineffectual instructional techniques, and student outcomes. To reiterate, only when we synthesize the planning of content, instruction, and assessment can we construct the educational experiences we intend for students.

## ■ SECTION SUMMARY

The manner in which you define curriculum will most certainly have an impact on the decisions you make and the options you consider in choosing how to help students achieve educational outcomes. If you restrict yourself to a narrow conception of the curriculum as restricted to what you teach in the classroom, you may pass up many opportunities to teach students important processes, skills, and knowledge. Broader conceptions of the curriculum not only open up multiple avenues or contexts in which to teach but also provide you with many other people who can support those efforts. When you think of the curriculum as part of an interactive instructional model, it prompts you to remember the integral role that assessment and instruction play in the planning, delivery, and evaluation of school experiences. The next section explores the

dilemmas that special educators have faced in trying to define the scope of the curriculum within special education.

## Current Curricular Approaches in Special Education

Although there exists no overarching framework for a comprehensive special education curriculum, special educators have developed and implemented curricula using five primary approaches. These divergent, if not competing, conceptual orientations to the planning and delivery of curricula in special education programs have included (1) basic skills approaches that primarily emphasize the remediation of developmental or academic deficits, (2) developmental approaches that focus on "speeding up" a student's attainment of "typical" developmental milestones, (3) learning strategies that focus on teaching students how rather than what to learn, (4) functional approaches that target the development of context-specific skills and repertoires of behavior, and (5) career education orientations that emphasize vocational training and adult independent-living skill outcomes (Bigge, 1982; Clark, 1994; Polloway, Patton, Epstein, & Smith, 1989). Table 9.1 summarizes the details of these approaches.

The development and use of special education curricula have been criticized heavily in recent years (Goldstein, 1986; Halpern & Benz, 1987; Jenkins, Jewell, Leicester, O'Connor, Jenkins, & Troutner, 1994; O'Neil, 1988; Pugach & Warger, 1996a). The five approaches to special education curricula described in Table 9.1 are either simply criteria for judging the curriculum (in the case of functional and developmental approaches) or narrow elements of the curriculum that lack comprehensive curricular frameworks (such as career education, remedial, and learning strategy approaches). In fact, many professionals believe that special education has neglected curricular issues because it has (1) emphasized individual education (Forness, cited in O'Neil, 1988; Kavale, 1990; Pugach & Warger, 1996a) and (2) overemphasized the identification and establishment of effective instructional strategies (Gable, Hendrickson, & Mercer, 1985; Pugach & Warger, 1996a). Consider the learning strategies approach. Although learning strategies enhance the capacity of

| TABLE 9.1 | Curricular Approaches in Special Education | |
|---|---|---|
| **Approach** | **Characteristics** | **Concerns** |
| **Remedial** | The focus is on academic or subject area (math, English) deficits.<br><br>Student deficits are identified and then broken down into component or prerequisite skills, and students are drilled until those skills develop. Children with disabilities are "broken," and the purpose of education is to remediate or fix the ability area or skill that is deficient.<br><br>Children with disabilities develop according to the same sequence and milestones of children without disabilities. | The focus on students' weaknesses typically reinforces their sense of failure and dilutes their motivation to learn.<br><br>Skills often are taught in isolation, and students typically have problems transferring what they have learned to other environments or contexts. Focusing only on deficits ignores holistic instruction and students' strengths, which may inadvertently cause them to have additional gaps in their overall achievement or to lose current skills. A prolonged focus on remedial skills often puts students behind in other content or domain areas, increasing the gap between their achievement and that of their age-appropriate peers (Adelman & Taylor, 1993; Deschler, Schumaker, Lenz, & Ellis, 1984; Polloway et al., 1989; Reid, 1991). |
| **Developmental** | Grounded in beliefs similar to those of the remedial model, the focus is on students' deficits in cognitive, affective, communicative, and physical skills.<br><br>The goal is for students with disabilities to demonstrate the same developmental milestones (sequencing, walking, speaking, playing, tying shoes, saying the alphabet) as their nondisabled peers (Falvey, 1986). | Children with disabilities do not necessarily develop in the same sequence or manner as children without disabilities.<br><br>Concerns with this model are similar to those for the remedial model.<br><br>Professionals often fail to understand that milestones are indications of certain cognitive, affective, communicative, or physical capacities and instead treat them as absolutes that are necessary for children to demonstrate. This can lead to students working on skills that are not appropriate for their age and missing opportunities to develop and apply other critical capacities and skills. |
| **Learning strategy** | The focus is on teaching students to think about how they learn and to use what they have learned (Baur & Shea, 1989; Cooney, 1991; Zigmond, 1993). The goal is to improve student strategies for pacing and timing, thinking and questioning, organizing, structuring, and integrating information, and solving problems (Adelman & Taylor, 1993). For example, students are taught explicit strategies for note taking, paraphrasing, memory retention, studying, test taking, organizing materials, self-monitoring, self-regulation, and self-reinforcement. | Although learning strategy instruction has proved beneficial to students typically labeled as learning disabled, mentally retarded, emotionally disturbed, and low achieving (Deschler & Schumaker, 1984; Palinscar & Brown, 1984; Pressley, Goodchild, Fleet, Zajchowski, & Evans, 1989; Scruggs & Mastropieri, 1988), the application of these technologies is not widespread among special educators (Klenk & Palinscar, 1996; Sands, Adams, & Stout, 1995). |
| **Functional** | The focus is on the development of skills and behaviors that permit or allow individuals to perform in arenas of | These curricula are based, to a great extent, on a behavioral model, so the emphasis is on the acquisition of repertoires of behaviors |

| Approach | Characteristics | Concerns |
|---|---|---|
| | everyday life, including the home, the community, the workplace, and recreation and school environments (Falvey, 1985; York & Vandercook, 1991).<br><br>The emphasis is on the acquisition of age-appropriate skills that increase an individual's capacity to exist independently and to participate in activities of typical life. | that may not be generalizable to other environments.<br><br>Students exposed to functional curricula frequently are unable to participate in typical classroom environments because their instruction occurs outside of the school environment or targets skills not usually addressed in general education environments, such as riding the bus or shopping. |
| Career education | The focus is on vocational and adult outcomes, to preparing students to assume adult roles and responsibilities across multiple contexts, including the home, school, workplace, and community.<br><br>The curriculum addresses daily living skills, occupational awareness, specific work habits, and community access skills.<br><br>Models of career education identify associated knowledge and skills that should be addressed in elementary, middle, and high school programs (Brolin, 1992; Clark, 1994; Clark, Carlson, Fisher, Cook, & D'Alonzo, 1991). | Large numbers of students with special education needs are not exposed to curricula in this area (Frank, Sitlington, Cooper, & Cool, 1990; Sands, Adams, & Stout, 1995; Wagner, 1989).<br><br>With the trend toward discouraging special education outcome data and recent legislation mandating functional, integrated secondary curricula, there is renewed attention to this important curriculum area (A concern about, 1992).<br><br>Although multiple efforts to develop curricula in these functional life areas and to integrate these teachings within the scope and sequence of general education curriculum across grade levels have been documented, few teachers adopt these techniques (Brolin, 1982, 1992; Falvey, 1991; Helmke, Havekost, Patton, & Polloway, 1994; McGinnis & Goldstein, 1984). |

**TABLE 9.1** *(continued)*

individuals to make meaning of content, learning strategy approaches, in and of themselves, are not sufficient. Teaching students to monitor their own learning and to evaluate the effectiveness of their learning strategies is important. But teaching students learning strategies without embedding these strategies within content ultimately may not help students advance academically. Similarly, career education is one component of a complete curriculum, but students need more than career education to achieve the outcomes of inclusive school communities.

Remedial approaches are curricular strategies rather than content areas. The notion of curricular strategies defines many of the so-called curricula in special education. Indeed, Morrison (1993) refers to multisensory approaches, **precision teaching,** and direct

instruction (all examples of remedial approaches) as curricular strategies. In discussions about collaborative curricula in inclusive school communities, special educators can contribute ideas about learning strategies and career education, their curricular strategies, and their knowledge of learner characteristics taught to all learners. General educators can then contribute their in-depth knowledge of content to those discussions. In the chapter-opening vignette, Pam Kniss discusses how she came to similar conclusions about the possibilities for collaborative curriculum decision making between special educators and general educators. By merging special education curricular strategies and knowledge of learner characteristics with the general education curriculum, we can achieve coherent instructional and curricular decision making and practices.

As part of an inclusive curriculum, diverse students work together to operate a distant robot.

## ■ SECTION SUMMARY

The field of special education has focused much of its attention on understanding individual student characteristics and instructional strategies as opposed to the curriculum. As a result, many students with disabilities often have limited exposure to academic content in areas such as math, science, social studies, and language arts. Obviously, this can limit the choices and opportunities of students as they progress through school and, equally importantly, as they graduate and pursue postsecondary and employment experiences. In inclusive school communities, special educators work closely with their general education colleagues to help make the general education curriculum accessible to all students.

## An Inclusionary Approach to the Curriculum

### (A) Understanding the Need for Curriculum Reform

Nationally, discussions about school restructuring, program content, structure, and accountability have put the curriculum at the forefront of reform efforts in the fields of general and special education (Elmore & Fuhrman, 1994; Reynolds, Wang, & Walberg, 1992; U.S. Department of Education, 1994). School professionals need to work to ensure that the curriculum is no longer a barrier to inclusionary practices (Warger & Pugach, 1993). Curriculum reform across both general and special education provides a unique opportunity for collaboration among school professionals, support personnel, students, families, and community members. In fact, curriculum deficits, not student deficits, can become the common ground from which representatives of these groups work collaboratively (Pugach & Warger, 1996b). As you read this section think about questions 3–6 in Box 9.1.

What are necessary reforms? In some cases, recommendations for reform are specific. For example, organizations and initiatives such as the Secretary's Commission on Achieving Necessary Skills (SCANS), the National Council on Education and Standards, and Goals 2000: Educate America set a platform and put forth recommendations for standards-based education (U.S. Department of Education, 1994). Standards are explicit expectations for student outcomes. Standards or directives for education nationally have been proposed in the areas of science (Bybee, Buchwald, Criss-

**BOX 9.2**

## Guidelines for Curriculum Reforms to Meet the Needs of All Students

1. Provide in-depth coverage of content with less emphasis on facts.

2. Challenge students to think critically and creatively and to solve problems.

3. Embed the acquisition of skills in more meaningful and authentic activities.

4. Provide students with the skills necessary to work collaboratively and foster peer relationships.

5. Foster high self-esteem and self-management skills.

6. Provide experiences that address affective, physical, cognitive, and communicative skills.

7. Integrate key concepts across subject areas.

8. Tap student's prior learning, cultural background, and interests.

9. Involve high-interest, nonsexist, multicultural experiences.

10. Establish a clear focus and essential long-term outcomes for all students.

11. Allow for differences in the manner in which students interact with and learn the curriculum and demonstrate their learning.

12. Expand opportunities for student learning in their current and future lives (home, community, vocational, recreational, and postsecondary environments).

Source: Pugach & Warger, 1996b.

man, Heil, Kuerbis, Matusumoto, & McInerny, 1989), math (National Council of Teachers of Mathematics [NCTM], 1989), social studies (Bradley Commission on History in Schools, 1988; National Commission on Social Studies in Schools, 1989), and literacy (Monda-Amaya & Pearson, 1996). Proponents of standards-based education are explicit regarding their beliefs that all students, including those with disabilities, can be held to higher educational standards and can learn at levels higher than previously thought. Within the broad framework of educational reform, there is a call for curriculum options to focus on (1) whole-person education, (2) ethnic, linguistic, ability, and cultural diversity, (3) personalized learning, (4) process learning, and (5) transdisciplinary education (Benjamin, 1989; Slavin, Madden, Dolan, & Wasik, 1994; Willis, 1994). Thus, flexibility, choice, and personalization are the driving forces behind curriculum reform. The characteristics of curriculum that meet these challenges are presented in Box 9.2. To incorporate these characteristics, we must expand the content of schools to include a focus on areas such as **process instruction,** self-determination, career education, and social skills.

School professionals from general education bring in-depth knowledge of content areas and insight into curriculum frameworks that can be applied to provide greater access for larger and more diverse groups of students. School professionals from special education bring additional important knowledge about (1) learner variance, (2) the interdependence of students' physical, affective, cognitive, and communicative needs, and (3) the need to broaden curriculum experiences to encompass life in the home, community, and work environments. Helping school professionals to understand the need for curriculum reform is a critical first step; empowering them to achieve such reform is the next step.

## Empowering School Professionals to Drive Curriculum Reform

One of the most important variables in any attempt to reform the curriculum is teacher beliefs. "While beginning teachers are usually content to follow prepared curriculum, with experience, teachers become confident in their own judgment and assume control of the curriculum in their own classrooms" (Walker & Soltis, 1997, pp. 4–5). This influence is often overlooked. First, we need to distinguish between the formal curriculum, which is formulated at the national, state, or district level, and the planned curriculum, which involves what teachers actually say and do. Teachers translate and interpret the formal curriculum in order to design units of study or daily lesson plans. At this point of interaction, teachers' beliefs and practices strongly influence the content experiences of all students.

For example, Tanya's third-grade teacher, Ms. Nelson, believed that all of her students needed to take primary responsibility for monitoring their own learning. This included knowing when they needed help, being able to accurately describe the problems they were having, and knowing when the help they received was sufficient to carry on with their work. Student self-management skills were not a part of any curriculum document she had received from the school district or the building. However, because of Ms. Nelson's belief in the importance of this set of skills, whenever she began a new lesson or introduced new material, she prepared students to monitor their learning by asking a series of questions, such as "How will you know if this information is making sense to you?" and "What are three strategies that you could use if you get confused?" Although very few persons would argue against what Ms. Nelson chose to do, teacher decisions may not always match the expectations of others. Therefore, despite intense efforts at the national, state, district, and even building level to construct curricula, "by their decisions and actions, teachers determine whether policy is implemented, transformed or ignored" (Cuban, 1988, p. 33). Because teacher beliefs are a critical component in curriculum design, use, and accountability, those beliefs are important to understand, develop, and support (Ross, Cornett, & McCutcheon, 1992).

School professionals play an integral role in designing students' school experiences. It is important that teachers be empowered to make curriculum decisions because they are most aware of the diverse needs of students. To make the best decisions possible in terms of students' needs, interests, and goals, teachers should be educated and supported through collaborative frameworks. Minimizing teacher decision-making power merely serves to reduce the responsiveness of the curriculum to student needs and, ultimately, the potential quality of students' education.

To illustrate, consider the following scenario: Kurume's third-grade teacher, Ms. Link, was provided with the district's elementary curriculum manual. The curriculum was designed in a manner that set forth topics and associated broad outcomes by grade level. Each topic had a recommended unit length and suggested activities, although there was much room for teacher discretion. One unit, on simple machines, was to be covered over a five-week span and included concepts such as magnetism, leverage, balance, and coordination. Suggested unit activities included getting students to experiment with pulleys, small motors, and home appliances. Because Ms. Link took the time to assess her students' current knowledge of and interest in these concepts, she determined that they had not only sufficient but advanced understanding of these concepts. This group of students had had multiple opportunities not only in school but also through their home, recreation, and community experiences, to learn and apply information about the concepts. After all, these children were skilled in roller-blading, roller-skating, skateboarding, playing Game Boy, and so on. Ms. Link decided that spending five weeks on this unit would be a waste of everyone's time. Therefore, she decided to cut the unit back to one week and then to move on to a unit that she and her students had developed on the theme of reflection.

Ms. Link's decision was in the best interest of her third-graders. Curriculum designers at the district or state level simply do not have access to the information that building-level professionals do when they design the formal curriculum. We are not suggesting that teachers openly sabotage district- or building-level curricular materials. In fact, many beginning teachers use the curriculum in a more prescribed manner because they lack the experience or confidence to make adaptations. Over time, however, teachers do, and should, modify prescribed curricula to better match the strengths and needs of individual students (Bingham, 1995; Pugach & Warger, 1996a).

For teachers to make the best curriculum decisions possible, they need to develop the skills associated with recommended practice (Pugach & Warger, 1996b). For example, curriculum integration frameworks are increasingly recognized as an approach to curriculum development that supports the ideals and goals of inclusive school practices (Grenot-Scheyer, Abernathy, Williamson, Jubala, & Coots, 1995; Jorgensen, 1996). Because few teachers have had training in developing and using integrated, thematic units, they will require professional development support to adapt that methodology. Successful efforts to revitalize and change teachers' curriculum behaviors have been found to follow a particular sequence. Change initially involves informal behavior patterns (bottom-up) at the individual and small-group level and then is reinforced and further propelled by changes in formal design and procedures in the organization (top-down) (Beer, Eisenstat, & Spector, 1990). Studies of school curricula reveal that both bottom-up and top-down initiatives are necessary for adoption and implementation of innovative content practices (Fullan, 1994). As schools adopt curriculum principles and practices necessary to support inclusive school communities, the organizational structures and professional practices needed to support their use must be developed as well.

## ■ Section Summary

The curriculum is a focal point of inclusionary school practices. School professionals from general and special education have skills that, when joined, put them in a position of creating curricula that take into account students' diverse ethnic, linguistic, cultural, and socioeconomic backgrounds, as well as their individual learning needs and capacities. A critical first step is to empower school professionals to seek and support necessary curriculum reform. Support for school professionals to come together to face these challenges can begin through curriculum decision-making activities at the building level.

# Building-Level Curriculum Decisions in Inclusive Schools

Refer back to question 7 in Box 9.1, which deals with the role of building-level curriculum decisions in inclusive school communities. Now refer back to questions 8–11, which address issues about school outcomes and the relationship of outcomes to curriculum and individual student needs. Keep these questions in mind as you read about building-level curriculum decisions in inclusive school settings.

As inclusive school communities become more widespread, critical curriculum decision-making responsibilities, which traditionally have rested at the district level, need to be transferred to the building and classroom levels (Sage, 1996; Sailor, 1991). Only when we fully understand the personal needs, goals, and interests of our students can we formulate and support responsive school experiences. In this section, we discuss formal curriculum planning from a building-

based level, but the reality is that, in many cases, this planning may take place at both the building and the district levels (Jackson, 1994). Ultimately, the hope is that decision makers at the building level are empowered to provide direction through formal curriculum planning to respond to the unique needs of their students, families, and local community members (Wang, Reynolds, & Walberg, 1994/1995).

## Identifying Elements of Building-Level Decisions

Kniep and Martin-Kniep (1995) describe seven elements that should serve as the basis of and purpose for building-based curriculum discussions: (1) shared vision, (2) goals, (3) outcomes, (4) standards, (5) curriculum and assessment frameworks, (6) standards for professional practices, and (7) organizational structures (see Table 9.2). These elements serve to articulate and document the basic values and guidelines for building-level and classroom-level curriculum activities. The elements are not necessarily linear; that is, they do not need to progress from element 1 to element 7. For example, the new standards project starts with teachers developing assessments, not a vision. The assessment helps them clarify decisions about content, methods, expectations, tests and tasks, and so on. The elements build upon and reinforce one another, such that decisions made about one element should inform and guide decisions about the others.

For example, suppose members of a school community hold a common vision that all students have a right to participate and make choices about significant life (school) events. This vision closely resembles one of our recommended school outcomes—that students be able to act in self-determined ways. An associated goal might be that, when provided with a personally relevant life choice, students will apply skills and strategies necessary for making informed decisions. This basic value would continue to be played out across all other curriculum decisions made at the building (and eventually the classroom) level.

Discussions at the building level should involve representative school professionals, support personnel, student body representatives, family members, and community members. When a group meets to formulate curriculum guidelines at this level, members can consult models of curricula from the national,

| TABLE 9.2 | Elements of Building-Level Curriculum Decisions |
| --- | --- |

■ *Shared vision.* The foundation of the blueprint is the community's shared vision of the kinds of schools and schooling its children will need to prepare them for the 21st century.

■ *Goals.* Based on the shared vision, goals represent the community's most fundamental educational values, describe a desired state or condition for all students, and answer the question "Prepared as or for what?"

■ *Desired learning outcomes.* Outcomes are derived from and define the goals. Stated as the desired measurable or observable results, effects, or consequences of schooling, outcomes describe what students must know, be like, and be able to do to achieve the stated goals. Outcomes are broad enough to be interdisciplinary and to permit flexibility.

■ *Standards.* Based on and derived from the desired learning outcomes, standards specify the levels and types of knowledge or performance we expect from students. Standards describe the knowledge, characteristics, and levels of performance embedded in the outcomes.

■ *A framework for curriculum and assessment.* The framework guides the development of curriculums in schools and classrooms and ensures that all students have the opportunity to achieve the outcomes adopted by the district. The framework comprises three main elements:

  □ *Curricular strands,* derived from the outcomes and standards adopted by the district, give direction to what is taught.

  □ *Benchmarks* for selected age or grade levels set targets for measuring students' progress toward meeting the standards.

  □ *Assessment and curriculum strategies* suggest appropriate methods for assessing students' performance within each strand. Teaching and curricular suggestions geared to helping students meet the benchmarks and standards are tied to assessments.

■ *Standards for professional practice.* These standards reflect a belief system for how children learn and the best of what we know about effective teaching. The standards set out the criteria for how professional roles and preferred practices are carried out by teachers, administrators, support staff, and others involved in the learning process.

■ *Organizational structures.* These structures facilitate an organization plan for decision making, communication, and allocation of resources. The plan supports everyone in helping all students meet the desired goals and outcomes.

Source: Kniep, W., & Martin-Kniep, G. O. (1995). Designing schools and curriculums for the twenty-first century. In J. Beane (Ed.), *Toward a coherent curriculum: The 1995 ASCD yearbook* (pp. 87–100). Alexandria, VA: Association for Supervision and Curriculum Development. Reprinted by permission.

state, and district levels. For example, in 1989, the National Council of Teachers of Mathematics published their Curriculum and Evaluation Standards for School Mathematics (National Council of Teachers of Mathematics, 1989). These guidelines urged schools to support math education in a manner that encouraged student involvement and application of critical-thinking skills. But curriculum decision makers at the building level also must ground their work closer to home. To formulate their own building's guiding vision and desired outcomes, goals, standards, and frameworks, they must articulate their beliefs about what is important to learn, how learning takes place, what sorts of curricular guidelines should be established, and what principles should drive curriculum planning, implementation, and evaluation.

## Defining a Vision, Goals, Outcomes, and Standards

In defining their vision, goals, outcomes, and standards, building-level curriculum decision makers must agree on what is important for students to learn. Four approaches have guided investigations into what is important to learn in school: (1) traditional subject area disciplines, (2) back-to-basics, (3) child-centered, and (4) social reform (see Table 9.3). Understanding each view and its implications for the curriculum helps school professionals engage in meaningful dialogue about their school's curriculum. Most importantly, adherence to one view over another impacts curriculum experiences and how they relate to the goals, interests, and needs of students.

| TABLE 9.3 | Traditional Views on What Is Important to Learn |
|---|---|
| **Approach** | **Characteristics and Implications** |
| **Traditional subject area disciplines** | The use of traditional subject area disciplines (versus interdisciplinary or cross-disciplinary ones) such as math, history, language arts, and philosophy is a curricular approach that is rooted in the past. |
| | Proponents believe that there is a universal knowledge and value base that should be passed on from one generation to another; they focus on Western European and American (white) history, typically ignoring other cultures, multiculturalism, and gender issues. |
| | As "experts," teachers transmit their knowledge to students through common, core subject area curricula. Student interests are not integrated into the curriculum, and subjects such as art, music, PE, homemaking, and vocational instruction are viewed as frivolous (Ornstein & Hunkins, 1988). |
| **Back-to-basics movement** | Heavily related to the traditional subject area disciplines, the back-to-basics movement takes a more moderate stance, looking not only to the past but to the needs of the future. |
| | Definitions of the core curriculum and teacher and student roles, the focus on cognition, and the overt disinterest in the affective needs of students are shared by proponents of both the back-to-basic and the traditional discipline approaches. |
| | Back-to-basic proponents concede that (1) "frilly" subjects (art, PE, vocational education) could be considered as minor subjects (though much more expensive to support than academic courses), and (2) accommodations must be made for less able students (minimum competencies). |
| **Child-centered curriculum** | The child-centered curriculum grew out of educational, political, and social rejections to the prescribed, authoritarian nature of the discipline-based and back-to-basic movements. |
| | This curriculum is linked to constructivist psychology, with an emphasis on interdisciplinary knowledge, hands-on learning, multiage grouping, and developmentally appropriate practice. |
| **Social reform** | A spin-off of child-centered curricular approaches, social reformists view the problems of society as reflected in and perpetuated by schools. Therefore, by changing schools, we change society. |
| | The social reform curriculum advocates a more global, social agenda for education, as opposed to focusing primarily on the needs of individuals or any one class of citizens. The purpose of the curriculum is to support teachers and students in learning the skills necessary to assume the role of change agents. As change agents, it is then their responsibility to provoke and facilitate social, economic, and political reform platforms to combat problems such as racism, gender inequality, poverty, teen pregnancy, substance abuse, unemployment, welfare, pollution, disease, and hunger. |
| | Curriculum experiences allow for the generation of alternative solutions to social issues. |

For example, those who subscribe to a traditional subject area approach believe that subject areas such as English, math, science, and social studies are the most important content to cover in school. They probably believe as well that the teacher's primary role is to convey in-depth knowledge of those subjects to students, and they oppose spending resources or time on topics such as prosocial skills, art therapy, and music education.

What might strict adherence to academics mean for students like Annie, Kirk, and Kurume? If the language arts curriculum had focused on reading the "classics," Annie might not have learned how to use her augmentative communication system. And given the severity of her mental retardation, an emphasis on the classics would hardly have responded to her needs. Similarly, Kirk's teacher would not have been as able to respond to Kirk's affective need to learn more acceptable ways of dealing with anger. In contrast, if Kurume's teacher had approached curriculum from a social reform standpoint, the curriculum might have provided him with an opportunity to research the deaf rights activism movement. Through his research, he could have developed his own skills in advocating for, say, improved accommodations from his local bank so that people who were hearing impaired could access banking services easily. The debate between proponents of traditional subject area designs and those favoring social reform focuses on how time is spent in the curriculum. Traditionalists argue that foundational knowledge is critical; social reformists counter that knowledge without connection to personal meaning and current events may never be operationalized.

These debates can polarize school professionals unless they share a common vision for the outcomes of schooling. Recall that in Chapter 1 five broad outcomes for schooling were proposed: (1) development and support for families, (2) choice and self-determination, (3) lifelong learning, (4) socioeconomic security and productivity, and (5) community participation and support. To achieve these outcomes, schools need to borrow principles from several of the major views on curriculum, while focusing on individual student's cognitive, affective, communicative and physical needs. An eclectic approach borrows elements from each approach and emphasizes (1) the importance of the knowledge bases of traditional disciplines, (2) the changes that are taking place in our generation of knowledge and content, (3) the need to involve students in problem-solving and self-directed learning experiences, and (4) the holistic nature of the learning process.

## Formulating a Vision, Goals, Outcomes, and Standards

When decisions are made at the building level about what students need to learn, school professionals will be in a position to set a vision and to define the goals, outcomes, and standards that guide curriculum design, implementation, and evaluation. Remember, the curriculum is a primary vehicle for helping students achieve that vision and associated goals, outcomes, and standards.

Each school community must define these elements in a way that best meets their needs. For example, the Jefferson County school district formulated curricular outcomes whereby each student would be (1) a complex thinker, (2) an effective communicator, (3) an ethical person, (4) a quality worker, (5) a responsible citizen, and (6) a self-directed learner (Jefferson County Public Schools, 1995). Grade-level benchmarks and proficiency levels (standards) were delineated through the district curriculum guidelines. The school community members in one building in the district adopted these same student outcomes but personalized the formal curriculum when they drafted the following belief statement:

> *We Believe:*
>
> *All children can learn.*
> *Children learn best by doing.*
> *When children have choices, they take responsibility for their learning.*
> *Children deserve to be surrounded by good books.*
> *After successes, children are ready to take challenges and risk occasional failure.*
> *Children learn best through trial and error.*
> *Children enlarge their vocabularies when they learn new words in context.*
> *Children need a variety of kinds of experiences.*
> *(Perez, 1991, p. 5)*

The vision, goals, outcomes, and standards defined by a building (or district) should apply to all the students in that school community—those with and without disabilities and those from diverse cultural, linguistic, ethnic, and religious backgrounds. However, as Eisner (1991) suggests, learners bring a personal lens with which they act upon, filter, process, and construct meaning from their learning experiences. Due to differences in their capacities, interests, motivations, and backgrounds, the ways in which students ultimately achieve school outcomes will differ. For example, students with severe limitations in their motor abilities, like Annie, might direct their own learning by signifying choices through an augmentative communication system as opposed to verbal communication. Student abilities to be responsible citizens also could be expressed in a variety of ways. For example, Tanya's volunteer work as a candy striper at the local hospital is one way of contributing to her community; Kurume's campaign to educate young, deaf adults about their rights to vote is another. Each makes a contribution to their community, but in a personally relevant and meaningful way. Because of the individual nature of the learning process, school professionals cannot guarantee that students will achieve the same outcomes, but they can ensure that students have the same opportunities to achieve the same broad outcomes. The frameworks you apply to organize and manage your curriculum will support or detract from your ability to accomplish this task.

## Creating Frameworks to Organize and Manage the Curriculum

The next phase of building-level decisions is to create a framework for organizing and managing the curriculum that guides both building-based and classroom-based efforts to help students achieve stated outcomes, goals, and standards. This framework becomes the formal, building-level curriculum guide and serves several functions. First, it helps to clarify the explicit means by which curriculum experiences will be supported throughout the school community. For example, in Kirk's middle school, there was a buildingwide effort to support students' development and use of prosocial skills. That effort was spurred by discussions about the type of buildingwide curriculum experiences that were important for all students to receive.

As indicated by Kniep and Martin-Kniep (1995) a second function of a building-level curriculum framework is to set forth curriculum strands, standards, benchmarks, and strategies. National or state standards can be used to inform and drive the definition of curriculum frameworks (Jorgensen, 1997). In some locales, district-level planning defines curriculum frameworks, and individual buildings will then personalize the elements to meet community, family, and student needs. In other locales, planning of curriculum frameworks takes place at the building level. Curriculum

strands emerge from the outcomes and goals that have been determined for a building. These strands help to clarify the topics, subjects, skills, and processes that are important for students to develop and master. In some cases, buildings may decide to include a recommended sequence or order in which the strands will be covered. This is often done to address the developmental needs of children and to prevent unnecessary overlap in students' curriculum experiences.

Remember the six student outcomes from Jefferson County? Consider, for example, how in their science strand, those outcomes are supported through the following elementary-level benchmarks:

*1.1 Students learn science by actively taking part in the process: asking questions, manipulating materials, working as an active member of a team, making observations, analyzing data, and designing their own experiments.*

*Grades K–2—students will be able to raise personally relevant questions; make predictions; describe and compare things in terms of shape, color, size, texture, weight, numbers, and motion; use data to construct explanations; explore the concept of "representativeness," provide reasoned explanations; experience teamwork; and cooperatively share results.*

*Grades 3–5—students will be able to raise questions about the natural world; predict and investigate answers to those questions; apply investigative processes (observing, describing, comparing, classifying, questioning, and recording); follow written procedures; effectively manage teamwork; complete a full investigation, comparing predictions to conclusions; and consider outside influences that affect their results. (Jefferson County Public Schools, 1995)*

In Jefferson County, the strategies to accomplish these benchmarks are the prerogative of classroom-level curriculum decision makers.

There are three critical notions to keep in mind as you create building-level curriculum frameworks, benchmarks, or standards. First, remember that there should be a direct relationship between the building-level curriculum frameworks you design and the agreed-upon vision, outcomes, goals and standards. That is, there must be a match between what you state is important for students to learn and the types of experiences you then structure for them. For example, if collaboration is important to you, then teaching the

BOX 9.3

## Examples of Close-Ended Curriculum Benchmarks or Standards

All students will:

1. Orally recite their multiplication tables using the numbers 0–10.
2. Write and correctly spell 300 of the most commonly used vocabulary words.
3. Diagram and illustrate the grammatical structure of fifty compound sentences.
4. Write a five-page paper on the history of the United States.

skills of collaboration and providing opportunities to apply those skills across many contexts is necessary. If you believe that the ultimate goal of school is to provide students with the knowledge, skills, attitudes, and processes necessary to carry out adult roles and responsibilities, then planned curriculum experiences should incorporate opportunities for students to learn across multiple contexts, including their home, school, community, and work environments.

Second, as you design building-level curriculum benchmarks or standards, pay attention to the amount and degree of specificity you include. The amount of specificity and direction you provide within building-level curriculum frameworks influences the degree of flexibility you have as you make decisions in the classroom regarding what, how, when, and to what degree a particular skill or concept will be addressed. For exam-

ple, refer to the examples of close-ended curriculum frameworks in Box 9.3 and then think about Kurume. Suppose he was expected to diagram and illustrate the grammatical structure of fifty compound sentences. Because of Kurume's deafness, he has trouble with the formal structures of the English language. Does the ability to communicate one's needs effectively demand that one be able to diagram and illustrate the structural components of the English language? What is more important—communicating one's needs effectively or diagramming sentences?

Now look at Box 9.4, which contains examples of more open-ended curriculum benchmarks or standards. Designs that are broadly defined or open-ended allow schools and teachers great flexibility as to what will be covered and when and how it will be covered (Stainback, Stainback, Stefanich, & Alper, 1996). For example, students can access information in a variety of ways. Michael likes to interview people; Kurume prefers to read; Kirk likes to surf the Web; Annie manipulates her environment and looks at pictures; Tanya likes to listen and then read about the topic.

Open-ended curriculum frameworks and assignments facilitate school professionals' abilities to respond to and support diverse, individual student needs within whole-group instruction (Bingham, 1995). In contrast, designs that are more prescriptive, detailed, or close-ended tend to limit the flexibility of schools and teachers. When the curriculum specifies uniform expectations for how, what, and when students learn, school professionals are restricted in their ability to support student diversity and address individual needs. Thus, the degree and amount of flexibility that is supported through the formal, building-level cur-

BOX 9.4

## Examples of Open-Ended Curriculum Benchmarks or Standards

All students will be provided with:

1. Knowledge about themselves (as learners) and the world in which they live.
2. Skills to both regulate themselves and interact with others across multiple, changing environments.
3. Opportunities to develop attitudes that support a positive self-image and that value, embrace, and understand human diversity and interdependence.
4. A process for understanding how to use their knowledge and skills in order to maximize their capacities, achieve their life goals and objectives, and solve meaningful everyday problems.
5. A system for communicating their needs, interests, and goals.
6. Knowledge that will help them solve difficult life problems.
7. Skills in literacy, technology, and numeracy.

**BOX 9.5**

## Strategies for Planning Curriculum Frameworks

1. Create a match between your stated outcomes and planned experiences.

2. Build in flexibility and provide options.

3. Keep it broad and open-ended.

4. Remember your outcomes, and provide alternative vehicles as needed. It is more important that students achieve the outcomes than that they complete your curriculum.

riculum framework can directly influence the school's or teacher's ability to respond to individual student's capacities, interests, and needs. A narrowly defined curriculum may exclude many students from the educational experiences they need to become contributing members of a democratic society. Therefore, the goals of inclusive school communities are best accomplished through broad, flexible curriculum designs (Grenot-Scheyer et al., 1995; Jorgensen, 1996).

Finally, in creating building-level curriculum frameworks, remember that, even though you may apply a systematic process for determining the curriculum of your building, your formal curriculum is merely a "best guess" as to the types of knowledge, skills, and experiences that will lead students to your stated outcomes. While you hope that students can access and make meaning from the curriculum you plan, what is important is that students achieve your stated outcomes. Your stated outcomes are not that children will learn everything in the formal curriculum. It is the outcomes, not the curriculum per se, that are most important. For many students, large chunks of the same curricular experiences may in fact move them in those directions (Ferguson, Ralph, Meyer, Willis, & Young, 1993). However, when it becomes obvious that students are not able to assimilate or accommodate those experiences in a manner that allows them to achieve intended school outcomes, we need to provide them with more individually tailored experiences. The process of accommodating, modifying, and, in extreme cases, substituting the curriculum to meet individual student needs must maintain the integrity of school outcomes. Thus, the curriculum involves an ongoing

process of negotiating among individual student needs and intended school outcomes. School professionals need to organize and manage the curriculum so that it is flexible and meets the individual needs of all learners. Box 9.5 summarizes strategies that can be applied to achieve this flexibility and responsiveness to individual needs. Standards for professional practice guide those management decisions.

## Articulating Standards for Professional Practice

When you have defined your vision, outcomes, goals, standards, and curriculum framework, it is important to establish a set of standards for professional practice. The term *professional practice* must be applied broadly to include the school professionals, support personnel, peers, family members, and community members involved in the curriculum experiences of a school community. Standards for professional practice help guide how various professional and support roles are fulfilled and how assessment, curriculum, and instructional practices are implemented. These standards reflect beliefs about how children best learn and what constitutes effective teaching (Kniep & Martin-Kniep, 1995).

Earlier, we suggested that curriculum reform may serve as a context for general educators and specialists to pool their respective expertise and skills. Interestingly, a review of two texts, one from special education and one from general education, indicates that the recommendations for standards of professional practice in the curriculum are consistent across the two systems (Falvey, 1995; Zemelman, Daniels, & Hyde, 1993). Table 9.4 summarizes the corresponding standards. Note that although the phrasing may vary, the conceptual and applied aspects of the standards are highly compatible.

Each school community must develop a set of principles or standards to guide the roles and practices of its school professionals, support personnel, peers, family members, and community members. These standards should then be modeled, practiced, and applied to building- and classroom-level curriculum design, implementation, and evaluation. For example, Box 9.6 clarifies how the standards of "functional" and "partial participation" were applied for Tanya, Kurume, Kirk, Michael, and Annie. Furthermore, as

**TABLE 9.4** Professional Standards for the Development and Use of the Curriculum

| Special Education Principles | General Education Principles |
| --- | --- |
| *Functional*—Looking at the environments in which people are expected to function and making sure that people have the skills necessary for participating and supporting themselves in those environments. Domain areas include home, school, work, community, and recreation/leisure. Functional reading, then, could be considered to move from reading basic signs (women, men, exit, danger) that are within the student's immediate school, home, community, and leisure environments to reading shopping lists, recipes, newspapers, bus schedules, job listings, and so on. | *Authentic*—Dividing pizza or cake rather than working on odd-number problems in math book—purposes that make sense to children and that they can ultimately use in their lives. |
| *Based on needs, wants, preferences, and culture of student*—Determining what is important to the student. What do they think would help them learn? What do they want to learn? What are the cultural expectations that they bring to the school environment? | *Child centered and democratic*—Taking cues from students' interests, concerns, and questions; exercising choice, negotiating conflicts, working together, and valuing differences. |
| *Natural cues, consequences, and environments*—Providing information that is typically available to persons in natural environments that is equivalent in intensity, duration, and frequency to that which is naturally occurring. | *Experiential*—Using real-world experiences through direct or simulated immersion rather than through a transmission model. |
| *Integrated, normalized with nondisabled peers*—Providing opportunities across all domain areas for students with disabilities to interact with their nondisabled peers and participate in similar activities. | *Social relations and collaborative learning*—Allowing children to learn from and with others, working toward the ability to develop problem-solving, social, and communication skills. |
| *Partial participation*—Allowing students access to environments and activities even when the individual is not fully capable of carrying out all of the required skills or activities independently. | *Cognitive experiences*—Moving children into experiences that support their understanding of concepts and help them become self-regulated learners. |
| *Chronologically age-appropriate*—Teaching activities that are performed by nondisabled, same-aged peers but that recognize and respond to the student's developmental capacities. | *Developmental*—Providing experiences that reflect an understanding of the stages that guide children's cognitive, affective, physical, and communicative abilities over time. |
| *Transitions*—Orienting students toward the future and preparing them for future environments, expectations, norms, and rules. | *Holistic*—Incorporating whole-to-part in addition to part-to-whole approaches, providing children with the "big picture" so that they can understand. |
| *Self-determination*—Promoting self-regulation and self-management over significant life choices and preferences without undue interference. | *Reflective*—Providing students with opportunities to look back on what they've done to consider how well it went, what worked, what didn't work, and how they managed themselves and their learning opportunity. |

Source: Falvey, 1995; Zemelman, Daniels, & Hyde, 1993.

**BOX 9.6**

## Applying Professional Standards to Support Students' Needs

### What's "Functional" for Tanya?

When Tanya was young, Juanita and her teachers tried unsuccessfully to teach her how to tie her own shoes. These efforts kept them from addressing other skill areas. At one point, Juanita asked, "If Tanya doesn't learn to tie her shoes, will she have to depend on someone else to do that for her?" The answer was no, given the technological advances with Velcro and the option of slip-on shoes and boots. Juanita and Tanya's teachers decided it was time to abandon "shoe tying" and move on to a more functional skill for Tanya.

### What's "Functional" for Kirk?

When Kirk was in junior high, he had a choice of taking geometry or a consumer's economics class. Because he was unsure about his postsecondary plans for education, he didn't necessarily need geometry. And, given that he was constantly running out of money and incurring debt, he decided that the consumer course, which covered topics such as using credit, establishing and maintaining a savings account, and getting insurance, would better suit his immediate and future needs.

### What's "Functional" for Kurume?

When Kurume was in eleventh grade, his English teacher decided to approach the development of his language and reading skills using functional tasks as a primary vehicle. She connected Kurume with a pen pal in Florida, and the two boys used the Internet to communicate with each other through e-mail. This relationship was highly motivating to Kurume and

offered him an authentic means by which to further develop and refine his communication skills.

### What's "Functional" for Michael?

When Michael was 8 years old, he was still having problems solving one-digit addition problems. This meant that he was unable to keep up with his peers during third-grade math. So, during math, his classroom teacher had Michael work in the lunchroom sorting knives and forks for each of the classes. He also had to anticipate the number of lunch trays needed for each lunch period. Michael's teacher tried to find as many ways of exposing Michael to grouping numbers of items as she could. By the end of the first quarter of third grade, Michael was able to group items up to sets of ten.

### What's "Functional" for Annie? How Can We Help Her "Partially Participate"?

When Annie was 12 years old, many of her same-aged peers spent their after-school time at the community recreation center. In order for Annie to have opportunities to access similar environments and strengthen friendships with her peers, Annie's teachers arranged to provide her with instruction at the recreation center. They taught her to present her identification card, to use the women's locker room, and to access the gymnasium and swimming pool. Because Annie could not fully participate in games such as basketball, she was taught how to make tic marks on a piece of paper to keep track of the score for her peers (partial participation).

school experiences are constructed at the building and classroom levels, these standards can be used to assess the responsiveness of curriculum design, implementation, and evaluation strategies. If you applied the standards described in Table 9.4, you could ask the following types of questions:

■ Have students been allowed to explore the topics and ask the questions they want to?

■ Are we teaching students the skills that they need to function today and in the future?

■ Are we using real-life experiences to help students connect and elaborate on the concepts, knowledge, and skills that they are developing?

■ Have we considered how the cultural experiences of our students may influence our curriculum expectations?

- Are we maximizing the extent to which each child, despite individual capacities and needs, participates in all school experiences?

How you organize and manage your building and the decision-making processes you institute will influence the degree to which school professionals, support personnel, students, and family and community members can practice and model professional standards of practice.

## Creating Responsive Organizational Structures

Last, but certainly not least, the building-level curriculum must identify the organizational structures that will allow desired curriculum outcomes to occur for all students. Organizational structures facilitate and support effective and efficient (1) use of human, fiscal, and material resources, (2) operational structures, (3) role definitions and expectations, (4) communication and decision-making systems, and (5) human resource development. Organizational structures include teacher schedules, personnel roles, decision-making processes, and budgetary tasks.

No teacher, no matter how experienced or gifted, is likely to possess all of the knowledge and skills to design a curriculum for all the students in a given classroom (Ferguson et al., 1993). In inclusive school settings, building-level supports must be in place for school professionals to collectively respond to the individual needs of students (Sage, 1996; Stainback, Stainback, & Jackson, 1992). This could include structuring the school day to permit shared planning time between specialists and general education teachers. If your school community encourages parent participation in curriculum decision making, you may have to commit resources or make special provisions in scheduling such meetings. Schools committed to serving diverse communities of learners and to adhering to principles of democratic teaching and learning are increasingly refining their organizational structures to reflect that commitment. In other words, they practice what they preach. Their organizational structures reflect the values and beliefs that guide their decisions about their vision, goals, outcomes, standards, curriculum frameworks, and standards for professional practices. Box

---

**BOX 9.7**

### The Case of Central Park East Secondary School

In 1985, Central Park East Secondary School was established as an alternative high school. The curricular aims of the school were to stress mastery of a limited number of important subjects, and to teach students how to learn, how to reason, and how to investigate complex issues that required collaboration and personal responsibility. The school was guided by principles that included knowing some things well rather than many things superficially, personalization, high standards for all, and self-discovery and regulation. In order to support the curriculum outcomes, goals, and standards set for the school, the following organizational structures were created:

1. Half-day theme-centered classes, organized around math/science and the humanities

2. Small classes, accomplished through the elimination of roles such as department heads, guidance counselors, and deans with the responsibilities formally carried out by the people shifted to classroom-based instructors

3. Use of critical friends—professionals and community members external to the building who were brought in regularly to reexamine curriculum practices and standards, review portfolio products, or provide advice on a range of topics

4. Biweekly blocks of planning time allocated to groups of school professionals and support personnel, as well as monthly meetings, to discuss issues of race, class, and gender and to attend to school matters such as family conferences, report writing, and recommendations from working groups

Source: Meier & Schwarz, 1995.

9.7 discusses one school's attempts to align practices with beliefs. As that school community found, the attempt involved sacrifices and forced the community to make difficult choices (Meier & Schwarz, 1995).

## ■ SECTION SUMMARY

Although many of the decisions about the formal curriculum are made at the district level, those decisions increasingly must be shared at the building level in order to accommodate the different needs of learners. Even if decisions about student outcomes or curriculum targets are made at the district level, building-based school professionals, students, family members, and community members should have the flexibility to adapt those district decisions to meet the needs of individual schools and students. In inclusive school communities, building-level curriculum decisions set the tone, pace, and expectations for the planning, implementation, and evaluation of students' school experiences across a wide variety of contexts. The challenge to inclusive school communities is to create guidelines for building-level curriculum experiences that collectively consider, integrate, balance, and support the needs of students, families, the local community, and the greater school system. When a building has its vision, goals, outcomes, standards, curriculum frameworks, and organizational structures in place, it creates a healthy environment in which classroom-level curriculum decisions can take place.

# Classroom-Level Curriculum Decisions in Inclusive Schools

Clearly, many decisions must be made before the curriculum is actually documented. Your answers thus far to the questions posed in Box 9.1 should also help you appreciate the critical information you need and the roles you play in curriculum decision making as a school professional, student, family or community member. Once fundamental decisions have been made at the district and/or building level, the stage is set for the curriculum activities that must take place at the classroom level. As you read this section on those classroom decisions, you will be able to continue to elaborate on your responses to previous questions, as well as to question 12 in Box 9.1.

# Identifying Elements of Classroom-Level Decisions

School professionals continue to apply the principles related to building-level curriculum decisions to the curriculum activities that they plan for classrooms and other school environments. Specifically, they seek to create broad activities that offer multiple and flexible ways for students to access, make sense of, and demonstrate their understanding of the curriculum goals and objectives (Tomlinson, 1995). The emphasis on multiple and flexible ways is particularly important when the student body is as diverse as those found in inclusive school communities. One of the basic tenets of inclusive school communities is adaptable curriculum experiences that are accessible to the greatest number of students. This flexibility is achieved through the use of varied and multiple instructional strategies, materials, and content foci.

Classroom-level curriculum planning involves four main tasks: (1) applying and refining students' skills in the cognitive, affective, communicative, and physical domains, (2) supporting and developing skills to compensate for or support students' needs in each domain, (3) providing students with the knowledge, skills, and processes necessary to meet their goals and interests, and (4) helping students achieve broad school outcomes and apply their skills across many environments, including the school, home, community and workplace. To accomplish these goals, curriculum decision making at the classroom level has three features: (1) instructional frameworks such as **peer tutoring,** cooperative learning, circles of friends, and team teaching that empower both teachers and students to support one another, (2) activity-based, open-ended curriculum frameworks such as integrated or thematic units that allow for flexibility in student goals, objectives, performances, and outcomes, and (3) rules and expectations that promote acknowledgment of individual differences, fairness, equity, and mutual respect (Stainback & Stainback, 1996b; Stainback, Stainback, & Jackson, 1992).

Creating curriculum at the classroom level relies on two sources of information. First, classroom-level decisions draw heavily from the vision, goals, outcomes, standards, frameworks, and professional guidelines set at the building and district levels. For example, think about how the standards for functionality and partial participation were applied to Tanya,

Kirk, Kurume, Michael, and Annie (see Box 9.6). As you wrestle with the content that you are going to cover in the curriculum, you can use those standards to assist you in personalizing the curriculum and making it relevant to your students. But to do so, you must know your students well. For example, what are their physical, affective, cognitive, and communicative needs? What cultural expectations and values do they bring to the classroom? What are their strengths and preferences? In the chapter-opening vignette, Pam Kniss emphasized how important it is to include students in curriculum planning. Gathering this type of information and using it to define your classroom outcomes is critical to creating classroom curriculum activities that respond to the needs of your students. This leads to the second source of information that is critical to classroom curriculum planning—the students themselves.

Classroom-level curriculum decision makers must gather and use critical pieces of information about their specific group(s) of students. To reiterate, only when you synthesize the planning of content, instruction, and assessment can you truly construct the educational experiences you intend for students. This means that you must assess for the purpose of getting to know your students. For example, what do they know? What do they want to know? What is important for them to know? How do they learn best? What are their strengths and needs in the cognitive, affective, communicative, and physical domains? Table 9.5 lists possible curricular strategies in each domain.

For instance, if you had a student who needed to work on developing his or her memory skills, you might select one of the memory strategies such as visualization or rehearsal and teach that skill to the whole class. Or, if you were a second-grade teacher in Jefferson County, you might work on a science unit focusing on the use of data to construct explanations. Suppose you decided to use cooperative learning groups to look at various materials that sink or float in water (the concept of displacement). For students to function effectively in these groups, they would need some of the cognitive skills listed in Table 9.5, as well as some of the skills listed in the affective and communicative domains. Thus, you might remind students that they could begin their group work by identifying the roles that each student would perform in the group. Or you might ask students to pay attention to the voice tones

that they used to ask questions, make remarks, or disagree with one another's conclusions. In this way, you would integrate curriculum from each of the domain areas within the subject matter curriculum.

This level of planning helps you refine the decisions you make about how you will support your students to achieve important school outcomes. Once you know the types of content experiences that are important to your students, you can select the instructional strategies that will best help you communicate and facilitate that content. Then you have to perform another round of assessment to evaluate how well the strategies worked. Can the students do what was planned for them to do? What worked (for you and your students)? What didn't work (for you and your students)? The process of using assessment information, addressing specific content, matching instructional strategies, and evaluating the effectiveness of your interventions is critical to the classroom-level curriculum decisions that you make.

Classroom-level curriculum decision making typically entails three levels of planning: (1) units of study, (2) lesson plans, and (3) individualized adaptations and modifications. In this chapter, the focus is on creating a classroom curriculum that is both accessible to and responsive to the greatest number of students. The key is to tailor the curriculum for students who cannot be expected to do what the majority of their peers can. The skills of many school professionals and support personnel are required for effective classroom curriculum planning. In addition, students, their family members, and community members continue to play important roles at this level of curriculum decision making. Sometimes, school professionals at similar or across many different grade levels have these discussions. At other times, teachers and groups of students work to plan classroom curriculum.

## Creating Units of Study

Units of study help school professionals organize and map out the skills, processes, and knowledge that students need to achieve important school outcomes. Using building-level curriculum frameworks and broad annual outcomes, you delineate the specific skills, processes, or knowledge that students must master and

| TABLE 9.5 | Possible Curricular Strategies Across the Four Domains |
|---|---|
| **Domain Needs** | **Skills to Teach** |
| **Cognitive Domain** | |
| Attention | Listening, note taking, identifying environmental cues, outlining |
| Perception | Recognizing patterns, self-monitoring for understanding, questioning, organizing, sequencing, outlining, note taking, using reciprocal questioning, matching, using categorization, requesting help |
| Working memory | Using mnemonics, visualization, rehearsal, chunking, associations, elaboration, pairing; selecting salient features of a problem |
| Long-term memory—procedural | Sequencing, outlining, mediating, doing error analysis, problem solving, cultivating independent work habits, developing flexible reading rates, locating information, using books, following rules for comprehending and remembering, locating the main idea, self-questioning, mapping |
| Long-term memory—declarative | Generating questions; developing concepts, facts, and principles; inquiring; hypothesis testing; researching questions; mapping information; communicating information; evaluating information; linking information with other areas of knowledge |
| Long-term memory—organizational structures | Concept mapping, webbing, patterns, elaborations, relationships |
| Long-term memory—conditional | Comparing and contrasting ideals with actual practice; thinking precisely about thinking; using critical vocabulary; noting significant similarities and differences; examining or evaluating assumptions; distinguishing relevant from irrelevant facts; making plausible inferences, predictions, or interpretations; giving reasons and evaluating evidence and alleged facts; recognizing contradictions; exploring implications and consequences |
| Executive function | Questioning, judging, evaluating, refining, using self-talk, critiquing |
| Self as learner | Identifying personal learning styles, gaining knowledge of personal strategy use and rating effectiveness, understanding and stating personal learning preferences, understanding and stating personal cognitive style (formulator, implementer, or evaluator) |
| Self-reinforcement | Using self-talk, stating strengths, verbalizing why something went well, using self-recording strategies to monitor progress |
| Self-regulation | Self-monitoring, judging, evaluating, refining, questioning, requesting help, organizing |
| **Affective Domain** | |
| Self-concept | Understanding expectations and developing skills to carry out appropriate roles—student (following rules, listening skills, organization, cooperation), sibling, friend, child; identifying strengths and weaknesses; identifying needed compensatory skills |
| Self-regard | Developing and monitoring positive self-talk, developing skills in logical self-evaluation, developing the ability to compare oneself to a set standard or criteria |
| Self-awareness | Identifying and labeling emotions; controlling the expression of emotions; monitoring physiological manifestations of emotion, as well as voice tone, facial expressions, and body language |
| Self-control | Identifying salient features of social interactions, self-monitoring and -regulating, controlling anger, problem solving, delaying gratification, developing impulse control, planning skills, managing time, goal setting |

*(continued)*

| **TABLE 9.5** *(continued)* | |
| --- | --- |

| Domain Needs | Skills to Teach | |
| --- | --- | --- |
| **Affective Domain** *(cont.)* | | |
| Motivation | Identifying personal values, philosophies, locus of control; identifying, sustaining motivation; identifying likes, dislikes; practicing self-reinforcement, naming goals | |
| Social cognition | Identifying features of an environment; identifying social relationships and problems; generating and implementing solutions; checking for efficiency, quality, and effort | |
| Social skills | Turn taking, negotiating, developing self-advocacy, compromising, cooperating, greeting others, problem solving, initiating and sustaining conversations | |
| **Communicative Domain** | | |
| | *Receptive* | *Expressive* |
| Form | Recognizing the type of message conveyed (question vs. statement), as well as punctuation, spelling, voice tone markers, expression and intonation patterns, sound-symbol relationships | Oral and written grammar, word endings, writing strategies, verb tenses, sign language, augmentative systems, spelling |
| Use | Interpreting nonverbal cues, self-monitoring, self-questioning, identifying parts of speech and grammar, interpreting gestures and body language, developing reading rate and fluency, comprehension monitoring | Turn taking, gestures, proximity cues, self-talk, metalinguistics, verbal and written fluency, articulation patterns, social interaction |
| Content | Interpreting meaning, developing expansive vocabulary, developing reading strategies for decoding and comprehension, following directions | Concepts, word meanings, parallel constructions, vocabulary development, story forms, refusal skills, requesting skills, similarities and differences, relational words, directions, sequencing |
| **Physical/Health Domain** | | |
| Sensory system | Orientation, use of residual senses, alternative and augmentative communication systems, self-monitoring, care for hearing aids or mobility supports | |
| Musculoskeletal system | Prosthesis care and management, mobility, use of alternative modes of transportation such as wheelchairs or walkers, the development of lifelong patterns of exercise | |
| Central nervous system | Relaxation techniques, motor planning strategies, desensitization, sensory integration | |
| Respiratory system | Special diet routines, monitoring of physiological signs of distress, disease prevention. | |
| Cardiovascular system | Lifelong patterns of exercise, diet control | |
| Respiratory system | Environment management, reduced exposures to toxins and allergens, prophylactic use of medications, emergency care | |
| Digestive system | Special diet management and routines, health procedures such as care of feeding tubes or catheters | |

Learning extends out into the community as young students enjoy a field trip to a local salt marsh.

apply over time. Knowledge of the cognitive, affective, communicative, and physical domains can assist you in determining the kinds of knowledge, skills, or processes that students must learn over time. Table 9.5 also provides explicit ideas for what students may need to be taught to support their skills across each domain.

Once you know what you want students to learn, you can plan units of study. These units may take several days, weeks, or even months to complete. For example, if you are working toward a broad outcome of student self-determination, you know that there are several component skills that support students' ability to act in self-determined ways (Sands & Wehmeyer, 1996). Those skills include decision making, goal setting, needs advocacy, and self-regulation. You may decide to develop one or more units that, combined, help students acquire and apply these skills across multiple contexts. Because the component skills of self-determination are used in and across multiple contexts, you will be able to utilize many topical areas to help students learn how and when to apply their skills. For example, component skills of self-determination can be used to help students (1) complete homework, (2) set future employment goals, (3) improve their social

interaction skills, and (4) solve a local community problem.

As soon as you begin to plan units of study, you can address individual learner characteristics, needs, goals, and interests. Using a unit planning form, like the one shown in Figure 9.1, you can map out the content experiences that all students will share, those that most students will share, and those that some students will share. For example, when you consider what content some students will share, you might think about a learner who is gifted or one who has significant learning challenges, such as Annie. Once you are clear on the differentiated content elements of your unit, you will be better able to match the appropriate materials, resources, strategies, adaptations, products, and evaluations to individual students and to support the greatest numbers of students in terms of the planned curriculum. Thus, if you wanted to teach Annie and Kirk how to greet others, you might have the same curriculum expectation but employ differing instructional strategies. For instance, to teach Annie how to greet others, you might use a lot of physical, overt modeling and practice. In contrast, you might have Kirk observe his peers in multiple settings, such as in

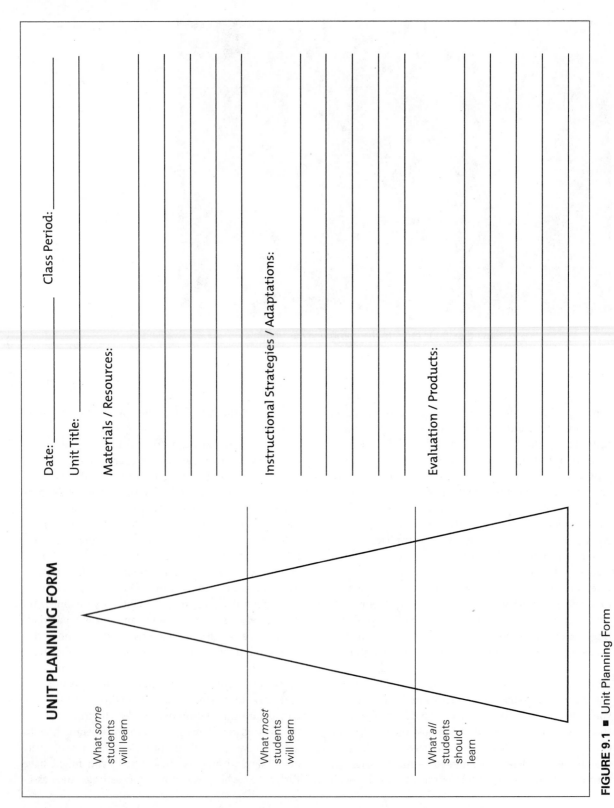

**FIGURE 9.1** ■ Unit Planning Form

*Source:* Bulgren, J., & Lenz, K. (1996). Strategic instruction in the content areas. In D. Deschler, E. Ellis, & B. Lenz, *Teaching adolescents with learning disabilities* (2nd ed.) (p. 429). Denver: Love. Adapted with permission.

the lunchroom, classroom, and hallway. Then you might have him analyze and generate a list of ways to greet others, select some to practice, and then have him self-evaluate how well he was able to model the behavior. In addition to varying instructional approaches, inclusive classrooms demand flexibility in assessing learning. For instance, while Michael may be able to write or talk about what he has learned, you must allow Tanya to demonstrate what she has learned through the use of concrete, real-life activities. To address student diversity, construct units in flexible ways.

**MODELS FOR UNIT DESIGN** Several models of curriculum design are used to guide unit planning. Curriculum designs tend to be organized by subject area, discipline structure, integrated designs, learner-centered designs, experience-centered designs, problem-centered designs, and life-situations designs (Armstrong, 1989; Morrison, 1993; Ornstein & Hunkins, 1988). As you read about these broad models in Boxes 9.8, 9.9, and 9.10, think back to the philosophical foundations of the curriculum discussed earlier in this chapter. What resemblances do you notice? Which design you choose depends on the central focus of your unit. Options and considerations include (1) subject matter areas or processes specific to a field of discipline, (2) themes, concepts, or process skills that transcend or are common across many disciplines or subject areas, and (3) the personal and social needs of your learners or the broader community or society.

While the subject area approach is the oldest, best-known, and most widely used curriculum design, it is increasingly coming under attack (Beane, 1995). Sub-

ject matter designs tend to foster narrow, lockstep approaches to the teaching/learning process although they need not. Teachers using subject area designs often depend on lectures, textbooks, worksheets, and drill-and-practice activities, but this combination of subject matter and teacher-centered instructional strategies prevents many students from being successful (Stainback & Stainback, 1996b). When classrooms have diverse student populations, multiple curriculum designs may be preferable because they lead to more variation in the content focus and instructional strategies. As with building-level curriculum frameworks, you want to design units that address the individual learning characteristics of your students.

**DESIGNS THAT ADDRESS DIVERSE LEARNER NEEDS** Integrated curriculum designs are the most consistent with the principles and beliefs of inclusive school communities (Grenot-Scheyer et al., 1995; Kovalik, 1993; Udvari-Solner & Thousand, 1995). Integrated curricula are characterized by a focus on information that is generated by students, that is relevant to their lives, and that helps them develop the skills necessary to be successful both in school and in later life. Furthermore, integrated curricula are designed to respond to the multiple ways in which students learn, to focus learning on concepts, and to increase opportunities for students to explore, discover, and apply information across many content areas (Kovalik, 1993).

Teachers are increasingly applying integrated unit designs in school settings that support students from diverse ethnic, cultural, linguistic, socioeconomic backgrounds and with differing ability needs (Educational

---

**BOX 9.8**

## Subject Area and Discipline Approaches to Curriculum Design

In this model, the curriculum is organized by subject areas or disciplines of knowledge. For example, the curriculum would be designed around math, science, language arts, English, biology, reading, and writing. Typically, the focus of subject area approaches is on dividing up the knowledge base within a particular area or discipline and transmitting that knowledge to students. The subject matter tends to be divided by grade level.

A variation of the subject area or discipline approach incorporates an emphasis on the structures or

techniques that are used to discover new information within a particular field (Doll, 1992). For example, students in science courses would be encouraged to master techniques such as inquiry or hypothesis testing in addition to remembering specific facts or concepts. Similarly, students in social studies courses would be expected to carry out research and discovery techniques and to demonstrate the ability to compare and contrast sets of information.

---

**BOX 9.9**

## Integrated Curriculum Designs

This model of curriculum design is organized around themes or concepts that relate to two or more subject or discipline areas. Various models of integrated designs have been documented, including multi-disciplinary, interdisciplinary, and transdisciplinary approaches (Burns, 1995; Drake, 1993; Jacobs, 1989). Multidisciplinary approaches use a common theme to connect content from each of the main disciplines (science, math, art, geography, and so on). Typically, these units are conducted such that each discipline is addressed distinctly, with efforts made to encourage links between both the content and the procedures of one discipline and the others. "The interdisciplinary approach shifts from an emphasis on applying the themes to subject areas to focusing on the commonalities across disciplines—usually turning to critical thinking skills as the organizing principle for order and structure of the unit" (Drake, 1993, p. 38).

When the interdisciplinary approach is used, content knowledge is regarded as more of a context for developing thinking skills, as opposed to constituting the primary outcome of a unit. In a transdisciplinary

approach to curriculum design, educators are encouraged to focus on real-life contexts for understanding concepts, skills, and knowledge. Within this framework, disciplines are transcended, and life contexts such as business, politics, economics, technology, and law are used to guide and direct student exploration of knowledge. Flexibility is key in the integrated curriculum design.

Integrated unit designs focus on broad concepts or themes. In addition, basic skills in areas such as literacy, computation, technology, cognition, and communication are infused in the process or serve as vehicles to learn about the particular concept or theme. Thus, students not only learn content (across multiple disciplines) but also develop and use important physical, affective, cognitive, and communicative skills. Integrated unit designs are intended to be carried out in a flexible manner that allows for active student engagement and for students to learn in different ways and at different paces and to demonstrate their learning in multiple formats (Sapon-Shevin, in O'Neil, 1995).

---

**BOX 9.10**

## Problem- or Needs-Based Curriculum Design Approaches

Several models for designing curriculum can be described broadly as problem- or needs-based approaches. Use of these approaches is often an "effort to move attention away from subject matter to the life needs of people" (Doll, 1992, p. 164). Extending from a social reconstructionist philosophy of education, one approach involves the use of life situations as a way of understanding and addressing major political,

social, environmental, and economic structures and forces. Another approach involves curriculum plans that are organized around personal and social needs of learners. This personal orientation approach assigns high priorities to learner interests, needs, and capacities (Armstrong, 1989). In addition, learner-centered designs begin with the student's own experiences as an initiating point for planning.

---

Leadership, December 1994/January 1995; Kucer, Silva, Delgado-Larocco, 1995; Ostrow, 1995). For example, one group of secondary school science teachers was highly concerned about their lack of success with two particular groups of students—those for whom English was a second language and those with disabilities (Drake, Hemphill, & Chappell, 1995). This group decided to apply an integrated curriculum framework known as the KISS model (Drake, 1995). The KISS

model takes school professionals through this series of steps:

1. State one to three cross-subject outcomes.
2. Decide what students will have to know and do to achieve and demonstrate the outcome(s).
3. Create a set of criteria (a rubric) or standards that will be used to judge the students' performance or final products.

## TABLE 9.6  Science Instruction Through an Integrated Unit Design

| | |
|---|---|
| *Unit outcome/goal:* | To be able to ask a meaningful question and answer it in a systematic way that shows respect for the environment as part of the problem-solving process. |
| *What students will have to know:* | The criteria for a meaningful question.<br>A systematic way to answer questions (such as the scientific method).<br>A way to answer a question that shows respect for the environment. |
| *What students will have to do:* | Develop a meaningful question.<br>Answer it in a systematic way.<br>Demonstrate a respect for the environment in the answer. |
| *Teacher key beliefs:* | Active learning is best.<br>All students can learn when/if they are motivated.<br>Students have different learning styles.<br>Acquiring skills that help students understand scientific principles is more important than content.<br>Producing students who will be our neighbors and who respect the environment is more important than creating scientists. |
| *Sample instructional activities:* | Webbing knowledge on green plants; webbing on the related legal, political, social, environmental, technological, and global issues; values clarification; journals; brainstorming "fat" (complex) and "thin" (simple) questions; library research; "bell-ringer" labs (students choose a series of labs that are intended to spark questions for study); experiments. |
| *Culminating activity:* | Hold a science symposium.<br>Invite parents and community members.<br>Have students deliver a video or live presentation, including a poster on their selected question/answer.<br>Conduct peer evaluations, self-evaluations, and unit evaluations. |

Source: Drake, 1995.

4. Choose a theme, topic, or issue and then brainstorm the real-life contexts or connections to this theme, topic, or issue.

5. Decide on a culminating activity in which students can demonstrate what they have learned.

6. Brainstorm a series of activities that will lead to and support the major outcome (Drake, 1995).

An abbreviated version of how this group of science instructors applied this unit design is summarized in Table 9.6.

How might the KISS model be applied to a student like Tanya? Would she be able to deal with a relatively sophisticated topic that requires high-level thinking skills? Yes, as long as she can conduct her activities in a way that is concrete and connected to her life. For example, she may choose to ask a question like, "What are all the ways I can get rid of my empty soda pop cans that won't hurt the earth?" Instead of having to rely on reading for all of her research, she might visit the local recycling center at the grocery store or to the recycling plant. As long as Tanya is provided with curriculum activities that respect her physical, affective, cognitive, and communicative needs, she can be expected to achieve outcomes similar to her peers. In fact, Drake, Hemphill, and Chappell (1995) found that, when they planned their curriculum using an integrated model, their students, some of whom had disabilities similar to Tanya's, experienced greater success than they did with more teacher-directed and close-ended approaches.

**MULTIPLE DESIGN APPROACHES**  Though there have been many successes with integrated curriculum

## Extending Your Learning

Look at the unit outcome/goal in Table 9.6. Would you classify the goal as open-ended or close-ended. Why?

designs (Apple & Beane, 1995), one design usually does not fit the needs of all learners at all times. Thus, some elementary schools offer a subject-oriented curriculum in the morning and integrated units across subjects in the afternoon. In addition, these elementary schools often schedule time for special course work in areas such as substance abuse or physical violence. But it is important to consider the relative benefits of one design over another in terms of the outcomes you hope to achieve in a particular unit. If you are not purposeful in the decisions you make about applying different curriculum designs, your approach may reflect a mindless eclecticism or denote a knee-jerk reaction to "political situations that are subject to external control, compromise, conflicting values, and unpredictable events" (Longstreet & Shane, 1993, p. 101). Your units of study should lead students to stated building-level and classroom-level outcomes and should address the needs, interests, and goals of your students (Ladson-Billings, 1995).

## Planning for Specific Teaching/Learning Experiences

The next step in classroom-level curriculum planning involves decisions about daily student activities. These lesson plans guide teacher-student interactions on a day-to-day basis, breaking large units of study into smaller, manageable increments. Lesson plans can be written to cover small portions of time, such as a ten-minute minilesson, or larger blocks of time spanning several days or more. In part, the timing for a lesson plan is dictated by the skill level of the students. For example, if students are working on a unit that involves using previously developed research skills, the classroom teacher might start each day with a minilesson on steps in the research process. But if the students have never been exposed to research skills, the classroom teacher, along with a library/media specialist, might prepare a lesson that spans several days and al-

lows for modeling, demonstrations, student practice, and teacher feedback on the steps necessary to conduct research.

Generally, lesson plans set forth the topic or theme of the lesson, the expectations or rationale, the specific activities, the objectives, and the evaluation criteria. Thus, the synthesis of curriculum, instruction, and assessment is documented through the lesson plan. Many forms can be used to plan lessons; Figure 9.2 shows a lesson planning form that is an extension of the unit planning form shown in Figure 9.1.

What concerns should drive your lesson planning? First, you want to create lessons that are accessible to the largest numbers of students possible. Following the logic that directed curriculum planning at the building level and for units of study, you should write lesson plans that accomplish the following:

1. Support a progression of skills or knowledge that lead to intended outcomes of the unit (and therefore school outcomes).

2. Reflect objectives that can be met and demonstrated in many ways.

3. Connect new information to previous knowledge or skills.

4. Engage students through multiple forms of learning.

5. Incorporate physical, affective, cognitive, and communicative skills and knowledge in the objectives.

6. Match instruction, content, and assessment.

In addition, in both your unit planning and lesson planning, you should analyze the demands of the tasks and activities that you plan to use and determine precisely what you want students to be able to do with the topic or information at hand. Curriculum decisions should account for (1) the point of entry in the learning sequence, (2) the structure and organization of each learning unit or task, (3) the best sequence for presenting the tasks and experiences, and (4) the developmental state of the learners. Three tools—task analysis, cognitive taxonomies, and a taxonomy of learning stages—can help you design lessons and units that address these concerns.

**TASK ANALYSIS** Task analysis helps us make curriculum decisions about the requisite skills that students might need before learning some new skill or knowledge or the components involved in a particular

Date: _____   Class Period: _____   Unit: _____

Lesson Objective(s):_____

_____

_____

Materials                                    Evaluation

In Class Assignments                  Homework Assignments

What *some* students will learn

What *most* students will learn

What *all* students should learn

Agenda

1 _____

_____

2 _____

_____

3 _____

_____

4 _____

_____

5 _____

_____

6 _____

_____

7 _____

_____

**FIGURE 9.2** ■ Lesson Planning Form

Source: Bulgren, J., & Lenz, K. (1996). Strategic instruction in the content areas. In D. Deschler, E. Ellis, & B. Lenz, *Teaching adolescents with learning disabilities* (2nd ed.) (p. 430). Denver: Love. Used by permission.

skill or knowledge domain. Box 9.11 outlines the steps in task analysis. Once the instructional objective is defined, the process of delineating the components is relatively easy if the task analyzer has a grasp of the subject or skill area. However, deciding on an instructional objective or learning target is a complex process. It involves consideration of the classroom curriculum, the needs of the learners, and the content to be taught. In particular, you have to be concerned with what you want students to be able to do with the information or skills to be taught. A cognitive taxonomy helps you categorize your learning targets.

 **COGNITIVE TAXONOMIES** The learning targets you specify in your unit and lesson plans can be categorized according to cognitive taxonomies. **Cognitive taxonomies** are classification schemes arranged in hi-

erarchical order (Biehler & Snowman, 1993). For example, Bloom and his associates (1956) developed a widely used taxonomy for categorizing the cognitive skills that students call into action when involved in learning opportunities and achieving learning targets (see Table 9.7). The higher you go on Bloom's taxonomy, the higher-order thinking skills the learner will use in order to reach the learning objective. An alternative classification system, proposed by Williams and Haladyna (1982), is illustrated in Figure 9.3. The premise of their system is that "any instructional objective, test item, or other environmental demand on an individual can be classified according to the information or content to be used and the intellectual operation or task to be performed" (Williams & Haladyna, 1982, p. 162). The check marks in Figure 9.3 indicate the interaction between the various cognitive tasks and content types. For example, according to Williams and Haladyna, prediction can be applied only when students are working with concepts and principles, not facts.

As you apply cognitive taxonomies in your unit- and lesson-planning activities, track whether you are introducing your students to increasingly complex skills and content. When learning objectives are set, students should be expected to demonstrate their competence across all levels of higher-order thinking skills and content types. For example, teachers sometimes reserve tasks that require synthesis, evaluation, or analysis for older students. Yet, even young children can activate skills that demonstrate these cognitive operations if they have information that is developmentally appropriate. For instance, when Tanya was young, Juanita had her set the table for dinner. To help Tanya evaluate how well she accomplished this task, Juanita

| **TABLE 9.7** | **Bloom's Taxonomy** |
|---|---|
| ■ *Knowledge:* | Recall or recognition of specific elements in a subject area |
| ■ *Comprehension:* | Translation, interpretation, or extrapolation of knowledge |
| ■ *Application:* | Use of principles and generalizations to solve novel problems |
| ■ *Analysis:* | Examination of a phenomenon in terms of its constituent elements so that the relationship among the elements and their effect on the phenomenon as a whole is made explicit |
| ■ *Synthesis:* | The creation of a novel pattern or structure from elements |
| ■ *Evaluation:* | Judgment of products or performance |

Source: Bloom et al., 1956.

| | CONTENT | | |
|---|---|---|---|
| **TASKS OR MENTAL OPERATIONS** | *Facts* Associations between names, other symbols, objects, and locations | *Concepts* Defines classes of objects or events that are grouped together | *Principles* Propositions such as if/then statements |
| *Reiteration*—individuals must recognize or produce information in the same form as it was received. | ✔ | ✔ | ✔ |
| *Summarization*—individuals report the substance accurately as opposed to verbatim. | ✔ | ✔ | ✔ |
| *Illustration*—individuals demonstrate understanding by recognizing or providing unfamiliar examples. | | ✔ | ✔ |
| *Prediction*—individuals employ rules to predict future change or changes in related situations. | | ✔ | ✔ |
| *Evaluation*—individuals use criteria to make a judgment or selection. | | ✔ | ✔ |
| *Application*—individuals employ other thinking skills to solve problems or think creatively. | | | ✔ |

**FIGURE 9.3** ■ Williams and Haladyna's Taxonomy
Source: Williams & Haladyna, 1982.

gave her a place mat showing pictures of a cup, plate, napkin, and silverware in their respective places. After she set the table, Tanya could go from one place setting to another matching the pictures on the place mat to the actual settings to evaluate whether she had completed her task accurately. In addition to tracking learning targets according to a cognitive taxonomy such as Bloom's or Williams and Haladyna's, lesson plans should reflect consideration of previous experiences of the learner with a skill or topic. A taxonomy that addresses learning stages can help you with this.

## Extending Your Learning

Using the classification system proposed by Williams and Haladyna (1982), describe the content and type of task involved in the following test item: What factors should be considered in deciding the degree of emphasis to be placed on nuclear generation of energy for the next ten years?

**A TAXONOMY OF LEARNING STAGES** Once a learning objective has been specified, curriculum planners must consider the previous experiences of the learners with a skill or topic. Haring, Liberty, and White (1980) categorize learning into five phases: (1) acquisition, (2) fluency, (3) generalization, (4) adaptation, and (5) maintenance. This learning hierarchy helps teachers to distinguish between those curriculum activities they might use if learners have no prior experience with a task or skill to be learned and those curriculum activities that might be used to make sure that students maintain their facility with a well-learned skill. The activities that are used to maintain skills are organized very differently from the activities that are used to teach students who are learning a skill for the first time. During acquisition lessons, teachers must present information clearly, provide lots of models, check for understanding frequently, and make sure that students can demonstrate basic knowledge before having them practice the skill on their own. When students can perform successfully under guided circumstances, then they are ready to move to a fluency phase.

During fluency, students practice a skill until they are able to perform it with some degree of automaticity (see Chapter 5). In other words, they no longer have to self-talk as they perform each step in the sequence. In generalization, students learn to apply the principles of one skill to another skill or to transfer the use of one skill from one environment to another. For instance, tying shoes may be generalized to tying large, secure knots to moor a boat or tying string on a package. Writing and debating provide another example of generalization. When students have learned a process for a particular form of written expression—say, argument—in the generalization phase, they may be asked to apply that same process to the development of a speech that promotes a particular viewpoint.

## Adapting the Curriculum for Students with Disabilities and Other Needs

There will be times, regardless of supports at the building and classroom levels, when the curriculum must be individualized to allow for one or more learners to experience success or to have their learning and social needs met. This stage of planning is often referred to as curriculum adaptation and modification. Although we strongly believe that the curriculum must be individualized, we do not intend to convey images of classrooms of thirty or more children with thirty or more corresponding individualized curriculum plans. As stated previously, for many students, large chunks of the same curricular experiences will provide the opportunities necessary for them to achieve school outcomes (Ferguson at al., 1993). Individualizing curricular experiences merely reflects the fact that, due to a variety of factors, children sometimes require alternatives. Table 9.8 provides an overview of both specific curriculum content and ideas for general curriculum adaptations and modifications that might be considered for students with disabilities. As you review this table, however, you must remember that each student is unique. Just because students might share the same type of disability does not mean they will have the same needs for curriculum content or for modifications and adaptations. Also, the general education curriculum should always be considered as the beginning place from which to evaluate and determine what students should know and be able to do. If a decision is

made to vary from that curriculum or to provide adaptations and modifications to that curriculum; the needs of each student must be determined on an individual basis, in concert with the student, family members, and school professionals. The IEP provides a vehicle to document student needs and provide teachers with information about the direction that their curriculum planning should follow.

The goal of curriculum adaptation and modification is to more closely align the cognitive, affective, communicative, and physical/health demands of the curriculum to the capacities, strengths, and needs of students. The curriculum is individualized if it allows students some choice in what they learn, how they go about learning it, what materials they use, and how they demonstrate their new knowledge and skills or apply them to solve problems. When possible, approaches to unit and lesson planning should incorporate this level of flexibility. Sometimes, however, student needs cannot be accommodated strictly through the models of curriculum design employed at the classroom level. Only through the use of adaptations and modifications will some students achieve the same curriculum goals (Van Dyke, Stallings, & Colley, 1995). In fact, as Pugach and Warger maintain, it is not necessary that all students achieve the same curriculum goals:

> Different students will learn the curriculum to different degrees. They will do so in different ways and use their learning for different purposes. Not everyone (so the saying goes) is going to become a rocket scientist, so why design all curriculum around the needs of budding rocketeers? The challenge for educators is to facilitate a learning environment that teaches students fundamental learning-how-to-learn skills and encourages thinking, social, and communication skills, so that students can tackle new content in ways that better their current and/or future lives. The job of educators is to refrain from the philosophical debate that pits elitists against egalitarians and to stay focused on providing all students with a rich set of learnings. (1996b, p. 228)

As such, there are several approaches to planning the curriculum that can assist teachers in individualizing curriculum, including the multilevel curriculum, curriculum overlap, and the substitute curriculum (see Table 9.9). These planning strategies directly affect the

| TABLE 9.8 | **Curriculum Concepts for Students with Disabilities** | |
|---|---|---|
| **Disability Label** | **Specific Curriculum Content** | **General Adaptations and Modifications** |
| **Mental retardation** | Attention skills<br>Memory skills<br>Functional academics (filling out job applications, learning survival words, using money, carrying on conversations)<br>Choice making<br>Learning strategies<br>Time management<br>Organizational skills<br>Generalization skills<br>Self-advocacy | Embed opportunities to practice functional life skills such as those needed to perform daily activities in home, school, work, or community environments (tying shoes, riding a bus, making the transition from one class to another, greeting people in an appropriate manner).<br>Use concrete, age-appropriate, real-life teaching materials.<br>Demonstrate new routines in a sequential manner, checking for understanding.<br>Use discrimination questions to check for understanding at each step.<br>Employ assistive technology.<br>Use visual (pointing, graphics or pictures, color) cues or auditory ("Get ready to . . . ," "Stop," "Look at me," "Listen") cues to help students work independently or to direct their own learning.<br>Use simple directions and language to communicate information.<br>Translate abstract information into something concrete that has relevance for students' lives.<br>Use if/then statements to help students explore viable alternatives to make decisions or solve their problems.<br>Use sufficient wait time (at least ten seconds) to let students organize their responses. |
| **Visual impairments** | Body image<br>Spatial concepts<br>Trailing techniques<br>Sighted guide techniques<br>Use of residual vision<br>Braille<br>Orientation and mobility skills<br>Learning strategies to acquire, remember, and demonstrate understanding of information<br>Self-advocacy | Maintain consistent class arrangements that allow for easy movement around furniture and equipment.<br>Provide large-print materials or software and/or Braille materials.<br>Provide audiotaped materials.<br>Use assistive technology devices (Perkins Braillewriter; magnifying lenses; computers with speech-to-print capabilities; Kurzweil reading machine, which scans print and reads it aloud; white board used with black or contrasting markers; talking calculators).<br>Offer manipulatives and tactile materials.<br>Provide low-glare, high-contrast-materials.<br>Use devices with audio output (clocks, calculators, scales).<br>Position students to take best advantage of natural and artificial light sources. |

*(continued)*

| TABLE 9.8 *(continued)* | | |
| --- | --- | --- |
| **Disability Label** | **Specific Curriculum Content** | **General Adaptations and Modifications** |
| **Hearing impairments** | Speech reading<br>Sign language<br>Finger spelling<br>Auditory training<br>Idiomatic expressions<br>Cultural aspects of deafness<br>Self-advocacy | Use amplification instruments (hearing aids, classroom amplification devices such as phonic ears).<br>Use speech patterns that are clear and natural, not exaggerated.<br>Face the audience when speaking and keep your whole face visible.<br>Write important information on a board or in notes provided to students.<br>Provide note-taking guides or peer note takers.<br>Use interpreters.<br>Adapt the curriculum for students with hearing impairments or deafness.<br>Use textbooks and worksheets with lower reading levels.<br>Translate abstract information into concrete forms.<br>Provide visual aids (text telephones, signaling systems such as sound or tactile doorbells, clocks, smoke alarms).<br>Use preferential seating arrangements. |
| **Specific learning disabilities** | Test-taking strategies<br>Note-taking strategies<br>Organizational skills<br>Summarizing skills<br>Mnemonic strategies<br>Learning strategies to acquire, remember, and demonstrate understanding of information<br>Self-advocacy<br>Risk taking<br>Auditory and visual perception skills<br>Communication skills<br>Problem-solving skills | Provide study guides, practice tests, textbooks to highlight, and taped books.<br>Allow alternative response forms, extra time, or alternative places to do work or take tests.<br>Use alternative grading criteria based on students' individualized goals.<br>Provide advanced organizers and cuing systems for important information.<br>Use textbooks and worksheets with lower reading levels.<br>Translate abstract information into concrete forms.<br>Organize information presented in textbooks, worksheets, testing materials, and assignments.<br>Provide visual coding of key operations and information.<br>Use evaluation alternatives that respond to the student's individual learning needs.<br>Focus on learning styles, with different mediums for presenting information, having students work with information, and assessing student outcomes.<br>Use technology such as Alpha Smarts, spell checkers. |

*(continued)*

| TABLE 9.8 | *(continued)* | |
|---|---|---|
| **Disability Label** | **Specific Curriculum Content** | **General Adaptations and Modifications** |
| **Emotional or behavioral disabilities** | Goal setting and decision making<br>Self-questioning<br>Self-monitoring<br>Self-evaluation<br>Self-adjustment<br>Self-reinforcement<br>Biofeedback<br>Language to express needs in positive ways<br>Social skills (initiating interactions, turn taking, perspective taking)<br>Anger management<br>Stress management<br>Self-advocacy | Cue students into desired performance.<br>Increase the number of times students can practice skills.<br>Model desired behaviors.<br>Expand opportunities for student choice and participation in daily decisions.<br>Structure opportunities for processing expectations and consequences with students.<br>Engage students in activities that allow them to assume control over their environments. |
| **Speech and language impairments** | Alternative and augmentative communication skills<br>Expressive language skills<br>Receptive language skills<br>Elaboration strategies<br>Remediation of speech and language problems<br>Learning strategies to acquire, remember, and demonstrate understanding of information<br>Relaxation techniques<br>Self-advocacy | Clarify and verify that messages are received correctly.<br>Use alternative communication systems (sign language, finger spelling).<br>Use augmentative communication devices and systems (individualized switch systems, hearing aids, auditory training units, voice amplification devices).<br>Use visual (pointing, graphics or pictures, color) cues or auditory ("Get ready to . . . ," "Stop," "Look at me," "Listen") cues to help students work independently or to direct their own learning.<br>Use technology (word prediction programs, alternative input methods).<br>Allow sufficient response time. |
| **Severe and multiple disabilities** | Functional academics (using money, locating items, learning survival words, sorting silverware in cafeteria)<br>Choice making (communicating preferences and honing refusal skills)<br>Self-management in environment<br>Self-care skills, especially those required within environments in which students participate<br>Social skills<br>Communication skills (initiating and sustaining interactive conversations) | Use of a variety of modes for expressive and receptive communication skills (gestures, verbal, nonverbal, augmentative, sign language, assistive technology).<br>Employ verbal, visual, or tactile cues and prompts.<br>Use systematic instruction.<br>Use natural cues.<br>Use adaptive equipment or devices (voice-activated computers, switches that allow individuals to independently activate electronic devices or reaching devices). |

*(continued)*

| TABLE 9.8 | *(continued)* | |
|---|---|---|
| **Disability Label** | **Specific Curriculum Content** | **General Adaptations and Modifications** |
| **Severe and multiple disabilities** *(cont.)* | Cause and effect<br>Leisure skills<br>Self-advocacy | Use task analysis to ensure that all steps are incorporated into systematic instruction.<br>Provide frequent feedback and reinforcement.<br>Arrange for breaks at regular intervals. |
| **Gifted and talented** | Critical and creative thinking skills<br>Research skills<br>Independent study skills<br>Self-advocacy | Integrate multiple disciplines in areas or themes of study.<br>Encourage choice through extended study activities, taking concepts in general education units and extending them by conducting in-depth studies of one or more topics of interest.<br>Provide advanced reading materials.<br>Accelerate the curriculum (through early admission to school, grade skipping, early admission to college).<br>Compress the curriculum.<br>Use mentorships or apprenticeships.<br>Provide enrichment activities. |
| **Physical disabilities** | Skills that will increase personal independence<br>Mobility, within classroom, school, home, workplace, and community environments<br>Self-care skills<br>Self-advocacy | Apply principles of proper and customized positioning and seating.<br>Make classroom materials and work areas accessible.<br>Modify the height, slant, or angle of work areas to meet individual student's needs.<br>Use materials to help stabilize work materials (tape, clamps, Velcro, suction cups).<br>Use technology and adaptive equipment (mobility aids, hand controls, arm/wrist supports, page-turning devices, modified keyboards, scanners, voice recognition programs, mouth-operated devices). |
| **Autism** | Attention skills<br>Memory skills<br>Functional academics (filling out job applications, learning survival words, using money, carrying on conversations)<br>Communication skills<br>Social interaction skills<br>Learning strategies<br>Time management<br>Organizational skills<br>Generalization skills<br>Facilitated communication | Embed opportunities to practice functional life skills in daily activities in the home, school, workplace, or community (tying shoes, riding a bus, making the transition from one class to another, greeting people in an appropriate manner).<br>Use concrete, age-appropriate, real-life teaching materials.<br>Demonstrate new routines in a sequential manner, checking for understanding at each step.<br>Use assistive technology.<br>Use visual (pointing, graphics or pictures, color) cues or auditory ("Get ready to . . . ," "Stop," "Look at me," "Listen") cues to help students work independently or to direct their own learning. |

*(continued)*

| **TABLE 9.8** | *(continued)* | |
|---|---|---|
| **Disability Label** | **Specific Curriculum Content** | **General Adaptations and Modifications** |
| **Autism** *(cont.)* | Self-advocacy | Use simple directions and language to communicate information. |
| | | Translate abstract information into something concrete that has relevance for students' lives. |
| | | Use a variety of modes for expressive and receptive communication skills (gestures, verbal, nonverbal, augmentative, alternative sign language, assistive technology). |
| | | Give verbal or manual prompts. |
| | | Provide systematic instruction. |
| | | Use natural cues. |
| | | Use adaptive equipment or devices. |
| **Deaf/blindness** | Body image | Use a variety of modes for expressive and receptive communication skills (gestures, verbal, nonverbal, augmentative, sign language, assistive technologies). |
| | Spatial concepts | |
| | Trailing techniques | |
| | Sighted guide techniques | Employ verbal, visual, or tactile cues and prompts. |
| | Use of residual vision | |
| | Braille | Use systematic instruction. |
| | Orientation and mobility skills | Use adaptive equipment or devices. |
| | Use of residual hearing | Use interpreters. |
| | Communication skills | Provide large-print or Braille materials. |
| | Sign language | Provide audiotaped materials. |
| | Finger spelling | Use assistive technology devices (Perkins Braillewriter; magnifying lenses; bright light; computers with speech-to-print capabilities; Kurzweil reading machine, which scans print and reads it aloud; white board used with black or contrasting markers; talking calculators). |
| | Auditory training | |
| | Functional academics (filling out job applications, learning survival words, using money, carrying on conversations) | |
| | | Supply manipulatives and tactile materials. |
| | Self-advocacy | Use low-glare, high-contrast paper. |
| | | Use preferential seating. |
| **Traumatic brain injury** | Test-taking strategies | Use computers for targeting the development of specific cognitive skills. |
| | Note-taking strategies | Keep instructional times short. |
| | Organizational skills | Use concrete, age-appropriate, real-life teaching materials. |
| | Summarizing skills | |
| | Mnemonic strategies | |
| | Learning strategies to acquire, remember, and demonstrate understanding of information | Demonstrate new routines in a sequential manner, checking for understanding at each step. |
| | Self-management skills | Use discrimination questions to check for understanding. |
| | Memory strategies | |

*(continued)*

| TABLE 9.8 *(continued)* | | |
| --- | --- | --- |
| **Disability Label** | **Specific Curriculum Content** | **General Adaptations and Modifications** |
| **Traumatic brain injury** *(cont.)* | Perception skills<br>Directions<br>Problem solving<br>Self-advocacy | Use assistive technology such as communication devices.<br><br>Use visual (pointing, graphics or pictures, color) cues or auditory ("Get ready to . . . ," "Stop," "Look at me," "Listen") cues to help students work independently or to direct their own learning.<br><br>Simplify directions and language used to communicate information.<br><br>Translate abstract information into something concrete that connects with students' lives.<br><br>Use advanced organizers and other strategies for aiding in organization of information.<br><br>Provide frequent breaks and rest periods as needed. |

planning of content in the classroom. Adaptations and modifications may also be required in assessment and instructional strategies.

**INDIVIDUALIZING THE CURRICULUM THROUGH THE IEP**  For students with disabilities, the IEP is a useful tool in determining curriculum adaptations and modifications (see Chapter 7). The function of the IEP is to document recommendations for (1) instructional strategies or curricular content that may not typically be represented in a student's educational experiences and (2) adaptations and modifications to existing instructional practices and curricular content (Adelman & Taylor, 1993; Falvey, Coots, Bishop, & Grenot-Scheyer, 1989). For example, when Michael was in sixth grade, his classroom teacher and special education teachers were concerned that, while he was successful in his day-to-day classroom activities, he often performed poorly on his quarterly exams. After a series of informal assessments, Michael and his teachers realized that he had few strategies for studying for those tests. After conferring with Michael's mother, they revised his IEP to include the goal that Michael would develop, use, and evaluate test-taking strategies. Although his sixth-grade teacher did not typically cover that type of information, she and Michael's special education teacher

worked together and designed a two-week mini-unit on test-taking strategies. The strategies included suggestions for skimming, determining relevant information, taking notes, and summarizing. The teacher then realized that the whole class could benefit from the information, and so she presented it to the entire sixth grade instead of arranging for Michael to have individual instruction. Michael's self-evaluation of his strategy use, in addition to his subsequent grades on quarterly exams, indicated that the unit was successful in meeting his needs.

Goals and objectives on an IEP "should be determined according to a student's unique interests, needs, and capabilities" (Falvey, 1986, p. 146). Using assessment data about a student's cognitive, affective, communicative, and physical/health needs, the IEP should set forth specific recommendations regarding both educational content and processes. For example, refer back to Table 9.5, which lists skills associated with learning needs in each of the four domain areas. Because students who receive special education services have specific learning needs that must be addressed to support their continued learning, the strategies listed in Table 9.5 become important elements of their IEPs. Review of students' IEPs can help classroom-level decision makers as they plan units of study or individualize daily lesson plans.

| TABLE 9.9 | Curriculum Approaches That Support Individual Needs | |
|---|---|---|
| **Approach** | **Description** | **Inclusive Example** |
| **Multilevel curriculum** | Using the same content focus, teachers have students working at differing levels.<br><br>This approach allows teachers to expand or enrich the curriculum or to narrow and personalize classroom content. | A unit deals with the theme of conflict. Kurume and a group of peers are exploring factors leading to major world wars. Tanya and other students are investigating a conflict at the local level involving the preservation or demolition of a building. Kirk is analyzing personal issues that impede his ability to work effectively with groups of peers. Michael is studying disability law to help explain why his mother and teachers often do not see eye to eye about his needs and supports. The concept of conflict remains the same, but the content that illustrates the concept and the relationship of that conflict to students' lives differs. Students have a choice in the products they turn in. Additionally, student products may reflect work that involves competencies at the knowledge, comprehension, application, synthesis, or evaluative levels. |
| **Curriculum overlap** | Teachers and students address more than one curriculum content area in a given activity or series of lessons.<br><br>The focus for any one student may involve one or both of the areas. | In Kirk's biology class, students are working in small groups on an experiment. For most students, the concepts and skills associated with the biology experiment are of importance. For Kirk, the opportunity to develop or practice his social skills is a secondary objective of the activity. In addition to contributing to his group's report on the experiment, Kirk has to hand in a self-evaluation of his collaborative group skills. |
| **Substitute curriculum** | Occasionally, a curriculum independent from what the majority of the group is working on may be provided to one or a small group of students.<br><br>The substitute curriculum may be delivered within similar or totally separate learning activities. | Because no other high school classes supported her needs and her peers had all mastered this skill, Annie was taken into her local community to work on using her augmentative communication system to order food and make purchases at local restaurants and department stores.<br><br>Annie participates with her classmates on writing a report on China. Annie may be expected to turn the pages of a *National Geographic* article on China while another student reads aloud about the Gobi Desert. The materials for instruction remain the same, but the expected output from students is different. Moreover, while the activity is the same, the curriculum is very different. Annie is learning to take turns, to read the language cues in a social interaction, and to develop physical strength by turning the slippery pages of glossy magazines. We are not sure if she understands the concept of China and its geography. The reader is making meaning from the text, gathering information, and culling important details for the group's report on China. These different curricular outcomes are valid because they meet the developmental and age-appropriate needs of each learner. |

**INDIVIDUALIZING THROUGH COLLABORATIVE PROBLEM SOLVING** School professionals should work collaboratively in order to ascertain the need for the nature and extent of adaptations, modifications, and devices that will support and benefit children with and without disabilities (Warger & Pugach, 1993). Recommended collaborative steps for identifying adaptations and modifications include the following:

1. Identify the learning targets for the whole class.

2. Identify the learning targets for the student in question.

3. Identify the cognitive, affective, communicative, and physical/health strengths and needs of the student (from the IEP if applicable).

4. Evaluate the cognitive, affective, communicative, and physical demands of the lessons or class activities.

5. Analyze discrepancies between student strengths and needs and the demands of the lessons or class activities.

6. Examine the range of choices for adaptations and modifications in content, assessment, or instructional strategies, and match those options to student needs.

7. Institute an evaluation plan to ensure that the strategy worked (Filbin, 1994; Ford, Toshner, & Fitzgerald, 1994; Stainback & Stainback, 1992; Udvari-Solner, 1995).

It is important that decisions to adapt and modify curriculum be based on individual student cognitive, affective, communicative, and physical/health needs.

School professionals should be leery of "recipe" approaches to adaptations and modifications. For example, one text recommends that, when a student has a problem with math, school professionals should provide the student with a calculator. But unless you assess the nature of the student's problems with math, you have no way of knowing whether a calculator would be of any assistance whatsoever. If the student is having problems with, say, long division, many cognitive and affective dimensions should be considered. Cognitively, the student may (1) lack a conceptual understanding of the nature and purpose of long division, (2) forget the procedural steps in doing long division, (3) lack accuracy in computing basic arithmetic facts, or (4) fail to employ self-monitoring and self-regulation strategies

to remediate execution or organizational errors in long division. In the affective domain, the student may have a long history of problems in the subject and so bring a sense of hopelessness or lack of interest to the task. And for all of these particular problems, a calculator may be of assistance in only one—lack of accuracy in computing basic math facts. It requires the collective skills of school professionals, support personnel, students, and family members to effectively determine the need for and the extent to which we employ curriculum adaptation and modification strategies.

## ■ SECTION SUMMARY

Inclusive school communities must create overarching curriculum frameworks that can then be tailored to accommodate the needs of individual learners. Accommodations must attend to the affective, cognitive, communicative, and physical/health needs of students and recognize that students' learning needs extend beyond the classroom or school to their home and community environments. Increasing the capacities of schools so that they can better accommodate diverse student characteristics and provide instructional interventions that improve every student's ability to choose from a menu of experiences is the primary goal (Wang, 1989).

## Chapter Summary

Upon completing a historical review of the traditions and legislation that have guided our nation's educational system, Goodlad (1984) offered the following conclusion:

*The charge to public schools emerging from these complex, connected developments is formidable. First, they are to provide free elementary and secondary education in a "common" school embracing grades one through twelve, or in many states, kindergarten through grade twelve. Second, they are to utilize every possible means to assure optimum access to this expanded common school for an increasingly diverse student population. Third, each school is to both provide a reasonably comprehensive program of studies and assure a balance of academic, vocational, social, and personal instruction for each student. Fourth, each school is to provide such special instructional provisions as are needed to assure that individual differences, particularly those stemming from economic, and racial or ethnic circumstances, will interfere minimally with access to such a program. Equality and quality are the name of the game. These two concepts will frame dialogue, policy, and practice regarding schooling for years to come. (p. 45)*

Goodlad captures what we have maintained throughout this book—that our schools are faced with the challenge of providing comprehensive educational services to an increasingly diverse population of students. Philosophically, as stated in Chapter 1, we must incorporate and capitalize on this diversity in order for our

educational system to respond to the social, political, and economic agendas of the future. By answering the questions that were posed in Box 9.1, you are well on your way to being able to create curricula in inclusive school communities. By combining the skills of general and special education school professionals, students, their families, and community members, we are in a unique position to work collaboratively to design and implement curricula for diverse student populations. When the curriculum is open and flexible, the need for highly individualized or separate curricular structures is decreased. Instead, the resources that have traditionally been used to separate general and special education can be combined to increase the opportunities for students to learn from one another in inclusive classrooms.

---

**INSTRUCTIONAL ACTIVITY**

## Creating Your Own School

### Objectives

- Through a cooperative learning activity, to apply the seven elements of building-level curriculum decisions in creating a vision, goals, learning outcomes, standards, curriculum frameworks, standards for professional practice, and the organizational structures of a new school
- To communicate elements of the new school through a school brochure

### Materials

- Desktop publishing and graphic design technologies

### Product

- A school brochure that communicates a vision, goals, desired learning outcomes, standards, curriculum frameworks, standards for professional practice, and the school's organizational structures

### Agenda

- Your instructor will divide you into groups of no more than five persons.
- Imagine that you have just been elected to serve on a team to create a new school in your local neighborhood. One of your first official jobs is to plan the curriculum of your school. Using the seven elements of building-level curriculum decisions as suggested by Kniep and Martin-Kniep (1995), create a brochure that communicates how your school will approach curriculum.
- Work in or out of class to plan each element and how it will be presented on the brochure. Feel free to use clip art and other creative design features.

### Evaluation

- All of the information should fit on one piece of paper, set in brochure style using a one- or two-fold format.
- Graphics and copy must be consistent with the vision and goals of the school, and there must be coherence among each of the seven elements.
- Optional: Once all brochures have been developed, class members should vote on which school they would send their own children.

# Glossary

**Cognitive taxonomies** Classification models used to categorize differing cognitive skills or mental operations.

**Cooperative learning** A teaching strategy that involves placing students in groups whose members are expected to work together to carry out a task or assignment. Often, members fill a role such as timekeeper or recorder to assist the group in its task.

**Peer tutoring** Students teaching each other.

**Precision teaching** A precise method of accounting for how information is presented to students and how teachers respond to the correct and incorrect performances of students.

**Process instruction** Instruction that targets teaching students processes or procedures in addition to traditional content—for example, test-taking strategies, note taking, outlining, decision making, goal setting, and problem solving.

**Task analysis** A process whereby a task or activity is broken down into smaller steps or procedures.

## CHAPTER 10

# Developing Instructional Strategies for Diverse Learners

# Interview with a Student with Learning Disabilities

Amber, 16, goes to a school where the teachers provide a good model for ways of individualizing instruction for each student. Although Amber receives no special education services now, she was assessed and determined to be eligible for special education services in her previous school. However, Amber did not want to go to special education because the only service option offered to her was in a self-contained classroom. Along with her parents, she decided to go to a school that advertised itself as a place where all students could learn. Here, the classroom teachers assume responsibility for teaching both the content and the strategies that Amber needs to learn. The following interview was audiotaped and transcribed. In it, Amber discusses her own learning process and what teachers have done that has helped her to learn.

*Interviewer:* Tell me some of the things your teachers do that help you be an effective learner.

*Amber:* Well, we start the year by studying our own learning processes. I am a relater and a visual learner. So I get along better if I work in groups, relate ideas, and make pictures of what I learn. I don't learn as easily auditorally, so things I hear go in one ear and out the other. This is how they taught in my last school. They had lectures which just don't stick to me. So now, after I read a chapter or listen to a lecture, I use something we call "pegs"—to draw pictures.

*Interviewer:* Will you explain how this peg system works for you?

*Amber:* Well, when we studied the Bill of Rights, I used it to remember each of the rights. For example, the first one is a picture of a Jewish man holding a pen. That kicks off peg 1 and reminds me of freedom of religion. Then, he's signing a dog—that stands for freedom to petition. He's on an ironing board and that stands for freedom of the press. Peg 4—a guy standing with his hands on a car—a policeman putting on a glove that stands for freedom from unwarranted search and seizure. Peg 6 is a man driving in a car with a six-pack of beer (which stands for peg 6) and he's speeding, there's a sign that says "trial at work" so it stands for a speedy trial. Peg 10 is a girl standing in the state holding a balloon, which stands for the one and the zero and that stands for states' rights.

*Interviewer:* I notice here in your notes that you have written a strange word. What does this word—"oobleck"—mean?

*Amber:* That's an experiment we did during physical science. We had to do experiments with this stuff called "oobleck" to figure out what the qualities of the oobleck were, and we had to make a report about the oobleck. We worked in groups, and each of us took responsibility for certain parts of the report—like, I took the part about how it reacted to physical touch, like when we hit it, or gently touched it.

*Interviewer:* So, how were you able to discover the properties of the oobleck? How did you know what to try?

*Amber:* Well, the teacher gave us guidelines about what to try each day. One day we tried various acids, and the next day we tried bases, and we recorded the re-

actions each of those things had on a chart.

*Interviewer:* Did each group member have a chart?

*Amber:* No, the group had a chart, and we each had to contribute to the information by observing and using our own words to describe what we saw, smelled, felt, or heard.

*Interviewer:* Would you have been able to discover the things you did on your own, if the teacher hadn't told you what experiment to do that day? What would have happened if your teacher had just given you the stuff and told you to figure out what it was?

*Amber:* I probably wouldn't have learned as much as I did.

*Interviewer:* What made the difference?

*Amber:* Group activities helped the most, trying to figure out the one thing the teacher assigned, so we could all focus on the one thing and get different opinions from all different people. Kids have all different ways of thinking and seeing things.

*Interviewer:* When you're working in a group, does it help you to hear what the other kids are thinking, or is it distracting?

*Amber:* Oh, it helps. It helps to know what other people are thinking 'cause therefore you can combine them together and go further instead of just staying with one opinion. When you go together, you both have opinions you can work on and you can go further than you can go by yourself.

*Interviewer:* Did you ever find yourself saying, "Oh, I never looked at it that way!"

*Amber:* Oh, yeah! All the time. You go, "I never thought of that. My brain doesn't do that."

*Interviewer:* When you would do the discovery activities, did you have a worksheet to fill out, or did the group have to fill out a paper, or did you just say an answer out loud, or how did the teacher know you had stayed on task?

*Amber:* We wouldn't have worksheets, but we would have a hypothesis, an experimental part and a conclusion. Sometimes we had a group paper. Other times we had our own paper that we had to compare with other people and get their ideas. Then you just have to write it up yourself. Mine came out a little different than some, but everybody went through and said, "Maybe you held yours in there longer."

*Interviewer:* So, you hypothesized why your answers were a little different than others' answers? Wasn't it cheating to compare your answers with your group mates' answers?

*Amber:* No, it wasn't cheating. The teacher told us to ask each other about why our answers might be the same or different.

*Interviewer:* Did you get individual grades or group grades on these?

*Amber:* Sometimes individual and sometimes group grades.

*Interviewer:* Which do you like better?

*Amber:* Group grades, because you can work together and succeed together and get better grades.

*Interviewer:* What happened if one group member didn't contribute? Or what if they just sat back and let everyone else in the group do all the work? What happened to your grade?

*Amber:* That did happen sometimes. You know, all different kinds of people go to our school. Some kids just don't care as much about learning, and they would just sit around and act cool.

*Interviewer:* So, what did you do about it?

*Amber:* First, we would go, "Hey, ah . . . it's your turn to contribute." And if they didn't, then we would go talk to the teacher. The teacher would talk to the student. The teacher walks around stopping by all the groups to check on everybody, anyhow. But then the teacher would talk to the student to find out what was going on.

*Interviewer:* What about a subject that's really hard for you—reading?

Amber: I can always use the peg system when I'm reading literature. I always do that to help myself remember what I've read. I have a lot of trouble with reading comprehension. But, if I make notes and pictures, it helps me remember. There are a few other things that I should tell you about that also help me. One is "THRILD." When you use THRILD what you do is for the T you read the title of a chapter, then for H you read all the headings, for R you read the first paragraph, for I you look at the illustrations, L stands for reading the last paragraph, and D for discuss the ideas. Another method I've learned to use when I'm reading someone else's opinion is the meaning "TEST." That's where I ask myself these questions: First, what does the person mean—what is the other person's point of view? Then I go through TEST. T stands for true. Is the argument true? Are there

errors of thinking? Like that. Then E stands for evidence. I look to see if they used any ways of backing up what they say. Then S stands for "So what," or what are the implications of the argument? Finally, T is for take, so I take a look at the outcomes of the argument. Another thing I do is use a pencil to trace very lightly under the line I'm reading. It helps me keep my place and not get the lines mixed up. I also make little notes in the margin by using "ACID." A lot of times you get a literature book that has light pencil marks and notes from other people in the margin. See, as I read along I put an A if I agree with what it says, a C if I'm confused, I if I think it's interesting, and D if I disagree with what it says.

*Interviewer:* Tell me about some of the things that will help you be a more independent learner when you go to college. Will you be able to independently apply these methods—the peg system, the ways of organizing your ideas, taking margin notes, what you know about how you learn best—when you go to college?

*Amber:* Oh, yes. Now that I know how to do these methods, I can always use them whenever I need them. I don't need any special accommodation from a professor to do that now that I know how to do it.

*Interviewer:* But will you use them? Some kids think that the kinds of techniques you describe are just too much work.

*Amber:* Well, I need them or I don't learn it very well. You see, I'm a relater, and I have to be able to relate everything to something else or it just doesn't stick. I've learned how to use these things and now I just automatically do.

# Introduction

Teaching requires a thorough understanding of learners through accurate assessment, careful selection of curricular content, and competent implementation of instruction. Several national groups working on standards for various teaching and related-services personnel reinforce this notion. Groups such as the National Board for Teaching Standards, the Council for Exceptional Children, and the Interstate New Teacher Assessment and Support Consortium have developed standards that reflect the belief that teaching requires knowledge of the students and their individual needs and of the interaction among content, instruction, assessment, environment, and resources. These types of standards apply regardless of whether you are preparing to be a special education teacher, a general education teacher, an early childhood specialist, a school psychologist, or other related-services personnel. In concert with other chapters in this text, this chapter proceeds from the perspective that good teaching is good teaching and that the instructional environment is a key element in teaching.

Throughout Part Two, which translates theory into practice, we have maintained that opportunities to learn occur as a result of the interaction among the classroom context, assessment, curriculum, and instruction. Chapters 6–9 explored the dynamic relationships among the classroom environment, assessment, and curriculum. This chapter addresses the instructional environment. As Figure 10.1 shows, the instructional environment is dynamic, with planning, implementing, and assessing continuously occurring elements in the instructional cycle. As school professionals reflect on each element of the cycle, they are able to improve the opportunities for learning in the classroom. Learning needs are revealed through the dynamic interaction of the cognitive, affective, communicative, and physical domains. And learning outcomes point the way to future instructional activity based on individuals' needs. Box 10.1 lists questions that reflective teachers ask as they construct the instructional environment.

Inclusive school communities and their classrooms are places where diversity abounds. When you think about providing instruction to a classroom full of diverse students—taking into account the needs discussed in Chapter 5, as well as cultural and linguistic diversity—the answers to the questions in Box 10.1 involve complex issues. These questions, and others like them, start you on the path to informed decisions about how you make the curriculum accessible and

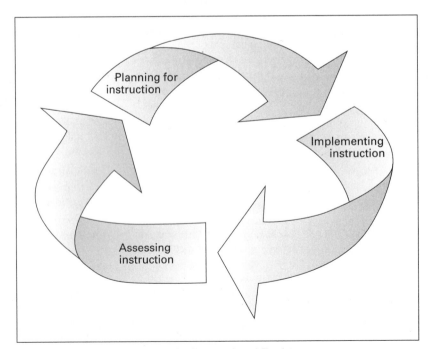

**FIGURE 10.1** ■ Constructing the Instructional Environment

**BOX 10.1**

## Questions That Reflective Teachers Ask

1. How can we meet the needs of all our students?

2. How can we be strategic in the way that we plan for the individual needs of all students?

3. What types of instructional methods will address the needs of our students?

4. Are our instructional approaches helping students reach important school and curriculum outcomes?

meaningful for all your students. They also help to keep you focused on the long-term outcomes of schooling that we outlined in Chapter 1: (1) exercising choice and self-determination, (2) pursuing lifelong learning, (3) participating in school and neighborhood communities, (4) supporting families, and (5) achieving economic security and productivity. In Chapter 1, we also discussed how, organizationally, inclusive school communities should operate as adhocracies, in which groups of people work collaboratively to solve problems of practice. The processes of designing, implementing, and evaluating instruction involve various school professionals, support personnel, students, families, and community members.

Think of this chapter as a compass that will provide direction for your selection and use of appropriate instructional methods for students. Like a compass that is set for true north, your instructional path should be guided by targeted learning outcomes. The families of instruction discussed here can be analyzed and selected based on the learning principles in Chapter 5. As you head out in the direction of your learning outcomes, you will ask yourself many questions. For instance, do your instructional strategies support the development of self-regulated learning (a facet of self-determination)? Do your instructional strategies give all students meaningful opportunities for task engagement? Do these strategies relate to your curriculum goals? When observers look into your classroom, are students like Annie, Tanya, Michael, Kurume, and Kirk engaged in meaningful tasks alongside their classmates? Have you considered the cognitive and metacognitive needs of

your learners? Have you addressed their motivational and affective needs? Did you consider the developmental and social issues that your students bring to the teaching/learning process? Do you understand the individual differences that exist among your students?

Too often, school professionals and community members assume that instruction involves the use of a few tried-and-true techniques. But we argue, along with other researchers, that "business as usual" has not worked and will not work for increasingly diverse groups of students (Carbo, 1996; Slavin, 1996; Villa & Thousand, 1995). Thus, even experienced teachers will find themselves adopting unfamiliar methods of instruction that better match the needs of their current group of students. Managing the instructional environment is a complex task that begins with an understanding of the nature of each learner and the content to be taught. Because instruction in the classroom involves all class members in various configurations— from the whole class working on the same activity to individual learners focused on their own projects—we discuss techniques that work with large and small groups and with individuals.

When it comes time to choose instructional strategies, you have many options. One of the purposes of this chapter is to provide you with information and a set of guidelines to assist you in instructional decision making. First, to help organize your understanding, we provide information on three families of instruction. The "family" organization is useful because each family emerges from different theoretical foundations and targets different functions of the learning process. It's important to choose methods and apply techniques from each of these families, because they work in concert to address the cognitive, affective, communicative, and physical/health needs of students. Next, we examine the process of matching learner needs, content, and instructional strategies. Finally, because our best plans and implementation may or may not result in reaching the targets that we intend, we discuss how to evaluate instruction in order to make the necessary adjustments and modifications.

## Families of Instruction

In this section, we review three approaches to structuring learning opportunities. Like Joyce, Weil, and Showers (1992), we call these approaches "families of instructional models." These families include the social, behavioral, and information-processing families. The distinctions that we make among these three families are based primarily on their respective theoretical bases and on the domain areas that are emphasized through their use in classrooms. Theoretical explanations for why these approaches may be beneficial for learning range from behavioral orientations to social constructivist views. However, none of these approaches are mutually exclusive, nor are they necessarily competing (Good & Brophy, 1994). In fact, in inclusive school communities, given students' diverse learning preferences and needs, school professionals must draw on strategies from all three families as they plan, implement, and evaluate instruction (Stone & Reid, 1994).

Currently, technology can be used to support social, information processing, and behavioral approaches to learning opportunities. For example, from a social perspective, interactive technologies involve teachers and learners in the development of computer-assisted modeling, creation of linked hypertext (see Box 10.2), and dialog and problem solving through the Internet.

As you read these overviews about the families of instruction, think about the types of curriculum goals that might be a good match with strategies from each family. More than likely, when you plan instruction, you will choose strategies that fall in one or more of these approaches in order to respond to student needs and accomplish your curriculum targets. In fact, in a recent discussion of effective reading instruction, Harris and Graham (1996) elaborate on how and why strategies from both the social, information processing, and behavioral families must be used in concert in order to provide for the needs of all students.

## The Social Family

The social family of instructional models has allegiance to the work of social constructivists. Social constructivists subscribe to the following tenets of learning:

- Knowledge is constructed and continuously reconstructed by individual and groups of learners.

- Cognitive and affective domains are inextricably linked.

- Reflection on problems of the physical and social world is critical to the construction of knowledge.

---

**BOX 10.2**

### What Is Hypertext?

Hypertext is a body of text and graphics that can be connected and read in a nonlinear manner, permitting readers to move from topic to topic based on their personal interests and needs. For example, a local special education teacher developed a hypertext program for creating IEPs. She wrote the program so that, when she reached certain components on the form, she could access detailed information on that section. For instance, in one section of an IEP, she was supposed to list the student's cognitive strengths and needs. With a click of a button, she was able to bring up a series of screens that allowed her to look up information on attention, perception, memory, and so on. In addition, she could access screens that gave her examples of student behaviors that indicated strengths or weaknesses for each cognitive component.

---

- Understanding the perspectives of others is important to our own understanding of the world.

According to social constructivists, learners reconstruct what they see or experience in the world, with experiences mediated first between people and then internally, through an individual's cognitions (Vygotsky, 1978). Because of this dual-stage process, the social family of instructional approaches is based on creating active, meaningful learning opportunities in which interpersonal interactions precipitate the construction of internal, mental schemata. The social family of instructional approaches supports learning through the cognitive, affective, and communicative domains.

In addition to learning theory, the social family is connected to philosophies that promote the application of democratic principles to schooling (Dewey, 1916). These educational philosophers suggest that the essence of democracy is the negotiation of problem definitions and solutions. Classrooms provide a natural opportunity for students to practice the principles of democracy through shared decision making and collaborative learning activities. As a result, students are prepared in school to assume future responsibilities of citizenship.

In the social family, the role of the teacher is conceptualized in terms of responsibility for structuring learning opportunities and then facilitating and coaching students through those experiences. The role of the student is conceptualized in terms of responsibility for active mediation of his or her own and others' learning. Social constructivists promote learning as a natural process that is active, volitional, and internally mediated. Additionally, social constructivists view the learner as an active participant in the creation of meaningful, coherent representations of knowledge.

## SOCIAL FAMILY INSTRUCTIONAL APPROACHES

There are many instructional approaches that find their home within the social family. These approaches include, but are not limited to, cooperative learning, peer-mediated instruction, peer tutoring, group investigation, role play, jurisprudential inquiry, and activity-based projects. Cooperative learning groups are distinguished from other types of groupings in the social family by five components: (1) positive interdependence, (2) face-to-face interaction, (3) individual accountability, (4) interpersonal and small-group skills, and (5) group processing (Johnson, Johnson, & Holubec, 1991). Plans for cooperative lessons must attend to each of these five elements, as well as to specific academic and social objectives. With activity-based projects, students engage actively in learning experiences that require them to solve problems and think critically. Activity-based instruction can involve research-based projects, field trips, experimentation, or internships. Peer-mediated learning shares many features of cooperative learning; however, it typically holds individuals rather than groups accountable for grading purposes. With role play, students dramatize a situation, for a variety of purposes. Role play can be used (1) to evaluate students' conceptual understandings of events, phenomena, and problem-solving strategies in many subject areas; (2) to teach routines and procedures; and (3) to develop and practice interpersonal skills (Goldstein, 1988).

There are many variations on these approaches found in the social family—for example, informal and formal cooperative learning techniques. Informal cooperative groups are temporary, ad hoc groups that form for anywhere from a few minutes to an entire class period. In contrast, formal cooperative learning groups last longer—from one class period to several weeks of instruction focused on one specific task or project. In Appendix 10.1, we describe variations on cooperative learning and peer-mediated approaches to

learning, along with ideas about when to apply these strategies.

**BENEFITS OF STRATEGIES WITHIN THE SOCIAL FAMILY** Proponents of inclusive school communities advocate increased use of strategies within the social family when working with students from diverse ethnic, linguistic, cultural, socioeconomic, and ability backgrounds (Alper, Schloss, Etscheidt, & Macfarlane, 1995; Krich, 1994; Udvari-Solner & Thousand, 1995). Research on the use of strategies within the social family with students who have diverse learning needs provides evidence of several benefits. For example, research on cooperative learning indicates that use of this model (1) results in higher academic achievement (Slavin, 1990; Slavin & Karweit, 1985), (2) promotes active learning (Johnson & Johnson, 1989), and (3) develops social skills (Putnam, Rynders, Johnson, & Johnson, 1989). Research indicates that activity-based learning and a focus on higher-order thinking skills result in increased comprehension and the development of skills in the areas of analysis, synthesis, and evaluation across subject area content such as math, social studies, science, and reading (Anderson & Roth, 1989; Blumenfeld, 1992; Hiebert & Wearne, 1992; Savoie & Hughes, 1994; Slavin, Madden, Dolan, & Wasik, 1994). Peer-mediated activities, like those listed in Appendix 10.1, may be incorporated into traditional, lecture-type, individualistic, or competitive lessons, in any subject area, and address multiple domain areas simultaneously. For example, in one study, students with and without disabilities were put in reciprocal peer-teaching pairs. These pairs engaged in three reading activities typically addressed during teacher-directed instruction: (1) partner reading with retell, (2) paragraph summary, and (3) prediction relay. The study indicated that reading achievement was highest among students involved in the peer-teaching classroom as compared to students in a control group who received their instruction in the typical fashion (Fuchs, Fuchs, Mathes, & Simmons, 1997). Equally important, the power of peer teaching is that it engages each learner as an active participant in the learning process and provides significantly more opportunities to respond (Delquadri, Greenwood, Whorton, Carta, & Hall, 1986; Gartner & Riessman, 1994). Furthermore, studies that have incorporated peer teaching activities for students with and without disabilities have concluded that academic achievement is enhanced for all learners.

In the chapter-opening interview, Amber comments on the positive effects of cooperative learning: "It helps to know what other people are thinking 'cause you can combine them together and go further instead of just staying with one opinion. When you go together, you both have opinions you can work on." Amber's point is that cooperative work among peers provides opportunities for them to model for one another and thus expand their individual repertoires of problem-solving strategies.

**THE USE OF TECHNOLOGY IN THE SOCIAL FAMILY** In the social family, technology becomes another way for students to construct meaning from their experiences with others. Computers provide a medium for the social construction of knowledge that we are just beginning to understand. By learning to program in hypertext, students have a vehicle for creating their own models or schemata of knowledge through the way they link hypertext together. Communicating with other computer users around the world via e-mail and the Internet provides new access to information and social interaction. One advantage of this social interaction is that it may not be bound by the usual judgments that individuals make about one another based on social class, culture, gender, and ethnicity (Herring, 1993).

## The Behavioral Family

Instructional models in the behavioral family are also based on a set of principles and beliefs about the way that learning occurs. Behaviorists believe that behavior—and in this case, learning—is lawful and responsive to structure, organization, and feedback from the environment. Recall that reinforcement, modeling, and antecedents (stimuli) can be used to shape students' behaviors (see Chapter 6). These same conditions can be varied in order to teach academic skills. Therefore, instructional models in the behavioral family provide teachers with strategies to structure, organize, and provide feedback within learning opportunities. For example, to help structure learning opportunities, behavioral models incorporate task analysis to break down what is to be taught into small, sequentially ordered steps that specify requisite skills in the task to be learned. Recall from Chapter 9 that task analysis begins with the learning target and then iden-

A young girl receives hand-over-hand prompting from her mother to learn some basic play skills.

tifies the component skills or knowledge required to meet that target. Once the learning target is established, the process of delineating the components is relatively easy if the task analyzer has a grasp of the subject or skill area.

Behavioral approaches to teaching and learning focus on the activities of the teacher in ensuring that learning occurs. For example, teachers can vary antecedents and consequences for behavior by (1) providing a model of the learning target, (2) prompting or assisting the learner to perform the target, or (3) modifying the materials used to achieve the learning target (Wolery, Bailey, & Sugai, 1988). Behavioral approaches are prescriptive in specifying what teachers should do before, during, and after instruction occurs, which helps explain their wide appeal.

**BEHAVIORAL FAMILY INSTRUCTIONAL APPROACHES** Many teaching techniques apply principles from the behavioral family, including mastery learning, direct instruction, **discrete trial**, and prescriptive teaching. Here, we focus on mastery learning and direct instruction. The tenets of **mastery learning** are basic: (1) Criteria for mastery of any task are specified; (2) students are informed of teachers' objectives; (3) teachers must use diagnostic tools to understand what learners still need to master and intervene at that point; and (4) teachers provide specific feedback and opportunities to reteach information until it is mastered.

Mastery learning proponents suggest that time, not individual ability, is the key variable in ensuring that students achieve mastery. From the perspective of mastery learning proponents, when time and instructional methods are made constant, some students will fail, most students will make progress, and a few students will achieve mastery. Mastery learning is based on the premise that, given enough time, almost all learners can achieve competent performance or mastery of a learning task (Bloom, Madaus, & Hastings, 1981). According to this view, Michael, Kurume, and Kirk might all be able to write persuasive arguments for and against the use of nuclear power. However, the time that it takes each student to accomplish this target will differ. The amount of time that it takes learners to reach competent performance levels can be increased or decreased by the use of instructional techniques that are matched to the needs of individuals.

Direct instruction is a second member of the behavioral family. Here, direct instruction refers to a systematic, teacher-directed instructional strategy. But the term can also be framed as Direct Instruction—"a comprehensive system that integrates curriculum design with teaching techniques to produce instructional programs in language, reading, mathematics, spelling, written expression, and science" (Tarver, 1992, p. 141). While the conceptions and definitions of direct instruction are varied and not altogether mutually exclusive (see a review by Kameenui, Jitendra, & Darch, 1995), essentially direct instruction is a teacher-guided method of teaching and Direct Instruction is an instructional design system.

Direct instruction can be used to deliver instruction to an individual or to groups of students. Typically, direct instruction consists of breaking a skill or concept down into component steps or parts, teaching those steps to a student or group of students, involving students in controlled application of the concepts or skills,

---

**BOX 10.3**

## Steps in Direct Instruction Procedure

1. Motivate students by linking lesson objective to at least one of three rationale:
   a. the importance of achieving success on the task because of personal needs fulfillment.
   b. the intrinsic enjoyment of the task—fun, opportunities for socialization, reflection, and so on.
   c. utility value—task success will be a step toward a future goal.
2. Provide a model of the performance or product.
3. Isolate and teach the steps in the performance or product development:
   a. check for understanding of each step.
   b. assure that students can perform each step.
4. Provide guided practice.
5. Provide independent practice.
6. Assess and reteach (if necessary).

---

and scheduling further practice through independent seatwork or out-of-classroom homework. Box 10.3 summarizes the steps of a direct instruction procedure.

**BENEFITS OF STRATEGIES WITHIN THE BEHAVIORAL FAMILY** To help teachers organize their work, behavioral models use strategies like modeling, prompting, and **shaping** to transform approximations of desired outcomes into an accurate performance. "Shaping consists of reinforcing successive approximations or improved 'attempts' at the target response" (Snell, 1994, p. 131). The following example illustrates the use of shaping to teach new behaviors. Initially, Annie's mother gave her a drink of water each time she put her hand near her mouth. Then she made the reward (having a drink) a little more difficult to get, so that Annie could only get a drink when she moved her hand near her mouth and shaped her hand into a cuplike shape. Finally, when Annie had mastered both the arm movement and the hand shape, her mother raised the target once more. Now, Annie could only get her drink when her hand in the cuplike shape actually touched her lips. Performance tasks like writing, reading out loud with youngsters, and pausing while they

| TABLE 10.1 | Drill-and-Practice Software That Helps Develop Language Skills |
|---|---|

**Apple Learning Series: Early Language**

- Provides practice in letter, number, shape, and color recognition and the matching of upper- and lowercase letters.
- Teaches the concept of one-to-one correspondence.
- Uses voice synthesizers to develop letter/sound correspondence.
- Teaches writing and composition skills through word processing and programs that allow children to hear the letters, words, and sentences they've written.

Source: Drexler, Harvey, & Kell, 1990.

say one of the words in a sentence and physical tasks like skipping rope are often taught by successive approximations. As is evident in the use of rewards for Annie's use of new behaviors, systematic, consistent feedback is a hallmark of instructional models within the behavior family.

A number of researchers have promoted the practices of direct instruction for teaching math, reading, strategy skills (test taking, studying, problem solving, and so on), and academic learning (Carnine, Silbert, & Kameenui, 1990; Deshler & Ellis, 1995; Gersten, Woodward, & Carnine, 1987; Gersten, Woodward, & Darch, 1986; Harris & Graham, 1996; Kameenui & Simmons, 1990; Lovitt, 1995). These researchers have shown that, for many students, with and without disabilities, who face challenges in learning, behavior, and/or social/emotional development, structured, explicit, direct forms of instruction help to develop skills, processes, strategies, and understandings. For students with the most significant needs, direct instruction procedures like the discrete trial format have been shown to result in the development of skills for daily living (bathing, brushing teeth), communication acquisition (greeting others, requesting help), transportation in the community (bus riding), and academic tasks (writing names, selecting printed materials) (Snell, 1994).

**THE USE OF TECHNOLOGY IN THE BEHAVIORAL FAMILY** Because computer software provides consistent, immediate feedback and endless repetitions, it can offer intense, individualized support to students who need practice, repetition, and clear feedback. Consistent with instructional models in the behavioral family, technology can be used to reinforce skills or to introduce content by providing one-on-one direct instruction through carefully sequenced learning software.

*Reinforcing Skills* Drill-and-practice activities on the computer help students develop automaticity with math facts, spelling words, definitions, sight vocabulary, and other declarative knowledge. Approximately 85 to 90 percent of computer use in schools focuses on drill and practice (Wirth, 1993). Although drill and practice represents a primitive use of computers, drill-and-practice software is a patient tutor (see Table 10.1). When Michael used a computer in elementary school, he liked the way the computer afforded him the privacy to correct his mistakes and to monitor his own progress. It did not seem like work to him; no one saw his mistakes, and he could try the same problem over and over again until he got it right. He also found it motivating to try to beat his high score from the previous session.

*Introducing Content* Computers are effective tutors for introducing certain content through a combination of graphics, text, and exercises. They provide immediate feedback to the person at the keyboard. For example, Kirk took high school accounting and used a computer to learn about the concept of "depreciation." The program first gave him the definition "depreciation = cost/expected life" and then asked questions like "If a bread-making machine costs $300 and is expected to last 6 years, what is the annual depreciation?" In response to the answer "$50," the computer would say, "Good," and go on to the next problem or concept. If Kirk had typed "$30," he might have been told, "Sorry, but you're probably not ready to work for H&R Block. Thirty dollars would be the depreciation if the machine lasted 10 years. To find annual depreciation for a machine that lasts 6 years, divide the cost by the expected life of 6. Please type the correct answer." Hassett (1986) described this program as one example of how computer tutorials can adapt without being redundant. Thus, if Kirk had already understood the concept of depreciation, the computer would have moved him on to the next concept. This feature allows faster students to move ahead while providing additional help for students who need it.

## The Information Processing Family

The information processing family of instructional models is based on an understanding of how we think that is both a metaphor (the brain as a computer) and a description of internal cognitive mechanisms (Swanson & Watson, 1990). In Chapter 5, we explored information processing in detail in the section on the cognitive domain. Here, we will merely remind you that the information that an individual acts on moves through several processes (attention, perception, working and long-term memory, executive control) so that it can become part of the individual's knowledge bank. Also, information and skills can be thought of as one of three types: declarative, procedural, or conditional. Instructional models that account for these different ways of knowing **scaffold,** or provide support to, learners as they process information and develop competent performance levels (see Box 10.4).

Instructional models within the information processing family are concerned with how children know about their learning and how they know how to know (Brown & Campione, 1986). Because learning involves making associations between new and previous understandings and experiences, instruction must develop students' thinking and self-regulation skills. Self-regulation refers to the degree to which individuals are metacognitively, motivationally, and behaviorally active participants in their own learning process (Zimmerman, 1986). Instructional models within the information processing family address one or more functions. For example, some models help to teach students to think critically about issues, performances, and theories and to predict events across content or disciplines. Other models teach the procedures involved in global and task-specific learning skills.

To teach students how to think and be more strategic in their learning, teachers must structure, direct, model, and facilitate overt opportunities for students to develop, use, and evaluate their own critical thinking and learning strategies. Through instructional

### BOX 10.4
### What Is Scaffolding?

Scaffolding refers to forms of temporary and adjustable supports that teachers give students that help students move from their current abilities to the intended goal (Monda-Amaya & Pearson, 1996; Rosenshine & Meister, 1992). Forms of supports can include prompts, cues, questions, error analyses, metaphors, elaboration, and cognitive modeling (as a teacher models the task, he or she talks out loud, sharing his or her own thinking). For example, if you are helping students learn to read, you might summarize the main ideas, remind them to use strategies for developing and monitoring their comprehension (identifying key ideas, summarizing, taking notes, questioning themselves), or provide them with an advanced organizer (Good & Brophy, 1994). Use of scaffolding allows students to engage in complex tasks that they might not otherwise be able to manage on their own, until they can understand how to do it and when to apply it (Monda-Amaya & Pearson, 1996).

models based on the information processing family, students are taught to direct and manage their own learning. This means that students not only set goals for their own learning but also assume responsibility for attending to the internal regulation of their learning processes. Recall Amber from the chapter-opening interview. Amber's teachers helped her understand that it would be easier for her to learn when information was presented visually and when she overtly related new information to her existing knowledge base. They provided many strategies to support Amber's needs. Now that Amber is equipped with these skills and, more importantly, understands how these strategies help her to be a more competent learner, Amber is prepared to direct her own learning and to advocate for her own learning needs.

**INFORMATION PROCESSING FAMILY INSTRUCTIONAL APPROACHES** Common instructional approaches in the information processing family include critical thinking, **concept attainment,** memory strategies, advanced organizers, inquiry training, cognitive behavior modification, reciprocal learning, strategy instruction, and scaffolding. Here, we focus on three:

critical thinking, advanced organizers, and strategy instruction.

*Critical Thinking*  Thinking critically is a complex, higher-order thinking process that is essential in developing the capacity of learners to gather and act upon information independently. Critical thinking skills include prediction, analysis, analogical reasoning, and evaluation. For students to be successful critical thinkers, they need skills in forming concepts, comparing and contrasting, recognizing micro- and macro-level patterns, and synthesizing information. Some approaches to teaching critical thinking require students to engage in increasingly complex thinking processes; other models in the information processing family influence the ways in which students retrieve, store, connect, extrapolate, evaluate, and make decisions about information (Marzano, Brandt, Hughes, Jones, Presseisen, Rankin, & Suhor, 1988).

*Advanced Organizers*  The use of advanced organizers is an instructional strategy that supports the presentation of new information to students. Think of advanced organizers as cognitive maps that help learners associate new information to their existing cognitive schemata and anticipate relationships between prior and new knowledge. Advanced organizers signal to learners that they may need to change their internal maps to accommodate new information. According to Ausubel (1963), advanced organizers not only aid students in their organization and processing of new material information but also activate student participation in traditionally passive instructional activities such as lectures and reading. Other forms of organizing information and activating student participation include the use of lesson organizers, chapter survey routines, unit organizers, and course organizers (Lenz, Bulgren, Schumaker, Deshler, & Boudah, 1994; Lenz, Marrs, Schumaker, & Deshler, 1993; Schumaker, Deshler, & McKnight, 1989).

*Strategy Instruction*  Other models within the information processing family provide students with explicit instruction in improving their own strategic approaches to learning. An individual's approach to a task is called a strategy when it reflects how that person thinks and acts in planning, performing, and evaluating task performance (Lenz, Ellis, & Scanlon, 1996). Cognitive strategies are deliberate, planned processes

**BOX 10.5**

**Guidelines for Teaching Stragegy Use**

1. Assess current strategy use.
   a. Does the student currently use a strategy? Is it helpful?
   b. Does the student have necessary prerequisite skills?
2. Help students understand what the strategy will help them accomplish and how and when to use it.
3. Model strategy use within the appropriate context.
   a. What is the student thinking?
   b. What is the student doing?
4. Provide guided and independent practice.
5. Provide specific feedback and encourage self-evaluation and self-reinforcement.
6. Help students to generalize strategy use.

learners use to process information. Box 10.5 provides guidelines for teaching strategy use.

There are two main classes of strategy instruction: global and task-specific. Learners employ global strategies to sequence approaches to tasks and activities. For example, Kurume needs to use the same set of strategies in any new social situation. Specifically, he needs to determine who should know about his deafness, how best to communicate that information, and what kinds of assistance will help him participate effectively in the communication demands of the setting. This is a global strategy because it applies to many situations. It is strategic because it allows Kurume to participate successfully without having to create novel responses in each new situation. Global strategies assist us in automatizing our problem solving. In that way, we can allocate more of our mental processes to higher-order thinking and less to procedural demands. Amber's interview provides us with many examples of her use of learning strategies. For instance, she uses the peg system to help her remember information; she applies the steps of THRILD to help her reading comprehension; and she applies the TEST strategy to evaluate the logic of others' arguments or opinions. Table 10.2 provides a list of common global learning strategies that are useful across a variety of academic and social learning

| **TABLE 10.2** | **Global and Task-Specific Learning Strategies** |
|---|---|
| **Global Strategies** | **Task-Specific Strategies** |
| Prediction | Reading |
| Attention |   Decoding |
| Visualization |   Comprehending |
| Summary | Writing |
| Error analysis |   Planning |
| Self-reinforcement |   Composing |
| Self-evaluation |   Revising |
| Memorization | Math |
| Help seeking |   Procedures |
| Organization |   Concepts |
|   Arranging materials, tasks, and space | Study skills |
|   Managing time and stress | Test taking |

tasks. Also, Appendix 10.2 provides specific information on several strategies for enhancing students' memory skills.

Task-specific strategies also capitalize on benefits of automaticity. Task-specific strategies might involve procedures that students learn to employ when reading new material. For example, Michael has learned to skim new reading material to determine the story structure. By knowing that he will be reading a mystery instead an expository essay on, say, the development of metal and its use in warfare, Michael can regulate his reading rate in anticipation of language and information that he will encounter.

*Cognitive Behavior Modification* **Cognitive behavior modification** occupies an interesting theoretical position. It belongs in the behavioral family because it targets specific problems and uses principles of reinforcement or feedback to guide and support performance. Because it focuses on the internal regulation of the thinking process, however, it also belongs in the information processing family. This is an example of how, when married, models from all the families improve the opportunities for learning for all students. Cognitive behavior modification is an approach to teaching strategies that relies on the use of small, carefully sequenced steps in teaching students to use internal language to influence and mediate their behavior (Meichenbaum, 1979). Cognitive behavioral strategies

are used to teach students (1) global and task-specific problem solving approaches like those listed in Table 10.2 and (2) self-monitoring strategies, including monitoring academic performance and emotions (Goldstein, 1993). The guidelines in Box 10.5 can also be used to teach cognitive behavioral strategies; Box 10.6 lists the steps for modeling and guiding students as they modify their behavior.

Using a cognitive behavioral approach, students have been taught to use specific procedures to guide their behavior in social and academic settings. For example, Box 10.7 describes the development of a self-monitoring strategy.

**BENEFITS OF STRATEGIES WITHIN THE INFORMATION PROCESSING FAMILY** Research is accumulating on the effectiveness of the application of strategies from within the information processing family. Most of the research in teaching students to think critically suggests that these skills are progressive. That is, students need practice in content-specific areas to develop generalized skills in concept formation, comparison and contrast, pattern recognition, and other higher-order thinking skills (Hyde & Bizar, 1989; Joyce, Weil, & Showers, 1992). Research in the area of reading instruction has shown that the application of critical thinking skills to the process of reading has resulted in increased reading comprehension for students from the elementary through the college levels (Cook &

---

**BOX 10.6**

## Steps for Modeling and Providing Guided Practice in Behavior Modification

1. Perform the task while talking out loud, providing instructions in how to approach and complete the task.
2. Write the instructions down so that the student can see and remember the language used to guide performance.

3. Have the student perform the same task while using the language guide to talk out loud.
4. Have the student whisper the guiding language while completing the task.
5. Have the student perform the task while using the guiding language silently.

---

Mayer, 1988; Paris, Wasik, & Turner, 1991; Pressley, El-Dinary, Gaskins, Schuder, Bergman, Almasi, & Brown, 1992). To apply critical thinking skills to the reading process, competent readers prepare to read text by anticipating what information or ideas they will en-

---

**BOX 10.7**

## Tanya's Self-Monitoring Strategy

Tanya struggled to stay on task during her independent seatwork, especially during math. Although there were many reasons for her inattentiveness, her classroom teacher, together with the special educator, decided to teach Tanya to monitor her own on-task behavior. The special education teacher came into Tanya's class one day with an egg timer, a set of math manipulatives, several math worksheets, and two index cards. She told Tanya that she could stay on task if she could remember to do two things: (1) pay attention to time and (2) ask herself, "Do I think I can do this?" The special educator modeled completing a math worksheet while the grains ran through the egg timer on the desk before them. When the egg timer ran out of sand at the top, the special educator stopped and said, "Am I doing my math?" Tanya said yes. Then, on one of the index cards, Tanya put a check mark. The two of them practiced this strategy for about thirty minutes, until Tanya was able to complete at least two cycles accurately. Then the special educator gave Tanya both index cards. On one, she wrote the self-monitoring question "Am I doing my math?" On the other, she listed the next three days of the week. Tanya's task was to maintain or increase the number of checks she received over the next three days.

counter. Furthermore they constantly monitor their own thinking throughout their reading, analyzing, and synthesizing what they read by comparing it to what they know.

Recent research on the use of advanced organizers suggests that explicit references to the purpose and use of advanced organizers is necessary in order for students to activate their own prior knowledge (Lenz, Alley, & Schumaker, 1987). Box 10.8 lists some guidelines for effective use of advanced organizers.

A broad research base also supports the benefits of strategy instruction, particularly in areas such as reading, writing, test taking, study skills, self-monitoring, and self-reinforcement (Schunk & Zimmerman, 1994). In particular, researchers have noted that, though many low achievers, students at risk, and students with disabilities fail to activate strategic approaches to learning (Swanson, 1991), when these students learn to use these processes, academic performance and social skills improve (Palinscar, David, Winn, & Stevens, 1991; Schunk & Cox, 1986; Schunk & Swartz, 1993; Wong, 1991). For example, teaching poor readers to adopt specific prereading techniques helps them to establish a purpose, heightens motivation, and activates thinking (Kameenui & Simmons, 1990). These prereading activities are based on the presumption that reading and thinking are related and that reading comprehension is enhanced when critical thinking skills, like prediction, are activated prior to the act of reading. Examples of predictive questions that readers might use prior to reading include the following:

1. What might the story be about?
2. Where might the story take place?
3. What might the problem be in this story?
4. What kind of story might this be?

**BOX 10.8**

## Guidelines for Effective Use of Advanced Organizers

1. Tell learners the purpose of the advanced organizer.
2. Identify the topic of the activity.
3. Provide students with background information.
4. State the concepts to be learned through the activity.
5. Motivate students through a rationale for the activity.
6. Introduce or review new terms or words.
7. Provide an organizational framework for the activity.
8. State desired outcomes.

Source: Lenz, Alley, & Schumaker, 1987.

**THE USE OF TECHNOLOGY IN THE INFORMATION PROCESSING FAMILY** Technology supports instructional models in the information processing family through the use of software that prompts steps in critical thinking, problem solving, the use of self-regulatory strategies, and the development of cognitive maps or webs. Computers are thought to hold great potential for enabling problem solving (Thornburg, 1986; Woodward, Carnine, & Gersten, 1988). For instance, some simulation programs are promising, including Gertrude's Secrets and Gertrude's Puzzles (Learning Company). By manipulating objects on the screen, students discover the criteria for placement. Another publisher (Wings for Learning/Sunburst Communications) has created several programs designed to foster experimentation with and discrimination of characteristics, attributes, and rules.

## Extending Your Learning

Observe several class sessions in a local school or university. Note the types of techniques that are incorporated during the course of a lesson. Would you classify any as belonging to the social family of instruction, the behavioral family, or the information processing family? Did you see evidence of strategies combined across two or more of the families?

## ■ SECTION SUMMARY

To reinforce how important it is that you become skilled in a variety of instructional strategies, consider Michael's seventh-grade science class. To help students prepare for a final exam on the unit on the skeletal system, the teacher (1) used direct instruction to introduce topics, (2) used cooperative learning groups for guided practice, and (3) taught strategies for learning and remembering new material so that, by the time the students were expected to perform on their own, they had the skills and supports to do so. Similarly, Amber's history teacher combined several models of instruction. Specifically, her teacher paired lectures with the use of mnemonics (memory strategies), combining direct instruction with information processing, enabling Amber both to gain access to information and to have a way to remember and retrieve it over the long term.

The critical question is when, and under what conditions, you might choose among the three broad approaches to structuring learning opportunities. For example, successful outcomes for direct instruction to large groups rely on the homogeneity of the group. But as classrooms become more heterogeneous, school professionals must balance the amount of time they spend in large-group, direct instruction and increase the use of methods that allow them to address the individual differences of their students. This means that instruction in inclusive classrooms must use a variety of methods and approaches. Planning for instruction requires that you be able to make competent and reflective choices that match learner needs, curricular content, and instructional implementation. The next section discusses a framework for selecting among these approaches. While choosing a strategy or a series of strategies is your primary focus in instructional planning, how you make those choices involves many levels of decision making.

# Instructional Planning Using RSVP

As the discussion of the social, behavioral, and information families suggests, there are many effective ways to teach. There is no single, right strategy or model to teach the curriculum of a school (Falvey & Grenot-Scheyer, 1995; Joyce, Weil, & Showers, 1990). In fact, as mentioned earlier, Harris and Graham (1996) maintain that successful instruction demands that teachers apply the learning principles from all three approaches in order to support diverse student needs. Being able to consider strategies from each of the three families of instruction is a good starting point in instructional planning, but the process demands additional decisions. But you also need a framework to make judgments about which approaches to use to achieve a particular instructional goal. This section introduces you to the RSVP framework for instructional planning.

## Selecting Instructional Strategies Using the RSVP Framework

RSVP is a common acronym used on invitations to remind recipients to let the host know whether they will attend the event. Here, we use the RSVP acronym as a mnemonic device to help you remember the set of questions that you can use to test the "goodness of fit" between your learning approaches, student needs, and instructional strategies (see Figure 10.2). As you read this section, think of the RSVP criteria as a decision process that will help you to select instructional approaches that transform your classroom into a true community of diverse learners.

**REASONABLENESS** You can judge reasonableness in two ways: (1) Consider whether the instructional approach uses time, money, materials, and human resources efficiently, or (2) debate whether the approach to instruction will meet the needs of most of the students in the learning situation. In responding to either criterion, school professionals must be able to anticipate the demands of the task and the capacities of the learners, as well as specify the learning outcomes. Using resources and equipment efficiently means that the planning and implementation of an activity should not consume all of the teacher's mental and physical re-

---

# You're Invited!

## To Select Instructional Strategies for Diverse Learners in Inclusive Classrooms
### *Please RSVP*

### *R* Is it Reasonable?

Can I use this method even if I don't have a big budget? Can I manage it with the human and material resources available to me? Does it meet the needs of most students?

### *S* Is it Sound?

Can I do it with an entire class, or does it only work for one child at a time? Is it consistent with the principles of human learning and development? Does it help to make information meaningful to students? Is it useful at different developmental stages? Does it incorporate different personal approaches and expressions of learning? Does it promote the functional aspects of the knowledge or skill?

### *V* Is it Valid?

Does it do what it says it will do? Is it grounded in a theoretical base?

### *P* What Power does it have?

Can it be used for different subjects? Can it be used for different age groups? Does it address multiple domains simultaneously? Can it be varied to allow for differences in students' needs? Does it allow for individual variations or adaptations and still work for the whole group?

**FIGURE 10.2** ■ An Invitation to Teach

sources, because time and energy must be available for crises, for future planning, and for evaluation. Schools, like most public institutions, have limited budgets. Instructional activities need to be planned so that all students have access to the materials they need to complete tasks.

Teachers also must make sure that the learning needs of students are being met through the instructional activity. A reasonable approach to teaching in inclusive classrooms assumes that, in any given situation, the teacher can expect all students to accomplish at least one learning target, most students will accomplish several learning targets, and some students will achieve all learning targets. This is reasonable because inclusive classrooms contain students with a broad range of cognitive, affective, communicative, and physical skills. The unit and lesson planning sheets that were provided in Chapter 9 prompted you to set multiple instructional objectives so that learning opportunities are in place for all students.

**SOUNDNESS**  The test of soundness requires that the teaching strategies you use (1) work with groups of students, (2) be sensitive to the developmental needs and differing learning styles of students, and (3) reflect the cognitive, affective, communicative, and physical domains. Selecting among sound strategies allows you to address the entire group, break a large group of students into smaller learning teams, or provide a process for directing learners to work independently. The extent and degree to which you address the group as a whole, in smaller teams, or as individual learners will depend on how diverse the learners are in their learning needs. For instance, the length of time that students are able to attend to one kind of activity has implications for the choice among, say, lecture, activity-based learning, or silent reading. If your class, like most inclusive classrooms, has learners who operate at several different developmental levels, then the test of soundness will guide you to choose strategies that support multiple learner needs. In this chapter, we focus on the types of teaching strategies that work best with groups of students because sound instruction for large groups will decrease the amount of time required for highly individualized, one-on-one tutoring or remedial instruction.

As discussed in Chapter 9, the curriculum should be student-centered and based on the needs, wants, learning preferences, and cultures of learners. In addi-

tion to these criteria, the test of soundness requires that instructional methods be based on the principles of learning and acknowledge development in each of the domains. Depending on the cognitive needs of your students, an instructional strategy may be sound if it helps learners to attend to a particular feature of a lesson, to interpret and use information, or to store and organize information for future use. Table 10.3 lists a broad range of strategies that support learning across all of the components of cognition. Similarly, there is an array of strategies that support components of affect, communication, and physical/health needs. For instance, methods that support affective needs assist students to become more self-aware, to self-regulate their interactions with others, and to practice the skills necessary to collaborate with others. Methods that support communicative needs provide opportunities for students to engage in discourse with other children, as well as with adults. Finally, methods that support physical needs have sufficient flexibility to allow for individual needs in terms of variations in physical movement, student positioning (standing, sitting), and materials or equipment.

The strategies in Table 10.3 can be embedded within the instructional context to enhance the opportunities for successful learning by all students. For example, the use of tape recorders can enhance Michael's access to a lecture on solving equations, but taped teacher lectures can be helpful to other learners as well as they do their homework. By using multiple strategies to support learning, you increase the potential for all students to learn. Later in this chapter we will return to these strategies for supporting the individual needs of learners.

**VALIDITY**  Valid methods are theoretically grounded and result in intended learner accomplishments. For example, inquiry methods are theoretically grounded in constructivism. Behavioral approaches to teaching learning strategies meet the test of validity because research shows that they result in the acquisition of strategic approaches to learning in content areas (Kameenui & Simmons, 1990). Validity can be confirmed through research in your own school by collecting student assessment data that reveal learner accomplishments. (Chapter 8 provides methods for curriculum-based assessment.) Validity is also demonstrated through the research you read about in professional journals and scholarly books. When you select an instructional

| TABLE 10.3 | Possible Instructional Strategies for Supporting Learning in the Cognitive Domain |
|---|---|
| **Cognitive Component** | **Instructional Strategies** |
| Attention | Using tape recorders |
| | Writing down what you say |
| | Using lots of visuals with auditory information |
| | Using auditory cuing systems |
| | Checking for understanding frequently |
| | Providing models |
| | Offering systematic, direct instruction |
| Perception | Listing no more than five items on an overhead |
| | Giving no more than three steps in any set of directions before you check for understanding |
| | Using at least two modalities to present information |
| | Providing frequent opportunities for student participation |
| | Checking for experience with content |
| | Being redundant |
| | Giving clear examples |
| | Increasing the size of salient information |
| | Underlining, boldfacing, and/or italicizing critical information |
| | Pointing to key information |
| | Circling key information |
| Working memory | Giving no more than three steps in any set of directions before you check for understanding |
| | Using at least two modalities (visual, auditory, smell, taste, touch) to present information |
| | Providing frequent opportunities for student participation |
| | Offering systematic, direct instruction |
| Long-term memory— procedural | Scaffolding |
| | Making strategies clear and specific |
| | Building new strategies on old strategies |
| | Applying strategies directly to tasks |
| | Emphasizing transfer and generalization |
| | Emphasizing self-regulation |
| Long-term memory— declarative | Anchoring instruction by linking it to learners' previous experiences |
| | Using media, computer data bases |
| | Facilitating reading of sources |
| | Assigning interviewing tasks |
| | Using a journal to write down students' understandings and questions |
| | Using activity-based experiments |

*(continued)*

| **TABLE 10.3** *(continued)* | |
|---|---|
| **Cognitive Component** | **Instructional Strategies** |
| | Employing application-level testing whereby students have to use information to do something |
| | Holding students accountable for information shared through testing and portfolio assessment |
| **Long-term memory— organizational structures** | Forming cooperative learning groups |
| | Using exemplars and nonexemplars to list attributes of categories |
| | Sequencing the order of assignments to parallel problem-solving steps |
| | Using discovery learning |
| | Posing problems and interventions with paradoxes, dilemmas, and discrepancies |
| **Long-term memory— conditional** | Giving long-term assignments that require problem solving and the use of other critical thinking skills |
| | Using jigsaw approaches to build from one form of understanding to another |
| | Holding debates |
| | Giving essay exams |
| | Doing performance assessments |
| | Assigning readings from competing points of view |
| | Posing novel problems to cooperative learning teams |
| | Holding tournaments |
| **Self as learner** | Using cognitive behavior modification |
| | Modeling |
| | Promoting self-questioning |
| **Self-reinforcement** | Cuing, self-monitoring |
| **Self-regulation** | Teaching self-instructional strategies |
| | Promoting self-questioning |

approach, ask yourself what you know about its effectiveness with students who are similar to yours.

**POWER**  Good teaching also demands that the instructional models selected match the demands of the tasks that are to be taught. This matching of task demand and instructional model increases the power of an instructional interaction. For example, during a lesson on photosynthesis, the teacher may choose to demonstrate the effect of light on the production of food in plants. By choosing to demonstrate at the beginning of the lesson, the teacher provides a concrete example of the results of photosynthesis. The demonstration supports the needs of a variety of learners who

range from concrete to abstract problem solvers. The demonstration becomes the focal point of discourse and problem solving. Some students might describe what they saw; others might predict possible reasons for the effects they observed; still others might attempt to represent symbolically the relationships between light and plant food production. The use of demonstration not only meets multiple students' needs, but also addresses the other element of power. Demonstrations or problem-based learning can be used in multiple subject areas such as reading, math, and social studies (Carpenter, Fennema, Peterson, Chiang, & Loef, 1989; Rugen & Hartl, 1994). A method has power if it can accomplish learning outcomes in more than one of the four domains and across many subject areas. A method is also considered powerful if it can meet simultaneously multiple students' needs.

## Applying RSVP to the Classroom

Now, let's apply the RSVP framework to a real classroom. First, read about Ms. Barnsley and her high school class in Box 10.9. Then we'll use the RSVP framework to critique her instructional choices.

**REASONABLENESS** By considering the developmental needs of her students, Ms. Barnsley is increasing the probability that they will be able to immerse themselves in the topic. The developmental needs of students drive other instructional considerations. You will notice that Ms. Barnsley selected several different

---

**BOX 10.9**

### A Visit to a High School History Class

Ms. Barnsley was pleased to see that her first-period European history class was a diverse group of learners. In addition to Kurume and Michael, she will be teaching Brendan, who has spina bifida and uses a wheelchair. Brendan has difficulty remembering and comprehending abstract information. He uses speech to communicate, although his expressive semantic and pragmatic skills are not as developed as his peers. For example, Brendan sometimes offers ideas or thoughts in class without reference to the current topic of conversation, and he rarely waits for a pause in the conversation to speak. The other 28 students represent a wide variety of experiences and backgrounds. Four students are at risk for dropping out of high school and have been on a variety of discipline contracts. Three students are National Merit semifinalists and plan on attending universities. Fifteen of the students are Hispanic-Americans, six are Euro-Americans, five are African-Americans, and the remaining five represent Asian-Americans and Native Americans.

Ms. Barnsley will be covering sixteenth-century British history, and she must make some choices about what she will teach. A few students need knowledge about British history to understand the powerful forces that shaped Western civilization. Most of her students need to be able to connect the study of history to contemporary, informed decisions as citizens in their own communities. Ms. Barnsley has chosen to teach one unit that focuses on the separation of the Church of England from the Catholic Church. She made this choice because this religious split has important implications for the development of self-determination on a personal and community level. Furthermore, this separation provides opportunities to discuss important concepts involving auton-

omy and family. After selecting the concepts that will anchor this unit, Ms. Barnsley also considers the kinds of study skills that her students can develop and apply as they explore the topic. For instance, the school recently connected to the Internet. Through the Internet, students can discuss key points with historians and peers and can do on-line literature searches for references. So, Ms. Barnsley's students need skills in accessing and using the Internet. Additionally, they need skills in organizing their knowledge, connecting it to their lives, and applying the concepts to personal issues. Skills in expressing their knowledge, creating arguments that support a particular position, referencing critical theorists, and rebutting the opinions of others complete the opportunities for skills development that Ms. Barnsley has targeted.

She has set her compass: All students will be able to access and interact on the Internet; most students will be able to apply these events and concepts to contemporary religious and political issues; and a few students will be able to construct and apply a knowledge base that connects key events and concepts in the separation of church and state. Ms. Barnsley has decided that she will organize her class into cooperative groups to carry out the research and writing activities associated with this unit. As a culminating activity, each cooperative group will develop a brief on a contemporary issue that parallels the issues of the separation of church and state encountered in sixteenth-century Great Britain. The brief must be explicit both in drawing parallels and in taking a position on the issue selected. These briefs may be written, orally presented, taped and presented on video, or graphically depicted. Individual students will receive grades for the unit based on the product their ways of involving her students in learning. Because she had students with limited abilities to attend to for extended periods of time, she chose to deliver instruction to the whole class only twice during her six-week unit.

By allowing her students to use multiple methods for collecting information about the sixteenth century, she increased the probability that most of them would develop or improve their research skills. For example, Brendan had the opportunity to develop skills using the mouse and the computer screen. Michael learned how to construct meaning from text by questioning experts through written discourse on the computer. Kurume enhanced his ability to access libraries across the country and to develop a system for archiving research information by both on-line computer searches and the use of a relational data base on the computer.

Ms. Barnsley chose direct instruction to teach her students how to use the Internet—a reasonable choice

group develops. They will also receive a grade for individual portfolios that display the results of their own research, as well as other artifacts of their participation in their team. These artifacts might include meeting notes, diagrams, charts, copies of research reports found on the Internet, and a journal of their own thoughts and reactions to their group work.

With her curriculum targets in mind, Ms. Barnsley chooses a set of instructional strategies that anchor the instruction to the experiences of her class. Ms. Barnsley developed many different lessons and used a combination of approaches from all three families. The descriptions of the following three activities were preceded and followed by other instructional activities:

1. *Behavioral family.* Before she sent groups off to do independent research, she conducted two days of direct instruction on the use of the Internet and ways of accessing and organizing research data. Each day, Ms. Barnsley prepared a visual advanced organizer that laid out the steps for accessing, traveling through, and quitting the Internet.

2. *Information processing family.* Ms. Barnsley spent one day teaching a strategy for expository writing because the culminating activity for this unit was writing a brief. She used the DEFENDS strategy (Ellis & Friend, 1991). The DEFENDS strategy is a mnemonic cuing strategy that sequences the steps for writing an argument: (1) Decide on goals and themes, (2) Estimate main ideas and details, (3) Figure the best order for main ideas and details, (4) Express the theme in the first sentence, (5) Note each main idea and supporting points, (6) Drive home the message in the last sentence, and (7) Search for errors and correct.

3. *Social family.* Using the students' experiences to anchor the points that she wants to make, Ms.

Barnsley assigned a set of activities for cooperative groups to work on for the next week. One group of students works on researching the political environment; another group researches the religious teachings of the church; a third group researches the cultural aspects of marriage and family; a fourth group researches the life of Henry VIII; and the final group analyzes the economic conditions of the times. At the end of the week, Ms. Barnsley reorganizes the groups. She puts a member of each research team into a new group so that each group has at least one member from each of the teams. She then asks them to produce responses to a set of questions. These responses can be written, they can be lectures, or they can be video clips. This knowledge will provide students with a broader basis from which to prepare their briefs.

Ms. Barnsley gives the groups a week to answer these questions. She schedules meeting times with each group on a daily basis. Individual students are held accountable for keeping a journal of their contribution to the group's work. Ms. Barnsley uses pop quizzes, a group organization and accomplishment rubric, and a leadership rubric to evaluate how the groups are doing on a daily basis. At least three times each week, she spends about fifteen minutes debriefing projects with the whole class. She makes comments about how groups are doing, perhaps offering a few tips on how to access the on-line research tools. She makes some materials available and asks the groups to provide feedback to individual members about their contributions.

To bring the unit to a close, Ms. Barnsley schedules meeting times with each of the groups. Each group presents the results of their research and products. Based on evaluations of group and individual work, Ms. Barnsley assigns each student and group a grade.

because it saved time. Students had a chance to learn a basic set of skills so that they knew what to do when they sat down to work on the computer. By providing instruction in the fundamentals of the Internet, Ms. Barnsley created the opportunity for herself to work as troubleshooter and coach, rather than having to visit each student individually to make sure he or she knew what to do. Although members of a dyad or cooperative learning group might be effective in helping one another to solve issues they encounter on the Internet, they will work more efficiently in groups when they have basic information to work from. Many students may have experience with computers and operating systems. However, because different operating systems have slight variations, Ms. Barnsley has decreased the chance that a student will generalize the wrong problem-solving procedures to the computers her class must use. Using a visual organizer at the beginning of each class session helped her students to focus on the procedural nature of the lesson content. By using both visual information and oral explanations, Ms. Barnsley increased the probability that many of her students would remember the steps needed to use the Internet successfully.

Her social family choice also meets the test of reasonableness. When the classroom consists of students with a wide range of needs, teachers find they have little time to attend to every student. The suggested remedy for this difficulty has often been smaller class size, but rarely is that solution enacted for various economic and political reasons. Cooperative learning is a time-effective alternative. Cooperative learning groups allow the teacher to attend to small groups of students (Maheady, Sacca, & Harper, 1988). In Ms. Barnsley's class, if cooperative groups are composed of four students per group, she has eight groups to visit rather than thirty-one individuals. The writing strategy that Ms. Barnsley chose is also reasonable. Students have a concrete model to follow when they begin to write their briefs and a list of criteria (DEFENDS) to apply as they compose their briefs.

**SOUNDNESS** The use of cooperative learning groups for researching sixteenth-century British history increased the possibility that more students would be involved in developing their research skills and gathering information about another period of time. Cooperative learning as a vehicle for instruction was a sound choice because it allowed students to proceed

through the learning activity according to their own developmental level. And because students would be involved in active learning through cooperative groups, Ms. Barnsley used a method that will work for all her students, although the degree of mastery of learning outcomes may vary. By setting tangible outcomes for each group, Ms. Barnsley increased the likelihood that students would engage in activities like problem solving that are prerequisites for performances or written products. Group problem-solving strategies can be more varied, fine-tuned, and powerful than those produced by individuals (Udvari-Solner & Thousand, 1995). Depending on how quickly different students develop efficient strategies for the research and writing process, different groups will move at different paces according to their own needs. In doing so, they do not disrupt the learning rates of students in other groups. Finally, Ms. Barnsley's product was a functional task that asked learners to integrate their new knowledge with their existing beliefs about and dispositions toward the relationship between government and religion.

**VALIDITY** An empirical research base suggests that basic skills are acquired through direct instruction of the kind that Ms. Barnsley used when she taught about the Internet and when she taught the DEFENDS writing strategy. For example, Kameenui and Simmons' (1990) method for teaching textbook prose comprehension contains a series of procedural skills that have shown to be successful with students with mild-to-moderate disabilities, with at-risk students, and with students who do not have identified disabilities.

Many characteristics have been attributed to students who have problems in school. The first set has to do with academic work–related skills, such as note taking, problem solving, reading comprehension, written expression, study skills, and test-taking skills (Carlson & Alley, 1981; Schumaker, Sheldon-Wilgren, & Sherman, 1980). The second set has to do with passivity toward learning and a lack of active involvement in learning (Torgeson, 1982). The third set has to do with levels of activity, interpersonal interactions with adults and peers, attending, impulsivity, and organization (Forness & Walker, 1992; Zentall, 1993). Ms. Barnsley's use of the DEFENDS strategy is supported because it addressed the first set of characteristics that distinguish students who have problems in school. She used cooperative learning and activity-based instruction to address the second set of characteristics and, by doing so, improved students' engagement in learning and their interpersonal skill development.

Proponents of cooperative learning have demonstrated that it frees up the teacher to spend more time working individually with students. Because cooperative learning groups also empower students to help teach one another, students are able to get quicker responses to their questions. Also, students are more likely to have their questions answered completely because a whole group is not held up while the teacher attempts to clarify a point for an individual. Groups allow students to be involved in more forms of expression and choice making (Harmin, 1994). Remember the discussion of Bloom's taxonomy in Chapter 9? Although not all students bring the same sophistication to their problem solving, all students can engage in analysis, synthesis, and evaluation—the higher-order thinking skills. Cooperative learning groups create opportunities for students to contribute to the work of the group in varied ways. Through their contributions, they demonstrate their facility with these thinking skills. For all these reasons, Ms. Barnsley's use of cooperative learning groups was a sound choice.

**POWER** Ms. Barnsley chose instructional approaches from all three families. She was also careful to match her approaches to her content. In Chapter 9, we discussed several levels of curriculum decision making. For the purposes of this discussion, we assume that curricular decisions have already been made at the district/building level. For example, Ms. Barnsley knew that she was responsible for teaching sixteenth-century British history. However, she had a great deal of flexibility in the selection of content within this curricular area and in the instructional approaches that she would use. Because Ms. Barnsley knew that adolescents are enmeshed in issues of emancipation and self-determination, she selected content areas that applied to the developmental needs of her students. If she had had responsibility for this curriculum at the middle school level, she might have chosen events that highlight group cohesion and identity, such as the conflict between the loyalists of Mary, queen of the Scots, and those of Elizabeth I, queen of England.

This example of unit development is predicated on several decisions that Ms. Barnsley made. First, she thought about the abilities and interests of her class. She knew that few of her students understood or were motivated to learn historical events. She also knew that most of her students had difficulty sustaining attention during lectures. And she knew that more than a few of her students produced low-quality written reports. Using Bloom's taxonomy, she made the decision that her students were capable, at least, of engaging in the content at an application and analysis level. However, traditional products that history teachers require—such as research papers, oral presentations, and objective tests—might not have been the best choice for evaluating her students' learning. Nor would lecturing have been the most efficient form of conveying all or most of the information.

To address the issue of power, we will look at the three strategies that were identified in the description of Ms. Barnsley's class to see how they match the content of her unit (see Box 10.9). First, her use of direct instruction had power because she could use direct instruction to provide a knowledge base about specific skills. Direct instruction can work with young children, with children who have diverse learning needs, and with adult learners when it is offered in short segments, with time for students to practice or apply the content under guidance. By varying the complexity of her language, by including visual and oral information, and by sequencing instruction in small steps, Ms. Barnsley helped most of her students gather and retain information through direct instruction. For instance, when she checked for understanding, she had some students write a sentence that described elements of a procedure. She also had other students tell someone what they had just learned. A third way of checking for understanding involves having students organize written procedures by arranging strips of paper on which one step of the procedure is written per strip. By having all three of these checking-for-understanding activities going on simultaneously, Ms. Barnsley was able to differentiate and meet the needs of many of her students.

Second, Ms. Barnsley's use of the DEFENDS strategy had power because instructional strategies have been shown to support the learning activities of many kinds of students. For example, although Brendan may not have been able to complete all of the steps of the DEFENDS process on his own, he could participate in selecting the goals and theme of the brief his group was putting together. Because he needed someone to read text to him, he became a particularly effective editor, as his listening skills allowed him to pick up lapses in logical arguments, as well as grammatical errors.

Finally, Ms. Barnsley's use of cooperative learning had power because it allowed students like Brendan to develop critical thinking skills and to learn new skills in logical argument while also meeting the learning needs of students who were working at a more complex level. The power criteria demonstrates how Ms. Barnsley, like other reflective teachers, had to make decisions about what content to provide, how to deliver it, and how to evaluate student performance based on student skills rather than her own teaching mode preferences.

## ■ SECTION SUMMARY

Planning instruction is a critical element of the instructional process. In Chapter 9, you were introduced to important criteria to guide your choice of curriculum. Concepts like age appropriateness, partial participation, holism, developmental appropriateness, functionality, and reflective practice should guide your critical evaluation of potential curricular choices. In the same way, RSVP provides a set of criteria to help you make choices about the vehicles for instruction that you use in your classroom. You should be able to apply the RSVP criteria—reasonableness, soundness,

validity, and power—to choices that you make in your own teaching. Matching curricular activities and content to learner characteristics requires thoughtful analysis. Avoid the tendency to pick an instructional method that is being touted as a panacea for overcoming learner difficulties. Remember that engaged learners are a product of reflective, not reactive, planning.

Of course, you will inevitably make mistakes in matching learner needs with curriculum targets. You will discover this as you teach and assess student progress. Accordingly, you will need to adjust your instructional strategies, your curricular activities, or even the content that you have chosen to teach. In the next sections, you will read about some ways to improve your teaching and some processes to help you monitor and adjust to the needs of your students.

## Implementing Instruction

Planning instruction is a complex and reflective process; implementing instruction is an interactive, dynamic process that requires high levels of energy, continuous thinking, and quick decision making. The ways that school professionals orchestrate the instruc-

A student benefits from large letters on the computer screen.

tional environment influence the probability that student effort will result in learning (Bellamy, 1994). You may think implementing instruction is a matter of carrying out the specific steps of the strategy or strategies that you planned to use. But as Ayers (1995a) suggests, competent school professionals move beyond routines and established patterns of behavior to respond to the unique needs of their students. There is no formula that can encompass all of the possible permutations and responses that teachers must be able to create in order to ensure that each child has an opportunity to learn. However, as classroom research reveals, not only is there a strong, empirical knowledge base about the fundamentals of good teaching (Evertson, Emmer, Clements, Sandford, & Worsham, 1993), but good teaching is good teaching regardless of the shapes, sizes, and abilities of your students (Algozzine, 1993).

In an inclusive classroom, with students of varying abilities and from diverse linguistic, cultural, ethnic, and socioeconomic backgrounds, school professionals and support personnel must be accomplished at carrying out the elements of good teaching (Bingham, 1995; Kucer, Silva, & Delgado-Larocco, 1995; Ostrow, 1995). The need for precise, consistent teaching techniques is particularly true in inclusive classrooms because the diversity of the students demands careful execution of instructional techniques. Exposed to proper teaching techniques, students are better able to focus their attention on the content of the curriculum and to spend their time engaged and on-task, rather than being confused about what is to be learned or completed in any given activity.

Good and Brophy (1994) have identified elements of the instructional delivery process that are commonly seen in classrooms in which students make gains in their achievement test scores. These include (1) high teacher expectations, (2) many opportunities to learn, (3) curriculum pacing through routines and procedures, (4) active teaching, and (5) achievement motivation. Effective teachers motivate their students by setting and communicating high expectations for all students. Effective teachers ensure that time in classrooms is spent on learning activities and interactions. A key component of task engagement is creating explicit connections between the current lesson or activity and learners' backgrounds and previous experiences. Learners need to be engaged in the lesson or activity, to have opportunities to practice new or emerging skills, and to receive feedback on their performance (Ayers, 1995b). Students whose teachers engage in active teaching by demonstrating skills, explaining concepts, facilitating activities, and conducting reviews (Good & Brophy, 1994; Good, Grouws, & Ebmeier, 1983) learn more than students who interact primarily with curriculum materials. Ensuring that students work through the phases of acquisition, fluency, and mastery results in higher achievement for students. When teachers create supportive learning environments, as we discussed in Chapter 6, students can focus on learning. Furthermore, these elements of effective teaching apply whether the teacher chooses an instructional approach from the social, behavioral, or information processing families.

## Teacher Expectations

Many studies have shown that student achievement is related to teacher expectations and, more importantly, to specific types of teacher behavior that communicate teacher expectations to students (Beez, 1968; Eden & Shani, 1982; Rosenthal, 1974; Schrank, 1968). Teacher behaviors that communicate high expectations to students include (1) more opportunities to perform publicly on meaningful tasks, (2) more opportunities to think, (3) more assignments that deal with comprehension and understanding, (4) more autonomy and choices, and (5) fewer teacher interruptions (Good & Weinstein, 1986). Conversely, when teachers have low expectations for students, they (1) rarely wait for students to respond to a question before calling on someone else, (2) criticize more often and praise less often, (3) pay less attention to low-achieving students, and (4) seat low-achieving students farther away from them.

Teachers can keep their expectations for individual students current by monitoring their progress closely and emphasizing students' present performance. By stressing progress that individual students have made, teachers relate students' personal effort to their growth. Feedback also provides students with specific information about what they can do to improve performance. Finally, teachers can minimize their differential expectations by assuming more responsibility for student misunderstanding and difficulty in grasping concepts. When students struggle with new information, teachers can diagnose why they are having difficulty understanding the explanation and then think of a different way to reteach the idea. For instance, Ms. Barnsley, our secondary history teacher from Box 10.9, often reteaches using pictures and diagrams rather than words. Sometimes, instead of providing a detailed description, she transforms her explanation into an analogy to a simple process or familiar experience like driving a car or watching a movie. Other times, she reteaches a concept or process by breaking her original description into smaller, more discrete pieces. She checks for understanding by summarizing after explaining each step in the process to make sure that her previously confused students continue to follow the new, more detailed description.

## Opportunities to Learn Through Classroom Management and Organization

Students tend to master more curriculum targets when they are in classrooms in which time spent on-task is maximized and classroom interruptions or bureaucratic details are minimized. But many unanticipated events happen daily in classrooms—for example, students arriving late, fighting, or getting sick, or a fire drill or an assembly being called. In addition, not every lesson goes as you plan. You may not have anticipated the questions that your students ask. You may have assumed that your students had more prior knowledge than they have. You may have planned a fluency lesson when the students are still in the acquisition phase of learning. These unplanned events complicate the delivery of your lessons. As a result, you may need to adjust your lesson plan on the spot, to omit something you had planned to cover, or to assign independent work to your students while you deal with the problem. Every classroom has the potential for these distractions to occur, and teachers who anticipate these events can do many things to lessen their effects.

Teaching requires that you attend to and manage multiple features within the classroom environment, as well as perform the specific steps of your instructional activities. Fluent execution of instruction helps you to maintain an environment that optimizes learning opportunities for all students. Whether teachers work with large or small groups of students, one of their primary jobs is to keep students engaged in learning. Kounin (1970) suggests that teachers who achieve instructional fluency share several skills: (1) "withit-

ness," (2) overlapping, (3) smoothness, (4) momentum, and (5) coherence. We use Ms. Barnsley's high school class to illustrate some of these skills. However, the same skills are needed in classrooms at the preschool, elementary, and middle school levels.

**"WITHITNESS"**   "Withitness" refers to the teacher's ability to be aware of all activity occurring in the classroom (Evertson et al., 1993; Kounin, 1970). When Ms. Barnsley works with one of her research teams, she needs to let the rest of the class know that she is aware of what is going on. She does this by consciously scanning the classroom, checking on each of the other groups, providing feedback, and reacting to incidents that may interfere with opportunities to learn. Initially, she may prompt herself to scan the environment every time she says "yes" in her small group or turns a page or picks up a pencil. Scanning is something teachers must teach themselves to do. Most of us come to teaching with skills in remaining focused, not in dividing our attention. As Ms. Barnsley scans, she needs to provide feedback. She may simply comment, "It looks like Tom's team is on track" or "Tanya, are you adhering to your agenda?" These kinds of remarks let students know that you are paying attention. When minor disruptions occur, Ms. Barnsley uses surface management techniques that redirect students to their learning tasks. She may stand up when she sees some off-task behavior, or she may move closer to a group of students who seem distracted. If she senses that the whole class seems restless, she may suddenly shift activities: "Okay, class, that's enough research for today. I'd like all of you to stand up and form two lines. We are going to have a knowledge bee. Harry, you be the captain of the Elizabethans. Celeste, you take the Papists." "Withitness" allows you to keep minor distractions from becoming major distractions.

**OVERLAPPING**   Kounin (1970) also noticed that students were more productive in classrooms in which teachers were skilled in overlapping. That is, the teachers were able to attend simultaneously to the curriculum activity and to student behaviors. So, while Ms. Barnsley is leading one group through a problem-solving exercise, she also is working with Michael on his editing. She moves back and forth between these two coaching activities without diminishing her value to either the group or the individual student. Many teachers who find themselves in this situation during

## Extending Your Learning

In elementary schools, lining up, taking attendance, carrying scissors across the classroom, getting materials off the shelf, and straightening out desks are all procedures that can become routines. Observe a preschool, elementary, middle, or high school classroom, and identify all the daily tasks that can become routines. How many routines are completed without teacher intervention or prompting?

lessons end up being frustrated and conveying their frustration to their students. These teachers need to regard overlapping as an important skill. Students will benefit from your facility with this skill.

**SMOOTHNESS** Another characteristic of competent teachers is smoothness. As they teach, they stay on topic, avoiding peripheral topics and side conversations. In elementary classrooms, this means maintaining a focus on reading during reading time, even if the teacher remembers that she left out an important explanation during the math lesson that she just finished teaching. Instead of asking the students to stop reading and to think about math computation, the teacher makes a note to herself to correct the omission or mistake during the next math session. Smoothness involves keeping on track. Of course, logical links between what is being taught and other lessons help learners to make connections between subject areas. Smoothness is also characterized by a summary of each activity as it comes to a close. This helps students to make the transition from one task to the next. Smoothness is maintained through routines and procedures and through careful transitions between activities and events.

## Routines and Procedures

When comparing the classrooms of novice and expert teachers, Good and Brophy (1994) note that expert teachers spend more time in developing, teaching, and ensuring that routines and procedures are in place to make the mundane tasks of everyday life in the classroom automatic. Many tasks in classrooms are routine—for instance, turning in papers or products.

Creating a routine for performing these tasks entails deciding when, where, and how papers will be turned in. For example, Ms. Barnsley has an agreed-upon rule: All papers are due when the bell rings at the beginning of a period. When the bell rings, Ms. Barnsley goes to the basket that she keeps next to the door, picks up all the papers that have been deposited there, puts them in a red file folder (all sixth-period materials are kept in red file folders), and puts them in her grading bag to take home to grade. She does not say anything, and she is not interrupted by students asking if they should hand in their papers. Everyone knows what will happen, and it does, like clockwork, every day. This kind of automaticity means that Ms. Barnsley can spend more time on teaching and students can spend more time engaged in meaningful learning. Teaching routines may take some time to establish, but in the long run it saves time.

## Transitions

Transitions are times during the day when one activity is coming to an end and another activity is about to occur. In preschools, these transitions happen when children take off their coats and join circle, when they move from circle to activity centers, and when they go from activity centers to recess. In elementary classrooms, transitions occur when students shift between subjects or move from activities at their desks to those on the floor, or from class to lunch, recess, or physical education, music, and art. Each bell signals a transition in middle and high schools. Transition times can be complicated if students don't know what to do when they move from one activity to the next. School professionals find themselves directing traffic, prompting confused students, and acting as referees for students who may respond to the increased activity and confusion with problem behaviors. You teach routines and procedures for transitions just as you do for other routine activities in classrooms. This means providing prompts such as "We will be moving into the hallway in about one minute. What three rules guide our behavior when we walk down the hall?" It means giving students cues such as "When you move from your desks to the floor for author's corner, please bring a pencil and the current story you are working on, and think about the kinds of questions that you will ask our next author."

**MOMENTUM** Momentum involves the maintenance of an evenly distributed flow of instruction from the beginning to the end of an activity or lesson. When distractions arise, they should be addressed quickly and directly, with no time spent in trying to teach values. The task at hand is to keep everyone's attention on the learning target. If you need to debrief a student, do it later, when you are not taking up the time of the other learners.

Suppose you need to remind students about the materials they need to complete a task; have samples on hand so that you can use visuals to remind them, rather than wasting valuable class time discussing the materials. Also, because momentum is broken when explanations or directions are too long, try to limit your directions to three-step procedures. And be sure to check for understanding: "Are we going upstairs before we expose our film?" Finally, be aware that students will always have more questions than you have time to answer. Evaluate how your answer to a question will help the whole group get started, stay engaged, or finish a task. If the answer to the question keeps the class from becoming engaged, try to answer it individually, at a later time. Large groups need to focus on the topic so that all learners can become engaged, and momentum helps this process. Managing surface behaviors adeptly means that the momentum of a lesson or activity can be maintained.

**SURFACE MANAGEMENT** Surface management techniques keep the class involved without undue disruption (see Box 10.10). Ms. Barnsley used surface management techniques such as proximity, the surprise factor, and reliance on routine to keep her history students on task, but she chose not to use ignoring or antiseptic bouncing. Choosing to ignore certain kinds of behavior is a judgment call. For example, if a commotion is simply a case of students settling their own dispute, you may decide that the behavior will not be contagious. However, if you see two students engaged in a game that is not part of their assignment, you may want to intervene. Ignoring is efficient when it works but disastrous when it does not.

Sometimes, a student may arrive in class with personal problems from home or from a peer interaction. The student is emotionally charged, and if a minor stress occurs in class, it may be enough to cause the student to express emotions in disruptive ways. By paying close attention to your students, you can some-

---

**BOX 10.10**

### Surface Management Techniques

1. Ignore the student behavior.
2. Give signals (like a head shake) to interrupt off-task behavior.
3. Move toward students engaged in off-task behaviors.
4. Boost motivation by introducing novel activities.
5. Use humor to reduce anxiety or tension.
6. Use routines to keep students participating in class activities.
7. Remind students of their ethical principles.
8. Remove disruptive objects.
9. Use antiseptic bouncing.

Source: Long & Newman, 1971.

---

times avert these emotional blowups by creating a diversion. Recall from Chapter 4 that antiseptic bouncing means finding a way to get a student out of a class before he or she is so emotionally charged that a confrontation with the teacher or a peer is inevitable. In Chapter 4, we described the use of antiseptic bouncing with Michael. His teacher, Ms. Pope, had Michael take notes to the school secretary, Charleen, when she needed a nonconfrontational way of getting him back on task. Sometimes, sending a student who is having difficulty on an errand creates enough nonstressful time that the student can return to class and finish his or her work without a blowup. Teachers can then schedule time to talk with the student individually to sort through the problem.

## Active Teaching

In Chapter 9, we discussed the selection and sequencing of curriculum, but we want to remind you that the selection and use of curricular content can be enhanced through the choices you make in instruction. For instance, when Tanya's teacher introduced information about electricity, she wanted to connect the notion of electricity to the lights that Tanya used at home when it got dark. Connecting new information to learners' experiences and current knowledge helps them to grapple with new or complex ideas. Similarly, when Annie's classroom teacher introduced a unit on the family, she began with her students' families. Then, by sequencing sets of information about families, Annie's teacher gradually increased the complexity of the notion of family. Michael's math teacher knew that she needed to be prepared to teach any new math procedure in several ways so that Michael could understand the process as completely as possible. Active teaching means that teachers are involved in connecting new information with old, increasing the complexity of the information to be learned gradually, and planning to explain material in several different ways to meet the unique cognitive needs of all the students in a classroom. The elements of active teaching include (1) focusing attention, (2) presenting information appropriately, (3) maintaining coherence, (4) keeping students engaged, and (5) practicing.

**FOCUSING ATTENTION**  Helping students to focus their attention provides supports across several cognitive skills and components. For example, helping students to focus on what is important or on what they are expected to do helps them to direct their attention, activate their perception and long-term memory skills, and regulate themselves. Before starting a lesson or giving out directions, make sure you have the attention of the student or group. You might use a standard signal such as raising your hand or reciting a jingle such as "One, two, three, eyes on me." When you are in the middle of a lesson, you might alert the group by asking a question before calling on a student to respond. For instance, Ms. Barnsley might ask, "Explain the religious implications of choosing Anne Boleyn as Henry VIII's wife." Then she would look around the room for a respondent, picking a student at random: "This is a tricky question. [pause] Trina, I'd like you and Chris to answer this question." By letting the class know that it is a tricky question, Ms. Barnsley creates a positive bind. She implies that not everyone may be able to come up with a complete response. And by pairing Trina and Chris, she creates a support system for both of them and gets them both engaged in answering. Finally, Ms. Barnsley might pick up a pencil to take notes on their answer and announce to the rest of the class, "Pay attention to this answer, because I'm going to ask you to critique it." In this way, she provides a model for

the rest of the class to take notes and also alerts other students that they may be called on in connection with the answer that is about to be provided. Students attend when ambiguity is introduced into the teacher question. They continue to attend because they need to be able to comment on what is being discussed.

Getting the attention of younger students may also involve nonverbal signals—for example, holding a hand in the air, ringing a little bell, or sending a student to turn the lights on and off. All of these visual and auditory signals tell the group that it's time to attend to the teacher. Teachers train their students to respond to these signals at the beginning of the year. They practice the routine with the class several times a day, until students become accustomed to and respond rapidly to the signal.

**PRESENTING INFORMATION APPROPRIATELY**
Active teaching means modulating speech mechanics like the volume of your voice, the pacing of your sentences, your articulation patterns, and other speech mechanics (Good & Brophy, 1994). When you present information directly through lecture or demonstration, you need to follow some basic presentation guidelines. For example, you must focus your students' attention, orient them to the material to be covered, highlight new vocabulary, demonstrate or explain concepts in sequential order, ask students to replicate your demonstration or summarize the explanation, correct misconceptions, and then involve other students in activities that apply the principles you demonstrated. When leading discussions, you need to attend to the cognitive level of questions that you ask. Bloom's taxonomy can guide your question development (see Chapter 9). Try to keep your questioning at the analysis, synthesis, and evaluation levels. Make sure that your questions are clear, purposeful, brief, and natural, and allow students time to formulate their answers before you prompt or cue an answer.

**MAINTAINING COHERENCE**  Whenever possible, activities should be introduced and engaged in as a whole, rather than broken down into fragments. For instance, in teaching students to write a business letter, you should begin with examples of correctly constructed business letters that are drafted for specific reasons, like complaints, praise, or requests for information, rather than beginning with instructions on how to write salutations. Coherence in a lesson is also maintained when teachers have the whole group practice or engage in an activity, rather than having one student at a time take a turn. One or two students can demonstrate how to do an activity, and then the rest of the class can do it individually or in small groups as the teacher circulates to provide feedback. It is difficult to maintain everyone's attention when twenty-five students are waiting in line while one student completes an activity.

**KEEPING STUDENTS ENGAGED**  Maintaining the attention of the class and keeping large groups of students focused on learning activities require a repertoire of strategies. By varying the use of these strategies, teachers can keep their students' attention on-task and reduce the need for disciplinary measures. Students who are engaged in learning have little time to disrupt the class. Remember that the strategies you use need to be taught to students so that they know how to meet your expectations. Holding students accountable for the material in a lesson and assigning roles to students in a group helps them to focus on their role in the class. In kindergarten and early elementary school, a teacher might encourage the whole class by saying, "I can see you all have your thinking caps on" or "While Cal is answering this question, I want you to think hard about your own answer." Alternatively, a teacher might ask and answer her own question and then have students turn their thumbs up or down depending on whether they think it is the right or wrong answer. This enables the teacher to spot check on comprehension for the whole class and keeps all the students involved.

Other strategies for keeping students involved include fishbowls, opposing panels, dyads, and cooperative learning groups. In fishbowls, five to seven students sit in a circle in the middle of the class, while the rest of the class sits in concentric circles outside of the fishbowl. The teacher circulates around the perimeter, posing discussion questions to the group in the fish bowl as the students outside the fish bowl listen in on the discussion. Fish bowl members are interchanged with students outside the inner circle. Sometimes, the class can be divided into smaller groups that compete for points or recognition. Using dyads, teachers can structure brief dialogs between students to highlight a particular topic and keep the whole class involved. Pairing and grouping gives teachers the opportunity to break up groups of students (cliques) who have a tendency to pull the class off-task. In general, maintaining

attention means remembering not to focus all your attention on one student's response. As much as possible, you want to get the whole class engaged and involved in the material being presented.

**PRACTICING**  Students need opportunities to apply what they've learned under your guidance and to practice their new skills. Because you want them to practice skills correctly, you need to establish a practice pattern that is correct. Practice is a good time to create heterogeneous ability groups so students can monitor one another's skills and offer immediate feedback. You can visit with groups of students to make sure that their practice is accurate and also to answer any questions. Good practice involves authentic activities that mirror what students might encounter in the world outside school. Box 10.11 outlines some strategies for creating successful practice opportunities.

## Achievement Motivation

Teacher expectations, opportunities to learn through classroom management, active teaching, and teaching to mastery are essential elements of successful instruction. However, students themselves must be motivated to achieve. Without that motivation, the best-executed instruction will not result in intended outcomes. School professionals should remember that the motives, goals, and strategies that students develop in response to classroom activities depend on the nature of the activities themselves, as well as on how the teacher presents. Motivation can be promoted externally, through activities, events, and people in the environment, or it can be generated internally, by the individual, who may have highly goal-directed behavior, enjoy a particular activity, or feel as if success will be easy to attain (see Box 10.12). The source of most motivation is probably a combination of opportunities to receive positive feedback and the individual's need to be successful or achieve a goal. Notice that we use feedback, rewards, and praise as examples of external motivators. That is because each of these responses to student performance can result in performance improvement. Where external responses to student performance, during practice or in response to a completed activity, increase students' willingness to engage in tasks or improve task performance, we call this extrinsic motivation.

**BOX 10.11**

## Strategies for Creating Practice Opportunities

1. Be present to provide feedback and encouragement as students try out new skills.
2. Make sure students can complete activities in the homework.
3. Provide opportunities for students to role-play and practice questioning skills.
4. Provide feedback to students in writing as well as verbally.
5. Use transition times to practice new information.
6. Practice new skills daily, and practice learned skills frequently.

**BOX 10.12**

## Guidelines for Motivating Individuals

1. Link performance to at least one of three rationale:
   a. the importance of achieving success on the task because it will help to fulfill personal needs.
   b. the intrinsic enjoyment of the task—fun, opportunities for socialization, reflection, and so on.
   c. utility value—task success will be a step toward a future goal.
2. Provide specific, encouraging feedback during tasks.
3. Comment on task completion and the quality of the work completed, and make specific recommendations for improvement.
4. Ensure that students have time to reflect on and evaluate their own performance.

Extrinsic motivation is modulated by forces outside the student; both school professionals and peers can be primary sources of extrinsic motivation. Extrinsic motivators can help students to stay focused and on-task by providing external verification of their effort and achievement. As a result, much research has been directed at the effects of generalized and specific praise on student performance in the classroom. When teachers rely on extrinsic rewards like grades or points to motivate students, students are likely to adopt goals and strategies that help them meet minimum requirements (Good & Brophy, 1994). However, some students may need the concrete, on-going information that grades, points, or other basic forms of reinforcement provide. That is, extrinsic reinforcement helps students to know that they are producing behavior that meets the expectations of teachers. Annie, for instance, is able to sustain her attention in group activities when she gets frequent encouraging statements like "Annie, you're really looking at the problem!" Feedback, encouragement, or praise will improve student performance if it is specific, positive, and frequent. For example, when Tanya's teacher sees her forming letters with a pencil, she might say, "Tanya! Look at that *H* you wrote; it looks just like the picture. I'll bet all your *H*'s are going to have two lines down and one across." In contrast, feedback that details what is poorly executed without specific information on what to improve may discourage further effort. For instance,

Michael's third-grade teacher discouraged him from improving his cursive handwriting with remarks like "No, Michael, weren't you listening? That's not a *Q*, that's a *G*."

The choice to use extrinsic forms of motivation should be determined by student need, not teacher preference. In a heterogeneous classroom, many types of external motivators will be in use, because students will have differing needs based on their skill in an activity, their preference for the activity, and their belief that they can succeed at the activity. In some classrooms, differing responses to student performance confuse the students. It's best for the classroom teacher to inform students in advance that different students will get different kinds of feedback and encouragement. This awareness will help students interpret teacher encouragement.

In contrast, intrinsic motivation is internally generated. It can be affective or emotional (the activity is enjoyable), and it can be cognitive or intellectual (the activity is interesting or intellectually provocative, or it yields insight for the individual). Both extrinsic and intrinsic motivation support the effort that is required to learn. Motivation theorists believe that individuals expend effort if they expect to succeed at the task or performance and if they value the outcomes of the task or activity (Bandura, 1989; Schunk, 1991). This relationship between expectancy for success and value for an activity or skill to be learned comprise motivation (Good & Brophy, 1994). In order to increase the probability that their students will learn, teachers must support students' appreciation for the value of a task and ensure that students can achieve success in these activities.

## ■ SECTION SUMMARY

Instruction requires attention to many performance skills. Positive teacher expectations can have a strong effect on student performance. Classroom management strategies also support student involvement in learning tasks and lessen disruptions and distractions to learning. Good teachers employ skills like "withitness," overlapping, smoothness, momentum, and coherence that involve students in the learning process. Understanding how achievement motivation affects student performance reminds you to accentuate the value of learning specific skills and to make sure that you sequence skill building in such a way that students can succeed, most of the time.

# Evaluating Instruction

In Chapter 9, we discussed how even under the best of planning and implementation conditions, the curriculum will have to be individualized to allow for one or more learners to experience success or to have their unique needs addressed. The same is true for instruction. Even under the best of instructional planning and implementation circumstances, some students will need further individualization in order to have successful learning experiences. The way you implement instruction may be the source of difficulties learners experience. Therefore, you must be prepared to evaluate, adapt, and modify your instruction to create a better match between what the learner needs and what you do. As a school professional, you will play a crucial role in the process of evaluating your instruction and making decisions to adapt and modify instruction and curriculum. But do not forget that you have other valuable resources to tap for these processes. Decisions to adapt and modify instruction and curriculum are best

made by school professionals, related-services personnel, students, and their families working in teams.

In this text, we define accommodations as the broad umbrella under which both adaptations and modifications are organized (see Table 10.4). Accommodations are defined as changes made either in the way a lesson is taught or in the scope and sequence of what is taught in order to meet individual student needs. Adaptation refers to the changes to instructional procedures that can be made in order to ensure that all students have opportunities to learn in their classrooms. In contrast, curriculum modification refers to adjustments made in the content itself. We addressed modifications in Chapter 9; here, we focus on accommodations.

## A Framework for Guiding Adaptation Decisions

Information about when and how to make instructional adaptations comes from several sources. First, teachers learn to make adjustments to their curricular and instructional strategies based on informal classroom assessments. Chapter 8 provided several examples of assessments that would yield information as to whether your instructional strategies were supporting student learning. The use of informal assessment also gives students an opportunity to share their perspective on what is or isn't working for them. A second source of information about adapting instruction comes from a student's IEP. In Chapter 9, we discussed how Michael needed to be taught test-taking strategies. In addition to specifying the additional content that he required, his IEP included recommendations for instructional adaptations. Specifically, Michael was to be provided with a visual graphic of each step of the strategy he was presented with.

A framework for thinking about these adjustments can also assist teachers, in conjunction with their colleagues, students, and family members, to make changes in the way that lessons are designed, structured, and delivered (Udvari-Solner & Thousand, 1995). One such framework has six components to investigate: (1) the structure of the instructions, (2) the demands and evaluation criteria of the task, (3) the learning environment, (4) the materials used for learning, (5) the support structure, and (6) participatory activities. Box 10.13 lists the questions that can be asked within each category.

| TABLE 10.4 | **Instructional Accommodations** |
|---|---|
| **Areas for Instructional Adaptations** | **Examples** |
| Instructional groupings | Whole-group, small-group, one-to-one, independent seatwork |
| | Teacher-directed, partner learning, cross-age tutors, cooperative groups |
| Location of instruction | Different areas in the classroom |
| | Other school environments (playground, cafeteria, office, library) |
| Physical arrangement of the environment | Location of materials |
| | Lighting |
| | Noise levels |
| | Heights of desks or chairs |
| | Arrangement of furniture |
| Materials | Large-print books |
| | Calculators |
| | Recorded books |
| | Manipulatives |
| | Magnifying equipment |
| | Adaptive equipment such as pencil holders and name stamps |
| Presentation format | Modified language by simplifying, using common terms, or inserting symbols or pictures |
| | Graphics such as advanced organizers |
| Student response format | Pictures or graphics |
| | Templates for responding |
| | Responses marked in book |
| | Typewriter or computer |
| | Audiotaped responses |
| | Written instead of oral presentation |

## An Instructional Accommodations Framework

The questions in Box 10.13 are designed to help school professionals make the fewest changes possible while optimizing the learning environment for all students. The process of accommodating the diverse needs of learners does not need to be an additive process. That is, school professionals may be able to adjust their instructional plans to accommodate the varied needs of their students. If the existing instructional plan meets the RSVP criteria of reasonableness, soundness, validity, and power and some learners continue to struggle, then the instructional accommodation framework can guide school professionals in making adjustments to either instructional procedures or the curriculum.

The goal of instructional adaptation is to more closely align the learning preferences and needs of the student with the teacher's teaching style. Once again, it is important that you consider the student's cognitive, affective, communicative, and physical/health needs. In Table 10.3, we listed the instructional strategies that support learners who have needs in the cognitive domain. Where an individual student has particular needs in one or more of the need areas, school professionals will need to ensure that the appropriate instructional strategies are consistently used in all instruction.

In adapting instruction, the goal is to maximize the extent to which the students can access and participate in the learning opportunities of the classroom. For some students, more individualized approaches to

BOX 10.13

## Questions to Ask in an Instructional Accommodations Framework

### Structure of the Instructions

1. What can these students do well (in any and all domains)?
2. Can all students actively participate in the lessons without modification?
3. Can all students' participation be increased by changing the instructional arrangement?
4. Can all students' participation be increased by changing the lesson format?

### Demands and Evaluation Criteria of the Task

1. What specific needs (in any of the needs domains) do the students have that could be built into this lesson?
2. Will some students need adapted curricular goals?
3. What adjustments to performance standards, pacing, content, functional applications, evaluation criteria, or management techniques are needed?

### Learning Environment

1. How can students contribute meaningfully to the group's work?
2. What changes in the classroom environment or lesson location will facilitate participation?

### Learning Materials

1. Will different materials be needed?
2. Should the materials differ in size, number, or format?
3. Will different materials allow a different mode of input or output?
4. Will different materials reduce the level of abstraction?

### Support Structure

1. What needs to be incorporated into the group's reward structure to encourage all students to help one another contribute and learn as much as is possible and attainable for them?
2. Will personal assistance for some students be needed to ensure participation? From whom?

### Activities to Foster Participation

1. What changes should be made in teaching methods, in the directions given to all students, in the way they demonstrate their knowledge or learning, or in the ways they work together?
2. Will a different activity need to be designed and offered for some students and a small group of peers? In the classroom? In other school environments? In the community outside the school?

instruction may be needed to teach a specific skill. Providing specific prompts, such as full physical prompts to assist a student in performing the learning target, is one example of a highly individualized approach (Snell, 1994).

For instance, suppose that a second-grade teacher is creating a routine in her classroom whereby children will simply leave the classroom whenever they need to use the bathroom. The teacher establishes a routine for leaving the classroom that involves students finding their own magnet-backed photograph and placing it on the "out-of-class" board before leaving to go to the bathroom. They must go directly to the bathroom and return directly to the classroom. When students re-enter the classroom, they move their photos back to the attendance board. When one classroom teacher ac-

tually taught this routine, she taught it to the whole class and provided small-group practice time. For the first week that she instituted this procedure, she provided group rewards to each team in her class that was able to successfully complete the procedure each morning and afternoon. In the second week, she used a daily acknowledgment procedure. By the third week, she was randomly giving feedback to students who used the system correctly. Only Annie still had trouble with the routine because her working memory required more practice than most learners in order for her to produce a new skill without prompts and cues. The classroom teacher decided to set aside some individual instructional time with Annie. She used an instructional procedure called the "discrete trial" to teach Annie this routine (see Box 10.14). Like other forms of

**BOX 10.14**

## Steps in the Discrete Trial Procedure

**Before a Student Response**

1. Provide a clear, distinct stimulus for students to respond to.

2. Provide verbal, gestural, or physical prompts, if necessary, to guide the accuracy of student response.

3. Provide sufficient prompts to get an accurate student response.

4. Repeat and gradually reduce prompts until performance is maintained by rewards or responses from the environment.

**After a Student Response**

1. Provide specific praise or rewards for accurate responses.

2. Ignore incorrect responses, but assess what inputs the student needs to make a correct response.

3. Wait at least ten seconds before providing the stimulus again.

---

direct instruction, the discrete trial procedure begins by breaking tasks down into small components and then helps learners to practice routines by carefully inserting only the prompts necessary to successfully complete a step in the process.

Discrete trial is an example of an instructional accommodation that is designed to meet the unique needs of individual learners and requires one-on-one instruction. This process, like other forms of tutoring, requires the full attention of a teacher. If school professionals can anticipate that they or a support person may need to provide this level of assistance, they may choose to plan the instructional schedule so that all students are working in small groups or teams. This frees some instructional time to provide this level of assistance. There are other, intensive, procedure-based instructional models that require very small teacher-to-student ratios, such as graduated guidance, **differential reinforcement schedules,** cuing, and time delay (Snell, 1994; Wolery, Bailey, & Sugai, 1988). When students need these intensive levels of instruction to master skills, school professionals and support personnel must work collaboratively to plan and carry out instruction.

## ■ SECTION SUMMARY

Instruction in inclusive school communities must support the learning preferences and needs of students. Sometimes, despite a teacher's thorough planning and competent execution of instruction, one or more students will require more individualized approaches. As with curriculum modifications, evaluation of instruction will help you create instructional adaptations that attend to and consider the affective, cognitive, communicative, and physical/health needs of students. School professionals, related-services personnel, students, and their families should participate in the process of determining instructional adaptations. Through careful analysis, a match can be made between the student's needs and the system's responses.

## Chapter Summary

School professionals must be able to select and use teaching methods that provide students with the fundamental skills they need to become proficient learners. The use of sound instructional practices that are carefully designed to meet the needs of learners in a particular learning environment can diminish the need for separating students by ability groups. However, to accomplish this difficult task, school professionals must collaborate along with support personnel, students, families, and community members. Information about the unique learning needs of students will come from the students themselves, from their families, and from school professionals like the school psychologist, special education teacher, or counselor. Careful choices of instructional approaches, combined with attention to the organizational structures of the learning environments, will ensure that students have opportunities to learn. Using the assessment processes discussed in Chapter 8, school professionals can track and adjust their instructional and curricular strategies to meet the needs of all learners. Remembering that one activity can have multiple outcomes means that school professionals can focus their attention on creating activities that accommodate varying needs.

Because it is impossible to include all possible teaching methods in a single chapter, we have developed the RSVP rubric to guide school professionals in the selection of teaching methods. Typically, we have chosen to present only those methods that can be used in a classroom in which a single teacher works with support from other school professionals and, sometimes, a para-educator. Where school professionals work together to address the individual and unique needs of students, the RSVP criteria and the instructional accommodations framework are particularly valuable. Good planning is supported by competent instructional implementation. Skills like "withitness," smoothness, and overlapping help to focus students on learning tasks rather than on controlling behavior.

---

### INSTRUCTIONAL ACTIVITY

## Carousel Brainstorming

### Objective

- To create a series of lesson plans that reflect multiple instructional strategies for supporting the same curriculum objective

### Materials

- Packages of file cards of different colors for each group of students

### Product

- A collection of file cards that contain abbreviated versions of lesson plans for a curriculum objective

### Agenda

- Your instructor will assign you to groups of no more than four persons.
- Each group will receive a package of file cards (remember each group will have a different color).
- In your groups, begin by thinking of a skill or topic that you want to teach. You must specify the age group to whom you would teach this content. Write the skill or topic on one file card, and then on the same card generate an objective for one lesson.

- On a second file card, describe how you would teach the lesson—the instructional strategy or strategies you would use and the materials and evaluation methods you would incorporate.
- Hold onto your second card (describing how you would teach the lesson) while passing on your first card to another group.
- Look at the topic or skill card you received from another group. On a blank card, generate your own lesson for the same content. In essence, each group independently creates a lesson plan for each of the topics. When the topic cards have rotated among all groups, all cards of the same color should be returned to the original group.
- Review the lesson plans generated for your topic and report to the class the variations on lessons that can be used for a single topic. In addition, analyze the advantages and disadvantages of each lesson for learners with particular learning preferences.

### Evaluation

- Criteria include group ability to correctly analyze the similarities and differences among the lesson plans and to match and critique approaches to instruction and learner preferences.

# Glossary

**Cognitive behavior modification**  A teaching strategy that relies on the use of small, carefully sequenced steps in teaching students to use internal language to influence and mediate their behavior.

**Concept attainment**  A teaching strategy that provides students with a list of attributes that are then used to distinguish both examples and nonexamples of a targeted concept.

**Differential reinforcement schedules**  A technique that involves the deliberate reinforcement of a specific behavior when, and only when, it occurs under specific conditions.

**Discrete trial**  A systematic approach to instruction, typically used with students who have severe or profound learning needs, that requires the teacher to control the presentation of stimulus, prompts, and consequences.

**Jurisprudential inquiry**  A teaching strategy that engages students in case studies containing problems that can only be solved through values clarification and resolution of conflicts and competing demands.

**Mastery learning**  Instructional model based on the view that any learner can master a set of objectives if provided with sufficient time and appropriate materials.

**Scaffold**  Refers to when teachers provide supports such as cues or prompts to help students develop competent performance levels.

**Shaping**  Cuing or reinforcing students for progressively moving toward a target behavior.

# Examples of Strategies from the Social Family

## Informal Cooperative Learning Activities

| Approach | Description | Application |
|---|---|---|
| **Tell/retell 2-4-8** | A pair of students tell each other about an incident or experience they had. Then this pair of students joins another pair. Partner A tells partner B's story, partner B tells partner A's story, and so on. These two pairs now join four other students and recount short versions of another incident or experience. The group then comes to a consensus on two or three issues, benefits, or themes that are represented in the stories. Finally, a spokesperson tells the class about the group's conclusions. | This method gives rigorous attention to both receptive and expressive communication skills while promoting the cognitive processes of attention, perception, and working memory. |

## Formal Cooperative Learning Activities

| Approach | Description | Application |
|---|---|---|
| **Group investigation** | Students are assigned to heterogenous groups to study a designated topic. They seek information from a variety of sources inside and outside the classroom. Group members each contribute something to the group product. Central to the group's work is the planning of their inquiry. Together, members determine how they will investigate and present their completed project to the class. Often, there is a division of labor in the group that enhances positive interdependence among members. | Group investigation is appropriate for integrated study projects that deal with the acquisition, analysis, and synthesis of information in order to solve a multifaceted problem. The academic task allows for diverse contributions from group members but should avoid seeking only direct answers to factual questions. For example, it would be ideal for teaching about the history and culture of a country or about the biology of the rain forest, but it would not be appropriate for teaching map skills, multiplication facts, or the periodic table of the elements. |
| **Teams, games, tournaments (TGT)** | These methods consist of five major components: (1) whole-class teaching, (2) team practice, (3) assessment using quizzes (STAD) or tournaments (TGT), (4) scoring, and (5) team recognition. | These are related methods developed by Slavin (1983) that employ both a cooperative goal structure and an extremely fair form of competition. They can be used in any subject area from grades 2 through 12. If the teacher has done a good job of creating study teams that are truly heterogenous and if the bumping |

*(continued)*

## Formal Cooperative Learning Activities *(continued)*

| Approach | Description | Application |
|---|---|---|
| **Teams, games, tournaments (TGT)** *(cont.)* | Whole-class teaching occurs in a variety of ways depending on the preference of the teachers and the material. For example, students may read, listen to a lecture, view a video, or call on other human resources.<br><br>The team practice phase occurs in groups of four or five students who represent a cross-section of the class in terms of academic performance, gender, or ethnicity. The major function of the team is to prepare all its members to do well on the quizzes or in the tournaments. The team meets together after the initial presentation of the material to study worksheets, notes, outlines, or photos. Members discuss problems together, compare answers, and correct any misconceptions if teammates make mistakes.<br><br>In TGT, students participate in games and tournaments. Games are composed of content-relevant questions designed to test knowledge. Games are played at tables of three students, each of whom represents a different study team.<br><br>Scoring in STAD consists of comparing previous quiz scores with the current score to determine an improvement percentage. In TGT, the scoring system is more complex. Each student earns a score depending on how he or she placed in the game—first, second, or third place. The student then adds his or her score to the scores of the other study team members to get a team score. Study teams use the weekly score to rank themselves in the class. | process is done well, every student—no matter what his or her abilities or limitations—competes. Teams may earn certificates or other rewards for the highest scores in TGT. Recognition of accomplishments sets the competitive aspect of the methods up as a group motivator. In one variation, the teacher may use quizzes rather than tournaments to assess student learning. |
| **Jigsaw** | Each member of a threesome selects or is assigned a portion or piece of the group's task. Members must sort and synthesize their pieces of the "puzzle" by gathering, studying, and organizing information. Group members teach their critical findings to the other group members so they all know all the pieces of the jigsaw as well as they know their own. | The jigsaw method is particularly powerful because of its versatility. It can be used in any subject area, and it can employ modified materials that accommodate any level of learner needs. The basic premise of jigsaw is the same as in group investigation. The name "jigsaw" comes from the puzzlelike character of the arrangement. To participate in jigsaw, students need explicit instruction on how to share the information they have with others. Once mastered, the design can be varied endlessly to accommodate many different types of material. |

## Peer-Mediated Instructional Activities

| Approach | Description | Application |
|---|---|---|
| **Turn to Your Partner and . . . (TTYPA)** | TTYPA gets students to talk to one another as they explore personal connections to the topic under discussion. Telling one another about what they just learned seems to enhance their memory and learning (Weaver & Cotrell, 1986). | This method sets high expectations for students because it is next to impossible to turn to a partner and *not* say something. There is a built-in expectation for reciprocity and positive interdependence. It's hard to get left out of a twosome if one partner depends on the other to do his or her part. |
| **Paired partners: think aloud** | This design pairs students so that one becomes the problem solver and the other becomes the thinking monitor. The problem solver talks aloud while completing a task, giving a running monologue of thoughts, strategies, and ideas for solving the problem. The monitor cues the "think aloud" of the problem solver with appropriate questions: What is your purpose? What are you expecting? Does that make sense? Why? What are you thinking? Did you skip a step? | The focus of this method is on helping students make their thinking "visible" so they can correct faulty reasoning and strategies for doing tasks. This method requires intense, guided practice for effective partner work, but it is worthwhile because of its power to adapt to many subjects and to emphasize the self-reflective aspects of cognition, affect, and communication (Bloom & Broder, 1950; Whimbey & Whimbey, 1975). |
| **Dyads: think/pair/share** | This cooperative method, based on the work of Lyman (1981) and Lyman and McTighe (1988), is a multimode discussion cycle. Students first acquire some information by listening to a question or a presentation, watching a video, or reading a passage. They then take time to think individually, talk with each other in pairs, and finally share responses with the larger group. The teacher signals students to switch to think, pair, and share modes by using cues. | Cuing enables teachers to manage the amount of time students spend thinking about their forthcoming response (Rowe, 1986), thus combating impulsivity and improving the quality of responses. Cuing also assists students in knowing how to think about a particular topic. For example, the teacher may cue students to reach consensus, engage in problem solving, or assume the role of devil's advocate. |
| **Classwide peer tutoring** | This pairs students for brief but frequent periods of drill and practice of factual material. This method has been correlated with improved student achievement on weekly quizzes (Maheady, Sacca, & Harper, 1988). It helps focus students' attention for intense practice periods. | The teacher might have students work in pairs to practice the spelling of vocabulary words. The teacher would set it up this way: Partner A says one word at a time while partner B writes it. As partner B writes, partner A watches letter by letter. When partner B finishes the word, partner A either pronounces it "correct" and awards 2 points to partner B or says, "wrong" and then spells it correctly so partner B can write it correctly. Partner B follows this first correct spelling with two more correct copies of the word. When the remedial task is complete, partner A awards 1 point to partner B and goes on to the next word. Partner A cycles through all the words as many times as possible in the four-minute time frame. The partners then change roles, and partner B reads the words as partner A writes. |

*(continued)*

## Peer-Mediated Instructional Activities *(continued)*

| Approach | Description | Application |
|---|---|---|
| **Triads: observer feedback** | This variation of peer teaching is most useful when the purpose of the lesson is to have students examine their own thinking, processing of information, use of steps or procedures, or social behaviors. In this case, a third member is assigned to each pair—but strictly as an observer, not a participant. The role of the observer is to stand outside the activity, looking in, as it were, on the action. In this way, metacognitive processes can be fostered in the classroom. The observer records specific data during the partner interaction and then provides feedback when the partner interaction ends. | Mrs. Rahjad, the second-grade teacher from Chapter 5, used this method during her unit on creatures of the ocean. She assigned the task of creating a Venn diagram to compare and contrast the characteristics of sharks and dolphins. She directed the partners to try to share as many ideas as possible but to be sure to take turns doing so. The observer then tallied each partner's number of speaking turns. After the task was completed, the observer shared the data with the partners and discussed how many turns each person had and the sequence of speaking turns. Thus, Mrs. Rahjad was teaching pragmatic language skills, social skills, and cognitive skills simultaneously. For some children, this opportunity to practice is crucial to their continued communicative and social development. |

**A P P E N D I X   1 0 . 2**

# Examples of Strategies from the Information Processing Family

## Strategies for Enhancing Memory

| Approach | Description | Application |
|---|---|---|
| **Mnemonics** | Mnemonics are memory-enhancing devices that help students remember information.<br><br>For example, when trying to remember how many days there are in a given month, do you find yourself reciting the verse "Thirty days hath September, April, June, and November . . ."? Or do you count on your knuckles, with the "high" points the longer months and the "dips" between knuckles the shorter ones? Some people recall the colors of the visible spectrum using the device ROY G BIV—Red, Orange, Yellow, Green, Blue, Indigo, Violet. When asked to name the five great lakes, some people immediately remember HOMES—Huron, Ontario, Michigan, Erie, Superior. Even adults who haven't seen their piano teacher for years remember the notes on the lines of the treble clef by reciting, "Every Good Boy Deserves Fudge—EGBDF" and the notes in the spaces as FACE.<br><br>Mnemonic devices that use significant letters that form a word (like HOMES) are known as acronyms. FOIL is an acronym in which the letters tell the order of processes for solving quadratic equations—First Outside, Inside Last. Mnemonic devices that employ letters to stand for the words in a sentence are called acrostics. For example, some people remember how to spell the word *arithmetic* by reciting the acrostic "a rat in the house might eat the ice cream." | When faced with the task of remembering information, proficient learners do so by first thinking about the relevance of the information in their lives and about the relationship one bit of information has to another. When the relevance and connections are apparent, immediate, and important, no extra memory devices need to be employed (Carney, Levin, & Levin, 1993). But school professionals (and others) often ask students to remember information for which they have little background knowledge, experience, or other cognitive connections. When long-term memory structures are weak, partially formed, or unavailable, proficient students find that the use of a mnemonic device helps them remember the material (Eggen & Kauchak, 1992). Inefficient learners, in contrast, tend to overrely on rote rehearsal or repetition as a memory device but find that the results are inconsistent. |
| **FIRST-letter**<br>**(Nagel, Schumaker,**<br>**& Deshler, 1986)** | To use the FIRST-letter strategy, do the following:<br>1. *F*orm a word.<br>2. *I*nsert a letter(s).<br>3. *R*earrange the letters.<br>4. *S*hape a sentence.<br>5. *T*ry combinations. | Students can create mnemonic acronyms using the first letters from the words they need to memorize. |

*(continued)*

# Informal Cooperative Learning Activities

| Approach | Description | Application |
|---|---|---|
| **SAIL (Gearheart, DeRuiter, & Sileo, 1986)** | To use the SAIL strategy, do the following:<br>1. *S*elect the item to be learned.<br>2. *A*ssociate a familiar word (keyword) that sounds similar to the item to be learned.<br>3. *I*llustrate the association between the keyword and the item to be learned, including as much meaning as possible.<br>4. *L*earn the meanings by rehearsing and reviewing the illustrations. | Students can use SAIL to create their own keyword devices to remember individual words, phrases, and passages. |
| **Reciprocal teaching (Palinscar & Brown, 1984)** | Reciprocal teaching consists of ongoing interaction between two students about a particular reading passage they are working on. Each student assumes the role of teacher and asks questions of the other to assist the partner in critical analysis of the passage. | Reciprocal teaching is an instructional model that is associated with reading instruction. The use of questioning techniques are thought to activate higher levels of reading comprehension. |
| **SQ3R: survey question, read, recite, review (Robinson, 1946)** | To use SQ3R, students move through five interactions with the text:<br>1. *Survey* the material by reading quickly through the major headings and introductory and summarizing paragraphs. Once the survey is complete, they evaluate whether informational needs have been met. If so, the process stops. If not, they move to the second step.<br>2. Ask *questions* about each heading or subtopic and predict the content of each section.<br>3. Locate the answers to the questions and identify the main idea from each section.<br>4. *Recite* to answer the questions by speaking, outlining, making notes, or creating other visual representations of the information in a personalized manner.<br>5. *Review* to commit the information to memory using the words or representations created in the previous step. | Research suggests that self-questioning can be taught to all students using direct instruction, modeling, imitation, reinforcement, and reciprocal questioning (Palinscar, 1982; Wong & Jones, 1982). However, students tend to be better at self-questioning when the topic is somewhat familiar to them and when the reading material is not too difficult (Andre & Anderson, 1978–79; Miyake & Norman, 1979). Students who asked themselves higher-order questions (evaluation, comparison, problem solving, cause and effect) also showed better comprehension than those who asked lower-order (literal) questions. |
| **Solving unknown words (Ellis, 1996)** | These five steps can be taught to readers who lack strategies for figuring out unknown words they encounter during reading:<br>1. Use the context for clues.<br>2. Look for semantic clues.<br>3. Break the word into component parts. | The use of context clues involves guessing what the unknown word means based on the surrounding text. Semantic analysis involves looking for smaller, familiar words within the unknown word. Structural analysis involves breaking the word into component parts (prefixes, suffixes) to see if the root word is a familiar one. Word |

*(continued)*

## Informal Cooperative Learning Activities *(continued)*

| Approach | Description | Description |
|---|---|---|
| **Solving unknown words** *(cont.)* | 4. Identify word components that have specific meanings.<br>5. Use external sources. | components involves breaking down unknown words into smaller units that hold specific meanings in English. For example, *pre* means "before," and *ing* means "in the process of doing an action." External sources include asking another person and using the dictionary. |
| **Procedure sheets** | To use a note-taking "procedure sheet," follow the steps:<br>1. Pick out the most important and then the supporting ideas, and summarize them.<br>2. Write notes in your own words, using your own abbreviation system.<br>3. Use words that give structural clues, like "first" and "because" to help you remember the relationships between ideas. | Note taking requires the learner to identify the main ideas from an assortment of information bits offered either orally or in print. Younger students and those who have fine motor limitations tend to have more difficulty because the amount of energy they must devote to the formation of letters and symbols distracts them from the cognitive task of differentiating between main and lesser ideas. Brown and Day (1983) suggest that typically developing students should begin to learn note-taking skills by about the fourth grade. Many teachers who use holistic approaches to reading and writing instruction have much younger students taking notes as they read, even if those notes are not readable by others. Teaching students to take notes involves helping them to review a written passage (a sentence or a paragraph) and extract the fewest number of words that convey its meaning. |

# Putting It All Together

## CHAPTER 11

# Meeting the Needs of All Learners

# Four Frameworks for Dialog, Four Arenas for Action

### by Tom Bellamy

Not surprisingly, given the incessant press coverage of education, school professionals often feel they work at the center of a storm. Conflicting currents of public and professional opinion affect what they do, how it is perceived, and whether it is allowed to succeed. Practices that are praised as innovative one year are often criticized the next as outdated or out of step with some new philosophy. Success—indeed, even perseverance—in this context requires reflection and dialog about the issues affecting professional practice and a willingness to influence, and not merely accept, the direction of the storm.

But the issues are complex, and often what is intended as a dialog seems like talking into the wind. What starts as reflection often ends in confusion or too-eager acceptance of the next viewpoint or practice advocated by one of the many interest groups in the education community.

Over the years, as a special education teacher, researcher, teacher educator, federal program administrator, and, now, university dean, I have developed a simple but effective way to sort through complex issues in education and special education. Essentially, my approach rests on the belief that almost every issue worth working on in education has four critical vantage points, each structuring an important framework for dialog and an arena for action.

The first, where most school professionals spend most of their time, is what I call the professional/procedural vantage point. Conversations within this framework ask questions like these: What techniques and

procedures produce desired results for students? How does the school professional set priorities and organize materials to achieve those results? How can professional services and informal supports work in concert? This dialog is informed by a rich knowledge base of procedural research, process/product research, and qualitative studies that address day-to-day life in schools. Positive action within the procedural vantage point is often described as action research. Professional action has been extremely influential in demonstrating that limitations previously attributed to individual students and their disabilities could be overcome with better instructional methods—leading, in turn, to higher expectations, greater exercise of rights, and more opportunities for self-determination by individuals with varying abilities.

Of course, professionals work in organizations, with rules, roles, funding levels, policies, goals, and mandates—which give rise to the second vantage point. Conversations in this organizational framework address questions like the following: How should an organization be structured and managed to achieve its goals? How should resources be allocated to serve conflicting needs? What interpersonal and cultural features support or detract from the organization's mission? Can the defined goals of the organization be achieved within the available resources? Our knowledge base about the effectiveness of organizations in delivering education services expands through such efforts as program evaluation, scaled-up innovations, and studies in the theory and practice of leadership. The organizational vantage point of-

fers rich possibilities as an arena for positive action by school professionals. Demonstrations that particular programs work—that they achieve worthy goals for individuals with disabilities within normal resource constraints—can stimulate broad changes in the expectations of consumers and policymakers and create intense pressure for improvement in other services.

Organizations, in turn, exist within a policy context established by government action, giving rise to the third vantage point. Conversations within this policy framework explore whether the mandates, incentives, rights, and support systems established by state and federal governments have their intended effect. Do they, in fact, achieve the goals defined through the political process? Do they structure achievable goals for organizations responsible for actual delivery of the required services? The knowledge base in this area grows through legal research and policy analysis. Positive action by school professionals includes participation in the work of professional and advocacy organizations as they attempt to influence the political process and use the courts to clarify and support the rights of individuals, including those with disabilities.

The fourth vantage point addresses philosophical and cultural perspectives. What values underlie the public policies, organizational structures, and professional practices that affect individuals from diverse ethnic, linguistic, and cultural backgrounds, as well as those who have differing ability levels? How are conflicts among these values resolved? How strong is the commitment to these values among professionals and the general public? Our knowledge base in this area progresses through critical inquiry and ethics, and action strategies for school professionals involve personal persuasion, dialog, and public information.

What can you do with the four vantage points? I use them in three ways. First, I depend on them to help sort out the many facets of education issues. In this sense, they are a guide to productive conversations, helping to maintain a common focus as a problem is explored. Second, all four vantage points serve as a guide for reflection and analysis. Any position at one vantage point reflects assumptions about the other three. Making these assumptions explicit often challenges my earlier thinking on the topic. Finally, the four vantage points provide a guide to action. Progress in one arena often stimulates progress in the other three; lack of attention to any one arena can stifle creativity in the others. I look for opportunities for progress on all four vantage points, expecting change to proceed in different ways on different issues.

# Introduction

In this text, we have highlighted the changing face of education and promoted the use of inclusive school communities as a response to those changes. Using Tom Bellamy's four vantage points, we explored the organizational, philosophical, and policy perspectives in Chapters 1–4. For example, in Chapter 1, we introduced the concept of inclusive school communities as a logical response to our increasingly diverse society. In Chapter 2, we examined the values that have driven legislative mandates for inclusive educational practices. In Chapter 3, we traced the increased importance of involving families in the educational process. And in Chapter 4, we discussed the policy and organizational shifts required to support new roles for school professionals, support personnel, students, families, and community members. Chapters 5–10 primarily addressed Bellamy's fourth lens, professional/procedural knowledge. For example, in Chapter 5, we explored how cognitive, communicative, affective, and physical/health domains can inform our understanding of learning in individual children. And Chapters 6–9 outlined strategies for creating inclusive classroom environments through classroom management, assessment, curriculum, and instructional practices that acknowledge and accommodate diversity.

Making the kind of changes necessary to create and sustain inclusive school communities can be difficult and time-consuming. In this chapter, we introduce a framework for guiding the change process. First, we introduce a portion of this framework, based on the story model, which was designed as a tool for educators in training, school professionals, and concerned community members to analyze and respond to issues of educational change (Drake, Bebbington, Laksman, Mackie, Maynes, & Wayne, 1992). Second, we extend the story model by adding Bellamy's four vantage points to the framework (Bellamy, 1994). Through various vantage points, we analyze the values, policies and regulations, organizational structures, and professional behaviors and procedures that effect change in educational organizations. Finally, we examine the philosophical, policy, organizational, and procedural issues involved in creating and sustaining inclusive school communities.

# Changing Schools in a Diverse Society

## The Complexity of Issues That Face School Professionals, Students, Families, and Community Members

The issues faced by school professionals are not limited to the field of education. Not only do economic, political, and social issues impact school communities, but schools can serve as the catalyst for issues that take on national or global prominence.

For almost any issue that we face as a society, schools are viewed as a vehicle through which to educate children and youths. Consider the war on drugs, which impacts almost every element of our society. For example, the courts are overflowing with drug-related cases; law enforcement agencies devote considerable resources to fight drug crimes; the health care system must deal with the physical and emotional costs associated with substance abuse; and the media runs commercials about the dangers of drugs. Schools are asked to participate in efforts to combat drug abuse by sponsoring education programs such as Drug Awareness Resistance Education (DARE), targeted to communicate to students the perils of substance abuse. This is just one example of how schools are called upon to assist in issues of national import.

Issues that originate in schools can also serve as the basis for change in the larger society. For example, in Chapter 1, we mentioned the passage of the School-to-Work Act in 1995. This legislation opened the door for collaboration among school professionals, community members, and business leaders to more adequately support students' long-term career education needs. The movement toward inclusive school communities challenges typical societal responses to differences based on sex, ethnicity, and learning preferences and abilities (Turner & Louis, 1996). Thus, the many facets of our society are interdependent: Community issues become school issues just as school issues ultimately become community issues.

## Complexity and Inaction

The demands placed on schools by sweeping educational, social, political, and economic changes are unrelenting and overwhelming and, often, at cross purposes. Whether creating higher standards for student achievement or establishing programs to respond to crises involving teen pregnancy, gangs, violence, drug abuse, and day care, school professionals are called upon to respond to the needs of the greater society. With each change, complex issues emerge that challenge school professionals to examine and often modify their roles, functions, and instructional practices.

The changes required to create and sustain inclusive school communities are no different from what people have to do to support other types of changes (such as responding to high teen pregnancy rates or to gangs), so creating inclusive schools will involve complex issues. Many school professionals are unsure of how to organize and manage schools and classrooms in inclusive school communities; they are unclear about the complex, constantly evolving, systemic changes that are required (Sands & Wehmeyer, 1996). "Inclusive schooling cannot spontaneously or readily occur, regardless of what any one individual does. Changes involve multiple levels of the administrative system, including the central district structure, individual building organization, and classroom instruction" (Sage, 1996, pp. 105–106). In fact, many variables converge as school professionals try to deal with such change and to utilize the research and recommended practices presented throughout this text (Malouf & Schiller, 1995; Villa, Thousand, Nevin, & Malgeri, 1996).

Without global, prolonged, in-depth discussions on the changes needed in the purpose and conduct of schooling, educational reform in the form of inclusive school communities cannot become a reality (Noddings, 1995). Given the scope of the educational, economic, social, and political issues involved, change can occur only when a broad base of individuals representing various constituencies work collaboratively to analyze and formulate solutions to the controversies faced by our school communities (Skrtic, 1995; Villa et al., 1996). School professionals must be prepared to participate in these problem-solving activities.

## Using the Story Model to Organize Complexity

It will be difficult to build inclusive school communities without a systematic framework by which to sort,

### Extending Your Learning

Pick a topic such as pollution, deforestation, animal rights, or sex. Think about the ways in which that topic interacts with social components such as business, media, politics, law, technology, the economy, and the environment, as well as the interrelationships that exist among the various components. What implications do these relationships have for the curriculum of schools?

Now, pick a topic that is usually associated with schools, such as grading, discipline, or the curriculum. Again, think about the implications of this school topic for the constituencies outside of the school environment.

analyze, evaluate, and critically reflect on the issues important to the education of our children. "Employing a systematic process allows us to organize our thoughts and systematically solve problems of practice by: (a) reflecting upon the relative impact of varying perspectives; (b) considering and evaluating the sufficiency of our current knowledge base; (c) weighing the advantages and disadvantages of possible options; and, (d) formulating and evaluating plans of action" (Sands & Wehmeyer, 1996, p. 333).

The **story model** shown in Figure 11.1 was designed as a "model for understanding the process of change" (Drake et al., 1992, p. 9). At the heart of the story model is the belief that our behaviors are driven by basic sets of assumptions and values that exist at personal, cultural, and global levels. In other words, as individuals we ascribe to certain beliefs. These beliefs may be influenced by or independent of beliefs that are communicated through our cultural heritage. Global assumptions and beliefs are common among all

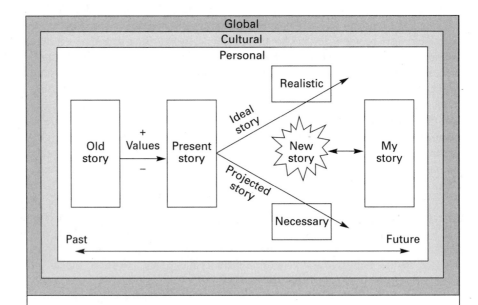

1. Identify why the present story is in a "state of flux" or change.

2. Identify the roots of the conflict by looking at the past or old story. Identify the explicit and implicit values in the old story.

3. Explore the future through:

   a. The projected story (if we continue to act according to the implicit values of the old story).

   b. The ideal story, which can be developed by examining alternative views of the future proposed by such groups as environmentalists, futurists, feminists, and holistic educators. Elicit the values inherent in these emerging stories.

4. Create a new story by integrating the *realistic* from the ideal story and the *necessary* from the projected story.

5. Develop a personal action plan that will facilitate the new story becoming reality.

**FIGURE 11.1** ■ A Guide to Using the Story Model
Source: Drake et al., 1992.

people. In order to understand, respond to, and resolve controversial issues, we must examine our own beliefs and the beliefs of others.

In using the story model, the roots of a current controversy, or "state of flux," are examined in light of - traditional ways of thinking or behaving and then current or emerging beliefs and values are considered. This usually clarifies the foundation of the current controversy or call for change. For example, changing knowledge of and assumptions about the effects of smoking have led many people to abandon this habit and promote stronger policies that limit or curtail smoking activities. Educationally, advances in our understanding of cognitive psychology and the nature and function of the brain have led to teaching technologies that support more **student-centered** and **student-directed strategies** (Caine & Caine, 1994; Schunk & Zimmerman, 1994). With a clear understanding of the past and the present, we can begin to formulate (1) a projected story (if we continue behaving the same way), (2) an ideal story (if we change and act the way we should or really want to), and (3) a new story (which is somewhere between the projected and the ideal). Based on these formulations, we can develop strategies for personal action. And by taking action, school professionals and local communities make real contributions to solving the many dilemmas we face in education.

## ■ SECTION SUMMARY

Changing schools to respond to the needs of an increasingly diverse student body will be a complex task requiring sustained work. School professionals, support personnel, administrators, families, students, and community members all must be involved. The story model provides a framework for understanding and implementing change. This model considers the importance of global, cultural, and personal values in the change process; it includes mechanisms for moving toward a new way of conducting business; and it provides an opportunity for individuals to consider how they may contribute to the process.

In the next section, we apply the story model to show how change can and does take place in our beliefs and practices. Specifically, we share our professional experiences and trace how changing values have shaped our commitment to expanding opportunities for all students to participate in inclusive school communities.

# A Personal Perspective on the Challenges of Diversity

Obviously, we are committed to creating inclusive school communities that can respond to and support the needs of children from diverse ethnic, linguistic, ability, and cultural backgrounds. We now know that schools need to examine and in some cases expand upon or change their current policies, organizational structures, and practices in order to support increasing diversity and to function in a manner that facilitates collaborative, caring communities for all learners (Apple & Beane, 1995a; Stainback & Stainback, 1996; Villa & Thousand, 1995).

A key component supporting school change is personnel and professional preparation (Villa et al., 1996). If we can alter the manner in which we prepare school professionals for their future jobs, we can support building-level efforts to create more responsive learning communities. Based on our experiences, we believe changes are needed in how we train school professionals. Here, we apply the story model in hopes of illustrating where we have been, where we are, and where we hope to be in the future with regards to this mission of creating inclusive school communities. We also hope to illustrate these key points: (1) Common ideas can emerge from diverse backgrounds and experiences; (2) values and beliefs can change over time or become more explicit with experience and new knowledge; and (3) systematic analysis allows for more pointed and responsive action.

## Our Pasts

We represent multiple and diverse backgrounds, personally and professionally, but we still ended up working on many of the same problems of school practice. An examination of our histories will help you understand how it is that we now find ourselves working toward common goals.

**DEANNA'S PAST** As a child, I had few experiences with people who had disabilities (later I discovered that my school district bused children with disabilities out of district to receive services). I had a very close friend whose parents were both deaf, but I never perceived them as "disabled" because they led "normal" lives—they were married, had children, owned a home, and were employed. I "fell" into education after initially planning to major in engineering or computer sciences. I earned an undergraduate degree in language and social science. My master's degree was in special education with an emphasis in deaf education. I earned two teaching certificates, one in elementary education and one in special education (K–12). As a result of my personnel preparation program, I left college believing (and didn't question) that the educational needs of children with disabilities were special and, for the most part, had to be addressed differently from those of children that were not identified as having disabilities. In fact, I believed that I was somehow better prepared than general educators to meet the needs of all children because of my "expertise" in students with learning problems.

My teaching career began at a state residential school for students with deafness, blindness, or deaf/blindness. These students lived on campus and went home for occasional weekends and during the summer. Many of the students I served had multiple disabilities, including cognitive, physical, communicative, and affective disabilities. At this school, children were grouped and served according to type and severity of disability. So, students with deafness and cognitive disabilities were served separately from students who had visual disabilities. In fact, there was a campus for students who were deaf, a campus for students who were blind, and a campus for students who had multiple disabilities.

Early in my career, I began to question many of the practices that my colleagues and I used to serve our students. For example, why were we taking children from their parents as early as 4 and 5 years of age and sending them to school, sometimes at distances of over 250 miles from home? Understanding that language is in a large part learned or constructed through social environments, how were students, many of whom had tremendous developmental lags in language, supposed to learn from peers who were functioning with the same developmental needs? I questioned our narrow, academic-oriented approaches to curriculum when one of my 16-year-olds approached me with tears in her eyes and said, "I just want to learn how to go to Kmart and buy my own clothes so that my mom and house-parents (residential staff) aren't always picking out what I have to wear."

After attending a professional conference, I began to push for community-based training opportunities for my students. I had come to the realization that in

many ways my students had been sheltered from the "real" world and had few skills by which to navigate the common, everyday experiences of most people, such as shopping or eating in a restaurant. Over time, with exposure, I began to realize that my students were learning from these community-based experiences—not necessarily because of anything I had ever taught them, but because they watched and mimicked people in the community. My students began to learn social skills even as they were picking up on academic skills such as math computation and reading. While we had worked diligently on these same skills in our classroom, our classroom lacked the relevance and social pressures that served to expedite their development almost overnight. I also began to observe how many of the inappropriate behaviors that my students would regularly demonstrate on our campus were nonexistent in the community.

I believed then, and still do today, that, once my students had the opportunities to interact with people who did not have disabilities, they no longer had the need to act out in inappropriate manners. I question the utility of self-contained, segregated educational environments for students with disabilities. Although I believe that the professionals in residential schools have the students' best interests at heart, I am not convinced that we adequately address the broad educational needs of students with disabilities when we teach them in segregated, isolated environments. Nor do we adequately address our own educational and social needs when we fail to teach students without disabilities to understand, support, interact with, and learn from those with disabilities. In recent years, I have extended these same beliefs to concerns for our broader school communities—inclusionary learning environments that value and support learners with diverse cultural, linguistic, socioeconomic, and ethnic backgrounds and with differing and ability levels.

**ELIZABETH'S PAST**  "Who are these children and how do they think? Why are they different?" Those were my thoughts as I looked outside the second-story window of my classroom at Franklin Elementary School. Below, on the playground (and it wasn't recess), were a group of nine or ten children who came from the "special" classroom. My mother had told me that these children were very sick. One of them, she said, was a "blue baby." I wanted more than anything to see a blue baby. But when I ventured past the classroom on my way to deliver a film projector to the kindergarten teacher, I couldn't see anyone who was blue. Later, as an adult, I realized that my mother was talking about a child with a heart defect. While this class of students was something of a novelty in our school at first, after a while their isolation from the rest of us made them fade into the background. They ate at a different time. They played outside at a different time. There was no opportunity for someone as curious as me to spend time with them.

Fortunately, I did get an opportunity to meet some children with disabilities at Camp Easter Seal. This camp provided opportunities for children without disabilities to go to camp with children with cerebral palsy, blindness, and deafness. Together, we bunked, swam, ate, and played. I learned how to tell another child about what was on her plate and where she could find her green beans (at 2 o'clock). I wheeled one boy up and down from the wheelchair cabin. I learned a little about a girl with mental retardation who looked like the rest of the kids but took a long time to understand directions.

But these were really the only opportunities that I ever had to interact with people with disabilities as a child. While they were interesting experiences, they didn't really inform my value system because I had such a limited time to be with children whose abilities were so different from mine. When I made a career choice as a high school student, ability differences did not even enter my decision-making process. I went to college to study political science with a goal of being in the diplomatic corps. But life interfered. I ended up dropping out of my undergraduate program and becoming a day care worker and, later, director.

The children who were the most fascinating to me were the ones with learning and social problems. Stephanie as a 4-year-old spent most of her day crying—what was she so afraid of? Eddie ran around that center faster than a greyhound and never stopped. Andy went to the bathroom everywhere except in the toilet. Virginia was sweet and wistful but never seemed to understand what was going on. These children were a great puzzle to me. I wanted to know how to help.

When I could, I went back to school. Imagine how disappointed I was to find out that I couldn't study special education until my master's program. But I was sure that I wanted to study and work with children with disabilities, so I got an undergraduate degree in early childhood education and a master's degree in special education with an emphasis on children with social and emotional disabilities. My first job was in a

segregated school that had been the campus for African-American students before desegregation. After desegregation, it became the school for all students with disabilities.

As a special education teacher in 1977, I was put in charge of an in-service program for teaching classroom teachers about the mandate for **mainstreamed** education. The irony, of course, was that my students were in the segregated school. When I moved to a new school district, I was employed to work with children with emotional and behavioral needs. My classroom was in a cute little brick house across the playground from the elementary school. I worked there for about a year and then transferred with some of my students to another school where we had a classroom inside the elementary school building.

Shades of Franklin Elementary School! After twenty years, I was no longer the child looking out on the playground where the children with disabilities played alone. I was the teacher taking the children with disabilities out. I realized that I could no longer work with my students in isolation from other children. So began the long process of creating opportunities for my students to be included in the rhythm and pace of life at my new elementary school. I believe that we diminish our potential for the development of connections, friendships, compassion, and fairness when we deny children the opportunities to know, understand, and value the broad spectrum of human experience: ability, linguistic, ethnic, gender, and cultural uniqueness.

**NANCY'S PAST**  I can trace the values that guide me back to 1960. The family that lived across the street from us took in a 6-month-old foster child who had come from a home where he had experienced physical abuse resulting in neurological damage. He was exactly my younger brother's age, but the developmental differences were obvious to all. Michael did everything later, with substantially more coaching and coaxing from his family—but there were some things he couldn't do at all. In 1965, my brother went to kindergarten as most 5-year-olds do. Michael wasn't invited.

I remember the grief the family experienced when they first faced the inevitable label "mental retardation." I watched that grief turn to determination to help Michael learn to do everything he possibly could to be an independent person. At age 7, his family taught him to make his own lunch because, by then, they had found a school that he could attend. Their uncommonly good sense was impressive to me. They had clear goals in mind. They believed that Michael should learn to do everything for himself that would have to be done by another person if he didn't learn how. For example, they were determined that he should learn enough about reading to distinguish canned peas from cranberry relish at the grocery store. And they insisted that he learn something about how to use money and get change.

Michael's first school was in a church basement. He and six other children were kept apart from other kids his age, but he had a real teacher and a real schedule that was similar to that of the neighborhood kids. As Michael grew older, the classes that were available to him were often what his foster parents called "envelope stuffing." They led only to complete dependence on family, charity, or the institutional system—always separated from the mainstream of life. Michael's family objected vigorously, consistently voicing their belief that every child, no matter how disabled, should be taught to be as independent as possible and that they should have a rich and varied set of friends and acquaintances in their community.

I was only a neighbor—Michael's baby-sitter at times—but I was already an avid student of special education. When I started college in 1965, having watched this family fight for their child's education, my decision about what major to pursue was easy. I needed to know more about special education. My disappointment grew as I took course after course that gave me so little information about how to educate children with disabilities in real schools. After four years, I had earned a dual degree in elementary and special education, but I had very little knowledge about how to provide the kind of education that Michael's family wanted for him.

I spent the 1970s teaching in an elementary classroom. I wasn't willing to spend my career in church basement classrooms. In the mid-1970s, state and federal laws were enacted that affected my school and classroom directly. For the first time, the kids from the church basement had a room in a regular school building. "Mainstreaming" became the buzzword of the decade, and I experimented with every available technique to meet the needs of children with diverse strengths and weaknesses. Unfortunately, I felt very alone in this endeavor. I had no colleagues who shared my perspective, nor did I have much support from special education teachers. Their job, they told me, was to stay in the special education room with the other kids while one or two children came to my classroom for

short periods of time. Other classroom teachers viewed special education as a way of relieving themselves of students who had difficulty learning.

In the 1980s, I tried negotiating with the special educators. I said, "Bring all the special education students to my room for math, and you come, too. We'll plan lessons for all the students and divide our instructional time among all of them." These early attempts to include all children on a small scale were alternately successful and frustrating. Inclusion of all children was still far from a reality. The kinds of schoolwide support and collaboration among professionals that I needed to accomplish my agenda were patently absent. The instructional technologies—classroom management, assessment methods, instructional methods, and curricular design—that we needed to make it all work were still in early stages of implementation.

Now, at the dawn of the twenty-first century, the instructional technologies are well developed. Many schools are working to establish the collaborative culture they need to support the diverse needs of all students. All this is too late for Michael—he is 35 years old now, living at home with his parents. He goes to work two or three days a week with his father (a retired policeman) at Disney World in Orlando, Florida, selling hats to park visitors. I think that the schools of the twenty-first century will be able to provide the kind of education Michael deserved. My mission is to help make that happen.

**MAKING MEANING FROM OUR PASTS** Interestingly, Deanna's early views of disability were centered in her analysis of whether individuals engaged in "typical" activities or had an actual disability. Those views served as a foundation that helped her to challenge and later dismiss many of the assumptions communicated through her teacher preparation program. Her teaching experiences helped her to develop a value for education that extended beyond traditional academics in order to prepare her students for critical life experiences. She also came to realize the importance of teaching students within real-life contexts.

The early explanations provided to Elizabeth about children with disabilities communicated commonly held beliefs at that time—that children with disabilities were sick and needed to be attended to in a manner that was distinct and separate from children without disabilities. Although her early, limited interactions with children who had disabilities were interesting, it was not until she had more long-term interactions with them that she began to understand them in a new way. Elizabeth's experience communicates how important ongoing, sustained interactions are to helping people come to truly understand and value our differences.

Early on in her childhood, Nancy was exposed to a family who, from the beginning, challenged commonly held views about and practices with children who had disabilities. These experiences had a direct influence on Nancy's career choice. Furthermore, those experiences instilled in Nancy a set of beliefs and values that helped her to pursue personal educational training that would prepare her to teach in a way that contested previous boundaries.

Our pasts represent the adventures of (1) a special education teacher with experiences primarily in separate, segregated schools, (2) a special educator with experiences in public schools but serving students in **self-contained classrooms,** and (3) a general educator who, without formal training, extended her instructional support systems to all children in her classroom, despite their varied learning capacities and needs. The predominant societal values of our pasts were that (1) disability was a condition that needed to be fixed and (2) students with disabilities required highly specialized and separate educational support systems. However, with experience, each of us began to question traditional views of disability and the nature of the special education system. Our independent pasts led us to share common beliefs and assumptions about the purpose of schooling and the manner in which we should address the needs of children who represent cultural, linguistic, ethnic, and socioeconomic backgrounds and have differing abilities.

## Our Present

Our pasts have converged, and the three of us are now involved in teacher preparation and professional development activities. This book grew out of a desire to influence the material presented in survey courses on exceptional children taught to undergraduate and graduate-level students in teacher preparation programs. These introductory-level courses, which are probably very similar to the ones that you are taking if you are reading this text, serve as a foundation to most initial teacher certification programs—in general and special education. The purpose of these courses is to introduce potential teachers to issues specific to edu-

cating youths with disabilities. Texts used in these courses typically are organized to provide, according to individual disability labels, **etiology, prevalence data,** groups of characteristics, and special education eligibility information. Those texts usually provide little information related to specific classroom instruction, curriculum, and management practices. Because general education teachers generally have to take only one course on students with disabilities, they often have no opportunities to learn specific strategies for working with such students. Students who plan to eventually become special educators must take additional courses to learn this information.

Examination of the content of texts used to provide teachers with information on students with disabilities left us wondering what people would do with information such as the numbers and characteristics of people with particular disability labels or the pathology/etiology of their conditions. It seemed as though we automatically set up students with disabilities with the teacher expectation that they were very different and, as a result, difficult to teach. Furthermore, few texts offered specific suggestions as to the types of instructional practices that would facilitate the participation of students with disabilities in general education classrooms. This meant that general educators were leaving their personal preparation programs with little idea as to how to support inclusionary practices for students with diverse needs.

We do not believe that students with disabilities or other students from varying cultural, linguistic, or economic backgrounds are all that difficult. Of course, there are children who challenge our ability to support and manage their educational needs. And it will take the work of teams of school professionals beyond the general education teacher to identify the learning needs of those students and to provide assessment, curriculum, instruction, and classroom management activities to support those needs. But to move toward school communities that can support the diverse needs of all students, changes are needed in our teacher preparation practices.

## Our New Story

According to the story model (Drake et al., 1992), new stories are derived through the interaction of the realistic components or beliefs from the ideal story and the necessary components or beliefs from the past story.

Personal actions then actualize the new story. Our new story emerges as we seek new ways of organizing content and implementing teacher preparation programs. Traditionally, persons pursuing careers in general and special education have been prepared in separate training programs—one for general educators and one for special educators. Furthermore, within special education, teachers often are trained in programs specific to a particular disability label. For example, if you want to work with students who are labeled "learning disabled," you take course work specific to that categorical label. If you want to work with students labeled "emotionally disturbed," you might take a different set of courses related to that categorical label. But, again, children with disabilities are more alike than different from children who are not labeled, and children with disabilities have a right to participate in general education classrooms with necessary supports and services. As long as we prepare teachers in a manner that leads them to believe that the needs of children from various backgrounds are so different from those of "typical" children (whoever they are), we perpetuate educational communities that are fragmented, disjointed, and, often, uncaring.

**OUR IDEAL STORY**  We share Hobbs' view that teachers must be committed to all children and to the proposition that all children can be helped by the process of education (in Kauffman, 1993). Ideally, all school professionals, support personnel, peers, and family and community members should share the responsibility for all students and be committed to work together to meet their needs. Students' needs should drive the organization and professional practices of schools, and building- and classroom-level supports should anchor the management, assessment, curriculum, and instruction practices. As such, school professionals should understand the contributions that can be made by generalists and specialists alike. General educators should expect and be ready to support students with disabilities in their classrooms. Special educators and related services personnel should be trained to extend the skills of generalists; they should also be prepared to support their colleagues to develop school and classroom practices in a manner that responds to the unique needs of students with cognitive, affective, communicative, and physical needs. Peers and family and community members should contribute to the daily routines and supports necessary to carry out those practices.

**OUR PROJECTED STORY**  Separate training programs engender a spirit of individualism, role boundaries, and, to some extent, competition. As a result,

A student intern gains valuable classroom experience working with diverse learners.

**BOX 11.1**

## Working with Kirk: The Old, Present, and Future Stories

Remember the interview between Kirk and his counselor, Mollie, that we discussed in Chapter 1? That interview was the first of many steps that Mollie decided to employ in order to change the way that she interacted with and planned for Kirk. After reaching a point of total frustration with her lack of progress with Kirk, she reflected on her own beliefs and typical actions with Kirk. She realized that, for the most part, she and Kirk's teacher always focused on what Kirk did that was disruptive or on his lack of progress. In addition, whenever they attempted new interventions, Kirk's teacher and Mollie were the ones who planned and executed those plans; no one else, not even Kirk, was involved. She wondered how this might feel to Kirk. She also wondered what Kirk might be thinking about school and his future. She realized that she had never really considered if Kirk had interests or goals for the future and what those might be.

Mollie decided to use the interview as a "jumping off" point for what she hoped would be a significant change in the way she attempted to respond to Kirk's needs and to get him more involved in his education. In the interview, Mollie found what she was looking for: Kirk was interested in music, he wanted to earn his GED before leaving school, and he had a strong need for friendships with peers. Mollie decided that these interests and needs would be the basis for discussion at Kirk's next IEP meeting. She would use these three areas to establish goals and objectives and to engage Kirk in a discussion about what he wanted to accomplish, what would need to happen, and who could help him meet these goals. Mollie envisioned Kirk running his own meetings in the future—setting the agendas, inviting the participants, and completing the necessary components of the IEP. She also envisioned a time when he could leave the residential care facility and return to his neighborhood high school or community college.

school professionals are not trained to work collaboratively to solve significant school problems of practice. When students demonstrate difficulties with learning, they are often isolated and taught in fragmented ways. Too often, students who are different are not prepared for life after school and lack quality-of-life outcomes. And if we continue to prepare professionals for roles that are narrowly defined, schools will continue to fail to provide educational access and opportunities for all students.

What is necessary? We cannot ignore the fact that students have unique needs. Our educational resources must be directed to helping students to identify their needs and to develop explicit ways of acquiring skills that they are missing. Box 11.1 explains how one counselor changed her approach to better serve Kirk's unique needs.

**A NEW STORY** Changes are taking place in our teacher preparation programs (Blanton, Griffin, Winn, & Pugach, 1997). For example, some programs are moving toward noncategorical special education teacher training, while others are combining courses taken by teacher candidates in general education and

special education. Increasingly, programs for general education teachers are based on the belief that children with disabilities should be served in those classrooms and are preparing teachers to support their needs. Yet, there are pressing realities that serve to stall and in some cases defeat those efforts. From the federal level on down through state departments of education and institutions of higher learning, programs supporting the professional preparation, ongoing development, and licensing of teachers are dominated by separate, specialized administrative and financial structures (Blanton et al., 1997). Until these barriers to inclusive education are removed, the types of changes in which we are currently involved will be, at best, slow in the making.

**OUR ACTIONS** To realize our ideal, we have created and are implementing, together with our general education and related-services colleagues, a teacher preparation program that allows school professionals to develop expertise through shared training opportunities. First, our personnel preparation program provides all teacher candidates with a foundation in broad general education content and instruction. These courses are co-taught by faculty with expertise in traditional general education content areas (math, science, literacy, social studies) and faculty from areas such as special education, mental health, and technology (Sands & Drake, 1996). Teacher candidates do not take separate courses on issues related to disability, gender, ethnicity, or culture. Through co-teaching, faculty expose students to classroom, instructional, and behavior management techniques and model teaching and curriculum strategies that are effective with diverse groups of learners.

A second feature of our preparation program that supports inclusive school practices is our use of the construct of "leadership areas." In our program, students must select an area of emphasis that they will pursue as they complete the requirements for their general education teaching license. Our program is organized around the following leadership areas: (1) literacy, (2) bilingual education, (3) technology, (4) mental health, (5) interdisciplinary curriculum, and (6) inclusionary practices. Instruction is provided through both special seminars and regular course assignments related to each area of emphasis. For example, if a teacher candidate is interested in bilingual education, in addition to general education course work, he or she attends seminars and serves a directed internship on issues relating to bilingual education. Upon completion of a general education certification program, candidates can develop further expertise by pursuing additional certification or teaching endorsements in their leadership area.

## ■ SECTION SUMMARY

We use the story model to illustrate how we can (1) analyze the roots of a current controversy or push for change and (2) begin to formulate a plan of action. This model helps illuminate the beliefs and assumptions that guided the writing of this text. This model

### Extending Your Learning

Refer back to Box 11.1. What beliefs and values were changing for Mollie? How were those beliefs changing the way Mollie was planning for Kirk's educational experiences? What changes would be required of Mollie and of Kirk for her to actualize her dream?

also can provide you with a vehicle for reflecting upon your values and beliefs at a macrolevel, as they relate to the types of educational experiences you are exposed to. You need to be aware of whether the values and beliefs that are either inherent in or overtly articulated in your program match your own. What do you believe about children and their learning? What information are you provided about children and learning? What do you believe about the sociocultural context of education? How would you actualize your beliefs in school policies, organizational structures, and professional/procedural practices? Only when you carefully reflect on questions such as these can you determine if your program is providing you with the kinds of information and practices that will allow you to act in a manner that is consistent with your beliefs.

# Using Multiple Vantage Points to Understand Educational Issues

At certain points in issue debates, it becomes necessary to examine at the microlevel specific elements within an organization or system that create or serve the basis for controversy. Recall that Tom Bellamy urges us to apply four vantage points in examining issues specific to educational organizations. Bellamy's framework elaborates on the story model by focusing on the interrelationships of four vantage points: (1) values and beliefs, (2) policy decisions, (3) organizational structures, and (4) procedural or programmatic practices. A schema for overlaying Bellamy's four vantage points onto the story model is illustrated in Figure 11.2.

## Four Interrelated Vantage Points

According to Bellamy (1994), each of the four vantage points provides (1) a unique set of questions to ask about an issue, (2) one or more paradigms from which to access or develop a research and knowledge base, and (3) a particular set of action strategies to influence change. The **philosophical vantage point** is grounded in questions regarding competing values and beliefs. Knowledge bases critical to this element include ethics, sociological data, opinion polls, and critical inquiry. Influencing change in philosophical views can be ac-

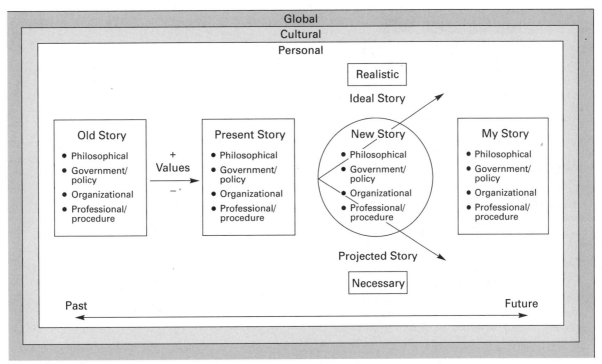

**FIGURE 11.2** ■ A Framework for Analyzing Complex Educational Issues
Source: Drake et al., 1992; Bellamy, 1994.

complished through persuasive communication, advocacy, sensitivity training, and the media. The **policy vantage point** allows us to examine the cultural and philosophical goals that are intended to be achieved through government policies and regulations. Policy analysis and evaluation, along with legal research, yield the knowledge base for this element, and lobbying, coalition building, and legal and political action support change at this level. The **organizational vantage point** enables us to question whether the goals of an establishment's programs, structures, and assignment of personnel are consistent with policy and regulations and whether the organization is effective in achieving stated goals. Results from program evaluation data and pilot studies of innovative designs form the knowledge base that can inform the need for organizational change, restructuring, and redesign. The **professional/ procedural level vantage point** lets us query the effectiveness of the organization's strategies, tools, and procedures in achieving organizational and societal goals. Model demonstration projects and research can yield information necessary to support the staff develop-

ment, peer support networks, and action research necessary to sustain change at this level.

The application of Bellamy's vantage points allows us to thoroughly analyze an educational issue by clarifying controversial questions and issues, identifying and reflecting on the existing knowledge base, and determining the need for and then generating a set of strategies to support change. In addressing an issue in a cogent and comprehensive manner, factors specific to each vantage point must be clearly outlined. When people intermingle discussion across vantage points prior to sufficiently identifying and operationalizing important variables, they compromise their ability to adequately understand and respond to issues. This makes it more difficult to take a personal stand and define a set of actions that can be carried out at one or more of the vantage points.

Consider the scenario in Box 11.2. This case illustrates the kind of day-to-day dilemmas that school professionals face as they move from traditional ways of serving students with disabilities to more inclusive school practices. At first glance, Denise's request might

## Extending Your Learning

1. *Philosophical vantage point.* A suburban school district implements a policy that allows for the establishment of collaborative teams to make decisions at the building level. At the end of one school year, one team votes unanimously to retain their school principal. The next day, however, the central administration fires the principal due to the building's reportedly low student scores on a standardized test. What competing values are at play in this scenario?

2. *Policy vantage point.* An urban district school board wants to implement policies and procedures that recognize the importance and contributions of its diverse student population. How might you address this concern in the development and refinement of existing school board policies?

3. *Organizational vantage point.* The faculty at a middle school recognizes that many of their students have ongoing personal and affective problems. The school psychologist runs crisis groups on an as-needed basis, but the demands on her to assess students for eligibility determination are excessive and leave her little time to implement the groups. While recognizing legal expectations for eligibility, the faculty believes that supporting and developing students' prosocial skills are important. How might you redesign the role of the school psychologist, and what supports would be necessary in order to institute these changes? What information would you need?

4. *Professional/procedural vantage point.* In an attempt to address problems of attendance, punctuality, school and classroom behavior, and homework, one local school implements a system of rewarding students with money for positive learning and social behaviors. Students use the money to purchase groceries in a school-administered store to take home to their families. What variables may influence the success of this program?

seem inappropriate and put Beth and her students in jeopardy by expecting them to support a student with such severe developmental delays. You might also wonder what makes Denise believe that Beth has any business working with Annie. It might seem that Denise is overstepping her boundaries and that Beth should simply decline. In fact, embedded in this scenario are multiple and complex issues that, unless carefully articulated and analyzed, could remain unresolved and set these two teachers up for a daunting future relationship. More importantly, unresolved, the issues embedded within this scenario could result in Annie not having her needs met. Use of the four vantage points can help to clarify the roots of confusion between

**BOX 11.2**

### Potential Barriers to Inclusive School Communities

As Beth was making her way to her third-grade classroom, Denise, the education specialist, approached her. Denise explained that she had just come from an annual review on one of her special education students and wanted to talk to Beth about the possibility of "including" Annie in Beth's classroom for several hours per day. To Beth, Annie was simply the little girl who appeared very different from other students—she couldn't talk, and she often made strange sounds in the hall. Beth thought to herself, "Why would Denise put a kid like that in my classroom—there isn't anything she could possibly do that the rest of my kids do?" As a first-year teacher, Beth had no experience working with children like that. She did remember learning on one of her teacher preparation classes about "syndromes"—their genetic etiologies and associated characteristics—but she certainly hadn't learned what to do with those children! More importantly, she thought, this was Denise's student, not hers! Maybe this was what Ms. Graham, the school principal, meant at the last faculty meeting when she mentioned the new district policy mandating that children with special education needs had to start going to their home school. It didn't occur to Beth that it might mean they would also start attending the general education classrooms in those schools!

Denise and Beth and the actions necessary to resolve their differences.

Philosophically, Denise seems to be operating from a view that Annie and other children with disabilities have the right to access general education classrooms, while Beth seems to disagree. From a governmental or policy standpoint, it is not clear if either teacher understands the regulatory or policy supports or barriers that may be relevant to this issue. Although Ms. Graham apparently conveyed a message leading teachers to believe that they now had to include children with special education needs in their classrooms, we do not have enough information regarding the actual nature of school policies or views on the topic. Organizationally, many questions remain concerning this issue. First, it is unclear if there is a stated goal in the school for including children with disabilities into the general education classrooms. Second, there don't seem to be any formal structures that allow teachers to cooperatively plan and make decisions about how to identify and support the needs of students with disabilities. Finally, Beth's reaction suggests that there may not have been sufficient staff development to support a mission of including students with disabilities in the general education classrooms. Procedurally, at this time, we know only that Beth does not believe she has the skills to carry out whatever supports Denise has in mind. In order to sort through and respond to each of these outstanding issues, the knowledge base across each of the vantage points must be examined systematically.

In addition to recognizing the many layers of issues that are embedded in this situation, consider also that Denise and Beth are operating from different vantage points. Denise is at the professional/procedural vantage point—ready to provide Beth with information on *how* to support Annie in her classroom. It may be that Denise is acting from the assumptions that Beth (1) believes children like Annie have the right to be educated alongside their peers, (2) has a well-grounded understanding of the district policy, and (3) has the professional capacity to carry out whatever supports she plans to recommend for Annie. In fact, although Beth agrees to meet with Denise, Beth is operating at a philosophical level. She wonders *why* Annie should be included in her classroom. She does not acknowledge Annie as one of her students, and she seems to think that it is Denise's job to provide her with an education. Conversations that evolve from multiple vantage points often lead to confusing discussions that are tar-

geted at cross purposes. Box 11.3 examines how two schools dealt with learners with special needs.

## Applying Multiple Vantage Points to Contrast the Old and the Present Stories

The inclusion of students with disabilities in the general education system poses challenges for today's schools and school professionals in both the general and special education systems (Barry, 1995; Fuchs & Fuchs, 1994; Gartner & Lipsky, 1987; Wang, Reynolds, & Walberg, 1995). According to the definition proposed in Chapter 1, inclusion involves school communities allowing students with diverse needs, including those with special education needs, to participate in their same-age classrooms with the necessary supports and services required to meet their individualized educational needs. Too often, proponents and opponents alike reduce discussions of inclusion to the simplistic "this is the right (wrong) thing to do" (O'Neil, 1995; Shanker, 1995). This oversimplification of a process that involves changes in current beliefs, policies, organizational structures, and professional practices typically results in exchanges of dogmatic doctrine.

In this section, we apply the Drake (Drake et al., 1992) and Bellamy (1994) models to illustrate how school professionals can systematically understand the many factors that must be addressed in order to resolve and respond to issues as complex as the notion of inclusionary practices. For each vantage point, we set forth the major questions that should be addressed, compare conventional and emerging or distinct viewpoints, and speculate on future concerns. Given the breadth of topics that are related to the issue of inclusionary practices, we will provide condensed examples for each vantage point and will refer to the various knowledge bases provided throughout this text.

**THE PHILOSOPHICAL VANTAGE POINT** For many, the movement toward including students with disabilities into general education classes is grounded in a set of beliefs and values. Specifically, proponents of full inclusion believe that children and youths with disabilities should "be educated in their neighborhood schools, in the 'regular classroom' with children their own age. The idea is that these schools would be restructured so that they are supportive, nurturing communities that really meet the needs of

## Extending Your Learning

Compare and contrast the approaches to establishing an inclusive school community recounted in Box 11.3. Specifically, hone in on how the values aspect of inclusive school communities was addressed. How might these differences contribute to the dilemma in which Denise and Beth are involved? What and how would you do things differently?

all the children within them: rich in resources and support for both students and teachers" (Sapon-Shevin, in O'Neil, 1995, p. 7).

Philosophically, the issue of inclusionary practices moves us to question the goals and objectives of education, the role of schools in addressing the needs of persons with disabilities, and core values about the relative contributions to or demands on schools by persons whose needs seem to differ substantially from the "norm." More specifically, discussions on the philo-

**BOX 11.3**

## Annie and Kurume—Contrasting Approaches to Change

Both Annie and Kurume are now attending schools that are working toward becoming inclusive school communities. But the roads these two schools have taken are different. Follow their progress as recounted here, and think about the factors that influenced where each building finds itself today.

As you'll recall, Annie went to Humphrey Elementary School. Dave and Debbie, Annie's parents, attended a weekend seminar for families of students with disabilities and were introduced to the concept of inclusion. They liked the idea of having Annie participate in activities with her peers at Humphrey and believed that she could learn things in environments other than her self-contained classroom. At the parent seminar, Dave and Debbie learned of an annual national conference that focused on strategies for building inclusive schools. They invited Annie's special education teacher, Denise, and the school principal, Ms. Graham, to attend the conference with them. These four adults returned from the conference more excited about educational possibilities than they had been in years. Dave and Debbie had real hope that Annie could actually experience the kinds of educational activities that her peers enjoyed each day. Denise began to see new possibilities not only for her students but for herself. She couldn't wait to begin to use some of the ideas she had gotten from the conference. For Ms. Graham, the conference helped to explain a district policy that had been implemented earlier that year on inclusive education. She was now prepared to move her building forward. She would announce the district's policy on inclusive education at her next faculty meeting and see that it was implemented.

Now consider how the move toward inclusive education was approached at Kennedy High School, Kurume's school. In that district, two central district administrators had gotten wind of a due process hearing related to inclusive school practices in a neighboring district. In addition, a third administrator and the special education services coordinator had been urging the district to move toward more inclusive school practices for about a year. These four individuals decided to learn more about inclusive school communities and to view their own practices in light of what they found. A task force was formed consisting of central district administrators, principals, general education teachers, special education teachers, parents, and local community members. They studied the notion of inclusive education for one year. Their study involved trips to other districts that were implementing inclusive school practices, reading and discussing professional literature, and talking to parents and students in the district about their views. At the end of the year, the members of the task force were committed to educational change in their district that would allow them to support inclusive school communities. Applying the information they had gained over the past year, the task force designed a five-year implementation plan. The plan involved work that needed to be done at the district, building, and community levels. It required that attention be paid to how people felt about the impending changes, district and school policies, organizational issues, and new roles.

sophical bases of inclusionary practices involve questions like the following:

1. What is society's goal in relation to persons with disabilities—treatment or access and change?

2. Who needs to change—the person with the disability or others in society?

3. What is the proper role of schools in promoting social change?

4. Is it the school's responsibility to change attitudes of students toward people with disabilities?

5. What are the social consequences of identifying and treating a group of children differently from others?

## Extending Your Learning

A seventh-grade classroom generated the following classroom constitution:

■ We appreciate our individual differences. We recognize that each person is unique.

■ All individuals will be treated with respect and dignity. There is no room for put-downs in our room.

■ We will be honest with one another in order to build trust.

■ We will learn to resolve conflicts, which may involve learning to live with nonresolution.

■ Each person will truly listen to every other person.

■ We will cooperate and collaborate with one another.

■ Learning will be meaningful.

■ We recognize that people learn in different ways.

■ Assignments, field trips, and hands-on experiences will be varied so that everyone can and will learn. If everyone tries, we ALL will succeed.

■ Having fun will naturally become part of our experiences.

■ All individuals will be organized and on time.

■ We will respect the right to pass (and not take a turn).

What behaviors might you expect to see or not to see in this classroom? How might this classroom operate as compared to classrooms in which you have participated?

Source: Adapted from Brodhagen, 1995, pp. 83–84.

6. What is the goal of education and special education—mastery of academic curriculum or quality of life after graduation?

Questions such as these generate differing responses that are indicative of diverse values and assumptions about (1) the political, social, and structural contexts of schooling, (2) individuals with differing abilities, and (3) school processes. Table 11.1 summarizes differing viewpoints that can influence educational decision making (Astuto, Clark, Read, McGree, & Fernandez, 1994). These viewpoints then serve as the basis for creating school missions, setting policies, organizing schools, and implementing school practices that may or may not be consistent with personal or professional goals and objectives. For example, if an individual believes that factors such as poverty, minority status, and affiliation with atypical families places a student at risk of failure in school (Astuto et al., 1994), that person may be cynical as to whether education can benefit those children and not be supportive of special programs targeted to their needs. If an individual believes that competition, as opposed to cooperation, nurturance, or support, provides the bases for higher levels of individual achievement, that person will probably resist efforts to incorporate cooperative learning instructional techniques within the context of school environments.

Differences of opinion stem from differing life experiences and knowledge bases. Unchallenged, these differences of opinion can serve as the basis for conflicting responses to the call for the inclusion of children with disabilities in general education classrooms. Understanding these varying perspectives allows us to persuade or otherwise influence those beliefs and values through advocacy, sensitivity training, provision of alternative experiences, and other persuasive techniques. As a school professional, the manner in which you respond to questions that target values and beliefs that are congruent or incongruent to inclusionary practices will certainly affect your attitude toward and decisions about supporting children with disabilities in general education classrooms (Fox & Ysseldyke, 1997).

**THE GOVERNMENTAL AND POLICY VANTAGE POINT** The governmental and policy vantage point allows us to analyze our laws, regulations, and policies to determine the underlying beliefs or philosophies meant to govern our behaviors. For example, with the

---

**TABLE 11.1** **Alternative Perspectives on Beliefs About the Political, Social, and Structural Contexts of Schooling, Individuals, and School Processes**

| Beliefs | Opposing Beliefs |
|---|---|
| The purpose of schooling in a democracy is to allow children and youths to progress and develop on the basis of their own ability and talent (meritocratically). | The purpose of schooling in a democracy is to extend the benefits of the society to all children and youths by preparing them to access those benefits. |
| The test of the efficacy of an educational system is its instrumental contribution to the goals of society. | The test of the efficacy of an educational system is the extent to which it allows all children to access the benefits of their society. |
| Achievement in school rests predominantly in the hands of the student. | Individual achievement in school is influenced greatly by the adjustment of the school to the student. |
| Educational achievement is enhanced by high standards, competition, and comparative assessment of students, schools, and school districts. | Educational achievement is enhanced by conditions of cooperation that reflect trust, confidence, support, and challenge between teachers and learners. |
| Additional resources in public education will not increase system performance and are unnecessary for reform. | Additional resources will increase system performance and will impact the rate and scope of reform. |
| Schools can effect only marginal, value-added gains in the education of students from differing economic and cultural backgrounds. | Schools can reduce the deterministic relationship of educational performance and socioeconomic status through interventions. |
| Goals, specification of task assignments, and decision making grounded in impersonality promote fairness, reduce conflict, and optimize organizational control. | Norms and ethics of professional practice and decision making grounded in values of social justice and responsibility promote equity, tolerate conflict, and optimize individual control. |
| Diversity should be controlled and irradicated so that systems and social institutions can function predictably. | Diversity should be respected and embraced because it supports creativity and innovation. |
| The purpose of assessment and evaluation is to sort, categorize, and select people who are capable of "competent" performance. | The purpose of assessment and evaluation is to provide feedback to individuals to support their continued growth. |
| Intelligence is a prediction of success in learning and is static; a narrow set of skills defines competence. | There are multiple intelligences; a broad range of skills define competence. |
| Education is best delivered in homogeneous groups of students. | There are great educational and social benefits to providing services to heterogeneous groups of students. |

Source: Astuto et al., 1994.

passage of the Rehabilitation Act Amendments of 1992, Congress communicated strong values and beliefs regarding the nature of disability and the rights of the disabled:

> *Congress finds that . . . disability is a natural part of the human experience and in no way diminishes the right of an individual to live independently; enjoy self-determination; make choices; contribute to society; pursue meaningful careers; enjoy full inclusion and integration in the economic, political, social,*
> *cultural, and education mainstream of American society. (P.L. 102-569, Section 2)*

Clearly, Congress is communicating the principle that disability is a naturally occurring human condition. In light of that condition, Congress sees no reason that persons with disabilities should be denied basic rights and access to activities that persons without disabilities enjoy. The language of this statute can be interpreted as strongly supporting inclusionary practices. At the same time, legislation and policy can serve as a barrier to a particular cause. For example, many people claim that the practice of having to label children as disabled in order to receive federal and state funding serves as a barrier to instituting school reform that would make it easier to serve students with disabilities within general education classrooms (Wang, Reynolds, & Walberg, 1995). As a result, the following kinds of questions address the appropriateness of existing policy:

1. Does IDEA define a distinguishable group of children who are eligible for special education services?

2. Do the benefits of labeling—identification for special education funding and rights—outweigh the harm of stigmatization and separation when special education is provided in separate settings?

3. What purpose do current educational categories—special education, compensatory education, migrant education, and bilingual education—serve?

On the one hand, our laws serve to protect and guarantee certain rights. On the other hand, implementation of those laws may not always reflect the spirit of a particular decree. For example, as we discussed in Chapter 2, in 1975, P.L. 94-142 set out to guarantee the rights of students with disabilities to a free and appropriate education in the least restrictive environment. An inherent assumption was that a distinct group of children could be identified as having disabilities and that those children might require instruction that varied from general education classroom practices. Over time, however, there has been reason to question these basic assumptions. For instance, researchers have discovered that, in practice, (1) there is little or no differentiation in the curriculum or instructional approaches used with students with disabilities, particularly those labeled as learning disabled, emotionally disturbed, and mildly mentally retarded, and (2) techniques prescribed as effective for students with disabilities are also successful with other groups of students, including those from diverse ethnic, linguistic, and cultural backgrounds (Barry, 1995; Epstein, Patton, Polloway, & Foley, 1992; Harry, 1992; Matute-Bianchi, 1986; Wagner, 1989). Thus, our knowledge base now puts us in the position to question whether certain assumptions underlying educational statutes protecting the rights of persons with disabilities are, in fact, correct. It is these sorts of irregularities that serve as the basis for proponents of inclusionary practices to initiate efforts to amend or change existing law.

As professionals, we must be knowledgeable about the policies and regulations that govern and influence the goals, objectives, and procedures of our organizations and practices. Thorough analysis and careful interpretation at the governmental or policy vantage point allow school professionals to take actions consistent with the accompanying values and beliefs.

**THE ORGANIZATIONAL VANTAGE POINT** Organizationally, the issue of inclusionary practices revolves around questions about the manner in which services are designed and delivered in school buildings and classrooms. This includes the roles of professionals, support service staff, students, and family members. Traditionally, special education has been organized around a separate system of administrative, financial, and personnel services delivered in a manner that largely bypassed the general education system. In Chapter 4, we discussed emerging practices that involve collaborative working structures and practice between special and general education school professionals and families and that allow students with disabilities to be served within the general education system. However, services such as consultation, collaboration, and co-teaching are difficult to support adequately within organizational structures designed for independent and separate service systems. If school communities are to respond to beliefs, values, and policies that promote inclusionary practices for students with disabilities, the following types of questions regarding their organizational practices need to be considered:

1. What benefit is gained by separate bureaucracies for each categorical program?

2. What are the necessary and appropriate uses of educational specialists?

3. Do specialists lead to segregation?

4. Do specialists add more value to overall school outcomes?

5. Are separate and pullout services effective?

6. Can regular education services be effective for students with disabilities?

7. What conditions are necessary for collaboration to work?

Organizational structures serve as the foundation for professional and procedural ways of behaving in school buildings. Without attention to organizational issues, we place school professionals and students at

Recall that, in our initial overview of Michael, we talked about the dilemma he and his mother faced with his high school class schedule. Michael was told that, to get the supports he needed, he would have to sign up for a course called "Learning Strategies." But if Michael took that class, he would have to give up one of his two electives—Spanish or music, classes that held the greatest interest for him. How can decisions at the organizational level create barriers for school professionals, students, and their families? If you were the principal in Michael's school, what questions would you ask if you wanted to eliminate these types of barriers? What process would you use to work through the issues? Whom would you involve?

risk for engaging in relationships and practices that are counterproductive and self-defeating.

**THE PROFESSIONAL/PROCEDURAL VANTAGE POINT** The professional/procedural vantage point is the element that is most pressing in the minds and hearts of school professionals. It is at this level that we deal with the day-to-day decisions and practices that support learning communities. Although it is critical that we address issues of professional practice, we must be careful not to focus on this element to the exclusion of those previously addressed. Remember Beth and Denise's dilemma in Box 11.2? Denise is ready to implement procedures that allowed Annie to participate in Beth's class, but Beth is not convinced that Annie should even be in her classroom. In Chapter 9, we discussed the impact of teacher beliefs on their classroom practices. If Denise presses Beth into employing practices to support Annie before she addresses Beth's basic concerns about Annie being in her classroom, Denise is likely to fail in her effort to include Annie in Beth's classroom.

At the professional and procedural level, we need to ask questions like these:

1. Are different educational treatments or procedures needed by children with different educational labels?

2. What collaboration and consultation strategies actually improve learning outcomes in regular classrooms?

3. When children with disabilities are educated in general education classrooms, is the achievement of typical learners affected?

4. What student information do teachers need in order to teach effectively?

5. Under what conditions does cooperative learning work for all students?

6. What curriculum frameworks allow teachers to respond to the diverse needs of their students?

7. Under what conditions should teachers use a remedial approach to instruction?

8. How can teachers organize and manage their classrooms in order to respond to the collective and individual needs of all students?

As stated previously, the knowledge base that informs questions at this vantage point extends from model demonstration projects and action research. Reports on schools that are striving to support and model inclusive communities give answers to many of the questions posed here (Educational Leadership, 1996; Falvey, 1995; Stainback & Stainback, 1996; Villa & Thousand, 1995).

## Creating a New Story

The issues involved in creating inclusive school communities must be addressed on a building-by-building, classroom-by-classroom, and person-by-person level. There are no quick and easy fixes or magic formulas to help us implement the educational practices that reflect the underlying values and beliefs that drive this movement. If we are to develop inclusive school communities, we must continue to work toward a knowledge base that informs those practices.

One of the final elements of the story model is to create a personal story that provides details of the types of action that you can take to make the new story happen. This component of the model encourages you to formulate strategies for action by responding to questions such as these:

1. What is the knowledge base?

2. What knowledge do I need?

3. Given my current knowledge base, where do I stand?

4. What can I do for the time being?

5. What can I do to change the future?

In addition to assessing ourselves temporally, we must attend to variables at each of the four vantage points. If you are trying to create inclusive school communities, this might involve (1) influencing values and beliefs for equality, access, and interdependence, (2) expanding and refining current laws to more accurately reflect and document those values and beliefs, (3) transforming current organizational structures to meet the goals of those policies, and (4) adopting professional practices that respond to the goals of the organization. Taking critically reflective action is thus based on knowing where you were, where you are, and where you want to be. This entails consideration of the impact you can make at the philosophical, policy, organizational, and professional/procedural levels.

## ■ SECTION SUMMARY

The four vantage points—philosophical, governmental/policy, organizational, and professional/procedural—are useful in classifying the multiple variables that can support or impede our ability to resolve complicated educational issues or controversies. Because the vantage points are interrelated, the goals and assumptions of one level typically are set by those above and the information base used to evaluate one level is supplied from the level below. For example, as Tanya was approaching the upper elementary grades, the special education consultant wanted to co-teach with Tanya's fifth-grade teacher. The two school professionals decided that the entire class could benefit from some of the work the special educator had done in the area of career education. The two teachers determined that information on career education would mesh nicely with the fifth-grade teacher's unit on "Essential Questions in My Life." The two teachers made attempts to engage in co-teaching activities, but after three weeks they were exhausted. At first, they thought they simply weren't skilled at co-teaching, but after going through a problem-solving exercise with their colleagues, they realized their need for common planning time. In this case, information from the procedural level revealed ineffective structures at the organizational level—lack of shared planning time. If school professionals are encouraged or expected to work collaboratively, then school structures must change in order to accommodate that process. Examples such as this reveal why change must be approached systematically and how change at one level must be examined in light of and be supported by change at other levels.

## Your Story

If you are reading this text, there is a good chance that you are thinking about or preparing for a career that involves working with children, youths, or adults with disabilities in the education, rehabilitation, or human services systems. According to the models of change proposed in this chapter, your values and beliefs will play a key role in preparing you to work in those systems. Many individuals argue that it is not the job of professionals, and in particular school professionals, to address issues of values and beliefs. However, beliefs and values influence our daily practices and behaviors, and we do not and cannot pretend that we function in a value-free environment. As such, we have written this book in part to influence your values and beliefs about the needs of persons with disabilities and to increase your knowledge about the kinds of educational practices that you can incorporate in order to allow these people, as well as those with diverse linguistic, ethnic, cultural, and socioeconomic needs, to access the general education system and to achieve quality-of-life outcomes.

At this point, you might be wondering what you can do to influence the types of changes that are necessary to create and sustain inclusive school communities? Ultimately, it takes many people to support the work of inclusive school communities, but it requires only one person to ignite the spark. That person can be a general educator, special educator, school principal, student, or family member; that person can be *you*. The point of entry can be the school science fair, a mission statement, literacy instruction, school friendships, team teaching, in-service training, or judicial mandate (Ercolano, 1994; Ford, 1994; Putnam, 1994). For example, as a general education teacher, you can open the door to inclusive school practices through the use of flexible curriculum targets, cooperative learning, peer-mediated instruction, and a classroom climate that values and supports diverse learners. As a special educator, you can help to modify and adapt the general education curriculum to meet the needs of individual students. You can team teach, or you can gain access for students with disabilities to typical education experiences when you coach the track team or sponsor the student council. Or, like Denise, you can foster inclusive school practices by approaching your colleagues on a one-to-one basis, supporting the needs of one student in a general education classroom and expanding from there. Remember, there is no one recipe. But you can be the first of the many active ingredients needed to create an inclusive school community.

# Chapter Summary

At this point in time, we invite you to reflect on how you can apply the information in this book to your professional beliefs and future practices. As you play out your story, we encourage you to continue reflecting on the critical role you may play in the education of our youth. Though specifically referring to persons working with youths who have emotional or behavioral disorders, we refer you again to Hobbs as he describes the ideal teacher of diverse students.

> *Most of all a teacher is a decent adult; educated, well-trained; able to give and receive affection, to live relaxed, and to be firm; a person with private resources for the nourishment and refreshment of his own life; not an itinerant worker but a professional through and through; a person with a sense of the significance of time, of the usefulness of today and the promise of tomorrow; a person of hope, quiet confidence, and joy; one who has committed him- or herself to all children and to the proposition that all children can be helped by the process of education. (in Kauffman, 1993, p. 498)*

Our best of luck to each of you.

## INSTRUCTIONAL ACTIVITY

## Making Sense of It All

### Objectives

- To use the components of the story model as a basis for creating a personal philosophy of education statement
- To defend a philosophy of education statement in light of established theories of learning and research

### Materials

- Readings from throughout the text and supplemental course materials

### Product

- A personal philosophy statement

### Agenda

- Using elements of the story model, reflect on your educational values and beliefs and how, over time, those have or have not changed.
- Based on those reflections and considerations of theoretical discussions throughout the text and supplemental course materials, develop a written "story" or personal philosophy statement of education. In this statement you should identify your theoretical values and beliefs about learning and then describe how those beliefs inform and define the role of school professionals and learners.
- In small groups, you should share their philosophy statements. When a group member has shared his or her statement, the remaining group members should pose questions that challenge the individuals' position.

### Evaluation

- A sound rationale for personal beliefs and values
- Congruence between beliefs and values and corresponding roles described for school professionals and learners
- Ability to defend your position with sound and logical reasoning
- Ability to pose challenge questions to others that elaborate upon and extend the quality and depth of the discussion

# Glossary

**Etiology**  The cause of a disability, impairment, or disease.

**Mainstreaming**  A term used early on to describe attempts to include students with disabilities in general education classrooms. Typically, students with disabilities were only allowed to be "mainstreamed" if they could participate in the general education classroom with little to no support or accommodations.

**Organizational vantage point**  A manner of examining the goals, structures, and program assignments of an organization.

**Philosophical vantage point**  A manner of analyzing the underlying values or beliefs of an issue or organization.

**Policy vantage point**  A manner of examining the cultural and philosophical goals of policies or regulations.

**Prevalence data**  Data on the number of people who have a particular condition or disease at a specific point in time.

**Professional/procedural vantage point**  A manner of examining an educational issue at the level of what happens on a day-to-day basis with students and school professionals.

**Self-contained classrooms**  A classroom in a public school that is designated for students with specific types of disabilities.

**Story model**  A framework for analyzing educational change.

**Student-centered strategies**  Teaching strategies that are targeted to meet student needs as opposed to externally imposed requirements.

**Student-directed strategies**  An approach to teaching that teaches and then holds the expectation for students to be more involved and responsible for their own learning.

# References

Abbott, D. A., & Meredith, W. H. (1986). Strengths of parents with retarded children. *Family Relations, 35,* 371–375.

Abery, B. H., & Fahnestock, M. (1994). Enhancing the social inclusion of persons with developmental disabilities. In M. F. Hayden & B. H. Abery (Eds.), *Challenges for a service system in transition: Ensuring quality community experiences for persons with developmental disabilities* (pp. 83–119). Baltimore: Brookes.

Achenbach, T., & Edelbrock, C. (1986). Child behavior checklist. San Antonio: The Psychological Corporation.

A concern about . . . Special education in school restructuring. (1992, March). *Concerns, 35,* 1–7.

Adelman, J. S., & Taylor, L. (1993). *Learning problems and learning disabilities: Moving forward.* Pacific Grove, CA: Brooks/Cole.

Affleck, G., Tennen, H., Allen, D., & Gershman, K. (1986). Perceived social support and maternal adaptation during the transition from hospital to home care of high-risk infants. *Infant Mental Health Journal, 7*(1), 6–18.

Affleck, G., Tennen, H., Rowe, J., Roscher, B., & Walker, L. (1989). Effects of formal support on mothers' adaptation to the hospital-to-home transition of high-risk infants: The benefits and costs of helping. *Child Development, 60,* 488–501.

Affleck, J., Edgar, E., Levine, P., & Kortering, L. (1990). Postschool status of students classified as mildly mentally retarded, learning disabled, or non-handicapped: Does it get better with time? *Education and Training in Mental Retardation, 25,* 315–324.

Agran, M., & Martin, J. E. (1987). Applying a technology of self-control in community environments for individuals who are mentally retarded. In M. Hersen, R. M. Eisler, & P. M. Miller (Eds.), *Progress in behavior modification* (Vol. 21, pp. 108–151). Newbury Park, CA: Sage.

Ainsworth, M. S. (1973). The development of infant-mother attachment. In B. Caldwell and H. Ricciuti (Eds.), *Review of child development research,* Vol. 3 (pp. 113–139). Chicago: University of Chicago Press.

Aleem, D., & Moles, O. (1993). *Review of research on ways to attain goal six: Creating safe, disciplined, and drug-free schools.* Washington, DC: OERI.

Allen, D. A., & Affleck, G. (1985). Are we stereotyping parents? A postscript to Blacher. *Mental Retardation, 23*(4), 200–202.

Allen, T. E. (1986). Patterns of achievement among hearing-impaired students: 1974 and 1983. In A. N. Schildroth & M. A. Karchmer (Eds.), *Deaf children in America* (pp. 161–206). San Diego: College Hill Press.

Alogzzine, R. (1993). Splitting hairs and loose ends: Answering special education's wake-up call (letter to the editor). *Journal of Special Education, 26,* 462–467.

Alper, S., Schloss, P. J., Etscheidt, S. K., & Macfarlane, C. A. (1995). *Inclusion: Are we abandoning or helping students?* Thousand Oaks, CA: Corwin Press.

American Association on Mental Retardation. (1992). *Mental retardation: Definition, classification, and systems of support—Workbook.* Washington, DC: Author.

American Psychological Association. (1997). *Learner-centered psychological principles.* Washington, DC: Author.

Anderegg, M. L., Vergason, G. A., & Smith, M. C. (1992). A visual representation of the grief cycle for use by teachers with families of children with disabilities. *Remedial and Special Education, 13*(1), 17–23.

Anderson, C. (1985). The investigation of school climate. In G. Austin & H. Garber (Eds.), *Research on exemplary schools*. New York: Academic Press.

Anderson, C., & Roth, K. (1989). Teaching for meaningful and self-regulated learning of science. In J. Brophy (Ed.), *Advances in research on teaching. Vol. 1: Teaching for meaningful understanding and self-regulated learning*. Greenwich, CT: JAI Press.

Apple, M. W., & Beane, J. A. (Eds.). (1995a). *Democratic schools*. Alexandria, VA: Association for Supervision and Curriculum Development.

Apple, M. W., & Beane, J. A. (1995b). The case for democratic schools. In M. Apple & J. Beane (Eds.), *Democratic schools* (pp. 1–25). Alexandria, VA: Association for Supervision and Curriculum Development.

Armstrong, D. G. (1989). *Developing and documenting curriculum*. Boston: Allyn & Bacon.

Armstrong, T. (1994). *Multiple intelligences in the classroom*. Alexandria, VA: Association for Supervision and Curriculum Development.

Asher, S. R., & Renshaw, P. D. (1981). Children without friends: Social knowledge and social-skill training. In S. R. Asher & J. M. Gottman (Eds.), *The development of children's friendships* (pp. 273–294). Cambridge: Cambridge University Press.

Association for Supervision and Curriculum Development. (1992). *Resolutions 1992*. Alexandria, VA: Author.

Astuto, T. A., Clark, D. L., Read, A., McGree, K., & Fernandez, L. (1994). *Roots of reform: Challenging the assumptions that control change in education*. Bloomington, IN: Phi Delta Kappa Educational Foundation.

Atkinson, R. C., & Shiffrin, R. M. (1968). Human memory: A proposed system and its control processes. In K. W. Spence and J. T. Spence (Eds.), *Psychology of learning and motivation* (Vol. 2). New York: Academic Press.

Au, K. H. (1980). Participant structures in a reading lesson with Hawaiian children: Analysis of a culturally appropriate instructional event. *Anthropology and Education Quarterly, 11*, 91–115.

Ausubel, D. (1963). *The psychology of meaningful verbal learning: An introduction to school learning*. New York: Grune & Stratton.

Ayers, W. (1995a). Reinventing schools. In W. Ayers (Ed.), *To become a teacher* (pp. 123–126). New York: Teachers College Press.

Ayers, W. (1995b). Thinking and teaching. In W. Ayers (Ed.), *To become a teacher* (pp. 59–77). New York: Teachers College Press.

Baddeley, A. D. (1981). The concept of working memory: A view of its current state and probable future development. *Cognition, 10*, 17–23.

Baddeley, A. D., & Hitch, G. (1974). Working memory. In G. H. Bower (Ed.), *The psychology of learning and motivation* (pp. 199–239). New York: Academic Press.

Bailey, D., & Simeonsson, R. (1988). Assessing needs of families with handicapped infants. *The Journal of Special Education, 22*, 117–127.

Baker, B. L. (1984). Training parents as teachers of their developmentally disabled children. In S. Salzinger, J. Antrobus, & J. Glick (Eds.), *The ecosystem of the sick child*. New York: Academy Press.

Baker, B. L., Seltzer, G., & Seltzer, M. (1977). *As close as possible*. Boston: Little, Brown.

Baldwin, D. (1994). As busy as we wanna be. *Utne Reader, 61*, 52–58.

Ballenger, C. (1992). Because you like us: The language of control. *Harvard Educational Review, 62*, 199–208.

Bandura, A. (1977). Self-efficacy: Toward a unifying theory of behavioral change. *Psychological Review, 84*, 191–215.

Bandura, A. (1986). *Social foundations of thought and action: A social-cognitive theory*. Englewood Cliffs, NJ: Prentice-Hall.

Bandura, A. (1989). Human agency in social cognitive theory. *American Psychologist, 44*, 1175–1184.

Bandura, A. (1991). Human agency: The rhetoric and the reality. *American Psychologist, 46*, 157–162.

Bandura, A., & Wood, R. (1989). Effect of perceived controllability and performance standards on self-regulation of complex decision-making. *Journal of Personality and Social Psychology, 56*, 805–814.

Barrera, M., Sandler, I., & Ramsay, T. (1981). Preliminary development of a scale of social support: Studies on college students. *American Journal of Community Psychology, 9*, 435–447.

Barrera, N., & Ainlay, S. (1983). The structure of social support: A conceptual and empirical analysis. *Journal of Community Psychology, 11*, 133–143.

Barry, A. L. (1995). Easing into inclusive classrooms. *Educational Leadership, 52*, 4–6.

Bartholomew-Lorimer, K. (1993). Community building: Valued roles for supporting connections. In A. N. Amado (Ed.), *Friendships and community connections between people with and without developmental disabilities* (pp. 169–179). Baltimore: Brookes.

Battan, F. K. (1994). Emergencies of accidents. In W. W. Hay, Jr., J. G. Groothuis, A. R. Hayward, & M. J. Levin (Eds.), *Current pediatric diagnosis and treatment* (pp. 344–363). Norwalk, CT: Appleton & Lange.

Baum, L. F. (1909). *The Road to Oz*. Toronto: Copp Clark.

Baur, A. M., & Shea, T. M. (1989). *Teaching exceptional students in your classroom*. Boston: Allyn & Bacon.

Bawrens, J., Hourcade, J., & Friend, M. (1987). Cooperative teaching: A model for general and special education integration. *Remedial and Special Education, 10*(2), 17–22.

Beane, J. A. (1995). Introduction: What is a coherent curriculum? In J. A. Beane (Ed.), *Toward a coherent curriculum* (pp. 1–15). *1995 Yearbook of the Association for Supervision and Curriculum Development*. Alexandria, VA: ASCD.

Beane, J. A., & Apple, M. W. (1995). The case for democratic schools. In M. Apple & J. A. Beane (Eds.), *Democratic schools* (pp. 1–25). Alexandria, VA: Association for Supervision and Curriculum Development.

Becker, F. (1981). *Workspace: Creating environments in organizations.* New York: Praeger.

Beckman, P. J. (1983). Influence of selected child characteristics on stress in families of handicapped infants. *American Journal of Mental Deficiency, 88,* 150–156.

Beer, M., Eisenstat, A., & Spector, B. (1990). *The critical path to corporate renewal.* Boston: Harvard Business School Press.

Beez, W. (1968). Influence of biased psychological reports on teacher behavior and student performance. *Proceedings of the 75th Annual Convention of the American Psychological Association, 3,* 605–606.

Beirne-Smith, M., Patton, J. R., & Ittenbach, R. (1994). *Mental retardation* (4th ed.). New York: Macmillan.

Bellak, L., & Bellak, S. (1974). Children's apperception test. San Antonio: Psychological Corporation.

Bellamy, G. T. (1994). *The whole-school framework.* Unpublished manuscript. Denver: University of Colorado at Denver.

Bellamy, G. T. (1994). The slow pace of change [Book review of *Integrating general and special education*]. *Journal of Teacher Education, 45,* 76–78.

Benjamin, S. (1989). An ideascape for education: What futurists recommend. *Educational Leadership, 7,* 8–14.

Benne, K., & Sheats, P. (1948). Functional roles of group members. *Journal of Social Issues. 4,* 41–49.

Bennis, W.G. (1989). *Why leaders can't lead.* San Francisco: Jossey-Bass.

Beukelman, D. R., & Yorkston, K. M. (1991). Traumatic brain injury changes the way we live. In D. R. Beukelman & K. M. Yorkston (Eds.), *Communication disorders following traumatic brain injury: Management of cognitive, language, and motor impairments.* Austin, TX: Pro-Ed.

Biehler, R. F., & Snowman, J. (1993). *Psychology applied to teaching* (7th ed.). Boston: Houghton Mifflin.

Bigge, J. L. (1982). *Teaching individuals with physical and multiple disabilities* (2nd ed.). Columbus, OH: Merrill.

Biklen, D., Bogdan, R., Ferguson, D., Searl, S., & Taylor, S. J. (1985). *Achieving the complete school: Strategies for effective mainstreaming.* New York: Teachers College Press.

Bingham, A. A. (1995). *Exploring the multi-age classroom.* York, ME: Stenhouse.

Blacher, J. (1984). Sequential stages of parental adjustment to the birth of a child with handicaps: Fact or artifact? *Mental Retardation, 22*(2), 55–68.

Blankenhorn, D. (1991). The American family is in big trouble. *Bottom Line: Personal, 12*(13), 7.

Blanton, L. P., Griffin, C. C., Winn, J. A., & Pugach, M. C. (1997). *Teacher education in transition.* Denver: Love.

Blase, J. J. (1986). A qualitative analysis of sources of teachers stress: Consequences for performance. *American Educational Research Journal, 23*(1), 13–40.

Blase, J. J., Blase J., Anderson, G. L., & Dungan, S. (1995). *Democratic principals in action: Eight pioneers.* Thousand Oaks, CA: Corwin Press.

Blatt, B. (1987). *The conquest of mental retardation.* Austin, TX: Pro-Ed.

Bloom, B. S., Englehart, M. B., Furst, E. J., Hill, W. H., & Krathwohl, D. R. (Eds.). (1956). *Taxonomy of educational objectives. The classification of educational goals. Handbook I: Cognitive domain.* New York: McKay.

Bloom, B. S., Madaus, G. F., & Hastings, J. T. (1981). *Evaluation to improve learning.* New York: McGraw-Hill.

Bloom, L., & Lahey, M. (1991). *Language development and language disorders* (3rd ed.). New York: Macmillan.

Blumenfeld, P. (1992). The task and the teacher: Enhancing student thoughtfulness in science. In J. Brophy (Ed.), *Advances in research on teaching. Vol. 3: Planning and managing learning tasks and activities* (pp. 81–114). Greenwich, CT: JAI Press.

Bodgdan, R. (1986). The sociology of special education. In R. Morris & B. Blatt (Eds.), *Special education: Research and trends* (pp. 344–359). New York: Pergamon Press.

Bradley Commission on History in Schools. (1988). *Building a history curriculum: Guidelines for teaching history in schools.* Washington, DC: Author.

Brainerd, C. J., & Kingman, J. (1984). On the independence of short-term memory and working memory in cognitive development. *Cognitive Psychology, 17,* 210–247.

Bredekamp, S., & Copple, C. (Ed.). (1997). *Developmentally appropriate practice in early childhood programs.* Washington, DC: National Association for the Education of Young Children.

Breslau, N., Staruch, K. S., & Mortimer, E. A. (1982). Psychological distress in mothers of disabled children. *American Journal of the Disabled Child, 136,* 682–686.

Brigham, T. A. (1989). *Self-management for adolescents.* New York: Guilford Press.

Bristol, M. M. (1987). The home care of children with developmental disabilities: Empirical support for a model of successful family coping with stress. In S. Landesman & P. Vietze (Eds.), *Living environments and mental retardation* (pp. 401–422). Washington, DC: American Association on Mental Retardation.

Brodhagen, B. L. (1995). The situation made us special. In M. Apple & J. Beane (Eds.), *Democratic schools* (pp. 83–100). Alexandria, VA: Association for Supervision and Curriculum Development.

Brolin, D. E. (1982). Life-centered career education for exceptional children. *Focus on Exceptional Children, 14,* 1–15.

Brolin, D. E. (1992). *Life centered career education (LCCE) curriculum program.* Reston, VA: Council for Exceptional Children.

Bronfenbrenner, U. (1973). Toward an experimental ecology of human development. *American Psychologist, 32,* 513–531.

Bronfenbrenner, U. (1979). *The ecology of human development: Experiments by nature and design.* Cambridge, MA: Harvard University Press.

Brooke, M., Uomoto, J. M., McLean, A., & Fraser, R. T. (1991). Rehabilitation of persons with traumatic brain injury: A continuum of care. In D. R. Beukelman & K. M. Yorkston (Eds.), *Communication disorders following traumatic brain injury: Management of cognitive, language, and motor impairments.* Austin, TX: Pro-Ed.

Brooks, J. G., & Brooks, M. G. (1993). *The case for constructivist classrooms.* Alexandria, VA: Association for Supervision and Curriculum Development.

Brooks, R. (1991). *The self-esteem teacher.* Circle Pines, MN: American Guidance Service.

Brophy, J., & Evertson, C. (1976). *Learning from teaching: A developmental perspective.* Boston: Allyn & Bacon.

Brown, A. (1975). The development of memory: Knowing, knowing about knowing, and knowing how to know. In H. Reese (Ed.), *Advances in child development and behavior.* New York: Academic Press.

Brown, A. D., Ash, M., Rutherford, K., Nakagawa, A., Gordon, & Campione, J. (1993). Distributed expertise in the classroom. In G. Salomon (Ed.), *Distributed cognitions: Psychological and education considerations.* New York: Cambridge University Press.

Brown, A. L., & Campione, J. (1986). Psychological theory and the study of learning disabilities. *American Psychologist, 14,* 1059–1068.

Brown, A. L., & Palinscar, A. S. (1987). Reciprocal teaching of comprehension strategies: A natural history of one program for enhancing learning. In J. Borkowski & J. D. Day (Eds.), *Intelligence and cognition in special children: Comparative studies of giftedness, mental retardation, and learning disabilities.* New York: Ablex.

Brown, J. M., Joseph, D. F., & Wotruba, J. W. (1989). Factors affecting employers' roles in the school-to-work transition of persons with disabilities. In D. E. Berkell & J. M. Brown (Eds.), *Transition from school to work for persons with disabilities* (pp. 187–226). New York: Longman.

Brown, L., & Hammill, D. (1985). Behavior rating profile. Austin, TX: Pro-Ed.

Brown, L., Long, E., Udvari-Solner, A., Davis, L., Van Deventer, P., Ahlgren, C., Johnson, F., Gruenwald, L., & Jorgensen, L. (1989). The home school: Why students with severe intellectual disabilities must attend the schools of their brothers, sisters, friends, and neighbors. *TASH, 14,* 1–7.

Brown, L., Sherbenon, R. L., & Dollar, S. L. (1982). Test of nonverbal intelligence. Austin, TX: Pro-Ed.

Bruer, J. T. (1993). The mind's journey from novice to expert. *American Educator, 6*(15), 38–46.

Bruner, J. (1986). Thought and emotion: Can Humpty-Dumpty be put together again? In D. Bearison & H. Zimilies (Eds.), *Thought and emotion: Developmental perspectives.* Hillsdale, NJ: Lawrence Erlbaum.

Bryan, T., Donahue, M., & Pearl, R. (1981). Learning disabled children's peer interactions during a small group problem-solving task. *Learning Disability Quarterly, 4,* 13–22.

Bulgren, J., & Lenz, K. (1996). Strategic instruction in the content areas. In D. Deshler, E. S. Ellis, & B. K. Lenz (Eds.), *Teaching adolescents with learning disabilities* (2nd ed.) (pp. 409–473). Denver: Love.

Bulgren, J. A., Schumaker, J. B., & Deshler, D. D. (1988). Effectiveness of a concept teaching routine in enhancing the performance of LD students in a secondary level mainstream class. *Learning Disability Quarterly, 11,* 3–17.

Burger, J. M. (1992). *Desire for control: Personality, social, and clinical perspectives.* New York: Plenum Press.

Burton, T. A., & Hirshhoren, A. (1979). The education of severely and profoundly retarded children: Are we sacrificing the child to the concept? *Exceptional Children, 45,* 598–602.

Buswell, B., & Martz, J. (1987). The meaning of partnerships: Parents' perspectives. *Mainstream.* Washington, DC: The Legal Center.

Butler-Nalin, P. (1989). *The effects of school characteristics and program participation on special education dropouts*

(Contract No. 300–87-0054). Menlo Park, CA: SRI International.

Butt, D. S. (1987). *The psychology of sport: The behavior, motivation, personality and performance of athletes* (2nd ed.). New York: Van Nostrand Reinhold.

Bybee, R., Buchwald, C., Crissman, S., Heil, D., Kuerbis, P., Matusumoto, C., & McInerny, J. (1989). *Science and technology education for the elementary years: Frameworks for curriculum and instruction.* Andover, MA: National Center for Improving Science Education.

Caine, R. N., & Caine, G. (1994). *Making connections: Teaching and the human brain.* Menlo Park, CA: Addison-Wesley.

Campione, J. (1989). Assisted assessment: A taxonomy of approaches and an outline of strengths and weaknesses. *Journal of Learning Disabilities, 22,* 151–165.

Carbo, M. (1996). Reading styles: High gains from the bottom third. *Educational Leadership, 53,* 8–13.

Carlson, E., & O'Reilly, F. E. (1996). Integrating Title I and special education service delivery. *Remedial and Special Education, 17,* 21–29.

Carlson, S. A., & Alley, G. R. (1981). Performance and competence of learning disabled and high achieving high school students on essential cognitive skills. (Research Report No. S3). Lawrence: University of Kansas Institute for Research in Learning Disabilities.

Carnine, D., & Kameenui, E. (1992). *Higher ordered thinking: Designing for mainstreamed students.* Austin, TX: Pro-Ed.

Carnine, D. W., Silbert, J., & Kameenui, E. J. (1990). *Direct instruction reading* (2nd ed.). Columbus, OH: Merrill.

Carnoy, M. (1974). *Education as cultural imperialism.* New York: McKay.

Catania, A. C., Matthews, B. A., & Shimoff, E. H. (1990). Properties of rule-governed behavior and their implications. In D. E. Blackman & H. Lejune (Eds.), *Behavior analysis in theory and practice: Contributions and controversies* (pp. 215–230). Hillsdale, NJ: Erlbaum.

Ceci, J. S., & Bronfenbrenner, U. (1985). "Don't forget to take the cupcakes out of the oven": Prospective memory, strategic time-monitoring, and context. *Child Development, 56,* 152–164.

Ceci, J. S., & Liker, J. (1986). Academic and nonacademic intelligence: An experimental separation. In R. J. Sternberg & R. Wagner (Eds.), *Practical intelligence: Nature and origins of competence in the everyday world* (pp. 119–142). New York: Cambridge University Press.

Cervone, D., Jiwani, N., & Wood, R. (1991). Goal setting and the differential influence of self-regulatory processes on complex decision-making performance. *Journal of Personality and Social Psychology, 61,* 257–266.

Cessna, K. K., & Adams, L. (1993). Implications of a needs-based philosophy. *Instructionally differentiated programming: A needs-based approach for students with behavior disorders* ([Monograph] pp. 7–17). Denver: Colorado Department of Education.

Chadsey-Rusch, J., Rusch, F. A., & Phelps, L. A. (1989). Social ecology of the workplace: Contextual variables affecting social interactions of employees with and without mental retardation. *American Journal on Mental Retardation, 94,* 141–151.

Chamberlain, P., & Medeiros-Landurand, P. (1991). Practical considerations for the assessment of LEP students with special needs. In E. V. Hamayan & J. S. Damico (Eds.), *Limiting bias in the assessment of bilingual students* (pp. 111–156). Austin, TX: Pro-Ed.

Chan, S. Q. (1986). Parents of exceptional Asian children. In M. K. Kitano & P. C. Chinn (Eds.), *Exceptional Asian children and youth* (pp. 36–53). Reston, VA: Council for Exceptional Children and Youth.

Chan, S. Q. (1990). Early intervention with culturally diverse families of infants and toddlers with disabilities. *Infants and Young Children, 3*(2), 78–87.

Charlson, E., Strong, M., & Gold, R. (1992). How successful deaf teenagers experience and cope with isolation. *American Annals of the Deaf, 136,* 339–343.

Chinn, P. C., Winn, J., & Walters, R. H. (1978). *Two-way talking with parents of special children.* St. Louis: Mosby.

Christenson, S. L., Ysseldyke, J. E., & Thurlow, M. L. (1989). Critical instructional factors for students with mild handicaps: An integrative review. *Remedial and Special Education, 10,* 21–31.

Clark, G. M. (1994). Is a functional curriculum approach compatible with an inclusive education model? *Teaching Exceptional Children, 26*(2), 36–39.

Clark, G. M., Carlson, B. C., Fisher, S. L., Cook, I. D., & D'Alonzo, B. J. (1991). Career development for students with disabilities in elementary schools: A position statement of the division of career development. *Career Development for Exceptional Individuals, 14,* 109–120.

Colorado Developmental Disabilities Planning Council. (1995). *The policy paper on inclusion.* Denver: Author.

Colvin, G. T., & Sugai, G. M. (1988). Proactive strategies for managing social behavior problems: An instructional approach. *Education and Treatment of Children, 11,* 341–348.

Combrinck-Graham, L. (1983). The family life cycle and families with young children. In J. Hansen & H. Liddle (Eds.), *Clinical implications of the family life cycle.* Rockville, MD: Aspen.

Commins, N. (1989). Language and affect: Bilingual students at home and at school. *Language Arts, 66,* 29–43.

Commins, N., & Miramontes, O. (1989). Perceived and actual linguistic competence: A descriptive study of four low achieving Hispanic bilingual students. *American Educational Research Journal, 26,* 443–472.

Condeluci, A. (1991). *Interdependence: The route to community.* Orlando: Paul M. Deutsch Press.

Cook, L., & Friend, M. (1991). Principles for the practice of collaboration in schools. *Preventing School Failure, 35*(4), 6–9.

Cook, L., & Friend, M. (1993). Educational leadership for teacher collaboration. In B. Billingsley (Ed.), *Program leadership for serving students with disabilities* (pp. 421–444). Richmond: Virginia Department of Education.

Cook, L. K., & Mayer, R. E., (1988). Teaching readers about structure of scientific text. *Journal of Education Psychology, 80,* 448–456.

Coots, J. J., Bishop, K. D., Grenot-Scheyer, M., & Falvey, M. A. (1995). Practices in general education: Past and present. In M. A. Falvey (Ed.), *Inclusive and heterogeneous schooling: Assessment, curriculum and instruction* (pp. 7–22). Baltimore: Brookes.

Correa, V. I., & Weismantel, J. (1991). Multicultural issues related to families with an exceptional child. In M. J. Fine (Ed.), *Collaboration with parents of exceptional children.* Brandon, VT: Clinical Psychology.

Covey, S. R. (1990). *Seven habits of highly effective people.* New York: Simon & Schuster.

Cramer, S., Erzkus, A., Mayweather, K., Pope, K., Roeder, J., & Tone, T. (1997). Connecting with siblings. *Teaching Exceptional Children, 30*(1), 46–51.

Crnic, K. A., & Leconte, J. M. (1986). Understanding sibling needs and influences. In R. R. Fewell & P. F. Vadasy (Eds.), *Families of handicapped children: Needs and supports across the life span* (pp. 77–98). Austin: TX: Pro-Ed.

Crockett, W. (1988). Schemas, affect, and communication. In L. Donohew, H. E. Sypher, & E. Tory Higgins (Eds.), *Communication, social cognition, and affect.* Hillsdale, NJ: Lawrence Erlbaum.

CTB/McGraw-Hill. (1985). California achievement test. Monterey, CA: Author.

Cuban, L. (1988). *The managerial imperative and the practice of leadership in schools.* Albany: State University of New York Press.

Cuban, L. (1996). Myths about changing schools and the case of special education. *Remedial and Special Education, 17,* 75–82.

Cummins, J. (1986). Empowering minority students: A framework for intervention. *Harvard Educational Review, 56,* 18–36.

Daggett, W. (1991). Lincoln High School. Videotape. Denver: Auraria Library. LC1045D34.

Davies, D. (1988). Low income parents and the schools: A research report and plan for action. *Equity and Choice, 4*(3), 51–59.

Davis, P. B., & May, J. E. (1991). Involving fathers in early intervention and family support programs: Issues and strategies. *Children's Health Care, 20*(2), 87–93.

Day, H. M., Horner, R. H., & O'Neill, R. E. (1994). *Journal of Applied Behavior Analysis, 27*(2), 279–289.

Deci, E. L., & Ryan, R. M. (1985). *Intrinsic motivation and self-determination in human behavior.* New York: Plenum.

Dede, C. (1989). The evolution of information technology: Implications for curriculum. *Educational Leadership, 47,* 23–29.

Delpit, L. (1995). *Other people's children: Cultural conflict in the classroom.* New York: New Press.

Delquadri, J., Greenwood, C. R., Whorton, D., Carta, J. J., & Hall, R. V. (1986). Classwide peer-tutoring. *Exceptional Children, 6,* 535–542.

Demands on single parents. (1984). *The Exceptional Parent, 14,* 44–46.

Dennis, R. E., Williams, W., Giangreco, M. F., & Cloninger, C. J. (1993). Quality of life as a context for planning and evaluation of services for people with disabilities. *Exceptional Children, 59,* 499–512.

Deno, E. (1970). Special education as developmental capital. *Exceptional Children, 37,* 229–237.

Deshler, D. D., Ellis, E. S., & Lenz, B. K. (Eds.). (1996). *Teaching adolescents with learning disabilities: Strategies and methods* (2nd ed.). Denver: Love.

Deshler, D. D., & Schumaker, J. B. (1984). An instructional model for teaching students how to learn. In J. L. Graden, J. E. Zins, & J. J. Curtis (Eds.), *Alternative educational delivery systems: Enhancing instructional options for all students* (pp. 391–411). Washington, DC: NASSP.

Deshler, D. D., Schumaker, J. B., Lenz, B. K., & Ellis, E. S. (1984). Academic and cognitive interventions for LD adolescents (Part 2). *Journal of Learning Disabilities, 17,* 170–187.

DeStefano, L., & Wagner, M. (1991). *Outcome assessment in special education: Lessons learned.* Menlo Park, CA: SRI International.

Dewey, J. (1916). *Democracy and education.* New York: Macmillan.

Dinkmeyer, D., McKay, G., & Dinkmeyer, D., Jr. (1980*). Systematic training for effective teaching.* Circle Pines, MN: American Guidance Service.

Doll, B., Sands, D. J., Wehmeyer, M. L., & Palmer, S. (1996). Promoting the development and acquisition of self-determined behavior. In D. Sands & M. Wehmeyer (Eds.), *Self-determination across the lifespan: Independence and choice for people with disabilities* (pp. 65–90). Baltimore: Brookes.

Doll, R. C. (1992). *Curriculum improvement: Decision making and process* (8th ed.). Boston: Allyn & Bacon.

Donnellan, A. M., Mirenda, P. L., Mesaros, R. A., & Fassbender, L. L. (1984). Analyzing the communicative functions of aberrant behavior. *Journal of the Association for Persons with Severe Handicaps, 9,* 201–212.

Drake, S. (1993). *Planning integrated curriculum: The call to adventure.* Alexandria, VA: Association for Supervision and Curriculum Development.

Drake, S. (1995). Connecting learning outcomes and integrated curricula. *Orbit, 26,* 28–32.

Drake, S. M., Bebbington, J., Laksman, S., Mackie, P., Maynes, N., & Wayne, L. (1992). *Developing an integrated curriculum using the story model.* Toronto: Ontario Institute for Studies in Education Press.

Drake, S., Hemphill, B., & Chappell, R. (1995). Creating a new story in grade 9 science. *The Green Teacher.*

Dreikurs, R., Grunwald, B., & Pepper, F. (1980). *Maintaining sanity in the classroom.* New York: Harper & Row.

Drexler, N., Harvey, G., & Kell, D. (1990). Student and teacher success: The impact of computers in primary grades. Paper presented at the annual meeting of the American Education Research Association, Boston.

DuFour, R. (1995). Restructuring is not enough. *Educational Leadership, 52,* 33–36.

Dunkle, M., & Usdan, M. D. (1993, March). Putting people first means connecting education to other services, *Education Week.*

Dunlap, G., & Kern, L. (1996). Modifying instructional activities to promote desirable behavior: A conceptual and practical framework. *School Psychology Journal, 11,* 297–301.

Dunst, C. J., & Paget, K. D. (1991). Parent-professional partnerships and family empowerment. In M. J. Fine (Ed.), *Collaboration with parents of exceptional children.* Brandon, VT: Clinical Psychology Press.

Dunst, C. J., Trivette, C. M., & Cross, A. (1986). Mediating influences of social support. *American Journal of Mental Deficiency, 90,* 403–417.

Dunst, C. J., Trivette, C. M., & Deal, A. (1988). *Enabling and empowering families.* Cambridge, MA: Brookline Books.

Dyson, L., Edgar, E., & Crnic, K. (1989). Psychological predictors of adjustment by siblings of developmentally delayed children. *American Journal on Mental Retardation, 94*(3), 292–302.

Eden, D., & Shani, A. (1982). Pygmalion goes to bootcamp: Expectancy leadership and trainee performance. *Journal of Applied Psychology, 67,* 605–606.

Eden-Piercy, G. V. S., Blacher, J. B., & Eyman, R. K. (1986). Exploring parents' reactions to their young child with severe handicaps. *Mental Retardation, 24,* 285–291.

Educational Leadership. (1996, February). *Students with special needs, 53.*

Educational Leadership. (December 1994/January 1995). *The inclusive school, 52.*

*Education Daily Special Supplement, 30* (1997, July), 137.

Eisenhart, M., & Graue, M. E. (1993). Constructing cultural difference and educational achievement in schools. In E. Jacobs & C. Jordan (Eds.*), Minority education: Anthropological perspectives.* Norwood, NJ: Ablex.

Eisner, E. W. (1988). The ecology of school improvement. *Educational Leadership, 45*(5), 24–29.

Eisner, E. W. (1991). What really counts in schools. *Educational Leadership, 10*–11, 14–17.

Eisner, E. W. (1994). *Cognition and curriculum reconsidered* (2nd ed.). New York: Teachers College Press.

Elias, M. J., Zins, J. E., Weissberg, R. P., Frey, K. S., Greenberg, M. T., Haynes, N. M., Kessler, R., Schwab-Stone, M. E., & Shriver, T. P. (1997). *Promoting social and emotional learning: Guidelines for educators.* Alexandria, VA: Association for Supervision and Curriculum Development.

Elliot, E. S., & Dweck, C. S. (1988). Goals: An approach to motivation and achievement. *Journal of Personality and Social Psychology, 54,* 5–12.

Ellis, A. K., & Fouts, J. T. (1994). *Research on school restructuring.* Princeton Junction, NJ: Eye on Education.

Ellis, E. S. (1994). An instructional model for integrating content-area instruction with cognitive strategy instruction. *Reading and Writing Quarterly: Overcoming Learning Difficulties, 10*(1), 63–90.

Ellis, E. S., & Friend, P. (1991). The adolescent with learning disabilities. In B. Y. K. Wong (Ed.), *Learning about learning disabilities.* Orlando, FL: Academic Press.

Ellis, E. S., Lenz, B. K., & Sabornie, E. J. (1987). Generalization and adaptation of learning strategies to natural environments: Part 1: Critical agents. *Remedial and Special Education, 8,* 6–20.

Ellis, H. C., & Hunt, R. (1983). *Fundamentals of human memory and cognition.* Dubuque, IA: Brown.

Ellis, N. R. (1970). Memory processes in retardates and normals. In N. R. Ellis (Ed.), *International review of research in mental retardation.* New York: Academic Press.

Elmore, R. F., & Fuhrman, S. H. (1994). Governing curriculum: Changing patterns in policy, politics, and practice. In R. F. Elmore & S. H. Fuhrman (Eds.), *The governance of curriculum: 1994 yearbook of the Association for Supervision and Curriculum Development* (pp. 1–11). Alexandria, VA: Association for Supervision and Curriculum Development.

Emmer, E., & Aussiker, A. (1990). School and classroom discipline programs: How well do they work? In O. C. Moles (Ed.), *Student discipline strategies: Research and practice.* Albany: State University of New York Press.

Emmer, E., Evertson, E., & Anderson, L. (1980). Effective classroom management at the beginning of the school year. *Elementary School Journal, 80,* 219–231.

Emmer, E., Evertson, C., Sanford, J., Clements, B., & Worsham, M. (1984). *Classroom management for secondary teachers.* Englewood Cliffs, NJ: Prentice-Hall.

Englehard, G., Jr., & Monsas, J. A. (1989). Performance, gender and the cooperative attitudes of third, fifth, and seventh graders. *Journal of Research and Development in Education, 22,* 13–17.

Epstein, M. H., Patton, J. R., Polloway, E., & Foley, R. (1992). Educational services for students with behavior disorders: A review of individualized education programs. *Teacher Education and Special Education, 15,* 41–48.

Ercolano, V. (Ed.). (1994). *Toward inclusive classrooms.* Teacher-to-Teacher Series. West Haven, CT: National Education Association.

Evertson, C. (1987). Managing classrooms: A framework for teachers. In D. Berliner & B. Rosenhine (Eds.), *Talks to teachers* (pp. 54–74). New York: Random House.

Evertson, C., Emmer, E., Clements, B., Sandford, J., & Worsham, M. (1993). *Classroom management for elementary teachers* (3rd ed.). Englewood Cliffs, NJ: Prentice-Hall.

Fairweather, J. S., & Shaver, D. M. (1990). Making the transition to postsecondary education and training. *Exceptional Children, 57,* 264–270.

Falvey, M. A. (1986). *Community-based curriculum: Instructional strategies for students with severe handicaps.* Baltimore: Brookes.

Falvey, M. A. (1986). Introduction. In M. A. Falvey, *Community based curriculum: Instructional strategies for students with severe handicaps* (pp. 1–12). Baltimore: Brookes.

Falvey, M. A. (1991). *Community based curriculum: Instructional strategies for students with severe handicaps* (2nd ed). Baltimore: Brookes.

Falvey, M. A. (Ed.). (1995). *Inclusive and heterogeneous schooling: Assessment, curriculum, and instruction.* Baltimore: Brookes.

Falvey, M. A., Coots, J., Bishop, K. D., & Grenot-Scheyer, M. (1989). Educational and curricular adaptations. In S. Stainback, W. Stainback, & M. Forest (Eds.), *Educating all students in the mainstream of regular education* (pp. 143–158). Baltimore: Brookes.

Falvey, M. A., & Grenot-Scheyer, M. (1995). Instructional strategies. In M. A. Falvey (Ed.), *Inclusive and heterogeneous schooling: Assessment, curriculum, and instruction* (pp. 131–158). Baltimore: Brookes.

Farr, R. C., Prescott, G. A., Balow, I. H., & Hogan, T. P. (1986). Metropolitan achievement tests. San Antonio: Psychological Corporation.

Featherstone, H. (1980). *A difference in the family.* New York: Basic Books.

*Federal Register,* 1992, p. 44848.

Fennema, E. H., & Peterson, P. L. (1985). Autonomous learning behavior: A possible explanation of gender-related differences in mathematics. In L. C. Wilkinson & C. B. Marrett (Eds.), *Gender influences in classroom interaction.* New York: Academic Press.

Ferguson, D. L., Ralph, G., Meyer, G., Willis, C., & Young, M. (1993*). Individually tailored learning: Strategies for designing inclusive curriculum* (Module 1d). The Elementary/Secondary System: Supportive Education for Students with Severe Handicaps. Specialized Training Program, University of Oregon.

Ferrari, M. (1986). Perceptions of social support of chronically ill versus healthy children. *Children's Health Care, 15,* 26–31.

Ferster, C., & Skinner, B. F. (1957). *Schedules of reinforcement.* New York: Appleton-Century-Crofts.

Fiedler, C. R. (1993). Parents and the law: Conflict development and legal safeguards. In J. L. Paul and R. J. Simeonsson (Eds.), *Children with special needs: Family, culture and society* (pp. 256–278). Fort Worth: Harcourt Brace Jovanovich.

Filbin, J. (1994). *Identifying learner outcomes within curricular activities: A performance-based model.* Denver: Colorado Department of Education.

Fimian, M. J. (1982). What is teacher stress? *The Clearing House, 56,* 101–106.

Fimian, M. J. (1986). Social support and occupational stress in special education. *Exceptional Children, 52*(5), 436–442.

Fisher, E. (1985). Educator examines myths, realities of LD students at college level. *Hill Top Spectrum, 3,* 1–8.

Fisher, R., & Brown, S. (1988). *Building relationships that get to yes.* New York: Houghton Mifflin.

Flynn, L. L., & McCollum, J. (1989). Support systems: Strategies and implications for hospitalized newborns and families. *Journal of Early Intervention, 13*(2), 173–182.

Ford, A., Davern, L., & Schnorr, R. (1992). Inclusive education: Making sense of the curriculum. In S. Stainback and W. Stainback, *Curriculum considerations in inclusive classrooms* (pp. 37–61). Baltimore: Brookes.

Ford, P. (1994). Something gained: A family's long road to inclusive schooling. In J. Rogers (Ed.), *Inclusion: Moving beyond our fears* (pp. 227–230). Hot Topic Series. Bloomington, IN: Phi Delta Kappa.

Forest, M., & Pearpoint, J. C. (1992). Putting all kids on the MAP. *Educational Leadership, 50,* 26–31.

Forness, S. R., & Walker, H. M. (1992*). Special education and children with ADD/ADHD.* NADDA Monograph Series. (Publication No. 110). National Attention Deficit Disorder Association.

Fox, N. E., & Ysseldyke, J. E. (1997). Implementing inclusion at the middle school level: Lessons from a negative example. *Exceptional Children, 64,* 81–91.

Fox, T., & Williams, W. (1991*). Implementing best practices for all students in the local schools.* Vermont Statewide Systems Support Change Project, Center for Developmental Disabilities, Burlington, Vermont.

Frank, A., Sitlington, P., Cooper, L., & Cool, D. (1990). Adult adjustment of recent graduates of Iowa mental disabilities programs. *Education and Training in Mental Retardation, 25,* 62–75.

French, J. R. P., & Raven, B. (1959). The bases of social power. In D. Cartwright (Ed.), *Studies in social power.* Ann Arbor: University of Michigan, Institute for Social Research.

French, N. K. (1991). Elementary teachers' perceptions of stressful events and stress related teaching practices. *Perceptual and Motor Skills, 72,* 203–210.

French, N. K., & Cabell, E. A. (1993). Are community college training programs for paraeducators feasible? *Community College Journal of Research and Practice, 17,* 131–140.

French, N. K., & Pickett, A. L. (1997). Paraprofessionals in special education: Issues for teacher educators. *Teacher Education and Special Education, 20*(1), 61–73.

Frey, K. S., Fewell, R. R., & Vadasy, P. F. (1989). Parental adjustment and changes in child outcome among families of young handicapped children. *Topics in Early Childhood Education, 8*(4), 38–57.

Frey, K. S., Greenburg, M. T., & Fewell, R. R. (1989). Stress and coping among parents of handicapped children: A multidimensional approach. *American Journal on Mental Retardation, 94,* 240–249.

Friedman, M. I., & Lackey, G. H. (1991). *The psychology of human control: A general theory of purposeful behavior.* New York: Praeger.

Friend, M., Reising, M., & Cook, L. (1993). Co-teaching: An overview of the past, a glimpse at the present and considerations for the future. *Preventing School Failure, 37*(4), 6–10.

Froyen, L. (1988). *Classroom management: Empowering teacher leaders.* Columbus, OH: Merrill.

Fuchs, D. (1994). Mainstream assistance teams: A prereferral intervention system for difficult-to-teach students. In G. Stoner, M. Shinn, & H. Walker (Eds.), *Interventions for achievement and behavior problems* (pp. 241–268). Silver Spring, MD: National Association of School Psychologists.

Fuchs, D., & Fuchs, L. S. (1987). Norm-referenced tests: Are they valid for use with handicapped students? *Exceptional Children, 54,* 263–271.

Fuchs, D., & Fuchs, L. S. (1994). Inclusive school movement and the radicalization of special education reform. *Exceptional Children, 60,* 294–309.

Fuchs, D., Fuchs, L. S., Mathes, P. G., & Simmons, D. C. (1997). Peer-assisted learning strategies: Making classrooms more responsive to diversity. *American Educational Research Journal, 34*(1), 174–206.

Fuchs, L., & Fuchs, D. (1986). Linking assessment to instructional intervention: An overview. *School Psychology Review, 15,* 318–323.

Fuchs, L., & Fuchs, D. (1988). The validity of informal reading comprehension measures. *Remedial and Special Education, 9,* 20–28.

Fullan, M. G. (1994). Coordinating top-down and bottom-up strategies for educational reform. In R. Elmore & S. Fuhrman (Eds.), *The governance of curriculum* (pp. 186–202). Alexandria, VA: Association for Supervision and Curriculum Development.

Fullan, M. G., & Stiegelbaur, S. (1991). *The new meaning of educational change.* New York: Teachers College Press.

Gable, R. A., Arlen, N. L., & Cook, L. (1993). But—let's not overlook the ethics of collaboration. *Preventing School Failure, 37*(4), 32–36.

Gable, R. A., Hendrickson, J. M., & Mercer, C. D. (1985). A classroom-based curriculum validation process for teaching the behaviorally disordered. *Teaching: Behaviorally Disordered Youth,* 1–11.

Gagne, R. M. (1984). Learning outcomes and their effects: Useful categories of human performance. *American Psychologist, 39,* 377–385.

Gardner, H. (1983). *Frames of mind: The theory of multiple intelligences.* New York: Basic Books.

Gardner, H. (1991). *The unschooled mind: How children think and how schools should teach.* New York: Basic Books.

Gartner, A. (1971). *Paraprofessionals and their performance: A survey of education, health and social services programs.* New York: Praeger.

Gartner, A., & Lipsky, D. (1987). Beyond special education: Toward a quality system for all students. *Harvard Educational Review, 57,* 367–395.

Gartner, A. J., & Riessman, F. (1994). Tutoring helps those who give, those who receive. *Educational Leadership, 52,* 58–60.

Gath, A. (1977). Effect of the abnormal child on the parents. *British Journal of Psychology, 130,* 405–420.

Gaustad, M. G., & Kluwin, T. N. (1992). Patterns of communication among deaf and hearing students. In T. N. Kluwin, D. F. Moores, & M. G. Gaustad (Eds.), *Toward effective public programs for deaf students: Context, process, and outcomes* (pp. 107–128). New York: Teachers College Press.

Gerrig, R. J., & Banaji, M. R. (1994). Language and thought. In R. J. Sternberg (Ed.), *Thinking and problem solving: Handbook of perception and cognition.* New York: Academic Press.

Gersten, R., Woodward, J., & Carnine, D. W. (1987). Direct instruction research: The third decade. *Remedial and Special Education, 8,* 48–56.

Gersten, R., Woodward, J., & Darch, C. (1986). Direct instruction: A research approach to curriculum design and teaching. *Exceptional Children, 53,* 17–31.

Getzels, J. W. (1982). The problem of the problem. In R. Hogarth (Ed.), *New directions for methodology of social and behavioral science: Question framing and response consistency.* San Francisco: Jossey-Bass.

Glasser, W. (1986). *Control theory in the classroom.* New York: Harper & Row.

Goldenberg, I., & Goldenberg, H. (1980). *Family therapy: An overview.* Monterey, CA: Brooks/Cole.

Goldfried, M. R. (1988). Application of rational restructuring to anxiety disorders. *The Counseling Psychologist, 16,* 50–68.

Goldstein, A. P. (1988). *The prepare curriculum: Teaching prosocial competencies.* Champaign, IL: Research Press.

Goldstein, M. (1986, Spring). Curriculum: The keystone for special education planning. *Teaching Exceptional Children,* 220–223.

Good, T. L., & Brophy, J. E. (1994). *Looking in classrooms* (6th ed.). New York: HarperCollins.

Good, T., Grouws, D., & Ebmeier, H. (1983). *Active mathematics teaching.* New York: Longman.

Goodlad, J. I. (1984). *A place called school: Prospects for the future.* New York: McGraw-Hill.

Goodwin, T. (producer), & Wurzburg, G. (director). (1992). *Educating Peter.* USA: State of the Art.

Graden, J. L., Casey, A., & Bronstrom, O. (1985). Implementing a prereferral intervention system: Part II. The data. *Exceptional Children, 51,* 487–384.

Graham, S., & Harris, K. R. (1993). Self-instructional strategy development: Programmatic research in writing. In B. Wong (Ed.), *Intervention research with students with learning disabilities: An international perspective.* New York: Springer-Verlag.

Graham, S., Harris, K. R., & Reid, K. (1992). Developing self-regulated learners. *Focus on Exceptional Children, 24,* 3–15.

Grant, L. (1984). Black females' "place" in desegregated classrooms. *Sociology of Education, 57,* 98–110.

Gredler, M. E. (1992). *Learning and instruction: Theory and practice* (2nd ed.). New York: Macmillan.

Greenwood, C. R. (1991). Longitudinal analysis of time, engagement, and achievement in at-risk versus non-risk students. *Exceptional Children, 57,* 521–535.

Grenot-Scheyer, M., Abernathy, P. A., Williamson, D., Jubala, K., & Coots, J. J. (1995). Elementary curriculum and instruction. In M. Falvey (Ed.), *Inclusive and heterogeneous schooling: Assessment, curriculum, and instruction* (pp. 319–340). Baltimore: Brookes.

Grossman, H. (1983). Manual on terminology and classification in mental retardation (Rev. ed.). Washington, DC: American Association on Mental Deficiency.

Grossman, H. (1991). Special education in a diverse society: Improving services for minority and working-class students. *Preventing School Failure, 36,* 19–27.

Grossman, H. (1995). *Classroom behavior management in a diverse society.* Mountain View, CA: Mayfield.

Grossman, H. (1995). *Special education in a diverse society.* Boston: Allyn & Bacon.

Gursky, D. (1990). On the wrong track? *Teacher Magazine, 1,* 43–51.

Halliday, M. A. K. (1975). *Learning how to mean: Explorations in the development of language.* London: Edward Arnold.

Halpern, A. S., & Benz, M. R. (1987). A statewide examination of secondary special education for students with mild disabilities: Implications for the high school curriculum. *Exceptional Children, 54,* 122–129.

Hamre-Nietupski, S., Branston, M. B., Ford, A., Gruenewald, L., & Brown, L. (1978). Curriculum strategies for developing longitudinal interactions between severely handicapped and non-handicapped individuals in school and non-school environments. In L. Brown, S. Hamre-Nietupski, M. B. Branston, M. Falvey, S. Lyon, & L. Gruenewald (Eds.), *Curricula strategies for developing longitudinal interactions between severely handicapped students and others and curricular strategies for teaching severely handicapped students to acquire and perform skills in response to naturally occurring cues and correction procedures* (Vol. 8). Madison, WI: Madison Metropolitan School District.

Hanson, M. J., Lynch, E. W., & Wayman, K. I. (1990). Honoring the cultural diversity of families when gathering data. *Topics in Early Childhood Special Education, 10*(1), 112–131.

Hanson, N. (1990). *Final report: California early intervention personnel study project.* San Francisco: San Francisco State University, Department of Special Education.

Hardman, M., & McDonnell, J. (1987). Implementing federal transition initiatives for youths with severe handicaps. The Utah community-based transition project. *Exceptional Children, 53,* 493–498.

Haring, N. G., Liberty, K. A., & White, O. R. (1980). Rules for data-based strategy decisions in instructional programs: Current research and instructional implications. In W. Sailor, B. Wilcox, & L. Brown (Eds.), *Methods of instruction for severely handicapped students* (pp. 159–192). Baltimore: Brookes.

Haring, T. D., & Kennedy, C. H. (1992). Behavior analytic foundations of classroom management. In W. C. Stainback & S. B. Stainback (Eds.), *Controversial issues confronting special education: Divergent perspectives* (pp. 210–212). Boston: Allyn & Bacon.

Harmin, M. (1994). *Inspiring active learning: A handbook for teachers.* Alexandria, VA: Association for Supervision and Curriculum Development.

Harris, K. R., & Graham, S. (1996). Memo to constructivists: Skills count, too. *Educational Leadership, 53,* 26–210.

Harrison, A. O., Wilson, M. N., Pine, C. J., Chan, S. Q., & Buriel, R. (1990). Family ecologies of ethnic minority children. *Child Development, 61*(20), 347–362.

Harry, B. (1992). *Cultural diversity, families and the special education system: Communication and empowerment.* New York: Teachers College Press.

Harter, S. (1982). Perceived competence scale for children. Denver: University of Denver.

Harter, S. (1983). Developmental perspectives on the self system. In P. Mussen (Ed.), *Handbook of Child Psychology* (pp. 275–385). New York: Wiley.

Hasazi, S .B., Gordon, L. R., & Roe, C. A. (1985). Factors associated with employment status of handicapped youth exiting high school from 1979–1983. *Exceptional Children, 51,* 455–469.

Hass, G., & Parkay, F. W. (1993). *Curriculum planning: A new approach* (6th ed.). Boston: Allyn & Bacon.

Hassett, J. (1986). *Computer technology in the classroom.* New York: Horizon Technologies.

HEATH (1990). *Americans with disabilities act,* Vol. 9, No. 2. Washington, DC: National Clearinghouse on Post-secondary Education for Individuals with Handicaps.

Heath, S. B. (1983). *Ways with words: Language, life and work in communities and classrooms.* Cambridge, England: Cambridge University Press.

Heath, S. B. (1986). Socio-cultural contexts of language development. In Bilingual Education Office, California State Department of Education, *Beyond language: Social and cultural factors in schooling language minority students* (pp. 141–186). Los Angeles: Evaluation, Dissemination and Assessment Center, California State University.

Helmke, L. M., Havekost, D. M., Patton, J. R., & Polloway, E. A. (1994). Life skills programming: Development of a high school science course. *Teaching Exceptional Children, 26,* 49–53.

Hendrick Hudson District v. Board of Education, 458 U.S. 176, 181 (1982).

Herring, S. C. (1993). Gender and democracy in computer-mediated communication. *Electronic Journal of Communication, 3,* 1–17.

Heward, M. L., & Orlansky, M. D. (1992). *Exceptional children* (4th ed.). New York: Macmillan.

Hiebert, J, & Wearne, D. (1992). Links between teaching and learning place value with understanding in first grade. *Journal for Research in Mathematics Education, 23,* 98–122.

Hieronymus, A. N., Hoover, H. D., & Lindquist, E. F. (1986). Iowa tests of basic skills. Chicago: Riverside.

Hiskey, M. (1966). Hiskey Nebraska test on learning aptitude. Lincoln, NE: Author.

Hobbs, N. (1975). *The futures of children.* San Francisco: Jossey-Bass.

Hocutt, A. M., & Alberg, J. Y. (1995). Case studies of the application of categorical and non-categorical special education. *Exceptionality, 5,* 199–222.

Hodgkinson, H. (1991). Reform versus reality. *Phi Delta Kappan, 73*(1), 9–16.

Hodgkinson, H. (1992). *A demographic look at tomorrow.* Washington, DC: Institute for Educational Leadership.

Horner, R. H. (1994). Functional assessment: Contributions and future directions. *Journal of Applied Behavioral Analysis, 27,* 401–404.

Horner, R. H., & Day, H. M. (1991). The effects of response efficiency on functionally equivalent competing behaviors. *Journal of Applied Behavior Analysis, 24,* 719–732.

Hourcade, J. J., Parette, H. P., & Huer, M. B. (1997). Family and cultural alert! Considerations in assistive technology assessment. *Teaching Exceptional Children, 30*(1), 40–44.

House, J. (1981). *Work stress and social support.* Reading, MA: Addison-Wesley.

Hoy, C. (1986). Preventing learned helplessness. *Academic Therapy, 22,* 11–18.

Hresko, W. P., & Parmar, R. S. (1991). The educational perspective. In D. K. Reid, W. P. Hresko, & H. L. Swanson (Eds.), *A cognitive approach to learning disabilities* (2nd ed.) (pp. 3–44). Austin, TX: Pro-Ed.

Hull, J. M. (1990). *Touching the rock.* New York: Pantheon Books.

Hulsebusch, P. L. (1989). *Significant others: Teacher perspectives on relationships with parents.* Paper presented at the annual meeting of the American Educational Research Association, San Francisco.

Hunt, D. E. (1975). Student conceptual level and models of teaching: Theoretical and empirical coordination of two models. *Interchange, 5,* 19–30.

Hunt, D. E. (1979). Learning styles and teaching strategies. *Behavioral and Social Science Teacher, 2,* 22–34.

Hunt, D. E., & Gow, J. (1984). How to be your own best theorist II. *Theory into practice, 23,* 64–71.

Hyde, A. A., & Bizar, M. (1989). *Thought in context: Teaching cognitive processes across the elementary school curriculum.* New York: Longman.

Irving Independent School District v. Tatro, 468 U.S. 883, 104 S. Ct. 3371, 82 L. Ed. 2d 664 (1984).

Iwanicki, E. F., & Schwab, R. L. (1981). A cross validation of the Maslach Burnout Inventory. *Educational and Psychological Measurement, 41,* 1167–1174.

Jackson, B. T. (1994). Forward. In R. Elmore & S. Fuhrman (Eds.), *The governance of curriculum* (pp. v–vi). Alexandria, VA: Association for Supervision and Curriculum Development.

Jacobs, H. H. (1989). *Interdisciplinary curriculum: Design and implementation.* Alexandria, VA: Association for Supervision and Curriculum Development.

Janicki, M. P. (1990). Growing old with dignity: On quality of life for older persons with a lifelong disability. In R. L. Schalock (Ed.), *Quality of life: Perspectives and issues* (pp. 115–126). Washington, DC: American Association on Mental Retardation.

Jefferson County Public Schools. (1995). *Exit outcomes and proficiencies.* Golden, CO: Author.

Jenkins, A. H. (1982). *The psychology of the Afro-American: A humanistic approach.* New York: Pergamon Press.

Jenkins, J. R., Jewell, M., Leicester, N., O'Connor, R. E., Jenkins, L. M., & Troutner, N. M. (1994). Accommodations for individual difference without classroom ability groups: An experiment in school restructuring. *Exceptional Children, 60,* 344–359.

Jewell, G. (1985). *Geri.* New York: Ballantine Books.

Johnson, D. W., Johnson, R. T., & Holubec, E. J. (1991). *Cooperation in the classroom* (Rev. ed.). Edina, MN: Interaction Books.

Joint Committee on Teacher Planning for Students with Disabilities. (1995). *Planning for academic diversity in America's classrooms: Windows on reality, research, change, and practice.* Lawrence: University of Kansas Center for Research on Learning.

Jones, K. H., & Bender, W. N. (1993). Utilization of paraprofessionals in special education: A review of the literature. *Remedial and Special Education, 14*(1), 7–14.

Jones, V., & Jones, L. S. (1995). *Comprehensive classroom management: Creating positive learning environments for all students* (4th ed.). New York: Allyn & Bacon.

Jorgensen, C. M. (1996). Designing inclusive curricula right from the start: Practical strategies and examples for the high school classroom. In S. Stainback & W. Stainback, *Inclusion: A guide for educators* (pp. 221–236). Baltimore: Brookes.

Jorgensen, C. M. (1997). Curriculum and its impact on inclusion and the achievement of students with disabilities. *Policy Research Issue Brief, 2*(2), 1–14.

Joyce, B., Weil, M., & Showers, B. (1992). *Models of teaching* (4th ed.). Englewood Cliffs, NJ: Prentice-Hall.

Joyce, B., Wolf, J., & Calhoun, E. (1993). *The self renewing school.* Alexandria, VA: Association for Supervision and Curriculum Development.

Kail R., & Bisanz, J. (1992). The information-processing perspective on cognitive development in childhood and adolescence. In R. J. Sternberg & C. A. Berg (Eds.), *Intellectual Development* (pp. 229–260). New York: Cambridge University Press.

Kameenui, E. J., Jitendra, A. K., & Darch, C. B. (1995). Direct instruction reading as contronym and economine. *Reading and Writing Quarterly, 11,* 3–17.

Kameenui, E. J., & Simmons, D. C. (1990). *Designing instructional strategies: The prevention of academic learning problems.* Columbus, OH: Merrill.

Karagiannis, A., Stainback, S., & Stainback, W. (1996). Historical overview of inclusion. In S. Stainback & W. Stainback (Eds.), *Inclusion: A guide for educators* (pp. 17–28). Baltimore: Brookes.

Karagiannis, A., Stainback, W., & Stainback, S. (1996). Rationale for inclusive schooling. In S. Stainback & W. Stainback (Eds.), *Inclusion: A guide for educators* (pp. 3–15). Baltimore: Brookes.

Karen, O., Lambour, G., & Greenspan, S. (1990). Persons in transition. In R. Schalock & M. J. Bogale (Eds.), *Quality of life: Perspectives and issues* (pp. 85–92). Washington, DC: American Association of Mental Retardation.

Karpinski, M. J., Neubert, D. A., & Graham, S. (1992). A follow-along study of postsecondary outcomes for graduates and dropouts with mild disabilities in a rural setting. *Journal of Learning Disabilities, 25,* 376–385.

Kauffman, J. M. (1993). *Characteristics of emotional and behavioral disorders of children and youth* (5th ed.). New York: Macmillan.

Kauffman, J. M. (1997). *Characteristics of emotional and behavioral disorders of children and youth.* New York: Merrill.

Kaufman, A., & Kaufman, N. (1983). Kaufman test of educational achievement. Circle Pines, MN: American Guidance Service.

Kern, L., & Dunlap, G. (in press). Assessment-based interventions for children with emotional and behavioral disorders. In A. C. Repp & R. H. Horner (Eds.), *Functional analysis of problem behavior: From effective assessment to effective support.* Monterey, CA: Brooks/Cole.

Kerr, M., & Bowen, M. (1988). *Family evaluation: An approach based on Bowen theory.* New York: Norton.

Kinzie, J. D. (1985). Overview of clinical issues in the treatment of Southeast Asian refugees. In T. C. Owan (Ed.), *Southeast Asian mental health: Treatment, prevention, services, training and research* (pp. 113–135). Washington, DC: U.S. Department of Health and Human Services, National Institute of Mental Health.

Kissam, B., & Lenz, B. (1994). *Pedagogies for diversity in secondary schools: A preservice curriculum.* Lawrence: University of Kansas.

Klein, S. D. (1993). The challenge of communicating with parents. *Developmental and Behavioral Pediatrics, 14,* 184–191.

Klenk, L., & Palinscar, A. S. (1996). Enacting responsible pedagogy with students in special education. In M. C. Pugach & C. L. Warger (Eds.), *Curriculum trends, special education, and reform: Refocusing the conversation* (pp. 179–199). New York: Teachers College Press.

Kniep, W., & Martin-Kniep, G. O. (1995). Designing schools and curriculums for the 21st century. In J. Beane (Ed.), *Toward a coherent curriculum: The 1995 ASCD yearbook*

(pp. 87–100). Alexandria, VA: Association for Supervision and Curriculum Development.

Kounin, J. (1970). *Discipline and group management of classrooms.* New York: Holt, Rinehart & Winston.

Kovalik, S. (1993). *Integrated thematic instruction. The model* (2nd ed.). Oak Creek, AZ: Books for Educators.

Kozleski, E. B. (1993). Reflections on "Taylor's story: Full inclusion in her neighborhood elementary school." *Exceptionality, 4,* 193–198.

Kozleski, E. B., Cessna, K., Bechard, S., & Borock, J. (1993). Lessons from policy decisions: Politics and services for students with emotional and behavioral disorders. *Behavior Disorders, 18,* 205–217.

Kozleski, E. B., & Sands, D. J. (1992). The yardstick of social validity: Evaluating quality of life as perceived by adults without disabilities. *Education and Training in Mental Retardation, 27,* 119–131.

Kozleski, E. B., Sands, D. J., French, N. K., Moore, E. D., & Roggow, R. (1995). *A systematic approach to supporting inclusive learning communities.* Denver: TRL Associates.

Kozol, J. (1991). *Savage inequalities: Children in America's schools.* New York: Crown.

Krich, L. P. (1994). Everyone can be a scientist. In V. Ercolano (Ed.), *Toward inclusive classrooms* (pp. 25–37). Teacher-to-Teacher Series. National Education Association of the United States.

Kucer, S. B., Silva, C., & Delgado-Larocco, E. L. (1995). *Curricular conversations: Themes in multilingual and monolingual classrooms.* York, ME: Stenhouse.

Kunc, N. (1992). The need to belong: Rediscovering Maslow's hierarchy of needs. In R. Villa, J. Thousand, W. Stainback, & S. Stainback (Eds.), *Restructuring for caring and effective education.* Baltimore: Brookes.

Ladson-Billings, G. (1994). *The dreamkeepers: Successful teachers of African-American children.* San Francisco: Jossey-Bass.

Ladson-Billings, G. (1995). A coherent curriculum in an incoherent society? Pedagogical perspectives on curriculum reform. In J. Beane (Ed.), *Toward a coherent curriculum: The 1995 ASCD yearbook* (pp. 158–169). Alexandria, VA: Association for Supervision and Curriculum Development.

Lamb, I. E., Pleck, J. H., Charnov, E. L., & Levine, J. A. (1987). A biosocial perspective on paternal behavior and treatment. In J. Lancaster, J. Altmann, A. Rossi, & L. Sherrod (Eds.), *Parenting across the life span.* New York: Aldine de Gruyter.

Lambie, R., & Daniels-Mohring, D. (1993). *Family systems within educational contexts.* Denver: Love.

Landis, L. J. (1992). Marital, employment, and childcare status of mothers with infants and toddlers with disabilites. *Topics in Early Childhood Special Education, 12,* 497–507.

Larson, C. E., & LaFasto, F. M. J. (1989). *Teamwork: What must go right/what can go wrong.* Newbury Park, CA: Sage.

Laszlo, E. (1972). *Introduction to systems philosophy: Toward a new paradigm of contemporary thought.* New York: Harper & Row.

Lave, J. (1988). *Cognition in practice.* Cambridge: Cambridge University Press.

Lehr, E. (1990). *Psychological management of traumatic brain injuries in children and adolescents.* Rockville, MD: Aspen.

Leigh, (1987). Parenting and the hearing impaired. *Volta Review, 89*(5), 11–21.

Lenz, B. K., Alley, G. R., & Schumaker, J. B. (1987). Activating the inactive learner: Advance organizers in the secondary classroom. *Learning Disability Quarterly, 10*(1), 53–67.

Lenz, B. K., Bulgren, J. A., Schumaker, J. B., Deshler, D. D., & Boudah, D. J. (1994). *The content enhancement series: The unit organizer routine.* Lawrence, KS: Edge Enterprises.

Lenz, B. K., Ellis, E. S., & Scanlon, D. (1996). *Teaching learning strategies to adolescents and adults with learning disabilities.* Austin, TX: Pro-Ed.

Lenz, B. K., Marrs, R. W., Schumaker, J. B., & Deshler, D. D. (1993). *The content enhancement series: The lesson organizer routine.* Lawrence, KS: Edge Enterprises.

Leung, E. K. (1988, October). *Cultural and acculturational commonalities and diversities among Asian Americans: Identification and programming consideration.* Paper presented at the Ethnic and Multicultural Symposia, Dallas. (ERIC Document Reproduction Service No. ED 298 708.)

Lipsky, D., & Gartner, A. (1989). *Beyond separate education: Quality education for all.* Baltimore: Brookes.

Lipsky, D., & Gartner, A. (1996). Inclusion, school restructuring, and the remaking of American society. *Harvard Educational Review, 66,* 762–795.

Lipsky, D., & Gartner, A. (1998). Taking inclusion into the future. *Educational Leadership, 56,* 78–81.

Lloyd, L. L., & Karlan, G. R. (1984). Non-speech communication symbols and systems: Where have we been and where are we going? *Journal of Mental Deficiency Research, 28,* 3–20.

Lombana, J. (1983). *Home-school partnerships.* New York: Grune & Stratton.

Long, M. J. (1988). *Handbook of rights to special education in Colorado: A guide for parents.* Denver: Legal Center.

Long, N., & Newman, R. (1971). Managing surface behaviors of children in school. In N. Long, W. Morse, & R. Newman (Eds.), *Conflict in the classroom* (4th ed.). Belmont, CA: Wadsworth.

Longhurst, T. M. (1996). Career pathways for related service paratherapists working in early intervention and other education settings. *Journal of Children's Communication Development, 18*(1), 23–30.

Longhurst, T. M., & Witmer, D. (1994). Initiating paratherapist training in Idaho. *New Directions, 15*(3), 1–5.

Longstreet, W. S., & Shane, H. G. (1993). *Curriculum for a new millennium.* Boston: Allyn & Bacon.

Lovitt, T. C. (1995). *Tactics for teaching* (2nd ed.). Englewood Cliffs, NJ: Prentice-Hall.

Luria, A. R. (1982). *Language and cognition* (J. V. Wertsch, Ed.). Washington, DC: Winston.

Lynch, E. W., & Hanson, M. J. (1992). *Developing cross-cultural competence: A guide for working with young children and their families.* Baltimore: Brookes.

MacKinnon J. D., & Brown, M. E. (1994). Inclusion in secondary schools: An analysis of school structure based on teachers' images of change. *Educational Administration Quarterly, 30,* 126–152.

Magai, C., & McFadden, S. H. (1995). *The role of emotions in social and personality development.* New York: Plenum.

Maheady, L., Sacca, K. M., & Harper, G. F. (1988). Classwide peer tutoring with mildly handicapped high school students. *Exceptional Children, 55*(1), S2–S10.

Mahoney, G., Finger, I., & Powell, A. (1985). Relationships between maternal behavioral style to the developmental status of mentally retarded infants. *American Journal of Mental Deficiency, 90,* 296–302.

Malouf, D. B., & Schiller, E. P. (1995). Practice and research in special education. *Exceptional Children, 61,* 425–439.

Marzano, R. J. (1992). *A different kind of classroom: Teaching with dimensions of learning.* Alexandria, VA: Association for Supervision and Curriculum Development.

Marzano, R., Brandt, R., Hughes, C., Jones, B., Presseisen, B., Rankin, S., & Suhor, C. (1988). *Dimensions of thinking: A framework for curriculum and instruction.* Alexandria, VA: Association for Supervision and Curriculum Development.

Mash, E. J., & Terdal, L. G. (1981). *Behavioral assessment of childhood disorders.* New York: Guilford Press.

Maslow, A. (1970). *Motivation and personality* (2nd ed.). New York: Harper & Row.

Mason, E. J., Kruse, L. A., & Kohler, M. S. (1991). Exceptional children and their siblings: Opportunities for collaboration between family and school. In M. J. Fine (Ed.), *Collaboration with parents of exceptional children*. Brandon, VT: Clinical Psychology Publishing.

Matute-Bianchi, M. E. (1986). Ethnic identities and patterns of school success and failure among Mexican-descent and Japanese-American students in a California high school: An ethnographic analysis. *American Journal of Education, 95,* 233–255.

May, J. (1993, October). Images of fathers. *Exceptional Parent,* pp. 49–50.

McCann, C. D., & Higgins, E. T. (1988). Motivation and affect in interpersonal relations: The role of personal orientations and discrepancies. In L. Donohew, H. E. Sypher, E. T. Higgins (Eds.), *Communication, social cognition, and affect.* Hillsdale, NJ: Lawrence Erlbaum.

McGinnis, E., & Goldstein, A. P. (1984). *Skill-streaming the elementary school child: A guide for teaching prosocial skills.* Champaign, IL: Research Press.

McLinden, S. (1990). Mother's and father's reports of the effects of a young child with special needs on the family. *Journal of Early Intervention, 14,* 249–259.

McLuhan, M. (1962). *The Gutenberg galaxy: The making of typographic man.* Toronto: University of Toronto Press.

McWhirter, B. T., & McWhirter, J. J. (1990). University survival strategies and the learning disabled college student. *Academic Therapy, 25,* 345–357.

Meece, J. L., Blumenfeld, P. C., & Hoyle, R. H. (1988). Students' goal orientation and cognitive engagement in classroom activities. *Journal of Educational Psychology, 80,* 514–523.

Meese, R. L. (1994). *Teaching learners with mild disabilities.* Pacific Grove, CA: Brooks/Cole.

Mehan, H. (1993). Beneath the skin and between the ears: A case study in the politics of representation. In S. Chaiklin & J. Lave (Eds.), *Understanding practice: Perspectives on activity and context.* Cambridge: Cambridge University Press.

Meichenbaum, D. (1979). Teaching children self-control. In B. B. Lahey & A. E. Kazden (Eds.), *Advances in clinical pyschology* (Vol. 2). New York: Plenum.

Meier, D., & Schwarz, P. (1995). Central park east secondary school: The hard part is making it happen. In M. W. Apple & J. A. Beane (Eds.), *Democratic schools* (pp. 26–40). Alexandria, VA: Association for Supervision and Curriculum Development.

Melaville, A. I., & Blank, M. J. (1993). *Together we can: A guide for crafting a profamily system of education and human services.* Washington, DC: U.S. Government Printing Office.

Meyer, D., Vadasy, P., Fewell, R., & Schell, G. (1982). Involving fathers of handicapped infants: Translating research into program goals. *Journal of the Division for Early Childhood, 5,* 64–72.

Meyer, L. H. (1987). A validation of program quality indicators in educational services for students with severe disabilities. *Journal of the Association for Persons with Severe Handicaps, 12*(4), 251–263.

Meyer, L. H. (1991). Advocacy, research, and typical practices: A call for the reduction of discrepancies between what is and what ought to be and how to get there. In L. H. Meyer, C. A. Peck, & L. Brown (Eds.), *Critical issues in the lives of people with severe disabilities* (pp. 629–649). Baltimore: Brookes.

Miller, R. J., LaFollette, M., & Green, K. (1990). Development and field-test of a transition planning procedure, 1985–1988. *Career Development for Exceptional Individuals, 13,* 45–55.

Mills v. Board of Education, 348 F. Supp. 866 (D.D.C. 1972).

Mintzberg, H. (1979). *The structuring of organizations.* Englewood Cliffs, NJ: Prentice-Hall.

Mire, S. P., & Chisholm, R. W. (1990). Functional communication goals for adolescents and adults who are severely and moderately mentally handicapped. *Language, Speech and Hearing Services in Schools, 20,* 57–58

Mirenda, P., & Locke, P. A. (1989). A comparison of symbol transparency in nonspeaking persons with intellectual disabilities. *Journal of Speech and Hearing Disorders, 54,* 131–140.

Mithaug, D. (1996). The optimal prospects principle: A theoretical basis for rethinking instructional practices for self-determination instruction. In D. Sands & M. Wehmeyer, *Self-determination across the life span: Independence and choice for people with disabilities* (pp. 147–165). Baltimore: Brookes.

Mithaug, D., Horiuchi, C., & Fanning, P. (1985). A report on the Colorado statewide follow-up survey of special education students. *Exceptional Children, 51,* 397–404.

Mithaug, D. E., Martin, J. E., & Agran, M. (1987). Adaptability instruction: The goal of transitional programming. *Exceptional Children, 53,* 500–505.

Monda-Amaya, L. E., & Pearson, P. D. (1996). Toward a responsible pedagogy for teaching and learning literacy. In M. Pugach & C. Warger (Eds.), *Curriculum trends, special education, and reform: Refocusing the conversation* (pp. 143–163). New York: Teachers College Press.

Montague, M., & Applegate, B. (1993). Mathematical problem-solving characteristics of middle school students with learning disabilities. *The Journal of Special Education, 7,* 175–181.

Moore, E. D., & Kozleski, E. B. (1993). *The needs that drive our behavior.* Niwot, CO: TRL Associates.

Moore, W. L., & Cooper, H. (1984). Correlations between teacher and student background and teacher perception of discipline problems and disciplinary techniques. *Psychology in the Schools, 21,* 386–392.

Moores, D. F. (1987). *Educating the deaf: Psychology, principles, and practices* (3rd ed.). Boston: Houghtin Mifflin.

Moran, M. A. (1985). Families in early intervention: Effects of program variables. *Zero to Three, 5,* 11–14.

Moran, M. R. (1987). Options for written language assessment. *Focus on Exceptional Children, 19,* 1–19.

Morra, L. (1994). *Special education reform: Districts grapple with inclusion programs.* Testimony before the Subcommittee on Select Education and Civil Rights, Committee on Education and Labor, House of Representatives.

Morrison, D., & Collins, A. (1996). Epistemic fluency and constructivist learning environments. In B. G. Wilson (Ed.), *Constructivist learning environments: Case studies in instructional design.* Englewood Cliffs, NJ: Educational Technology Publications.

Morrison, G. S. (1993). *Contemporary curriculum K–9.* Boston: Allyn & Bacon.

Morrow, R. D. (1987). Cultural differences—Be aware! *Academic Therapy, 23*(2), 143–149.

Morse, W., Ardizzone, J., Macdonald, C., & Pasnick, P. (1980). Affective education for children and youth. Reston, VA: Council for Exceptional Children.

Mullins, J. B. (1983). The uses of bibliotherapy in counseling families confronted with handicaps. In M. Seligman (Ed.), *The family with a handicapped child: Understanding and treatment* (pp. 235–251). New York: Grune & Stratton.

Mundschenk, N. A., & Foley, R. M. (1994). Collaborative relationship between school and home: Implications for service delivery. *Preventing School Failure, 39*(1), 16–20.

National Association of State Boards of Education Study Group on Special Education. (1992). *Winners all: A call for inclusive schools.* Alexandria, VA: Author.

National Center on Educational Restructuring and Inclusion. (1994). The "full inclusion" court cases: 1989–1994. *NCERI Bulletin, 1,* 1–8.

National Center on Educational Restructuring and Inclusion. (1995). *National study of inclusive education.* New York: City University of New York Graduate School and University Center, Author.

National Commission on Social Studies in the Schools. (1989). *Charting the course: Social studies for the 21st cen-*

*tury.* Washington DC: National Commission on Social Studies in the Schools.

National Council of Teachers of Mathematics. (1989). *Curriculum and evaluation standards for school mathematics.* Reston, VA: Author.

National Education Association. (1994). *Toward inclusive classrooms.* NEA Teacher to Teacher Series. Washington DC: National Education Association of the United States.

National Transition Network. (1993, Winter). IDEA: Its impact on transition regulations. *Policy Update.* Minneapolis: Institute on Community Integration.

Neel, R. S., & Cessna, K. K. (1993). Behavioral intent: Instructional content for students with behavioral disorders. In K. K. Cessna (Ed.), *Instructionally differentiated programming: A needs based approach for students with behavior disorders* (pp. 31–40). Denver: Colorado Department of Education.

Neisser, U. (1976). *Cognition and reality.* San Francisco: Freeman.

Nelson, R. O., & Hayes, S. C. (1986). The nature of behavioral assessment. In R. O. Nelson & S. C. Hayes (Eds.), *Conceptual foundations of behavioral assessment* (pp. 3–41). New York: Guilford Press.

Ness, J. E. (1989). The high jump: Transition issues of learning disabled students and their parents. *Academic Therapy, 25,* 33–40.

Nevin, A. (1993). Curricular and instructional adaptations for including students with disabilities into cooperative groups. In J. W. Putnam (Ed.), *Cooperative learning and strategies for inclusion* (pp. 41–56). Baltimore: Brookes.

Newell, A. (1980). Reasoning, problem solving and decision processes: The problem space as a fundamental category. In R. Nickerson (Ed.), *Attention and performance VIII.* Hillsdale, NJ: Lawrence Erlbaum.

Newland, T. E. (1969). Blind aptitude test. Champaign, IL: Author.

NICHCY. (1993). Including special education in the school community. *News Digest, 2*(2), 1–7.

Noddings, N. (1992). *The challenge to care in schools.* New York: Teachers College Press.

Noddings, N. (1995, January). A morally defensible mission for schools in the 21st century. *Phi Delta Kappan,* 365–368.

Novaco, R. W. (1975). *Anger control: The development and evaluation of an experimental treatment.* Lexington, MA: Heath.

Nunes, T., Schliemann, A. D., & Carraher, D. W. (1993). *Street mathematics and school mathematics.* New York: Cambridge University Press.

O'Connor, R. E., & Jenkins, J. R. (1996). Cooperative learning as an inclusion strategy: A closer look. *Exceptionality, 6,* 29–51.

O'Day, J. A., & Smith, M. S. (1993). Systematic school reform and education opportunity. In S. Fuhrman (Ed.), *Designing coherent education policy: Improving the system* (pp. 250–312). San Francisco: Jossey-Bass.

Ogbu, J. U. (1978). *Minority education and caste: The American system in cross-cultural perspectives.* New York: Academic Press.

Ogbu, J. (1993). Frameworks—Variability in minority school performance: A problem in search of an explanation. In E. Jacob & C. Jordan (Eds.), *Minority education: Anthropological perspectives* (pp. 83–111). Norwood, NJ: Ablex.

Ogbu, J. U., & Matute-Bianchi, M. E. (1986). Understanding socio-cultural factors: Knowledge, identity, and school adjustment. In Bilingual Education Office, California State Department of Education, *Beyond language: Social and cultural factors in schooling language minority students* (pp. 73–140). Los Angeles: Evaluation, Dissemination and Assessment Center, California State University.

O'Leary, K. D., & Johnson, S. B. (1986). Assessment and assessment of change. In H. C. Quay & J. S. Werry (Eds.), *Psychopathological disorders of childhood.* New York: Wiley.

Oller, J. W., & Damico, J. S. (1991). Theoretical considerations in the assessment of LEP students. In E. V. Hamayan & J. S. Damico (Eds.), *Limiting bias in the assessment of bilingual students* (pp. 77–110). Austin, TX: Pro-Ed.

Olson, D. H., & Hanson, M. K. (1990). *Source 2001: Preparing families for the future.* Minneapolis: National Council on Family Relations.

O'Neil, J. (1988, September). How "special" should the special education curriculum be? *Curriculum Update.* Alexandria, VA: Association for Supervision and Curriculum Development.

O'Neil, J. (1995). Can inclusion work? A conversation with Jim Kauffman and Mara Sapon-Shevin. *Educational Leadership, 52,* 7–11.

O'Neil, J. (1995). On preparing students for the world of work: A conversation with Willard Daggett. *Educational Leadership, 52,* 46–48.

Ornstein, A. C., & Hunkins, F. P. (1988). *Curriculum: Foundations, principles, and issues.* Englewood Cliffs, NJ: Prentice-Hall.

Oster, A. (1984). Keynote address. In National Center for Clinical Infant Program (Ed.), *Equals in this partnership: Parents of disabled and at-risk infants and toddlers speak to professionals* (pp. 26–32). Washington, DC: National Center for Clinical Infant Programs.

Ostrow, J. (1995). *A room with a different view: First through third graders build community and create curriculum.* York, ME: Stenhouse.

Otis, A. S., & Lennon, R. T. (1989). Otis-Lennon school ability test. San Antonio: Psychological Corporation.

Owan, T. C. (Ed.). (1985). *Southeast Asian mental health: Treatment, prevention, services, training and research* (pp. 113–135). Washington, DC: U.S. Department of Health and Human Services, National Institute of Mental Health.

Paine, S. C., Radicchi, J., Rosellini, L. C., Deutchman, L., & Darch, C. B. (1983). *Structuring your classroom for academic success.* Champaign, IL: Research Press.

Palinscar, A. S., & Brown, A. (1991). Dynamic assessment. In H. L. Swanson (Ed.), *Handbook on the assessment of learning disabilities: Theory, research, and practice* (pp. 75–94). Austin, TX: Pro-Ed.

Palinscar, A. S., & Brown, A. L. (1986). Interactive teaching to promote independent reading from text. *Reading Teacher, 39*(8), 771–777.

Palinscar, A. S., David, Y. M., Winn, J. A., & Stevens, D. D. (1991). Examining the contexts of strategy instruction. *Remedial and Special Education, 12,* 43–53.

Palinscar, A. S., Ransom, K., & Derber, S. (1989). Collaborative research and development of reciprocal teaching. *Educational Leadership, 37,* 40.

Paris, S., Wasik, B., & Turner, J. (1991). The development of strategic readers. In R. Barr, M. Kamil, P. Mosenthal, & P. Pearson (Eds.), *Handbook of reading research* (Vol. 2) (pp. 609–640). New York: Longman.

Paterson, J. M., & McCubbin, H. I. (1983). Chronic illness: Family stress and coping. In H. I. McCubbin & C. F. Figley (Eds.), *Stress and the family: Coping with normative transitions* (pp. 5–25). New York: Brunner/Mazel.

Pearl, R., Bryan, T., Fallon, P., & Herzog, A. (1990). Learning disabled students' detection of deception. *Learning Disabilities Research and Practice, 6,* 12–16.

Pennington, B. F. (1991). *Diagnosing learning disorders: A neuropsychological framework.* New York: Guilford Press.

Pennsylvania Association for Retarded Citizens (PARC) v. Commonwealth of Pennsylvania, 334 F. Supp. 1257, 343 F. Supp. 279 (E.D. Pa. 1971, 1972).

Perez, J. (1991). What is whole language? *First Teacher, 12,* 5.

Perlman, R. (Ed.). (1983). *Family home care: Critical issues for services and policies.* New York: Haworth Press.

Peters, T. J. (1992). *Liberation management: Necessary disorganization for the nanosecond nineties.* New York: Knopf.

Peterson, R. (1992). *Life in a crowded place: Making a learning community.* Portsmouth, NH: Heinemann.

Phillips, P. (1990). A self-advocacy plan for high school students with learning disabilities: A comparative case study analysis of students', teachers', and parents' perceptions of program effects. *Journal of Learning Disabilities, 23,* 466–471.

Piaget, J. (1971). *Genetic epistemology* (E. Duckworth, Trans.). New York: Norton.

Pickett, A. L. (1984). The paraprofessional movement: An update. *Social Policy, 14*(3), 40–43.

Pickett, A. L. (1986). Certified partners: Four good reasons for certification of paraprofessionals. *American Educator, 10*(3), 31–34, 47.

Pickett, A. L. (1989). *Restructuring the schools: The role of paraprofessionals.* Washington, DC: Center for Policy Research, National Governors Association.

Pickett, A. L. (1994). *Paraprofessional in the education workforce.* Washington, DC: National Education Association.

Pickett, A. L., Vasa, S. F., & Steckelberg, A. L. (1993). *Using paraeducators effectively in the classroom.* Bloomington, IN: Phi Delta Kappa Educational Foundation.

Polloway, E. A., Patton, J. R., Epstein, M. H., & Smith, T. E. (1989). Comprehensive curriculum for students with mild handicaps. *Focus on Exceptional Children, 21*(8), 1–12.

Powell, T. H., & Ogle, P. A. (1985). *Brothers and sisters—A special part of exceptional families.* Baltimore: Brookes.

Pressley, M., El-Dinary, P. B., Gaskins, I., Schuder, T., Bergman, J., Almasi, L., & Brown, R. (1992). Beyond direct explanation: Transactional instruction of reading comprehension strategies. *Elementary School Journal, 92,* 511–554.

Pressley, M., Goodchild, F., Fleet, J., Zajchowski, R., & Evans, E. D. (1989). The challenges of classroom strategy instruction. *Elementary School Journal, 89,* 301–342.

Prutting, C. A., & Kirchner, D. M. (1983). Applied pragmatics. In T. A. Gallagher & C. A. Prutting (Eds.), *Pragmatic assessment and intervention issues in language.* San Diego: College Hill Press.

Pugach, M. C., & Warger, C. L. (1996a). Treating curriculum as a target for reform: Can special and general education learn from each other? In M. C. Pugach & C. L. Warger (Eds.), *Curriculum trends, special education, and reform: Refocusing the conversation* (pp. 1–22). New York: Teachers College Press.

Pugach, M. C., & Warger, C. L. (1996b). Challenges for the special education–curriculum reform partnership. In M. C. Pugach & C. L. Warger (Eds.), *Curriculum trends, special education, and reform: Refocusing the conversation* (pp. 227–252). New York: Teachers College Press.

Pullis, M. E. (1988). Affective and motivational aspects of learning disabilities. In D. K. Reid (Ed.), *Teaching the learning disabled.* Needham, MA: Allyn & Bacon.

Putnam, J. W. (1994). From the courtrooom to cooperation: Educating a child with autism in the regular classroom. In J. Rogers (Ed.), *Inclusion: Moving beyond our fears* (pp. 139–162). Hot Topic Series. Bloomington, IN: Phi Delta Kappa.

Putnam, J. W., Rynders, J., Johnson, R. T., & Johnson, D. W. (1989). Collaborative skill instruction for promoting positive interactions between mentally handicapped and non-handicapped children. *Exceptional Children, 55,* 550–558.

Quay, H. C. (1986). Classification. In H. C. Quay & J. S. Werry (Eds.), *Psychopathological disorders of childhood.* New York: Wiley.

Quay, H. C., & Peterson, D. R. (1987). *Manual for the behavior problem checklist.* Coral Gables, FL: Author.

Quay, H., & Peterson, D. (1987). Revised behavior problem checklist. Coral Gables, FL: University of Miami.

Quay, H. C., & Werry, J. S. (Eds.). (1986). *Psychopathological disorders of childhood* (3rd ed.). New York: Wiley.

Ramirez, M., & Castañeda, A. (1974). *Cultural democracy, bicognitive development and education.* New York: Academic Press.

Red Horse, J. (1988). Cultural evolution of American Indian families. In C. Jacobs & D. D. Bowles (Eds.), *Ethnicity and race: Critical concepts in social work* (pp. 86–102). Silver Spring, MD: National Association of Social Workers.

Reichler, R. J. (1980). *Diagnosis and implications.* Proceedings of the Annual Meeting of the National Society for Autistic Children. Washington, DC: National Society for Autistic Children.

Reid, D. K. (1991). Cognitive curriculum. In D. K. Reid, W. P. Hresko, & H. L. Swanson (Eds.), *A cognitive approach to learning disabilities* (2nd ed.) (pp. 297–315). Austin, TX: Pro-Ed.

Reschly, D. (1981). Sociocultural background, adaptive behavior, and concepts of bias in assessment. In C. Reynolds & T. Gutkin (Eds.), *Handbook of school psychology.* New York: Wiley-Interscience.

Reynolds, M. (1962). A framework for considering some issues in special education. *Exceptional Children, 28,* 367–370.

Reynolds, M. C., & Birch, J. W. (1982). *Teaching exceptional children in all America's schools* (rev. ed.). Reston, VA: Council for Exceptional Children.

Reynolds, M., Wang, M., & Walberg, H. (1987). The necessary restructuring of special and regular education. *Exceptional Children, 53,* 391–398.

Reynolds, M. C., Wang, M. C., & Walberg, H. J. (1992). The knowledge bases for special and general education. *Remedial and Special Education, 13,* 6–10.

Rhodes, L. (1993). *Literacy assessment: A handbook of instruments.* Portsmouth, NH: Heinemann.

Rifkin, J. (1997). Rethinking the purpose of education: Preparing student for the end of work. *Educational Leadership, 54*(5), 30–33.

Rioux, W. J., & Berla, N. (1993). *Innovations in parent and family involvement.* Princeton Junction, NJ: Eye on Education.

Roarty, R. (1989). *Contingency, irony, and solidarity.* New York: Cambridge University Press.

Robinson, E. L., & Fine, M. J. (1994). Developing collaborative home-school relationships. *Preventing School Failure, 39*(1), 9–15.

Robinson, F. P. (1961). *Effective study.* New York: Harper & Row.

Rogers, J. (Ed.). (1994). *Inclusion: Moving beyond our fears.* Hot Topic Series, Center for Evaluation, Development, and Research. Washington, DC: Phi Delta Kappa.

Rojewski, J. W. (1992). Key components of model transition services for students with learning disabilities. *Learning Disabilities Quarterly, 15,* 135–150.

Romski, M. A., Sevcik, R. A., & Pate, J. L. (1988). Establishment of symbolic communication in persons with severe retardation. *Journal of Speech and Hearing Disorders, 53,* 94–107

Rorschach, H. (1921). *Psychodiagnostics: A diagnostic test based on perception.* New York: Grune & Stratton.

Rosenshine, B., & Meister, C. (1992). The use of scaffolds for teaching higher-level cognitive strategies. *Educational Leadership, 49,* 26–33.

Rosenthal, B. W., & Bergman, I. (1989). Intracranial injury after moderate head trauma in children. *Journal of Pediatrics, 54,* 115–346.

Rosenthal, R. (1974). *On the social psychology of the self-fulfilling prophecy: Further evidence for Pygmalion effects on their mediating mechanisms.* New York: MSS Modular Publications.

Ross, E. W., Cornett, J. W., & McCutcheon, G. (Eds.). (1992). *Teacher personnel theorizing: Connecting curriculum practice, theory, and research.* Albany: State University of New York Press.

Rowe, M. B. (1986). Wait time: Slowing down may be a way of speeding up! *The Journal of Teacher Education, 31*(1), 43–50.

Rugen, L., & Hartl, S. (1994). The lessons of learning expeditions. *Educational Leadership, 52,* 20–23.

Rumelhart, D. E., & Norman, D. A. (1981). Accretion, tuning and restructuring: Three modes of learning. In J. W. Colton & R. Klatsky (Eds.), *Semantic factors in cognition.* Hillsdale, NJ: Lawrence Erlbaum.

Sage, D. D. (1996). Administrative strategies for achieving inclusive schooling. In. S. Stainback & W. Stainback (Eds.), *Inclusion: A guide for educators* (pp. 105–116). Baltimore: Brookes.

Sailor, W. (1991). Community school. In L. H. Meyer, C. A. Peck, & L. Brown (Eds.), *Critical issues in the lives of people with severe disabilities* (pp. 379–385). Baltimore: Brookes.

Salvia, J., & Ysseldyke, J. E. (1991). *Assessment.* Boston: Houghton Mifflin.

Sands, D. J. (1993). *SkilSak: Skills of Independent Living Screening and Assessment Kit.* Niwot, CO: TRL.

Sands, D. J., Adams, L., & Stout, D. M. (1995). A statewide exploration of the nature and use of curriculum in special education. *Exceptional Children, 62,* 68–83.

Sands, D. J., & Doll, B. (1996). Fostering self-determination is a developmental task. *Journal of Special Education, 30,* 58–76.

Sands, D. J., & Drake, S. (1996). Exploring a process for delivering an interdisciplinary preservice elementary education curriculum: Teacher educators practice what they preach. *Action in Teacher Education, 18*(3), 68–79.

Sands, D., Kozleski, E. B., & Goodwin, L. D. (1991). Whose needs are we meeting? Results of a consumer satisfaction survey of persons with developmental disabilities in Colorado. *Research in Developmental Disabilities, 12,* 297–314.

Sands, D. J., & Wehmeyer, M. L. (1996). Future directions in self-determination: Articulating values and policies, reorganizing organizational structures, and implementing professional practices. In D. J. Sands & M. L. Wehmeyer, *Self-determination across the lifespan: Independence and choice for people with disabilities* (pp. 331–344). Baltimore: Brookes.

Sands, D. J., & Wehmeyer, M. L. (Eds.). (1996). *Self-determination across the lifespan: Independence and choice for people with disabilities.* Baltimore: Brookes.

Santelli, B., Turnbull, A., Sergeant, J., Lerner, E. P., & Marquis, J. G. (1996). Parent to parent programs: Parent preferences for supports. *Infants and Young Children, 9*(1), 53–62.

Sarason, S. (1971). *The culture of the school and the problem of change.* New York: Allyn & Bacon.

Sarason, S. (1990). *The predictable failure of educational reform.* San Francisco: Jossey-Bass.

Sarason, S. (1993). *Letters to a serious education president.* Newbury Park, CA: Corwin Press.

Sarason, S. B. (1995). *A critical appraisal of teacher education.* Washington, DC: American Association of Colleges for Teacher Education.

Savage, T. V. (1991). *Discipline for self-control.* Englewood Cliffs, NJ: Prentice-Hall.

Savoie, J. M., & Hughes, A. S. (1994). Problem-based learning as classroom solution. *Educational Leadership, 52,* 54–57.

Scanlon, D. (1996). Social skills strategy instruction. *Teaching adolescents with learning disabilities: Strategies and methods.* Denver: Love.

Schaffner, C. B., & Buswell, B. E. (1996). Ten critical elements for creating inclusive and effective school communities. In S. Stainback & W. Stainback (Eds.), *Inclusion: A guide for educators* (pp. 49–65). Baltimore: Brookes.

Schapps, E., & Solomon, E. (1990). Schools and classrooms as caring communities. *Educational Leadership, 47,* 38–42.

Schelecty, P. C. (1990). *Schools for the 21st century: Leadership imperatives for educational reform.* San Francisco: Jossey-Bass.

Scherer, M. (1998). Discipline of hope. *Educational Leadership, 56,* 8–13.

Schreibman, L. (1988). *Autism.* Newbury Park, CA: Sage.

Schreibman, L., Koegel, R., Charlop, M. H., & Egel, A. L. (1990). Infantile autism. In A. S. Bellack, M. Herson, & A. Kazdin, *International handbook of behavior modification and therapy.* New York: Plenum.

Schumaker, J. B., Deshler, D. D., & McKnight, P. (1989). *Teaching routines to enhance the mainstream performance of adolescents with learning disabilities.* Final report submitted to U.S. Department of Education, Special Education Services.

Schumaker, J. B., Nolan, S. M., & Deshler, D. D. (1985). *Learning strategies curriculum: The error monitoring strategy.* Lawrence: University of Kansas.

Schumaker, J. B., Sheldon-Wilgren, J., & Sherman, J. A. (1980). An observational study of the academic and social behaviors of learning disabled adolescents in the regular classroom. (Research Report No. 22). Lawrence:

University of Kansas Institute for Research in Learning Disabilities.

Schunk, D. H. (1991). Goal setting and self-evaluation: A social cognitive perspective on self-regulation. In M. L. Maehr & P. R. Pintrich (Eds.), *Advances in motivation and achievement* (Vol. 7) (pp. 85–111). Greenwich, CT: JAI Press.

Schunk, D. H. (1996). Goal and self-evaluative influences during children's cognitive skill learning. *American Educational Research Journal, 33,* 359–382.

Schunk, D. H., & Cox, P. D. (1986). Strategy training and attributional feedback with learning disabled students. *Journal of Educational Psychology, 78,* 201–210.

Schunk, D. H., & Swartz, C. W. (1993). Writing strategy instruction with gifted students: Effects of goals and feedback on self-efficacy and skills. *Roeper Review, 15,* 225–230.

Schunk, D. H., & Zimmerman, B. J. (Eds.). (1994). *Self-regulation of learning and performance: Issues and educational applications.* Hillsdale, NJ: Lawrence Erlbaum.

Scruggs, T. E., & Mastropieri, M. A. (1988). Are learning disabled students "test-wise"? A review of recent research. *Learning Disabilities Focus, 3,* 87–97.

Seligman, M., & Darling, R. B. (1989). *Ordinary families, special children: A systems approach to childhood disability.* New York: Guilford Press.

Senapati, R., & Hayes, A. (1989). Sibling relationships of handicapped children: A review of conceptual and methodological issues. *International Journal of Behavioral Development, 11*(1), 89–115.

Senge, P. M. (1990). *The fifth discipline: The art and practice of the learning organization.* New York: Doubleday.

Serpell, R., & Boykin, A. W. (1994). Cultural dimensions of cognition: A multiplex, dynamic system of constraints and possibilities. In R. J. Sternberg (Ed.), *Thinking and problem solving: Handbook of perception and cognition* (pp. 369–408). New York: Academic Press.

Shaffer, D. R. (1993). *Developmental psychology: Childhood and adolescence* (3rd ed.). Pacific Grove, CA: Brooks/Cole.

Shanker, A. (1995). Full inclusion is neither free nor appropriate. *Educational Leadership, 52,* 18–22.

Shannon, S. M., & Hakuta, K. (1992). Challenges for limited English proficient students and the schools. In M. C. Wang, M. Reynolds, & H. Walberg (Eds.), *Handbook of special education: Research and practice* (pp. 215–233). Oxford: Pergamon Press.

Shapiro, J. (1983). Family reactions–coping strategies in response to the physically ill or handicapped child: A review. *Social Science and Medicine, 17*(14), 913–931.

Shapiro, J. (1989). Stress, depression, and support group participation in mothers of developmentally delayed children. *Family Relations, 38,* 169–173.

Shapiro, J. P., Loeb, P., & Bowermaster, D. (1993, December). Separate and unequal. *U.S. News & World Report,* 46–60.

Sharan, S., & Sharan, Y. (1976). *Small group teaching.* Englewood Cliffs, NJ: Educational Testing Publications.

Shelton, T., Jeppson, E., & Johnson, B. (1987). *Family-centered care for children with special health care needs.* Washington, DC: Association for the Care of Children's Health.

Shepard, L. (1987). The new push for excellence: Widening the schism between regular and special education. *Exceptional Children, 53,* 327–329.

Shrank, W. (1968). The labeling effect of ability grouping. *Journal of Educational Research, 62,* 51–52.

Siegel, H. (1995). What price inclusion? *Teachers College Record, 97,* 6–31.

Simeonsson, R. J., & Thomas, D. (1994). Promoting children's well-being. In R. J. Simeonsson (Ed.), *Risk, resilience, and prevention: Promoting the well-being of all children.* Baltimore: Brookes.

Skinner, B. F. (1969). *Contingencies of reinforcement: A theoretical analysis.* New York: Appleton-Century-Crofts.

Skrtic, T. M. (1991). *Behind special education: A critical analysis of professional culture and school organization.* Denver: Love.

Skrtic, T. M. (Ed.). (1995a). *Disability and democracy: Reconstructing [special] education for postmodernity.* New York: Teachers College Press.

Skrtic, T. M. (1995b). Special education and student disability as organizational pathologies: Toward a metatheory of school organization and change. In T. M. Skrtic, (Ed.), *Disability and democracy: Reconstructing [special] education for postmodernity* (pp. 190–232). New York: Teachers College Press.

Slavin R. E. (1990). *Cooperative learning: Theory, research, and practice.* Englewood Cliffs, NJ: Prentice-Hall.

Slavin, R. E. (1996). Neverstreaming: Preventing learning disabilities. *Educational Leadership, 53,* 4–7.

Slavin R. E., & Karweit, N. A. (1985). Effects of whole group class, ability grouped, and individualized instruction on mathematics achievement. *American Educational Research Journal, 22,* 351–367.

Slavin, R. E., Madden, N. A., Dolan, L. J., & Wasik, B. A. (1994). Roots and wings: Inspiring academic excellence. *Educational Leadership, 52,* 10–13.

Snell, M. (Ed.). (1994). *Instruction of students with severe disabilities* (4th ed.). New York: Merrill.

Soder, R. (Ed.). (1996). *Democracy, education, and the schools.* San Francisco: Jossey-Bass.

Solomon, D., Schapps, E., Watson, M., & Battistich, V. (1990). Creating caring school and classroom communities for all students. In R. Villa, J. Thousand, W. Stainback, & S. Stainback (Eds.), *Restructuring for caring and effective education: An administrative guide to creating heterogeneous schools* (pp. 41–60). Baltimore: Brookes.

Sparling, J., Biller, M., & Berger, R. (1992). Fathers: Myth, reality and Public Law 99-457. *Infants and Young Children, 4*(3), 9–19.

Sparrow, S., Balla, D., & Cicchetti, D. (1984*). Interview edition, survey form manual, Vineland Adaptive Behavior Scales.* Circle Pines, MN: American Guidance Service.

Spitz, H., & Webreck, C. A. (1972). Effects of spontaneous vs. externally-cued learning on the permanent storage of a schema by retardates. *American Journal of Mental Deficiency, 77,* 163–168.

Sprenger, M. (1999). *Learning and memory: The brain in action.* Alexandria, VA: Association for Supervision and Curriculum Development.

Stainback, S., & Stainback, W. (1989). No more teachers of students with severe handicaps. *TASH, 15,* 9–10.

Stainback S., & Stainback, W. (1992). *Curriculum considerations in inclusive classrooms: Facilitating learning for all students.* Baltimore: Brookes.

Stainback, S., & Stainback, W. (1996). Curriculum in inclusive classrooms: The background, In S. Stainback & W. Stainback (Eds.), *Inclusion: A guide for educators* (pp. 203–208). Baltimore: Brookes.

Stainback, S., Stainback, W., & Jackson, H. J. (1992). Toward inclusive classrooms. In S. Stainback & W. Stainback (Eds.), *Curriculum considerations in inclusive classrooms: Facilitating learning for all students* (pp. 3–17). Baltimore: Brookes.

Stainback, W., Stainback, S., Stefanich, G., & Alper, S. (1996). Learning in inclusive classrooms: What about the curriculum? In S. Stainback & W. Stainback (Eds.), *Inclusion: A guide for educators* (pp. 209–219). Baltimore: Brookes.

Stancliffe, R., & Wehmeyer, M. L. (1995). Variability in the availability of choice to adults with mental retardation. *Journal of Vocational Rehabilitation, 5,* 319–328.

Stark, J., & Goldsbury, T. (1990). Quality of life from childhood to adulthood. In R. Schalock & M. J. Bogale (Eds.), *Quality of life: Perspectives and issues* (pp. 71–84). Washington, DC: American Association of Mental Retardation.

Steen, L. A. (1989). Teaching mathematics for tomorrow's world. *Educational Leadership, 47,* 18–22.

Sternberg, R. J. (1986). *The triarchic mind: A new theory of human intelligence.* New York: Viking Press.

Sternberg, R. J. (1989). Intelligence, wisdom, and creativity: Their natures and interrelationships. In R. Linn (Ed.), *Intelligence: Measurement, theory, and public policy.* Urbana: University of Illinois Press.

Sternberg, R. J. (1994a). Intelligence. In R. J. Sternberg (Ed.), *Thinking and problem solving: Handbook of perception and cognition.* New York: Academic Press.

Sternberg, R. J. (1994b). Allowing for thinking styles. *Educational Leadership, 52*(11), 36–40.

Sternberg, R. J., & Smith, C. (1985). Social intelligence and decoding skills in nonverbal communication. *Social Cognition, 2,* 168–192.

Stoddard, B., & MacArthur, C. A. (1993). A peer editor strategy: Guiding learning-disabled students in response and revision. *Research in the Teaching of English, 27,* 76–103.

Stone, C. A., & Reid, D. K. (1994). Social and individual forces in learning: Implications for instruction of children with learning difficulties. *Learning Disability Quarterly, 17,* 72–86.

Stoneman, Z. (1985). Family involvement in early childhood special education programs. In N. H Fallen & W. Umansky (Eds.), *Young children with special needs* (2nd ed.) (pp. 442–469). Columbus, OH: Merrill.

Stoneman, Z., Brody, G. H., Davis, C. H., & Crapps, J. M. (1988). Childcare responsibilities, peer relations, and sibling conflict: Older siblings of mentally retarded children. *American Journal of Mental Retardation, 93,* 174–183.

Stowitschek, J. J., & Kelso, C. A. (1989). Are we in danger of making the same mistakes with ITP's as were made with IEP's? *Career Development for Exceptional Individuals, 12,* 139–151.

Sulzer-Azaroff, B., & Mayer, G. R. (1991). *Behavior analysis for lasting change.* Fort Worth, TX: Harcourt Brace.

Summers, J. A., Behr, S. K., & Turnbull, A. P. (1989). Positive adaptation and coping strengths of families who have children with disabilities. In G. H. S. Singer & L. K. Irvin (Eds.), *Support for care giving families* (pp. 27–40). Baltimore: Brookes.

Swanson, H. L. (1991). Information processing: An introduction. In D. Kim Reid, W. P. Hresko, & H. L. Swanson (Eds.), *A cognitive approach to learning disabilities* (2nd ed.) (pp. 131–159). Austin, TX: Pro-Ed.

Swanson, H. L. (1991). Introduction: Issues in the assessment of learning disabilities. In H. L. Swanson (Ed.), *Handbook on the assessment of learning disabilities: Theory, research, and practice* (pp. 1–20). Austin, TX: Pro-Ed.

Swanson, H. L., & Watson, B. L. (1990). *Educational and psychological assessment of exceptional children.* Columbus, OH: Merrill.

Swift, M. S., & Spivak, G. (1969). The assessment of achievement related classroom behavior: Normative, reliability, and validity data. *Journal of Special Education, 2,* 137–153.

Swift, M. S., & Spivak, G. (1973). Academic success in classroom behavior in secondary schools. *Exceptional Children, 39,* 392–399.

Swize, M. (1993). Colorado's needs-based model. In K. K. Cessna (Ed.), *Instructionally differentiated programming: A needs-based approach for students with behavior disorders.* Denver: Colorado Department of Education.

Sylwester, R. (1995). *A celebration of neurons: An educator's guide to the human brain.* Alexandria, VA: Association for Supervision and Curriculum Development.

Szymanski, E. M., & Trueba, H. T. (1994). Classification of people with disabilities: Potential disempowering aspects of classification of disability services. *Journal of Rehabilitation, 60,* 12–20.

Tarver, S. G. (1992). Controversial issues confronting special education: Divergent perspectives. In W. Stainback & S. Stainback (Eds.), *Direct instruction* (pp. 141–152). Boston: Allyn & Bacon.

Taylor, S. (1988). Caught in the continuum: A critical analysis of the principle of the least restrictive environment. *TASH, 13*(1), 41–42.

Taylor, S., & Racino, A. (1991). Community living: Lessons for today. In L. Meyer, C. Peck, & L. Brown (Eds.), *Critical issues in the lives of people with severe disabilities* (pp. 235–328). Baltimore: Brookes.

Thoits, P. (1982). Conceptual, methodological, and theoretical problems in studying social support as a buffer against life stress. *Journal of Health and Social Behavior, 23,* 145–159.

Thomas, A., Chess, S., & Birch, H. G. (1968). *Temperament and behavior disorders in children.* New York: New York University Press.

Thompson, J. M., & Somes, R. A. (1973). Education apperception test. Los Angeles: Western Psychological Services.

Thornburg, D. D. (1986). Restoring inductive reasoning. *A+, 4*(6), 77–81.

Thorndike, R., & Hagen, E. (1986). Cognitive abilities test. Chicago: Riverside.

Thorndike, R. L., Hagen, E., & Sattler, J. (1985). Stanford-Binet intelligence scale. Chicago: Riverside.

Tiedt, P. L., & Tiedt, I. M. (1990). Multicultural teaching—A handbook of activities, information, and resources (3rd ed.). Boston: Allyn & Bacon.

Timothy W. v. Rochester, No. 88–1847, 875 F.2d (1989).

Tindal, G. A., & Marston, D. B. (1990). *Classroom-based assessment.* New York: Merrill.

Tomkins, S. S. (1991). *Affect, imagery, consciousness. Vol. 3: Anger and fear.* New York: Springer.

Tomlinson, C. A. (1995). *How to differentiate instruction in mixed-ability classrooms.* Alexandria, VA: Association for Supervision and Curriculum Development.

Torgeson, J. K. (1982). The learning disabled child as an inactive learner: Educational implications. *Topics in Learning and Learning Disabilities, 2*(1), 45–52.

Trute, B., & Hauch, C. (1988). Building on family strengths: A study of families with positive adjustment to the birth of a developmentally disabled child. *Journal of Marital & Family Therapy, 14,* 185–194.

Tung, T. M. (1985). Psychiatric care for South East Asians: How different is different? In T. C. Owan (Ed.), *Southeast Asian mental health: Treatment, prevention, services, training and research* (pp. 5–40). Washington, DC: U.S. Department of Health and Human Services, National Institute of Mental Health.

Turbiville, V. (1994). *Fathers, their children and disability.* Lawrence: University of Kansas Press.

Turbiville, V. P., Turnbull, A. P., & Turnbull, H. R. (1995). Fathers and family-centered early intervention. *Infants and Young Children, 7*(4), 12–19.

Turnbull, A. P., Behr, S. K., & Tollefson, N. (1986). *Positive contributions that persons with mental retardation make to their families.* Paper presented at the annual meeting of the American Association on Mental Deficiency, Denver.

Turnbull, A. P., & Summers, J. A. (1987). From parent involvement to family support: Evolution to revolution. In S. M. Pueschel, C. Tingly, J. E. Rynders, A. C. Crocker, & D. M. Crutcher (Eds.), *New perspectives on Down syndrome* (pp. 289–306). Baltimore: Brookes.

Turnbull, A. P., & Turnbull, H. R. (1986). *Families, professionals, and exceptionality.* Columbus, OH: Merrill.

Turnbull, A. P., & Turnbull, H. R. (1990). *Families, professionals, and exceptionality: A special partnership* (2nd ed.). Columbus, OH: Merrill.

Turnbull, H. R., III. (1993). *Free appropriate public education: The law and children with disabilities.* Denver: Love.

Turnbull, H. R., Guess, D., & Turnbull, A. P. (1988). Vox populi and Baby Doe. *Mental Retardation, 26*(3), 127–132.

Turner, C. S. V., & Louis, K. S. (1996). Society's response to differences: A sociological perspective. *Remedial and Special Education, 17,* 134–141.

U.S. Bureau of the Census. (1998, March). Consumer income. *Current population reports* (pp. 60–201). Washington, DC: U.S. Government Printing Office.

U.S. Department of Education. (1991). *America 2000: An education strategy source book* (ED/0591–13). Washington, DC: Author.

U.S. Department of Education. (1993). *Reinventing Chapter 1: The current Chapter 1 program and new directions.* Washington, DC: Author.

U.S. Department of Education. (1994). *High standards for all students.* Washington, DC: Author.

U.S. Department of Education. (1995). *Seventeenth annual report to Congress on the implementation of the Individuals with Disabilities Education Act.* Washington, DC: Author.

U.S. Department of Education. (1997). *Eighteenth annual report to Congress on the implementation of the Individuals with Disabilities Education Act.* Washington, DC: U.S. Government Printing Office.

U.S. Departments of Education and Labor. (1994). *School to work opportunities fact sheet.* Washington DC: Author.

Udvari-Solner, A. (1995). A process for adapting curriculum in inclusive classrooms. In R. A. Villa & J. Thousand (Eds.), *Creating an inclusive school* (pp. 110–124). Alexandria, VA: Association for Supervision and Curriculum Development.

Udvari-Solner, A., & Thousand, J. S. (1995). Promising practices that foster inclusive education. In R. A. Villa & J. S. Thousand (Eds.), *Creating an inclusive school* (pp. 87–109). Alexandria, VA: Association for Supervision and Curriculum Development.

Unger, D., & Powell, D. (1980). Supporting families under stress: The role of social networks. *Family Relations, 29,* 566–574.

United Cerebral Palsy Association. (1994, February). *Education reform fact sheet.* Washington, DC: UCPA.

Urban, W. (1963). Draw-a-person. Los Angeles: Western Psychological Services.

Uzgiris, I., & Hunt, J. M. (1975). *Assessment in infancy: Ordinal scales of psychological development.* Urbana: University of Illinois Press.

Vadasy, P. F., Fewell, R. R., Meyer, D. J., & Greenberg, M. T. (1985). Supporting fathers of handicapped young children: Preliminary findings of program effects. *Analysis and Intervention in Developmental Disabilities, 5,* 125–137.

Van Dyke, R., Stallings, M. A., & Colley, K. (1995). How to build an inclusive school community: A success story. *Phi Delta Kappan, 76,* 475–479.

Vigilante, F. W. (1983). Working with families of learning disabled children. *Child Welfare, 62*(5), 429–436.

Villa, R., & Thousand, J. (1992). Restructuring public schools: Strategies for organizational change and programs. In R. Villa, J. Thousand, W. Stainback, & S. Stainback (Eds.), *Restructuring for caring and effective education: An administrative guide to creating heterogeneous schools.* Baltimore: Brookes.

Villa, R. A., & Thousand, J. S. (Eds.). (1995). *Creating an inclusive school.* Alexandria, VA: Association for Supervision and Curriculum Development.

Villa, R. A., Thousand, J. S., Nevin, A. I., & Malgeri, C. (1996). Instilling collaboration for inclusive schooling as a way of doing business in public schools. *Remedial and Special Education, 17,* 169–181.

Vincent, L. J. (1995). Preschool curriculum and instruction. In M. A. Falvey (Ed.), *Inclusive and heterogeneous schooling: Assessment, curriculum, and instruction* (pp. 285–308). Baltimore: Brookes.

von Oech, R. (1983). *A whack on the side of the head.* New York: Warner Books.

Vygotsky, L. S. (1962). *Thought and language* (E. Hanfmann & G. Vakar, Ed. and Trans.). Cambridge, MA: MIT Press.

Vygotsky, L. S. (1978). In M. Cole, V. John-Steiner, S. Scribner, & E. Souberman (Eds.), *Mind in society: The development of higher psychological processes.* Cambridge, MA: Harvard University Press.

Wagner, M. (1989). *Influences on the transition experiences of youth with disabilities: A report from the national transition study.* Paper presented at the meeting of the Division of Research, Council for Exceptional Children, San Francisco.

Wagner, M. (1989). *The transition experiences of youths with disabilities: A report from the national longitudinal transition study.* Menlo Park, CA: SRI International.

Wagner, T. (1997). The new village commons: Improving schools together. *Educational Leadership, 54*(5), 25–28.

Walker, D. F., & Soltis, J. F. (1997). *Curriculum and aims.* New York: Teachers College Press.

Walker, H. M., & Bullis, M. (1991). Behavior disorders and the social context of regular class integration: A conceptual dilemma. In J. Lloyd, N. N. Sign, & A. C. Repp (Eds.), *The regular class initiative: Alternative perspectives on concepts, issues, and models* (pp. 75–94). Sycamore, IL: Sycamore Press.

Wang, M. C. (1989). Adaptive instruction: An alternative for accommodating student diversity through the curriculum. In D. Lipsky & A. Gartner (Eds.), *Beyond separate education: Quality education for all* (pp. 99–119). Baltimore: Brookes.

Wang, M. C., Haertel, G. D., & Walberg, H. J. (1993–94). What helps students learn? *Educational Leadership, 51,* 74–79.

Wang, M. C., Reynolds, M. C., & Walberg, H. J. (1988). Integrating the children of the second system. *Phi Delta Kappan, 70,* 248–251.

Wang, M. C., Reynolds, M. C., & Walberg, H. J. (1989). A rebuttal to Vergason and Anderegg: Who benefits from segregation and murky water? *Phi Delta Kappan, 7,* 64–67.

Wang, M. C., Reynolds, M. C., & Walberg, H. J. (1995). Serving students at the margins. *Educational Leadership, 52,* 12–17.

Ward, M. (1996). Coming of age in the age of self-determination: An historical and personal perspective. In D. Sands & M. Wehmeyer (Eds.), *Self-determination across the lifespan: Independence and choice for people with disabilities* (pp. 3–16). Baltimore: Brookes.

Warger, C. L., & Pugach, M. C. (1993). A curriculum focus for collaboration. *LD Forum, 18*(9), 26–30.

Warren, F., & Warren, S. H. (1989). The role of parents in creating and maintaining quality family support services. In G. H. S. Singer & L. K. Irvin (Eds.), *Support for care giving families* (pp. 55–68). Baltimore: Brookes.

Wasserman, R. (1983). Identifying the counseling needs of the siblings of mentally retarded children. *Personnel and Guidance Journal, 61,* 622–627.

Watson, D. L., & Tharp, R. G. (1993). *Self-directed behavior: Self-modification for personal adjustment.* Pacific Grove, CA: Brooks/Cole.

Webber, J., & Scheuermann, B. (1991). Managing behavior problems: Accentuate the positive . . . eliminate the negative. *Teaching Exceptional Children, 19,* 13–19.

Wehmeyer, M. L. (1996). Self-determination in youth with severe cognitive disabilities: From theory to practice. In L. Powers, G. Singer, & J. A. Sowers (Eds.), *On the road to autonomy: Promoting self-competence in children and youth with disabilities* (pp. 115–133). Baltimore: Brookes.

Wehmeyer, M. L. (1996). Self-determination as an educational outcome: Why is it important to children, youth, and adults with disabilities? In D. Sands & M. Wehmeyer (Eds.), *Self-determination across the lifespan: Independence and choice for people with disabilities* (pp. 17–36). Baltimore: Brookes.

Weiner, B. (1979). A theory of motivation for some classroom experiences. *Journal of Educational Psychology, 71,* 3–25.

Weinstein, C. (1979). The physical environment of the school: A review of the research. *Review of Educational Research, 49,* 577–610.

Weinstein, C., & Mignano, A., Jr. (1993). *Elementary classroom management: Lessons from research and practice.* New York: McGraw-Hill.

Wentzel, K. R. (1991). Social competence at school: Relation between social responsibility and academic achievement. *Review of Educational Research, 61,* 1–24.

Weschler, D. (1993). *Weschler intelligence scale for children—3rd ed.* Cleveland: Psychological.

West, J. F., & Idol, L. (1987). School consultation (Part I): An interdisciplinary perspective on theory, models, and research. *Journal of Learning Disabilities, 20,* 388–408.

Wieseler, N. A., O'Neill, R. E., Horner, R. H., Albin, R., Sprague, J. R., Storey, K., & Newton, J. S. (1997). Functional assessment and program development for problem behavior: A practical handbook. *Research in Developmental Disabilities, 18*(16), 477–495.

Wikler, L., Wasow, M., & Hatfield, W. (1983). Chronic sorrow revisited: Parent vs. professional depiction of the adjustment of parents of mentally retarded children. *American Journal of Orthopsychiatry, 51,* 63–70.

Will, M. (1986). Educating children with learning problems: A shared responsibility. *Exceptional Children, 52,* 411–416.

Willette, J. (1987). Just an ordinary parent. *The Exceptional Parent, 17,* 12–13.

Williams, P., & Shoultz, B. (1982). *We can speak for ourselves: Self-advocacy by mentally handicapped people.* London: Souvenir Press.

Williams, R. G., & Haladyna, T. M. (1982), Logical operations for generating intended questions (LOCIQ): A typology for higher level test items. In G. H. Roid & T. M. Haladyna (Eds.), *A technology for test-item writing* (pp. 161–186). New York: Academic Press.

Williams, R. G., & McHenry, P. C. (1981). Marital adjustment among parents of mentally retarded children. *Family Perspective, 15*(4), 175–178.

Willis, S. (1994). The well-rounded classroom: Applying the theory of multiple intelligences. *Update, 36,* 1–9. Alexandria, VA: Association for Supervision and Curriculum Development.

Wirth, A. (1993). Education and work: The choices we face. *Phi Delta Kappan, 74,* 361–366

Wlodkowski, R. J., & Ginsberg, M. B. (1995). *Diversity and motivation: Culturally responsive teaching.* San Francisco: Jossey-Bass.

Wolery, M., Bailey, D. B., Jr., & Sugai, G. (1988). *Effective teaching: Principles and procedures of applied behavior analysis with exceptional children.* Boston: Allyn & Bacon.

Wong, B. Y. L. (1991). Assessment of meta-cognitive research in learning disabilities: Theory, research, and practice. In H. L. Swanson (Ed.), *Handbook on the assessment of learning disabilities: Theory, research, and practice* (pp. 265–284). Austin, TX: Pro-Ed.

Wood, D. (1988). *How children learn.* Oxford, UK: Basil Blackwell.

Wood, M. M., & Long, N. J. (1991). *Life space intervention: Talking with children and youth in crisis.* Austin, TX: Pro-Ed.

Woodward, J., Carnine, D., & Gersten, R. (1988). Teaching problem solving through computer simulations. *American Educational Research Journal, 25,* 72–86.

Woolf, H. B. (Ed.). (1979). *Webster's New Collegiate Dictionary* (8th ed.). Springfield, MA: Merriam-Webster.

York, J., & Vandercook, T. (1991, Winter). Designing an integrated program for learners with severe disabilities. *Teaching Exceptional Children,* 22–29.

York-Barr, J., Schultz, T., Doyle, M. B., Kronberg, R., & Crossett, S. (1996). Inclusive schooling in St. Cloud: Perspectives on the process and people. *Remedial and Special Education, 17,* 92–105.

Ysseldyke, J. E., O'Sullivan, P., Thurlow, M. L., & Christianson, S. L. (1989). Qualitative differences in reading and math instruction received by handicapped children. *Remedial and Special Education, 10,* 14–20.

Ysseldyke, J. E., Thurlow, M. L., & Gilman, C. J. (1993). *Educational outcomes and indicators for students completing school.* Minneapolis: National Center on Educational Outcomes, University of Minnesota.

Zeaman, D., & House, B. J. (1963). The role of attention in retardate discrimination learning. In N. R. Ellis (Ed.), *Handbook of mental deficiency.* New York: McGraw-Hill.

Zemelman, S., Daniels, H., & Hyde, A. (1993). *Best practice: New standards for teaching and learning in America's schools.* Portsmouth, NH: Heinemann.

Zentall, S. (1993). Research on the educational implications of attention deficit hyperactivity disorder. *Exceptional Children, 60*(2), 143–153.

Zimmerman, B. J. (1986). Development of self-regulated learning: Which are the key subprocess? *Contemporary Educational Psychology, 16,* 307–313.

# Photo Credits

# Index